The JLC Guide to

Moisture Control

Practical Details for Durable Buildings

From the Editors of

The Journal of Light Construction

A Journal of Light Construction Book

www.jlconline.com

hanley▲wood

First printing: October 2007 Second printing: May 2008

Project Editor: Steven Bliss
Editorial Direction: Sal Alfano, Don Jackson
Managing Editor: Emily Stetson
Editorial Assistance: Jody Ciano, Vicky Congdon, Elizabeth Patterson

Graphic Designer: Terence Fallon
Illustrator: Tim Healey
Cover Design: Colleen Kuerth
Production Director: Theresa Emerson
Cover Photo: Brett Hagstrom

International Standard Book Number:
ISBN 13: 978-1-928580-36-2
ISBN 10: 1-928580-36-X
Library of Congress Control Number: 2007933282
Printed in the United States of America

A Journal of Light Construction Book
The Journal of Light Construction is a trade name of Hanley Wood, LLC.

The Journal of Light Construction
186 Allen Brook Lane
Williston, VT 05495

Acknowledgments

We wish to thank the many *JLC* authors who contributed to this book, largely drawn from the pages of *The Journal of Light Construction*. *JLC*'s strength lies in its authors: They are among the best builders and designers working in the field and among the most generous in their willingness to share their hard-won knowledge. This book represents their collective wisdom, benefiting all throughout the building industry and ultimately the owners of the homes they build and remodel — all of us. For their contributions, we wish to thank the following: Terry Amburgey, Brent Anderson, Scott Anderson, Dennis Bates, William Baldwin, Jim Blahut, Paul Bourke, David Bowyer, Al Bredenberg, Tom Brewer, Howard Brickman, Stephen Bushway, John Carmody, Jerry Carrier, Harold Chapdelaine, Peter Craig, Ted Cushman, Michael Davis, Clayton DeKorne, Henri de Marne, Andrew P. DiGiammo, David Dobson, Paul Eldrenkamp, Bill Feist, Paul Fisette, Dave Frane, Doug Garrett, Charles Gilley Jr., Carl Hagstrom, David Hansen, Robert Hatch, Martin Holladay, Andrew Hutton, Don Jackson, Kim Katwijk, Gary Katz, Michael E. Kenney, Russell J. Kenney, Todd LaBarge, Steve Lentz, Joseph Lstiburek, Harrison McCampbell, Dennis McCoy, Patricia McDaniel, James Morshead, Wanda Olson, Charles Owens, Peter L. Pfeiffer, John Raabe, Robert Randall, Judy Roberson, Bill Robinson, William B. Rose, Marc Rosenbaum, Andrew Shapiro, Chuck Silver, Angus Smith, Stephen Smulski, Henry Spies, Quenda Behler Story, Jon Tobey, Jeff Tooley, Bruce Torrey, Gordon Tully, Charles Wardell. Our apologies to anyone we inadvertently left off the list.

Contents

Introduction

Water is a building's worst enemy, which is why we spend so much time and effort trying to keep it out of buildings. Despite our best efforts, however, water will eventually find a way in. If it can't drip through an obvious hole in the roof, it will blow sideways or even uphill to find a hidden entry point. It may back up behind an ice dam, flow in any direction by capillary action, or pass through the walls invisibly as water vapor. But one way or another, water invariably travels to where it doesn't belong and often causes damage.

The focus of this book is on how to build homes that can cope with moisture in all its forms. On the one hand, we cover materials and details designed to keep water out in the first place. But because these efforts are rarely 100% successful, most of the book is devoted to an even more important topic: creating durable buildings designed to tolerate an occasional wetting and to readily dry out afterward with no harm done.

While we all intuitively understand the principle of lapping flashings and building paper to shed water as it runs downhill, it's often easier said than done on a real job site — at a complicated corner, for example, or between mulled windows or around the perimeter of a rooftop deck. More perplexing is groundwater, which is hidden from view and is as likely to flow uphill as down. If water rises above our perfectly laid footing drains, only a house built like a boat has a chance of staying dry. Equally challenging is the invisible moisture passing in and out of walls, attics, and ceilings as water vapor. Based on the last 20 years of debate over vapor barriers, it's obvious that even the experts get headaches over that one.

Perhaps the biggest challenge is that the rules of the game keep changing. The materials we build with and the way we assemble them have changed dramatically over the past few decades. Nearly airtight, well-insulated buildings hold the heat better than older buildings but stay wet longer, too. New fast-growth lumber is more vulnerable to moisture, making it less durable, less stable, and less able to hold paint than the wood of a generation ago. And new paints, sheathing wraps, insulations, flashing membranes, plastics, and composites all require new ways of building and new ways of managing moisture.

To address these issues, we've gathered from *JLC* contributors what we think are the best techniques and details for managing moisture in today's buildings. The book contains job-tested details to handle moisture from footings to ridge, in cold and hot climates, using both traditional approaches and the newest materials available. While moisture problems will never be completely eliminated from buildings, we hope this information will give you the upper hand when confronting the mysteries of moisture and help you create dry, comfortable, and trouble-free homes built to stand the test of time.

Steven Bliss
Project Editor

Chapter 1: Drainage

- Foundation Drainage
- Installing Air-Gap Membranes
- Retrofit Drainage for Wet Basements
- Moisture-Free Basement Remodels

Foundation Drainage

by Brent Anderson

As a concrete contractor, I have a vested interest in how well the water on site is controlled. Underground water and runoff from rain and snow pose a threat both to the structural integrity of the foundations I build and to below-grade interior living space. Wet basements and cracked foundations are difficult to fix after the fact, but good perimeter drainage, both at grade and down at the footings, is a cheap and easy way to prevent problems. If you follow these rules of thumb for perimeter grading and drain tile, you'll sleep easy knowing that the water-control systems you buried today won't bubble up into a callback tomorrow.

Surface Runoff

Although some wind-driven rain strikes the siding and drains onto the ground, most surface runoff comes from the roof, and the amount of runoff varies according to the size and style of the roof. A gable roof deposits all runoff onto the ground under the eaves, with little runoff at the gable ends; a hip roof distributes the runoff more evenly on all sides (**Figure 1**). In addition, valleys at main roof intersections and dormers can concentrate runoff into a relatively small area on the ground. In cold climates, runoff increases significantly during spring rainstorms, when higher temperatures and rain combine to melt snow on both the roof and the ground, adding to the total amount of surface water that must be drained away from the foundation.

Sloped grade. Most basement water problems can be solved by properly sloping the ground around the house. The finish grade should slope away from the foundation at the rate of 1/2 to 1 inch per foot for 6 to 10 feet. A 2- to 4-inch cap of silty-clay material will keep runoff from percolating down through the backfill.

A sloped grade will not work for long, however, if the perimeter fill is not mechanically compacted, which is rare in residential construction. Instead, com-

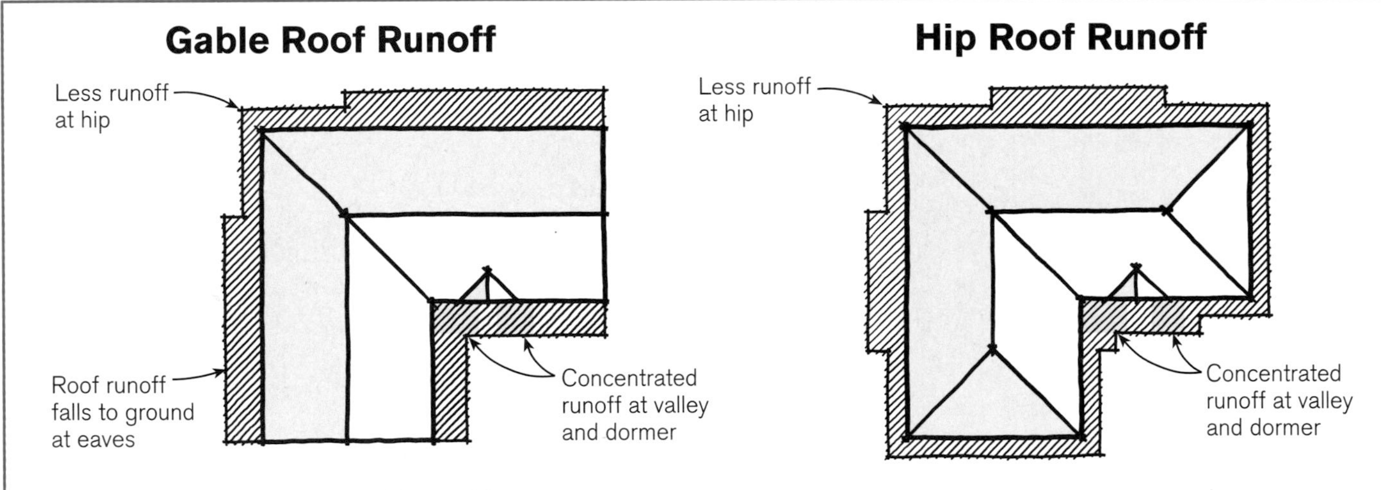

Roof Runoff
(from 2,500-sq.-ft. roof)

Rainfall Amount	Rainfall Rate	Volume (cubic ft.)	Volume (gallons)
1 in.	per hour	200	1,500
1 in.	per day	200	1,500
2 in.	per hour	400	3,000
2 in.	per day	400	3,000

Note: Every inch of rain, whether it falls during a one-hour downpour or an all-day rain, deposits 1,500 gallons of water onto the ground around a typical 2,500-square-foot roof surface. During a winter rainstorm, every foot of melting snow on the roof adds an additional 1,500 gallons.

Figure 1. Both of these roofs cover approximately 2,500 square feet. The gable roof deposits runoff along two sides of the house; the hip roof spreads the runoff more or less evenly along all sides. Main roof valleys and dormers concentrate the runoff into smaller areas on the ground.

Downspout with Sloped Leader

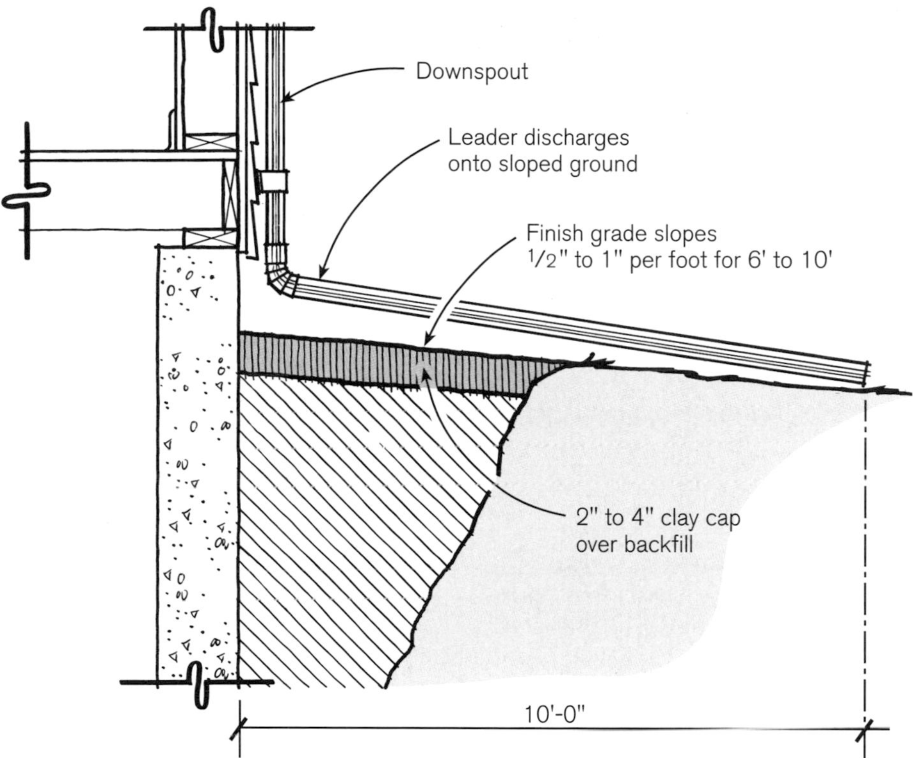

Downspout with Catch Basin

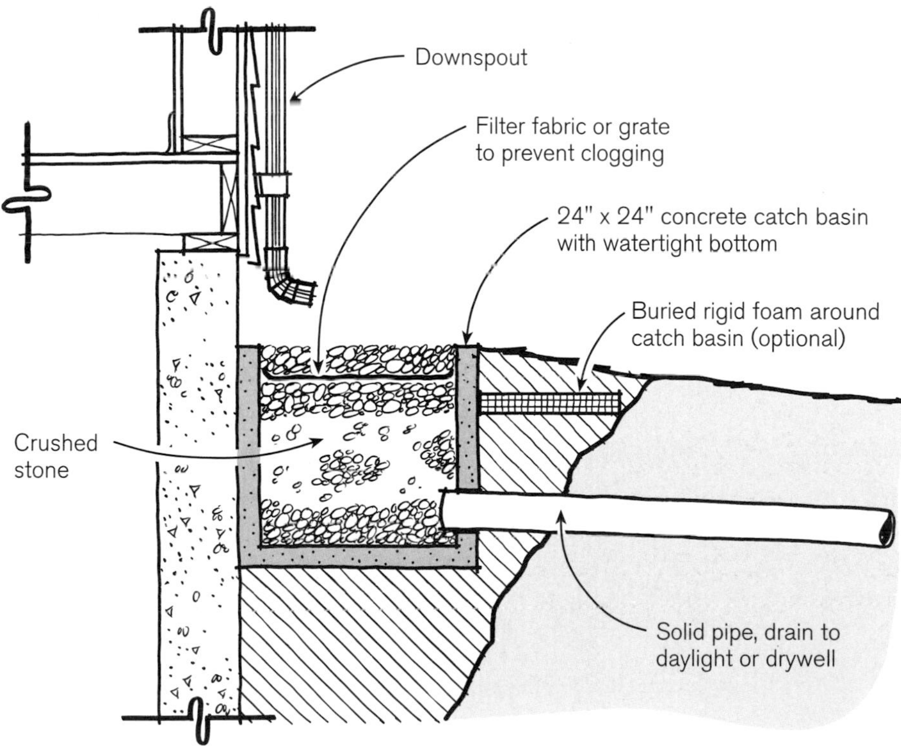

Figure 2. Sloped downspout leaders should discharge at least 10 feet away from the foundation wall (top). Use solid drainpipe to carry runoff from a concrete catch basin to daylight or a drywell (above).

paction is left to chance and occurs slowly over a period of months or years, depending on climate and the type of backfill used. Gravels and sands percolate faster and may reconsolidate more quickly — typically from three months to a year. Silts and clays, which have a much slower percolation rate, may not compact for several years.

In either case, though, the result is a negative grade that directs runoff back toward the foundation. Depending on the type of backfill, sooner or later the runoff will overwhelm the footing drainage system, and basement water problems will appear. Silt or clay fill, which hold water longer than gravel or sand, can make the foundation more susceptible to cracking from frost action; hydrostatic pressure may also develop with these types of fill, forcing water through the slab-footing joint. Rarely will any of these problems appear immediately, but down the road you'll be faced with a messy and expensive repair job.

Gutters. While gutters can dramatically reduce the total ground area onto which roof water drains, it is crucial to use a sloped leader to extend downspouts along the ground to carry water away from the foundation (**Figure 2**, previous page). Otherwise, a gutter-and-downspout system compounds the drainage problem by concentrating the entire roof runoff load

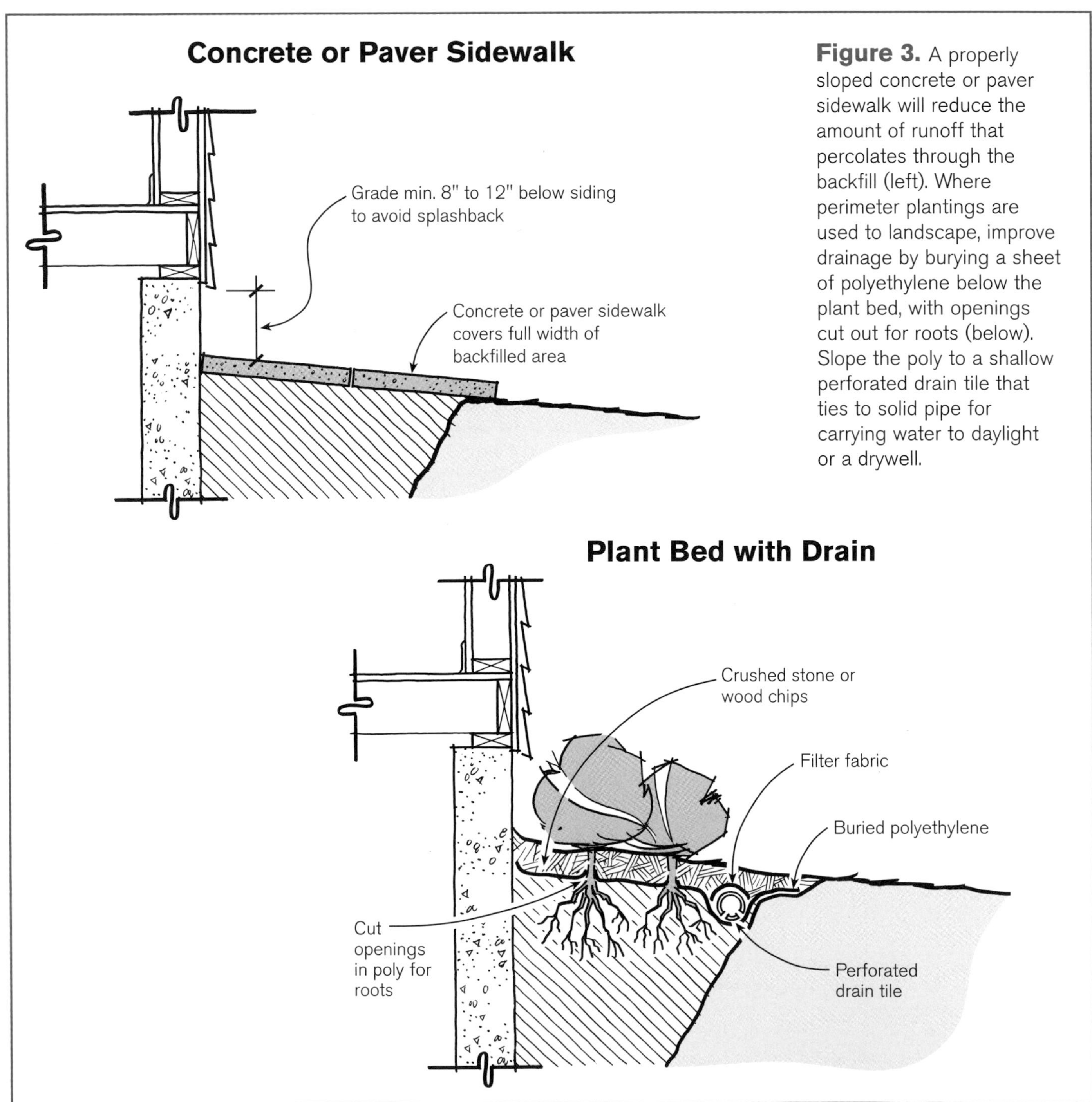

Figure 3. A properly sloped concrete or paver sidewalk will reduce the amount of runoff that percolates through the backfill (left). Where perimeter plantings are used to landscape, improve drainage by burying a sheet of polyethylene below the plant bed, with openings cut out for roots (below). Slope the poly to a shallow perforated drain tile that ties to solid pipe for carrying water to daylight or a drywell.

into a few small areas, usually at the house corners. Leaders should discharge onto sloping ground at least 10 feet from the foundation. If downspouts dump directly into a catch basin on the surface or underground, the collected runoff should be carried through a solid drainpipe to a drywell or to daylight.

Keep gutters clear of leaves, pine needles, and ice. Overflow from blocked gutters can follow the contour of the gutter and saturate the soffit and siding, often making its way into the wall and wetting the insulation, drywall, and floor. Similarly, gutters in cold climates can encourage ice damming, with the same damaging results.

Hardscape. Sidewalks built of concrete or paver block can also control percolation of runoff into the backfill (**Figure 3**) — I've measured reductions in runoff percolation of 75% to 85%. Again, the hardscape should be wide enough to cover the entire backfilled area, and the surface should slope away from the foundation walls.

A less expensive technique is to bury a sheet of polyethylene in a plant bed **(Figure 3)**. The poly should cover the backfilled foundation trench and slope to a perforated drain tile laid parallel to the foundation. Use solid pipe to carry runoff to daylight or to a drywell. In landscaped areas, cut openings in the poly to accommodate plant and tree roots.

Buried poly works well, as long as the backfill has been compacted. With a negative grade, however, the poly actually directs the water against the foundation wall. Plant and tree roots near the foundation can also compound problems with uncompacted fill, because their root systems absorb water and cause the soil to reconsolidate quickly. In a drought, tree roots can pull so much moisture out of the soil that the foundation may settle.

Perimeter Footing Drains

Foundation perimeter drains work in both directions. They not only carry rainwater percolating down through the backfill away from the foundation, but they also relieve excessive hydrostatic pressure from rising groundwater. By helping the backfill dry out more quickly, properly installed perimeter drains reduce lateral soil pressure, which in turn means that foundation walls can be designed to use more porous materials and less steel.

There's a right way and a wrong way to install perimeter drainage. Unfortunately, many foundation contractors and home builders labor under a false sense of security, reasoning that if complaints about leaky basements don't surface within the first year or two after a project is completed, their construction techniques must be working. In fact, basement water problems that occur within the first 12 months are usually related to waterproofing defects. Drain-tile problems typically take many years to develop. Thus, many contractors have buried time bombs that will eventually blow up in their faces.

Holes Down

Although porous cement-based tile is still in use today, most residential contractors would agree that perforated 4-inch-diameter plastic pipe produces tighter joints and is easier to work with. Not all would agree, however, on which direction the holes should face when installing footing drains.

The answer depends on the type of pipe. Flexible HDPE (high-density polyethylene) is slotted all the way around, and some rigid PVC has a pattern of holes around the entire circumference. With these types of drain tile, there is no "right" direction because there are openings on all sides. Plugged

Figure 4. Without a filter to keep silt from contaminating the surrounding stone, drain tile can be rendered useless within just a few seasons (left). Pipe that is prewrapped or "socked" with filter material (above) will prevent drain tile from becoming plugged.

holes on the bottom are cleared by water entering through the sides and top.

The most popular drain tile, however, is rigid PVC that has just two parallel rows of holes close together along its length. The classic approach is to lay this type of drain tile with the holes facing down, in the five-o'clock and seven-o'clock positions. This allows a rising water table to enter the pipe at its lowest point.

Filter fabric. While hydrostatic pressure helps to flush silt from the pipe, all buried drain tile should be surrounded with coarse gravel or crushed stone and wrapped with a filtering material. Without a filter, silt will contaminate the stone and eventually enter and plug the holes in the pipe (**Figure 4**, previous page). Various geotextiles are available in rolls, and prewrapped or "socked" pipe — pipe that is manufactured with a filter sleeve already in place — is also available.

Drain Tile Location

Filter fabric and properly oriented perforations, however, will not guarantee that drain tile will work. The pipe must also be installed carefully and in the right location with respect to the footing and any interior slab.

From an engineering point of view, the ideal place to lay exterior drain tile is alongside the footing, because water from a rising water table enters the pipe well before it reaches the level of the top of the slab (**Figure 5**). The drain tile does not need to be sloped, although a slight pitch helps keep the pipe clear of silt and clay (particularly when the pipe has just two rows of holes on the bottom). Avoid trying to slope flexible drain tile, however, because you can inadvertently create dips and sags that will eventually collect silt and clog the pipe (**Figure 6**). In fact, undulating drain tile can result in premature failure of the drainage system. This problem is more pronounced when trees are growing close to the foundation, because wet silt and

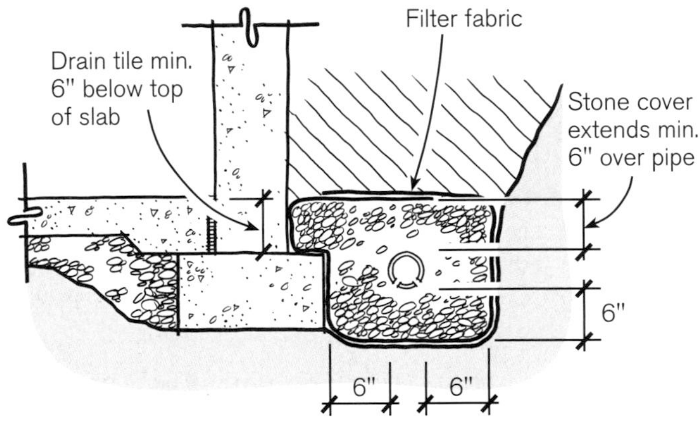

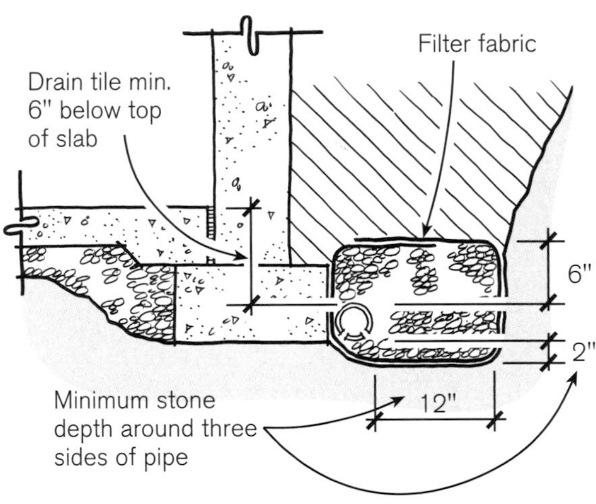

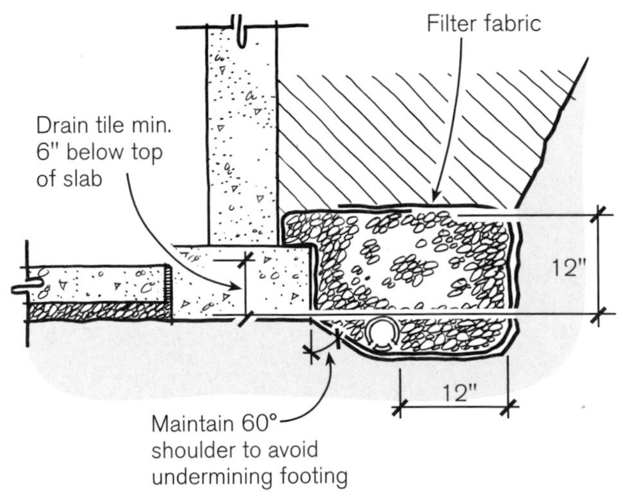

Figure 5. The best location for rigid drain tile is alongside the footing. Minimum requirements for stone cover depend on whether the tile is flush with the top of the footing (top left) or the bottom (above). In either case, the top of the interior slab should be at least 6 inches above the top of the drain tile. The pipe can be laid level or pitched slightly.

Where drain tile must be located lower than the bottom of the footing (left), avoid undermining the footing by keeping the pipe outside a 60° angle measured from the corner of the footing. This location also requires more stone cover for the pipe.

clay accumulating in low spots become targets for water-seeking tree roots in dry periods or in dry climates. In a relatively short period of time, tree roots can completely plug drain tile.

Some contractors create an even lower elevation for the tile by digging a small trench next to the footing. To avoid undermining the foundation, however, most codes require that the tile be placed outside a 60° angle from the footing.

Drain tile can also be placed on top of the footing. The advantage here is that the tile will be as level as the footing — a good strategy when using flexible pipe (**Figure 7**). But this higher placement doesn't control a rising groundwater table as effectively, and it may require raising the elevation of the interior slab.

Specialty drainage products. Today there are several products on the market, such as Form-A-Drain (CertainTeed Corp.), that provide both the footing form and the drain tile (**Figure 8**, next page). These systems ensure that the drainage system is level, and they often provide more flow capacity than traditional pipe systems as well.

On sites where an exceptionally high groundwater table creates intermittent hydrostatic pressure on the foundation walls, dimpled sheets can be used in conjunction with standard drain tile (see "Installing Air-Gap Membranes," page 9). These membrane systems provide a waterproof barrier while also directing excess water from higher up on the foundation walls into the perimeter drains.

Discharging Collected Water

Capturing groundwater in a perimeter drainage system is only half the battle — once you've collected water in the drain tile, you have to dispose of it somewhere. Discharging water into sanitary sewer systems is generally illegal, which leaves two basic ways to get rid of the water: On sloped sites, you can extend unperforated drain tile to daylight and discharge the water onto the ground; on flat sites, you can collect the water in a sump basket and pump it to a discharge area away from the basement.

Gravity discharge. Two elements are critical to proper function of a gravity drainage system. First,

Figure 6. Regardless of the type of pipe used or its shape, improperly positioned drain tile can easily be plugged with silt and clay (left). Water-seeking roots from trees growing too near the foundation can also clog perimeter drains (right).

Pipe Resting on Footing

Top of pipe should not be higher than top of slab

Filter fabric

12"

12"

2"

Flexible drain tile (slotted)

Figure 7. To keep flexible drain tile from developing low spots that will collect silt, place it on top of the footing, making sure that the top of the pipe is not higher than the top of the interior slab.

Figure 8. Form-A-Drain stay-in-place footing forms (left) ensure a level perimeter drain and have a larger capacity than pipe systems. To control hydrostatic pressure in areas with high groundwater, dimpled drainage panels can be fastened to the foundation wall to carry water from the backfill into the perimeter drains (right).

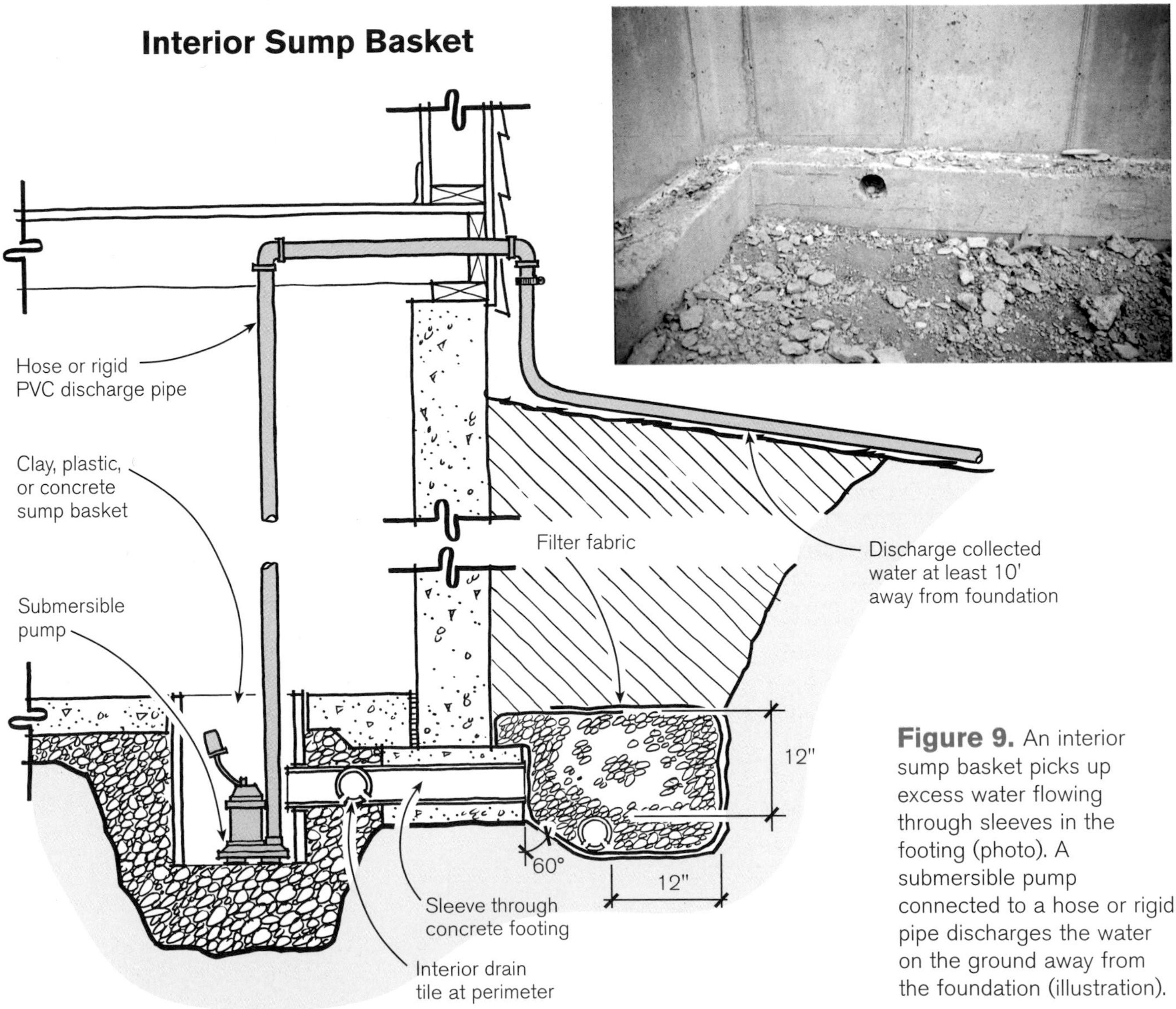

Interior Sump Basket

Hose or rigid PVC discharge pipe

Clay, plastic, or concrete sump basket

Submersible pump

Filter fabric

Discharge collected water at least 10' away from foundation

12"

12"

60°

Sleeve through concrete footing

Interior drain tile at perimeter

Figure 9. An interior sump basket picks up excess water flowing through sleeves in the footing (photo). A submersible pump connected to a hose or rigid pipe discharges the water on the ground away from the foundation (illustration).

although the perforated drain tile around the foundation itself may be level, solid pipe running from the foundation to daylight should slope at the rate of 1/16 to 1/8 inch per foot. Second, the open end of the discharge line should be designed to prevent entry by rodents, frogs, snakes, and reptiles. One method is to cover the exposed end of the pipe with 1/4-inch hardware cloth. Alternatively, you can bury the end of the pipe in crushed stone, which will allow the water to seep out below grade.

Pumped discharge. While gravity discharge to daylight is cheap and easy, I recommend installing a sump basket as a backup. A submersible sump in the bottom of the sump basket connects to a hose or rigid pipe system that carries the collected water out of the basement. If you provide for the collection sump at the time the foundation and slab are placed, the pump and discharge piping can be installed later if needed.

The sump basket should be located inside the foundation, where it can pick up groundwater that rises under the slab. On a flat site where all groundwater must be pumped away, water from perimeter drains should also be directed into the sump through drainage sleeves in the footing (**Figure 9**). To avoid having to excavate later, be sure to place sleeves before the footings are poured. Use 4-inch-diameter pipe, and space sleeves 6 to 8 feet apart around the entire perimeter of the footing. In special cases where the slab is placed a foot or more above the top of the footings, you can locate sleeves in the foundation wall. Although water passing through the sleeves or under the footing will generally find the sump basket on its own, I recommend an interior drainpipe at the perimeter, terminating in the sump basket.

Brent Anderson is a professional engineer and concrete consultant. His Minneapolis-area company provides concrete construction, investigation, and repair services.

Installing Air-Gap Membranes

by Don Jackson

Air-gap membranes have been used in Europe and Canada for years. Manufacturers claim that combined with a good footing drain, the membrane provides dry, odor-free basement living space. I had the opportunity to install one of these products on a new foundation in northern Vermont. The membrane, called Delta-MS, is made by Cosella-Dörken Products, Inc., a German company with North American offices in Ontario.

The membrane is a 6-mm-thick (24-mil) high-density polyethylene (HDPE) with a matrix of round dimples, about 5/8 inch in diameter, vacuum-formed into the sheet (**Figure 10**). The dimples are installed against the foundation and cause the membrane to stand off the concrete by about 5/16 inch, leaving an air space between the membrane and the concrete (thus the generic name, air-gap membrane).

The idea is simple: Moisture in the concrete foundation wall is able to "breathe" into the air space, where it can condense on the back of the membrane and run between the dimples down to the foundation drain. And because HDPE is impervious to water, any moisture in the soil will be stopped on the outside and will likewise fall to the foundation drain.

The membrane is designed to handle any foundation and finished grade level. It comes in 65-foot-long rolls in a variety of heights, from 3 feet 3 inches to 9 feet 9 inches (**Figure 11**, next page). The membrane is intended to be brought to within an inch or two of finished grade. It should last indefinitely if it's below grade and protected from UV exposure.

Installation Process

We were working with a stepped foundation, so we used three different-sized rolls. Whenever a roll is too

Figure 10. The Delta-MS membrane has dimples that hold it away from the wall, leaving an air space for the unhydrated water in the concrete to evaporate.

Figure 11. The membrane is available in several heights (left). Everything you need to know about installation is conveniently printed on the back of the wrapper (right).

Figure 12. Ramset's cordless TrakFast nailer works great for installing air-gap membranes. A special nosepiece (right) holds the plastic plugs (above right) that fit into the dimples in the membrane.

tall, it's easy enough to cut the entire roll or a portion of it with a circular saw or recip saw.

An 8-foot-tall roll weighs a little more than 60 pounds and is easily handled by one person. I worked with another carpenter to install the material. One of us would roll out the membrane along the top of the footing, smoothing out wrinkles and stretching it tight. The other would follow, making the attachment to the wall, using small plastic plugs that are part of the system. The plugs nest in the dimples and have a hole in the center to receive a concrete nail.

Attachment. An instructional video from the manufacturer shows workers nailing the membrane to the concrete with hammers. I guess this approach might work okay in green concrete, but it made my elbow ache just watching it. We were up against concrete that had cured for a month, so we used a Ramset TrakFast, a gas-fueled nailer like the Paslode Impulse, available from ITW Ramset/Red Head. Though the gun is a little heavy at 9.5 pounds, I can't imagine doing this job any other way. The TrakFast holds four strips of ten nails at a time. It never misfired, and one fuel cell took us through the entire job. Ramset makes a special nosepiece for the gun that holds the plastic plugs in place as the gun is fired (**Figure 12**). We were somewhat prone to dropping the plugs on the ground before we could get them nested into a dimple, but they're cheap, and it was no big deal to grab another one from the pouch.

Figure 13. At joints, the dimples of the overlapping membrane nest in the dimples of the bottom sheet. Butyl caulk provides the seal.

Fast Installation

The day we installed the material was the same day the excavator was scheduled to install the footing drain and backfill the foundation. We started work at 6:00 a.m. and had no problem keeping in front of the other work. The sound of the skid steer dumping gravel in the trench around the corner was good motivation, but the pace was never frantic.

We installed 188 linear feet of the membrane in around three hours. This included nailing a staggered double row of plugs 16 inches on-center along the top, caulking the overlaps between sheets, and shooting in a few extra plugs at corners and overlaps.

At joints, the manufacturer recommends a 6-inch overlap (**Figure 13**). Laps are quick: First you squirt a heavy bead of sealant on the underlying piece, then nest the overlying piece into the dimples of the bot-

Figure 14. A plastic termination strip is nailed along the flat tab at the top of the membrane (at right in photo). Where the flat tab gets cut off, as at this step-down, the cut edge is protected by a 2-inch-wide molding strip.

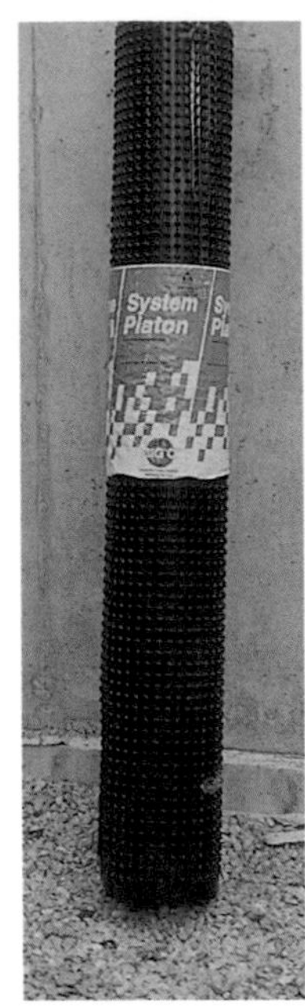

Figure 15. Similar to Delta-MS, System Platon air-gap membrane can also be installed with the TrakFast nailer.

tom sheet. A vertical row of plugs 8 to 10 inches on-center completes the lap.

With the membrane installed, we got out of the way while the excavator finished laying the foundation drain, gravel, and filter fabric. He then backfilled the trench to within a few feet of the top of the wall, leaving the top foot of the membrane exposed. We worked around the foundation perimeter using the TrakFast to nail off the Delta-MS's plastic termination strip along the top edge of the membrane (**Figure 14**, previous page).

Next, the instructions call for laying a heavy bead of sealant behind the top edge of the membrane just above the termination strip. The sealant helps to fill any gaps left along the top of the wall behind the termination strip, preventing soil from getting behind the membrane once the finish grading is done. Wherever the membrane was cut around windows or at elevation drops, we used a plastic molding strip to finish off the cut edge. The molding covers the dimpled cut edge, again keeping dirt out.

Another Product Option

Around the time we were to install the Delta-MS, I learned of a similar membrane called System Platon, manufactured by Armtec., also in Ontario, and was able to obtain a couple of rolls of that product to examine (**Figure 15**). The Platon membrane has half as many dimples as the Delta-MS but is otherwise similar and seems just as easy to install. Ramset also makes a TrakFast nosepiece for the Platon plugs. The System Platon calls for washered fasteners along the top edge instead of a termination strip. I think the Delta-MS termination strip might do a better job of keeping dirt out than the washered fasteners, but I have no evidence of this. Other than that, there seems to be no great difference between the two products.

Figure 16. For the air-gap membrane to work properly, there must be a working foundation drain (left) to carry off any water that condenses and runs down the back of the membrane. The riser that the worker is covering with his hand (center) later received a flush tube (right) for cleaning the drain where it exits toward daylight.

How Air-Gap Membranes Work

Eight years after installing the product, the basement remains dry and mold free. The perimeter drain outlet gushes water every spring because of both the air-gap membrane and the foot or more of stone placed at the bottom of the excavation. I might prefer a better-designed termination strip at the top, but, in general, the soil holds the membrane tightly against the foundation so that any small amounts of dirt that get in are negligible.

Based on my experience, I would definitely use the product again. For starters, the cost is reasonable. At around 35¢ to 40¢ per square foot, the material cost is about the same as the cost of spray-on dampproofing, which is the standard foundation treatment for new construction here in northern New England. Add in eight man-hours or so of labor, and the total cost is still much less than the cost of a bituminous foundation waterproofing system.

The air-gap membrane has two major advantages over spray-on dampproofing. Dampproofing provides a thin coating, so if a crack opens up in the concrete, the dampproof "skin" is cracked as well. The air-gap membrane is independent of the concrete, so the surface cracks typical of curing concrete make no difference. This also makes the membrane a good slip sheet for frost protection.

Dampproofing also seals the pores of the concrete, which prevents the water in the curing concrete from evaporating to the outside. Concrete will give up as much as 15 gallons of water per yard over three years after placement. With an air-gap membrane, that water has a chance to evaporate to the outside.

What I liked best about the air-gap membrane is the built-in tolerance. It's not meant to provide a watertight seal: If water happens to get behind the membrane, it has a way to get out. The membrane is plenty tough, but it is possible to puncture it during installation. Although a big tear would need to be patched (with more membrane, some sealant, and a few nails), an occasional small hole is not a problem. Any water that gets in will get out. The concept depends, of course, on a reliable footing drain to daylight, which every foundation should have in any case (**Figure 16**). It's common in this area to add an extra foot or two of gravel next to the foundation wall above the drain to ensure that groundwater has an easy path to the drain. With the air-gap membrane in place, however, the extra stone didn't seem necessary.

If this looks like a product you might want to try, I recommend giving the manufacturers a call first to request a sample of the material and installation instructions, including the video.

Don Jackson is chief editor of The Journal of Light Construction.

Retrofit Drainage for Wet Basements

by Scott Anderson

Damp or leaking basements are a common source of problems for homeowners. In fact, a nationally syndicated home-repair columnist I spoke with recently said that wet basements were the leading source of letters and e-mails sent to his weekly newspaper column.

Barrier System vs. Water Management

My company, Tri-State Basement Systems, based in Barre, Vt., concentrates on basement waterproofing. We always have plenty of work. Unlike most DIY efforts and "miracle coatings" that attempt to prevent groundwater entry with a barrier, our techniques don't try to stop the water but rather to manage it. Sometimes we use exterior perimeter drains and waterproofing, but more often we install water-management systems on the building's interior. Most homeowners prefer this approach because it costs less than excavating around the foundation and is less destructive to their landscaping.

One recent project involved a 1950s ranch home with a block foundation. The basement in this house was literally soaking wet. Water running down the walls accumulated on the floor, making the space virtually unusable — even for storage. And when you opened the basement door, you were greeted by a wave of humid air and the pungent smell of mold. The homeowner had tried numerous coats of waterproof paint, grading around the foundation, and a cheap sump pump illegally piped into the waste stack, but all these efforts were of little help. Another contractor suggested excavating around the foundation and installing a perimeter drain, but the plan was twice as expensive as ours and required removing a large deck.

So the homeowners decided to treat the problem using the WaterGuard system, one of the proprietary

Figure 17. Electric jackhammers are used to cut a trench around the slab's perimeter. The jackhammer makes less dust than a concrete saw and can break up rocks or other obstructions under the slab. Note the wet floor and mold on the walls.

basement-drainage systems manufactured and supplied by our franchiser, Basement Systems Inc. WaterGuard is a perimeter drainage system installed on the inside of the foundation. We dig a trench around the perimeter of the basement slab and install perforated pipe that drains to a sump. The collected water is pumped through a 2-inch pipe to the building's exterior. We give our customers a lifetime guarantee on the work we do, and we almost never get callbacks.

Trenching

The first step is to break up the floor at the edges of the concrete slab to create a 5- to 6-inch-wide trench around the perimeter. We use electric jackhammers instead of concrete saws because the jackhammers create less dust and can cut through slabs of almost any thickness (**Figure 17**). Also, the rough surface created by the jackhammer helps to key in the concrete patch at the end of the process. As we're running the demo hammers, we carry out the concrete rubble in five-gallon pails.

Once the slab is cut around the perimeter, we clean off the footing and, just inside it, use mattocks and hand trowels to dig a small trench about 4 inches deep. While one or two crew members are excavating the trench, another drills a series of weep holes in the base of the wall with a rotary hammer (**Figure 18**). Water stored in the cells of the concrete blocks often pours out of the wall for several seconds after a hole is drilled. We line the trench with 2 inches of crushed stone and install our proprietary WaterGuard drainage pipe, sloping it toward the sump ¼ inch over the length of each wall.

There are two styles of WaterGuard pipe (**Figure 19**). The standard version is placed directly against the foundation wall with a plastic flange extending up the foundation wall. The flange is designed to leave a small gap along the wall so any water flowing down the wall can reach the sub-slab drainage pipe (see "Basement Interior Drain," page 16). The other version works similarly but comes in two pieces. It's

Figure 18. The author's crew often uses mattocks and hand trowels to dig the trench along the inside of the footing (left). Next, workers drill a series of 3/8-inch weep holes along the base of the foundation wall with a rotary hammer (above). Water often pours out of the wall for several seconds after a hole is drilled. The bottom of the trench is lined with a layer of crushed stone.

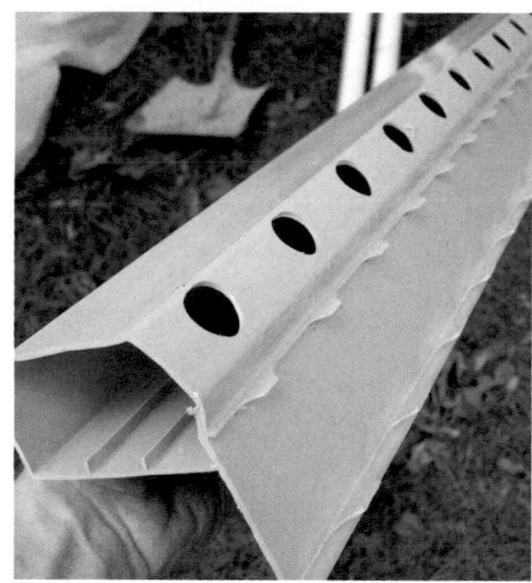

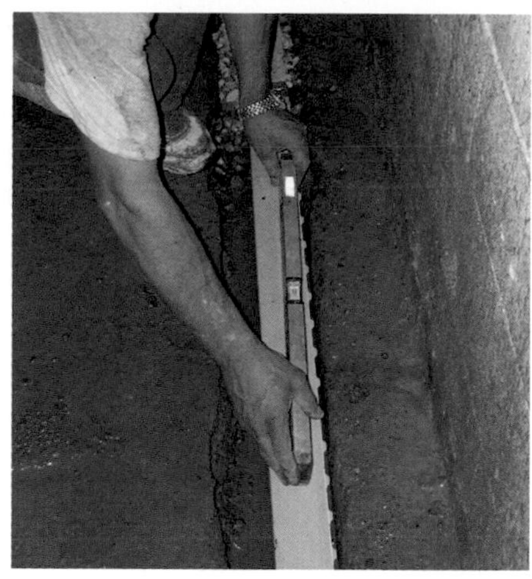

Figure 19. The author uses two styles of proprietary pipe. The standard type (left) is placed against the foundation wall. It has a toothed flange that creates a small gap between the basement wall and slab so any water seeping through the block and running down the wall is directed into the pipe. The job described here required the two-piece version (center) because the footing prevented placing the pipe against the wall. The piping is sloped toward the pump (right) — 1/4 inch over the length of the wall is usually enough.

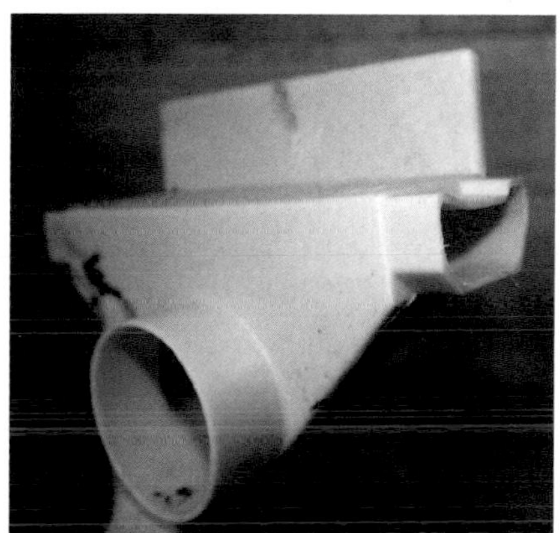

Figure 20. An adapter (left) connects the uniquely shaped WaterGuard footing drain to a length of 4-inch PVC pipe that runs into the sump basket. Workers use a jigsaw to remove the knockout in the sump basket (center); then they level the basket and backfill around it with washed stone (right).

used in applications where the footing prevents placing the drainage pipe against the foundation wall. The pipe comes in 10-foot lengths that we miter at the corners with an inexpensive miter saw.

Installing the Sump

While the drainage pipe is being installed, we start digging the sump pit. Water often fills the hole as we're digging, so we need to bail as we dig. Again, we use pails to carry out the rocks and muck.

When the hole is finished, we place a layer of washed stone in the bottom, insert the sump liner — making certain it's level — and then backfill around the basket with washed stone. We connect the sump basket to the WaterGuard pipe with a proprietary adapter and a length of 4-inch PVC (**Figure 20**).

The sump we use has features that improve its performance and durability, including a perforated basket to drain water from below the floor and heavy-duty plastic components. The high-quality Zoeller pump (Zoeller Pump Co.) is placed on a plastic stand, which prevents the pump from clogging with sediment (**Figure 21**, page 17). The sump basket has an airtight, two-piece, screw-down lid to prevent kids and pets from getting inside.

Running the Discharge Line

With the sump pump installed and the cover in place, we run the discharge line up the wall and across the ceiling to the exterior. Ordinarily we take

Basement Interior Drain

WaterGuard drainage pipe comes in one- and two-piece configurations. The one-piece pipe installs more quickly, but the two-piece version is needed where there isn't enough space to place the pipe between the slab and the top of the footing. Both types have a weep flange, which allows water seeping through the wall to reach the drainage pipe.

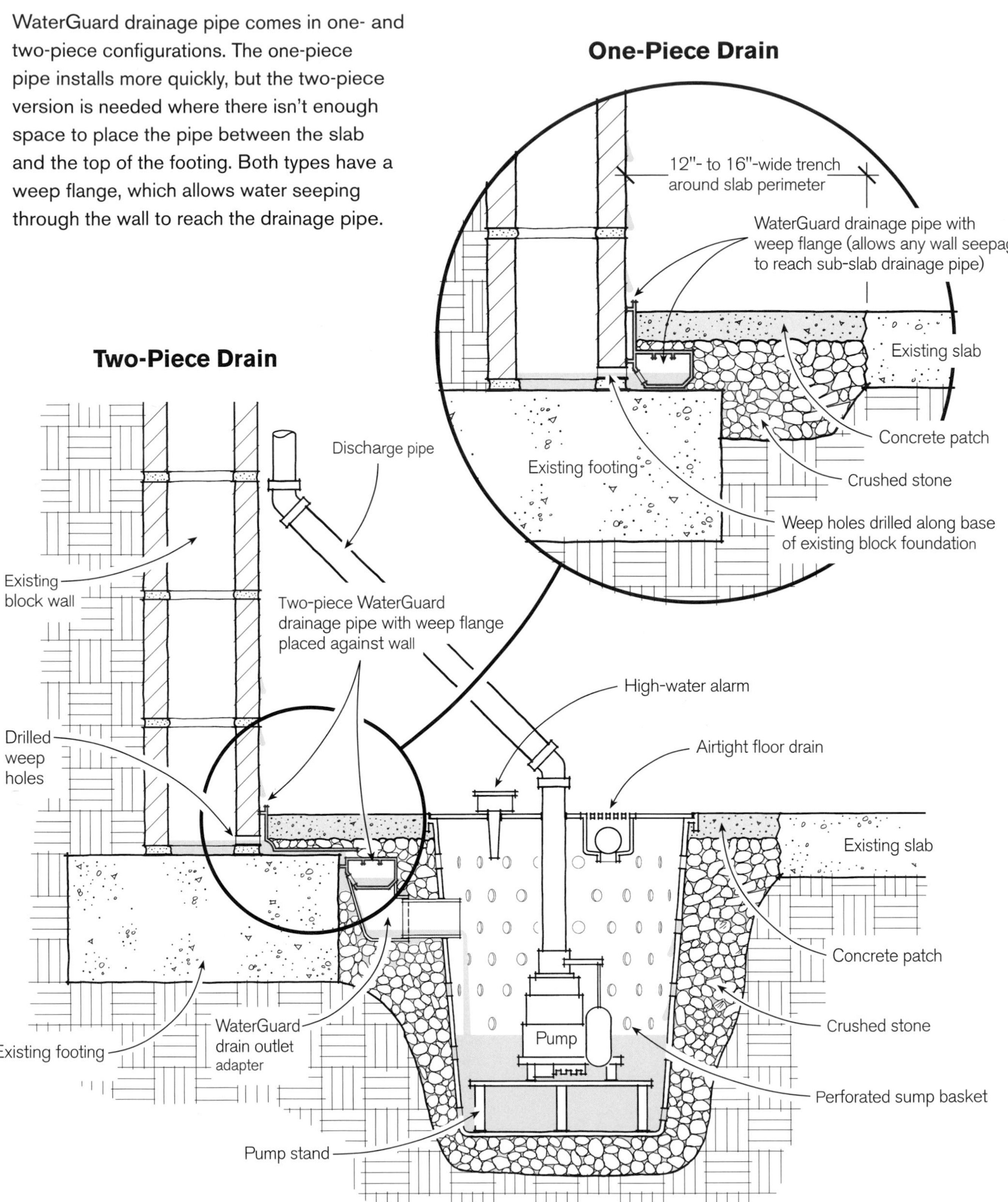

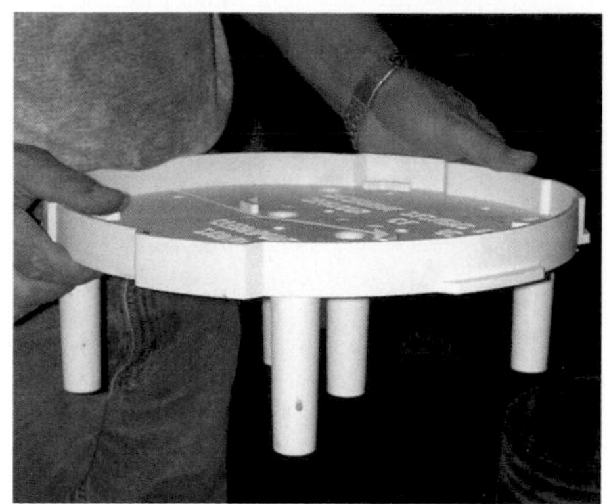

Figure 21. A plastic stand (above) raises the pump about 6 inches above the basket's bottom so it doesn't clog with sediment. Flexible couplings on the discharge line (right) and a two-piece lid (far right) allow the pump to be removed without cutting the pipe.

Figure 22. On this job, the discharge line was placed on the front of the house, since a large deck blocked access to the band joist in the rear where water is typically discharged. A proprietary IceGuard fitting allows discharge water to escape if the pipe freezes downstream. The fitting also acts as a coupling between the 2-inch pipe exiting the house and the 4-inch exterior pipe.

the most direct route, but sometimes we'll go out of our way to place the outlet in an inconspicuous spot on the home's exterior. The discharge pipe is tucked inside a joist cavity whenever possible so it won't interfere with finishing the ceiling.

Where the pipe exits the house, we seal the penetration with urethane caulk and install a plastic trim ring for a finished look.

Preventing the discharge line from freezing is an important consideration in our area, where winter temperatures can stay below 0°F for days. If the outlet were to freeze, the pump would still run, but the backed-up water could cause a flood or pump failure. We use a proprietary outlet called an IceGuard, supplied by our franchiser (**Figure 22**). It has openings that allow the water to escape even if the pipe below becomes clogged with ice or debris. We also slope the discharge pipe down toward the outside so water won't remain in the pipe near the outlet, where it's more vulnerable to freezing.

To direct the discharged water away from the foundation, we use a couple of methods. The least expen-

Figure 23. Because many properties may not have enough slope or a convenient spot to drain to daylight, running a pipe underground is not always an option. In these cases, a plastic tray called a RainChute is installed in a sloping trench to carry water away from the house (far left). It's placed slightly below grade so a mower can run over it (left).

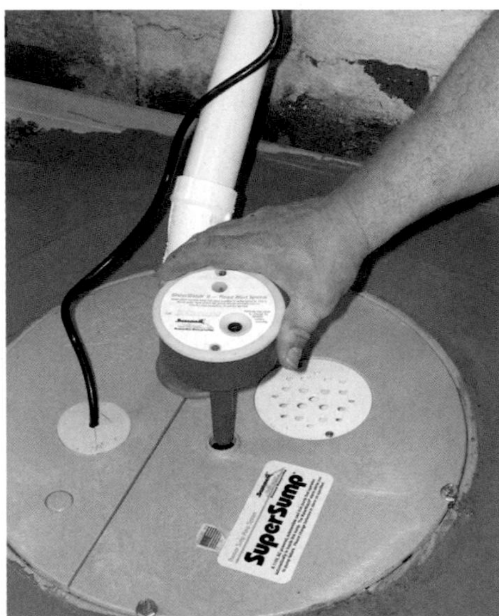

Figure 24. Final steps include patching the floor around the sump and basement perimeter (far left) and installing a high-water alarm (left) that sounds if the pump or discharge line malfunctions. An emergency floor drain handles leaks — plumbing mishaps, a broken washing-machine hose, and the like.

Figure 25. Many customers opt to finish the basement walls with white fiberglass-reinforced panels (left), a big improvement over the moldy masonry typically found in wet basements. The panels are fastened with drive anchors instead of adhesive, leaving space for seeping water to drain to the WaterGuard piping. These pictures were taken only a few days after the sump was installed. Note that the floor is completely dry (right).

sive and simplest option is to install a proprietary plastic tray called a RainChute (**Figure 23**). The chute has low-profiled sides so you can mow right over it, and it's placed in a sloping trench so the water is carried away from the house. We're mindful of where we locate the open-ended chute; we don't want the discharged water to pond in the yard.

Another option is to run an underground pipe to daylight, but some homeowners don't want to damage their lawns and some properties don't have enough slope for a daylight drain.

Finishing Touches

After the pipe is run and the system tested, we patch the concrete around the sump (**Figure 24**) and cover the WaterGuard pipe with at least an inch of concrete. The only part of the pipe that's visible is the vertical lip that catches water running down the wall. We also install a battery-powered high-water alarm that alerts the homeowner if the system is not working properly. Often we install fiberglass-reinforced panels over the interior basement walls as a final step. The plastic panels won't support mold growth, are easy to clean, and give the basement walls a better appearance (**Figure 25**).

Basement projects on small homes like this 1,200-square-foot ranch typically range from $1,500 to $8,000, depending on the extras selected by the client.

Scott Anderson owns Tri-State Basement Systems in Barre, Vt.

Moisture-Free Basement Remodels

by Paul Eldrenkamp

Turning a basement into pleasant, useful living space is always a challenge. My first task is to listen carefully to the customer's vision of the finished basement. Next, I take time to evaluate the existing conditions, looking for items that may affect the cost or feasibility of the project.

My first concern is, Can I make this basement dry? At best, the basements in my area have high humidity levels; at worst, there is actually standing water. I carefully assess the level of moisture and figure out the strategies I'll use to mitigate it. I look for mildew or water stains at the base of partitions, dampness or mildew under floor coverings, signs of rot where the stairs rest on the floor, or lally columns with rusty bases. Any efflorescence on the masonry walls is a sure sign of past and possibly current moisture problems.

On the exterior, I look for disconnected downspouts and grading that directs water toward rather than away from the house.

If the signs of moisture are severe enough, I'll explain to my customer the potential costs and uncertainties of attempting to eliminate the problem.

Mitigating Moisture

I've dealt with many wet basements, and my experience has been that roof runoff is responsible for most moisture problems. Clogged gutters, disconnected downspouts and leaders, and improper grading all contribute to the roof runoff being directed to the basement area. Two inches of rain falling on a 2,000-square-foot house can produce more than 2,600 gallons of runoff water. We repair any damaged or missing portions of the guttering system so that it's easy to monitor and maintain (**Figure 26**).

Figure 26. Always direct roof runoff away from the foundation. The author prefers to run downspouts into a dedicated PVC pipe that drains to daylight.

Basement leaks can also be caused by malfunctioning (or nonexistent) footing drains. Whatever the cause, a chronic water problem has to be fixed before proceeding with a basement remodel. You may have to wait a few months (or seasons) to make sure you've really solved the moisture problem.

If there is reason to believe that the surrounding seasonal water table is higher than the proposed finished basement floor, you may want to abandon the project. If you will be held responsible for any future moisture problems, the risk is probably not worth the reward.

Floating Subfloor System

We've had excellent results using a floating subfloor system that controls moisture, insulates, and provides a substrate for many types of finished flooring (**Figure 27**). We start by covering the existing slab with 6-mil polyethylene (turning up the edges 6 inches at the walls), followed by a layer of 1-inch extruded foam insulation. Using construction adhesive, we glue 1x3 furring to the foam at 16-inch centers, then glue and screw 3/4-inch T&G plywood to the furring strips, running a generous bead of adhesive in the T&G joint. This method avoids the costly and time-consuming mechanical fasteners that would otherwise be needed if the flooring system were attached to the concrete floor. To allow for expansion, the floor system is held back 1/2 inch from the foundation walls.

The plywood is a suitable substrate for just about any finished flooring material, including ceramic tile.

Retrofit Wall System

We apply 1 1/2-inch rigid foam to the basement walls using construction adhesive, and foil-tape all the joints. With the foam in place, we frame 2x4 walls. The 2x4s provide ample room for wiring and piping, and they're easier to install than furring that is fastened through the foam into the foundation wall. When we're faced with a stone foundation, we spray the walls with Icynene foam insulation (Icynene Inc.). It adheres to the irregular wall surface and provides the code-required R-value.

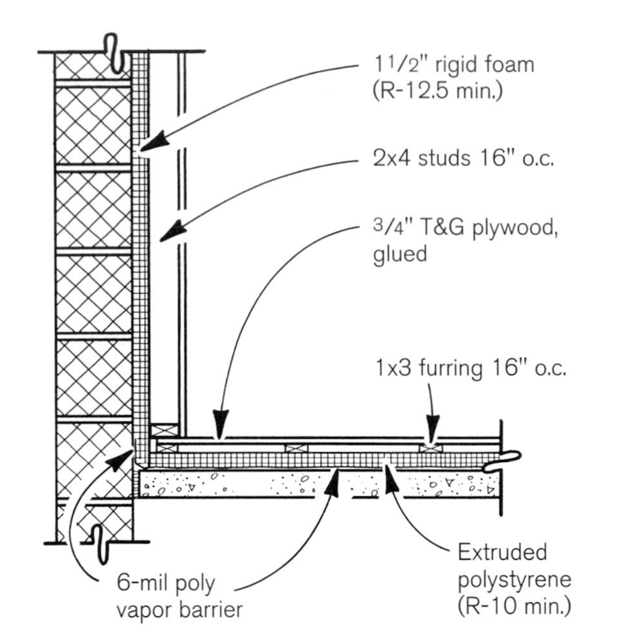

Figure 27. This floating floor system provides a dry base for the finish floor. Two-by-four walls over 1 1/2-inch rigid foam provide space for plumbing and wiring.

Paul Eldrenkamp owns Byggmeister Inc., a remodeling company in Newton, Mass.

Chapter 2: Dampproofing & Waterproofing

- Sub-Slab Vapor Barriers
- Waterproofing Options for Basement Walls
- Waterproofing ICF Foundations

Sub-Slab Vapor Barriers

by Peter Craig

The subject of vapor retarders beneath concrete slabs-on-grade has long been controversial. Some builders argue that slabs placed in direct contact with a vapor barrier or retarder are more susceptible to curling and other slab problems than those cast on a granular base. They consider a vapor barrier or retarder a downright nuisance.

Others have witnessed the devastating effect of moisture on modern floor coverings, adhesives, coatings, and a building's environment. They will justifiably argue that a vapor barrier or retarder beneath the slab can be an absolute necessity.

Not surprisingly, reaching consensus on this subject has been difficult. Both sides raise genuine arguments that cannot simply be dismissed. The fact is, a vapor barrier can be both a nuisance and a necessity. To better understand why moisture in concrete slabs has become such a problem, we must examine the sources of slab moisture, how moisture moves, and how it can adversely affect flooring materials, adhesives, and coatings (**Figure 1**).

Figure 1. Moisture can have a devastating effect on floor coverings, such as this failed gym floor.

Where Does the Moisture Come From?

Free water within the concrete itself is the first source of moisture that challenges a floor covering or coating.

To produce concrete of a workable consistency, more water is added to the mixture than that which merely satisfies chemical hydration of the cement. After the slab is placed, finished, and cured, some of this additional water-of-convenience must leave the slab in order for the concrete to reach the moisture requirements of the floor covering, adhesive, or coating. Most manufacturers of flooring materials currently require, before the product is installed, that the moisture emission rate from the concrete not exceed 3.0 pounds, or in some cases 5.0 pounds, of water per 1,000 square feet in 24 hours.

To understand how challenging it is to comply with these requirements, consider that a 4-inch-thick slab placed at a 4-inch slump with a 1:2, or .50, water-to-cement ratio can contain between 1,600 and 1,700 pounds of nonchemically bound water in a 1,000-square-foot area.

How quickly moisture is lost from a slab depends on the water-to-cement ratio, density of the concrete finish, ambient conditions above the slab, and moisture below the slab. The table at right summarizes the time necessary for laboratory-cast, 4-inch-thick concrete samples to reach the required moisture emission limit of 3.0 pounds per 1,000 square feet in 24 hours when exposed to 73°F and 50% relative humidity.

This drying study reinforces the benefit of using concrete mixtures with a water-to-cement ratio not exceeding 0.50 and the need to eliminate or significantly reduce sub-slab moisture from entering the concrete from below.

The times shown in the table should not be considered to begin until the slab is protected by a watertight roof and the curing period is completed. Rewetting of the slab by any means will significantly lengthen the drying time. Regardless of when the drying clock begins, it is important that the underside of the slab be sealed off from moisture below if a new

Days Drying Time to Reach 3.0 lb/1,000 sq. ft./24 hours

Water/ Cement Ratio	Bottom Sealed	Bottom Exposed to Water Vapor	Bottom in Contact with Water
0.40	46	52	54
0.50	82	144	199
0.60	117	365	>> 365
0.70	130	>> 365	>> 365
0.80	148	>> 365	>> 365
0.90	166	>> 365	>> 365
1.00	190	>> 365	>> 365

4-inch-thick specimen dried at 73°F and 50% relative humidity

Drying time, in days, required to reduce vapor emission to 3.0 pounds per 1,000 square feet per 24 hours.

ADAPTED FROM B. SUPRENANT, "MOISTURE MOVEMENT THROUGH CONCRETE SLABS," *CONCRETE CONSTRUCTION*, NOV. 1997.

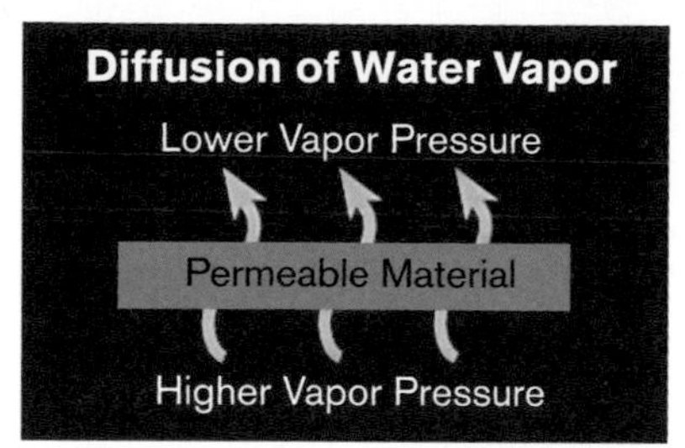

Figure 2. Diffusion of water vapor leads to moisture reaching the slab from below.

concrete subfloor is to dry to an acceptable level and remain dry thereafter. Once a nonbreathable floor covering is installed, moisture levels in the slab may rise again without an adequate vapor barrier below.

Moisture Migration

At some depth below most building sites, a natural source of water can be found. Because liquid water is often found beneath a failed flooring system, many people use the term "hydrostatic" to describe the condition. However, for a true hydrostatic condition to develop beneath the floor, the water table would have to be at or above the floor elevation. Such is seldom the case for a slab-on-grade.

There are two other ways in which water can rise upward through soils and contact a concrete slab-on-grade. The first method is capillary action, where water is drawn upward, well above the water table in fine soils. An example of capillary action is water rising to a higher elevation within a narrow straw placed into a beaker of water.

Capillary action can be interrupted by a "capillary break" layer of coarse gravel or crushed stone between the slab and the subgrade. However, while a capillary break can be effective in stopping the rise of water in a liquid state, it does not eliminate the potential for moisture to reach the slab in vapor form.

Water changes from a liquid to a vapor as it evaporates. Water as a vapor will move from areas of high vapor pressure to low vapor pressure by the natural process of *diffusion* (**Figure 2**). Diffusion of water vapor occurs in both soils and concrete.

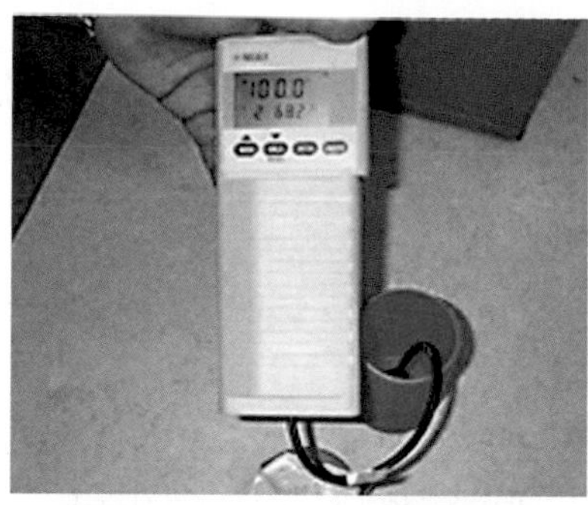

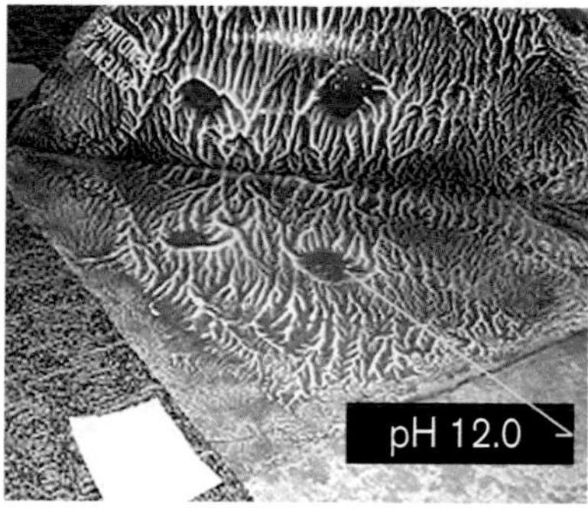

Figure 3. High moisture levels in the concrete cause soluble alkalis to enter into solution, raising the pH and leading to adhesive breakdown.

Numerous investigations show that the relative humidity in the base and subgrade material beneath covered slabs will generally test close to 100% regardless of the depth of the water table or the moisture content of the subgrade materials. Without effective moisture protection directly beneath the slab, this water vapor will enter the slab by the process of diffusion and raise the moisture content of the concrete over time.

The Effects

Liquid moisture can cause soluble alkalis within the concrete to enter into solution. When an alkali solution develops within the top surface of a slab, pH levels can rise to 11 to 12, well above the 9 to 10 pH limit of most modern adhesives. The high pH levels can cause the breakdown or re-emulsification of the flooring adhesive and lead to total failure of the bond (**Figure 3**).

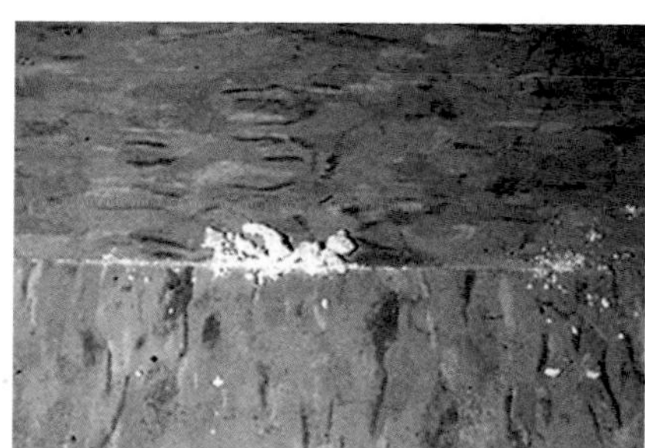

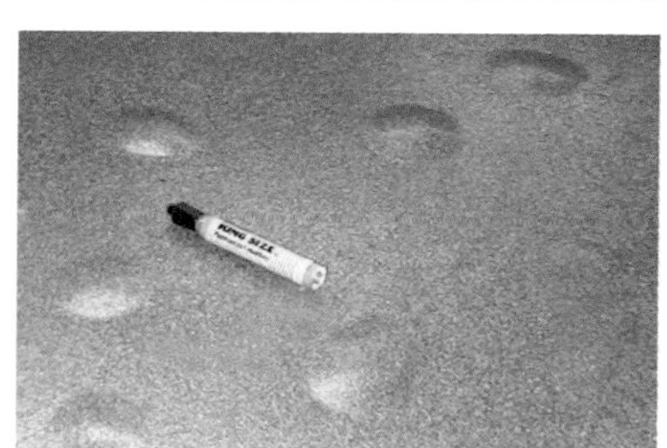

Figure 4. The effects of elevated pH levels can be seen in these examples of re-emulsified adhesive (left), soluble salts (center), and blistered floor coating (right).

Figure 5. Mold problems affecting indoor air quality can begin with moisture migration through concrete slabs-on-grade.

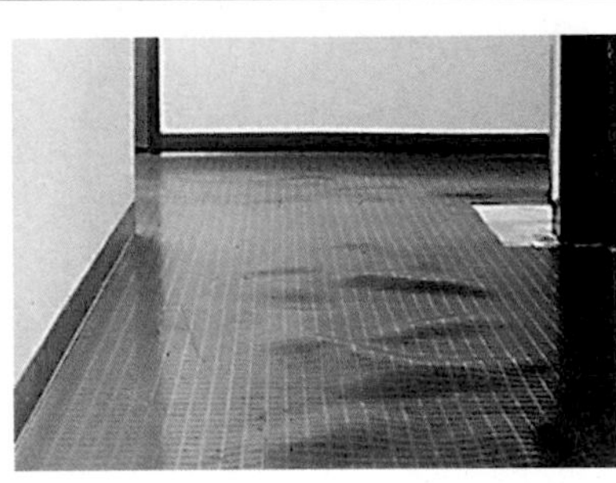

Figure 6. It can take months or even years for flooring problems to develop.

High moisture levels can also lead to blistering of coating systems (**Figure 4**, previous page). Beneath a flooring installation, high moisture in the slab can lead to cupping, bulging, or swelling of many flooring materials. To prevent these problems, moisture from beneath the slab must not be allowed to enter the concrete once it is covered.

Moisture migration through soils and concrete slabs-on-grade can also contribute to indoor air quality issues. At normal building temperatures, moisture beneath floor coverings or within adhesives or carpets can provide a suitable environment for mold, mildew, and other potentially harmful microbial growth. That in turn may adversely affect indoor air quality (**Figure 5**). An effective vapor barrier or retarder directly beneath the concrete can help reduce the amount of moisture available to such growth.

Barrier or Retarder?

A vapor barrier or retarder is a material designed to block or slow down the transfer of moisture from the ground into a concrete slab. Such materials are typically sheeting materials based on polyethylene or polyolefin technology. For many years, all such materials were called *vapor barriers*. However, very few can truly be considered an actual barrier. The term *vapor retarder* is a more accurate description of most materials used for sub-slab moisture protection.

How low should the permeance of below-slab moisture protection be? Current ASTM E-1745 class A, B, & C standards allow a vapor-retarder material to have a water-vapor permeance up to 0.3 perm. When tested in accordance with ASTM E 96 Method B, a 0.3-perm material would allow the passage of approximately 18 gallons of water per week in a 50,000-square-foot area. Although this may not seem like too much, and the actual transmission rate in field conditions will typically be lower, even a small amount of moisture entering the slab over time can significantly affect the moisture content of the slab.

Based on more than 150 flooring investigations, it seems that the performance of low-permeance, adhered floor coverings, such as sheet vinyl, PVC- or urethane-backed carpet tiles, or rubber flooring, warrants restricting moisture transfer to well below 0.3 perm. Other moisture-sensitive flooring materials, such as linoleum and wood, will also benefit from a high level of protection.

In short, if the material on top of the floor is considerably less permeable than the material protecting it below, the potential exists for moisture to increase within the slab over time. In such cases, it can take months or even years for problems to develop (**Figure 6**). Considering the extremely high cost of a flooring failure and the difficulty of drying concrete to an acceptable level in the first place, it makes sense to take ground moisture completely out of play.

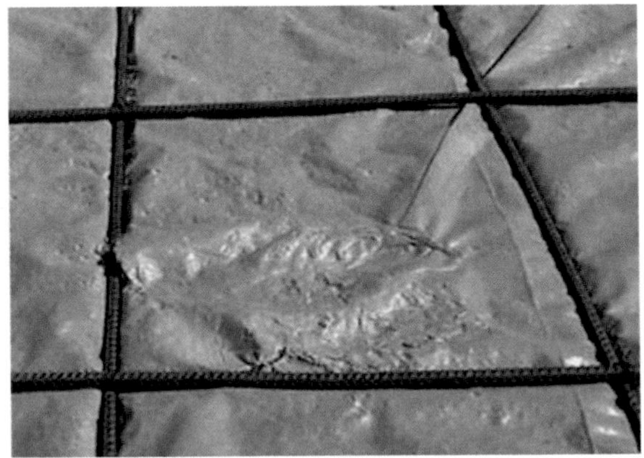

Figure 7. A thicker vapor barrier is required where there will be equipment traffic or with angular base materials. Note the example of torn 6-mil poly (right).

Moisture Control Tips for Slabs

Although each project should be considered individually, the following recommendations have proved helpful in overcoming moisture-related problems with concrete slabs-on-grade:

1. *Vapor barrier.* An effective, low-permeance vapor barrier or retarder is necessary to protect many modern floor coverings, adhesives, coatings, and building environments, and to conform with published guidelines from the floor-covering industry.

2. *Capillary break.* Whenever possible, a capillary break should be included as a sub-slab component. A capillary break will not, however, prohibit moisture from reaching the slab in vapor form.

3. *Concrete mix.* A water-to-cement ratio between 0.45 and 0.50 is a practical range that considers workability as well as reduced drying time. Lower water-to-cement ratios may be used to further hasten drying times, but special considerations should be given to placement size, workability, and curing. Pozzolonic materials such as fly ash or ground granulated blast-furnace slag added to the concrete mixture may help in reducing soluble alkali content within the slab.

4. *Placement beneath slab.* For most floor covering or coating applications, the vapor barrier or retarder should be placed directly beneath the slab (see flow chart, next page). Additional slab design considerations such as continuous reinforcement may be needed to offset the potential increase in curling stresses within the slab.

5. *Permeance rating.* For moisture- or alkali-sensitive flooring applications, including sheet vinyl, rubber-, PVC-, or urethane-backed carpet tile, wood, or linoleum, consider the benefit of vapor-retarder materials of extremely low permeance (0.01 perm or lower).

6. *Durability.* Homogeneous vapor-retarder materials should be not less than 15 mils thick when they will receive direct traffic from ready-mix trucks, concrete buggies, or laser screeds.

7. *Installation.* There is only one opportunity to select the level of below-slab moisture protection, and that is before the slab is placed.

8. *Curing.* To help minimize the drying time of the slab and surface preparation costs, consider moisture-retaining, seven-day cover curing methods rather than membrane or chemical curing compounds, which may adversely affect adhesive bond and require removal before installing the flooring material.

9. *Drying.* It is difficult enough to sufficiently dry free-water from within the slab without exposing it to additional moisture from below.

10. *Take the ground out of play!* — *P.C.*

In the past, selecting an extremely low permeance material was costly. Today, below-slab moisture protection as low as 0.01 perm is commercially available with little if any premium over conventional materials of far greater permeance.

Additional research is needed to establish exactly where new permeance levels should be set. Until such work is complete, designers, engineers, specifiers, and users are encouraged to select below-slab moisture protection with extremely low permeance levels, well below current industry standards. The purpose of a vapor barrier or retarder beneath a concrete slab is to stop below-slab moisture from entering the slab and becoming a problem.

Durability Also Important

While permeance is most important in evaluating a vapor barrier or retarder, the ability of the material to withstand construction activity is also important. A punctured, torn, or incomplete vapor retarder provides an open avenue for moisture to enter the slab from below.

Currently, the American Concrete Institute's "Guide for Concrete Floor and Slab Construction" (ACI 302) recommends a minimum thickness of 10 mils for vapor retarders. Puncture studies of 6- to 20-mil materials have demonstrated that 10 mils is the absolute minimum thickness that should be considered, and that a thicker material may be necessary over more angular base materials. A minimum thickness of 15 mils is recommended when ready-mix trucks or laser screeds drive directly on the vapor retarder (**Figure 7**).

Concrete's Role

In general, concrete permeability increases with an increase in the water-to-cement ratio. Concrete with a water-to-cement ratio below 0.50 is often considered to be watertight. But even watertight concrete is not impermeable to the passage of moisture. Once the floor is covered, the total moisture within the slab will increase over time without adequate protection. Also, without continuous moisture protection directly below the slab, sawed contraction joints and random cracks provide open passageways for moisture to rise through the slab.

Certainly concrete slabs to receive floor coverings or coatings will benefit from a reasonably low water-

Figure 8. A vapor retarder placed under granular fill (far left) may trap rainwater, leading to such moisture problems as were later seen with this tile floor (left).

to-cement ratio. However, depending solely on the concrete to provide protection from moisture migration places the flooring installation at serious risk. Omitting an effective vapor barrier or retarder may also result in liability for a flooring failure, since a vapor barrier or retarder is a published requirement in guidelines from the floor-covering industry and many flooring manufacturers.

Where to Place the Vapor Retarder

Until 2001, published guidelines from the American Concrete Institute (ACI) led slab designers and specifiers to place a 4-inch layer of granular fill atop a required vapor retarder. This detail has been successful on many projects, but has caused problems on others (**Figure 8**).

In April 2001, ACI published an update on vapor-retarder location in *Concrete International*. The update describes instances where fill courses above the vapor retarder have taken on water from rainfall, curing, or saw-cutting and may have subsequently contributed to flooring problems. As a result, the flow chart shown at left was developed to recommend where to place the barrier under different conditions. The chart will be published in the next revision of ACI 302.

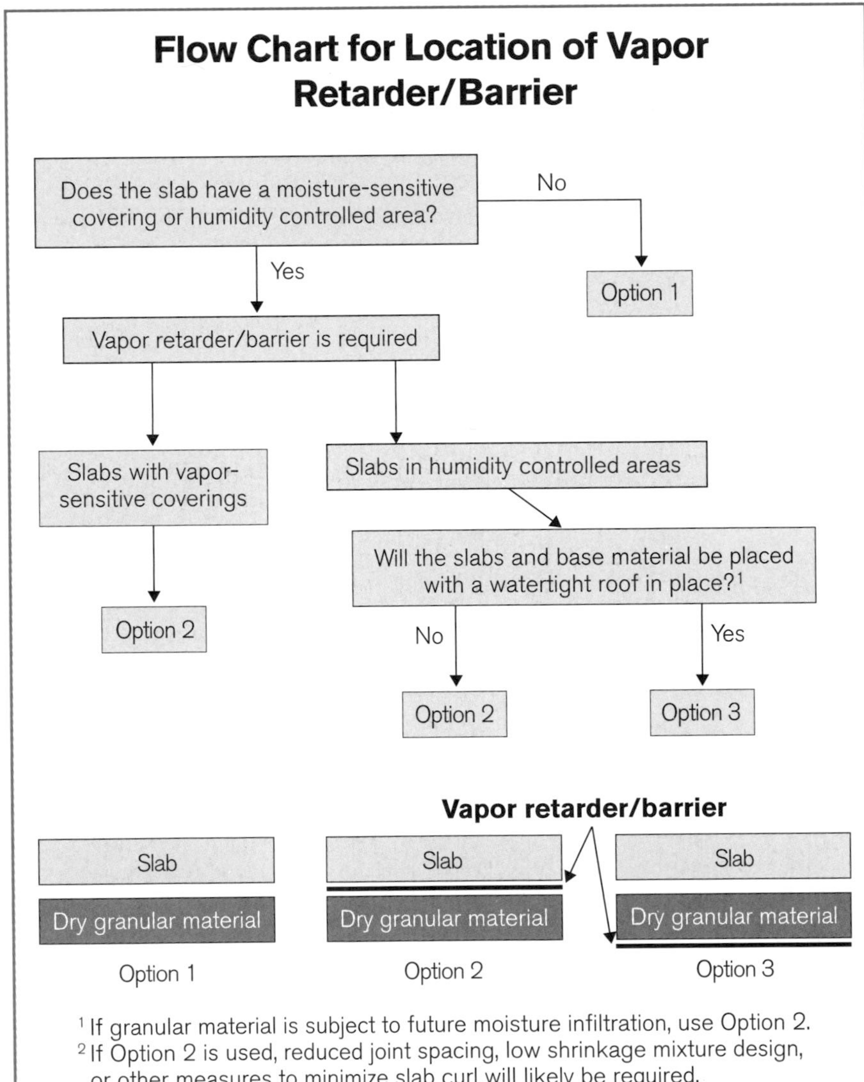

Source: Chart adapted from ACI 302. Courtesy of the American Concrete Institute.

The debate over vapor retarders will not be resolved overnight. However, with the cost of floor coverings over concrete slabs now estimated at more than a billion dollars a year in the United States, far greater attention must be given to the issue of moisture within and below concrete slabs-on-grade.

Peter Craig is a principal with Concrete Constructives and a member of ACI Committee 302, Construction of Concrete Floors. Photos by the author except where noted.

Special thanks to Herman G. Protze, Dennis Pinelle, and Ned Lyon for their review and comments.

Waterproofing Options for Basement Walls

by David Frane

As one manufacturer of waterproofing systems put it, most builders paint the foundation black and move on. He was referring to builders who do the minimum required by code, which is dampproofing the walls. However, dampproofing a foundation won't necessarily keep the water out. Residential codes don't require dampproofing to meet any performance standards. The only requirement is that it be some kind of bituminous (asphalt) coating.

Waterproofing vs. Dampproofing

Dampproofing can stop water vapor but won't bridge cracks or resist water pressure. Waterproof membranes are designed to be flexible, so they can span small cracks and resist static pressure. Most waterproofing systems are intended for use on block and poured concrete walls, but some also work on foundations made from pressure-treated wood or insulating concrete forms (ICFs).

It's cheaper to dampproof a basement than to waterproof it. The typical installed cost for dampproofing the walls of a 30x40-foot foundation is about $300. But it would cost around $1,200, or $1.25 per square foot of wall, to waterproof the same basement.

It's hard to fault a spec builder for going with a cheaper product when there's no guarantee a customer will pay more to get something better. On the other hand, cheap products aren't so cheap if they lead to callbacks. And the recent wave of lawsuits over toxic mold has given builders an added incentive to do whatever it takes to avoid moisture problems. According to one manufacturer, about 25% of new houses with basements now get waterproofing.

A waterproof membrane is part of a bigger system. Foundation coatings are designed to work in conjunction with footing drains, gutters and downspouts, and proper grading (see Chapter 1: Drainage). The idea is to keep water away from the foundation. Any water that does reach it should be prevented from entering until it can drain away **(Figure 9)**.

Figure 9. Waterproofing products are intended for use with a properly installed foundation perimeter drain.

Liquid Membranes

Most waterproofing systems rely on liquid coatings that dry to form seamless membranes. Materials come in different grades for different application methods. Most waterproofing is sprayed on, but you can use a roller, brush, or trowel. Liquid membranes are popular because they go on quickly and easily.

These products won't work if they aren't installed properly, however. Every manufacturer has specific requirements for filling rod holes and cracks, and for precoating or creating fillets at inside corners. Each coating must be applied to a specified thickness, usually 40 to 60 mils. (By way of comparison, a dime is about 40 mils thick; dampproof coatings are typically about 10 mils thick.) The actual thickness of the membrane depends on the skill of the applicator and the number of coats applied. Unskilled applicators apply material unevenly, which leaves thin spots in the membrane.

Most contractors sub out this work to companies that specialize in waterproofing. Some products require specialized application equipment, and most aren't covered by warranty unless the work is done by a certified applicator.

Figure 10. Water-based asphalt emulsion coatings are far less toxic than solvent-based formulations but must be protected from freezing during application.

Modified-Asphalt Coatings

Dampproofing is made from unmodified asphalt, which is not elastic enough to bridge the hairline cracks that develop in foundations as they dry. Also, pure asphalt tends to dry out and get brittle with age.

Asphalt-based waterproofing, on the other hand, contains rubber or rubberlike additives that increase initial elasticity and prevent it from drying out over time.

Modified-asphalt formulations typically contain solvents such as xylene, toluolene, or mineral spirits. This allows them to be applied over a wide range of temperatures, even well below freezing. But it also means they produce fumes and tend to be flammable and toxic until they dry. Modified asphalt should not be used on green concrete, and you can't use it on ICFs because the solvents will dissolve the foam.

Mar-flex 5000 (Mar-flex Waterproofing and Basement Products) is a modified asphalt that has a 24-hour cure time and can be applied anywhere between 0°F and 150°F. Another modified-asphalt option is #229 AR-Elastomeric (Karnak Corp.), a single-component rubber-reinforced asphalt.

Asphalt emulsions. Asphalt emulsions are water-based versions of the more traditional modified-asphalt coatings (**Figure 10**). Most asphalt emulsions can be applied to green or damp concrete, which makes it easier to schedule the job. These materials aren't flammable, produce little in the way of fumes, and can be cleaned up with water. They're usually compatible with ICF foundations because they don't contain the kind of solvents that dissolve foam insulation.

But asphalt emulsions aren't perfect. They take a long time to dry when it's cold and can get washed off the wall if it rains before the membrane has set. Water-based coatings should be protected from freezing before application and can't be applied at the same low temperatures as modified asphalt. Typically, you can't apply an emulsion below 20°F, or, in many cases, 40°F.

A large number of companies produce asphalt emulsion waterproofing material. Some of the better-known products are Tuff-N-Dri and Watchdog (Tremco Barrier Solutions), W.R. Meadows' Meadow-Pruf Seamless (W.R. Meadows), Ecobase (Epro Waterproofing Systems), and TruDry (HouseGuard).

Nonasphalt coatings. Some liquid waterproofing membranes contain little or no asphalt. Modified asphalt might be 20% rubber, but these nonasphalt coatings contain a much higher proportion of rubber or other polymers (**Figure 11**). It's hard to generalize about this category, because it covers such a wide range of materials, but typically these coatings are described as urethane, polyurethane, or rubber. These materials produce some of the most flexible membranes you can get. But many of them break down in sunlight, so it's often recommended that you backfill within two or three weeks of application. In most cases, they should not be applied to green or wet concrete.

Among the better-known rubber coatings are Rub-R-Wall and Graywall (Rubber Polymer Corp.). Grace Construction Products makes Procor, a two-part synthetic rubber that can be applied to green concrete. Two of the better-known polyurethane products are Tremproof 60 (Tremco Global Sealants) and Duramem 500 (Pecora Corp.).

Sheet Membranes

Sheet membrane — or peel-and-stick, as it's often called — is about 60 mils thick and comes in rolls

Figure 11. Rubber membranes, like Rub-R-Wall, shown here, are extremely flexible, so they can withstand shrinkage cracking in concrete better than other types of membrane.

Figure 12. Sheet membranes, like Grace's Bituthene, shown here, apply like peel-and-stick eaves membranes. Inside corners are first coped with proprietary sealants (left), then the membrane is pressed into place (center). Most sheet membranes are around 60 mils thick, or about one and a half times as thick as a dime (right).

about 3 feet wide (**Figure 12**). It's made by bonding a layer of rubberized asphalt to a cross-laminated sheet of polyethylene. Installing sheet membrane is kind of like hanging wallpaper. But instead of using paste, you peel off the release sheet and press the sticky inner face onto the foundation.

Adjoining sheets overlap by about 2 inches. Running a roller over the joints seals the seams. Some brands have an additional strip of adhesive along the edge of the outer face to create extra adhesion at the laps. In order to ensure a continuous bond, masonry walls should be primed before the membrane is applied. A good bond helps limit the amount of water that can enter through punctures by preventing water from migrating behind the sheet.

The big advantage of sheet membranes is that they'll stand up to an enormous amount of static pressure. And unlike spray-applied materials, you can be certain there aren't any thin spots. On the other hand, it takes more time and skill to apply sheet material than to spray it on with a gun. As a result, the installed cost of sheet membranes is much higher than liquid membranes.

Sheet membranes are more common on commercial projects. It's easier to justify an expensive waterproofing job when you're building a multistory building or one that goes 50 feet underground. House foundations rarely go that deep, and most residential builders avoid sites that have high water tables.

The best-known sheet membrane is Bituthene, made by Grace Construction Products. Comparable products include Mel-Rol (W.R. Meadows), Duramem 700-SM (Pecora Corp.), and SubSeal (MFM Building Products).

Insulation, drain board, and protection board. Waterproof membranes are frequently used in conjunction with drain board, protection board, or rigid insulation (**Figure 13**). Sometimes the board is added on to improve the performance of the membrane, but often the board is an integral part of the water-

Figure 13. Protective insulation and drainage boards are often incorporated into foundation waterproofing systems. Shown here are Tremco's Tuff-N-Dri (far left), which includes a foundation board from Owens Corning; and HouseGuard's TruDry (left), which uses a Dow Styrofoam insulation and drainage board.

proofing system. Many liquid membranes are designed to remain tacky so insulation and protection boards will stick. Tougher versions of these products are often available for use without added board.

Foundations can be insulated by gluing rigid foam insulation to the outside of the wall. In addition to lowering energy costs, insulation prevents the membrane from being damaged by backfill.

Drainboard performs the same protective function as insulation board and also speeds the movement of water into footing drains. It comes in many shapes and sizes and is made from a variety of materials. Hydroduct (Grace Construction Products) has an expanded polystyrene core that's bonded to a sheet of filter fabric. Water passes through the fabric and drains down through the hollow core. Enkadrain is a similar product manufactured by Colbond Geosynthetics.

Owens Corning makes Warm-N-Dri, the rigid fiberglass board that's used in Full System Tuff-N-Dri, marketed by Tremco. Installed over the membrane, the rigid fiberglass drains and insulates at the same time. Mar-flex uses similar insulating drain panels in its Mar-flex 5000 system.

Figure 14. Air-gap membranes, like Cosella-Dörken's Delta-MS (left) and System Platon (below), have raised dimples that allow any water that gets past the membrane to fall to the footing drain.

ThermaDry insulating drainage panels (TClear Corp.) consist of a grooved extruded polystyrene core bonded to filter fabric. The foam insulates, and the fabric allows the water to pass into the grooves and fall into the drain.

Air-Gap Membranes

Air-gap membranes have been used in Europe for 30 years but are relatively new to the North American market (**Figure 14**). Instead of coating the foundation with a waterproof membrane, you use a dimpled sheet of high-density polyethylene to create a small air space between the foundation and the backfill. Any water that gets into that space is supposed to fall to the footing drain before it has time to soak into the wall (see "Installing Air-Gap Membranes," page 9).

Two companies sell these products in the U.S. Cosella-Dörken makes Delta-MS, and Armtec makes System Platon. Both materials come in rolls and are installed in long continuous sheets. Delta-MS is nailed directly to the wall, and vertical seams are caulked with sealant. To keep dirt from getting in and clogging the air gap, the top edge of the sheet is covered with a nail-on molding strip. It takes fewer nails to fasten Platon because it's fastened to the building with metal clips. No caulk is used at the vertical laps, but the top edge is caulked to keep the dirt out.

Air-gap membranes can be installed over liquid membranes, but the manufacturers claim that you get a drier basement if you skip the coating. A poured foundation takes about three years to dry out, and the moisture has to go somewhere. Makers claim that with a traditional membrane, moisture goes into the building. If an air-gap membrane is used, the moisture is said to move outward until it hits the back of the dimpled sheet membrane, condenses, and falls to the drain.

The materials for an air-gap membrane cost about 40¢ per square foot; installed price is about 80¢ per square foot. These membranes can be installed over green or wet concrete and will bridge any nonstructural crack. The only downside to an air-gap system is that it's absolutely dependent on a properly functioning footing drain. That said, remember that every waterproofing system is designed to work with a drain.

Bentonite

Bentonite is a clay-based waterproofing material that's used as the basic ingredient in cat litter. For waterproofing purposes, it's formed into thin sheets by sandwiching it between layers of Kraft paper, filter fabric, or polyethylene. You install the material by nailing or gluing it to the wall.

Bentonite doesn't do much of anything until it gets wet, at which point it swells to 15 times its dry volume and fills nearby cracks and voids. Once the material reaches maximum volume, it remains that size and forms a permanent barrier to water. Such membranes are self-healing and can be installed at any temperature.

But bentonite is expensive and can be ruined if it gets wet before the foundation is backfilled. Architects sometimes specify it for residential projects, but it's more common in commercial construction.

Cementitious Waterproofing

These portland cement–based materials are mixed in the field and applied by brush. In the past, you mixed the dry material with water, but these days many take acrylic additives. One of the best things about cementitious waterproofing is that you can buy it anywhere. It also sticks well and is easy to apply.

The problem with cementitious coatings is that they don't stretch much. The specs for most membranes contain a rating for elongation, which is a measurement of how much they will stretch before they fail. Most liquid waterproofings have elongations between 500% and 1800%. Sheet membranes spec out between 300% and 500%. Cementitious coatings are not nearly as flexible. For example, Thoroseal 551 (BASF Building Systems) has an elongation rating of 20%, and the specs for the widely used Thoroseal Foundation Coating don't even list elongation.

Waterproofing Warranties

Warranty periods for waterproofing run between five years and the lifetime of the building. A longer warranty may sound better, but it's worth reading the fine print to check the ifs, ands, and buts. For example, a number of manufacturers mentioned that leaks and dampness can lead to toxic mold, but every warranty I looked at specifically excludes coverage for damage caused by that problem.

Most companies say that if there's a leak, they'll excavate the affected area and reapply the coating. Some agree to repair damage caused by the leak but limit the cost of repairs to $2,500. A few will go as high as $10,000. They all promise to backfill the trench when they finish patching the leak, but they won't replace lawn or landscaping that's damaged in the process. And all bets are off if the leak was caused by improper backfilling, a nonfunctioning footing drain, or a crack that's more than 1/16 inch across.

David Frane is a senior editor at The Journal of Light Construction.

Waterproofing ICF Foundations

by Todd LaBarge

Whenever possible, I persuade my customers to use insulating concrete forms (ICFs) for their foundations — particularly if they intend to use the basement as a finished living space. I like ICFs because they can be assembled by the on-site crew, there are no heavy forms to haul and set, and rebar is easy to place. ICFs also have a high built-in insulating value and, unlike retrofitted rigid foam board, they align with the framing above.

Membrane System

As with a conventional basement foundation, ICFs must be waterproofed below grade. Because of the joints between the blocks, foam forms alone won't prevent water penetration. In the past, I've used Tuff-N-Dri (Tremco Barrier Solutions), a dealer-applied spray-on elastomeric coating that cures very quickly. But I wasn't completely happy with the coverage, and wanted to control the waterproofing process myself. So, on a recent job, I decided to install a sheet membrane waterproofing system over the ICFs, figuring that it would block water as well as act as a barrier to termites and carpenter ants. To get into the foam, the bugs would have to chew through the waterproofing membrane first, a serious obstacle for any pest.

For this job, I chose the MiraDrain 860 sheet membrane waterproofing system (Carlisle Coatings & Waterproofing), a 56-mil self-adhesive rubberized asphalt membrane with a 4-mil poly facing. The system includes the sheet membrane, installed over primer, which is optional on rigid foam, a couple of proprietary mastic fillers and termination sealants, and transition flashing "tapes." Part of a family of coatings and sealants compatible with rigid foam, this membrane system would enable me to seal even the smallest gaps. Believe it or not, termites can find their way into a building at this joint, so sealing between the concrete footings and the base of the foundation wall is a real benefit.

Dual-Purpose Footing Forms

An important part of any foundation waterproofing strategy is a perimeter footing drain, which ensures that any entering water gets safely carried off to daylight or to a drywell. Rather than use round perforated drain tile, I like to form the footings with stay-in-place Form-A-Drain components (CertainTeed Corp.). These lightweight perforated vinyl forms install easily and do double duty as a permanent perimeter drain. After pouring the footings, we steel-trowel the concrete to ensure a smooth surface for the membrane.

Prepping the Corners

It's difficult to force the membrane into a sharp 90° corner without leaving unsupported voids behind it. Since any unsupported areas might rupture from backfill pressure, the first step in applying the membrane is to form a 3/4-inch cant strip, or fillet, by applying sealant at vertical wall junctions and at the footing. This eases the 90° transition for the membrane and seals the most vulnerable part of the wall against leaks (**Figure 15**). The manufacturer gives the option of forming a 1 1/2-inch concrete cant to ease the transition, but I chose the sealant because I thought it would be more leakproof and easier to apply. The sealant is a trowel-consistency two-component polyurethane that is mixed on site with a paddle chucked in a drill. Each one-gallon container must be mixed and used all at once; you can't save unused material or mix partial batches. We applied the sealant with putty knives and tooled it with a rounded mason's trowel to form the fillet. This method worked well enough, but a bulk caulking gun would probably be faster and waste less material.

Priming for Better Adhesion

According to the manufacturer, the membrane can be applied to fresh, clean rigid foam without priming, unlike concrete, which must always be primed first. But because the surface of foam blocks becomes dusty with prolonged exposure to sunlight, it seemed like a good idea to prep the ICFs to ensure a good bond. After a light wire-brushing to remove the dust, we used a roller to coat the foam and the exposed concrete of the footing with water-based Carlisle primer. On the first pass, we neglected to brush out

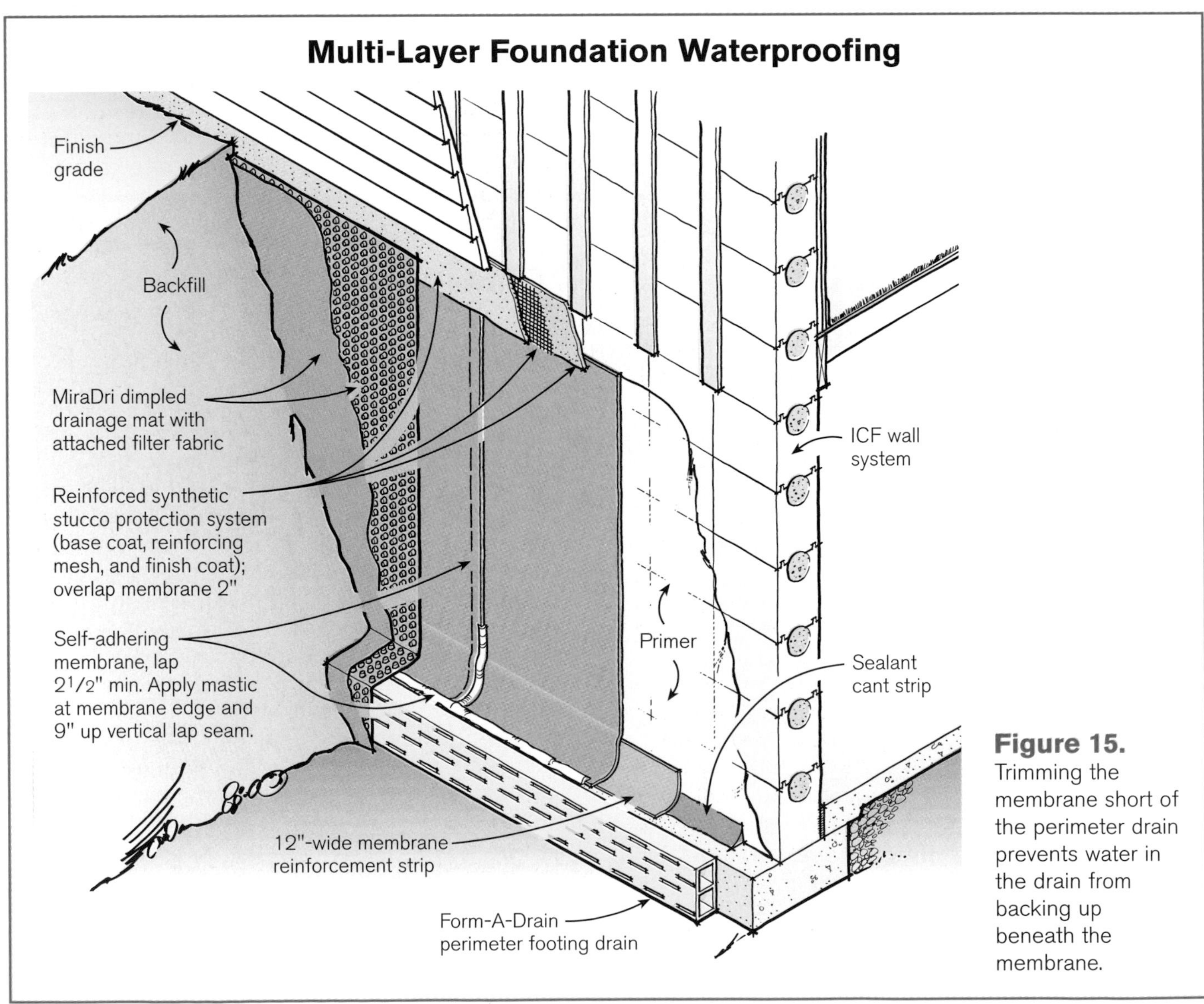

Figure 15. Trimming the membrane short of the perimeter drain prevents water in the drain from backing up beneath the membrane.

Figure 16. Twelve-inch-wide membrane strips reinforce vulnerable corner transitions and ensure a good bond over the cant strip.

the accumulated primer that dripped onto the footing from the roller. These spots didn't dry as quickly, and since the membrane wouldn't stick to the wet primer, we had to back up and brush out the excess, then wait for it to dry. After this, we made sure to brush out all of the drips after rolling each section.

Having applied a similar membrane to concrete before, I found that the primer really improved adhesion. The primer is considered cured when it's dry to the touch, but the open time is only about 12 hours, so it's best to coat only what you can cover with membrane in the same day. If there's any problem, though, you can always recoat.

Reinforced Corners

The installation instructions call for cutting lengths of membrane into 12-inch-wide by 3-foot-long strips. After the sealant fillet has cured (about 24 hours), these strips are applied to the wall-to-footing and wall-to-wall intersections, 6 inches on either side, around the entire foundation perimeter (**Figure 16**). The strips ensure a good bond for the membrane over the fillet and reinforce the corners. We primed an area of wall and footing to be covered that day and let it dry. Then we worked the reinforcement strip from the wall onto the sealant and out over the footing. To ensure a good bond, we overlapped the ends of the strips 2 1/2 inches, and rolled them down with a 2-inch-diameter rubber roller. For this phase of the job, the foundation perimeter measured about 203 linear feet, and it took two people about three days to complete.

Applying the Membrane

The next step was to apply the full-height sheets of membrane to the wall, from about 6 inches below finish grade to 2 inches beyond the edge of the footing. This would later be coated with stucco. Whenever possible, we tried to work on the shady side of the building, to keep the sun off the black membrane. Whenever a sheet heats up, it tends to soften and stick to itself, making it nearly impossible to separate.

The easiest way to apply the 8-foot-tall sheets was to work in teams. One person would attach the first 12 inches of the membrane to the upper wall and hold it there, while a helper peeled away the protective paper backing and smoothed the sheet down the wall and over the footing. The long edge of the membrane is premarked on the outside face with a yellow guideline for a 2 1/2-inch overlap, and it has a plastic release strip that covers a 1/2-inch-wide sticky edge. With the first sheet in place, we attached the next sheet like the first one, beginning at the top and aligned with the yellow line. After peeling the paper and bonding the membrane to the wall, we lifted the long edge and removed the release strip. Using a rubber seam roller on the overlap ensured a firm bond between sheets.

We trimmed the excess just short of the inner edge of the Form-A-Drain to make sure that groundwater couldn't come up behind the drain and get under the membrane.

Applying the membrane to the inside corners was pretty tricky: Not only does the membrane have to be folded into the corner but also out over the footing in two directions. After first completely removing the paper backing and then folding the sheet lengthwise, sticky face out, two of us worked the membrane out from the corner onto the wall and footing. An

Figure 17. Where the membrane meets a door or window buck, special flashing tape (not yet installed in photo) seals the transition into the opening.

Figure 18. Membrane overlaps are pressure-bonded using a hand roller, then treated from bottom to top with proprietary sealant. Horizontal membrane terminations are caulked with mastic to complete the barrier system.

unbacked sheet tends to flop around and stick to itself, so we lost a couple of lengths before we got the hang of it.

Sealing Details

The foundation on this job included a 6-foot slider. The opening was formed with pressure-treated 2x10s, which remained in place after the concrete cured to serve as nailing backers (**Figure 17**, previous page). To seal the edges of the opening, I applied a Carlisle through-wall flashing tape (a 32-mil version of the membrane) over the face of the 2x10 and folded it out onto the wall membrane to seal the opening. The vinyl flange on the door unit was then spread over this flashing layer, with a second layer of flashing tape on top to seal the fins to the wall.

After all the sheets were bonded, we sealed the edges with system mastic, using a quart-size caulking gun. Mastic is required at the horizontal top and bottom terminations, as well as 9 inches up the vertical seams from the footing. To be safe, we ran it continuously from bottom to top (**Figure 18**). It's extremely important to make sure the seam overlap bonds tightly, never depending on the mastic alone for the seal.

To seal around electrical service penetrations, I made an X-shaped incision in the membrane covering the holes and folded back the flaps. Then I ran PVC conduit sleeves through from the inside, troweled sealant into the voids around the conduit, and stuck the membrane flaps to the conduit on the outside. I wrapped a 6-inch-wide "wristband" of membrane over these and caulked the remaining gaps and membrane edges with the seam sealant. To guard against water entering through the conduit itself, I made sure to pitch it to drain, and packed more sealant around the electrical cables for good measure. We brought water lines in later, and thoroughly packed them in with sealant on both sides of the wall (**Figure 19**).

Positive Drainage

To complete the system, I installed MiraDri (Carlisle Coatings & Waterproofing), a flexible plastic dimple sheet with an attached ground-filter fabric (see "Installing Air-Gap Membranes," page 9). MiraDri forms the primary water barrier by directing groundwater down the wall to the Form-A-Drain, and protects

Figure 19. Water lines, drilled through the wall at a later date, are sealed with two-component urethane adhesive sealant, which cures to form a tough, elastic plug.

Figure 20. To direct groundwater to the perimeter drain and protect the membrane from impact during backfill, fabric-filtered drainage mat is applied over the membrane.

Figure 21. Backfill pressure holds the drainage mat firmly in place. Stucco protects the exposed portion of the ICF foundation and covers the upper edge of the membrane.

Figure 22. Using a stainless steel trowel prevents rust stains in the stucco.

the membrane from impact during backfill. The membrane manufacturer requires MiraDri or a similar drainage mat over the membrane. We installed the MiraDri over the membrane just below finish grade, extending down the wall and out over the perimeter drain (**Figure 20**). The installation instructions direct you to bond the MiraDri to the membrane using contact cement, but I wasn't thrilled with the results — in the end, I just held the dimple sheet in place with the backfill and temporary wood braces.

I worked with the excavator during the backfill operation, making sure that the dimple sheet stayed tight against the wall, and fishing out roots, branches, and large stones from the backfill to prevent damage.

Above-Grade Protection

The above-grade portion of an ICF foundation needs to be protected from physical impact and UV degradation. I used Coraflex (Sealoflex Waterproofing Systems), a reinforced synthetic stucco system with an elastomeric top coat, made for EIFS applications. I applied the stucco before installing the siding to make the process as simple as possible and to eliminate the need to protect the siding.

Base coat. We shoveled excess backfill away from the foundation, exposing the top 12 inches of the foundation and the upper edge of the membrane. After roughing up the surface of the foam and taking out any irregularities with a rasp, we formed the base coat using Corabase Onepack, which comes dry in 50-pound bags and is mixed with water to a trowel consistency. With one person mixing and two people using 1/4-inch-square notched stainless steel trowels, we coated one 3x10-foot section of the wall at a time. While the base coat was wet, we embedded reinforcing fabric mesh, making sure to press it thoroughly into the compound. Each embedded section overlapped the previous one by at least 2 inches to ensure continuity of the reinforcement.

We also extended the base coat about 2 inches over the Carlisle membrane (**Figure 21**). The base coat adhered firmly to the membrane, adding redundant protection to the upper membrane edge.

Finish coat. After the base coat cured for 24 hours, we applied Coraflex, a premixed colorized elastomeric top coat containing a fine aggregate for texture. To prevent rust stains, we used a stainless steel trowel (**Figure 22**). To apply the top coat, pull the material as thin as the aggregate size permits without dragging (about 1/8 inch thick), and catch the waste with a hock for redistribution. The result is a hard, protective, attractive surface that will remain impervious to water and resistant to pests for years to come.

Todd LaBarge is a residential contractor and structural engineer in Harwich, Mass.

Chapter 3: Crawlspaces

Building a Sealed Crawlspace

by Jeff Tooley

Recent research provides plenty of evidence that vents for crawlspaces don't work, and that sealed and conditioned crawlspaces are a better choice. But my business, the Healthy Building Company, is the first I know of to specialize in applying that science in the field. We've been sealing up crawlspaces in houses with moisture and mold problems for years, and we're taking on an increasing volume of work building dry crawlspaces for new homes.

We've developed a set of simple, effective, and repeatable methods that produce predictable results. I describe our system here, as well as how we deal with various obstacles that may crop up along the way.

In general, our installations have four phases. The first is the builder's job: Waterproof the foundation and install good foundation drains. Next, we come in and apply poly and rigid foam insulation to the foundation walls. As soon as there's a roof on so that rain won't get into the crawlspace, we come back a second time and put down a sacrificial layer of poly to keep the ground vapor out for as long as it takes to finish the house. Then, in the final two weeks of the job, we come back to take out this temporary "construction poly" and install a permanent version, carefully sealing all seams and securing it to the ground. At the same time, we also install a quiet ventilation fan that runs continuously to provide the newly sealed space with a steady supply of conditioned air.

Figure 1. Perimeter drains around the foundation footing are necessary to prevent groundwater from rising above the crawlspace's poly vapor barrier or penetrating its mastic-sealed seams.

Managing Bulk Water

My vapor barriers are sealed with mastic, and they're watertight and airtight as well as vapor-tight. But I don't intend for them to cope with pressure from groundwater. Since I work as a sub on the job, I hold the builder totally responsible for managing bulk water. I tell him that if he lets groundwater come up

Figure 2. Managing bulk water is essential for success in a sealed crawlspace. The author ties a backwater valve (detail, right) into the foundation drain system at the low spot in the crawlspace, so that any water from a plumbing leak will be able to drain out through the perimeter drain.

under my poly, presenting the risk of flooding the crawlspace, I won't guarantee the results. Our mastic joints are very tough, but they can fail under pressure. One good rip in the poly, and bulk water intrusion could completely bypass our vapor barrier.

So I need to see waterproofing, or at least dampproofing, on the foundation walls starting at the finish grade and extending down to the footing. I want a perimeter drain at the level of the footing, sloped to one corner of the building (**Figure 1**). An exterior footing drain is the minimum; even better is to have drains on both sides of the footing, connected across the footing at the low corner.

The crawlspace floor is also sloped to that low corner, so that if a pipe breaks and floods the space, water will drain that way on our poly. To provide the water with an escape route, we install a backwater valve in that low corner (**Figure 2**). The valve is connected to the perimeter drains; when we later install the final poly, we cover the inlet with a grate that's sealed to the poly with mastic. When the crawlspace is dry, the valve stays closed and keeps the groundwater out. But if water collects in the corner of the crawlspace, the valve flapper opens and allows the water to drain out through the footing drain. You can get these from your local plumbing supply or from D.A. Fehr, a distributor of plumbing supplies. The crawlspace floor isn't usually graded perfectly smooth. In the event of a flood caused by a plumbing leak, little dips and hollows might collect puddles, but that much water can evaporate out without wrecking our crawlspace. What we're trying to avoid is 10 inches of standing water, and this setup does it.

Complete dampproofing. At the time this was written, the North Carolina code called for dampproofing only where the exterior grade is higher than the interior crawlspace floor. This means that if I have a 4-foot block wall with 2 feet of earth inside it and 3 feet backfilled against the outside, dampproofing is required only on the 1-foot portion where the exterior

Figure 3. The author brushes mastic onto the block wall (left), then applies 6-mil black poly (below, left and right). Mastic creates a strong adhesive seal on many different materials, even if the surfaces are dirty.

Figure 4. The author attaches foam board to the foundation wall using powder-actuated nails (five nails per piece of foam). Although some building departments have required foil-faced polyisocyanurate foam (left), he generally uses extruded polystyrene (right). Either way, the R-10 foundation insulation meets the energy code without the need to insulate floor cavities with fiberglass. But air sealing and vapor sealing, not insulation, are the main reasons sealed crawlspaces reduce the load on the HVAC system.

soil is higher than the interior soil, not all the way to the footing. This seems to assume that water won't come through a block wall if there is soil on the other side. I don't see anything to prevent it, so I say use the belt and the suspenders: Coat the foundation all the way to the footing, and install drains inside and out.

Wall Poly and Insulation

Once the builder has the foundation wall built and the drainage installed, I install the poly and foam on the inside face of the wall. We attach the 6-mil black plastic to the wall with a water-based adhesive mastic (**Figure 3**, previous page), then fasten the foam board over it with powder-driven masonry nails (**Figure 4**). The wall poly extends onto the ground about a foot, leaving an edge flap for us to seal the floor poly to later.

Figure 5. The author carefully fits poly around a pipe that runs through the foundation wall, then seals the poly to the pipe with mastic. All penetrations through the crawlspace wall must be sealed.

No batts in the floor. Under the energy code, insulating the foundation to R-10 means we don't have to insulate the floor under the living space. We get rid of the usual fiberglass batts in the joist bays, where their performance is hindered anyway by air movement, poor fit, and interruption by wires, pipes, and bridging. Instead, we locate the thermal boundary of the house with the air-pressure boundary, where it should be. People concerned about indoor air quality are glad to see the fiberglass go, because it means no irritating fibers will be floating around to get sucked into the ductwork.

Side-wall penetrations. Where pipes or wires go through the side wall, we have to fit the foam board to them carefully and seal the vapor barrier around them (**Figure 5**). I'm working right now on a lot of houses with package heat-pump units, which add another large penetration for us to fuss with.

Detailing the duct penetration is just patchwork. Where the builder runs flex duct from the unit through the wall, we have to cut a half circle on one piece of foam board and a half circle on the other, then piece them together around the duct and seal the joint.

We use a water-based, nontoxic duct-sealing mastic called PS-1 (RCD Corp.) for all our sealing work because it is so effective. It sticks to all kinds of materials, rough or smooth, and even to dirty surfaces. It dries in hours and is tough and strong; once a mastic joint in poly sets up fully, two men can't pull it apart with all their strength.

Sealing the Floor

We install our sacrificial floor poly as soon as the house is dried in. Once the house is enclosed, vapor that enters the crawlspace will start to accumulate, so delaying this step can spell big trouble.

For example, I was called by a builder who wanted me to seal up his crawlspace, but it soon became clear that he had built his foundation almost a year earlier with no vents, ground vapor barrier, or wall poly. "What's it like down there now?" I asked him. "I don't know," he said. "I haven't looked."

A lot of bad things can happen in 10 months in a sealed crawlspace with no vapor barrier and no conditioned air supply — and in this case, they had. When I took a look, I found the floor joists covered in a thick fur of white fungus filaments. It wasn't mold, but the kind of rot you find under dead trees in the woods. This type of decay can seriously weaken wood before it's even visible. The necessary fix might go well beyond a simple cleanup.

Mold will grow on surfaces at 70% relative humidity, but wood rot means that the framing was saturated from long exposure to 90% or higher relative humidity. Vented crawlspaces don't usually get that damp, but an unvented one with no ground cover can. That's why it is so crucial to get your construction poly in place at the earliest possible moment. Without it, your whole project is at risk.

Installing the sacrificial poly. We place temporary ground poly as soon as there is tar paper on the roof. We lay the sheet out to completely cover the floor area but don't seal the seams. We use the same poly for the temporary cover as for the permanent installation — it's just the 6-mil all-purpose black plastic sheeting that you can pick up at any building supply outlet in 50-foot or 100-foot rolls, in widths of 15, 20, or 24 feet.

Drying the framing. The temporary ground cover prevents soil moisture from evaporating into the crawlspace. But by the time the poly goes down, the floor framing may already have absorbed quite a bit of moisture from the soil beneath and from rain falling on the still unroofed structure. To promote rapid drying, we temporarily install a small dehumidifier in the crawlspace at the same time we install the poly. So we don't have to count on anyone remembering to dump the reservoir, we rig the drain tube to discharge outside the crawlspace.

Dehumidifiers are rated on the basis of cubic footage, and most crawlspaces are low enough in volume to make a large unit unnecessary. We use a 25-pint model made by Whirlpool for most of our houses. The dehumidifier stays in place until we remove the sacrificial poly and replace it with the permanent, sealed ground covering — anywhere from a few weeks to several months, depending on the construction schedule.

Permanent floor covering. A week or two before the house is ready for the owners to move in, we take out the temporary poly and put down a nice, clean final floor.

By this time, the construction poly has generally been damaged and disturbed by the mechanical subs and other people who have been working in the space. I suppose we could just cover it up with the new poly, but it's better to take it out because it's almost always sprinkled with chunks of wood, sawdust, cardboard, and other scraps. We just bundle all that termite bait into the poly and haul the whole mess out. It's a quick cleanup.

Lapping and sealing. Next, we place the new permanent poly floor covering, sealing the seams at the wall

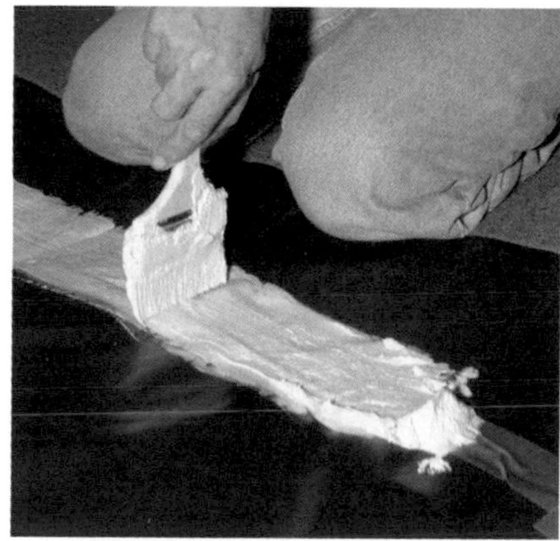

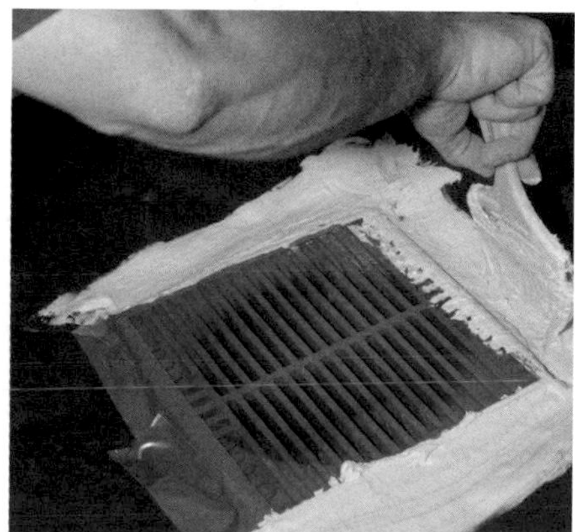

Figure 6. After removing the temporary poly, the author rolls out a new layer of 6-mil poly, carefully sealing the seams with duct tape and mastic (left). He also makes a duct-tape-and-mastic seal where the poly laps up onto piers (center) and around the grate that covers the backwater-valve floor drain (right).

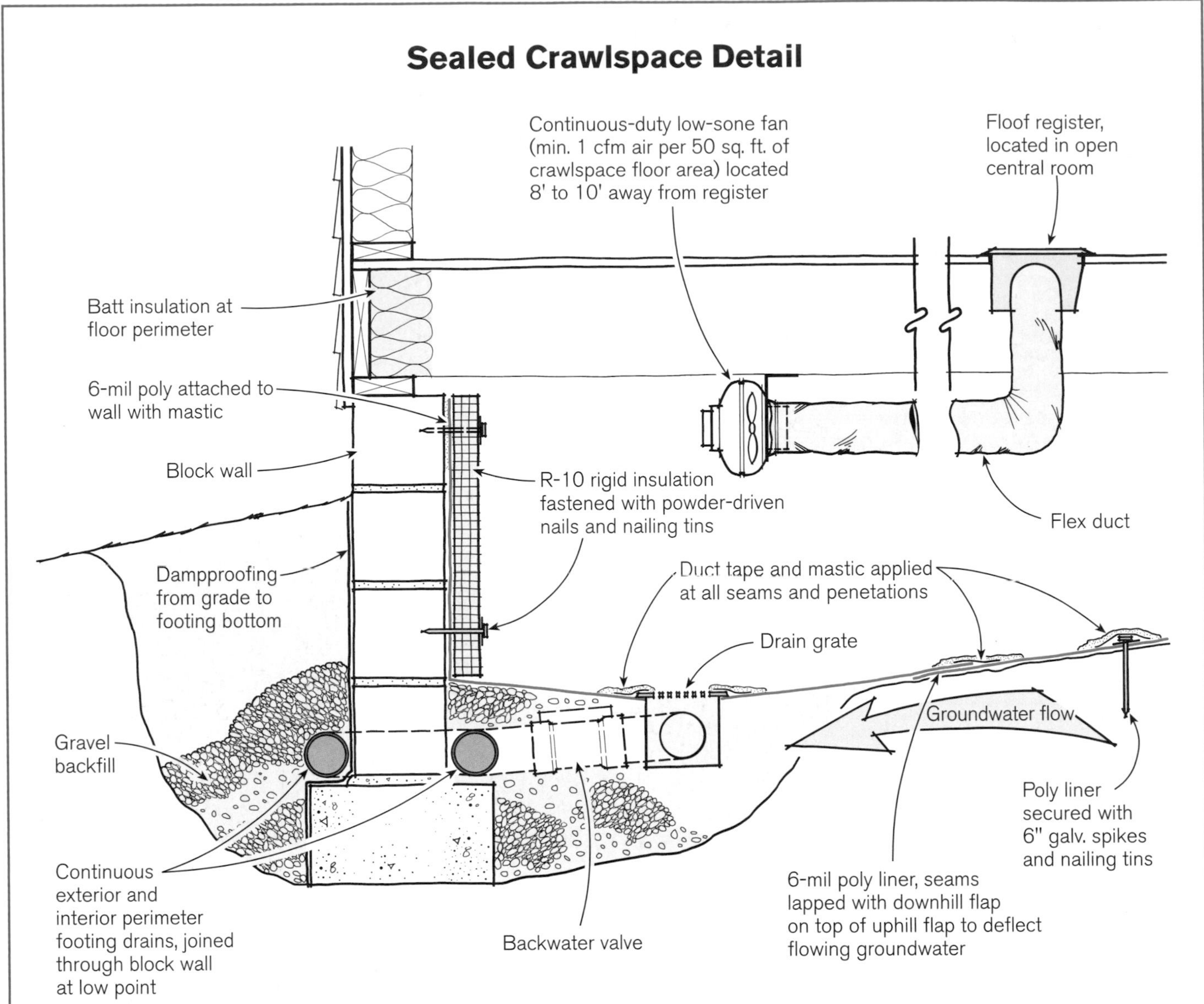

Figure 7. The components of a sealed crawlspace must address the issues of bulk water, air sealing, vapor sealing, and thermal insulation. Dampproofing and perimeter drains are necessary, because the poly ground cover is not designed to handle constant water contact. The author prefers drains both inside and outside the footing, joined at the low point. He ties a floor grate into the interior footing drain and protects the link with a backflow preventer valve. Floor poly is lapped reverse-shingle fashion to direct water flowing in the soil beneath the plastic. For maximum resistance to air and vapor infiltration, seams in the poly and at penetrations are sealed with mastic. R-10 insulation is placed at the foundation wall, aligning the air, vapor, and thermal boundaries of the space in the same plane. Finally, the fan ventilates the space with conditioned house air.

poly with duct tape and mastic, and also sealing every joint in the field (**Figure 6**, previous page). Each joint is secured with duct tape that is then coated with a brushed-on layer of mastic. The stripe of mastic extends at least an inch beyond the tape on each side.

It matters how you lap the poly at joints: You need to create a shingle effect to handle flowing water, but you're shingling upside down. You're placing poly on a slope, and water will run down the ground surface beneath the poly. If you lap the joint one way, it will allow the water to flow past, but if you lap it the other way, the lap will scoop water and hold it against the seam, threatening your mastic seal (**Figure 7**). It's a small thing that matters — mastic handles incidental water beautifully, but like any material, it may not perform so well if you let it get continuously soaked.

Floor spikes. To make sure the ground cover lasts and stays put, we nail the poly to the underlying soil with 6-inch spikes and washers (**Figure 8**). We use a lot of spikes — 5 to 10 per 100 square feet of poly — but it's well worth the time and effort. Imagine a worker in the

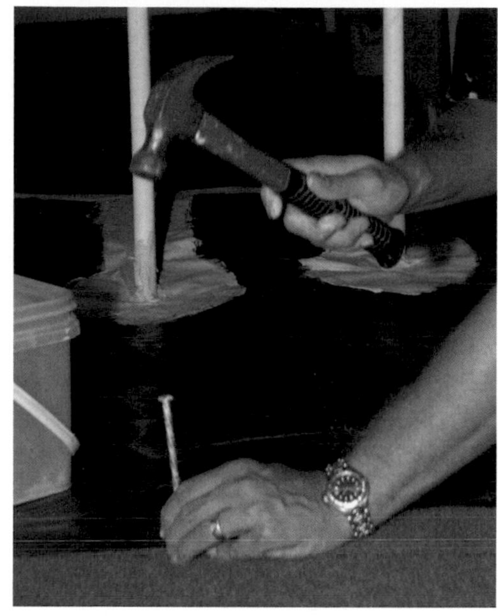

Figure 8. The author secures poly to the underlying soil with 6-inch galvanized spikes through nailing tins (far left). He then applies duct tape and mastic over the tins for reinforcement and a tight seal (left).

crawlspace dragging a toolbox along. If the corner of the box snags on the poly and the poly is not secured, he could pull out most of the ground cover at one time. If it's nailed down, he might rip a 10-foot piece off, but the rest of it would stay intact.

In case of accidents as described above, we always leave behind a patch kit consisting of a 250-square-foot piece of poly, a roll of tape, a brush, and a gallon of mastic. The homeowner can fix 250 square feet with our kit by simply laying down some poly, fastening it with tape, and brushing mastic over the tape.

Preventing future damage. To protect the permanent poly, we lay carpet runners in the space as a path for service technicians, running from the access door to the water heater, furnace, and any other appliance (**Figure 9**). One of the builders I work with doesn't put any equipment in the crawlspace; for that company, we just set a 10x10-foot square of carpet right inside the access door, in case the homeowners want to store something.

Some builders like to make crawlspace storage a selling point, but our crawlspace is virtually inside the house — it's just like the family's living room, and they have to treat it that way. That means the builder has to inform the homeowners that they can't store lawnmowers, pesticides, fuel, and the like in their sealed crawlspace.

Ventilation and System Monitoring

At this point, the crawlspace is clean, dry, well insulated, and both airtight and vapor-tight. All that's missing is a steady supply of conditioned air. Builders always expect me to install the fan, but, unfortunately, my hands are tied. Although installing a ven-

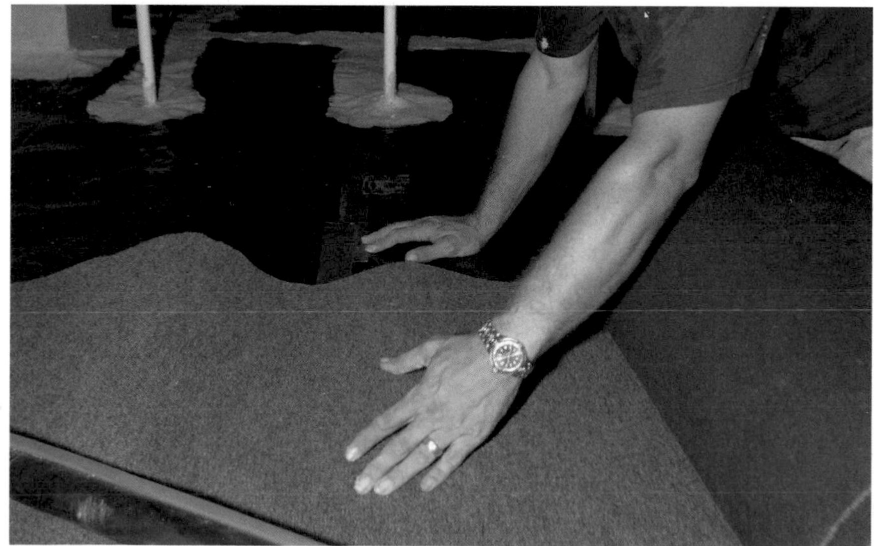

Figure 9. The author installs carpet runners over the poly as a pathway for tradespeople servicing basement appliances (left). He posts a sign warning workers not to rip the poly (below), but he also leaves a patch kit in case the poly does get damaged.

Sealed Crawlspaces and the Code

The International Residential Code is less than crystal clear about how to detail an unvented crawlspace. The main text requires vents of a calculated size in all crawlspace walls. Ventless crawlspaces are allowed under two different exceptions, both of which require some additional interpretation.

Taking exception. The first of these, Exception 4, says vents can be eliminated if continuous mechanical ventilation is provided at a rate of 1 cfm per 50 square feet of crawlspace floor area, but it doesn't say where the air has to come from or mention insulation. The second, Exception 5, says that vents aren't required as long as the space is supplied with conditioned air. How much air, though, and how it should be delivered, is not specified. Unlike Exception 4, Exception 5 does call for insulation of the perimeter walls to meet the energy code.

There's a lot of room in that language to make mistakes. In our hot, humid climate, we definitely don't want a continuous ventilation fan to pull in outside air. And we don't want it to pull air from the crawlspace and push it outdoors, either, because that would depressurize the crawlspace and draw moist outdoor air in through cracks and seams. Any fan you install should take air from the house and add it to the crawlspace. In theory, this will slightly pressurize the crawlspace and cause air to move away from the crawlspace in all directions. Whether or not the crawlspace becomes pressurized in practice depends on a variety of factors, including wind pressure and the tightness of the subfloor and ductwork.

In practice, subfloors in real homes are so full of holes, and ductwork located in crawlspaces is typically so leaky that the uncontrolled air exchange between the crawlspace and the house far exceeds the amount moved by our fan. The fan is not really necessary, as I know from all the existing crawlspaces I've fixed without one. But bringing conditioned air below the floor is the right idea, and it can't hurt. I like the belt-and-suspenders approach, so I don't mind the fan.

Basement or bedroom? Our application actually satisfies the provisions of both exceptions: We provide the 1 cfm of continuous ventilation required under Exception 4, and we do it with conditioned air, as required under Exception 5.

But that brings up another potential problem. Once you've conditioned the crawlspace, the code people aren't sure how to treat it. Some of them want to call it a plenum, while others want to consider it habitable space, like an additional bedroom. Either way, exposed wiring and plumbing can be an issue, even though there's no sensible way to cover up those elements inside a crawlspace.

Fortunately, most code people end up willing to think of our crawlspace as a very short basement. They've seen regular basements with all the same details, and they haven't treated them as habitable space.

Inspection guidelines. When you change from an accepted method to an alternative one, building inspectors don't automatically jump on board. We still run into problems occasionally. For example, I've been using extruded polystyrene rigid insulation on crawlspace walls for years, but on one project the building department decided that because the space was conditioned, we couldn't leave that foam exposed. We had to switch to foil-faced polyisocyanurate, which isn't used much in our area and had to be specially ordered.

But we find that when we make the effort to educate and inform code officials in advance, most of them accept our approach. For example, we have a one-page detail sheet that the building department can use to inspect our work. This document provides plenty of specific information, down to the five mechanical fasteners per sheet of foam board. We try not to leave them guessing about anything. The detail sheet itself is backed by a letter from an engineer, which endorses all the specifications and reassures the inspectors that they won't be blamed if something goes wrong.

Finally, we have one big thing going for us: What we're doing works. When building inspectors compare our dry, clean crawlspaces to the dank, moldy pits under most houses, it's hard for them to complain. Over time, they're going to start taking our methods for granted.

— J.T.

Figure 10. A quiet fan placed in the crawlspace runs continuously, drawing air from the main living space through a floor register and a short run of flex duct. The steady supply of conditioned air keeps crawlspace humidity levels close to that of the main house.

tilation fan is a simple job, my state won't let me do it because I'm not a licensed mechanical contractor.

Ducted fan. We do recommend a specific approach to ventilation that we've found to work well. We first install a floor register in an open central room that can't be closed off from the main body of the house (this prevents our fan from having to compete with the home's HVAC system). We have the mechanical contractor place a continuous-duty low-sone fan under the floor 8 or 10 feet away. Vent and fan are then connected with a run of flex duct (**Figure 10**). Separating the register and the fan in this way makes for quieter operation.

Our remote fan setup under the floor isn't the only way to provide ventilation. You could also locate the fan in the above-floor room and duct it to the crawlspace through a stud bay, for example. The code doesn't specify this detail one way or the other. Code officials make various judgment calls on the forced-air supply to crawlspaces. Some North Carolina municipalities, for example, now require an air conditioning supply register for the crawlspace; a dedicated fan is not considered acceptable. Where I've been working, it's the other way around — the fan's okay, but not a duct register.

In reality, it probably doesn't matter much either way. Fan or no fan, there's going to be constant air movement between the crawlspace and the rooms above. I've seen this countless times in houses with moisture problems. Humidity readings in upstairs rooms are always virtually the same as those in the crawlspace.

Monitoring humidity. When we've finished sealing a crawlspace, we install a humidity sensor under the floor; the sensor is wired to a digital readout and alarm located upstairs. Homeowners tell us the readout tends to settle at a relative humidity of around 50% to 55%. Mold starts to grow at around 70% relative humidity, so we set the alarm close to the top of the safe range, at about 65%. This prevents nuisance alarms when the whole family gets together at Thanksgiving and spends the day cooking, temporarily causing the indoor humidity (including that of the crawlspace) to spike.

We've yet to hear of an alarm going off at that 65% threshold, which seems to confirm that sealed crawlspaces do control moisture. The state of the floor framing is another good indicator. While the normal moisture content of joists in a vented crawlspace is around 16% to 18%, ours are running at 10% to 12%.

Costs and Benefits

My company is currently charging production builders about $1.75 per square foot to seal up a crawlspace, including materials. Custom builders pay more like $1.95. But there are offsetting reductions in other construction costs.

Up-front offsets. First of all, my price includes insulating the foundation walls, so you can subtract the cost of the floor insulation you don't have to put in. That's 40¢ per square foot in our market. You can subtract the cost of buying and installing foundation vents as well. So from $1.75, you're now closer to $1.25.

Also, by sealing the crawlspace, we cut the heating and cooling load on a house substantially. This has an especially pronounced effect on the air conditioning load, because dehumidification accounts for much of the work an air conditioner has to do in our area. By eliminating all the soil moisture and a big chunk of the infiltrating humid air, we drastically reduce that latent cooling load. On an average house, our work lets you downsize the equipment by 1/2 to 1 ton of cooling and reduce the ductwork accordingly. By the time you add up those direct offsets, our crawlspace work is almost free.

Callbacks and customer satisfaction. That reduction in load translates to lower energy bills for the homeowner, year in and year out. But the builder also gets a long-run benefit: Houses with sealed crawlspaces are much more stable from season to season, which means that some of the callback money you now spend caulking trim joints or rehanging doors will stay in your pocket.

Finally, there's liability. As anyone who's spent some time in a crawlspace knows, conventional vented crawlspaces are often musty and moldy. A well-sealed crawlspace, on the other hand, typically contains less mold than the outside air. In today's legal climate, that can't hurt.

Contractor and consultant Jeff Tooley is owner of the Healthy Building Company, based in Bear Creek, N.C.

Fixing a Wet Crawlspace

by Jeff Tooley

In North Carolina, where I live and work, enclosed crawlspace foundations with small vent openings are very common. Most of those crawlspaces experience high humidity, and many have problems with mold and rot.

My contracting firm, the Healthy Building Company, specializes in sealed and insulated crawlspaces, which the International Residential Code now allows. Instead of vents, a sealed crawlspace has a continuous vapor barrier to keep ground moisture out of the space.

Part of my company's business is detailing crawlspaces for new homes, as I described in a "Building a Sealed Crawlspace," page 38. The rest consists of fixing crawlspace problems in existing homes. Here I'll show how we cured severe moisture problems in the crawlspace under a four-year-old house in the Blue Ridge Mountains.

This job came our way when we got a call from the retired woman who had recently purchased the home. She was happy with the house in general, but a tradesman working on her deck had looked under the house and advised her to have the crawlspace checked out. Once on site, it didn't take long to see that this crawlspace was in bad shape — about a nine on a scale of one to ten. What I found was a disaster — a dank, dripping, moldy space, totally infested with bugs.

Figure 11. Upon opening the crawlspace door, the author saw large, obvious patches of white wood rot and black mold (above, left and right). The OSB ceiling looks considerably better at the end of the job (left), after the crew has scrubbed it with a borate solution.

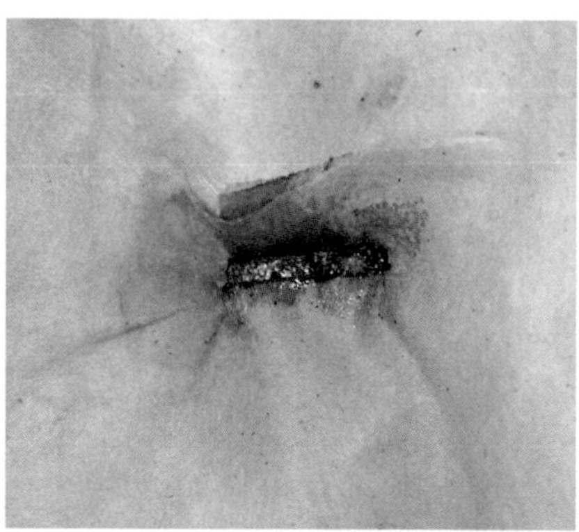

Figure 12. Every surface in the crawlspace was dripping wet, including electrical outlets (left). Even the staples holding insulation batts in place were rusty and gleaming with moisture (center). Droplets of water were also visible on the filaments of this white fungus (right).

As bad as it was, we were able to fix this space, in spite of the owner's limited budget, by cleaning up and sanitizing the mold-covered materials, installing a vapor barrier, sealing up the two small vents, and dehumidifying the newly enclosed space until the structure was well dried out. I also advised the homeowner that some other changes should be made: Some wood infill walls at the crawlspace perimeter should be replaced with a better system, or they might eventually rot. But that's the nice thing about the way we seal up crawlspaces — when the owner is ready, all someone has to do is cut the poly back, do the work, then install new poly, sealing it to the old with the same kind of mastic and tape that we used.

Bugs, Mold, and Rot

The sources of moisture around this cabin were plentiful and obvious. A nearby creek and pond had saturated the air and soil. In a location like this, any crawlspace needs to have a fully effective vapor barrier or there will be problems.

Those problems were evident as soon as I looked under the house (**Figure 11**). The mold and wood rot were everywhere. With water dripping from every surface (**Figure 12**), it was obvious that the crawlspace was at the dew-point temperature more or less continuously.

The concrete block columns supporting the house at the perimeter were exposed to the outside temperature, so their inside faces in the saturated crawlspace stayed constantly wet with condensation (**Figure 13**). Moisture from the block was wicking into the adjacent wood-frame, batt-insulated infill walls, built to close up the space and trap warmth during the winter. The pressure-treated wall plate was set directly on the damp earth, where it also wicked moisture into the air and into the wall framing above it.

When you assess a crawlspace, one thing to check

Figure 13. Moisture condensing on the cold masonry columns (left) on the perimeter of the crawlspace was wicking into the adjacent cripple wall framing and insulation batts. There was fungus even on the surface of the treated wood wall plate (right).

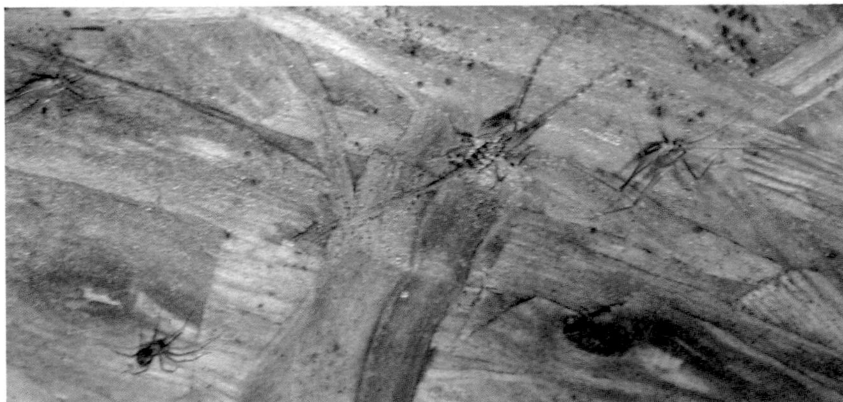

Figure 14. In the worst parts of the crawlspace, wood and insulation facings were covered with slick black coatings of wet, slimy mold (above, left and right). The presence of mole crickets (left) also indicated that the space was constantly damp.

out is what kind of insect life it supports. In my experience, a sealed, dry crawlspace will support only spiders. Millipedes, ladybugs, and potato beetles, for example, aren't found in a correctly detailed sealed crawlspace.

The crawlspace under this house was packed with mole crickets (**Figure 14**), a species that thrives in damp conditions. That told me that this crawlspace had been wet all the time, for a long time. In a sealed crawlspace, you'll never see a mole cricket. It was interesting to see that the spiderwebs under this house, as well as the electrical outlets and even the filaments of fungus, were beaded with moisture condensation.

At the back of the crawlspace, things looked really bad. The OSB on the ceiling and the paper face of the insulation were both glistening with moisture and coated with black, slimy mold. If left unattended, these materials would have completely decomposed within a very short time.

Figure 15. The entire crawlspace was equipped with just two small vents. One is shown here as viewed from outside the crawlspace under the exterior deck.

A Beach House in the Mountains

To cure this crawlspace's problems, we had to understand why they had gotten so bad. Generally, these wet conditions mean that there's a lot of moisture getting into the home and no way to remove it. In this case, the source was the ground, and the crawlspace details were trapping the incoming ground moisture. The two small vents in the crawlspace walls were totally ineffective at taking moisture out (**Figure 15**); that's not surprising, considering that the air outside the crawlspace was also nearly saturated most of the time.

The difficulties started when the builder constructed a beach house in the mountains. The home sits on columns, with insulation between the floor joists and OSB nailed up underneath the whole house. But in the mountain climate, the floors were too cold in the wintertime, so he went back and closed up the under-floor space with framed wood walls between the columns. I guess he thought this was a good way to trap heat in wintertime — which it is, in principle. But the enclosure also trapped moisture, because he didn't put down a poly ground cover.

What saved this house was the OSB under the floor joists (**Figure 16**) and the Tyvek under it (there is also insulation between the joists). Those details kept air infiltration from bringing the moisture right into the floor assembly and destroying the joists. The Tyvek didn't make sense at all as a vapor barrier in this application, of course — it's designed to let moisture through. But with the OSB on top of it, the assembly seems to have blocked both diffusion and air transport of moisture. The OSB was heavily attacked by mold and rot, but the joists didn't seem to have been significantly damaged.

Figure 16. OSB and Tyvek between the crawlspace and the floor protected the floor structure from damage, saving the floor (and perhaps the house) from total ruin. The OSB was heavily attacked by fungus, but it could still be cleaned up using stiff bristle brushes and a borate solution.

The Remedy

This job was as bad a case as you would ever want to see. But the solution is pretty much standard: Clean it up, dry it out, and seal it.

We first removed the insulation from the cripple walls, bagging it for disposal. We also had to excavate the crawlspace floor in places to gain access to back portions of the space (**Figure 17**). The builder had never scraped the organic soil from the site, he just dug trenches for a few center post footings.

I decided to leave the OSB in place, though. Structurally, it was garbage after being chewed on by rot for several years. But it was there as an air barrier, not for structural reinforcement. However, the mold and rot needed to be cleaned up. So we brought in a sprayer and saturated the OSB with a solution of borate (**Figure 18**, next page). We use either Tim-bor or Bora-Care products (Nisus Corp.); they are familiar to our clients (Grandma used borate), they don't harm people, and they are about the most effective thing available for killing mold and rot. Borates also kill insects, so we're getting rid of the bugs at the same time that we're cleaning up the mold. In this case, we used Tim-bor, because it comes as a powder that is convenient to mix up and put in our small sprayer.

Figure 17. The remedy included excavating the crawlspace floor to gain access to back portions of the space. The builder had just dug trenches for a few center post footings, so the organic soil had never been scraped from the site.

Figure 18. The author's old battery-powered sprayer (left) is small enough to drag into hard-to-access spaces, and allows him to saturate the underfloor OSB with a solution of Tim-bor borate, killing mold, rot organisms, and insects without toxic risk to people (right).

Figure 19. To finish off the space, the author's crew seals the vent openings with duct tape and mastic (top left), and applies a poly ground cover, sealed to the base of the crawlspace wall (above). Carpeting protects the 6-mil poly (left) in the area near the access, creating the perception of a space that should be treated with care.

Any small sprayer or power-washer can handle this work. Mine is an old one that runs off a 12-volt car battery. Its portability helps when we need to access crawlspaces through rear or side doors in houses that are far back from the road.

We saturated the OSB thoroughly with the borate solution — I wanted it completely soaked — and scrubbed the surface with stiff bristle brushes. Then we laid down temporary construction poly and set up our dehumidifier. It took a week of constant operation for the dehumidifier to dry out the OSB.

On a less severe case — the typical crawlspace with just a few spots of mold and wood moisture content of 14% to 18% — I would just put down the permanent sealed poly, then dehumidify. But the 25 gallons of water I added to the OSB is my responsibility, and I needed to pull that out before I sealed anything for real. If I hadn't, it would have come out by itself and ended up causing mold.

In the week it took for the OSB to dry, all the bugs and flakes of fungus rained down onto the construction poly. When we pulled out the poly, all that debris came with it.

Next, we installed our final poly (**Figure 19**). We used the same methods as in our new crawlspaces: lay down 6-mil black poly, overlap it a foot, duct tape the seams, and apply nontoxic duct mastic over that. In this case, we used PS-1 mastic from RCD Corporation as our usual preferred product. We sealed up the vents with duct tape and mastic.

Unfortunately, I couldn't run my poly up the crawlspace walls as I usually do. That would be like putting the wood wall in contact with the moisture conditions under the poly, and it would have quickly rotted out the untreated framing. So we ran the poly up onto the side of the treated-wood plate, adhered it with mastic, and nailed a 1x2 batten over it for protection.

We install the final poly wearing socks because we don't want to scuff up the poly even a little bit. When I give the crawlspace back to the homeowner, I want it to have that new-car shine and smell. In fact, some of what we do is mainly to influence the perception of anyone who looks in. That's part of the idea behind the carpet runners we install before we leave, for instance. I want the people to see the carpet and recognize that this is a conditioned space, not your average crawlspace.

When we left this job, we hadn't exactly created a formal living room, but we did accomplish our goal: We got rid of a mold and rot problem that could have destroyed the whole floor, we provided a boundary between the home and the soil that will improve energy efficiency and maintain good air quality in the home, and we created an underfloor space that people can enter and work in as needed without risking their health and safety.

Contractor and consultant Jeff Tooley is owner of the Healthy Building Company, based in Bear Creek, N.C.

WATER VAPOR CONTROL

Chapter 4: Vapor Retarders

Vapor Barrier Q&A: Principles

by the *JLC* Staff

Barrier vs. Retarder

Q. *What is the difference between a vapor barrier and an air barrier? Between a "barrier" and a "retarder"?*

A. A *vapor barrier* is a material or coating that significantly reduces the passage of water vapor by diffusion through wall, ceiling, and floor materials. In general, its purpose is to keep moisture from getting into exterior wall and ceiling cavities, where it can condense on framing members and sheathing.

Diffusion is the transfer of moisture through tiny pores in building materials. The amount of moisture that passes through a material depends on the material's permeability (*perm rating*) and the vapor pressure that pushes the moisture through. It's a scientific fact that moisture always moves from areas of higher temperature and relative humidity (higher vapor pressure, to be precise) to areas of lower temperature and humidity. The greater the pressure difference, the greater the push.

In cold climates, the vapor pressure is always higher indoors during the winter, so the moisture wants to move toward the outside. In hot, humid climates, the reverse is true — the moisture wants to move indoors if the building is air conditioned.

In climates with both heating and cooling, the vapor flow changes according to the seasons and weather, but it's usually the strongest during colder weather, when it's heading from the building's interior to the outside.

An *air barrier*, on the other hand, blocks the passage of *air* through leaks in the walls, ceiling, or other building components. Because air often carries a lot of moisture, air barriers and vapor barriers work together to keep moisture out of building cavities. In fact, a single material such as polyethylene often performs both tasks, and hence is often called an *air/vapor barrier*.

Currently, most codes do not recognize the distinction between an air barrier and a vapor barrier. Most codes require a vapor barrier of one perm or less. Researchers, however, have shown that air leakage generally moves a lot more moisture than diffusion. Therefore, the air barrier is usually more important than the vapor barrier. So if you're concerned about really keeping moisture out of your wall and ceiling cavities, you ought to be paying close attention to the air barrier. That means using either (1) a continuous, airtight membrane, such as poly, or (2) a lot of caulk, foam sealant, and gaskets to block up any significant leaks.

As to the difference between a *barrier* and a *retarder*, there is no difference. It's just that some people like to be super-precise so they call it a retarder, since no barrier is perfect. At best, a material will only slow down the passage of moisture or air but will never stop it completely.

The bottom line: You need both a vapor retarder and a continuous air barrier, and the colder the climate, the more you need them.

Is Perfection Required?

Q. *Does a vapor retarder need to be installed perfectly to be effective?*

A. No. At a given vapor pressure, the amount of diffusion you'll get is directly proportional to the surface area that is exposed to the moisture. So if you have only 90% of your walls covered with poly, your vapor retarder will still be 90% effective.

This is *not* true of an air barrier, however, because under pressure a great amount of air can leak through even a small crack in a building — just as a lot of air can rush out of a small hole in a balloon. How fanatical you need to be about vapor-retarder installation and air sealing depends on (1) how moist the interior of the building will be and (2) how cold the climate is.

An office building that is unoccupied at night and where no cooking or bathing takes place generally has pretty low indoor humidity levels, whereas a small house with three teenagers each taking two showers a day will likely have quite high levels.

As for climate, a house in northern Minnesota is much more prone to moisture problems than one in southern California, where it is both mild and arid. So you'll need to pay attention to local codes and practices, or talk to an experienced local energy consultant.

The bottom line: Don't knock yourself out with the vapor retarder, but do a thorough job with the air barrier — particularly in cold climates.

Interior vs. Exterior Location

Q. *Should the vapor retarder always go on the inside of a building?*

A. In most of the continental United States, code requires you to put a vapor retarder of 1 perm or less on the interior side of the wall. That's because the strongest vapor flows are from the interior to outside during cold weather. With an interior vapor retarder, the exterior side of the wall should be sufficiently permeable to allow drying toward the outside.

In mixed climates with both significant heating and cooling loads, the vapor retarder typically goes on the interior, since vapor pressures are usually greater during cold weather. An alternative strategy is to use insulating sheathing to warm the wall cavity enough to prevent high levels of condensation (see "Controlling Moisture in Mixed Climates," page 91).

In very hot and humid climates, such as south Florida and along the Gulf Coast, the dominant vapor flow is reversed: It's from the outside toward the building's interior. In those areas, locate vapor retarders on the outside of the wall assembly (see "Controlling Moisture in Cooling Climates," page 88).

In hot, humid climates, use vapor-permeable materials for the interior portions of the wall, such as unfaced fiberglass batts and drywall with permeable paint. This allows any moisture within the wall system to dry out by migrating to the cooler and drier interior of the building. Vapor-retarding materials on the interior, such as polyethylene or vinyl wallpaper, could inhibit this drying and could also lead to condensation on the back (exterior face) of the poly or wallpaper.

The bottom line: Put the vapor barrier on the inside except in very hot, humid climates.

Rating Materials

Q. *Is paint a vapor retarder? How about felt paper, DuPont's Tyvek, and plywood?*

A. A material's *perm rating* indicates the ability of moisture to diffuse through the material. The lower the perm rating, the better a material's resistance to moisture diffusion. In general, building codes call a material a "vapor retarder" if it has a perm rating of one or less.

From the table "Vapor Resistance of Common Building Materials," below, you can see that a couple of coats of oil-based paint can act as a pretty effective vapor retarder. However, #15 asphalt-impregnated felt is not a vapor retarder. Plywood is technically a vapor retarder, but it usually has enough cracks between sheets to allow moisture to escape from the wall.

A useful rule of thumb in cold climates is to *keep the outside of the wall five times more permeable than the inside.* To calculate the added value of two or more layered materials, you need to add the inverse of their perm ratings. This inverse figure is called a *rep* and is a measure of a material's resistance to vapor transmission.

The bottom line: In cold climates, keep the outside of the walls significantly more permeable to moisture

Vapor Resistance of Common Building Materials

Material	Perms	Reps
3/4" plaster on wood lath	15	0.067
1/2" drywall	37.5	0.027
1/2" 5-ply plywood	0.36	2.8
1" extruded polystyrene	1.2	0.83
1" expanded polystyrene (beadboard)	2.0 to 5.8	0.5 to .17
Aluminum foil	0.0	–
6-mil polyethylene	0.06	17
#15 asphalt felt	5.6	0.18
Kraft paper laminated with asphalt (used on insulation batts)	0.3	1.8
1 coat latex primer (vinyl-acrylic)	8.6	0.12
1 coat latex semi-gloss enamel (vinyl-acrylic)	6.6	0.15
1 coat latex vapor-retarder paint	0.45	2.22
2 coats of oil enamel on smooth plaster	0.5 to 1.5	2 to 0.66

Note: A *perm* is a measure of a material's permeability — the capacity for water vapor to pass through by diffusion. A *rep* is the reciprocal of a perm, and it measures a material's resistance to water vapor. Most codes define an interior "vapor barrier" as any material with a perm of one or less. However, because some exterior sheathing materials are not very permeable, there is a risk of trapping moisture in the wall cavity. To avoid problems, keep the outside of the wall five times as permeable as the inside.

than the inside and you'll avoid trouble. In hot, humid climates, keep the interior more permeable than the exterior.

Vapor Barriers and Housewrap

Q. *If the house is covered with a housewrap such as Tyvek (DuPont) on the outside, do I still need a tight air/vapor barrier on the inside?*

A. Yes. Housewrap on the outside will not keep interior air from leaking into the wall and ceiling cavities. Housewrap functions primarily as a wind barrier, preventing air from blowing through the gaps in the sheathing and around the band joist. It also acts as a secondary rain barrier during construction, and it later protects against any water that might leak behind siding and trim.

As it's typically installed, housewrap does not form a continuous envelope around the house. You still need to seal the most prominent air leaks in a house — around doors and windows, along the mudsill, behind tubs and cabinet soffits, and at all penetrations through the ceiling.

The bottom line: Install a continuous air/vapor barrier on the inside even if you use housewrap on the exterior.

Basement Moisture Control

Q. *Where should the vapor retarder go in a finished basement?*

A. Moisture control in finished basements is tricky, because the vapor drive between the soil and the basement is small and could go either way, depending on conditions.

The most common practice is to place the vapor retarder behind the wall finish as you would with an above-grade wall. For example, with a wood-frame wall, place the vapor retarder between the insulation and the interior finish. Under most conditions, this ensures that the vapor retarder is above the dew point of the air in the cavity between the wall and the concrete. This also keeps heated basement air from contacting the cool basement walls, where it might condense. Foam board is a good option for basement walls as it provides both insulation and a vapor barrier.

Reducing the moisture load is also important. Dampproofing or waterproofing the basement wall on the exterior helps keep soilborne moisture from migrating into the building. A low-permeability coating on the interior of the basement wall can also help. The floor slab should also be protected with a vapor retarder below and/or a layer of polyethylene above the slab and below the finished floor.

The bottom line: Treat below-grade walls the same as above-grade walls.

Effect of Foam Sheathing

Q. *How does foam insulation on framed walls affect moisture problems?*

A. When placed on the interior face of a wall, foam insulation is usually okay in cold climates, since it serves as an interior vapor retarder, similar to poly. However, there is one important difference. Because of the high R-value of the foam, the wall cavity is now significantly colder, and moist air that does get past the foam is more likely to condense inside the wall. So it's important to seal the foam board well against air leaks with construction tape and foam sealant.

When foam board is used on the exterior, it usually contradicts the old rule of thumb — to keep the outside of the wall five times as permeable as the inside. Yet it rarely causes problems. Here's why: Although the foam will tend to trap moisture in the wall, it also warms the wall cavity, making it less prone to condensation. Using this "warm wall" approach, water vapor in the wall cavity does not condense and is therefore harmless to the building.

To allow some drying to the exterior in cold climates, it's best to use a relatively permeable foam such as beadboard or extruded polystyrene rather than the foil-faced products. Also, the colder the climate, the higher the R-value you'll want on the exterior foam to keep the wall cavity warm. In cold climates, use at least 1 inch of foam in conjunction with R-11 batts; 2 inches of foam is better (see "Where Does the Dew Drop?").

The bottom line: If you put foam on the interior, seal it well. If you're going to put foam on the exterior, use an adequate thickness for the climate.

Retrofit Vapor Retarders

Q. *Do you need to add a vapor retarder when you retrofit insulation into walls or ceilings?*

A. An uninsulated leaky wall is generally not prone to moisture problems for two reasons: (1) the wall cavity is relatively warm from leaking household heat, and (2) the wind blows through and clears out any moisture that gets in. Once you insulate, however, the wall becomes colder at the outside sheathing and ventilation in the wall cavities is reduced. That means there may be more condensation on the back of the sheathing or siding, potentially leading to paint problems or other moisture problems. There's a fair amount of anecdotal evidence linking retrofit insulation with peeling paint. Therefore, it's a good idea to add as good an air and vapor barrier as is practical.

Where Does the Dew Drop?

To figure out how much insulating foam sheathing you should install on the exterior of a building, you need to know the dew point of the interior air during winter. The *dew point* is the temperature at which water will condense out of the air — either by cooling the air to the dew point or by exposing the air to a cold surface at or below the dew point (example: moisture that forms on a chilled beer mug on a humid summer day).

First, look at the psychrometric chart at right to figure out what the dew point is for a given air temperature and relative humidity. Say you have a maximum indoor relative humidity of 50% at 70°F. On the horizontal scale, locate the temperature and move up to the curve that represents 50% relative humidity, as shown. Then move left to the "saturation curve", and down to find the dew-point temperature: 50°F in this case.

Moisture must condense on a solid surface (it won't condense in midair and is unlikely to condense in fiberglass), and the inside surface of the sheathing is where the condensation is most likely to occur. The objective is to put enough foam on the wall so its inside surface remains *above* the dew point (in this case, above 50°F) for the average winter temperature at the site.

You can find the temperature at any point inside the wall if you know the R-values of the wall components you are using. The temperature change at any point within the wall is in direct proportion to that R-value on either side of that point. For example, for an outdoor temperature of 32°F, the temperature on the inside surface of the 1-inch foam sheathing in Wall A will be 7/18 (R-7 over R-18) of the way from 32°F to 70°F, or 47°F. This is below the dew point, so condensation is likely to form on the inside of the foam sheathing if moist indoor air leaks into the wall cavity.

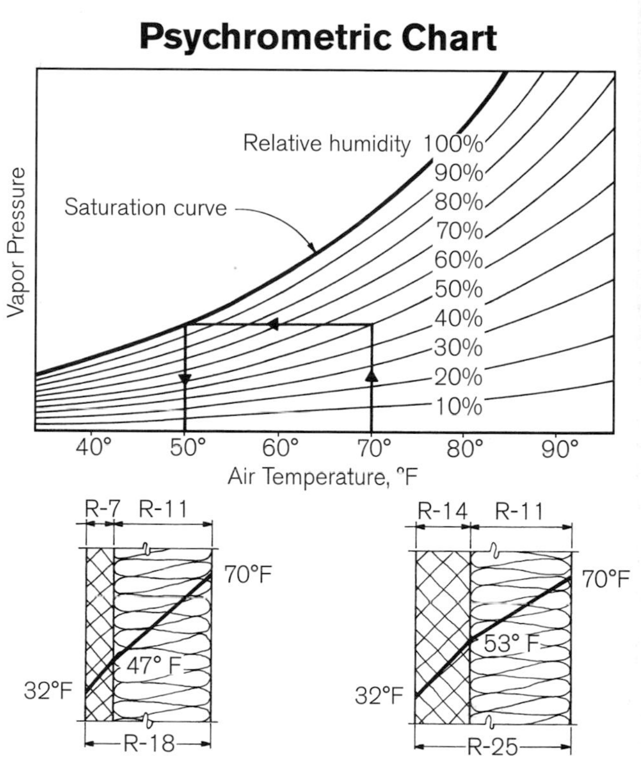

In Wall B, with 2 inches of foam, the temperature at the inside sheathing surface is 14/25 of the way, or 53°F — safely *above* the dew point. This thicker insulating sheathing would be your safest bet in climates with an average winter temperature of 32°F or less. Lower indoor humidity levels and effective interior air and vapor barriers will also help prevent moisture problems.

If the wall is older, it probably has more than a couple of coats of oil-based paint on the plaster, so the vapor retarder is already there. As for the air barrier, caulk as many cracks as you can find at baseboards and other trim, and seal electrical outlets with foam and gaskets. When sealing an old house, it's worth working with someone who has a blower door. By pressurizing the house with a blower door, you can pinpoint leaks that might be quite significant but are not immediately obvious. Most public utilities can put you in touch with a blower door contractor.

The bottom line: You should try to seal the walls against moisture transport whenever you retrofit insulation. Pay particular attention to air sealing on the interior.

Remodeling and Additions

Q. *Does it do any good to have a vapor retarder only in an addition? Or only in the ceiling?*

A. If a modern addition has modern insulation, it ought to have modern air and vapor barriers. As for ceiling-only vapor retarders, it's not something we recommend for new construction. But because the ceiling — particularly cathedral ceilings — is one of the most likely places to have moisture problems, ceilings are the best place to concentrate your air- and vapor-sealing efforts. Ceilings and attics are more vulnerable to moisture damage than walls because convection currents carry lots of warm, moist air into those spaces.

The bottom line: When you add on, add a vapor retarder throughout — not just in the ceiling.

Air-Quality Issues

Q. *Do vapor retarders contribute to moisture problems or air-quality problems inside a home?*

A. No, but air barriers might, since a good air barrier will prevent moisture and indoor toxins from dissipating. Remember, however, that the best way to reduce moisture problems in the walls is to reduce excess moisture in the home and vent it directly at its source.

That means you should install good bathroom and kitchen exhaust fans; vent the dryer outside; eliminate uncovered crawlspaces; and don't air-dry laundry or store firewood indoors.

Similarly, the best way to reduce air-quality problems is to keep strong toxins out of the home or ventilate them directly. For example, avoid products with a high formaldehyde content, such as cheap wood paneling, and ventilate hobby areas, such as a photo darkroom, directly outdoors. With very tight construction, a whole-house ventilation system, such as an air-to-air heat exchanger, might be required.

The end result will be a home with low energy use, high comfort levels, and excellent air quality regardless of the weather conditions.

The bottom line: Build tight and ventilate right. The tighter the home, the more you'll need to reduce moisture and pollution sources and add mechanical ventilation.

Vapor Barrier Q&A: On the Job

Where's the Dew Point?

Q. *What's the dew point and how do I find it?*

A. *Andrew Shapiro responds:* The dew point is not a location; it is the temperature at which water will condense out of the air. Since the dew point changes with the amount of humidity in the air, as well as the air temperature, the dew point for a particular temperature and relative humidity is best looked up in a table or a psychrometric chart (see "Where Does the Dew Drop?," previous page).

Water from the air will condense on building components when they are below the dew point of the air that's in contact with them. For example, in hot, humid summer weather, cold water pipes condense water and drip. In summer, uninsulated basement floors are often below the dew point of the hot, moist outside air, so water condenses on the floor if the basement is open to the outside. In an air-conditioned building in a warm, moist climate like the southeastern U.S., the drywall can be below the dew point of the outside air for months on end.

Just because a building component is below the dew point doesn't mean there will be a problem. Vinyl window frames and copper tubing aren't bothered by a little moisture. On the other hand, wood window components and drywall can't handle much moisture, especially if the wetting is prolonged and there is no opportunity for the components to dry out.

Determining whether a component in a wall assembly will ever get cold enough to permit condensation — that is, be below the dew point — can be complicated. If each element of a wall acted as a solid (which fiberglass doesn't), then the calculation of the temperature at any point in the wall assembly would be fairly easy. Halfway through the insulation value of the wall, the temperature would be halfway between inside and out.

In reality, such static calculations can be misleading. More accurate calculations, called *dynamic calculations*, take into account many additional factors but are so complex that they are best performed with computer software.

The good news is that this type of dynamic calculation is usually not needed — as long as builders employ good building practices that keep inside air out of walls in cold climates and outside air out of walls in hot, moist climates. In all climates, walls and roofs should be designed so they can dry out if they occasionally get damp. One good source for building details that avoid moisture damage is the Builder's Guide series from Building Science Consulting (www.buildingscience.com).

Andrew Shapiro is an energy and sustainable design consultant, and principal of Energy Balance in Montpelier, Vt.

Is a Vapor Barrier Necessary?

Q. *Our drywall contractor argues that installing a poly vapor barrier behind the drywall will trap moisture, where it will condense and cause the drywall to degrade. Is there any truth to this claim?*

A. *Clayton DeKorne responds:* The poly isn't the problem. Moisture in wall cavities is only a problem if it condenses into liquid water. To condense on the poly, the humidity would have to be very high (over 50% relative humidity), and the poly very cold (due to poor or missing insulation or lots of cold outside air leaking into the wall). In this case, you'll have condensation problems, with or without poly.

To understand this, let's look at a few principles. Vapor retarders, such as poly, are installed on the warm side of walls to prevent moisture diffusion into the wall cavity where it can condense and cause moisture damage. *Diffusion* is the movement of moisture through the tiny pores in a material and is only a problem in homes with high indoor moisture levels. For example, if a homeowner dries laundry or stores firewood in the basement, boils lots of pasta water, has many pets and houseplants, or houses a large number of family members who take frequent showers, the indoor humidity will be high, especially in a small house.

The best way to prevent moisture problems under these conditions is to remove the source — install a vented clothes dryer, build a wood shed, and install good bath fans and a range hood. A vapor retarder, such as poly, is a second line of defense to keep moisture from seeping into the wall cavity and condensing.

In the vast majority of cases, however, moisture problems in homes are caused by *air leakage,* rather than diffusion. Warm, moist indoor air that leaks into a wall or ceiling cavity can condense in cold weather when it reaches a cold surface — typically the back side of the exterior sheathing. Or, cold outside air leaking into a house can cool interior surfaces such as drywall, causing moist interior air to condense on the inside surfaces — often leading to mildew growth.

Wet areas, such as bathrooms, corners in unheated closets, and wall or ceiling areas near band joists, soffits, windows, and doors, are among the most vulnerable areas. To prevent these problems, concentrate your efforts on installing adequate wall insulation, providing good ventilation in wet areas, and sealing air leaks at the gaps around windows, doors, electrical outlets, and the band joist. One way to do this, of course, is to install poly under the drywall, carefully caulking or taping the edges around penetrations. In this case, the poly serves as *both* an air barrier and a vapor barrier.

Clayton DeKorne is the editor of Coastal Contractor *magazine. He is also editor of the* JLC Field Guide to Residential Construction *and a former senior editor at* The Journal of Light Construction.

Ceiling Vapor Barrier — Yes or No?

Q. *I build in a cold climate, where many longtime builders swear that you shouldn't put a ceiling vapor barrier in. The reasons go something like, "Because you have to let the moisture escape," or "Because the house has to breathe out the top." Are they correct?*

A. *Joseph Lstiburek responds:* Plastic vapor barriers should be installed in vented attics in climates with more than 8,000 heating degree-days (see chart, next page). You can forego the plastic and use a vapor retarder (Kraft-faced insulation or latex ceiling paint) in all other climates except hot-humid or hot-dry climates.

In hot-humid climates, attics should not be vented and vapor retarders should not be installed on the interior of assemblies. In hot-dry climates, a vapor retarder should also not be installed, but attics can be vented.

All attics — vented or unvented — should have an *air barrier* (a properly detailed airtight drywall ceiling, for example) regardless of climate. Continuous, sealed poly can also serve as the air barrier.

Omitting a ceiling vapor barrier by arguing that "you have to let the moisture escape" is actually correct, in a way. It's also incorrect, in a way. Now, I'm a real fan of controlled mechanical ventilation to limit interior moisture levels in cold and mixed climates, as well as to limit other interior contaminants in all climates. In other words, all houses require controlled mechanical ventilation in order to "breathe." It is also my view that this necessary air change should *not* happen because of a leaky attic ceiling, attic vents, or even leaky walls — hence, the requirement for an air barrier *and* controlled mechanical ventilation in all houses regardless of climate.

Having said that, I do not have a problem with relieving some of the moisture load in the house via diffusion. This can be achieved through a roof assembly designed to handle it, such as a vented attic in a moderately cold or mixed climate. It's important to understand that this is a *climate-specific* recommendation. In a well-insulated attic in a very cold climate (more than 8,000 heating degree-days), there is not enough heat loss into an attic from the house to allow for much moisture removal through ventilation. That's because attic ventilation requires heat loss to remove moisture from attics. Cold air can't hold much moisture. So ventilating a heavily insulated attic with outside air when it is really cold does not remove moisture. We do not want any moisture to get into an attic in a severely cold climate for this reason. As you move south into regions where it is not so miserably cold, this changes — hence, the recommendation for a vapor *barrier* in a severely cold climate but only a vapor *retarder* in most other locations.

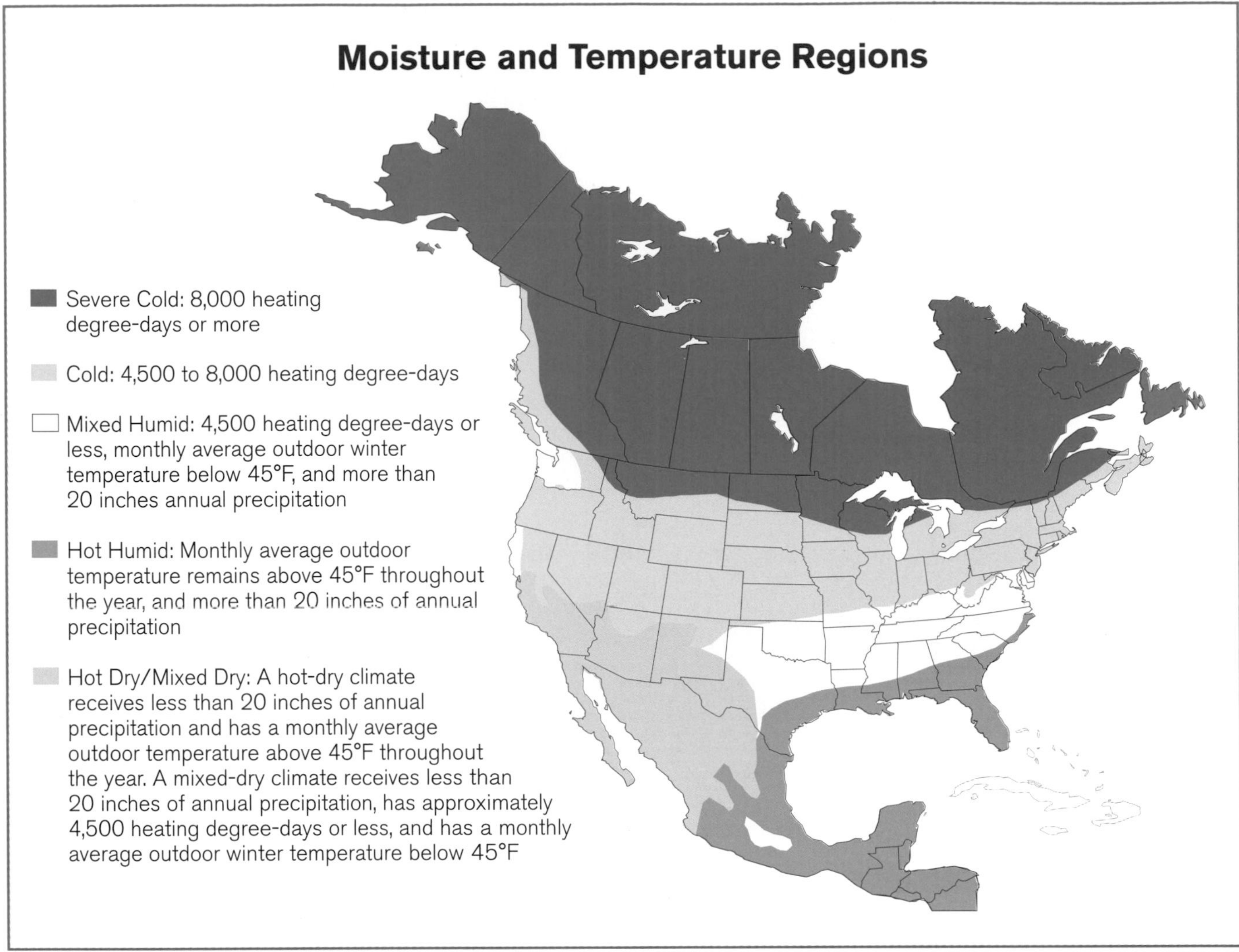

In the old days in severely cold climates, where attics were poorly insulated, it was okay to omit a plastic ceiling vapor barrier. The heat loss from the house warmed the attic sufficiently to allow attic ventilation to remove moisture from the attic. Cold outside air was brought into the attic and warmed up by the escaping heat loss, giving this air the capacity to pick up moisture from the attic and carry it to the exterior. This worked well until we added large quantities of attic insulation. With the added insulation, the attic stayed cold and so did the ventilating air from outside, which was now unable to effectively remove attic moisture — hence the need nowadays to reduce moisture flow into the attic and the need for a vapor barrier.

There's one other important qualification. Vapor moves in two ways: by diffusion through materials, and by air leakage through gaps and holes in building assemblies. Between the two, air leakage moves far more moisture than vapor diffusion. A vapor barrier in an attic assembly in a severely cold climate with the absence of an air barrier will likely be ineffective. On the other hand, an air barrier (a properly detailed airtight drywall ceiling, for example) in the absence of a vapor barrier *can* be effective, since it stops the flow of vapor-laden air. You can't just install plastic in a ceiling and assume it is also an air barrier. For plastic to be an air barrier, it needs to be continuous, meaning all joints and penetrations must be taped or caulked.

Joseph Lstiburek, PhD, PE, is a principal of Building Science Consulting (www.buildingscience.com) in Westford, Mass., and an investigator of moisture-related building problems.

Band-Joist Vapor Barriers

Q. *Is it necessary to make the vapor barrier and insulation continuous at the band joist?*

A. *Chuck Silver responds:* This detail has confounded builders since the dawn of energy-efficient construction. As for insulation, you should protect this area as you would any other section of exterior wall. In fact, this area may be particularly vulnerable to heat loss due to ductwork in the joist system and the fact that the warmest air is likely to lie on the ceiling, which is often penetrated by electrical boxes and recessed lights.

Non-Insulative Sheathing

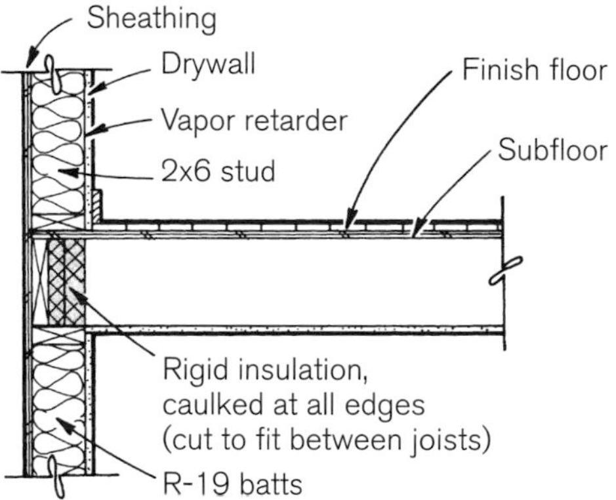

Figure 1. With standard platform framing, cut rigid insulation to fit between the joists and caulk each section in place.

Exterior Foam Sheathing

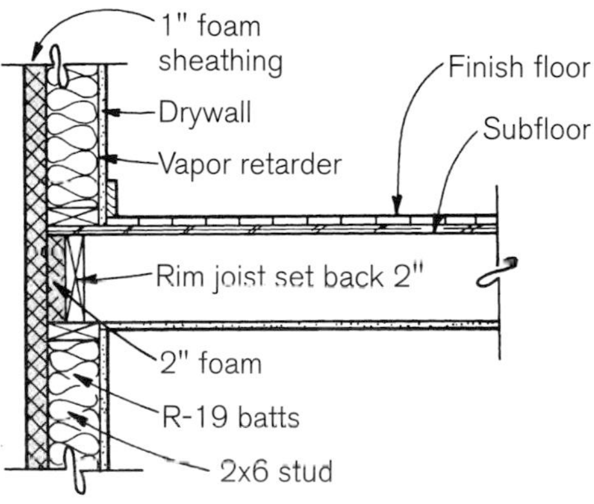

Figure 2. With exterior insulating sheathing, offset the band joist 2 inches and install long strips of foam on the exterior (this keeps the band joist warm enough so that moisture will not condense on it). Some framers, however, find this awkward.

Interior Foam Sheathing

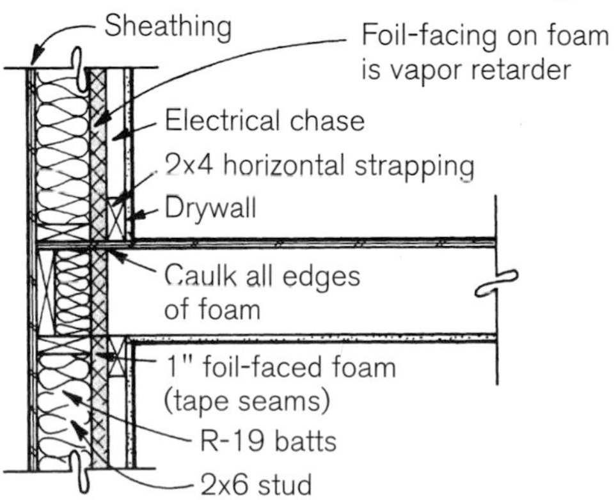

Figure 3. With interior foam sheathing, the foam board can be easily notched and slid up between the joists.

To control water vapor, a continuous air barrier on the warm side of the wall is desirable, since most moisture exits a building with leaking air. The barrier can be poly, drywall, rigid foam, or any material that will stop airflow.

Creating a perfect barrier at the band joist — particularly where it runs perpendicular to the floor joists — is probably impossible. As with the rest of the building shell, it is less critical if excess household moisture is removed by mechanical ventilation. Details that I've used successfully are illustrated at left (**Figures 1** to **3**).

Chuck Silver designs energy-efficient homes and conducts training seminars for builders in New Paltz, N.Y.

Condensation on Windows

Q. *A customer with insulated-glass windows has a problem with excessive condensation on the interior of the windows. What is the likely cause?*

A. *Andrew Shapiro responds:* Two factors affect the humidity level in a house: how fast water is being introduced and how fast it is leaving. A very tight house doesn't need a lot of moisture input to result in high humidity and condensation on the windows, while the same amount of water introduced into a very leaky house won't raise the humidity much.

You can use a blower door to check the house air leakage rate, though your wet windows may already be telling you that it is relatively tight. You can also check the humidity in the house with a Radio Shack temperature-humidity indicator. The windows should tolerate 40% relative humidity without condensing in cold weather. If they don't, then they are part of the problem — they're not well enough insulated at the edges. If the homeowner isn't willing to upgrade the windows or add storms, then you'll have to lower humidity levels further.

Showering contributes a lot of moisture to a home. A bath exhaust fan should take care of it, but often the fan is undersized, little used, or ineffective because of long ductwork with too many twists and turns. Drying clothes indoors also releases a lot of water. (Dryers should always be ducted outside.) Every drop of water that goes to houseplants ends up as moisture in the air. Drying firewood in the basement can add quite a lot of water. Cooking, particularly if the occupants don't use a range hood that is vented to the outside, can also generate a lot of moisture.

If the house is new, the construction materials contain literally tons of water that will evaporate over the first winter. Therefore, condensation problems that show up the first winter may not show up again. Poor basement drainage on a wet site can also be a major source of water. (Your nose will tell you if there is water in the basement — you can usually smell the damp or the mold.) Consistently bringing wet or snowy cars into an attached garage that is not adequately sealed from the house can also bring in a lot of water.

To solve condensation problems, first reduce the sources of moisture and then ventilate to get the humidity down to acceptable levels. I recommend powered ventilation for all houses. An inexpensive ventilation approach is to install a quiet, efficient bathroom exhaust fan, like those made by Panasonic. The fan can either run continuously or be wired to a control like the Airetrak (Tamarack Technologies), which runs the fan at a constant adjustable speed and has a push button for 20 minutes of high speed.

Andrew Shapiro is an energy and sustainable design consultant, and principal of Energy Balance in Montpelier, Vt.

Mildew in Closets

Q. *Why does mildew grow in a closet?*

A. *Marc Rosenbaum responds:* To control mildew growth, we must first consider the relationship between air, water vapor, and relative humidity (RH). The warmer the air, the more water vapor it can hold; the colder the air, the less water vapor it can hold. RH is a measure of how much water vapor is in the air compared to the maximum amount of water vapor the air can hold at that temperature. As air cools, its RH goes up. As the air continues to cool, it reaches the point where the water vapor it contains is all that it can hold — this is 100% RH. Cooling the air any further will result in condensation as some of the water vapor changes to liquid.

Mildew can grow only on surfaces where the RH of the surrounding air exceeds 70%. Closet surfaces tend to be colder than adjacent rooms because of poor air circulation from the heated room to the closet and because, relative to their size, they often have more exterior surface area for heat to escape. A corner or cold wall section lacking proper insulation is particularly vulnerable. These areas are colder but have just as much moisture in the air as adjacent rooms, so they have higher RH and are prone to mold and mildew (**Figure 4**).

To control the mildew, we have to lower the RH of the closet below 70%. To do this, we either have to raise the closet air temperature or lower the amount of water vapor present in the air.

When troubleshooting a closet mold problem, measure the temperature and RH in the adjacent room with a sling psychrometer. If the room RH is 30%, then it will be difficult (and hard on the occupants' respiratory systems) to reduce RH much, so look for ways to raise the closet temperature. Either increase heat flow into the closet (in some cases, louvered doors may permit enough heated room air to circulate; in other cases, you may have to put in some heat directly), or cut heat loss from the closet by adding insulation or sealing air leaks in the closet walls.

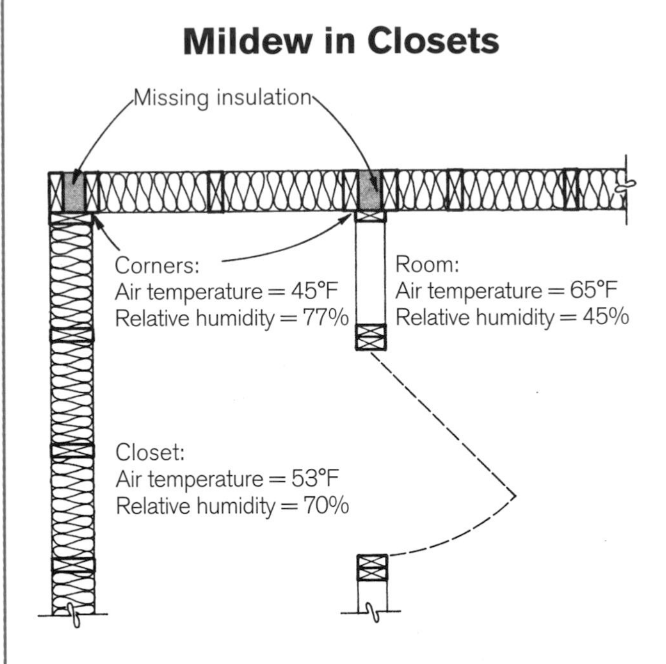

Figure 4. Mold and mildew often grow in closets because the colder temperatures there raise the relative humidity above 70%. Missing insulation at corners and framing intersections is often to blame.

If the room RH is 50% or greater, look for ways to reduce the amount of moisture in the air. First, control the moisture at its source. Is it coming from a hot tub, lots of plants, or a gross of gerbils? Is it coming from the six cords of firewood drying in the basement? Next, if the problem occurs in the heating season, increase ventilation levels to replace humid house air with cold outdoor air holding little moisture. As a last resort, use mechanical dehumidification.

Closet mildew problems often occur with other moisture problems that the homeowner is not aware of, so a comprehensive "footing to ridge" assessment may be in order.

Marc Rosenbaum, PE, owns Energysmiths, in Meriden, N.H., a company specializing in energy-efficient, environmentally sound homes.

Double-Sided Vapor Barriers

Q. *As part of the gut remodel of a 1940s house near Houston, Texas, we installed 3/4-inch rigid foam over the exterior wall sheathing, followed by vinyl siding. On the interior, we exposed the 2x4 studs and installed fiberglass batts. Then we installed 1/2-inch foil-faced rigid foam followed by drywall. In that climate, will these "foam sandwich" walls trap moisture?*

A. *Joseph Lstiburek responds:* Installing a vapor barrier on both sides of a wall is never a good idea in any climate. In the Houston climate, a vapor barrier should be located on the exterior, so your choice of exterior foam sheathing was a good one. The concern is the foam sheathing you installed on the interior.

The good news is that because of the thermal resistance of the interior foam, the wall cavity will rarely be below the dew point temperature of the exterior air (see "Where Does the Dew Drop?," page 57). The bad news is that if moisture ever gets into the wall — say, via a window flashing leak or because of negative pressure caused by leaky attic ductwork — it won't be able to get out easily.

Should you remove the foam sheathing on the inside? I wouldn't recommend it. If possible, however, watch the walls over the next few years; each year, cut open a small hole in several spots and look. If you did a careful job with exterior rain control and window and duct installation, the walls probably won't develop mold. But don't build a wall this way again.

Joseph Lstiburek, PhD, PE, is a principal of Building Science Consulting (www.buildingscience.com) in Westford, Mass., and an investigator of moisture-related building problems.

Exterior Vapor Barrier in Hot Climates

Q. *I'm considering using a waterproof membrane such as Grace Ice & Water Shield (Grace Construction Products) as a housewrap on the building's exterior. These materials are more expensive than Tyvek (DuPont) or felt paper but can't be beat when it comes to the wind-driven rain we get here in the Florida Panhandle. Could this "cold-side vapor retarder" cause problems?*

A. *Paul Fisette replies:* Climate has a definite impact on the specification of a weather-barrier system. In a heating climate, I would *not* recommend covering large areas of the wall sheathing with a rubberized membrane like Grace's. It is impermeable, and it forms a powerful cold-side vapor barrier. If water or vapor leaks into a wall cavity that has an airtight "rubberized" covering on the exterior surface and an impermeable vapor retarder installed on the wall's interior, the moisture will be trapped there.

But in your hot, humid climate, a low-perm membrane applied facing the warm exterior could work. It is important to build the wall so that it's able to dry toward the inside when conditions dictate — in other words, don't apply a poly vapor barrier or vinyl wallpaper to the interior.

However, given the expense of rubberized membranes, I think I would choose #30 felt. It's stiff and a bit difficult to work with, but it's more forgiving if you get water on the wrong side of the membrane. If you are building in a very exposed location where "sideways" rain is common, I would consider a rain-screen design, which balances air pressure and creates a drainage plane. This option is not cheap, but I think it's more effective for severe exposures.

Paul Fisette is a wood technologist and professor with the Building Materials and Wood Technology program at the University of Massachusetts in Amherst.

Installing a Polyethylene Air/Vapor Barrier

by Steve Lentz

Since 1984, I have been building energy-efficient homes with special attention to air sealing. Most conventional new homes, when tested with a blower door, show an infiltration rate of 4 to 8 air changes per hour; my homes are rated at 0.48 to 1.0 air changes per hour at 50 Pascals (ACH50), equivalent to a natural infiltration rate of less than 0.1 ACH. My package of energy-saving details costs my customers only about $1.25 per square foot, and they often make back the extra cost with just three to five years of energy savings. Because satisfied customers tell their friends about their low energy bills, my homes have been in steady demand.

Building a tight home does require training your subcontractors. But subs who do quality work may be eager to learn about air sealing, since those skills make them more attractive to other energy-efficient builders.

Below-Grade Moisture Control

Most builders install a poly vapor barrier under their basement slabs. But it's also important to include poly under the wall footings to prevent the foundation walls themselves from wicking up water (**Figure 5**, next page). Eliminating this source of moisture lessens the chance of mold and improves indoor air quality.

After my foundation contractor coats the exterior

Figure 5. Installing polyethylene under a concrete footing prevents ground moisture from wicking up the basement walls.

Figure 6. In preparation for pouring the basement slab, a layer of 1-inch-thick polystyrene insulation is installed over 6-mil polyethylene and 8 inches of crushed stone.

of the basement walls with dampproofing, I install 2 inches of extruded polystyrene foam from the footing to the mudsill. All of my basement footings have perimeter drain tile on the interior as well as the exterior. Finally, I backfill with 3/4-inch crushed stone up to 2 feet of finish grade.

To protect the rigid foam above grade, I use a tough fiberglass material called Ground Breaker (Nudo Products), which comes in 50-foot rolls in widths of 12 and 24 inches. These panels are tough — I've never put a hole in one. The top edge of the material is fastened to the mudsill with 3-inch roofing nails driven through the rigid foam, while the bottom is kept in place by the dirt backfill.

Our basement slabs are poured over 8 inches of 3/4-inch crushed stone covered with a layer of 6-mil poly (**Figure 6**). For the poly, we prefer a brand called Tu-Tuf (Sto-Cote Products) — a high-density, cross-laminated white polyethylene. Since the poly under the slab is a vapor barrier, not an air barrier, there's no need to tape the seams. Over the poly we install a layer of 1-inch rigid foam. If the basement is getting radiant floor heat, I increase the depth of the under-slab foam to 2 inches.

Air Sealing Begins at Framing

The most important factor in building an energy-efficient house is the installation of a continuous air barrier. Our company uses polyethylene, which also serves as the vapor barrier. As an air barrier, the poly needs to be as airtight as possible, as it snakes its way up from the mudsill, around the band joist, under the wall plates, up the interior edge of the studs, and under the ceiling joists.

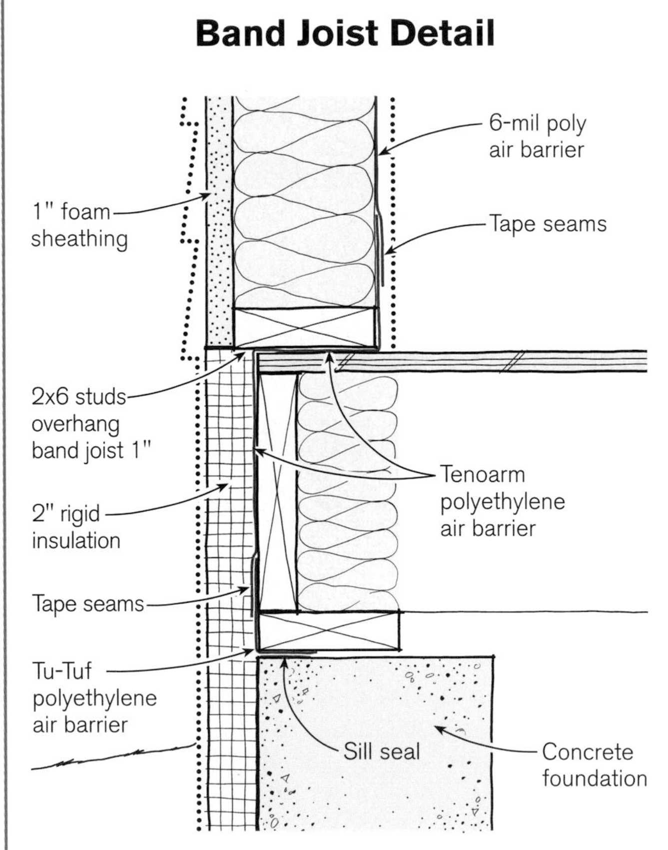

Figure 7. The key to the author's airtight shells is the continuous polyethylene air barrier, which starts beneath the mudsill. Every seam is taped or sealed with acoustical sealant.

Figure 8. Before installing the mudsill, a 6-inch-wide strip of poly is embedded in Tremco sealant and stapled to the underside. A 2 3/4-inch-wide strip of foam sill seal is stapled over the poly, and then the sill is flipped over and bolted in place. The poly flap faces the exterior.

If you wait until the framing is complete to think about air sealing, it's already too late. Unless the framers take time to install narrow strips of polyethylene between framing members in key areas, there's simply no way to keep the air barrier continuous.

For the polyethylene to serve as a true air barrier, all seams must also be sealed with either 3M contractor's tape or Tremco acoustical sealant (Tremco Global Sealants). Since Tremco is a sealant, not an adhesive, there must be a solid framing member behind it for it to work effectively. When sealing a seam without solid backing, we use tape. The red tape from 3M is tenacious and long lasting. I've opened up walls six years after completion and found the tape to be as good as the day it was installed.

Band Joist Details

We frame our floor system so that the band joist is flush with the foundation, while the walls are framed to overhang the band joist by 1 inch. When the band joists are later covered with 2-inch foam, they end up flush with the 1-inch foam wall sheathing (**Figure 7**).

On my houses, the poly air barrier starts under the mudsill. We staple a length of 6-inch-wide Tu-Tuf polyethylene, embedded in Tremco sealant, to the bottom of the sill before it is installed, with about half the width of the poly extending beyond the sill toward the exterior. Every seam gets sealed with Tremco or tape.

I cut the 5 1/2-inch-wide roll of sill seal in half lengthwise before I staple it to the sill, because I find that the narrower 2 3/4-inch-wide strip squashes down better and provides a better seal. Once the sill seal is stapled over the poly, the sill is flipped over and bolted down (**Figure 8**).

After the subfloor is nailed down and the lines are snapped for the exterior walls, we wrap the exterior of the band joist with poly. Since a band joist gets a lot of abuse during construction, we wrap it with Tenoarm (Resource Conservation Technology), a tough 10-mil polyethylene from Sweden. Unlike Tu-Tuf, Tenoarm is transparent, so we can see the chalk lines through it where it laps onto the subfloor.

The Tenoarm strips are about 16 inches wide, so they span the band joist and the 5 1/2-inch width of the bottom plate with at least an inch left for overlap. We seal the Tenoarm to the poly sticking out from under the mudsill with tape or Tremco, then fold it over onto the plywood subfloor (**Figure 9**).

Figure 9. The band joist is wrapped with Tenoarm, a very tough, transparent polyethylene. The Tenoarm is taped to the white polyethylene (which was stapled earlier to the bottom of the mudsill) and then wrapped up onto the subfloor.

Figure 10. After the walls are raised, the transparent Tenoarm polyethylene sticks out from under the bottom plate, facing the interior. This flap will later be taped to the wall poly.

Figure 11. To keep the air from the soffit vents from disturbing the attic insulation, flaps of poly are stapled between the heels of the attic trusses. The vent channel needs to extend only above the expected depth of attic insulation.

Next, we extend the 2-inch-thick basement wall insulation up to cover the exterior of the band joist. On the inside, we insert a piece of R-19 fiberglass batt insulation up against the band joist in each bay. The 2-inch exterior foam keeps the band joist warm enough to prevent condensation on the poly.

We frame our exterior walls with 2x6s spaced 16 inches on-center, since 24-inch spacing doesn't provide adequate nailing for siding. Once the walls are raised, the Tenoarm should peek out from under the bottom plate of the exterior walls, facing the inside of the house (**Figure 10**). On a two-story house, the second-floor band joist is also wrapped on the exterior with Tenoarm. In this case, the Tenoarm extends from the interior over the top plate, up over the exterior of the band joist, and back onto the second-story subfloor.

Insulation

Back in the 1970s, I used to pay an insulation contractor to blow 10 inches of cellulose into my attics. When I inspected the attic of one of my homes a few months after completion, I noticed that the cellulose barely covered the bottom chord of the trusses. My insulation sub explained, "It must have settled." So in 1979, I decided to get my own cellulose-blowing equipment. Now I install 22 inches of cellulose in every attic, so that even after settling, my attics have a minimum of 16 inches of insulation.

Eaves. To be sure there's enough room at the eaves for attic insulation, I specify raised-heel trusses. To get the necessary R-value on a stick-built roof, where the rafters come down too low at the attic perimeter, I install several layers of rigid foam insulation between the rafters above the wall plates.

To prevent wind-washing of the attic insulation above the soffit vents, we install wind breaks between the attic trusses. These are scraps of 6-mil poly, housewrap, or Tu-Tuf, stapled to the wall top plate and the roof trusses (**Figure 11**).

Cathedral ceilings. For cathedral ceilings, my minimum rafter size is 2x12, although I've installed wood I-joist rafters as deep as 18 inches. In my experience, when cathedral-ceiling rafters are densely packed with cellulose insulation, no ventilation channels or soffit vents are required. As cheap insurance against possible moisture problems, I include ridge vents above my cathedral ceilings. Although this "hot roof" construction is controversial, I have done it this way successfully for years. I've had several opportunities to open up the ridges of cathedral ceilings completed years earlier, and in every case the rafter bays were dry and free of mold. None of the houses I've built have ever had a problem with ice dams or ceiling condensation. Be careful, though: This approach works only if your ceiling air barrier is airtight.

Blowing walls. To retain the cellulose insulation blown between the studs, I use a translucent permeable fabric called InsulWeb (Hanes Industries). InsulWeb is a spunbonded polypropylene fabric full of tiny holes that allow excess air pressure to escape; it is not intended to act as a vapor or air barrier.

After stapling InsulWeb to the studs, we make one hole in each stud cavity, about 4 feet up from the floor. We start filling the cavity from the bottom, using a 2-inch rigid or flexible hose. When the stud bay is almost full of cellulose, we direct the hose to the top of the cavity to ensure that the top gets well filled.

When we finish blowing the walls, we count the bags of cellulose to be sure we've used enough. At the recommended density of 3 pounds per cubic foot, a 30-pound bag of cellulose should fill one and two-thirds 8-foot wall cavities framed with 2x6s on 16-inch centers. We also check the density by pounding on the installed cellulose: If the cellulose moves, it's not tight enough. If necessary, we go back and squeeze a little more.

We use fiberglass batts in a few areas, such as behind a tub located on an exterior wall. In this case, the batts and the poly air barrier need to be installed before the tub goes in. The poly behind the tub is taped to the flanges of poly protruding from the bottom plate and the intersecting partition walls (**Figure 12**).

Electrical boxes. Despite what some insulation contractors will tell you, dense-pack cellulose does not stop airflow — it just slows it down. If you have a leaky electrical box, you can feel the air moving right through the cellulose during a blower-door test. When I started building energy-efficient homes, I was frustrated that there weren't any decent airtight electrical boxes on the market, so I decided to design and manufacture my own.

For more than 20 years, I've been selling the Lessco box (Low Energy Systems Supply Company), an airtight plastic box large enough to accommodate a standard electrical box inside of it (**Figure 13**).

Lessco boxes are simple to install, so it shouldn't take long to train your electrician; they are installed at the same time as standard electrical boxes. After the walls have been blown, we insulate the Lessco boxes by hand with scraps of fiberglass.

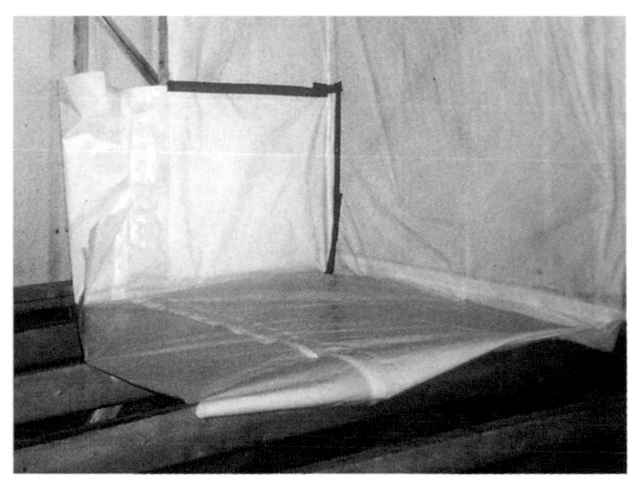

Figure 12. If a tub/shower unit is located against an exterior wall, fiberglass insulation and the poly air barrier need to be installed before the tub. All seams in the poly air barrier are taped with red contractor's tape from 3M.

Interior Air Barrier

Once our walls are insulated, we install a layer of Tu-Tuf poly over the InsulWeb on the inside of the exterior walls, sealing the seams with tape or Tremco. This layer is also sealed to the flap of Tenoarm sticking out from under the bottom plate. (We don't continue the Tenoarm up the walls, because it's too thick to form neat inside corners.) Where partitions intersect exterior walls, we install a 2x6 or 2x8 backing stud as a drywall nailer, followed by a strip of Tu-Tuf, which is also taped to the Tenoarm flap (**Figure 14**, next page).

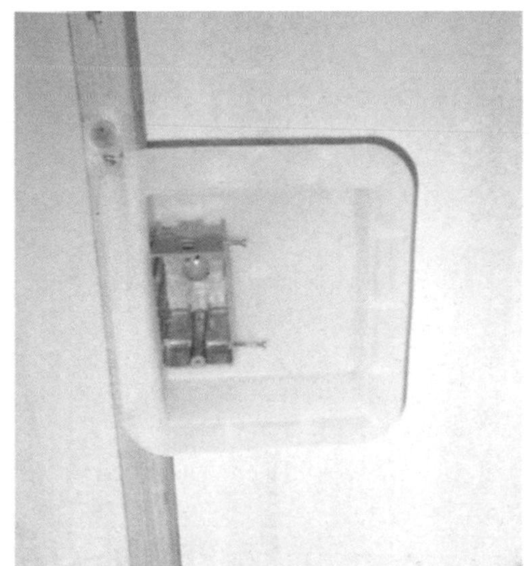

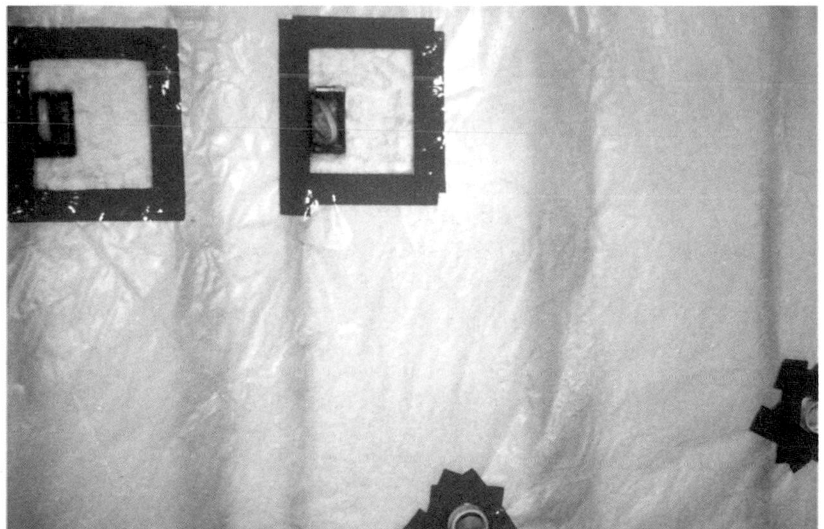

Figure 13. The Lessco box is a 6 1/2 x 7 1/2 x 2 7/8-inch airtight plastic box that's installed at the same time as a regular electrical box (left). After a wall is insulated, the poly air barrier is taped to the flange of the Lessco box (right), and the Lessco box is insulated with scraps of fiberglass or cellulose. Note that all plumbing penetrations in the wall are sealed with contractor's tape.

On the top floor, we prefer to install a continuous layer of poly on the entire ceiling before the partitions go up. To minimize damage to the ceiling poly, we carefully position the partition top plates against the ceiling joists and drive the bottom plates home with a sledge. Any accidental tears in the ceiling poly get repaired with tape.

Cut the ceiling poly. Once all of the interior partitions are installed, I go to the second floor and cut the ceiling poly around the perimeter of each room on three sides, leaving the poly hanging from the uncut side. Considering the care with which it was installed, this may seem strange — but if I don't cut it, I know the electrician will. After cutting the ceiling poly, I roll up the plastic and leave it hanging against the wall on the uncut side. I leave enough plastic at the perimeter of the room to give us something to tape to when it's time to put the ceiling poly back up — when all electrical and mechanical work in the ceiling is finished.

In a home with a bearing wall, where it's not possible to install the ceiling poly in one piece, we install

Figure 14. Where a partition intersects an exterior wall, a strip of poly is installed along the 2x8 drywall nailer before the partition is built. Note that the wall poly is taped to the Tenoarm poly that protrudes from under the bottom plate.

Figure 15. In homes where the ceiling poly can't be installed in a single sheet, it's installed room by room. When building the top-floor partitions, the framers must install a strip of poly between the top plates and the ceiling joists. Later, the ceiling poly in each room will be taped to the perimeter flaps.

Figure 16. A conventional recessed can fixture can be installed in a site-built foam box. The box, which is sized to provide 2 inches of free air on all sides of the fixture, is assembled with Tremco to seal the seams.

Figure 17. When planning for a light fixture above a tub, it sometimes makes sense to lower the ceiling to keep the electrical box from penetrating the poly ceiling barrier.

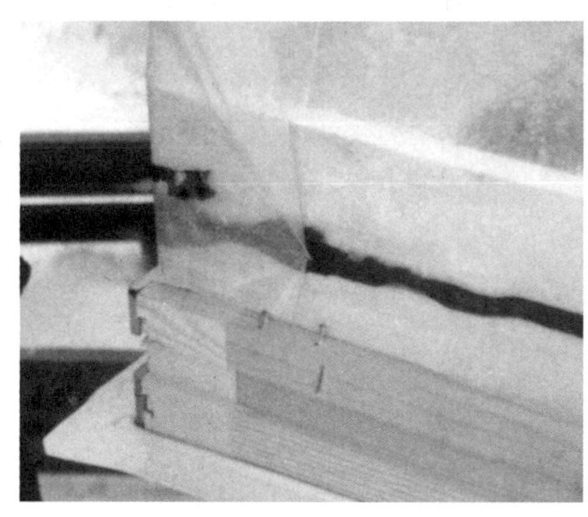

Figure 18. A polyethylene "bib" is added around the exterior of each window before it's installed. Several extra pleats of poly are provided at the window corners (far left), so that it can later be folded flat against the interior of the studs. A strip of duct tape over the poly (left) provides reinforcement for the staple heads.

it room by room. Each partition needs to have a strip of poly above the top plate (**Figure 15**), and any penetration of the ceiling poly needs to be carefully sealed with tape or aerosol foam.

Chimney penetrations. A gas or wood-fired zero-clearance fireplace can work well in a tight home, as long as the fireplace has glass doors and ducted combustion makeup air. Equally important, the customer needs to understand that the fireplace is there to look at, not to serve as a significant heat source.

Where a metal chimney penetrates the ceiling poly, we install the chimney manufacturer's metal fire-stop collar. We cut the poly 2 inches away from the chimney and seal it to the metal collar with tape. The gap between the chimney and the fire-stop collar is sealed with high-temperature GE silicone caulk, available from fireplace dealers. High-temperature caulk is rated for use up to 400°F or 500°F.

Ceiling-mounted electrical boxes. I stopped using commercially available "airtight" recessed can fixtures when blower-door testing showed that they leak like sieves. Now I use standard recessed can fixtures and install them in a site-built foam box made from scraps of 1-inch or 2-inch rigid foam with seams sealed with tape or Tremco (**Figure 16**). I size these boxes to provide at least 2 inches of free air space on all sides of the recessed fixture. We seal the ceiling poly to the edge of the foam box with Tremco. In the attic, we blow 22 inches of cellulose over the top of the box. We have never had a light fixture overheat using this system.

Another way to keep ceiling-mounted electrical boxes from penetrating the poly air barrier is to frame a secondary ceiling below the poly. A closet ceiling or the ceiling above a tub/shower unit can often be lowered to 7 feet or 7 feet 6 inches (**Figure 17**).

Attic access hatch. I make my attic access hatches out of 3/4-inch plywood with 8 inches of foam glued to the top. The hatch sits on the jamb, which is fitted with rubber bulb-type weatherstripping. Each hatch is closed with two casement window latches, which I buy from my local Weather Shield dealer.

Windows and Doors

My minimum spec for window glass is 5/8-inch insulated low-E argon-filled glazing. I've had good success using Pella aluminum-clad wood windows. If the customer chooses optional removable interior glazing panels, the windows are effectively triple-glazed.

Before installing a window, we put a bead of Tremco around the outside of the frame or the extension jambs. Then we attach a 6-inch-wide strip of 6-mil poly to the window frame, stapled through the Tremco every 6 or 8 inches. Adding a 1-inch strip of duct tape over the poly helps prevent the staples from pulling through. It's important to provide a generous bunch of poly at the corners of the window so the poly can later be folded back flat. To provide slackness at the corners, we extend the strip of poly around a window corner, double back around the corner, and then return a third time. This provides a kind of poly bib around the window frame. The bib extends toward the interior and is folded flat against the studs when the window goes in (**Figure 18**).

Later, we install Tremco between the bib and the main poly wall air barrier. The pressure of the drywall against it makes an effective seal. An exterior door gets the same type of bib, except that it is installed on three sides, not four. Before the door gets installed, we put down a bead of Tremco under the sill. Later, we squirt some aerosol foam under the sill as well.

Sheathing, Housewrap, and Siding

I sheathe my houses with 1-inch rigid foam — either polystyrene or polyisocyanurate, depending on current foam prices. In my area, the code allows walls to be braced with metal T-bracing, although code officials in many areas of the country require plywood or OSB sheathing, at least at corners.

I attach plastic housewrap through the foam sheathing with 1 1/2-inch staples into the studs. After losing a lot of Tyvek to wind, I switched to Rufco-Wrap (Raven Industries), which is both cheaper and stronger.

Most of our buildings get vinyl or horizontal cedar siding, nailed through the foam sheathing to the studs. Since windows with wide exterior casing can be hard to integrate with foam sheathing, I have developed a detail that works well for me: I butt the cedar clapboard to the window frames and install the wide casing on top of the siding. Because this detail requires no caulk, it looks better to my eye than butting the siding to the casing.

HVAC

These days, most customers want central air conditioning, so all of my homes use ducts for heat distribution. I have had good success using the Lennox CompleteHeat (Lenox International), a hydro-air system that provides both domestic hot water and space heat. The heating unit consists of a water heater coupled with a fan-coil unit to distribute hot air through a duct system.

We try to keep as much of our ductwork inside the building envelope as possible. When ducts must run through the attic, we use insulated flex duct buried under 22 inches of cellulose. Where a duct penetrates the ceiling poly, we carefully tape the air barrier to the flex duct. Every metal duct joint gets sealed with duct mastic.

A tight home requires good mechanical ventilation. All of my homes include a heat-recovery ventilator. My favorite HRVs are those made by Venmar because they are so quiet.

My customers are usually delighted to live in a tight, well-ventilated home with low energy bills. Word-of-mouth referrals from satisfied customers make up a large percentage of my leads and keep me as busy as I want to be.

Steve Lentz is a builder from Campbellsport, Wis. He is a life member of the Energy and Environmental Building Association (EEBA) and a past president of the Builders Association of Fond du Lac and Dodge Counties.

Chapter 5: Air Sealing

- Air-Sealing a New Home
- Rx for Common Air Leaks

Air-Sealing a New Home

by Paul Bourke

Over the years, I've developed a simple system to control random air leaks in the energy-efficient houses I build in Massachusetts. Of all the possible energy-saving upgrades, air sealing is the most cost effective, since about 30% of the heat loss in a typical home is the result of uncontrolled air leaks. Using the techniques described here, we build houses with consistently low infiltration rates — 0.6 square inches (or less) of leakage per 100 square feet of shell area, well under the Energy Crafted Homes standard of 2.0 square inches.

Creating a Tight Air Barrier

If you are committed to minimizing air leaks in the houses you build, you need to be sure that everyone on the job site, including the framing crew and the subcontractors, understands the basics of air sealing and understands your expectations for maintaining a tight air barrier.

In the colder parts of the U.S., builders typically install polyethylene under the drywall, calling it the "vapor barrier." But the most important function of polyethylene is as an air barrier. Moisture follows air leaks, moving through holes in a house at much greater rates than it passes through solid surfaces as a vapor. Most of the problem-causing moisture that condenses in attics and building cavities is transported by interior air leaking through holes in the air barrier.

An air barrier should be continuous with the thermal insulation. In most cases, the air barrier will be on the warm side of the thermal insulation, but it doesn't have to be. In some cases, it makes sense to establish the air barrier on the outside of the thermal insulation.

Assemble your materials. For a careful air-sealing job, you'll need to be sure you have a few important materials on hand:

- Reinforced polyethylene. Examples include Tu-Tuf (Sto-Cote Products), par/PAC and Good News Reused (parPAC, Inc.), or Tenoarm (Resource Conservation Technology).
- Tremco acoustical sealant (Tremco Global Sealants), a multipurpose air-sealing caulk that sticks to polyethylene
- 3M Builders' Sealing Tape, also called "contractor's tape" used for polyethylene and housewrap
- Airtight electrical boxes (from LESSCO)
- A good urethane foam gun

Keeping the Basement Warm

We always install 6-mil polyethylene and at least 1 inch of rigid foam insulation under all of our basement slabs. Besides saving energy, the foam keeps the slab warm, greatly increasing comfort and helping to minimize condensation. After installing crushed stone to the depth of the footing, we lay down the poly and then the rigid foam. We also install a strip

Figure 1. Installing 1 inch of rigid foam insulation under the basement slab keeps the slab warm enough to prevent moisture from condensing on it. The perimeter insulation between the slab and the colder concrete wall provides a thermal break.

of 1-inch foam at the perimeter of the slab, between the slab and the foundation wall, as a thermal break (**Figure 1**). If the basement floor is getting radiant heat, we'll increase the thickness of the under-slab insulation to 2 inches.

Insulating basement walls. We no longer insulate our basement walls from the exterior, because exterior foam is vulnerable to insect damage, and above-grade foam is difficult to protect. Instead, we frame up 2x4 walls inside the basement, leaving a 2-inch gap between the back of the studs and the basement wall. This allows enough room for the installation of R-19 fiberglass batts, which we cover with flame-retardant poly from Poly-America. One advantage of interior insulation: With the 2x4 perimeter walls installed, all it takes is wiring and drywall for a customer to finish the basement.

Most basement walls have few penetrations, so they are relatively simple to air-seal. But be careful of bulkhead doors, which are often leaky. The area between the door and the band joist, especially, needs to be sealed and insulated.

Figure 2. Recessing the band joist 2 inches provides room for exterior rigid foam insulation. To provide an air barrier, the foam is carefully caulked in place with Tremco acoustical sealant.

Preventing Drafty Floors

Many houses leak a lot of air through gaps at the perimeter of the floor system. To keep this area tight, four critical areas need to be addressed: under the mudsill, along the band joist, between the band joist and the subfloor, and between the subfloor and the wall plate.

Tight sills. Between the foundation wall and the mudsill, we use regular polyethylene foam sill seal, folded in half lengthwise. Doubled sill seal does a better job of air sealing than a single layer. Any gaps that are too big for the sill seal to handle are filled later, using our urethane foam gun.

Warm band joists. On many houses, the band joists are poorly insulated, so condensation forms on the cold interior surface of the lumber. Keeping the band joist warm with exterior foam insulation prevents condensation that can lead to rot.

Since we frame our walls with 2x6s, we can recess our band joists 2 inches. We attach 2-inch-thick rigid foam to the band joist with continuous beads of Tremco acoustical sealant (**Figure 2**). The rigid foam, once it is caulked in place, becomes the air barrier. Although Tremco sealant can be messy to apply (hence its nickname: "black death"), it's the best caulk to use for air-sealing a wide variety of materials, including most types of plastic.

From inside the basement, we stuff a piece of R-19 Kraft-faced fiberglass batt into each joist bay, behind the band joist. Finally, when we put the subfloor down, we put a continuous bead of construction adhesive along the band joist to prevent any air leaks at the perimeter of the subfloor.

Gasketed bottom plate. We install regular foam sill seal under the bottom plates of our exterior walls. To make the sill seal go twice as far, we usually cut it in half lengthwise. We roll out the foam and hammer-tack it to the subfloor just before we stand up our walls. Instead of foam sill seal, you can also use sticky-backed foam weatherstripping in this location.

Cantilevers. Cantilevered floors are particularly difficult to air-seal, especially if wires or pipes create an air path through the floor and up the exterior wall. At the point where the cantilever begins, we install solid blocking between each cantilevered joist. The edges of the blocking, as well as any penetrations through the blocking, get carefully caulked. Because the plywood subfloor over a cantilever is the air barrier, be sure the subfloor is installed with construction adhesive. Finally, the bottom of the cantilevered joists need to be wrapped with housewrap.

Keeping Walls Tight

Most of our walls are framed with 2x6s, 16 inches on-center. If the studs are spaced wider than 16 inches, the dense-pack cellulose insulation pillows out, interfering with drywall installation. If the customer is willing to pay for an upgrade, we space the 2x6 studs at 24 inches on-center and then install horizontal interior 1x3 strapping at 16 inches on-center (**Figure 3**, next page). The strapping restrains the cellulose and also provides a thermal break between the drywall and the studs.

When it comes to sheathing, we prefer to use plywood or OSB, unless the homeowner insists on foam. Foam sheathing causes several headaches: The walls need special bracing against racking; window and door openings need to be furred out; and siding can

Figure 3. When the budget allows, 2x6 studs are spaced 24 inches on-center, and 1x3 strapping is installed horizontally at 16 inches on-center. The air space provides a thermal break between the studs and the drywall. Red 3M tape is used to seal seams and tears in the poly air barrier.

be attached only to the studs.

We always install Tyvek (DuPont), which we consider the best available housewrap. We tape all seams with Tyvek tape, following the manufacturer's instructions.

Where an interior partition meets an exterior wall, we install a vertical 1x8, 1x10, or plywood piece as a drywall nailer. This nailer needs to be continuous (not a collection of scraps), and it needs to be wide enough to provide room to tape the poly air barrier in the corner.

Insulating Rafter Heels

In many houses, the insulation is thin at the rafter heels, where adequate space for insulation is lacking. This thin insulation can contribute to melting snow and ice dams. On the interior, thin insulation leaves the drywall cold at the corner, encouraging condensation and mildew.

One way to increase the R-value at the rafter heels is to install rigid foam insulation between the rafters. This is fussy work — first, installing 3/4-inch strips of plywood against the top of the rafter faces to maintain a ventilation channel, then cutting each piece of foam for a snug fit.

If the roof is being framed with rafters, an easier solution is to install a band joist and raise the rafters (see "Raised Rafter Plate Connections," page 273). Raising the rafters leaves plenty of room for insulation. If the roof is framed with trusses, use raised-heel trusses, which don't cost much more than regular trusses.

Windows and Doors

We build insulated door and window headers out of two 2x10s, a piece of 1/2-inch plywood, and 2 inches of rigid foam. The gap between a window and the rough opening should be sealed using a urethane foam gun or with backer rod and caulk, not fiberglass insulation. (Fiberglass insulation is not an air barrier.) We plan our rough openings for a 3/8-inch gap all around the window or door — just the right gap for a foam gun

Figure 4. When a tub/shower unit is located on an exterior wall, the poly air barrier is installed before the tub goes in. To create a tight air barrier, the poly needs to be taped to the bottom plate of the wall.

nozzle. We use Pur Fill low-expansion foam (distributed by Energy Federation Inc. or Todol Products), which won't distort the frame and pinch the sash.

Attic hatches. Since an attic access hatch is just an exterior door located in a ceiling, it needs to be carefully insulated and weatherstripped. A piece of drywall dropped into the opening is obviously inadequate. In winter, hatches without weatherstripping are often ringed with ice and deteriorated attic insulation.

We build our attic hatches from plywood and glue 4 inches of rigid foam insulation on top. Around the perimeter of the plywood hatch, we screw steel connector strapping. Along the top of the stop, we install magnetic door gasketing, which sucks that hatch down and seals it. When these magnetically sealed hatches are tested with a blower door, they are virtually leak-free.

Think Ahead

We've learned to recognize several areas that can be tricky to seal: walls behind tubs, interior soffits, recessed can lights, attic ductwork, zero-clearance fireplaces, chimney chases, dryer vents, and electrical boxes. If you plan the air-sealing details at the framing stage, sealing these areas will be much easier.

Tubs and showers. If a tub is located on an exterior wall, we install the poly air barrier, taped to the bottom plate, before the tub goes in (**Figure 4**). Then the area behind the tub is sheathed with plywood, which protects the poly and prevents the cellulose insulation from pillowing out. After the tub is installed, the stud bays can easily be filled with blown-in cellulose from the top.

Interior soffits. If the house has a second-floor soffit, don't forget to install the poly air barrier before the soffit is framed. The poly sheeting should be oversized with enough extra to allow it to be taped later to the rest of the poly air barrier.

Figure 5. Poorly sealed light fixtures in the ceiling continuously leak interior air into the attic. When the warm, moist air hits a cold surface, the moisture condenses, leading to mildew or rot.

Recessed cans. In many houses, recessed can lights act like little chimneys, constantly leaking interior air into the attic (**Figure 5**). If we have to install a recessed can light in an insulated ceiling, we make sure it is an airtight unit rated for insulation contact. We mount the can fixture on a piece of plywood that spans two joists; the plywood provides a surface for taping the poly air barrier.

Figure 6. Here, an HVAC register is installed in a piece of 3/4-inch plywood where it penetrates the attic air barrier. The register boot is caulked to the plywood, ensuring an airtight seal.

Figure 7. Where this dryer vent penetrates the exterior wall (at bottom of photo), a plywood block provides a surface for taping the poly air barrier. This house has horizontal wall strapping, so there was no need to recess the plywood block between the studs. Note that where the partition meets the exterior wall, the penetrations for the plumbing vent and electrical cable are sealed with urethane foam. The photo also shows an airtight electrical box.

Wherever possible, especially in bathrooms, we install recessed cans in soffits or dropped ceilings. Because the poly air barrier is installed at the bottom of the joists before the soffit is built, above the electrical fixtures, it remains intact.

Attic ducts. Most of our houses have some ductwork in the attic. At each ceiling register, and wherever a duct penetrates the ceiling poly, we install a section of 3/4-inch plywood spanning two joists. We usually provide the HVAC sub with a stack of 24-inch-wide pieces of 3/4-inch plywood for this purpose (**Figure 6**, previous page). The gap between the plywood and the duct or the flange on the register boot is sealed with a liberal amount of silicone caulk. The ceiling poly gets taped to the plywood.

All of the attic ducts are sealed with mastic or aluminum tape. After the HVAC sub has installed the ducts, we always go into the attic to inspect the work to be sure all penetrations of the ceiling air barrier are well-sealed. New subs usually take some training before they get it right.

Fireplaces. Zero-clearance fireplaces provide many opportunities for air leaks. Usually, we stop the air barrier one stud short of the fireplace, to keep the poly away from high temperatures. We tape the poly to that stud, and then install 1/2-inch cementitious backerboard between the stud and the fireplace. To maintain the air barrier, the backerboard is caulked in place with high-temperature silicone caulk, which we purchase at an auto supply store. The backerboard eventually gets covered with marble or brick.

Chimney chases. Most chimney chases allow interior air to rise to the attic through the 2-inch gap between the chimney and the ceiling joists. In many parts of the country, inspectors are being more stringent about enforcing the requirement for chimney fire stops. That's good, because fire stops improve energy efficiency.

For masonry chimneys, we make our fire stops out of 8-inch-wide aluminum flashing, bent on a brake. Our mason cuts a 1/2-inch kerf into the masonry to insert the fire stop, which doubles as an air barrier. Each chimney gets four pieces of flashing. We nail the flashing onto the framing, with a continuous bead of high-temperature silicone caulk under the flashing. We also install caulk at all of the flashing seams.

Metal chimneys require fire-stop kits provided by the chimney manufacturer. All of the gaps and cracks in these fire stops need to be caulked with high-temperature silicone.

Dryer vents. Where a dryer vent goes through an exterior wall, we usually install a plywood block between the studs, so that the vent duct has something to rest on (**Figure 7**). The plywood is attached to small 1x1 nailers and is mounted flush with the edge of the studs. We apply urethane foam between the dryer vent and the plywood, and tape the poly air barrier to the plywood.

Electrical boxes. We use one- or two-gang airtight electrical boxes, which don't cost much more than regular electrical receptacles. These boxes have a removable wide flange with a foam gasket designed to seal against the drywall. When we install the poly air barrier, we cut an X at each box and stretch the poly over the box. We tape the poly to the box, and then fit the flange on the box, locking the poly in place.

When we need three- or four-gang boxes, we buy airtight electrical boxes made by LESSCO.

Foam the gaps. After the framing is complete and the rough mechanicals are in — but before the insulation and poly — we inspect the house for gaps that need to be filled using the urethane foam gun. Places to check include between the foundation wall and the mudsill; where wires go through partitions that intersect exterior walls; and where wires and pipes penetrate the top plate into the attic.

Locating the Thermal Envelope

The continuous barrier formed by the insulation and air barrier is called the *thermal envelope*. Where to locate the thermal envelope depends, to some extent, on builder preference. Should it follow a flat ceiling or the sloping rafters? Should it include the crawlspace? In many cases, there is no single right answer to these questions. However, it is important to make a choice and stick with it, and then explain to your framing crew and subcontractors where the thermal envelope is located.

In the past, many builders excluded basements and crawlspaces from the thermal envelope. However, building scientists now recommend sealing and insulating crawlspace walls.

In cold climates, the prescriptive requirements of the Model Energy Code mandate basement wall insulation. Including the basement inside the building's thermal envelope is usually simpler and no more expensive than building an uninsulated basement, because insulated basements do not require ceiling insulation, duct sealing, duct insulation, or pipe insulation.

In a typical Cape, the second-floor knee walls are insulated, as well as a portion of the first-floor ceiling (see illustration). But when the thermal envelope is located at the knee walls, air sealing becomes very difficult. Interior air can escape through the first-floor ceiling into the cold area behind the knee walls. Exterior air from the soffit vents, which should rise above the insulation in the rafter bays to ventilate the roof, often enters the living area through gaps in the knee wall. An access door in an insulated kneewall is awkward to build, because it needs to be carefully insulated and weatherstripped.

Air sealing is easier when the rafter insulation is extended down to the plates, bringing the triangular crawlspace behind the knee walls within the building's thermal envelope. This also permits the area behind the knee wall to be used for storage without the need for an airtight access door. — *P.B.*

Air-Sealing a Cape Knee Wall

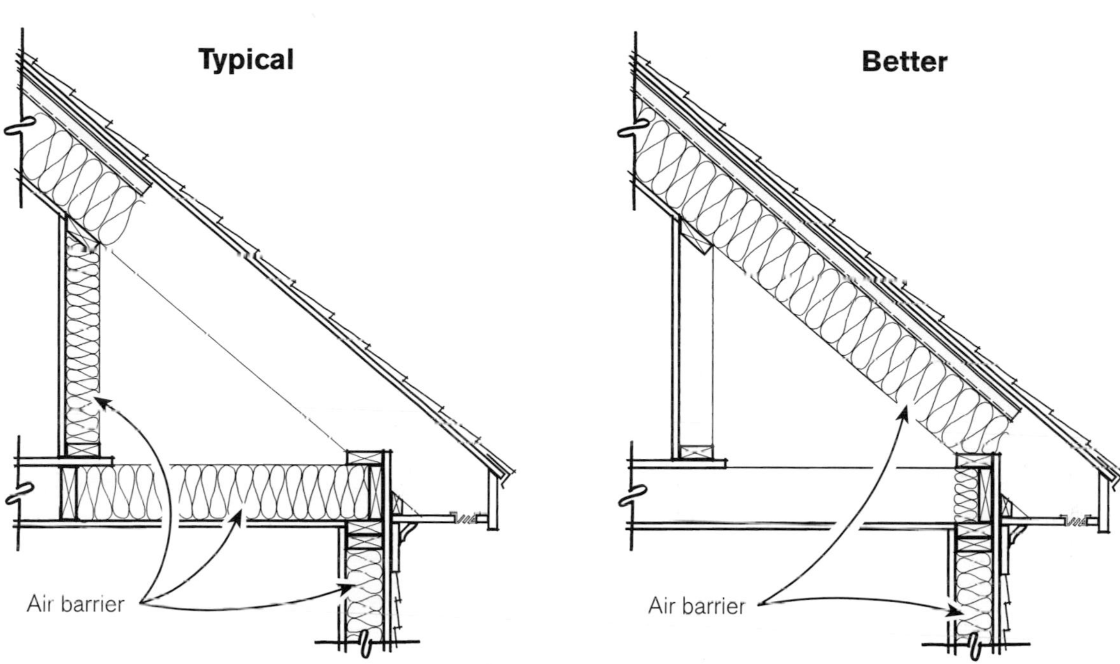

Creating a tight air barrier in a Cape knee wall is much more difficult if the knee walls and a portion of the first-floor ceiling are insulated (left). Air sealing is easier if the rafter insulation is brought all the way down to the wall plates (right).

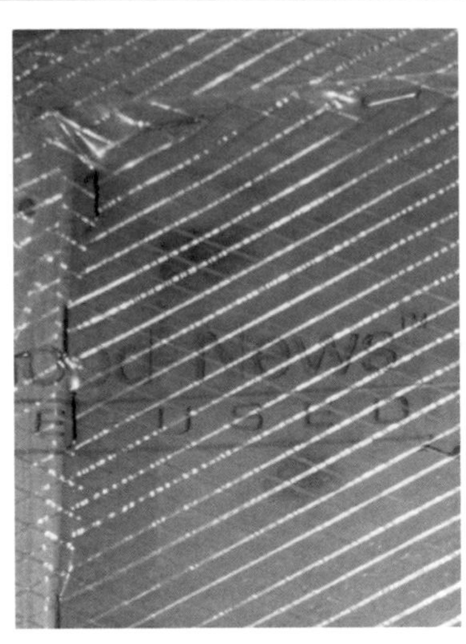

Figure 8. Most dense-pack cellulose systems require the installation of a reinforced polyethylene air barrier. Stapling the poly on the side rather than the edge of the studs helps keep the poly from bulging when the cellulose is blown in place.

Polyethylene Air Barrier

Some builders of energy-efficient homes advocate the Airtight Drywall Approach (ADA), creating their air barriers with gaskets installed under the drywall rather than with polyethylene. But because drywall contractors in our area are not familiar with ADA techniques, and because a poly barrier typically accompanies the installation of our preferred insulation — dense-pack cellulose — we don't use the ADA method.

Our insulation sub installs the reinforced poly air barrier according to our requirements. The poly gets stapled with 3/4-inch staples using an electric staple gun. For walls that won't receive interior horizontal strapping, the staples are driven into the side face of the stud, about 1/4 or 1/2 inch back from the interior edge (**Figure 8**).

Although a vapor barrier with a 2% gap is still 98% effective, the same is not true for an air barrier. An air barrier needs to be continuous, since small gaps can lead to big problems. All seams and gaps in a poly air barrier must be taped or caulked. For a typical building, we'll use about 12 rolls of 3M red contractor's tape, which costs about $12 a roll. Where the air barrier is being sealed to a top plate or bottom plate, or at the rough opening for a window or door, the poly can be sealed with either 3M tape or Tremco acoustical sealant.

We have experimented with installing the poly air barrier on the entire second-floor ceiling before we put up the interior partitions. But since that makes it more difficult for our mechanical subs to access the attic, we don't do it anymore. Usually, our ceiling poly is installed room by room and is carefully taped to the top plates of the walls. At the exterior walls, the ceiling poly gets taped to the wall poly.

Ceiling strapping. We usually strap our ceilings with 1x3s. In most cases, we install the poly air barrier on the bottom of the joists, before the strapping goes up.

Time to Insulate

Any insulation material can work well, as long as it is installed carefully. But if you expect fiberglass batts to match the performance of a blown-in insulation like dense-pack cellulose, you need to install the batts meticulously, without voids. How many fiberglass installers actually take the time to split the batts at every pipe and wire in the walls, much less in the attic?

Our preferred insulation is dense-pack cellulose, installed at a density of 2 1/2 pounds per cubic foot. Dense-pack cellulose helps reduce air infiltration and fills in especially well around mechanicals, wires, plumbing, and odd-shaped or tight spaces.

Because blowing cellulose in an attic is relatively

Figure 9. Cellulose insulation effectively fills all of the spaces around the bottom chords of roof trusses. Because cellulose is cheap, it can be piled on deep.

inexpensive, you can pile it deep (**Figure 9**). Before insulating an attic, we install sections of fiberglass batt insulation against the ventilation baffles, to prevent the cellulose from blowing into the soffits. When using blown-in cellulose in a cathedral ceiling, we install extra-rigid ventilation baffles (Durovent from ADO Products), as the cellulose pressure can cause standard baffles to collapse.

Our insulation sub slits the poly air barrier at each stud bay to insert the 2-inch blowing hose. It is the sub's responsibility to patch each hole with 3M tape. When the insulation job is complete, I check that the slits have all been taped. I also check the insulation density by feel, especially near the top of the stud bays. Well-installed cellulose should feel as firm as a car seat, not soft like a down pillow. The poly air barrier should be taut.

Build Tight and Ventilate Right

A tight house, which can't depend on random air leaks for ventilation and combustion makeup air, needs mechanical ventilation and sealed-combustion appliances. We ventilate many of our houses with Panasonic bathroom exhaust fans, which are quiet fans designed for continuous operation (see "Installing Simple Exhaust Ventilation," page 340). We follow the guidelines of ASHRAE 62-1989, which requires 15 cfm per person. Depending on the size of the house, this requirement is easily met with one or two Panasonic bathroom exhaust fans, each controlled by an Airetrak timer/fan-speed controller (Tamarack Technologies).

Multiple Benefits

The package of air-sealing details we provide adds between 2% and 2 1/2% to the cost of our homes — about $4,000 to $5,000 in construction costs on a $200,000 house. However, these details also result in savings. The houses require smaller heating and air conditioning units, as well as fewer radiators or less ductwork. Because we use sealed-combustion appliances, there is no need for a chimney. In many cases, these savings pay for the cost of the air-sealing measures.

Besides lowering the customer's heating bills, an energy-efficient house is less drafty and therefore more comfortable than a conventional house. During the winter, the indoor air will not be as dry as the air in a leaky house, so residents will have fewer bouts of respiratory infections, asthma, and allergic rhinitis. With fewer air leaks, there is less chance that warm, moist indoor air will leak into cold walls or the attic, where moisture can condense. Because of this, a tight house will be especially durable.

So if you build energy-efficient houses, your customers will be healthier. And they'll be pleased to know that their durable, comfortable, energy-efficient house will have a higher-than-average resale value.

Paul Bourke is a builder based in Leverett, Mass. He is a former instructor in the Energy Crafted Homes program and a member of the New England Sustainable Energy Association.

Rx for Common Air Leaks

by Bruce Torrey

As a GC who also specializes in diagnosing home energy performance, I receive a steady stream of calls from homeowners, property managers, and other builders requesting help. Common problems include drafty interiors, frozen pipes, high heating bills, ice dams, and comfort complaints. Surprisingly, most of these problems occur in new or newly renovated homes.

What's happening is a breakdown in the building sequence at the point where the framer stops and the insulation contractor starts. At that point, at least when air sealing is involved, the typical construction plan becomes vague or incomplete. This lack of continuity increases the likelihood that thermal and air bypasses will get built in to the project.

Tight Framing with Gaskets

To eliminate this disconnect, my company handles both framing and insulation in-house. Our goal is not to make the building absolutely airtight — an elusive goal at best — but to reduce the aggregate amount of leakage and to manage the flow of air entering and exiting the shell. Our typical target is a building with a passive rate of exchange of about 1/10 ACH per hour (.1 ACH). After we insulate a job but before the drywall is hung, I perform a blower-door test to measure how tight the insulated shell is (**Figure 10**, next page).

Over time, the test results have shown us where to concentrate our air-sealing efforts during framing. Fortunately, what's required adds little time or effort to the standard workflow. Instead of ordinary sill

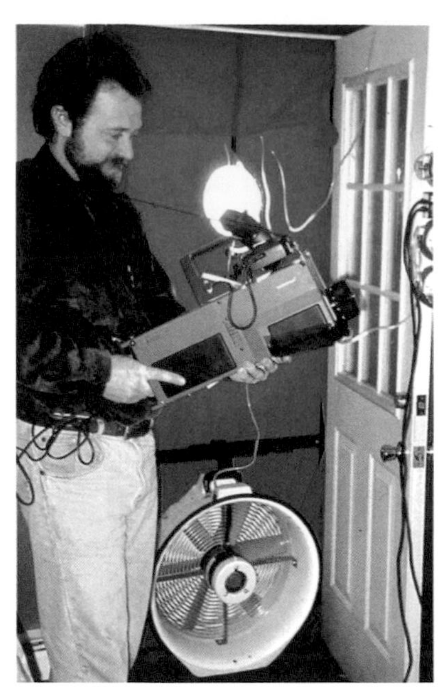

Figure 10. A blower door is a calibrated, variable-speed fan used to depressurize a house, creating a pressure difference between indoors and out. By measuring airflow through the fan, the total volume of air leakage through the building envelope can be determined.

sealer, we use a rubber (EPDM) gasket between the foundation and mudsill (**Figure 11**). The 5 1/2-inch-wide gasket is designed to provide a positive seal under a heavy structural load; it also serves as a moisture barrier between the concrete and wood.

After setting, stringing, and squaring the rim joists, we run a bead of construction adhesive over the joint between rim and mudsill. We've tried EPDM gaskets under the rim, but they tend to get in the way. Adhesive is less expensive and nearly as effective. It's important to take this step before rolling the floor joists into position; otherwise, rim sealing becomes a long, hard slog.

Glue-and-nail subfloor installation has become standard industry practice. However, not everyone glues the edge of the rim joist on the assumption that the walls hold the subfloor down at the edges. In fact, this is a common point of air entry, which we handle with a continuous bead of adhesive.

We frame and sheathe the walls on the deck before standing them on a rubber gasket tacked around the perimeter of the deck (**Figure 12**). I buy my gaskets from Resource Conservation Technology and Denarco Inc. These companies carry a good selection of gaskets designed for sealing a variety of framing configurations.

Because I'm convinced that air doesn't move through plywood, I sidestep the whole housewrap debate. Instead, shortly before installing the siding, we tape all the horizontal seams and any other cuts in the sheathing that aren't backed by framing. We use either DuPont Contractor Tape, 3M Builder's Sealing Tape, or both (**Figure 13**).

Gaps and Penetrations

Once the shell is tightened and weathered in, we turn our attention to interior air gaps and passages. Plumbers and electricians create their share of holes between bays and between floors. Expanding-foam caulk does a good job of sealing around wire and pipe penetrations. If left open, these holes become interconnected convective air conduits to the roof soffits and attic.

Packing fiberglass around the jambs of a window or door isn't particularly effective at stopping drafts, especially when the gap's too narrow to stuff. Expanding foam doesn't move with the frame's expansion and contraction cycles, and it runs the risk

Figure 11. EPDM rubber building gaskets, such as this sill sealer (left), are designed for heavy structural loads. The author uses several different configurations to seal various framing components. Between the rim joist and the mudsill, a continuous bead of subfloor adhesive provides an effective and inexpensive seal (right).

Sealing the Deck

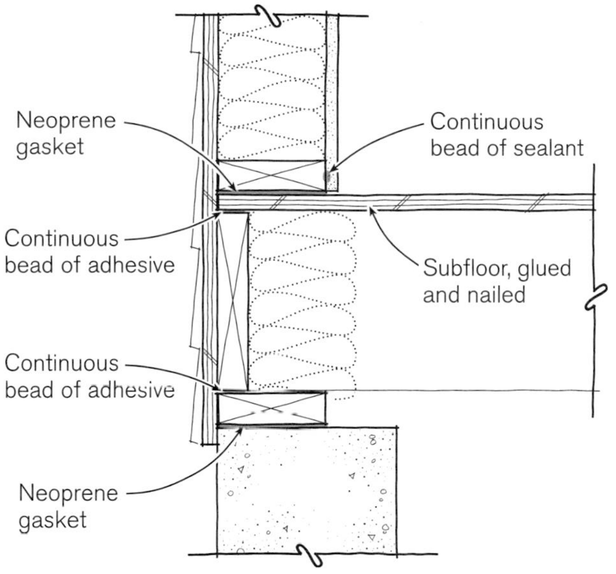

Neoprene gasket
Continuous bead of sealant
Continuous bead of adhesive
Subfloor, glued and nailed
Continuous bead of adhesive
Neoprene gasket

Figure 12. Bottom-plate gaskets may be tacked to the deck or the underside of the plate before sheathing and standing exterior walls.

of distorting the jambs on installation. Instead, we use another EPDM gasket configuration made for the task. The soft rubber slides into narrow cracks without undue force and provides a positive seal that moves with the framing (**Figure 14**). Cracks too narrow to slide a gasket into get caulked with silicone.

It's a good idea to size rough openings slightly larger than standard to ensure that the gasket has sufficient space to expand and seal.

Sealing the Ceiling

Balloon-frame configurations and open plumbing and mechanical chases provide prime conduits for cold attic air to enter the heated space. In new construction, these types of through-the-floor gaps are required to be fire-stopped with some form of noncombustible material, typically sheet metal. But fire stopping alone isn't so tight that moisture-laden air can't find its way into the attic. So we seal all the seams between fire stop and flue or chimney with a high-temperature silicone caulk.

Ceiling strapping, a typical framing detail in New England, can create a common air bypass, and a big one at that. The 3/4-inch-wide gap introduced by the strapping between batt-type insulation and a drywall ceiling can allow cold soffit air to travel between the two, effectively short-circuiting the insulating layer (**Figure 15**, next page). Even in ceiling configurations that aren't strapped, batt insulation is unlikely to lie in absolute contact with the ceiling board and can permit the same kind of infiltration. The result is a cold ceiling and a customer comfort callback. In this situation, adding another layer of insulation to the attic does little but waste money.

To reduce soffit air infiltration, we direct incoming air above the insulating layer into the attic, using custom-cut soffit blockers of 1-inch rigid foam board that fit snugly between the ceiling joists or rafters, as shown in the photo in Figure 15. The top edge of the soffit blockers is contoured to fit tightly against a typical foam insulation baffle, and the seams are sealed with expanding foam.

Frozen pipes. Infrared photography can reveal some surprises. The leakiest areas of a building may not be the exterior walls but interior partitions that conceal hidden air pathways to the attic. Ceiling drywall, an otherwise effective air barrier, typically stops short at either side of an interior partition, leaving the top plate

Figure 13. Instead of using housewrap, the author relies on plywood seam tape to block wind penetration. Tape installs easily just prior to siding.

Figure 14. A compressible dual-tube rubber gasket, forced into the shim gap around windows and doors with a drywall knife, provides a highly effective air seal.

Unblocked Ceiling Joists

Without end-blocking, outdoor air flows through batt insulation, wicking heat from inside

Figure 15. If ceiling bays aren't end-blocked, soffit vent air can travel along the ceiling and bypass the insulation. Piling on more insulation does nothing to correct a cold ceiling complaint (left). Rigid foam blockers, cut to fit around standard insulation baffles, direct ventilation above the ceiling insulation and prevent cold air infiltration (above).

exposed to the attic space. Loose-fitting and air-permeable attic insulation can allow cold attic air to flow past the plate into the wall cavity through continuous narrow gaps between the drywall and the framing (**Figure 16**). A convective air loop results, with cold incoming attic air replacing warm indoor air drawn through electrical outlets and other drywall gaps.

More than once, I've responded to seemingly freakish complaints of frozen pipes within an interior partition in a brand-new "well-insulated" home. In new construction, we make sure that all interior and exterior partitions are sealed at the top and bottom plates, using either drywall adhesive or a continuous rubber gasket along both sides. To correct an existing problem wall, we expose the top of the partition in the attic and seal the plate with a layer of expanding foam.

Insulating with Dry-Blown Cellulose

Fiberglass batts are widely regarded as the most cost-effective insulation. But it's difficult to properly detail batts around obstacles like wires, plumbing, and electrical boxes and in irregular framing configurations. Chemical smoke testing also shows that fiberglass provides little resistance to air movement. For us, the answer is cellulose; we've had good results dry-blowing cellulose in both new and retrofit work. Blown-in cellulose effectively fills very small voids and hard-to-access areas at a competitive cost per square foot. Its R-value is 3.5 per inch, and when installed at the proper density of 3.5 pounds per cubic foot, it is highly effective at reducing air infiltration. The fact that cellulose is a recycled product (newspaper) makes it even more appealing to my clients.

Settling not a problem. Complaints that cellulose is prone to settle after installation are based on a common misconception. Voids found in an existing cellulose job are invariably due to faulty installation. If the wall bay isn't filled at the minimum density, or is incompletely filled, voids will occur, regardless of the insulating material. Blown at a minimum density of 3.5 pcf, cellulose is installed at a density greater than its own natural settled density, which eliminates future voids.

Walls first. The best way to blow cellulose into a new home or addition is to treat walls and ceiling separately, at different stages. Flat ceilings are best blown after the drywall has been hung. Drywall provides containment, a built-in air barrier, and unyielding support for a 16-inch-deep layer of cellulose.

For walls, we use a reinforced plastic membrane for containment. In an ordinary wall installation, I use par/PAC reinforced poly membrane (ParPac, Inc.). The membrane is tacked up, then stretched taut over the edges of each stud and stapled to its side face. Stapling the membrane like this prevents the cellulose from "migrating" across the stud face when blown, trapping lumps that interfere with drywall installation.

Proper density. The difference between good and poor cellulose installation is about 15 seconds per stud bay and some basic technique. To ensure complete, void-free filling, I use a rigid PVC wand tubing at the end of the feeder hose. By inserting the wand through

Sealing Interior Partitions

Ceiling joists and strapping

Air-permeable attic insulation allows cold air to flow through gaps between drywall and top plate (and any wire/pipe penetrations) into wall cavity

Drywall typically stops short of either side of top plate

Convective loop within wall cavity contributes to heat loss and radiant cooling

Cold incoming attic air replaces warm indoor air, drawn through electrical outlets and other gaps in drywall

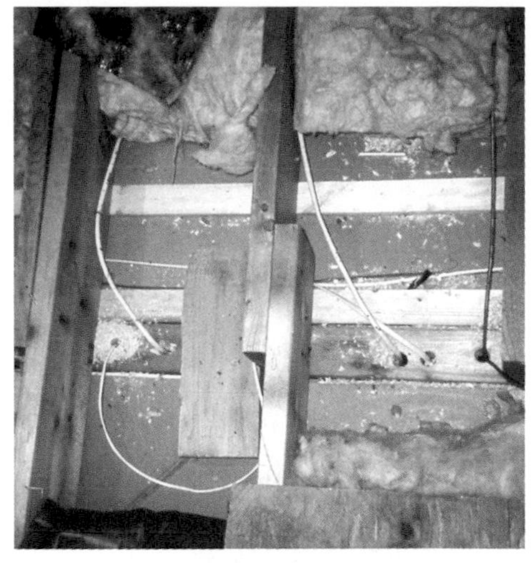

Figure 16. Interior partitions can be leakier than exterior walls, as cold attic air bypasses the top plate through cracks behind drywall, and through wire or pipe penetrations (drawing and top photo). In remedial work, the author seals the plate with two-part expanding foam to prevent convective loops inside the wall (bottom photo).

Figure 17. Blowing the wall from the center down, then up, ensures complete filling. A rigid extension wand enables the author to blow to the extremes and gradually withdraw the tube as the cavity fills.

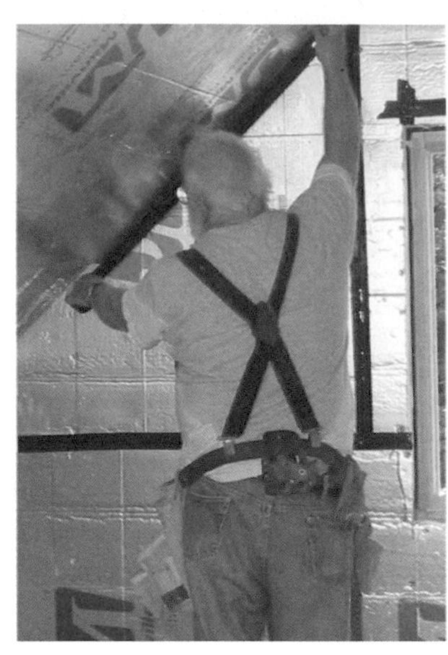

Figure 18. Foam board applied to the interior face of the exterior walls breaks thermal bridging through the studs and provides an effective air and vapor retarder.

Figure 19. A narrow access strip in the middle of a cathedral ceiling insulated with rigid foam allows the author to view the bays as he fills them.

a slit in the middle of each stud bay, I first fill from the bottom, withdrawing the wand as the cellulose fills to slit level (**Figure 17**, previous page). I then reverse direction and fill from the top of the bay down. To blow the cellulose into narrow and hard-to-reach areas, I switch to a smaller-diameter, flexible adapter, made from a length of vinyl tubing. The membrane is designed to literally take a beating. As the bay fills, I vigorously slap the membrane to help condense the cellulose and flatten the face, which otherwise bulges from the fill. With experience, you develop an accurate feel for the proper fill density.

Upgraded wall system. My preference, where the budget allows, is to sheathe the interior wall, using 3/4- or 1-inch-thick foil-faced foam board, after filling the cavity with cellulose. The foam board provides a thermal break over the studs, reducing convective heat loss through the framing. This application virtually guarantees that there are no "cold spots" on the wall where moisture might condense and support mold growth. The foil facing, with all seams and fastener penetrations taped and sealed, creates an effective air barrier that also retards the convective movement of moisture into the wall cavity (**Figure 18**). To retain the cellulose, I use a less costly, vapor-permeable membrane such as 100% polypropylene InsulWeb (Hanes Industries) or MemBrain (CertainTeed Corp.), a polyamide film whose permeability changes with ambient humidity conditions. Both products claim to avoid the potential moisture-trapping problems of conventional vapor retarders.

Figure 20. Two-component expanding foam seals and insulates in one step, making it an ideal solution for awkward configurations like this overhanging second-floor rim joist.

Figure 21. The author uses full-width vapor-permeable cardboard chutes in cathedral ceilings rather than rigid foam baffles. A bend in the bottom piece allows it to act as a wind stop at the top plate.

Sloped Ceilings

On sloped ceilings, we nail up 1-inch-thick foil-faced foam board but leave a narrow "window" near the middle of each slope for blowing access (**Figure 19**). Before installing the board, we cover the window area with a strip of containment membrane; elsewhere, the board holds the cellulose in place. After we blow the rafter cavities, the window is closed with foam board. All the seams and fastener penetrations are then sealed with housewrap tape.

Intricate or hard-to-reach framing transitions like tray ceiling perimeters, floors behind cathedral knee walls, and cantilevered rim joists are difficult to properly seal and insulate. We've had good success using Zerodraft two-component polyurethane foam (Zerodraft Division, Canam Building Envelope Specialists), especially in remedial applications where initial air sealing was never properly done. The two-component pressurized system is a rapid high-expansion foam, packaged with a 30-foot hose and applicator, with a 600-board-foot coverage capacity. The foam cures in 45 seconds and makes it simple to seal otherwise challenging configurations in short order (**Figure 20**). At around $400 per pack, it's too expensive to use as the primary insulation, but it's unbeatable for tricky areas and sealing leaks. I typically get about four average houses out of a pack.

Rafter chutes. In a sloped ceiling design, soffit-to-ridge ventilation is critically important to ensure continuous removal of moisture-laden air that finds its way through the ceiling insulation. We use cardboard "chutes," purchased from insulation wholesalers, rather than the ubiquitous polystyrene insulation baffles, which don't fully cover the underside of a rafter bay or prevent soffit air from moving under and through ceiling insulation (**Figure 21**). The chute has a smooth, flat face and prekerfed stapling flanges that automatically space the panel an inch away from the sheathing as it's installed. The cardboard is vapor-permeable but durable enough to be permanent. Installation begins at the top plate as a soffit blocker, then transitions to follow the slope of the roof to the ridge vent. I've recently acquired a rapid-firing pneumatic stapler that makes chute installation a breeze.

Bruce Torrey is a consultant with Building Diagnostics in East Sandwich, Mass.

WATER VAPOR CONTROL

Chapter 6: Warm & Mixed Climates

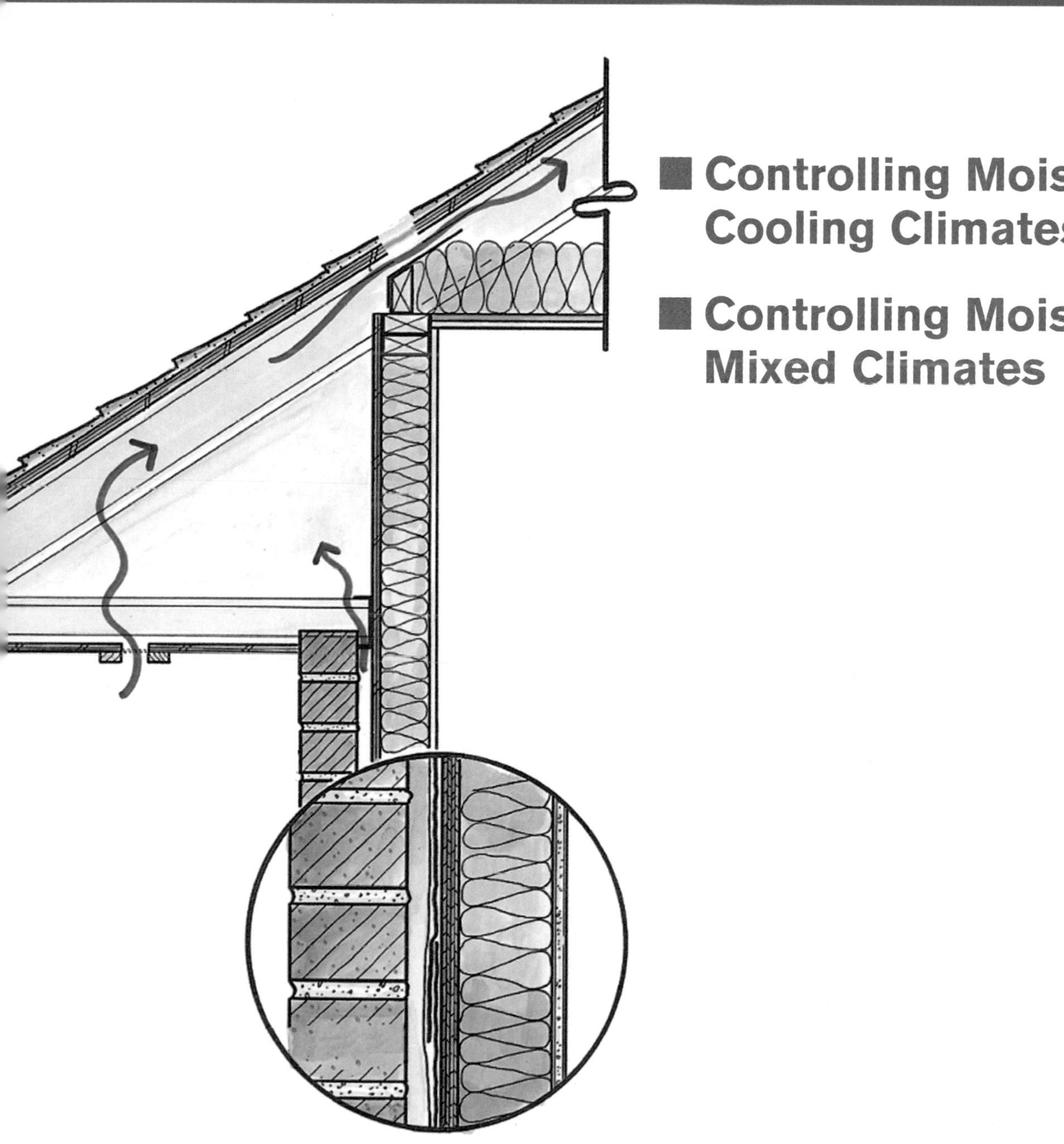

- Controlling Moisture in Cooling Climates
- Controlling Moisture in Mixed Climates

Controlling Moisture in Cooling Climates

by Peter L. Pfeiffer

To build long-lasting, energy-efficient, healthy houses in the Florida peninsula and Gulf Coast regions of the United States, builders must take into account the unique climatic conditions of the area. Code guidelines are not always helpful, since the International Residential Code and the Model Energy Code are mostly written for heating climates and offer little guidance on cooling climates or, in some cases, advocate construction practices that are the opposite of what should be done in cooling climates.

In the summertime along the Gulf Coast and Florida, the outside air is hot and moisture-laden, so most homes are air conditioned (**Figure 1**). Under these conditions, code-approved building practices such as ventilated crawlspaces or the use of vapor diffusion retarders on the interior side of exterior walls can be disastrous. My focus here is on the moisture-control techniques my company has learned during 18 years of building and designing homes in hot, humid Texas.

Concrete Slab Foundations

The soil is a constant source of moisture, so we use a sturdy vapor barrier such as 6-mil poly beneath slabs to prevent ground-based moisture from migrating up through the concrete by capillary action or diffusion. We lap the joints liberally and use tape on any tears and around pipe penetrations. We also use a minimum 1 1/2-inch sand base under the slab to further reduce water problems (see "Sub-Slab Vapor Barriers," page 22). In addition, the poly helps reduce mineral efflorescence on the slab surface, a common cause of discoloration on stained and patterned concrete floors.

Figure 1. Moisture-control practices for hot, humid climates (shaded area) are almost the exact opposite of recommended building practices for cold climates, because moisture is more likely to enter wall cavities from outside rather than from the building's interior.

Unvented Crawlspaces

Despite what the code books say, in our geographical area I strongly recommend against ventilating crawlspaces unless I suspect there is an underground water source beneath the foundation. If you think about the goal — keeping the crawlspace dry and inhospitable to mold — the last thing you want is to encourage the infiltration of warm, moist air into a cool, dark space. This would lead to condensation on all crawlspace surfaces, making them vulnerable to decay.

We do not specify vents for crawlspaces, and we make any access doors fit snugly. We also recommend carefully installing a 6-mil poly vapor diffusion retarder over the entire dirt floor. Spreading a few inches of gravel over the poly helps to keep it in place and protects it from damage. A sealed crawlspace also stays warmer on the few cold winter days we have here, minimizing the chance that warm, moist household air will create a problem when it finds a condensing surface within the crawlspace.

With a sealed crawlspace, it is imperative that standing water be kept out. This means that the finish grade must slope away from the building at a minimum of 1/4 inch per foot. Avoid sites where the seasonal water table is above the elevation of the crawlspace.

Wall and Framing System

Unlike most U.S. regions, in the hot, humid South, we cool our houses and buildings more than we heat them. Because the warm outside air usually has more moisture in it than cool inside air, moisture most often migrates from the outside of the structure to the inside. If you have a vapor diffusion retarder on the underside of the gypboard (a common detail in cold climates), or an impermeable vinyl wall covering over the gypboard, there is a good chance that warm, moist outside air migrating through the wall system will condense once it hits the relatively cool gypboard. This trapped moisture not only reduces the thermal performance of the wall insulation; it also creates potential problems in the wall cavity — from unhealthy mold and mildew to structural wood decay.

Drainage Plane Detail

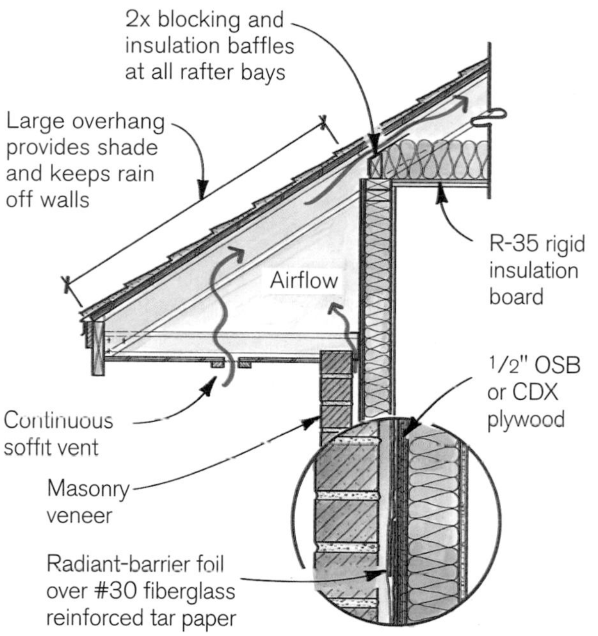

2x blocking and insulation baffles at all rafter bays

Large overhang provides shade and keeps rain off walls

Airflow

R-35 rigid insulation board

1/2" OSB or CDX plywood

Continuous soffit vent

Masonry veneer

Radiant-barrier foil over #30 fiberglass reinforced tar paper

Figure 2. For exterior sheathing, the author prefers to use plywood or OSB rather than rigid foam. A carefully lapped and tightly sealed layer of #30 building paper over the sheathing creates a drainage plane that directs water down and away from the wall. In addition, all cracks and wall penetrations are sealed on both sides using expanding foam and caulk.

Contrary to code, do not use a vapor diffusion retarder on the interior of the wall system, because walls in the hot, humid South dry to the *inside*, not to the outside. Especially avoid placing a sheet of poly under the gypboard or covering the gypboard with vinyl wallpaper. The only place where we use poly is on the interior side of walls around tub and shower enclosures that do not abut an outside wall. In these localized areas, we feel it's prudent to protect the partition wall cavity from the high humidity generated in the bathroom.

Exterior sealing. Houses in humid cooling climates do need to be sealed on the exterior, but careful detailing is critical. I am wary of tightly sealed exterior cladding systems, such as synthetic stucco, that are applied over impermeable rigid foam sheathings. These stucco systems are never perfect, and rainwater eventually penetrates through cracks around windows and doors. Even when the foam is well taped or covered with housewrap or building paper, the surface is often accidentally punctured during installation, allowing rainwater and water vapor to penetrate the foam and eventually find its way into the walls.

Whether a building is clad with stone, brick, traditional stucco, wood, or synthetic siding, we prefer to use plywood or OSB sheathing covered with 30-pound building paper and a layer of heat-reflecting foil. This provides a sturdy drainage plane behind the cladding that sheds water down and away from the wall cavity (**Figure 2**). Where the exterior cladding stands away from the wall, as with masonry veneers, use weep holes and flexible Moistop (Fortifiber Building Systems Group) flashing at the base to direct water out of the cavity.

Use common sense when installing sidewall flashing and housewrap or building paper. Because water drains downward, always lap the uppermost layers of flashing or housewrap over lower layers. Finally, provide ample roof overhangs: They not only shade windows and walls, but they help keep rainwater off as well.

Infiltration control. To create a barrier to airflow, seal all holes, cracks, and other penetrations through walls, ceilings, and floors after framing is complete, then again after the drywall work is done. Use expanding foam and a good-quality caulk to seal around window and door frames. I also insist on using foam-rubber or neoprene gaskets under all electrical switch and outlet plates mounted in exterior walls.

At the joint between wall plates and the foundation, I find that using a continuous roll of foam sill sealer does a better job of sealing than simply caulking the joint. In our experience, concrete tends to reject the caulk over time.

Roof Systems

In our area, attic spaces can heat up to 130°F or more on a hot summer day. Eventually, that heat transfers through the ceiling insulation into living spaces

Figure 3. Foil radiant barriers can reduce unwanted attic heat gain by up to 40%. The foil barrier should be installed on the underside of the sheathing and should be cut at the ridge vent to allow heated air in the attic to escape. At least one side of the foil barrier must face an air space for it to work.

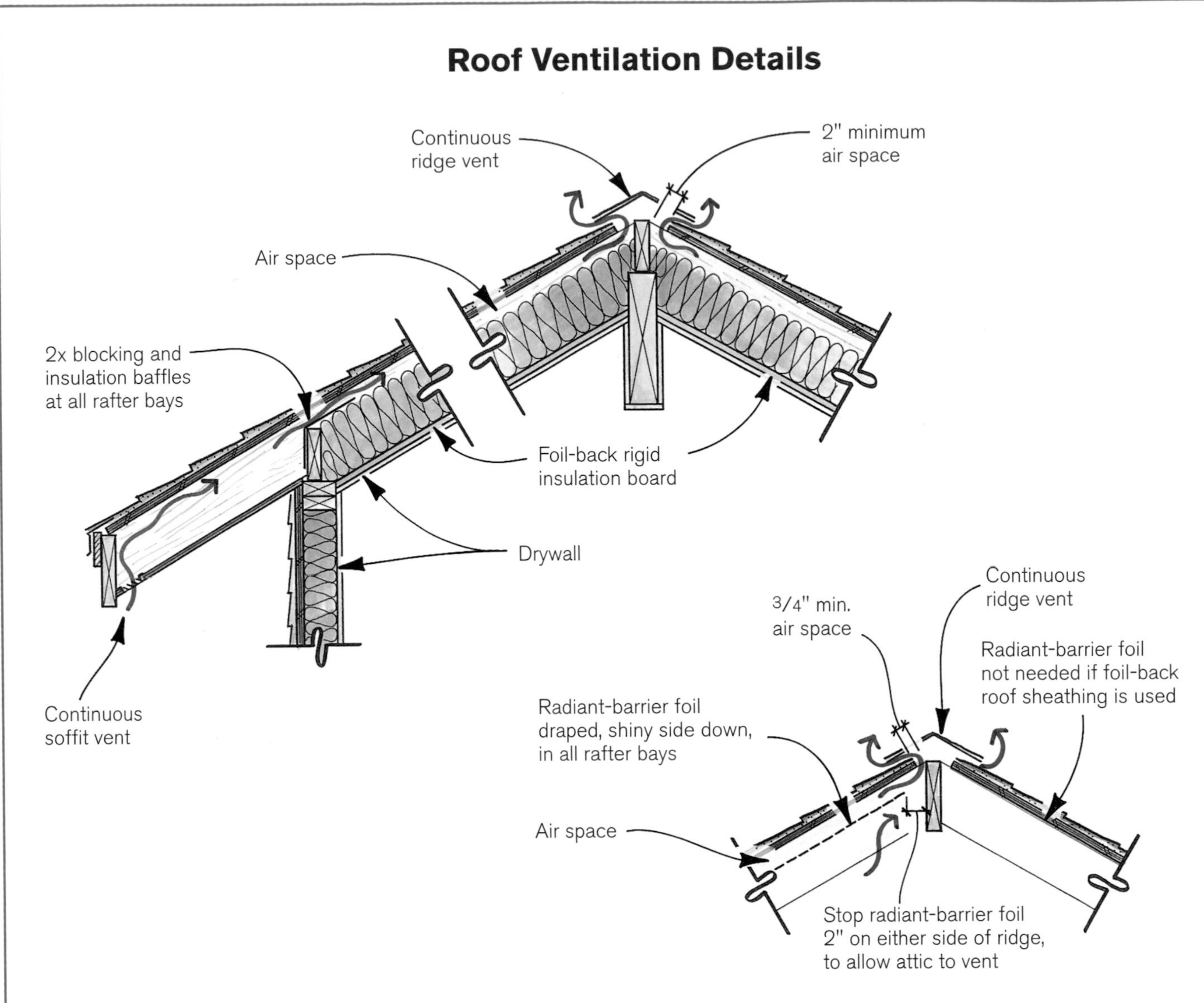

Figure 4. The author recommends doubling the net ventilation area in both attics and vaulted roofs. He prefers passive venting to power vents, which may draw conditioned air out of the living space.

below, increasing the cooling load. To counter this problem, we not only suggest twice as much roof ventilation as most codes recommend, but we also use a radiant barrier, such as Insul-Foil or Aluma-Foil (Advanced Foil Systems). You can also use Kool-Ply (Louisiana-Pacific), a labor-saving roof sheathing with foil laminated directly to it. The radiant barrier blocks the transfer of heat from the hot roof to the attic. Apply the radiant barrier to the underside of the roof, not on the attic floor, and make sure to cut open the radiant barrier along the ridge and below the low-profile vents so that attic air can exhaust (**Figure 3**, previous page).

We use continuous ridge and soffit venting wherever possible. I double the FHA code formula for attic venting (1:144 instead of 1:300), providing one square inch of net venting area at both the ridge and the soffits for every square foot of attic or vaulted ceiling area (**Figure 4**). Where this can't be done with continuous ridge venting, such as on hipped roofs, I supplement the ridge venting with low-profile vents on the roof itself. These should be located on the side of the roof opposite the direction of prevailing summer breezes. Don't substitute power attic vents for the passive venting techniques just described. They not only consume power, but often draw conditioned air from the living space by depressurizing the attic.

Duct Sealing

Mechanical air distribution systems, including ducts and air handlers, must be installed with minimum air leaks. Otherwise, a vacuum can occur in the living space, creating an imbalance that will draw in moist outside air. Consider this scenario: The air handler is pulling air from the house through a short return air duct or well-sealed chase. But because not all the supply-duct joints and seams are equally well sealed, not all of that air gets delivered back into the living areas of the house. Rather, it gets lost to the attic or someplace other than the building's occupied zone, creating a negative air pressure, or vacuum, in the conditioned zone. As a result, moisture-laden outside air from the attic — or worse yet, moist and chemically laden air (from insecticides and rat poisons) from the crawlspace — is drawn into the house through cracks and poorly sealed pipe penetrations.

To eliminate the imbalance that creates this negative air pressure, we seal all duct joints and transitions with fibrous mastic rather than duct tape (**Figure 5**). We use Versa Grip (Carlisle Hardcast) or RCD #7 Mastic (RCD Corp.). Sealing ducts this way is important both to maintain indoor air quality and to minimize moisture and mildew. I even suggest setting up the HVAC system to provide slightly positive pressure in the house. This can be done in a controlled way via a small outside-air intake duct to the return-air chamber of the air handler. It will provide outside makeup air and create a positive pressure difference between the inside and outside. Positively pressurizing the interior also keeps unwanted moisture from infiltrating the living environment. In addition, this outside air is dehumidified by the air handler before it reaches the home's interior.

Figure 5. Properly sealing ductwork with mastic will prevent HVAC systems from creating negative pressure in conditioned living space, which could draw unwanted moisture from the outdoors.

Educate the Homeowner

Using a little common sense, homeowners can keep humidity levels down inside the house, which will decrease the chance of mold and mildew growth during the summer and minimize condensation on windowsills during the winter. Builders can help by explaining why clothes dryers and kitchen exhaust fans must be vented directly to the outside, and by providing bathroom fans with timer switches so the owners won't have to remember to turn them off.

Homeowners will "buy into" these preventive techniques if you explain how they will prolong not just the hidden structural elements, but the interior paint job, windows, drywall, and other finishes as well.

Peter L. Pfeiffer, AIA, is a principal of Barley & Pfeiffer, an Austin, Texas, architectural firm specializing in sustainable architecture, planning, and energy consulting.

Controlling Moisture in Mixed Climates

by Joseph Lstiburek and John Carmody

Controlling moisture problems is difficult in climates where seasonal changes necessitate both heating and cooling of interior spaces. In addition to common concerns about rain penetration through exterior cladding, builders in a mixed climate must take special precautions to prevent moisture from becoming trapped in wall and roof cavities — a problem that is complicated by high humidity levels both inside and outside the structure.

Infiltration and Exfiltration

During heating periods, when interior vapor pressure is high, humid air inside the building is driven outward, either by exfiltration (air leaks into wall and roof cavities) or by diffusion (passage of water vapor through permeable materials). If roofs are not properly ventilated and if walls are not allowed to dry, this moisture can cause decay in structural framing members.

The situation is reversed during cooling periods.

Mechanical cooling and dehumidification cause the vapor pressure to be higher outdoors than indoors, driving humid outside air inward (infiltration). In fact, vapor pressure differences during cooling periods in this climate can be more significant than those found during heating periods. The high inward flow of moisture during cooling periods can increase cooling loads and the corresponding energy costs as well as increase building deterioration.

Moisture problems during cooling periods are compounded by cladding systems such as brick, wood, and stucco, which can absorb significant amounts of rain. As solar radiation warms exterior wall surfaces, lower temperatures on interior wall surfaces serve to drive moisture inward, where it can condense on surfaces cooled by air conditioning. An example of this effect is the damage caused to interior drywall covered with vinyl wallpaper. The vinyl wallpaper forms a vapor barrier that traps water in the wall. Interior vapor barriers such as vinyl wallpaper or polyethylene should be avoided.

Construction moisture — moisture present in the building materials themselves — merits special attention in mixed climates. Building assemblies constructed with wet lumber (greater than 19% moisture content by weight) or employing wet-applied insulation (wet-spray cellulose or blown fiberglass) must be designed so that they can dry to the interior or exterior.

Condensation

Improved airtightness of buildings in mixed climates tends to reduce the number of air changes during the heating season. This can lead to elevated interior levels of moisture, which not only contribute to condensation within walls and roof spaces but cause condensation on window surfaces and give rise to surface mold and mildew as well.

During the heating months, interior surfaces cooled by thermal bridges or other thermal defects (such as wind blowing through insulation) create high relative humidity at these interior surfaces. The result is localized mold and mildew growth, typically where exterior walls intersect insulated ceilings, at exterior corners, and at uninsulated or poorly insulated window lintels or headers.

Each of the five wall assemblies illustrated is designed to address the special moisture problems associated with a mixed climate (**Figure 6**), including rain penetration and absorption, air movement, water-vapor diffusion, drying, and interior finishes.

Rain Penetration

All but one of the five wall assemblies recommended for this climate use a rain screen to back-ventilate claddings. All of the wall assemblies rely on drainage.

With a brick veneer (Wall 3, page 94), the rain screen is created by providing a 1-inch air space between the brick veneer and the exterior sheathing and building paper. The air space should be clear of mortar droppings and should be vented at both the bottom and top of the wall. The vents (or "weep holes") at the bottom of the wall provide drainage as well as ventilation.

To direct cavity moisture to the exterior through the weep holes, extend flashing at the base of the wall to the back of the rain-screen cavity and integrate the flashing with the exterior building paper by extending the building paper over the top of the vertical leg of the flashing.

Stucco. With stucco (Wall 5, page 95), rain penetration is controlled by using drainage — the drainage occurs between two layers of building paper. The outer layer of building paper is a bond break between the stucco rendering and the inner layer of building paper, which acts as the drainage layer. To control cracking, use control joints.

Wood-based siding. With wood and wood-composite sidings, you should create a rain screen by installing the siding over furring strips. The wood-based siding should be back-primed or back-painted to control capillary wicking of water between the siding laps.

Rain Absorption

With vinyl or aluminum siding, the building paper keeps the exterior sheathing from taking on moisture, either directly through absorption or through capillary suction. Where rigid insulation is used as sheathing, its impermeable surface serves the same purpose, so building paper is not required.

With stucco cladding, the formulation and material properties of the stucco itself are important. In traditional three-coat stucco, each successive layer to the

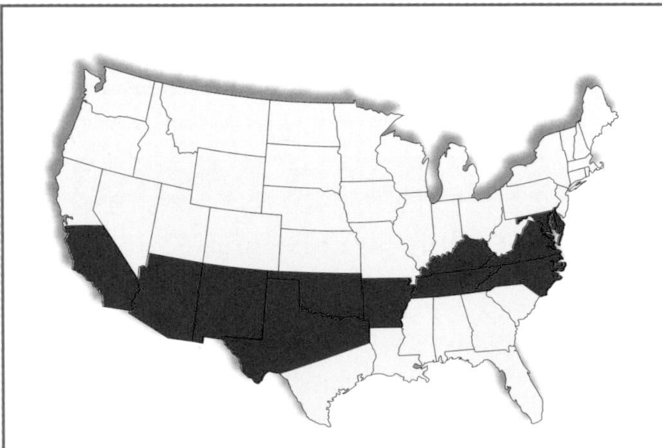

Figure 6. The need for both heating and cooling in homes built in "mixed climate" states (shaded area) complicates construction details used to control moisture.

Wall 1: Plywood Sheathing — Drying to Exterior and Interior

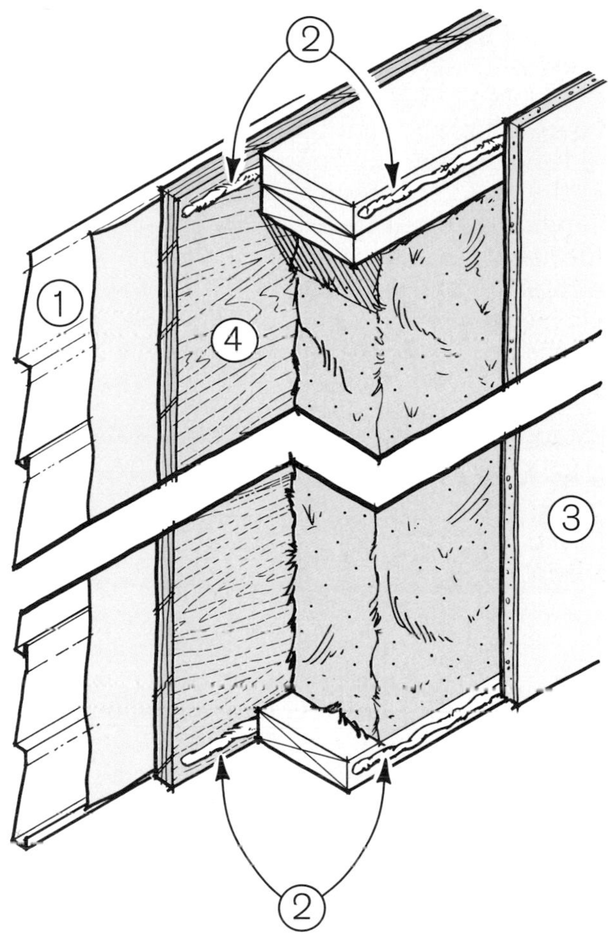

Wall 2: Fiberboard or Gypsum Sheathing — Drying to Exterior and Interior

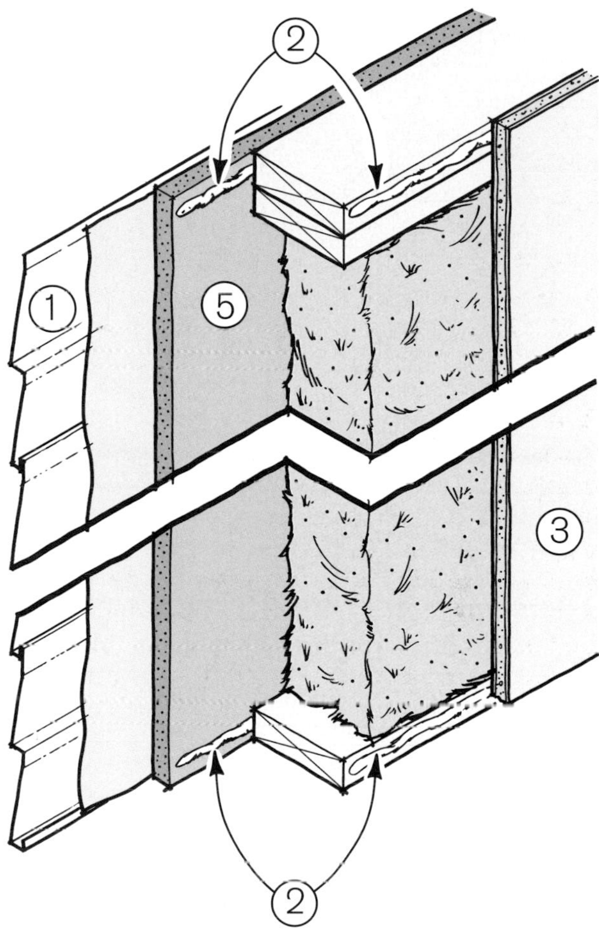

Both Walls:

- The rain-screen principle controls rain penetration when vinyl or aluminum siding is used. Building paper controls rain absorption into the sheathing. ①
- Air movement is controlled by an air barrier on both the exterior and interior of the wall, formed by sealing the interior gypsum board and exterior sheathing to the framing with caulking. ②
- Latex (acrylic) paint is used on the interior drywall to act as a vapor diffusion retarder. This slows down outward vapor flow from the interior during the heating season but still permits inward drying to the interior during summer cooling. ③

Wall 1:

- Uses semi-impermeable, noninsulating sheathing (plywood or OSB). ④
- Drying of the wall is to both the exterior and interior.

Wall 2:

- Sheathed with vapor-permeable asphalt-impregnated fiberboard or gypsum. ⑤
- Drying of the wall is to both the exterior and interior.

Wall 3: Brick Veneer — Drying to Exterior and Interior

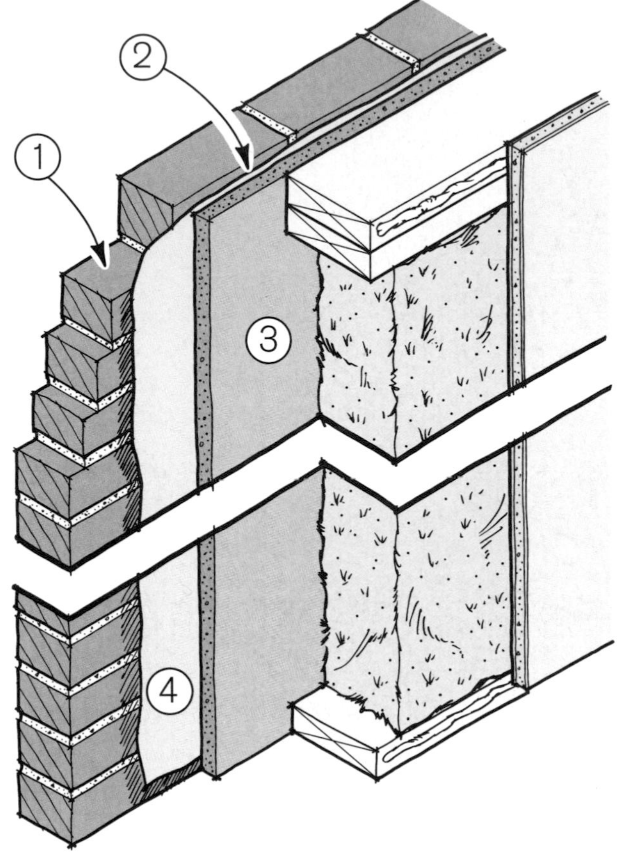

- Brick veneer covers wood-frame wall. ①
- A 1-inch air space between the brick and the wood-frame assembly is a receptor for capillary moisture and absorbed moisture driven inward by solar radiation. ②
- Drying is to the exterior and interior. ③
- Building paper. ④

exterior is weaker and more permeable than the layer under it. The result is that the farther water penetrates into the wall, the more resistance it meets; and once water has penetrated the stucco, this layered effect makes it easier for moisture to migrate toward the exterior than to penetrate any farther to the interior.

For the same reason, any paint or sealant should be more permeable than the outermost surface of the stucco itself. This is very difficult to achieve in practice, however, so you will have more success with stains or colorants added to stuccos during application than with paint films applied after the stucco cures.

With a brick veneer, the air space behind the brick controls both rain absorption and capillary suction. The air space also acts as a receptor for moisture driven inward by incident solar radiation. (The same principles are at work in wood-based siding applied to furring.) To further protect the sheathing, install a layer of building paper over the sheathing.

Air Movement

In a mixed climate, air can transport moisture inward from the exterior during the cooling season and outward from the interior during the heating season. To control this moisture, install an air barrier on the interior or exterior of the wall — if possible, on both sides of the wall. The most practical interior air barrier is drywall glued to the top and bottom plates of exterior walls. Plastic vapor barriers such as 6-mil polyethylene should be avoided. The most practical exterior air barrier is a continuous "housewrap" or exterior sheathing that is taped or sealed.

Vapor Diffusion

Water vapor can also move by diffusion both from the inside outward and from the outside inward, depending on the season. To protect against vapor diffusion from the interior during heating periods, limit interior moisture levels using controlled ventilation. Do not install interior vapor barriers, as they will prevent inward drying during air conditioning periods.

Walls with insulating sheathing work well in mixed climates because the insulating sheathing raises the temperature in the wall cavity during the heating season. When water vapor from the interior enters the wall cavity during the heating season, it does not accumulate, because the higher temperature in the wall assembly limits condensation. If the exterior sheathing does not provide adequate insulation value, condensation can occur on the cavity side of sheathing.

It is recommended that the thermal resistance of the insulating sheathing be R-5 or greater and that indoor moisture levels be limited to less than 40% relative humidity during heating season by using ventilation inside the home.

Cooling periods. Semi-permeable sheathings such as plywood or OSB act as effective vapor diffusion retarders and control vapor diffusion from the exterior during cooling periods. Rigid foam insulation installed on the exterior serves the same purpose.

Joseph Lstiburek, PhD, PE, is a principal of Building Science Consulting (www.buildingscience.com) in Westford, Mass. John Carmody is director of the Center for Sustainable Building Research at the University of Minnesota. This article was adapted with permission from Moisture Control Handbook *(1993, John Wiley and Sons).*

Wall 4: Rigid Foam Sheathing Without Vapor Retarder — Drying to Interior

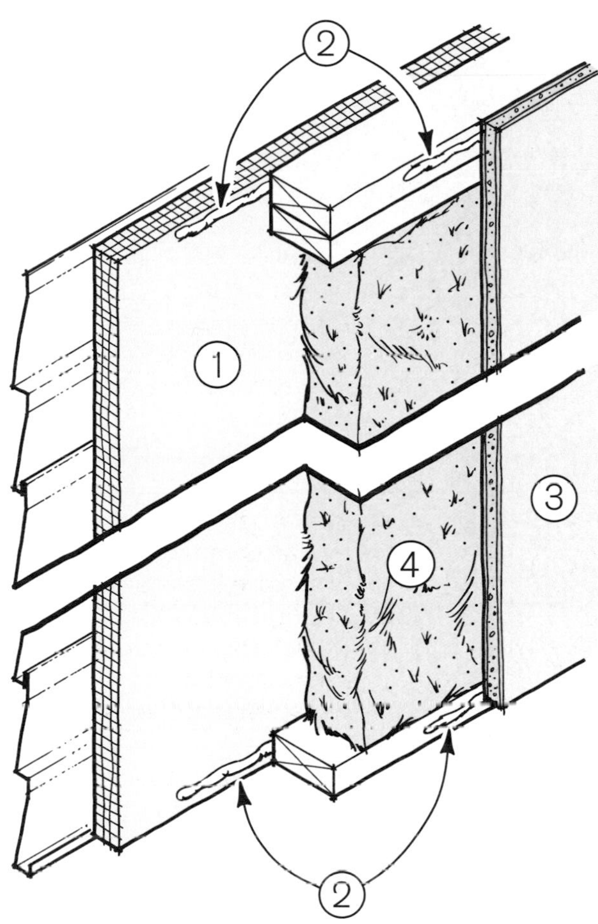

Wall 5: Stucco Over Foam — Drying to Interior

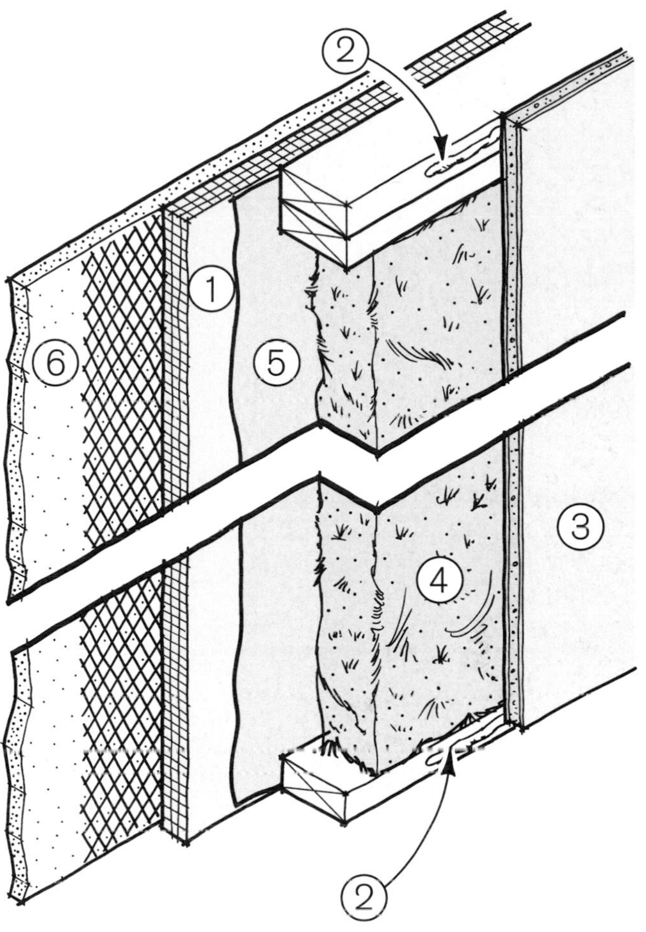

Both Walls:

- Exterior rigid insulation used as sheathing raises wall-cavity temperatures, controls or limits winter condensation, and controls inwardly driven moisture during summer cooling. ①
- Air movement is controlled by creating an air barrier using caulk to seal the interior drywall to bottom and top plates. ②
- Permeable latex paint on the gypsum board permits interior vapor to enter the wall and then dry to the interior. No vapor diffusion retarder is needed on the inside of the wall. ③
- Drying depends on several factors:
  - 2x4 wall construction.
  - Interior relative humidity must not exceed 40% at 70°F during heating periods.
  - Cavity insulation must be limited to R-11, while the rigid insulation must be at least R-5. ④

Wall 4:

- Building paper is not needed to control rainwater entry when foam sheathing (with joints taped) is used with a rain-screen cladding.

Wall 5:

- Building paper is needed to provide a drainage layer between the wall framing and the exterior foam insulation. ⑤
- Exterior cladding is stucco over galvanized lath, applied over rigid foam sheathing. ⑥

EXTERIORS

Chapter 7: Housewrap & Felt

- Water-Managed Wall Systems
- Choosing a Sheathing Wrap
- Choosing Flexible Flashings
- Housewrap Do's & Don'ts

Water-Managed Wall Systems

by Joseph Lstiburek

In the photo below (**Figure 1**), I'm testing the rain holdout characteristics of a brick-veneer garage wall by spraying it with a garden hose. I have a wager going with people inside the garage — I'm asking them to guess how long it will take, under the conditions of this test, for water to pass through the brick veneer. It's a multiple-choice test: (a) seconds, (b) minutes, or (c) hours.

The correct answer is (a) seconds — between 15 and 30 seconds, to be exact. Brick veneers are essentially transparent to water. We like to think, "Hey, brick is strong. It can handle water." And it can — in the sense that the water doesn't damage the brick. But brick is just like a sponge: It sucks water in by capillary action, holds some of it, and lets the rest drool out everywhere. Brick can protect our walls from many things, but water is not one of them.

Wood clapboards, fiber-cement siding, and vinyl siding also leak, each in its own special way. People continue to put their faith in every kind of cladding material, but in the real world all claddings leak sooner or later. They always have, and they always will.

The common fallback strategy is to use caulks and sealants. But that's not the answer, either. Sealants do not span cracks, they cannot withstand movement, and they will degrade from sunlight, temperature, and oxidation. Caulks dry up, they shrink, they freeze and crack, they decompose — in other words, they fail. When your cladding leaks, neither caulking nor sealants will keep water out of your building.

So if all claddings leak, and all sealants and caulks fail, how can we keep buildings dry? By creating a water-management system *beneath* the cladding: a continuous drainage plane with integrated flashings and weep holes, with an air space between the cladding and the drainage plane where water can flow (**Figure 2**). We overlap everything to direct water down and out, and we let gravity do the work.

Unlike caulks and sealants, gravity is free. Gravity does not wear out, and it does not require maintenance. Gravity is predictable: It always acts downward. In water-managed wall systems, gravity is one thing we can trust.

You can build a water-managed wall system with any cladding and with many different kinds of drainage plane and flashing materials. It will work as long as you follow certain basic principles. Human beings discovered those principles thousands of years ago, but some people still don't follow them.

Elements of a Rain-Managed Wall

There are four fundamental requirements for water-managed assemblies:

- ***Drainage plane:*** some water-repellent material that's continuous over the whole building exterior and overlapped to drain downward. "Continuous" is the key word here. All it means is that you should connect your windows and doors to the drainage plane, as well as connect your deck, your roof-wall intersections, any service penetrations —

Figure 1. In this hose test (left), water penetrated brick veneer in less than a minute (right). The wall behind brick veneer must be designed to drain.

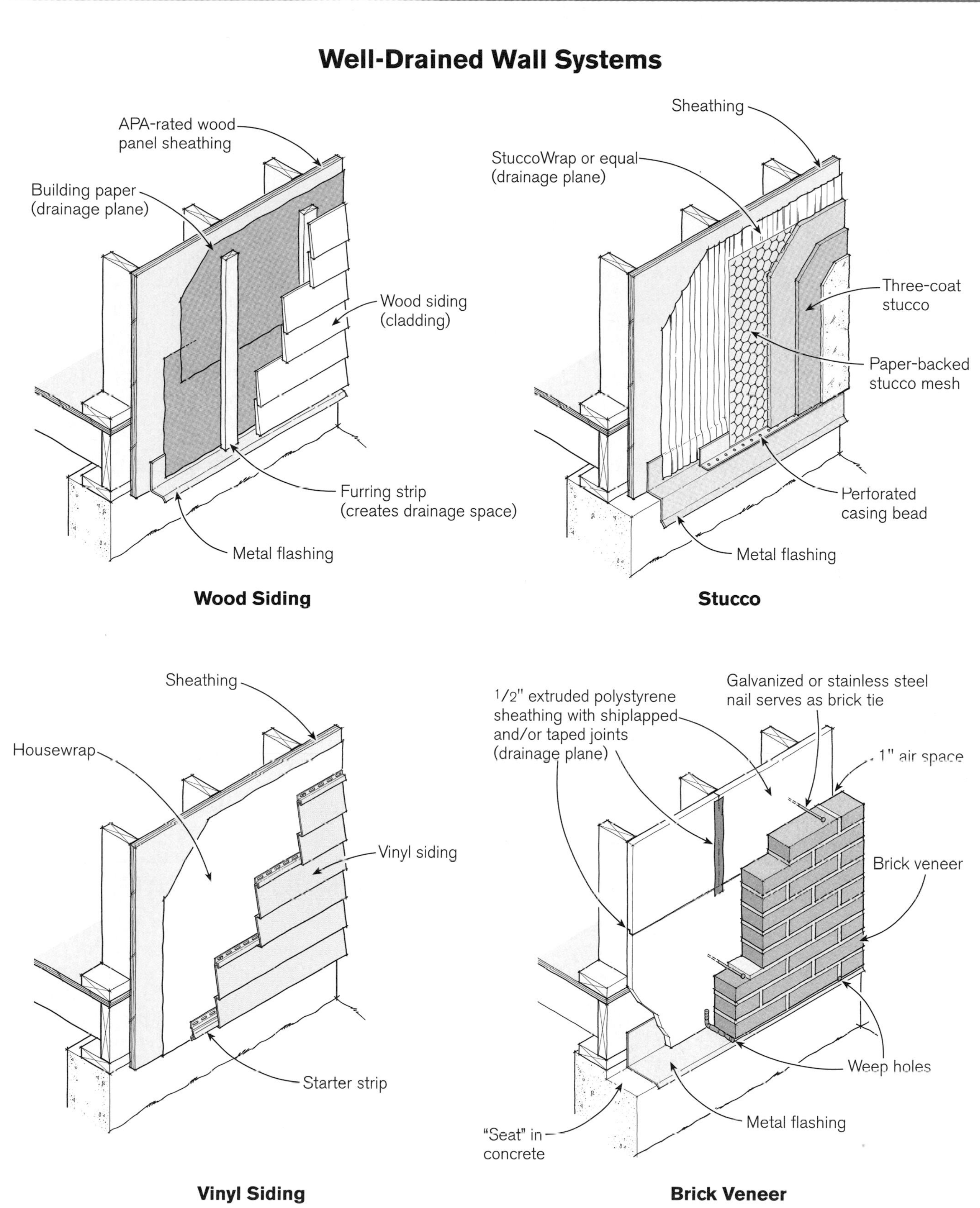

Figure 2. The key elements in rain control are a drainage plane, a drainage space under the cladding, flashings that integrate with the drainage plane, and weep holes to allow water to escape. These principles can be applied with any cladding system and with many different drainage plane and flashing materials.

Figure 3. Portland cement stucco bonds tightly to modern asphalt felts, denying water the drainage space it needs to flow down and escape the wall. Moisture that penetrates stucco will saturate the paper and destroy its water repellency, wetting the wall structure beneath unless an air space is somehow created.

everything. Every single flashing must tie into the drainage plane and dump on top of it, not behind it. There are no exceptions: One reverse lap or unflashed penetration can ruin your whole wall.

- ***Drainage space*** between the cladding and the drainage plane (the space can be very narrow, but it must be there). Water needs space to move.
- ***Flashings*** at every opening, penetration, or intersection, designed to kick water out and down.
- ***Weep holes:*** openings to allow water to escape to the outside.

If you have those four elements, you have a water-managed system. If you're missing any one, or you do any of them incorrectly, you can expect trouble.

Drainage Planes and Air Spaces

There are many choices of drainage plane material, and there's a lot of discussion over which is best. The most common drainage planes on houses are still the various building papers — asphalt-saturated felt, plastic housewraps, and coated papers. Housewrap makers like to stress the advantages of their brands, but the difference between one paper and another is really a minor issue. It's how you use them that counts, and the key factors are the air space and the flashings.

Let's take an example. **Figure 3** shows a classic drainage plane: tar paper installed shingle fashion behind the cladding. In this case, the cladding is stucco. Do you see the air space? No, because there isn't one. But there's supposed to be one, and in the old days there usually was. The reason we often don't get a drainage space behind stucco today is that tar paper has changed.

Decades ago, there was a product called 15-pound felt — asphalt-impregnated rag felt paper that weighed 15 pounds per 100 square feet. Today, in its place we have "#15 felt," which weighs less than 7 pounds per 100 square feet. In place of the old 30-pound felt, we now have #30 felt, which weighs 16.5 or 17 pounds. The papers are lighter and contain less asphalt.

The old heavy felts absorbed water and swelled up when we applied a scratch coat of stucco over them. They were intended to swell. Then as the felt paper dried, it wrinkled, shrank, and debonded from the back of the stucco, creating a thin, convoluted drainage space. If you tear into an old stucco wall, you'll see the space. But that process doesn't happen with modern asphalt felt papers — instead, the paper bonds to the stucco and sticks. It gets wet and stays wet, there's no drainage, and the paper starts to rot. Then your wall is unprotected.

West of the Mississippi, they figured it out. Many Western stucco applicators use two layers of Type D coated paper under their stucco instead of one layer of asphalt felt, and drainage occurs between the two layers of paper. The stucco might bond to the top layer, but the layer underneath stays free. Some brands of Type D paper even come with pieces of grit stuck on them, which helps to hold the two layers of paper apart.

My point is that any building paper will fail if it bonds to the cladding, and the system can't drain without an air space. With stucco, we create the air space by using two layers of paper.

Building Papers and Drainage Planes

A group of building scientists set up an eight-sided test building in my backyard at Building Science Consulting (**Figure 4**). We tested 21 different configurations of cladding-and-building-paper combinations for water leakage: 14 different combinations of vinyl siding over various sheathings and papers, and 7 combinations of hard-coat stuccos over various sheathings and papers. The holes in the wall are viewports that let us see what happens when we add water.

We depressurized the enclosure to simulate a 100-mph wind pressure, but we needn't have bothered: Any system that leaked, leaked with no pressure difference. A garden hose, it turns out, is plenty high powered.

We added a measured amount of water each time. That way, you can measure how much goes in and how much comes out; you can find the difference; and, if you want, you can even weigh the different materials before and after to find out how much water was absorbed. Remarkably, no one had done this kind of test for most of the wall systems on the market. With all the changes we've made in materials, no one had ever checked some of these systems to see if they work. So we tried this experiment with a few

Figure 4. The author and his colleagues tested 21 different combinations of building papers and claddings on this eight-sided structure (top left). Measuring the added water (above) provided a basis for comparing results across wall systems. The blower door apparatus (right) turned out not to matter, because leaks were apparent without any air pressure difference.

Figure 5. Portland cement stucco stuck tightly to housewrap (far left) and felt paper (left) in the author's tests, destroying the effective water repellency of the building papers.

systems, and we learned some interesting things.

Stucco and housewrap. In **Figure 5**, we see what happened when we applied hard-coat stucco over housewrap. The stucco bonded so tightly to the housewrap that when we peeled the paper back, the advertising transferred to the back of the stucco.

That tight contact destroys the water repellency of housewrap, which works like a tent in a rainstorm: If you touch the wall of the tent, you cause a leak. Here, the stucco has established what we call "capillary continuity" by bonding to the housewrap, and water repellency is lost. That's why you should never

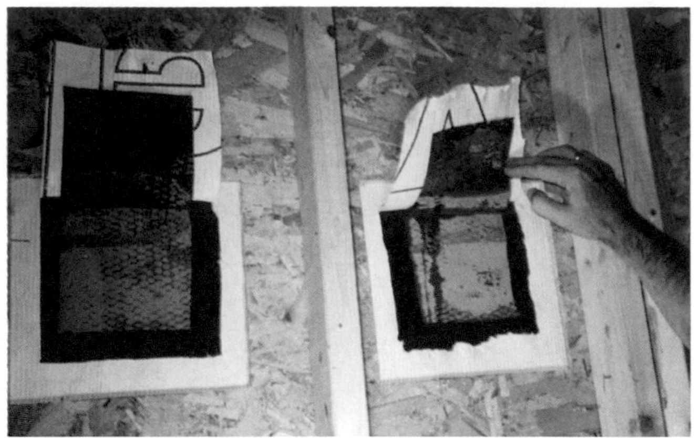

Figure 6. Wrinkled StuccoWrap adhered as tightly to stucco as did the other papers in the test, losing its ability to hold out water (left). However, the wrinkles worked effectively when a layer of inexpensive felt was installed over the StuccoWrap before the stucco was applied (right). The two papers in combination provided outstanding drainage and water protection. For stucco walls, the author recommends paper-backed stucco lath over wrinkle wrap as a drainage assembly.

put hard-coat stucco on any plastic housewrap — the stucco defeats the housewrap's intent.

Figure 6 shows DuPont's StuccoWrap, which is a wrinkled Tyvek. In spite of the name, the only product StuccoWrap doesn't seem to work with is stucco. When the stucco bonds to the StuccoWrap, drainage is lost along with water repellency. Stucco applied to StuccoWrap produced the second-worst performance of the systems in our test (the worst was stucco applied directly to a nonwrinkled plastic housewrap).

But StuccoWrap was also part of the best-performing system we tested. When we added a cheap felt paper over the StuccoWrap and then applied the stucco, the system worked perfectly. The cheap paper was a bond break, the StuccoWrap remained free, and then we saw tremendous drainage in the grooves.

So whenever somebody asks me, "How do you apply stucco to a building on the East Coast?" I tell them this: Put up OSB, staple up DuPont Tyvek StuccoWrap, and then put a paper-backed stucco lath over it — a product such as Tilath (Alabama Metal Industries Corporation) metal lath that comes with the paper stuck to it. The paper backing creates a bond break to provide the drainage. The difference between total success and major failure is that top layer of low-grade, 2¢-per-square-foot paper.

Comparing housewraps. In general, it's no use comparing one housewrap to another, at least in terms of water holdout characteristics. It's how you use them that counts.

The housewrap marketing people love to compare performance. But they do it based on a meaningless test. The standard test method is to fasten the housewrap over the bottom of a glass cylinder and see how high a column of water you can pour into the cylinder before the water comes through the wrap (every inch of water is equivalent to 250 pascals of wind pressure). The lab comes up with some figure, and then the marketing people go out and brag about it.

In the real world, however, we don't build houses with little glass cylinders. We staple the housewrap to the wall and nail siding over it. We put thousands of holes in it. That means the real performance of the system is about the holes — and regardless of the advertising claims made about housewrap performance, when you put nail holes in them, they're all the same.

For the system as a whole, the key thing to understand is that the air space makes all the difference. Water is like a politician: It always does the easiest thing possible. Whatever housewrap you have, and however many nail holes there are in it, if water can flow downward, it will go down, instead of sideways through the nail holes. As long as there is an air space, every housewrap and every felt paper works. So forget about comparing housewraps: Make sure there's an air space, and then concentrate on the flashings.

Insulated Sheathing as a Drainage Plane

Housewrap and felt are not the only drainage plane materials. Foam sheathing also works well, if you detail it carefully. In the Building America program (www.buildingscience.com/bsc/buildingamerica/overview.htm) we've had good success using foil-faced rigid polyisocyanurate as the drainage plane, taping the joints with red Tyvek tape. We've also used extruded polystyrene boards such as Dow Styrofoam the same way. It's an economical way to build a well-insulated wall that performs well.

As in any water-managed system, with foam sheathing the drainage space is critical. Foam-sheathing drainage planes work well with vinyl, because you create the air space just by putting the vinyl up. Vinyl is also self-ventilating — whether or not you like the way it looks, it performs beautifully. Brick also works well over foam sheathing.

Wood siding will not work well over a foam drainage plane unless you space the wood away from the wall with furring strips. In fact, you should fur out wood clapboards over housewrap and asphalt paper as well. It's the only way to allow the wood to dry evenly and to prevent substances in the wood from degrading the building paper. Wood siding should also be primed on the back and ends, not just painted on the weather surface.

I have a bias against tapes and sealants. I don't like to rely on adhesives. So we have developed a way of building a foam-sheathing drainage plane where you don't have to tape the joints. We use a shiplap vertical joint where the boards butt together, and at the horizontal joints we attach a strip of poly that acts as a Z-flashing (**Figure 7**). That poly, with the help of gravity, keeps the water on top of the drainage plane.

Flashings

In **Figure 8**, next page, we see a system using housewrap as the drainage plane. The builder has attached the window to the drainage plane with a membrane strip over the nailing flange. Looks rainproof, right? Wrong.

In America, we build as if windows don't leak. We assume that if we seal the window flange to the building paper, we're done. But in fact, most of the window leakage happens behind that seal, because the windows themselves come from the factory leaking. All windows leak at the joints. The only things that leak worse than windows are doors — especially sliding doors.

My colleagues and I conducted a survey of more than 3,500 vinyl windows that were less than two years old — all factory manufactured and precision engineered. We found that 20% of them had already begun to leak. So if you build a house with 20 vinyl windows, the odds are that four will leak right away (others will leak later). Which four windows do you want leaking into the wall? None of them, of course. So we have to assume that every window leaks and build accordingly.

But what is the common practice? Cut a big X in the housewrap and wrap it into the window. And where does that leave a hole? Right at the corner, just where the window leaks.

That's obviously not going to work. What we need is some kind of gutter under the window that collects the water dripping onto the sill and kicks it to the outside. There are a couple of good ways to do this.

Flexible peel-and-stick. In the photo on the lower left in Figure 8, we're demonstrating a really neat product, Tyvek FlexWrap (DuPont). It's a formable flashing — sort of an elastic ice and water shield that you can stretch under a window and mold into a flashing. It sticks beautifully. You put it in the opening and then install a window. Now your wall's protected when the window inevitably leaks. Ordinary, nonflexible peel-and-stick membranes can be used for the same purpose, but it takes some cutting and patching. In the upper right photo in Figure 8, the builder has used a membrane called Blueskin (Bakor Inc.).

With foam sheathing, it's particularly important to drain all water on top of the foam, not behind it, because the foam can trap the moisture inside the wall. In Figure 8, we're showing how to install FlexWrap over foam. Tyvek doesn't recommend that, maybe because if you stick the flashings right to the

Figure 7. Extruded polystyrene or foil-faced polyethylene can be an effective drainage plane material. Joints in the foam can be taped with red Tyvek tape (left). To reduce reliance on tape or sealant, the author likes to apply the foam with shiplap joints at the vertical seams and a black poly strip as a Z-flashing at horizontal joints (right).

Figure 8. Sealing window flanges to the housewrap (far left) is a common practice, but it does not protect against the predictable leakage within the window assembly itself. Only a pan flashing that dumps on top of the drainage plane will effectively keep water out of the wall. Peel-and-stick membrane applied over the top of the building paper and wrapping the sides and bottom of the rough opening (left) accomplishes the task. Another option is Jamsill Guard (Jamsill), an injection-molded plastic sill pan with seamless corners, shown below. The author highly recommends Tyvek FlexWrap for pan flashings, whether the drainage plane is housewrap or rigid foam (below left).

foam, you might not buy any Tyvek. But I recommend FlexWrap as a window pan flashing with foam-sheathing drainage planes (it also works with other brands of housewrap).

Even water puddled on the sill will dry out better than water absorbed by the wall. Some builders tack a small strip at the back of the opening to block water from moving into the interior, which is a good idea (**Figure 9**). But it would be best to slope the sill, so the water will flow out over the drainage plane. A quick trick is to tack a piece of beveled siding over the sill to create a slope to the outside, then apply the flexible membrane. If you need a flat spot for your window to rest on, you can take small pieces of the same beveled material and reverse them to create small level pads on top of the membrane. The membrane seals around nail holes.

Another option is what I call a "window booty." It's a premade metal pan flashing that might cost $10 from a metal fabricator's shop. In my opinion, windows should come with a preformed plastic flashing in this shape. But for now we have to make our own.

When you attach the pan, don't nail down through it into the sill: Fasten it through the vertical ears. Then wrap peel-and-stick over it around the window jacks. (With the FlexWrap pan flashings, I don't wrap the window sides. That's not the big leak point anyway, so I trust the seal to stick to the housewrap.)

Integrating the window. When we install the window, we integrate it into the drainage plane. The housewrap or felt above the window must lap over the top flange or the top window flashing; we tape the side flanges of the window to the housewrap on the side. But we don't seal the bottom flange to the wall. That's the weep hole: We want water to come out there if it has to. We will also provide weeps at the bottom of the wall.

A window placed in a wall should have redundant drainage systems. The window itself should drain, the opening the window is in should drain, and the wall the opening is in should drain. At every joint, flashings should kick water to the exterior. If you don't provide drainage but trust in caulks and sealants instead, you're asking for trouble.

Water-Shedding Windowsill

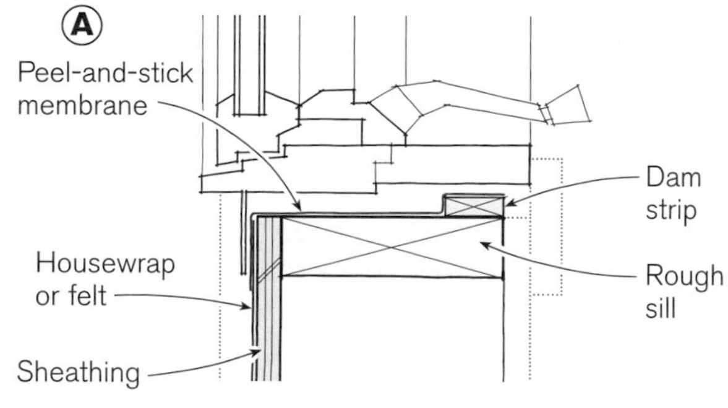

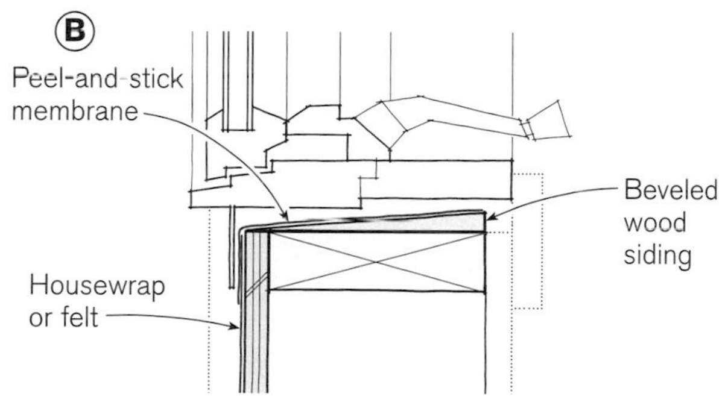

Figure 9. A strip of wood nailed at the back of the rough-opening sill forms a dam to prevent water from escaping to the interior (A). Even better is a piece of wood bevel siding nailed over the sill to create positive drainage toward the exterior (B).

Figure 10. This wall shows characteristic damage from leaks at the window frame joints. Good flashings and a drainage plane would have saved the structure.

Drainage Pan Formed Into Slab

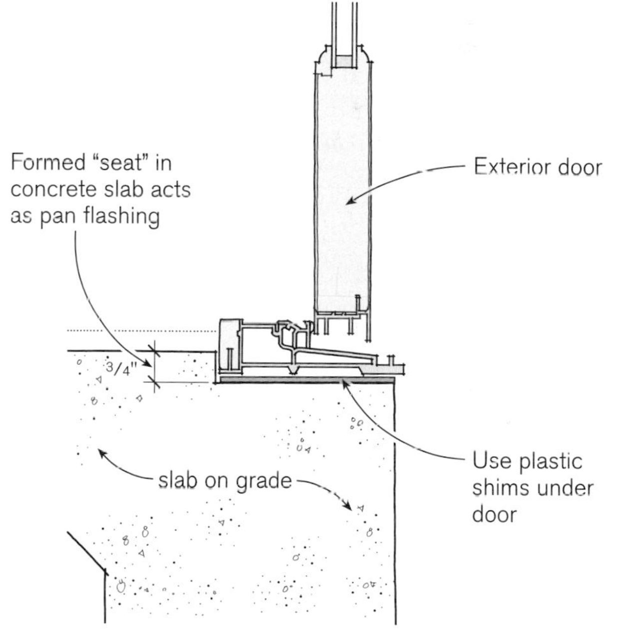

Figure 11. Forming a depression in a cast-in-place floor slab creates a built-in drainage pan for mulled entry doors and sliders, which are prone to leakage at joints.

Figure 10 shows what I'm talking about. We've torn the cladding off beneath a window, exposing terminal rot in the wood structure. It's evident from the dark decay pattern that the water intrusion originated at the window's corner and center mullion joints, then spread laterally and downward to soak the whole wall area beneath the window. Areas away from the window were not affected.

This is an adhesively attached EIFS wall, where the foam board is a cladding and not a drainage plane. EIFS is a classic nightmare, of course, but the drainage details and not the cladding are to blame. EIF systems that use a drainage plane and good flashings beneath the foam board are quite effective and reliable, and wood or vinyl siding installed without good drainage systems can be a disaster just like EIFS.

Pan flashings for doors. I have large builder clients who have experienced thousands of callbacks and claims because wood floors were damaged by leaking doors. When they started using pan flashings like the metal one in Figure 8, the problem went away. Any door with sidelights, and any sliding door, should have a good pan flashing — don't rely on the guarantee.

Here's a trick from the commercial building industry. For the exterior doors of a slab-on-grade house, form a 1/4-inch depression in the slab to create a seat (**Figure 11**). You're building a preformed pan flashing right into the edge of your slab. When that mulled front door or that slider leaks, this little step-down will kick the water outside and save your floors. The key is to shim the door up — don't set it down where it will be sitting in the puddle. (Use plastic shims, not wood.)

Rain and Vapor

Rain is the most important wetter of walls, but it's not the only one. Occasionally, walls get wet from condensation, and sometimes they start out wet because they're built with wet materials. And sometimes our rain management systems aren't perfect. So walls have to be designed to dry out — to the interior, to the exterior, or to both. To understand that, we'd have to take a close look at the vapor permeability of building materials and at the way vapor interacts with buildings.

In any case, no matter how well a wall is detailed for drying, there will be trouble if the wall is repeatedly subjected to wetting by rain. On the other hand, if we eliminate rain as a source of wetting, most walls will be fine. That's why it's so important to drain everything and to focus on every element of rainwater management: the drainage plane, the drainage space, the flashings, and the weeps. If we pay proper attention to those key details, we will have done most of what is necessary to provide our buildings with dry walls.

Joseph Lstiburek, PhD, PE, is a principal of Building Science Consulting (www.buildingscience.com). A forensic engineer who investigates building failures, he is internationally recognized as an authority on moisture-related building problems and indoor air quality.

Choosing a Sheathing Wrap

by Martin Holladay

What should you be using — asphalt felt, building paper, or housewrap? There is no shortage of opinions when it comes to these products, which I'll refer to as "sheathing wraps" in this article. (They're also called weather-resistive barriers.) Builders following the sheathing wrap debates may feel like they're being whipsawed back and forth, as manufacturers and building science experts announce the latest claims or laboratory findings.

Some professionals who have made noble attempts to clarify the muddy waters appear to be failing. In an effort to make it easier to compare the products, an ASTM task force has been working with scientists and manufacturers' representatives in hopes of developing common standards and test procedures for plastic housewrap, asphalt felt, and building paper. "We hoped we could write a specification, with tests to measure the performance of any of these products, but it's just not going to happen," says Thomas Butt, an architect from Richmond, Calif., who chairs the committee. "There are a lot of competing interests from some very economically powerful manufacturers. There is a lot of political pressure for something not to happen that would make one product look better than another," he notes.

Code Requirements

In many areas, building codes do not require any sheathing wrap at all, except under stucco, brick, stone, and composition sidings. In areas where the Model Energy Code is in force, a vapor-permeable housewrap is required, unless special measures are employed to reduce air infiltration.

Where codes do not require sheathing wrap, some builders may be tempted to omit it (**Figure 12**). However, studies have shown that houses without sheathing wrap tend to have damp walls. In the late '80s, George Tsongas, a professor of mechanical engineering at Portland State University and a consultant on moisture problems, opened up walls in 86 homes in Washington State and Montana and took moisture measurements of the wall cavities. "We found that in homes with no building paper or housewrap, there was a higher sheathing moisture content," says Tsongas. "In general, the use of a building paper or housewrap does tend to keep the sheathing drier."

What a Wrap Needs to Do

Most moisture problems in walls are water-entry problems, not vapor condensation problems. Sheathing wrap needs to resist any liquid water that gets behind the siding. In theory, at least, a sheathing wrap should also be a drainage plane. But in practice, most sheathing wraps can't drain.

Many experts, including George Tsongas, doubt that sheathing wrap, as typically installed, permits much drainage. "People think of housewrap or building paper as a drainage plane," says Tsongas. "But drainage is not possible with a siding that sits flush up against the building paper."

In order to function as a drainage plane, a sheathing wrap needs an air gap between the wrap and the siding. Partly in response to the widespread failures of EIFS (exterior insulation and finish systems), at least three manufacturers have responded to the drainage-plane problem by developing wrinkled

Figure 12. Studies have shown that, on average, houses without a wrap under the siding are more likely to have damp sheathing than houses with felt, Kraft paper, or housewrap.

sheathing wraps that are said to be self-draining (see "Ventilating Housewraps," below). Products currently on the market include Home Slicker (Benjamin Obdyke), StuccoWrap (DuPont), and Senergy drainage mat (Senergy).

Controlling vapor diffusion. If a wall cavity gets wet, either because of leaking flashings or condensing water vapor, a sheathing wrap should be vapor permeable so that the wall can dry to the exterior (see "Making Sense of Housewrap Specs," next page). Yet the ideal sheathing wrap would prevent water vapor from being driven into a wall by vapor pressure. Unfortunately, no one has yet developed a material that has "one-way permeance," allowing vapor out but not in. High vapor permeance is probably a desirable feature in a sheathing wrap during cold winter weather, but may be undesirable during hot, humid weather, when the action of the sun on saturated siding can cause vapor to be driven into a wall (**Figure 13**, page 109). Even in moderate climates, highly permeable sheathings and sheathing wraps can cause problems (see "The Air Conditioning Effect," page 109).

Does permeance matter? Surprisingly, some experts feel that the need for high vapor permeance in sheathing wrap has been overstated. "I think vapor permeance is totally irrelevant," says Wesley Page, a retired waterproofing consultant from Novato, Calif. "I have never seen a building where water vapor was the cause of failure, but I've seen hundreds where liquid water was." Consultant Joe Lstiburek of Building Science Consulting in Westford, Mass., also downplays the importance of permeance in a sheathing wrap, saying it "matters very little."

Most types of sheathing, including OSB and plywood, are not very vapor permeable, at least when dry. "Asphalt felt is rated at 5 perms, and the housewraps have ratings that range from 5 to 50," says Brad Allshouse, vice-president of marketing for Simplex Products, a housewrap manufacturer. "But commonly

Ventilating Housewraps

by Clayton DeKorne

Many researchers (but only a handful of builders) push the drainage concept to the extreme, advocating a "rain screen" method of siding. This typically involves installing siding over vertical strapping, or otherwise creating an air space behind siding to allow the siding assembly to dry. Home Slicker (Benjamin Obdyke), for example, provides a dense synthetic mat that presumably provides this air space, while adding only about 3/8 inch to the thickness of the wall, thereby eliminating the need to pack out windows and doors. Most EIFS products also have gone to a rain-screen-type system to avoid moisture problems.

While the theory of a rain screen is sound, strapping is rarely used under wood, vinyl, or fiber-cement siding in practice — primarily because of the added expense and the difficulty of furring out windows and doors. And while more and more builders in coastal and other harsh climates are beginning to experiment with Home Slicker, especially now that it is available preattached to Typar (Fiberweb) for a one-step weather-barrier installation, the jury is still out on whether this dense material allows moisture to drain or creates enough airflow to actually allow the siding assembly to dry.

A study by the Canada Mortgage and Housing Corporation (CMHC) to measure the drying potential of various wall systems, including a wall using Home Slicker, is now underway. Until the results are in, most contractors are putting their efforts into carefully lapping housewrap and flexible flashings, and allowing clear pathways beneath windows, doors, and other horizontal building elements to allow water to drain to the outside.

Clayton DeKorne is the editor of Coastal Contractor. *He is also editor of the* JLC Field Guide to Residential Construction *and a former senior editor at* The Journal of Light Construction.

Making Sense of Housewrap Specs

by Paul Fisette

In 1998, ASTM (the American Society of Testing & Materials) convened a task force on weather-resistive barriers — asphalt-treated Kraft paper, asphalt-saturated organic felt, and housewrap — in an effort to bring some consistency to the performance criteria by which these products are measured. A memo from the chairman of the group states that the three materials, any of which may meet the code criteria for "building paper" or "weather-resistive barrier," are "described by different ... standards" and that "there is no way to compare materials by a common set of criteria." The memo goes on to list no less than 24 test standards that manufacturers may pick and choose from to gain code approval for their products.

Air infiltration. Even if two manufacturers use the same test, the results can't be compared because the tests are often set up differently. For example, ASTM E 283, commonly used to test resistance to air infiltration, requires that the weather barrier be stretched over an 8x8-foot wall frame. However, the manufacturer can instruct the testing lab to put the wrap over anything from an open-stud wall to a fully sheathed, sided, insulated, and drywalled frame. To make a comparison, you would have to buy a copy of the code report for each product. Unless the test assemblies were exactly the same, a comparison of the specs would be meaningless.

Water resistance. There are many test procedures that can be used to qualify wall wraps as water resistant, but ASTM D 779, commonly called the "boat test," is recognized as the industry standard. In this test, a small sample of wall wrap is folded like a piece of origami and floated on water in a petri dish. A powdered substance, called an "indicator," is sprinkled on top of the wrap in a fine-layered, 1-inch circle. As water soaks up through the wrap, the indicator begins to change color. When an observer determines that the indicator is changing color at the fastest rate — a sign that water is passing through the wrap at the most rapid rate — the test is over and the elapsed time is noted. To qualify as a Grade D wrap, it must take at least 10 minutes for the color to change at its fastest rate. If a wall wrap claims a rating of 60, that means it took 60 minutes.

A problem with the boat test is that water vapor can also trigger the indicator's change of color — meaning that a highly vapor-permeable wrap like Tyvek fails. As an alternative, DuPont put Tyvek through AATCC 127, the "hydro-head" test, to prove its water resistance. In this test, the material is subjected to a 22-inch column of water — approximately the force exerted by a 200-mph wind — and must not leak a drop for 5 hours. This is a far more demanding test for water resistance than the boat test, yet as far as I know, among the plastic wraps, only Tyvek and R-Wrap have passed. Some researchers claim that felt has also passed, though inconsistently.

Here again, product literature can be misleading. Some manufacturers may list hydro-head test values like "186 cm." This is the height that the water column reached before the material began to leak.

Permeance to water vapor. One tested value that actually can be compared between brands of housewrap is vapor permeance, which is usually tested according to ASTM E 96, with the results expressed in perms. The higher the value, the more permeable the material. A material with a perm rating of 1 or less is considered a vapor barrier. The codes require wall wraps to match or exceed Grade D building paper, which has a minimum perm value of 5.

Unfortunately, the wide spread in perm ratings among brands — from 5 perms to over 200 perms — makes it a little difficult to assess the importance of this number. In addition, there are two common testing procedures under ASTM E 96 — procedure A (the dry-cup test) and procedure B (the wet-cup test) — which yield somewhat different results.

To complicate things, the permeance of felt paper is a moving target. Felt paper absorbs water and ranges from a low of around 5 perms when it's dry to more than 60 perms when it's exposed to relative humidity above 95%. The perm values of engineered wall wraps, however, are moisture-stable. Although high permeance is generally desirable in a wrap, excessively high ratings are not as important as resistance to air and water.

Paul Fisette is a wood technologist and a professor with the Building Materials and Wood Technology program at the University of Massachusetts in Amherst.

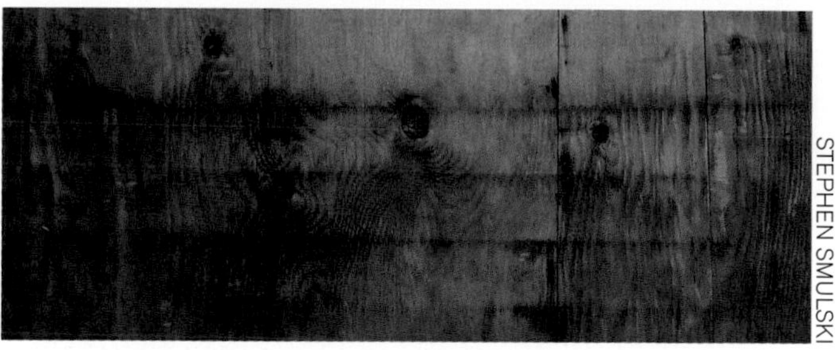

Figure 13. Highly permeable housewraps allow water vapor to escape to the exterior, helping walls to dry. However, in some circumstances, they can also allow water vapor to be driven inward, wetting the sheathing. Sun shining on damp wood siding can drive water vapor through a housewrap into the wall. These photos show water stains on the housewrap (left) and the sheathing (right) of a house with clapboard siding that had not been back-primed. The back side of the sheathing was dry, indicating that the moisture had traveled from the outside in. Although none of the sheathing on this house had rot, the siding paint peeled prematurely.

used sheathings have a permeance rating of less than 1. So the permeance of the housewrap is a moot point. A housewrap with a perm rating more than the code minimum of 5 is overkill," Allshouse says.

Controlling airflow. In the days of board sheathing, felt or paper was used under siding to slow wind down. Now that plywood and OSB are standard, the role of a sheathing wrap in reducing air infiltration is much less important, in spite of the energy claims made by plastic housewrap manufacturers. These days, most air leaks occur in ceilings and floors, not walls, so they are best addressed from inside a building, using gaskets and caulk.

Asphalt Felt

There are three basic types of sheathing wrap: asphalt felt, Grade D building paper, and plastic housewrap. Asphalt felt, which has been around for over a hundred years, was originally a true cloth felt. However, since present-day asphalt felt is a paper product, consisting largely of recycled corrugated paper and sawdust, the term "felt" is now somewhat of a misnomer.

Over the years, asphalt felt has also gotten lighter. In the old days, 15-pound felt used to weigh 15 pounds per 100 square feet. Manufacturers now call their product "number 15" (or #15) felt instead of 15-pound felt, and it weighs anywhere from 7 to 14 pounds per square.

ASTM has established two standards for asphalt felt. The less stringent standard is ASTM D 4869, which requires Type 1 (#15) felt to weigh at least 8 pounds per 100 square feet. The more rigorous standard, ASTM D 226, requires a minimum weight of 11.5 pounds per square.

Most lumberyards stock only lightweight asphalt felt with no ASTM rating. There are a few regions, however, such as Florida, where ASTM-rated felt is widely available because of code requirements. In Florida, roofing felt must carry an ASTM D 4869 label at a minimum.

The Air Conditioning Effect

Recent research shows that if a house with absorbent siding is air conditioned, solar-driven inward vapor movement can cause problems. Types of siding that can act as water reservoirs include brick, stucco, fiber-cement, and wood. "Inward vapor drive occurs everywhere, in almost any climate," says Mark Bomberg, a building science researcher and editor of *Journal of Thermal Envelope and Building Science*. Consultant Joe Lstiburek of Building Science Consulting in Westford, Mass., agrees. "I'm seeing a lot of problems with reservoir claddings — brick, cedar shingles nailed on felt without an air space, and stucco without an air space," says Lstiburek. "In all of these cases, the problems are caused by the solar-driven vapor phenomenon."

The problems are not restricted to the Deep South. "There is not much doubt that solar-driven vapor can damage walls," says John Straube, professor of civil engineering at the University of Waterloo in Ontario, Canada. "I have opened buildings and seen it. It can be a problem almost anywhere where there is air conditioning, including Toronto, Ontario."

Sheathings that are highly vapor permeable, like fiberboard and gypsum, are much more vulnerable to inward vapor-drive problems than sheathings that are relatively vapor impermeable, like OSB, plywood, or rigid foam. Back-priming wood or fiber-cement siding reduces problems from inward vapor drives. Finally, a simple way to avoid inward vapor drive problems is to choose a siding that can't act as a water reservoir, like vinyl siding. — *M.H.*

Asphalt felt is also available in a heavier version, commonly called 30-pound felt. This #30 felt is available in both the unrated grades and the ASTM-rated felts. ASTM standards refer to #30 felt as Type 2. The lightest unrated #30 asphalt felt is still heavier than the heaviest ASTM-rated #15 felt (see "How Much Does It Weigh?"), making it a logical choice for concerned builders.

Asphalt felt has a permeance of only 5 perms when dry, but a much higher rating of 60 perms when wet. Fans of felt note one of its advantages over housewrap: If water gets behind felt — either due to a flashing leak or condensation from solar-driven moisture — the felt can soak up the liquid water and gradually dry to the exterior. Plastic housewrap is not absorbent; any water trapped on the wrong side of plastic housewrap can only pass through to the exterior as vapor.

WESLEY PAGE

Figure 15. If Grade D building paper stays wet without the ability to dry out, it can rot. Rotting Grade D paper changes color from black to light brown. Here, flashing errors contributed to the failure of Grade D paper installed under stucco.

Grade D Building Paper

Builders in the western U.S., especially in areas where stucco is common, are familiar with Grade D building paper. However, in many areas of the country, including most of the East Coast, Grade D building paper is virtually unknown. Although Grade D paper is most often used under stucco, manufacturers point out that it can be used under any kind of siding.

Grade D building paper is an asphalt-impregnated Kraft paper that looks like a lightweight asphalt felt (**Figure 14**). The Grade D specification, which originated with the Uniform Building Code standard 14-1, requires that the paper have a minimum water-resistance rating of 10 minutes, and a minimum permeance rating of about 5 perms.

The water-resistance rating is based on a test, ASTM D 779, usually called the "boat test." If a piece of building paper or housewrap folded into a boat can float in a dish of water and withstand soaking for at least 10 minutes, it meets the water-resistance requirements of the Grade D specification. Many Grade D manufacturers choose to exceed the minimum water-resistance rating, and produce 20-minute, 30-minute, or 60-minute papers. Although the UBC calls these Grade D papers "waterproof," even a 60-minute paper is, at best, only water resistant.

FORTIFIBER

Figure 14. Grade D building paper is similar to asphalt felt, but lighter. It is made from virgin wood pulp, while asphalt felt is made from recycled cardboard.

Like asphalt felt, Grade D building paper is an asphalt-saturated paper. It differs from asphalt felt in two ways: It uses a lighter-weight paper, and the paper is made from new paper pulp rather than recycled cardboard. Since Grade D paper weighs less than asphalt felt, it also costs less. Manufacturers of Grade D paper like to point out that because it is lighter, it is easier to crease and install in inside corners.

Some experts note, however, that the added thickness of #15 felt is one of its virtues. If Grade D paper gets wet and stays wet, it can rot (**Figure 15**). Although asphalt felt can also rot, it holds up better in extreme conditions, because it is heavier. Because a single layer of Grade D paper may not hold up well to repeated wetting, the use of two layers of building paper has become a standard detail under three-coat stucco in many areas.

But in areas that get a lot of rain, even two layers of building paper can be overcome by regular soakings. "I've seen building paper rot, even if you have two layers," says building scientist Joe Lstiburek. "Grade D paper rots faster than roofing felt. The best paper for a wall is a roofing felt."

Those who have successfully used layers of Grade D paper under stucco, however, feel that building paper is being blamed for moisture intrusion problems that are best addressed with proper flashing details. All experts agree that any paper or felt will be less likely to rot if it is installed behind an air space that permits drainage.

Plastic Housewrap

Plastic housewraps are made from one of several available polyolefin fabrics, generally either polyethylene or polypropylene. Because there is no standard method for measuring vapor permeance, it is difficult to compare the permeance ratings of housewraps across brands. In general, housewraps have permeance values that range from 6 to 59 (see "Vapor Permeance of Plastic Housewraps," next page).

Housewraps can be divided into two categories, perforated and nonperforated. Nonperforated housewraps allow water vapor to pass between the fibers of the plastic fabric, while perforated housewraps are made from vapor-tight plastic films that are needle-punched with small holes to allow the passage of water vapor. Laboratory tests have shown that the non-perforated housewraps resist liquid water better than the perforated housewraps.

Some surfactants, which are chemical extractives that can leach out of wet cedar or redwood siding, have the potential to degrade a plastic housewrap's water resistance. However, surfactants can also degrade asphalt felt. "There have been problems with cedar and redwood sidings leaching wood sugars or surfactants," says Lstiburek. "This has occurred with all the plastic housewraps and the felts. Everything is affected. But the plastics seem to have more of a problem than the felts," he says. Back-priming of the siding is recommended to help minimize this problem.

Plastic housewraps are rarely used under stucco. "You can't stick stucco to any plastic housewrap, because if the stucco is in direct contact with a housewrap, the housewrap loses its water repellency," says Lstiburek. Frank Nunes, an officer with the International Institute of Lath and Plaster, has also seen problems using housewrap behind stucco. "Some housewraps are very reactive to surfactants in the cement plaster," says Nunes. "In one case I observed, the resins of the housewrap dissolved, leaving the fibers. It looked like a silkscreen — there was no material left."

Choosing a housewrap. If a wall is well designed and well flashed, any of the plastic housewraps will do the job. If you're concerned about inward vapor drives, you may want to avoid a high-permeance housewrap, especially when using a siding material that can hold water, like brick, stucco, or wood. The plastic housewraps with permeance ratings at the lower end of the range — from 5 to 15 — are comparable in permeance to asphalt felt. Since the most important function of a sheathing wrap is to resist liquid water, you may feel more comfortable with a non-perforated housewrap, especially if you are building in an area with a lot of rain.

In general, housewraps cost more than building paper or asphalt felt. Most builders find that housewrap is easier to install than paper or felt, because it comes in wide rolls (usually 9 or 10 feet wide) and it weighs less. On the other hand, builders working alone or working on a very high building may find a wide roll of housewrap more awkward than a narrow roll of paper or felt.

Housewraps stay more flexible in cold temperatures than paper or felt, and they resist tearing better. However, asphalt felt is better able to seal around fastener holes than housewrap. In the real world, housewrap is almost never installed as carefully as it is when tested in a laboratory. Researchers from the Pennsylvania Housing Research Center performed a field survey of installed plastic housewrap, and reported, "In the majority of the houses where staples have been installed with an automatic staple gun, tears and holes in the housewrap were common" (**Figure 16**, next page).

Frank Nunes points out, "As you wrap a building with housewrap and staple the material off, and keep rolling it out and tugging it, you will see an oval-shaped hole opening at the fastener. Moisture may

How Much Does It Weigh?

		Weight per 100 Square Feet
Plastic Housewraps		1.2 to 1.9 lb.
Grade D Building Papers	20-minute Grade D	3.3 lb.
	30-minute Grade D	3.7 to 3.9 lb.
	60-minute Grade D	5.6 to 6.4 lb.
#15 Asphalt Felts	Unrated (non-ASTM) #15	7.6 to 8.8 lb.
	ASTM D 4869 #15	8.0 to 9.7 lb.
	ASTM D 226 #15 (Type 1)	11.5 to 12. 5 lb.
#30 Asphalt Felts	Unrated (non-ASTM) #30	15.7 to 19.9 lb.
	ASTM D 226 #30 (Type 2)	26.4 to 27.3 lb.

Vapor Permeance of Plastic Housewraps

Type	Brand	Perms	Test Method
Perforated Housewraps	AmoWrap (PinkWrap) from Pactiv	15	A
	AmoWrap-VW from Pactiv	15	A
	Barricade from Covalence Coated Products	9	A
	Energy-Wrap from Fiber-Lam	9.7	B
	FirstWrap from Firstline Corp.	47.5	
	PinkWrap Plus from Owens Corning	34.7	A
	Typar from Fiberweb	22	A
	Valéron from Valéron Strength Films (Johns Manville ProWrap, Raven Industries Rufco-Wrap, Weyerhaeuser ChoiceWrap)	9	A
Non-perforated Housewraps	AmoWrap Ultra from Pactiv	48	A
	R-Wrap from Covalence Coated Products	59	A
	Tuff Weather Wrap from Celotex	6	B
	Tyvek from DuPont	58	B

These vapor permeance ratings, provided by the manufacturers (per 2000 stats), are based on one of two test methods described under ASTM standard E 96, method A and method B. Because the standard warns that "agreement should not be expected between results obtained by different methods," the permeance values in this table are not strictly comparable. However, these numbers do help to differentiate low-permeance housewraps like Barricade, Tuff Weather Wrap, and Valéron from high-permeance housewraps like R-Wrap and Tyvek.

be able to penetrate that hole." One solution to this problem is to switch to plastic-cap nails, which provide much better sealing than staples.

Virtually all plastic housewraps have been reviewed by the model code organizations and have been accepted as equivalents to #15 asphalt felt and Grade D building paper. Nevertheless, if you intend to substitute a plastic housewrap for code-required asphalt felt or building paper, it is always best to check for approval from your local building department.

Wrapping Up

There is no evidence that one type of sheathing wrap is disproportionately associated with moisture problems in walls. George Tsongas's research in the late 1980s confirmed this. "As long as the house had either building paper or housewrap, there was no significant difference in sheathing moisture content between the different types of paper or housewrap," says Tsongas.

When it comes to resisting liquid water, the nonper-

Figure 16. Damage from ladders (far left) and tears at staples (left) can undermine an otherwise careful housewrap installation.

forated housewraps appear to be the most waterproof, closely followed by asphalt felt. But neither asphalt felt nor Grade D paper nor perforated housewraps can keep water at bay for long. "Everyone seems to think of building paper as a moisture barrier," says George Tsongas. "In fact, they are not moisture barriers. If you get any significant amount of water behind the siding, the building paper will not hold back water — not even 15-pound felt. All the papers will allow liquid water to go through them in one day."

Moisture problems in walls, which are rare, are best avoided by good wall design and proper flashing. Which sheathing wrap to use is a secondary concern. If you're building in a location that gets a lot of rain, you may want to consider installing siding over a rain screen, since virtually all moisture problems in walls are lessened or eliminated when there's an air gap between the siding and the sheathing wrap.

Martin Holladay is the editor of Energy Design Update.

Choosing Flexible Flashings

by Martin Holladay

In recent years, builders have been paying more attention to the importance of keeping water out of walls. News of construction-defect lawsuits in California, EIFS failures in North Carolina, and the "leaky condo" crisis in British Columbia have all driven home the point that leaking buildings can cause major headaches for builders. One result of the focus on waterproof walls is the growing use of peel-and-stick membranes and other types of flexible flashing.

The term "flexible flashing" is used to describe a broad category of nonmetallic flashings, including both peel-and-stick and nonstick flashings. Manufacturers have not yet agreed on a generic term for these products, which are referred to as self-adhering bituminous tapes, flashing tapes, waterproofing tapes, flexible window flashings, flashing membranes, and wall tapes.

Only in the past few years have these flashings become common on residential job sites. Flexible flashing is rapidly replacing traditional felt splines for sealing the perimeter of finned windows. Some flexible-flashing manufacturers promote the use of these products at other locations as well: to cover below-grade concrete cracks, at roof penetrations, under exterior door sills, over deck ledger boards, at inside and outside corners of wall sheathing, under stucco shelves and parapets, and over sections of wall sheathing susceptible to splashback. But by far the most common use of flexible flashing is at window and door perimeters.

These new materials have some significant advantages over traditional flashing materials. Unlike most metal flashings, for example, peel-and-stick flashings conform easily to unusual shapes. Most types of flexible flashing can be folded to form a waterproof end dam on a rough windowsill, where making the same shape with copper would require soldering the flashing at the corners. Manufacturers claim that peel-and-stick flashings, unlike metal flashing, can form a waterproof seal between the flashing and the substrate.

These flashings are versatile and easy to install. But before slapping peel-and-stick over every exterior crack, you need to be sure you've chosen the right product for a given application. It's also important to know about potential compatibility problems and to avoid accidentally creating a wrong-side vapor barrier.

Rubberized Asphalt

Most peel-and-stick flashings are made from rubberized asphalt, also known as modified asphalt, modified bitumen, or rubberized bitumen. Rubberized-asphalt membranes were originally developed to protect roofs from ice dams. As builders recognized new uses for the product, several manufacturers began selling it in narrow rolls — typically between 4 and 12 inches wide — for a variety of flashing applications (**Figure 17**, next page).

Rubberized asphalt used for flashing is made by modifying asphalt with styrene butadiene styrene (SBS), which makes the asphalt more rubber-like. SBS-modified asphalt, being elastic, can accommodate thermal expansion and contraction in building components. Because of its "cold flow" characteristics, rubberized asphalt can also seal around fastener penetrations.

Sticky stuff. As long as the surface is clean and warm, rubberized asphalt sticks to a wide variety of substrates: dimensional lumber, plywood, steel, aluminum, hard vinyl, asphalt felt, and plastic housewrap (**Figure 18**, next page). Some manufacturers of rubberized-asphalt flashing advise that their products may not stick well to concrete, masonry, or OSB unless these substrates are first primed.

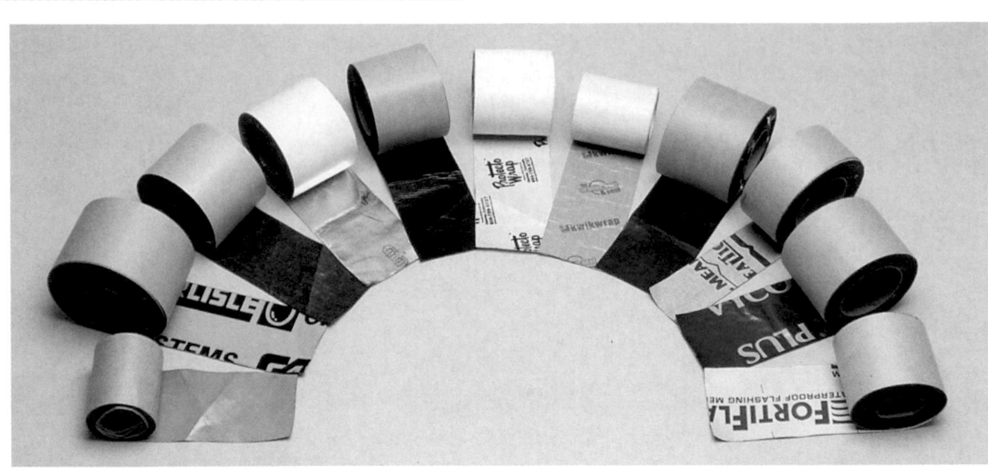

Figure 17. Self-adhering rubberized-asphalt flashings are made of the same material as the eaves membranes used to prevent ice dam leaks.

Figure 18. Rubberized-asphalt flashings, like Grace's Vycor Plus, stick well to unprimed plywood. Some manufacturers of rubberized-asphalt flashings warn that adhesion to OSB can be difficult unless the OSB is first primed.

Figure 19. Since foil-topped flashings like Peel 'N' Stick from Polyguard Products can be left exposed to the weather for a longer period than polyethylene-topped flashings, they are a good choice when siding installation may be delayed.

To make it possible to handle such a sticky substance, one side of the rubberized asphalt is laminated to a thin sheet (usually about 8 mils) of cross-laminated high-density polyethylene, and the other side is protected with a siliconized paper release sheet. Instead of polyethylene, some manufacturers laminate a thin layer of aluminum foil to the top of their rubberized-asphalt flashings (**Figure 19**).

Stickiness is a double-edged sword. In warm temperatures, when rubberized asphalt is at its stickiest, it can be impossible to readjust a flashing once it has touched a surface.

Keep it covered. Rubberized-asphalt flashings, except for those laminated with aluminum foil, should not be left exposed to the weather. Eventually, ultraviolet light breaks down the polyethylene, exposing the modified asphalt, which then begins to oxidize. Most manufacturers recommend that their flashings be covered within 30 days of installation, although one manufacturer, Protecto Wrap, says that its building tape can be left exposed for up to 120 days.

Butyl Rubber

Several manufacturers make peel-and-stick flashings from butyl, also called butyl rubber (**Figure 20**). Butyl flashings are usually black, resembling their rubberized-asphalt cousins. However, butyl flashings lack the asphalt smell that distinguishes rubberized-asphalt products, and they feel more rubbery. Like rubberized-asphalt flashings, butyl flashings are available with a top surface of either polyethylene or aluminum foil. Those with a top surface of polyethylene should not be left permanently exposed to the weather. FlexWrap, a butyl flashing from DuPont, has a top layer of corrugated Tyvek that enables it to conform to curved shapes, like the heads of archtop windows.

In general, butyl flashings cost about twice as much as rubberized-asphalt products (see "Flexible-Flashing Costs," page 116). However, DuPont's FlexWrap is significantly more expensive than other butyl flashings; it costs about six times the price of the average rubberized-asphalt product. Manufacturers claim that butyl has several advantages over rubberized asphalt: longer-lasting stickiness, less staining, less high-temperature

Figure 20. Self-adhering butyl flashings, like rubberized-asphalt flashings, can have a top layer of either polyethylene or aluminum foil. Butyl flashing, although more expensive than rubberized-asphalt flashings, can be installed over a wider temperature range.

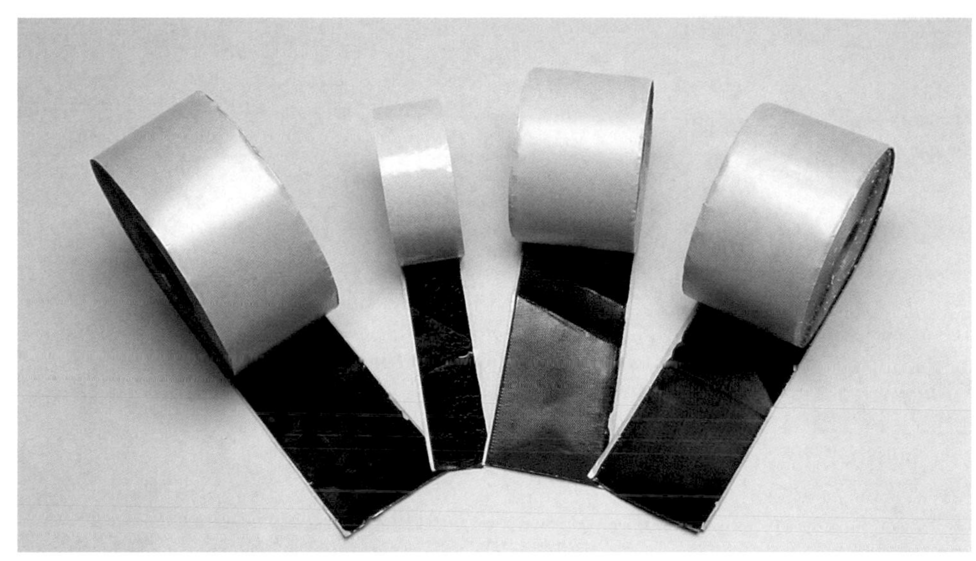

Figure 21. Butyl flashings with a top layer of EPDM are called cover tape or flashing tape and are commonly used to flash single-ply roofs. The EPDM layer protects the butyl from degradation by ultraviolet rays.

oozing, and a wider temperature range for installation.

Butyl rubber has a reputation for long-lived tackiness: One *JLC* editor has 21-year-old butyl glazing tape in his greenhouse that is still as pliable and tacky as the day it was installed. According to manufacturers, butyl is a more high-performance adhesive, providing better waterproofing and the ability to adhere to difficult surfaces. Although butyl's bond is aggressive, it is slower acting than the bond of rubberized-asphalt products. Butyl manufacturers tout this as an advantage, because it allows readjustment of the flashing during installation.

Although rubberized asphalt can be formulated for low-temperature installation, butyl flashings, on average, can be applied at colder temperatures than most rubberized-asphalt flashings.

Butyl laminated with EPDM. Some butyl flashings are laminated to a top layer of EPDM to make a type of flexible flashing called cover tape or flashing tape (**Figure 21**). EPDM, a rubbery membrane used for roofing, is very resistant to weather exposure. Because EPDM flashings are relatively expensive — costing about six times as much as the average rubberized-asphalt flashing — they are rarely used anywhere except on roofs, where the ability to resist ultraviolet light is essential.

Moreover, EPDM flashings are so thick (usually about 70 mils) that they would be awkward to use under siding. Rubberized-asphalt flashings are typically much thinner — between 20 and 40 mils thick — and are therefore easier to fold and tuck.

Variations on a Theme

Although most peel-and-stick flashings have a top layer of polyethylene, some are topped with aluminum foil. A few manufacturers sell flexible flashings that are not self-adhering and require the use of fasteners (**Figure 22**, page 117).

Foil-faced flashings. Flashings that are topped with a thin layer (2 mils) of aluminum foil can be left exposed to the weather. These flashings, which include an adhesive layer of either butyl or rubberized asphalt, are promoted for a variety of uses, including repair of rooftop ducts, metal chimneys,

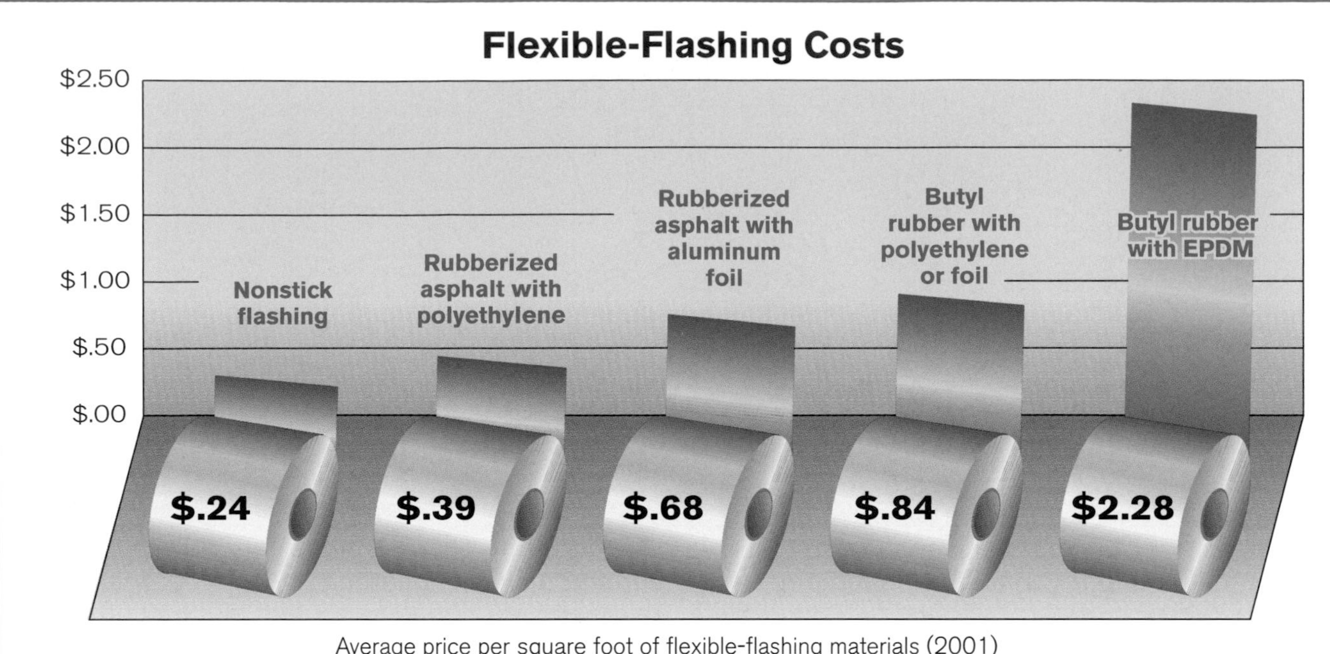

Average price per square foot of flexible-flashing materials (2001)

gutters, and trucks.

Because the long-term durability of these flashings is open to question, their use is usually limited to temporary roof repairs. One manufacturer, Tyco Adhesives, recommends its aluminum-foil flashing, Polyken 626-20 Window Flashing Tape, for use at window perimeters. If siding installation is delayed, even for many months, the aluminum foil layer will still protect the flashing from deterioration.

Nonstick flashings. At least two manufacturers make nonstick flexible flashings designed to be attached with staples or nails. Although nonstick flashings may appear unsophisticated compared to peel-and-stick products, they have their advocates. Some building-science experts feel that using a nonstick flashing (or even plain asphalt-felt splines) is preferable to using peel-and-stick flashings, which may be more likely to trap moisture in wall assemblies.

MFM's Future Flash is a nonstick flashing made from rubberized asphalt sandwiched between two films, a bottom layer of polyethylene and a top layer of metalized polyester. According to the manufacturer, Future Flash behaves better in very hot temperatures than most rubberized-asphalt flashings, because the metalized polyester layer helps reflect sunlight.

Fortifiber's nonstick flashing, called Moistop, is a relatively thin, 12-mil flashing made from Kraft paper laminated with two layers of polyethylene and one layer of fiberglass reinforcement. Moistop is inexpensive — about one-third the cost of the typical rubberized-asphalt product. Moistop shouldn't be used on windowsills, since the manufacturer warns that it is not intended for horizontal use. One disadvantage is that unlike Future Flash or other rubberized-asphalt flashings, Moistop can't seal around fastener holes. Moistop is also available in a version called E-Z Seal, which includes a narrow band of peel-and-stick adhesive along one side of the flashing.

Using Flexible Flashing

- Self-adhering flashings are particularly useful under windowsills and door thresholds, over deck ledger boards, and at horizontal projections and parapet walls that will be finished with stucco.
- To flash window and door perimeters, asphalt felt splines, nonstick products like Moistop, or self-adhering flashing can be used. Flashings should always be lapped to shed water.
- On wall sheathing, limit the use of self-adhering flashing to small areas in order to avoid creating a wrong-side vapor barrier.

Choosing the Right Flashing

Not surprisingly, manufacturers are eager to promote their flexible flashing products for a wide variety of applications. But not all manufacturers recommend the same applications, so it's important to read the installation instructions. Some manufacturers recommend using their products below grade or on roofs, while others specifically exclude those applications. In general, manufacturers of heavier 35-mil and 40-mil flashings are more likely to recommend roof or below-grade use than manufacturers of 20-mil products.

Figure 22. Not all flexible flashings are self-adhering. Future Flash from MFM Building Products (at left in photo) and Moistop from Fortifiber (photo center) are nonstick flashings that are installed with fasteners. Fortifiber's Moistop E-Z Seal (photo right) is similar to regular Moistop, but includes a 3-inch-wide adhesive band along one side of the flashing.

Thickness. Flexible flashings vary in thickness from 12 mils (Fortifiber's nonstick Moistop) to 79 mils (Illbruck Vapor Barrier Stucco Tape). Most self-adhering window and door flashings range in thickness from 20 mils to 40 mils. A thicker flashing may be more durable and better able to withstand abuse, but thinner flashing is easier to fold and conform to unusual shapes.

Hot locations. In very hot locations, butyl products are probably a better choice than rubberized asphalt, which can ooze at high temperatures. Oozing can occur when rubberized-asphalt flashing is installed under metal exposed to sunlight — for example, under metal roofing or on the nailing fins of south- or west-facing aluminum-clad windows. Grace Construction Products specifically prohibits the use of its Vycor Plus flashing in "hot desert areas in the southwestern U.S." Similarly, Carlisle Coatings warns that its product, Window and Door Flashing, is "not recommended in areas where flashing will be subject to continuous exposure to sunlight or to temperatures in excess of 180°F."

Cold-weather installation. Trying to install a peel-and-stick flashing on a cold wall can be frustrating. Both rubberized asphalt and butyl become less sticky as the temperature drops, and below 40°F some products just won't stick. One manufacturer, Ridglass Manufacturing (RGM Products, Inc.), ships different formulations of its Kwikwrap rubberized-asphalt flashing at different times of the year, with varying formulations to produce different levels of low-temperature stickiness. Unfortunately, there is no way to tell from the Kwikwrap label which product your local distributor has in stock.

The minimum application temperatures provided by flashing manufacturers vary from 10°F to 50°F (see "Flexible Flashing Specifications," pages 118 and 119). These recommendations should be taken as a guide, not as a guarantee. An installer can push the minimum application temperature somewhat by storing

Figure 23. Builders use a variety of methods for flashing windows. This installer has chosen a belt-and-suspenders approach, installing strips of FortiFlash, a rubberized-asphalt flashing, on top of strips of E-Z Seal, a Kraft-paper flashing laminated with polyethylene and fiberglass reinforcement.

Flexible Flashing Specifications

	Price per Square Foot*	Thickness	Available Widths (inches)	Min. Application Temperature	Priming of Substrate Required?	Roller Required for Installation?	Maximum Exposure Time
Rubberized Asphalt/Polyethylene							
Bakor Blueskin Weather Barrier	$0.80	25 mils	4, 6, 9	10°F	Recommended	Yes	42 days
Carlisle CCW-705 Window and Door Flashing	$0.44	40 mils	4, 6, 9, 12	25°F	Only for concrete, masonry, and some exterior gypsum	No	30 days
Dur-O-Wal Polytite PolyBarrier	n/a	40 mils	12, 18, 24, 36	25°F	Priming may be necessary	Yes	
Fortifiber FortiFlash	$0.29	25 and 40 mils	4, 6, 9, 12, 36	40°F	No	No	Cover as soon as possible
Grace Vycor Plus	$0.61	25 mils	4, 6, 9, 12	25°F	Only for concrete and masonry	No	30 days
Grace Vycor Weather Barrier Strips	n/a	40 mils	6, 9, 12	40°F	Only for concrete and masonry	No	30 days
Master Wall Weather Stop Flashing Tape	n/a	n/a	n/a	45°F	Yes	Yes	42 days
MFM Sub Seal	$0.40	45 mils	4, 6, 9, 12, 18, 36	50°F	Only for concrete, masonry, and OSB	Yes	45 days
MFM Window Wrap (polyester top)	$0.30	25 mils	3, 4, 6, 9, 12, 18	50°F	Only for "some wood composition panels as well as dirty, dusty or weathered surfaces"	Recommended	90 days
NEI Advanced Composite Homeseal	$0.32	30 mils	4, 6	40°F	Only for concrete and masonry	Yes	30 days
Polyguard WindowSeal	$0.24	20 mils	4, 6, 9, 12, 18, 36	45°F	Only for OSB	No	30 days
Protecto Wrap BT20XL Building Tape	$0.24	20 mils	4, 6, 9, 12	45°F	Only for concrete, masonry, Dens Glas Gold, and some OSBs	Yes	120 days
Ridglass Kwikwrap	$0.39	40 mils	4, 6, 9, 12, 36	40°F	No	Recommended	30 days
Sandell Presto-Seal	$0.42	40 mils	6, 12, 18, 24, 36	25°F	Yes	Yes	n/a
Tamko Moisture Wrap	$0.45	40 mils	4, 6, 9, 12	30°F	Recommended but not required for concrete and masonry	Recommended	n/a
Tremco Sealants Window/Door Wrap	n/a	20 and 40 mils	4, 6, 36	No limitation	Only for OSB	Yes	n/a
W.R. Meadows Sealtight Air Shield	$0.21	40 mils	4, 6, 9, 12, 16	25°F	Yes	No	n/a
Rubberized Asphalt/Aluminum Foil							
Illbruck Weather Barrier Tape	$0.73	41 mils	2, 3, 4, 6	41°F	Only for porous or wet surfaces	Yes	No limitation
MFM Peel & Seal	$0.73	50 mils	3, 4, 6, 9, 12, 18, 36	55°F	Only for OSB	Yes	No limitation
Polyguard Peel 'N' Stick	$0.70	45 mils	4, 6, 9, 12, 18, 36	45°F	No	Yes	No limitation
Ridglass Kwiksilver	$0.56	60 mils	2, 4, 6, 9	40°F	Only for concrete and some gypsum sheathings	No	No limitation

* based on average 2001 prices

the flashing in a warm location before use.

In consistently low temperatures, the best flexible flashing may be a nonstick flashing like Fortifiber Moistop or MFM Future Flash. Since these products are attached with fasteners, stickiness is not an issue. If you need a cold-weather self-adhering flashing, it's probably best to choose either a butyl product or Bakor Blueskin Weather Barrier, a rubberized-asphalt flashing that performs well at low temperatures. In a pinch, any flashing can be held up with roofing nails.

Compatibility problems. If you're using a flexible flashing anywhere near an asphalt product, it's best to choose a rubberized-asphalt flashing, because butyl flashings are incompatible with asphalt products. "There are oils that want to come out of the asphalt," says Jeff Winzeler, product manager for the roofing adhesive group at Ashland Chemical Co., a manufacturer of butyl tapes. "The butyl will suck them up and lose its adhesive properties."

Tyco Adhesives' instructions for installing one of its butyl flashing products, Polyken 627-35, warns, "Avoid contact with residuary asphaltic products such as coatings and other roofing products." A Tyco representative confirmed that its butyl flashings shouldn't be in contact with asphalt roofing cement. Since Tyco promotes the product for use on roofs, where asphalt roofing cement is often found, installers must be vigilant to avoid compatibility problems.

The jury is still out on whether butyl tapes should be allowed contact with asphalt felt. "If you are talking about 15-pound felt, there is not a lot of asphalt, because felts are relatively dry," says Winzeler. "You'll probably have fewer issues with compatibility than with roofing cement. But until you test, you can't be sure."

Rubberized asphalt is incompatible with some

Flexible Flashing Specifications

	Price per Square Foot*	Thickness	Available Widths (inches)	Min. Application Temperature	Priming of Substrate Required?	Roller Required for Installation?	Maximum Exposure Time
Butyl Rubber/Polyethylene							
DuPont Tyvek FlexWrap	$2.70	40 to 80 mils	8, 10	40°F	No	No	120 days
Illbruck Vapor Barrier Stucco Tape	$2.00	79 mils	2, 4, 6	41°F	Only for concrete, plaster, steel, dimensional lumber, and rough glass	Yes	90 days
MFM Butyl Window Wrap	$0.38	20 mils	4, 6, 9	25°F	No	Yes	n/a
Tyco Polyken 627-20 Window Flashing Tape	$0.28	20 mils	4, 6, 9	25°F	No	Yes	30 days
Tyco Polyken 627-35 Flashing Tape	$0.92	35 mils	3, 6, 9, 12	25°F	No	Yes	30 days
Tremco Sealants Tremlite Polyfoil	n/a	35 mils	4	40°F	No	Yes	No limitation
Butyl Rubber/Aluminum Foil							
Tyco Polyken 626-20 Window Flashing Tape	$0.38	20 mils	4, 6, 9	25°F	No	Yes	No limitation
Tyco Polyken 626-35 Foilastic Flashing Tape	$1.08	35 mils	2, 3, 4, 6, 9, 12	25°F	No	Yes	No limitation
EPDM Flashings							
ADCO ET-553 flashing tape	$2.14	n/a	6, 12	n/a	n/a	n/a	No limitation
Ashland Plioseal cover strip	$1.90	65 mils	5, 6, 7, 9, 12, 18	-20°F	Yes	Yes	No limitation
Ashland Plioseal flashing tape	$1.90	70 mils	5, 6, 7, 9, 12, 18	-20°F	Yes	Yes	No limitation
Avenco American Super Bond cover tape	$2.04	n/a	6, 9, 12	n/a	n/a	n/a	
Avenco American Super Bond flashing tape	$2.20	n/a	6, 12	n/a	n/a	n/a	No limitation
Geocel 9906 Flashing Tape	$3.50	70 mil	6	No limitation	May be required	No	No limitation
International Diamond Systems flashing tape	n/a	70 mils	6, 12	n/a	n/a	n/a	No limitation
Tremco Sealants uncured EPDM flashing	n/a	70 mils	6, 9, 12	No limitation	n/a	Yes	No limitation
Tremco Sealants cured EPDM cover strip	n/a	65 mils	6, 9, 12	No limitation	n/a	No	No limitation
Nonstick Flashings							
Fortifiber Moistop	$0.11	12 mils	6, 9, 12, 18	No limitation	No	No	Cover as soon as possible
MFM Future Flash	$0.29	25 mils	4, 6, 9, 12, 18, 36	No limitation	No	No	60 days
Other							
Fortifiber Moistop E-Z Seal	$0.32	35 mils	4, 6, 9, 12	40°F	No	No	Cover as soon as possible

* based on average 2001 prices

types of flexible vinyl, especially vinyl flashings that come in a roll. It doesn't appear to have any compatibility problems with hard vinyl, like the vinyl used for window fins.

Watch out for staining. Rubberized asphalt, like other asphalt products, can stain some materials, especially vinyl. According to Bob Sims, customer service manager at Bakor, such staining, called plasticizer migration, occurs when oils in the asphalt dissolve plasticizers in the vinyl. Since rubberized-asphalt flashings shouldn't be left exposed, staining is generally not a problem. The siding or other material used to cover the flashing usually hides any stains.

Installing Flexible Flashing

On most job sites, peel-and-stick flashings are installed without a lot of fuss. Typically, the flashing is cut to length, the release paper is removed, and the flashing is pressed in place by hand (**Figure 23**, page 117). But the easy way may not be the right way. Some manufacturers recommend that substrates should be primed before installing their peel-and-stick flashing, and that pressure should be applied with a roller, not the palm of the hand.

Is a primer necessary? Self-sticking flashings often adhere better to a primed surface than an unprimed surface. Manufacturers that recommend priming generally focus on concrete and masonry as the most problematic surfaces, partly because those surfaces can be dusty or damp. Other manufacturers specify that OSB and gypsum sheathing need to be primed, and a few recommend priming metal and plywood. Most manufacturers agree that in cold weather, a self-sticking flashing will adhere better to a primed than an unprimed surface. There is a catch-22, though:

Figure 24. Peel-and-stick flashing adheres poorly to dirty substrates or when applied in cold weather.

When it's too cold for peel-and- stick, it may also be too cold to apply primer.

In any case, few residential builders are likely to take the time to prime plywood or OSB sheathing before using peel-and-stick, which is one reason some manufacturers omit the recommendation. If you do decide to prime, remember to use the primer recommended by the flashing manufacturer, since the wrong primer may cause compatibility problems.

Hand pressure or roller? Many, but not all, manufacturers recommend that their flexible flashing should be installed with a steel or hard-rubber J-roller — the same type of roller used for gluing plastic laminate countertops. Many manufacturers' reps admit that this recommendation is widely ignored, but doing so carries some risk: When it comes to priming and using a roller, the bottom line is that builders who deviate from a manufacturer's recommendations can't expect any support from the manufacturer if something goes wrong.

Use With Care

Despite the versatility of flexible flashings, they have their limitations and must be used with common sense. Some builders have reported adhesion problems with peel-and-stick. Others note that too much peel-and-stick can create a wrong-side vapor barrier.

How tacky? Peel-and-stick doesn't always stick. "I've been to sites where I've seen the peel-and-stick already half falling off the housewrap," says Patricia McDaniel, owner of Boardwalk Builders in Rehoboth Beach, Del. Poor bonding can be due to a variety of factors, including low temperatures and dirty substrates (**Figure 24**). Manufacturers agree that the adhesive bond of peel-and-stick flashings varies over time. Initially, for the first month or so, the bond should actually get stronger. But no one really knows when, if ever, the bond strength may begin to fail.

Building scientist Joe Lstiburek urges caution. "A problem with these membranes is that they can peel away," says Lstiburek. "Don't rely on the adhesive property for waterproofing."

In an informal *JLC* test, 21 different peel-and-stick flashings were bonded to wood for 14 hours. About half of them failed to make a waterproof seal. Although further curing might have resulted in a waterproof bond, the test shows the need for caution when depending on an adhesive alone to seal out water.

Wrong-side vapor barrier. Peel-and-stick membranes should be used sparingly on wall sheathing, since they can create a wrong-side vapor barrier. "If you put a big hunk of peel-and-stick on the sheathing, interior moisture can condense behind it, causing rot," says Lstiburek. "It doesn't happen very often, but it happens occasionally. You've got to be careful not to get slaphappy with the stuff."

Several builders in British Columbia report finding sheathing rot behind peel-and-stick membranes, especially at window heads. But most investigators say that an important contributing factor in these cases was the use of damp framing lumber, and there don't appear to be any reports of such problems in other parts of North America. In fact, manufacturers of peel-and-stick membranes confidently recommend their use at window heads. "Clearly, vapor is an issue," says Rick Scruggs, technical service specialist at Grace Construction Products, a manufacturer of rubberized-asphalt flashing. "We wouldn't like to see you cover the whole wall, unless there are provisions for the vapor to get out. But if just a narrow strip of membrane is used around a window, the vapor can escape from other areas."

Many peel-and-stick manufacturers recommend the use of their products under siding at areas subject to splashback. However, because of the wrong-side vapor barrier problem, such an application is controversial. "The use of self-adhering membrane at splashback areas concerns me greatly," says Bob Switzer, of the Canadian Home Builders' Association of British Columbia. "You are far better off finding ways to prevent the splash, like replacing the soil with lava rock."

Yet many builders confidently use peel-and-stick to protect sheathing from splashback. "We use it at the splashback area all the time," says McDaniel. "I think you are much more likely to get water into a structure with bad flashing details than vapor problems, at least in our climate."

Over or under the housewrap? One debate that won't be settled soon is whether peel-and-stick should be applied directly to the sheathing or is best applied to the housewrap or felt. There are strong advocates for both positions.

Some manufacturers recommend that their peel-and-stick membrane should be applied directly to the sheathing. "In general, the membrane should be adhered directly to the wall sheathing, and not to a layer of felt or housewrap. What's the value of the membrane if it can't be fully adhered to the substrate to prevent water from getting behind it?" says Scruggs. McDaniel agrees. "Installing housewrap and then slapping windows in and then attaching peel-and-stick to the housewrap doesn't do anything," she says.

By contrast, builders who are worried about a wrong-side vapor barrier prefer to see a layer of building paper or housewrap between the sheathing and the peel-and-stick. "Rarely do I apply a piece of peel-and-stick directly to sheathing," says Randy Faustmann, president of Rainforest Envelope Protection Services, a consulting firm in Langley, B.C. "Usually, it is installed over the building paper. I think that having the layer of paper between the peel-and-stick and the sheathing allows a little bit more drying than it would without it."

No matter how you assemble your sandwich of flexible flashing, nailing fins, and building paper, everyone agrees on one point: Lap all the layers to shed water. "You have to lap your layers, because at some point the glue's going to give," says McDaniel. "Physics is going to win over chemistry."

Martin Holladay is editor of Energy Design Update.

Housewrap Do's and Don'ts

by Patricia McDaniel

To some extent, houses have always leaked. But in recent years, using new materials like panel sheathing, housewrap, and flanged windows, we've tightened up construction to the point that houses no longer dry well. During the same period, there's been a decline in traditional methods of carpenter training. One result is that houses are going up without proper attention paid to building paper and flashings. Once these new tight houses leak and the insulated framing cavities get soaked, they're more likely to stay wet and rot than the airy, "breathable" houses of the past.

In more than 20 years of building, repairing, remodeling, and inspecting homes, I've found that even the most critical flashing details are often installed wrong or overlooked altogether. These errors are common to expensive custom homes and inexpensive modular houses alike. Often, it's evident that the carpenters made a conscientious effort, yet still the details are wrong.

Again and again, flashing and papering mistakes come back to one overriding principle: Get the layers right so that water flows out on top, not behind, the housewrap and flashing. A second important principle: Don't rely on the siding to stop the water. I tell customers that the purpose of siding is to look good, and that, yes, it sheds most of the water off the house. But it also lets water past it, so the backup system of housewrap and flashings must deflect that water and allow it to weep or drain back out from behind the siding before it soaks the sheathing and framing.

Materials of Choice

We use Tyvek (DuPont) and Typar (Fiberweb) interchangeably (my carpenters tend to prefer Typar because it's quieter and easier on the eyes). Properly installed, we get good performance from either material.

The housewrap debate. There is some research that indicates that housewraps don't perform well when they're subject to persistent wetting. However, in my inspection work, I've never come upon a situation where there was rot behind housewrap that I couldn't trace to a water intrusion higher up — for example, a roof leak, a rip in the housewrap, a backwards lap, or a missing flashing.

I don't claim to have seen everything, but it's my strong opinion that if you get the details right, the brand of housewrap you use is not important. If you just can't bring yourself to trust housewrap, use tar paper — it's been around for a long time and still performs well.

Eaves membrane. Any areas subject to a lot of moisture — splashback zones, areas below intersecting roofs that dump accumulated rainwater, or tall beachfront houses, for example — can benefit from extra layers of tar paper or self-sticking eaves membrane (commonly referred to on the job site as "bituthene" or bituminous membranes) in addition to the housewrap. Wherever you use it, be sure the top edge of the membrane or tar paper is behind the housewrap above.

For the 36-inch-wide rolls of bituthene, we use one of several available brands, including Grace and CertainTeed. For the narrow flashing rolls, we prefer to use Grace's Vycor. Although this stuff is very sticky, it adheres best to clean surfaces, and sticks poorly to dirty housewrap.

Get a brake. If you're serious about keeping water out of the houses you build, you should invest in a metal brake and learn to use it. With a brake and a roll of coil stock on hand, we can bend the necessary flashings as we go, and not have to rely on a roofer or metalworking sub who may or may not be at the site when we need it.

Don't rely on chemistry. Don't substitute the stickiness of bituthene for proper layering. The same goes for housewrap tapes and caulks. In time, chemical bonds can break down, but properly lapped layers will not move.

Sequence Is the Culprit

The photos that follow illustrate common leak spots that occur from installing housewrap improperly. Some of these mistakes result from nothing more than carelessness. But a root cause of many problems is the construction sequence that's common on job sites today: The frame gets sheathed and wrapped, then everything else — doors, windows, decks, and flashings — gets put on top. Immediately you have a layering problem — unless you do something about it.

Incomplete Wrapping

All too often I see sloppy and incomplete housewrap installations; the housewrap is installed any which way, with no attention to proper layering.

Gable ends. For some reason, builders often think they can get away without wrapping the gable ends (photos **A** & **B**). This may be because they're thinking of the wrap only as an air infiltration barrier but not as a weather barrier, and figure there's no reason to worry about air leaking into the attic.

This is a mistake, because the gable is one of the most exposed parts of the house. Driving rain gets behind the siding, runs down the sheathing, and winds up behind the housewrap.

The problem often appears as drips along the top extension jamb of windows or sliders below. It may be hard to diagnose, because the leak may show up well below the point where the water runs behind the housewrap.

Band joist. Another problem area is the band joist. Walls may be sheathed and wrapped while they're lying on the deck. Then, when the wall is lifted, the band or mud sill remains unprotected (**C** & **D**). Splashback from below as well as water running down the housewrap from above can cause severe wetting. If you install wrap this way, make sure you go back and cover the band joist with a strip of housewrap, tucking it under the wrap above. Note that in photo **D** this would be difficult to do, because hold-down straps were installed over the wrap above and band joist below.

Outside corners. Often housewrap doesn't quite make it around the corners (**E**). Like gables, corners get a lot of weather exposure, and any water that enters at this intersection of trim and siding then has direct access to the structure. A leak at this point may never show up inside the house, but can nonetheless lead to rot over time. Make sure your housewrap extends all the way around corners. We typically add a layer of tar paper over the housewrap behind all corner trim boards.

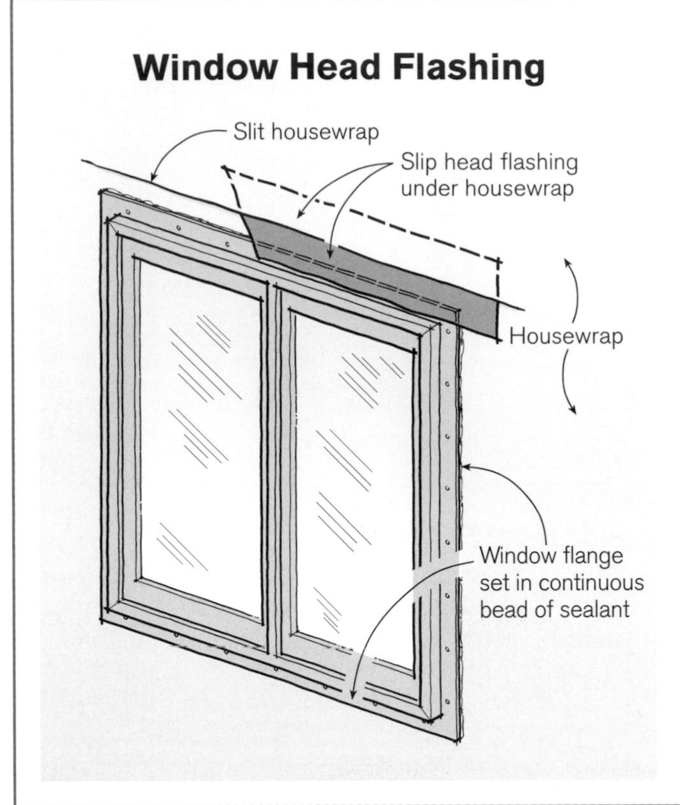

Wrapping Around Windows and Doors

Once in a while you see a window that's properly integrated with the housewrap, as in photo **F**. Here, the flanged window was installed over a strip of flashing paper at the bottom of the window, while flashing strips along the sides cover the flanges. At the top, the head flashing paper laps over the flange and was inserted into a slit in the housewrap above, then secured with tape. I don't have a lot of confidence that the tape will stick to the tarpaper for the long term, but since the lapping is correct, the installation should be weatherproof.

Around the corner on the same house, however, a door cased with brickmold was slapped into place right over the housewrap, with no effort to flash the head (**G**). This is a common problem both with cased doors and flanged units (**H**). Often the casing or flange is bedded in a bead of caulk. While this may help for a while to prevent water from entering at the window head, it does nothing to prevent the brickmold or wood head casing from soaking up water and eventually rotting. Once water gets behind the siding, it will run down the housewrap and pond on top of the head casing. This problem often shows up inside as water dripping from the head jamb extension.

Note in photos **G** and **H** the torn paper at the corners of the door head. This results when the installer is careless in making the conventional X-cut in the housewrap. The more common recommendation now is to make an I-cut (see "Flashing a Flanged Window," page 198), fold the sides in, and slip the top flange of the window behind the housewrap at the head. Or you can install the flanges on top of the housewrap, slice the housewrap above the window, and slip a piece of tar paper or flashing behind the housewrap at the top (see "Window Head Flashing," above). With wood brick mold, you should use a metal cap flashing, and slip the upper leg behind a slit in the wrap. In my opinion, these simple details will take care of 99% of the leaks around doors and windows.

Mulled windows. Mulled windows are another challenge. Many builders use the manufacturer's accessory mullion cover, but fail to provide a continuous head flashing across the top. The result is that water runs down between the units and often finds its way into the framing at the sill.

Photo **I** shows how someone went to a lot of trouble to seal a window wall tight to the weather, using Grace Ice & Water Shield between and around the windows. Unfortunately, the closeup shot (**J**) reveals some heartbreaking details. Despite the obvious effort, the lapping

is wrong: The top flanges of the windows lie on top of the membrane, allowing water to pass down behind the flange and into the framing. The messy caulk is an attempt to correct the situation, but for a beachfront house like this, it's a leak waiting to happen.

Photo **K**, shot elsewhere on the same house, shows a sticky flashing application already beginning to peel at the top. Grace Ice & Water Shield is probably overkill in this case anyway; it would have been better to use tar paper and tuck it into a slit at the top of the window.

The sloppy work shown here is indicative of the confusion that surrounds window installation in the industry today. Builders buy high-tech waterproof membranes, spend a lot of time fussing with the installation, and still end up with the basic details wrong.

Round windows. Half-round and full-circle windows are tricky to flash, because there's no practical way to lay the wrap on top of the flange, and metal flashings don't conform to the radius. Photo **L** (next page) shows an attempt to deal with the problem by taping the flange to the wrap. Unfortunately, the roof flashing at the bottom was installed on top of the bottom flange — again reverse layering. Some attempt was made to get it right by slicing the wrap at each side of the window and bringing it out on top of the metal flashing.

I would prefer to see Grace Ice & Water Shield used around radius windows rather than tape.

Roof Flashings

The layering problem with the roof flashing shown in photos **L** and **M** is all too common. It's rare for a roofer to take the time to lift the housewrap or building paper and tuck the upper leg of the flashing underneath. Water runs down the housewrap, behind the flashing, and shows up as a roof leak.

These simple shed roofs are easy to get right. Either hold the paper up until flashing is installed, or slit and tuck in a strip of tarpaper after the flashing goes in.

Trickier are the step-flashed areas where roofs meet walls. Photo **N** shows a fancy metal roof with lousy flashing details. Not only is the roof counterflashing on top of the housewrap, but it also delivers water right onto the deck rim joist below (as does the deck membrane above). Once the wood trim board gets installed over that deck rim joist, it's only a matter of time before rot sets in.

In photo **O**, the counterflashing on the upper roof was carefully tucked under the lifted housewrap,

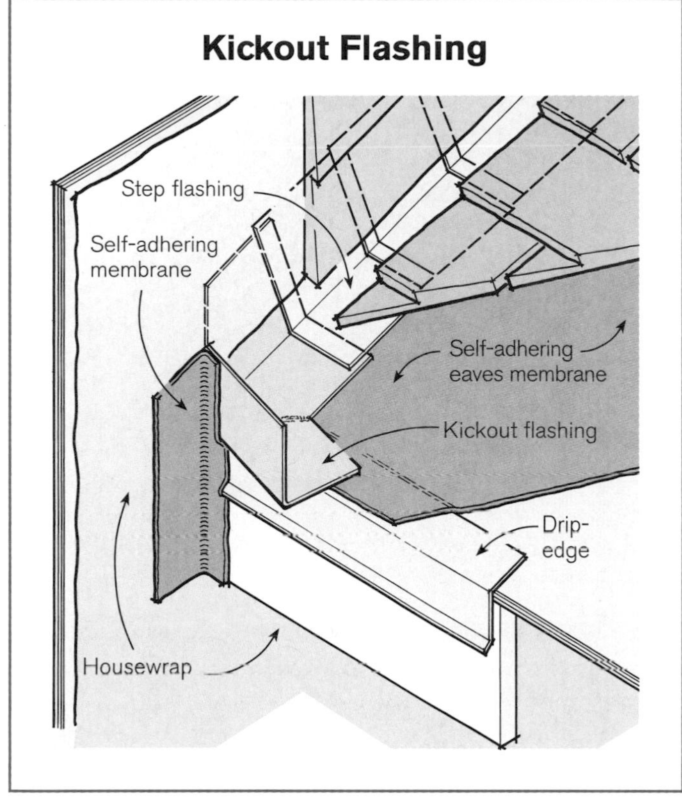

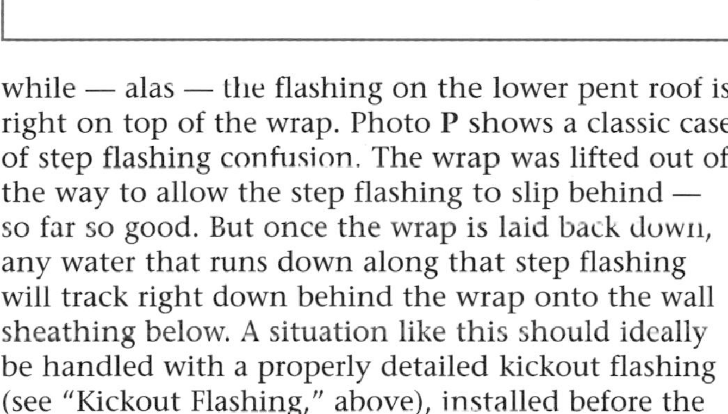
while — alas — the flashing on the lower pent roof is right on top of the wrap. Photo **P** shows a classic case of step flashing confusion. The wrap was lifted out of the way to allow the step flashing to slip behind — so far so good. But once the wrap is laid back down, any water that runs down along that step flashing will track right down behind the wrap onto the wall sheathing below. A situation like this should ideally be handled with a properly detailed kickout flashing (see "Kickout Flashing," above), installed before the eaves trim and roof shingles. If you don't use a kick-out, make sure that the housewrap is on top of the upper leg of the step flashing, but that the bottom piece of step flashing directs the water out on top of the housewrap below (and preferably, out on top of the siding). This requires careful slitting and weaving of the wrap and the metal, with Ice & Water Shield patches where necessary. In areas of severe wetting, an additional layer of tar paper on the lower wall is a good idea.

Deck Details

If you're not careful, deck ledgers can provide a direct path for water to enter the structure. Often — around here at least — the framing crew installs the deck ledger before the house is wrapped. In many cases, the band joist never gets sheathed at this point. The housewrap gets installed, but terminates just above the ledger. Unless the top of the ledger is properly flashed — which is not always the case — any water running down the wall gets channeled into the framing, leading to long-term saturation and rot.

Our framers always bring the sheathing down over the band joist, then install aluminum coil stock to separate the deck ledger from the house. We flash the top of the ledger, making sure this flashing is behind the housewrap (see "Deck Ledger Flashing," next page). Photo **Q** shows a sloppy wrapping job that leaves the band joist exposed. Because the deck is already in place, there's no practical way to flash the area. In photo **R**, the ledger flashing extends nicely up the wall, but is laid on top of the housewrap.

Attached rails. It's always a good idea to separate railing elements from the house walls when possible, to avoid pathways for water to enter the framing. Photo **S** shows what looks to be a nice detail: The railing is separated from the house wall, and the wrap passes behind. The only problem is that the eventual finish on this house was EIFS, meaning the wood railing post was buried under 1 1/2 inches of foam board.

Whenever we have to attach a post to a house wall, we separate the post from the sheathing with aluminum flashing. We bring the top of flashing 6 inches above the deck rail, and make sure it tucks behind the housewrap. Our preferred method is to install the siding first, and leave a gap of a few inches (code allows up to 4 inches) between the post and the house.

Stupid details. Some details defy common sense, and are best left to your competition (photo **T**). Rule of thumb: If you can't figure out how to flash it, don't build it.

Patricia McDaniel is the owner of Boardwalk Builders in Rehoboth Beach, Del.

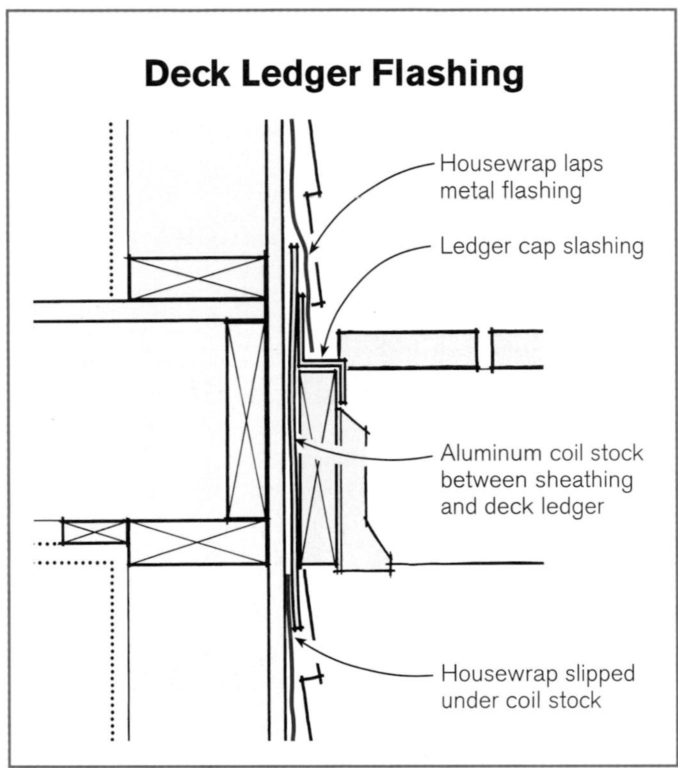

Chapter 8: Masonry

MIKE SLOGGATT

Keeping Water Out of Brick Veneer

by Jerry Carrier

There is little debate over brick's reputation as a durable, maintenance-free building material. Brick buildings that are hundreds of years old are still in use today. However, many people don't realize that the older brick buildings were not built like today's brick-veneered buildings. Historically, brick was used to create load-bearing walls, which were often four or more wythes of solid brick masonry. These walls prevented moisture penetration to the interior by their sheer mass.

The brick masonry in today's veneer wall is just one element of a drainage wall system, which typically consists of a single 4-inch-thick wythe of brickwork, an air space of 1 inch to 2 inches, and a separate wood, steel, or concrete block backup wall. When moisture-penetration problems occur, it is usually because the people building the wall didn't understand some of the basic principles of brick veneer construction.

Brick Veneer Is Not Waterproof

A common misconception, even among some masons, is that 4-inch brick veneer will stop all moisture penetration under all weather conditions. It is important to remember that brick is a porous absorptive material, and that water can penetrate a brick veneer wall wherever there is a gap in the material: at bond breaks, hairline cracks between brick and mortar, unfilled joints, movement cracks, and even unfilled line-pin holes.

There are all sorts of opinions about whether water that penetrates a brick veneer wall is coming through the brick, through the mortar, or through small cracks in the mortar. But it really doesn't matter how you visualize the moisture entering into the wall system. What matters is understanding the simple, inexpensive details and installation practices that can prevent water problems.

The Drainage Wall System

If you are installing brick veneer, you should expect water on the back face of your bricks (**Figure 1**). It is important to take steps to allow any moisture to drain from the wall, so that it can't enter the building's interior. The drainage wall concept is fairly simple: Water that penetrates the exterior wythe of brickwork travels down the back face of the brick until it's collected by through-wall flashing and led to the exterior through weep holes (**Figure 2**, page 132). There are three important elements in a drainage wall system: a clean air space, through-wall flashing, and weep holes (see "Brick Veneer Details," facing page).

Figure 1. Since wind-driven rain may penetrate brick veneer, it is best to assume that the backs of the bricks will be wet. Unless the water can drain to the exterior, moisture can damage framing or interior finishes.

A Clean Air Space

The purpose of a clean air space is to be sure that water can't get across to the backup wall. The Brick Industry Association (BIA) recommends a minimum 1-inch air space between the brick veneer and the backup wall system. (The International Residential Code also requires a minimum 1-inch air space, but allows the space to be fully grouted under certain conditions.)

Often, however, this 1-inch air space, which is little more than finger room for the mason, is reduced because of simple variation in the materials — sheathing that is not properly attached, framing that is out of plumb, or even variation in brick size. With a larger air space, mortar is less likely to bridge the air space, and masons can remove mortar more easily from the back face of the brickwork. Because a larger air space is less likely to become clogged, more and more designers and masons are including a larger 2-inch air space whenever possible.

It's also important to keep mortar droppings to a minimum. Dropped mortar can block weep holes and can also cause bridging that allows water to travel to the backup wall. Because some bridging across mortar droppings is inevitable (particularly with a small air space), it's also a good idea to install housewrap or #15 asphalt felt over the sheathing on wood-framed houses to help prevent moisture migra-

Brick Veneer Details

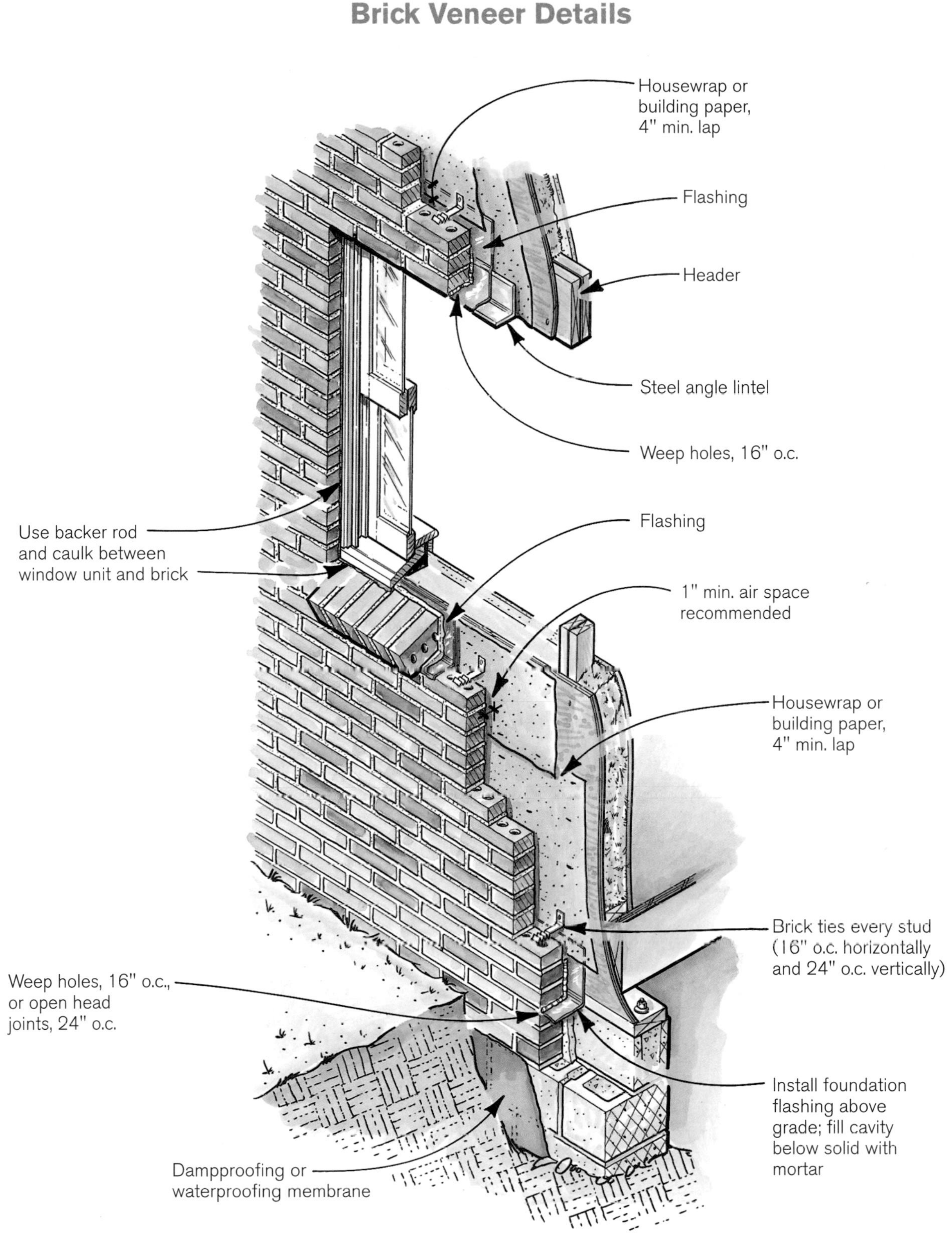

The brick veneer wall rests on a shelf at the top of the foundation and is anchored to the wood framing by galvanized metal ties at regular intervals. An air space (the Brick Industry Association recommends 1 inch) behind the brick allows any water that penetrates to drain down to the weep holes at the base flashing. Window and door heads are similarly flashed.

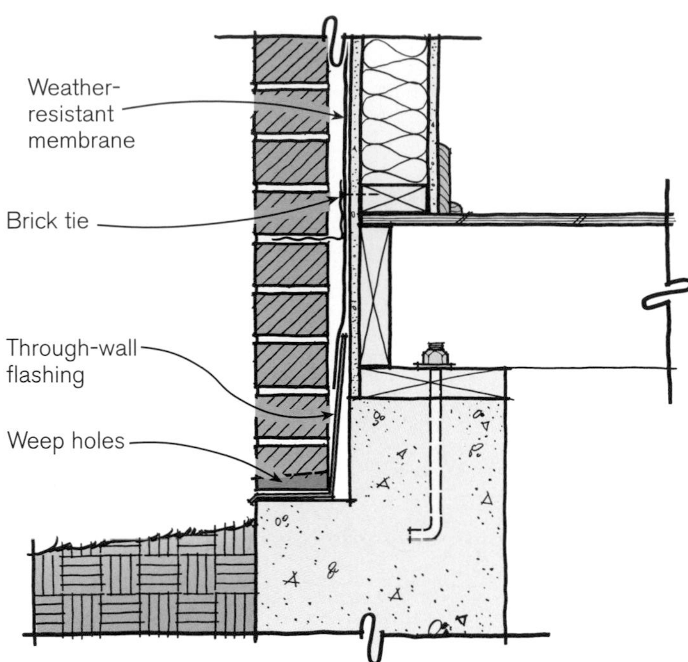

Figure 2. Through-wall flashing and weep holes direct water in the air space to the exterior.

tion. If housewrap or felt is installed, the BIA recommends that it be lapped at least 8 inches over the through-wall flashing (**Figure 3**).

Through-Wall Flashing

Through-wall flashing needs to be designed and installed to collect the water within the air space and to allow it to drain to the exterior. Through-wall flashing is not optional; it is required by most codes. The International Residential Code requires through-wall flashing at the base of a wall as well as above window and door lintels that are not self-flashing. The code also requires flashing when brick veneer is installed above a roof — for example, where a two-story brick veneer house rises above the roof of an attached one-story garage (**Figure 4**).

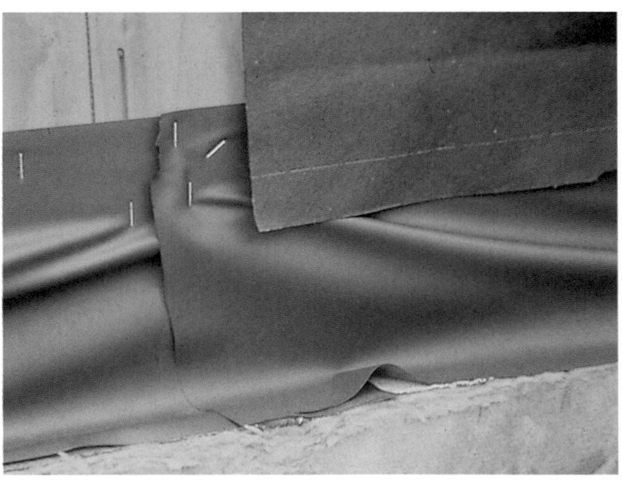

Figure 3. This through-wall flashing is properly tucked under the building paper, so that any water on the backup wall is directed onto the flashing. However, an overlap of at least 8 inches is recommended.

Is flashing necessary at windowsills? IRC requires flashing at windowsills only when the windows do not include a self-flashing flange. Regardless of window design, installing through-wall flashing under windowsills is always good practice, since any water hitting a window travels down the window and over the sill (**Figure 5**). In fact, self-flashing window flanges do not serve the same function as undersill flashing. Flashing below the sill prevents moisture from entering the wall system, while the self-flashing window flanges simply prevent moisture from entering the interface between the window and the backup wall.

Attach the flashing to the backup wall and install it carefully, so water can't find a route around it. For instance, if the backup wall behind the air space is concrete block, the flashing should be tucked into a mortar joint in the block wall to prevent water from getting behind the flashing. Where this is not possible, a reglet, pressure bar, continuous nailer, or self-adhesive type of flashing (such as rubberized asphalt) may be attached to the block wall.

When self-adhesive flashing is used in wood-frame

construction, it must be attached directly to the sheathing. Don't make the mistake of installing the flashing on top of the housewrap or building paper. If the housewrap is installed before the brick masonry, it should be detached along the bottom or slit horizontally with a knife, and the flashing tucked under it.

If the flashing is not one of the self-adhering types, and there is no housewrap or felt, then either the flashing must be installed before the sheathing, or the flashing must be attached to the sheathing with a continuous nailer. Both of these alternatives are awkward, however, and they are more likely to create discontinuities, holes, or tears in the flashing.

Lapping and sealing. At the base of the wall, through-wall flashing must be uninterrupted. At the joints and corners of a house, the flashing should be lapped at least 6 inches and sealed. This is easily done if you're using self-adhesive rubberized asphalt flashing. Otherwise, consult the flashing manufacturer for recommendations regarding the proper mastic or lap cement (**Figure 6**, next page). Note that some flashings react with certain mastics, drastically affecting the performance of the flashings.

Extend the flashing at least to the front face of the brick. Although the BIA recommends that the flashing should extend 1/4 inch beyond the brick face and turn down to form a drip, some of the flexible flashing materials can deteriorate when exposed to the weather. One solution with self-adhesive flashing is to install a metal drip in conjunction with the flexible flashing.

Flashing at Wall-Roof Intersection

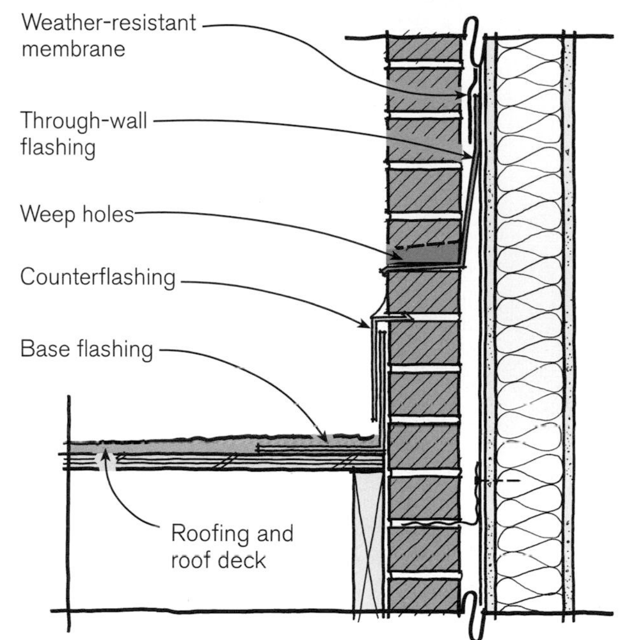

Figure 4. Where a brick veneer wall extends above a roof, through-wall flashing is required above the roof flashing. While the roof flashing prevents water from traveling between the roofing and the brick, the through-wall flashing stops any water that has entered the brickwork from above.

Window Head and Sill Flashing

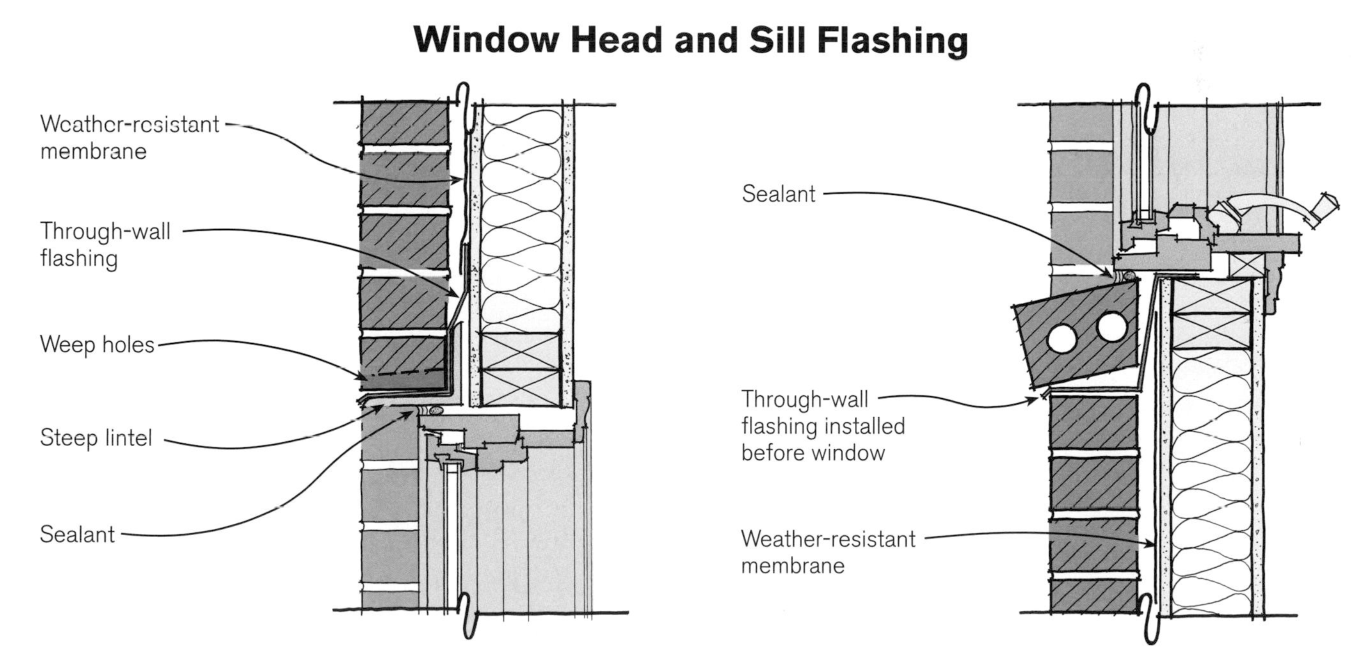

Figure 5. Flashing is required above the steel lintel at each window and door. Wherever flashing is installed, weep holes should be provided. It is a good practice to install flashing under a brick windowsill, since any rainwater hitting the window travels over the sill.

Figure 6. If the flexible flashing is not one of the self-adhering types, use mastic to seal any overlaps.

Figure 7. This flashing has been installed incorrectly, since it does not extend all the way to the front face of the brick. Any water is directed into the core holes of the brick instead of to the exterior.

If the flashing is installed sloppily — short of the face of the brick — then the collected water won't be delivered to the exterior. Remember, the core holes are typically only 1/4 inch back from the face. Even if care is taken to ensure that the flashing projects no less than 1/2 inch from the face of the wall, the flashing can scoot back when mortar and brick are laid over it, allowing water to enter the cores of the brick (**Figure 7**).

Because of these problems, many installers extend the flashing well past the face of the brick until the wall is complete, then cut the flashing flush with the face of the masonry. According to the BIA, this practice is acceptable, although it is not recommended.

Flashing Types

Although the choice of flashing material is often governed by price, other factors to consider are the ease of installation and the expected life of the material once it is embedded in the wall system. Metal flashings are often used on commercial jobs, but the two most common types of flashing for most residential jobs are EPDM and self-adhering rubberized asphalt. The BIA recommends that most nonmetal flashings should be at least 30 mils thick, which means polyethylene, housewrap, and #15 asphalt felt are *not* acceptable flashing materials. Aluminum is unacceptable because it corrodes when embedded in mortar, which becomes very alkaline when exposed to moisture. PVC flashing has been known to deteriorate as well, raising concerns about its expected life.

Remember that the drainage wall system works only if all the materials are properly installed, and if the flashing is designed to last as long as the wall itself. Consult the flashing manufacturers for recommendations on which product to use in a specific wall system.

End Dams

If through-wall flashing is not continuous around the whole building — for example, above a window, or wherever stepped flashing is needed — the flashing must include end dams (**Figure 8**). To create an end dam, turn the flashing up sideways, against the adjacent head joint, to create a pocket. An end dam will prevent moisture from traveling off the end of the flashing and into the adjacent air space. The BIA recommends that end dams should be at least 2 inches high.

Figure 8. End dams are required in any through-wall flashings that are not continuous, such as step flashings or window heads and sills.

Weep Holes

Most building codes require weep holes above all through-wall flashings. The sole purpose of a weep hole is to allow water that has been collected by the flashing to exit the wall system. Since it is impossible to eliminate all mortar droppings between the brick and backup, the weep holes must allow for drainage even when some mortar has dropped onto the flashing.

There are three common types of weep holes: open head joints, rope wicks, and weep inserts. Open head joints are formed by omitting the mortar from the vertical joints immediately above the flashing every 24 inches (**Figure 9**). They're simple, they're cheap, and they work. In standard-size brick, it takes 2$^1/_4$ inches of mortar droppings before an open head joint gets clogged. (A 2$^1/_4$-inch chunk of mortar creates more problems than just a clogged weep hole; the odds are mortar has also clogged the air space above, impeding the proper drainage of the wall system.)

Rope wicks are the next most popular type of weep hole. Although they do not allow as much flow as an open head joint, they are often chosen to avoid the appearance of an open hole or the shadow created by an open head joint. The best type of rope for this purpose is cotton rope, because nylon, polypropylene, and polyester do not wick. Wicks should be spaced 16 inches on-center — more closely spaced than open head joints, to make up for their smaller size. The rope should be a minimum of 10 inches long, so that when the outer end of the wick is installed flush with the exterior face of the brick, the excess can be draped in the cavity or attached to the backup wall. The extended length of wick in the air space will reduce the likelihood of mortar droppings covering the entire wick.

Figure 9. The most dependable type of weep hole is the open head joint.

There are also several different types of weep inserts available. These are typically made of plastic and are designed to fit into a head joint. The smaller the insert, the more easily it can be clogged. Plastic tubes should not be used, because the openings on either side of the tube are only $^1/_4$ to $^1/_2$ inch, which makes them easy to clog.

Weep holes must always be above grade to allow

Brick Coatings

Some people install brick veneer without flashings, thinking they can always fall back on the application of a coating if they have a water penetration problem. However, most coatings can't bridge bond breaks or hairline cracks. If you use a coating on bricks, remember that you are taking a chance that the coating won't work.

While clear coatings sometimes prevent moisture entry, coatings can also create problems. If the pores of the masonry are coated, and water gets into the brick from the back side, where the bricks aren't coated, then the water can't get out. When the saturated bricks freeze, the expansion of trapped moisture within the brick can cause severe deterioration.

Some coatings are breathable, which means that the coating allows moisture to exit the wall as vapor. But remember — if a coating is applied, the pore structure of the brick has been altered. The pore structure directly affects the durability of the brick. There must be enough pore space in the brick to allow any absorbed moisture to freeze and expand. If the pore structure is altered and the room for expansion is no longer available, the brick may deteriorate.

If you decide to try a coating, choose a breathable coating. While some types of silanes and siloxanes have been proven to reduce moisture penetration without reducing the durability of the masonry, siloxanes appear to be more successful with brick.

Siloxanes are fairly expensive, but you get what you pay for when it comes to coatings. If it costs $5 a can, you can do without it. In any case, properly installed brickwork should not require coatings to prevent moisture penetration. — *J.C.*

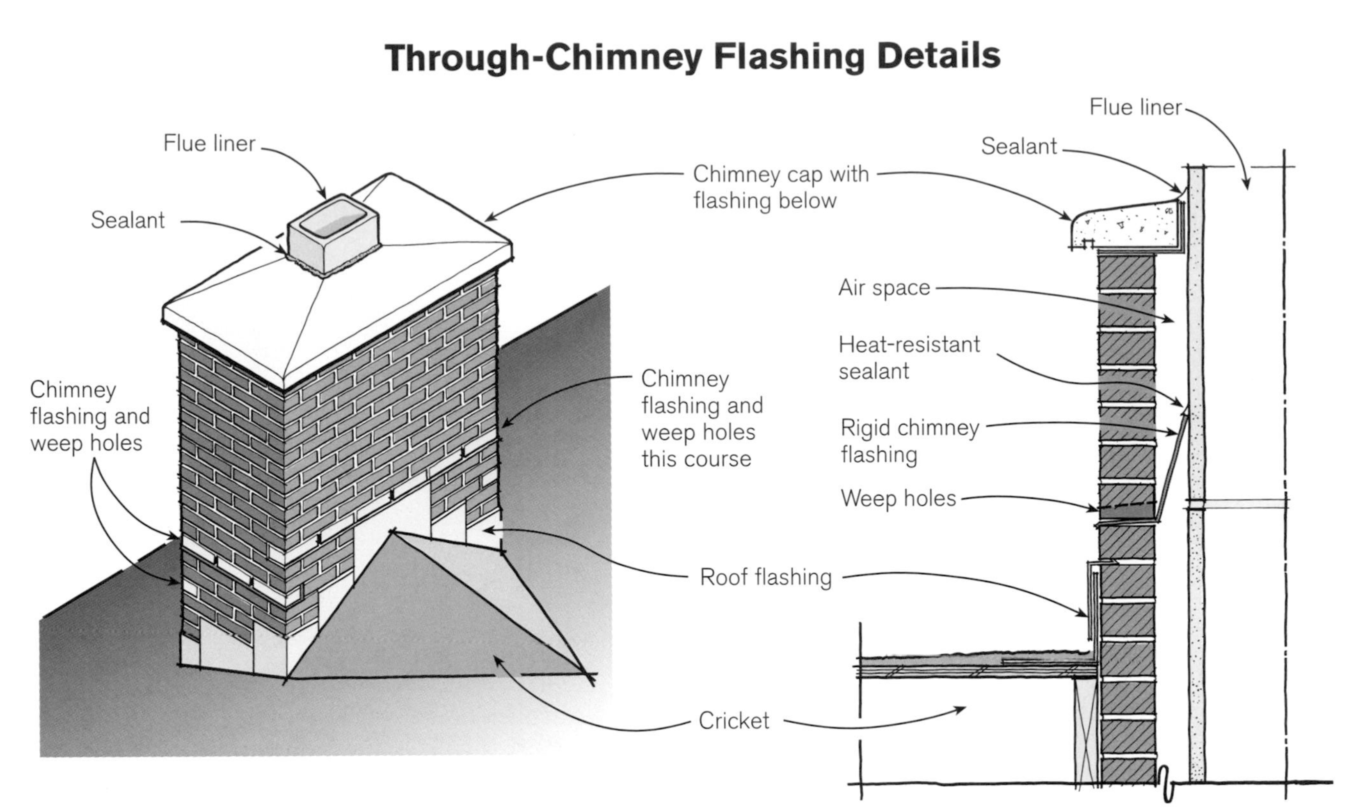

Figure 10. In addition to common roof flashing, a brick chimney requires flashing under the chimney cap and through-chimney flashing. The through-chimney flashing stops any water that has entered through the brickwork or cap. Through-chimney flashing is designed to collect any water that finds its way to the back side of the bricks.

Figure 11. If the flashing at the head of a bay window is placed directly above the lintel (left), it serves no purpose, since it directs water to the interior of the house. The correct location for through-wall flashing above a bay window is above the roof (right).

the wall to drain. Remember that the grade can change over time. For instance, when homeowners install several applications of mulch, the grade may end up above the weep holes, preventing proper drainage of the air space. In most cases, through-wall base flashing and weep holes should be 4 inches to 6 inches above grade. The air space below the base flashing should be filled solid with grout or mortar.

Through-Chimney Flashing

Most people are familiar with the visible base flashings and counterflashings that are installed where the roofing meets a chimney. These visible roof flashings prevent water from traveling between the roofing and the brick — but they don't stop any water that is already in the chimney, such as water that may enter through the brickwork or the chimney cap. Through-chimney flashing is designed to prevent moisture that has penetrated the chimney from traveling below the roof.

Through-chimney flashing operates on the same principles as through-wall flashing. Through-chimney flashing has to be installed above the roof flashing, even if that means putting it a few courses up, so that the collected water is led to the exterior (**Figure 10**).

Flashing should also be installed under a concrete chimney cap. This prevents moisture from entering the top of the masonry, and also prevents staining or contamination of the brick. The flashing can be laid in place above the top course of bricks, before the concrete cap is poured. A mortar wash does not form an adequate chimney cap.

A mortar wash will shrink and crack as it cures, especially when the mortar is brought to a featheredge. Mortar is very similar to concrete, only with smaller aggregate. Remember, concrete usually needs something to give it some tensile strength and to prevent cracking — for example, 6x6 mesh or other reinforcement.

For chimney applications, choose a flashing material that can hold up to the potentially high temperatures expected when the flue is in use. Use metal flashing at the chimney cap.

Bay Windows

A fairly common mistake when flashing brickwork above a bay window is to install the through-wall flashing too low. Although some building codes require flashing to be placed directly on steel lintels, this is of little use above a bay window, since the lintel is under the roof — which is to say, the lintel flashing is inside the building. The flashing and weeps can't direct the collected water to the exterior if the flashing is already indoors.

Figure 12. Omitting flashing and weep holes is risky. Water that penetrates brick veneer can saturate wood framing or enter the basement.

Above a bay window, install the flashing above the highest point of the roof flashing. This is similar to flashing a chimney. The flashing must continue over the entire length of the window area (**Figure 11**).

Getting By Without Flashing?

Some masons have built many brick veneer walls without flashing and weep holes, and claim that they haven't had any water penetration problems. This is risky. The amount of moisture penetration through brickwork depends on the degree of exposure to wind-driven rain. We have learned from experience that when more moisture is available, there is a greater likelihood of moisture penetration in any wall system. But the cost of correcting a moisture penetration problem will far exceed the cost of installing the flashing properly in the first place (**Figure 12**).

The concept of a drainage wall is simple: Any moisture that penetrates the veneer must be allowed to exit the wall before it travels to the interior. The proper materials are easily obtained, and the proper detailing and installation of a drainage wall is not difficult. When properly constructed, a brick veneer wall system is moisture free, fire resistant, and maintenance free.

Jerry Carrier works for Glen-Gery Corporation as a brickwork design adviser. He speaks frequently on brick masonry topics, provides brickwork technical assistance, and performs specification reviews and inspections.

Caulking Joints in Masonry

by Al Bredenberg

When it's done skillfully, caulking — or joint sealing — is almost invisible on a masonry exterior. But when it's botched, it can create a real eyesore. Worse, a poor caulking job can allow water into a building — with resultant damage, callbacks, lost time and money, and poor customer relations.

Masonry joint sealants are called for in three situations: in an expansion or control joint, in a joint between dissimilar materials, and at the perimeter of an opening in the masonry surface (**Figure 13**).

For the small general contractor, a single-family home or remodeling job that involves exterior masonry probably won't require enough caulking and sealing to make it worth hiring a specialty sub. But any joints, such as window and door perimeters or seams where brick meets wood siding, should be correctly sealed against water penetration. At least one person on your crew should understand the fundamentals of caulking.

While face brick is probably the most common masonry finish the caulker encounters, the same principles and similar procedures will apply for sealing joints in other materials — block, precast concrete, stone, stucco, and EIFS (exterior insulation and finish systems).

Size and Shape

A very tight joint — say, a joint less than 1/4 inch wide — is fairly easy to caulk, especially if it's a right-

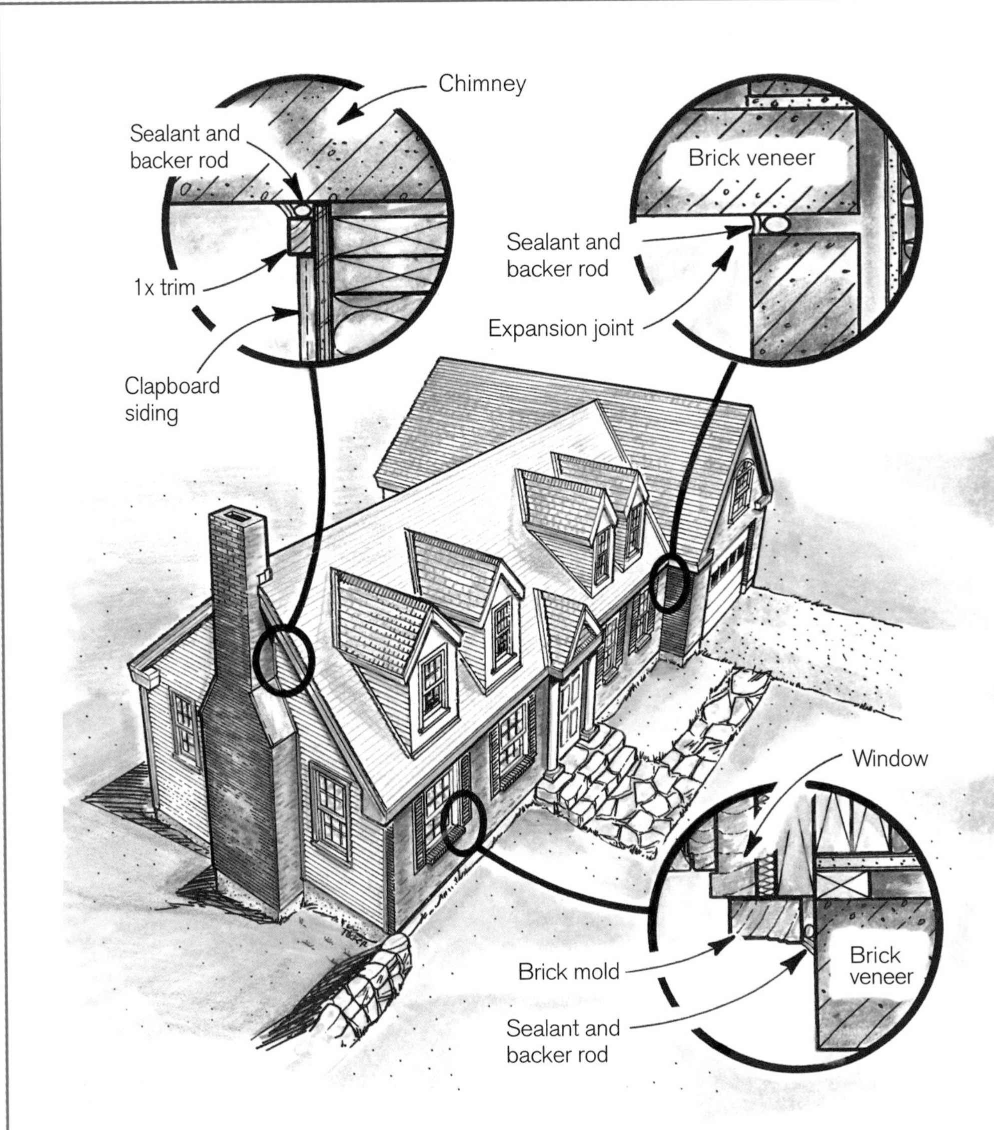

Figure 13. Joint sealants are needed at masonry expansion and control joints, where masonry meets another material, and at the perimeter of masonry openings.

C. BATES

Figure 14. Two-part bulk sealants have to be mixed with a drill and paddle (left). Using a bulk caulking gun (center and right) allows you to do high-volume caulking more cost effectively but is messy.

angle joint. This is usually the case with a window in a masonry opening. You are simply gunning the sealant and tooling it into a corner. The two perpendicular surfaces will guide the tip of your gun and your finishing tool.

However, because tight tolerances are hard to achieve in masonry work, you will typically encounter joints that are 1/2 inch wide or greater. And because a control or expansion joint needs to be fairly wide in order to tolerate the expansion, contraction, and movement in the masonry wall, it's not uncommon to come up against joints 3/4 inch, 1 inch, or even 1 1/2 inches wide. It's a real challenge to make a larger joint look good and provide a good seal.

The design of details should take joint sealants into account. If two dissimilar materials meet, there needs to be enough length of parallel return inside the joint so that backer rod will stay in place and so that the joint sealant will have sufficient bonding surface.

Joint Prep

To achieve proper bonding on the two sides of the joint, some surface preparation may be necessary. Joint surfaces should be dry, sound, and free of dust, dirt, and loose or foreign material. Be prepared to scrape, chip, and dust the inside of the joint or even blow it out with compressed air. Depending on the conditions and the manufacturer's instructions, you may have to clean the joint with solvent or apply a primer.

If you have the unenviable job of recaulking an older building, you will need to check with the sealant manufacturer for special procedures to thoroughly cut out the old caulk. Old caulk can be pretty stubborn stuff, so you may need a special saw and a machine grinder. You also might have to prime every surface to be sealed.

Joint Sealants

The joint sealants that are most often specified for construction work are polyurethanes, silicones, and polysulfides. Silicones usually come in tubes. Polyurethanes and polysulfides can come packaged in tubes or in bulk. All joint sealants should be finished with a steel tool.

If you're a beginning caulker, tube caulk is much easier to work with. Keep in mind, though, that masonry caulking can use up a large number of tubes. For a 1/2-inch or 3/4-inch joint you may only get about 10 feet per 10.5-ounce tube. Also, tube sealants are air-cured and can take a week or longer to cure.

Bulk sealants are mixed with an activator before application, so they are chemically cured and can cure in a day or two. To work with bulk materials, you'll need a bulk gun and a large drill (at least 1/2 inch) and special mixing paddle (**Figure 14**). Once you get it down, you can do a lot more caulking and save money on materials using bulk sealant. But you'll have a messier job and more cleanup, and you'll have to work with some unpleasant solvents.

Joint sealants come in a variety of standard colors. It's even possible to have the factory make up custom colors. Color decisions should be made well

Figure 15. Compressible foam backer rod fills the back of a joint and helps the caulk perform properly. Use a size slightly thicker than the crack and insert it gently with a blunt tool.

ahead of time, as some colors are hard to get and have to be special-ordered.

For a light-colored surface, I like a lighter sealant color; a darker surface calls for a still darker sealant color. For example, on a regular reddish brown brick wall, I often used a somewhat darker "redwood tan" sealant color to good effect. On a light gray block wall, a lighter "off-white" looks good. With this kind of scheme, the caulk line doesn't stand out so much.

Backer Rod

Backer rod is made out of foam and looks like long strings of spaghetti. It comes in sizes as thin as 1/4 inch and as thick as 2 inches and up. If you choose backer rod that's just a little larger than the joint you have to caulk, you can insert it under a slight compression so it will stay in place and allow you to control the depth of the sealant.

The main purpose of backer rod is to keep sealant off the back of the joint, thus preventing back-bonding, or three-sided bonding. To properly expand and compress, the joint sealant should be bonded to only two sides of the joint. If the joint is too shallow to fit backer rod, you can apply bond-breaker tape to the back of the joint to prevent back-bonding. Bond-breaker tape comes on a roll and looks like cellophane tape.

You can buy backer rod from joint sealant suppliers. Backer rod comes in open-cell and closed-cell form. Open cell compresses more and is easier to work with. However, some architects don't like it

Caulking Tips

Good caulking requires a great deal of skill and a certain amount of artistry. I've found that not just anyone can be trained to do caulking. You need aesthetic sense, patience, an eye for detail, and a real concern for the integrity and appearance of the finished product.

Here are some little tricks that might help your sealant work to go better:

For tube caulking: Cut the nozzle of your tube at an angle and slightly smaller than the size of the joint. If the joint size varies, have two or three tubes going at the same time, each with the nozzle cut at a different size.

Cold weather: Keep your material warm. You can even buy an electric heat chest to keep your tubes or bucket in. Use gloves with the fingers cut off to keep your dexterity.

Steel tooling: Use long, steady strokes. Attempt to tool every run only once rather than dabbing at it repeatedly. Rather than tooling toward your previous work (as if you were painting), pull away from the last section you tooled. Press the sealant firmly, so that it fills the joint and bonds to the sides.

Spatula: Provide yourself with a selection of various sizes. For any given run, choose a spatula slightly smaller than the width of the joint.

Keeping your tool clean: At the beginning of your workday, take a newspaper and rip it into pieces about 4x4 inches. Use these pieces to keep your tool clean.

Tools: Wear a toolbelt or nail apron to carry your various spatulas, scrapers, other tools, and your pieces of newspaper. Don't use your favorite carpenter toolbelt for caulking, as it will get pretty messy.

Sturdy caulking gun: Get a good sturdy caulking gun made for production work. Get a hook attachment so you can hang it on the staging or ladder. Use a gun with a release, so you can stop the flow of sealant quickly.

Backer rod: Rather than struggling to cram large backer rod into a small joint, keep a variety of sizes on hand for different sizes of joints.

Annoying details: When you're working on a section of a building, take note of things that weren't ready to be caulked the first time you went through. Have a plan for getting back to them later, especially if they are high up, hard to get to, and easily overlooked. — *A.B.*

Figure 16. Caulk should be applied to a joint in a smooth, even bead. When applying tube caulk to a joint whose thickness varies, carry several tubes with various size openings.

Figure 17. To properly finish a joint, smooth it in a continuous motion with a steel caulking tool or spatula. The author sometimes custom-fabricates a tool from a wooden tongue depressor.

because it's like a sponge and can absorb water, while closed-cell backer rod is impervious to water.

Whichever type you're using, push the backer rod into the joint gently, using a blunt tool that won't pierce or tear it (**Figure 15**). A piece of wood shingle makes a good backer-rod tool.

Applying Joint Sealants

Joint sealants have both a functional and an aesthetic purpose. In sealing a joint, you are trying to provide a seal against penetration by water and air, and you are applying a finish detail. The aesthetic aspect is affected mostly by your tooling method, but several factors will affect the watertightness of a joint.

In sealing joints, don't think of yourself as just filling a crack. Be aware that you are providing a flexible seal between the surfaces of two independent building components, which move and shift in relation to one another. The dimensions of that seal must be carefully controlled. It can't be just a thin skin, but neither can it be a thick gob.

If your joint sealant is not applied properly, it will not expand and compress with the movement of the joint. Instead, it may split or rip away from one of the two joint surfaces.

Most polyurethane joint sealants are designed to tolerate up to 40% extension and 25% compression. However, they will not achieve that degree of movement if the joint is too deep. For example, for a joint 1/2 inch to 2 inches wide, one sealant manufacturer requires that the joint depth be no more than 1/2 inch.

When gunning sealant into the joint, try to achieve a smooth, even flow (**Figure 16**). Don't just try to zip down a skin. Fill — but don't overfill — the joint, placing sufficient sealant to achieve proper joint depth.

Tooling

Correct tooling is critical to creating a sealant joint that's tight and looks good (**Figure 17**). The best tool is a steel spatula or sculptor's tool that is slightly smaller than the width of the joint. Try to achieve a smooth, even appearance, without squeeze-out on the sides. Good tooling takes a lot of practice.

For special circumstances, I have on occasion made a custom-sized wooden tool by whittling down a tongue depressor. I have also seen plastic joint tools. Unless the joint is very small, don't try to tool with your finger. It slows you down and makes a mess. Also, manufacturers' instructions usually discourage using water or solvent to tool a joint.

Planning a Caulking Job

On the surface, caulking can seem pretty simple. It's rarely on the "critical path" of a project plan. However, one key aspect of joint sealing guarantees complications: Often, the sealant is being used to treat the joint between two dissimilar materials, and these materials are often installed by different trades and at different times.

Just think of all of the various assemblies or materials that can go into a masonry opening or through a masonry wall. You could have a wood window installed by the carpenters, an aluminum-frame window installed by a window company, a hollow metal door installed by the carpenters, a metal louver installed by the HVAC crew, and even a pipe run by the plumbers.

Access is a key concern for joint-sealing work. Sometimes you can get everything from the ground or from a 6-foot stepladder. If the caulking work is to be done off the staging, make sure that it will be left up long enough. Because staging is often rented, there's a lot of pressure to get it off the job quickly.

Don't forget conditions on the ground. How steep is the grade — not the finished grade, but the grade as it will be when you're doing the caulking? Will it be safe for a ladder? Will a boom lift be able to operate in the area? Keep in mind that a boom lift won't work if the grade is too steep.

Identify the scope of work. What gets caulked and what doesn't? Will one party be responsible for all caulking on the job? Or will each trade be responsible for caulking its own work? (This is a strategy that often yields poor results, in my experience.)

Weather and temperature affect caulking work. You can't caulk a wet surface, so allow flexibility in the schedule. And, although you can caulk in cold weather (check the manufacturer's limitations), sometimes ice or frost will collect in a joint and can be very hard to detect.

The application of joint sealants is a little-known construction specialty. But it can make a big difference in the integrity and life span of a masonry building. If you take care to apply the materials properly and give attention to detail, this is a trade that can add to your profits — and give the satisfaction that comes with doing fine work.

Former contractor Al Bredenberg, of Cornwall, Conn., writes frequently on construction topics.

Concealed Water Damage from Manufactured Stone

by Dennis McCoy

As a contractor specializing in remediation and repairs, I've been concentrating for years on fixing failed applications of EIFS and traditional stucco. I've learned from experience that most stucco failures result from improper flashing and drainage details behind the stucco. Typically, houses that end up with rotten sheathing and framing under the stucco don't have properly installed building papers and flashings.

In recent years, I've been finding more and more cases of leaking and rot behind another material that is very similar to stucco: cementitious manufactured-stone veneer, or "cast stone," as it is sometimes called. The problems we are finding with cast stone

Figure 18. Where stucco (left and center) and cast stone (photos at right) have been installed on the same home, the author frequently finds more severe moisture and rot damage under the cast-stone portions of the exterior. One reason is that the stucco terminates at the bottom with a weep screed, while the cast stone sits in a bed of mortar and grout, directly on a foundation ledge, with no weeps or flashings.

are just like the problems we've seen with incorrectly applied stucco. But the weather detailing flaws we identify in artificial-stone jobs often cause even greater problems than the errors made with stucco. With cast-stone veneer, leaks and rot often show up sooner, progress more quickly, and cause more severe damage inside the wall (**Figure 18**).

After investigating and repairing at least a hundred examples, I've concluded that the problems with cast stone go back to a misunderstanding of the material. Installers as well as building inspectors have gotten used to thinking of cast stone as a masonry material, and they expect walls to get the kind of weather detailing behind the stone that is traditional with brick: a single layer of paper, lapped a couple of inches at the horizontal joints. But, unlike brick, cast stone is not installed with an air space between the cladding and the framed wall. Cast-stone veneers are cementitiously adhered to a stucco-like base coat that is applied directly to the wall. Like stucco, cast stone gets saturated with water in a rainstorm and holds that water right up against the framed wall. The papers and flashings under the veneer have to fend off that moisture load without the benefit of any drainage or drying space. One layer of paper isn't going to do the job — two layers, as specified under stucco, are necessary.

Painstaking Details Required

If anything, cast stone should in fact be backed up by even tougher details than stucco. That's because it has some characteristics that may help create a more stressful moisture load for walls during wet weather.

For one thing, manufactured stone is a cement-based product that absorbs and holds water like stucco, but cast stone is thicker than stucco and can thus store more moisture. Also, most of the cast-stone brands now have "ledgestone" versions of the product, which have a long, horizontal shape; the long, flat, shelflike ledges are often sloped toward the framing when installed, which provides a place for rainwater to puddle up and soak into the wall (**Figure 19**).

Figure 19. Long, flat "ledgestone" pieces like this create many horizontal shelves where water can stand and soak into grout joints.

The greater thickness of cast stone also complicates the task of fabricating and installing practical flashing components. The kickout or diverter flashing required where a roofline butts into a wall is a good example. On job after job, my company gets paid good money to go in after the fact, tear cast-stone veneer off a wall, and retrofit a larger kickout flashing to the wall because the original roofer's kickout flashing was too small to push water out beyond the plane of the cladding. If the diverter flashing is too small, it may

Figure 20. Undersized or omitted diverter — or kickout — flashings allow water to flow beneath the cast-stone facade (left). Window flanges that lap under instead of over building paper can bring rainwater into direct contact with the sheathing (right).

Under a Fine Surface, a Disturbing Discovery . . . and a Costly Repair

*The owners of this one-year-old custom home (**A**) reported moldy smells behind the drywall; a mushroom growing from the cast-stone veneer face was the only visible sign of trouble on the exterior (**B**). The gutter butting into the top of the wall seemed a likely source of moisture, while the bottom of the wall provided no way for moisture to escape (**C**).*

E

F

*Opening the wall (**D**) revealed severely rotted OSB sheathing and damage to the framing. While the row of soldier bricks at fascia height provided some protection (**E**), the water coming off the roof saturated the cast stone and soaked through the housewrap beneath, turning the sheathing at the base of the wall to compost in less than two years (**F**).*

G

*To repair the damage, the author's crew replaced the rotted wood members (**G**), but was able to leave the original drywall in place because it had been protected by the interior vapor barrier (**H**). Parts of the band joist were left in place but soaked with a copper-based wood preservative (**I**).* — D.M.

H

I

Destructive Investigation: Tracing a Leak to Its Source

*On this job, the original installer of the cast-stone veneer wall had tried unsuccessfully to stop leaks by spraying a clear sealer onto the stone and by removing the lowest courses to apply a membrane flashing where the wall meets the foundation. To assess the problem, the RAM Builders team first seals large openings inside the home (**A**) and sets up a blower door (**B**). With the blower door running to depressurize the house, the crew turns on a water-spray apparatus (**C**), thus simulating the effect of a 15-mph wind-driven rain. Within a short time, water finds its way into the house (**D**).*

as well not be there: All the water flowing and blowing against that spot will just get dumped into the wall system below (**Figure 20**, left photo, page 143).

Of course, all the other typical vulnerable spots in a stucco application are just as problematic, if not more so, in a cast-stone application. Window pan flashings, for instance, are a good idea in a manufactured-stone job. However, we are more likely to see a reverse-lap flashing error, with building paper run to the window edge in such a way that the window flange directs water beneath the paper instead of on top of it (**Figure 20**, right photo, page 143). And, as with stucco, brick, or any other cladding, a cast-stone veneer should be equipped with weeps of some kind at any bottom termination, whether at the foundation sill or above a window or abutting roof. Otherwise, water will pool longest at the lowest points, and those areas may stay continuously wet.

We also see problems when cast stone is paired with another material on the same wall. It's very common, for instance, for a single house to have stucco or EIFS as well as cast stone; if the joint where the two meet is detailed wrong, water can get to the wood-framed wall and cause trouble.

Investigating Problems

When my company is called to look at a building, the owners or the builder often have no conception of the severity of the problem they may be facing. Poly vapor barriers under the home's drywall often conceal wall framing that is sopping wet; on the exterior, the cementitious stone or stucco does not decay, so it never betrays the secret underneath. Homeowners may complain of just a few small leaks, or be worried about a moldy smell.

From experience, we know where trouble is likely to be found, and how bad it can be. By spraying a wall with water while we create negative pressure inside the house, we can find out how water is getting in, and by removing a few small sections of the cladding, we can get an idea of the extent of the damage (see "Destructive Investigation," above).

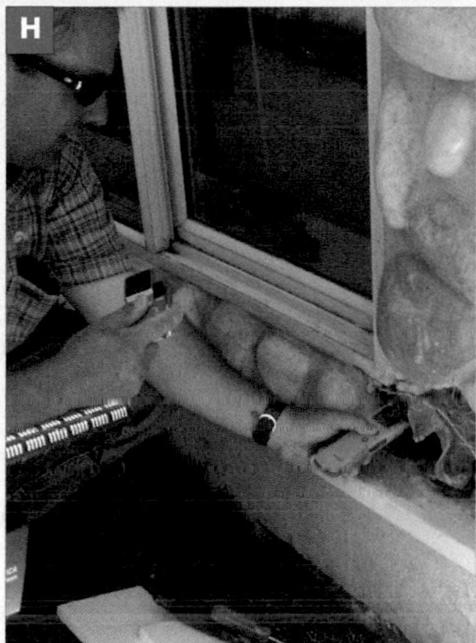

*After verifying that the cladding leaks, the team digs under the surface to find out why. Tearing off small areas of EIFS on the upper wall reveals that there is no building paper or window flashing installed where the EIFS meet the cast stone (**E**), or between upper and lower windows in the EIFS wall (**F**). Tearing off cast stone near a window (**G**), the team learns that water has wet the OSB sheathing. The author measures high moisture content even at the bottom of the wall, where no direct stream was applied (**H**). The retrofit flashing repair has proven ineffective because flaws higher in the wall dump water behind it.*
— D.M.

Repairing the Failures

On many occasions, our company has found a shocking amount of water damage and rot under the cast-stone cladding of homes less than two years old, or in some cases less than one year old. The amount of water that can be taken in and held by cultured stone is significant — enough to support robust growth of wood-destroying funguses. If rot organisms have water and they have wood, they will thrive until the wood is gone. Often, what we find under cast stone looks more like the ashes of a fire than like lumber (see "Under a Fine Surface, a Disturbing Discovery," pages 144 and 145).

If it's caught soon enough, the damage can be repaired. But this is far more costly than doing the job right the first time. Although I make my living from this kind of work, I wish that every builder and contractor who installs this material, as well as the building officials who inspect the jobs, could see some of the failures I have seen and learn how to avoid them. Too often, I've seen problems like these ruin a family's finances when they lead to the uninsured loss of much of a home's value.

Details That Work

Code provisions for cast stone can be confusing and murky. The product isn't mentioned in the body of the building code, and the evaluation reports and manufacturer instructions required for code acceptance can be contradictory or incomplete. But the basic methods required to succeed with the material are not that complicated. In essence, cast stone has to be treated as if it were stucco.

Before you apply lath to the wall, you need to be sure you have a weather-resistant paper barrier on that wall — and it needs to include two layers of paper, not just one. Wherever there are penetrations, or intersections between assemblies such as walls and roofs, or joints between cast stone and other materials like brick or stucco, there must be properly lapped flashings that keep kicking water away from the building. And at the bottom of the wall, there has to be a way for water to drain out. If all those precautions are observed, there is no reason cast stone should cause moisture problems.

When you're choosing your building paper, be careful. Grade D paper gets a "minute rating," based on the time the paper can be placed in direct contact with water before it soaks through. You can get 15-minute, 30-minute, or 60-minute rated paper, and the more severe the climate, the higher the rating you should choose. In dry and mild parts of Southern California or Arizona, for instance, two layers of 15-minute paper ought to be fine. In the valley-floor areas near Salt Lake City, we use two layers of 30-minute paper. But if we work up near the ski areas, where there is lots of wind and rain, we use two layers of 60-minute paper. Sixty-minute paper is very rugged stuff — it is more than twice as thick as 30-minute paper. In Houston, we use two layers of either 60-minute paper or sometimes a layer or two of asphalt felt paper applied over the top of a housewrap such as Tyvek (DuPont).

But no paper is intended to be absolutely waterproof for an indefinite period. That's why the flashings and weeps are so important. If you don't have them, water can pool at low points and stand against the wall for hours, days, or weeks. And if that happens, no paper, be it housewrap, asphalt felt, or Grade D Kraft, is going to save your wall from rot. So if you're applying cast stone, be smart: Use the papers, install the flashings, and provide the weeps. It will cost a little more, but it is a lot cheaper than hiring me and my crew to come back and fix the wall when the studs are decaying underneath the cast stone.

Dennis McCoy owns and operates RAM Builders, based in Lindon, Utah, which specializes in remediation and repair work in Utah, Texas, Colorado, and California.

Chapter 9: Stucco

Drainage Details for Stucco

by Dennis McCoy

As a kid helping my father on building projects in coastal California, and later as a construction supervisor and contractor myself, I have been around stucco for most of my life. Nowadays, the kind of stucco that I grew up with is known as "conventional" or "traditional" stucco.

Good old stucco is still around, but it's not alone. There are now at least 35 different modified, proprietary hard-coat stucco systems on the market and more than 30 varieties of exterior insulation finish systems (EIFS) that have the look of stucco. With products continually leaving and entering the market, and new hybridized systems coming along that combine characteristics of EIFS and hard-coat systems (or go on over some other base like fiber-cement board), it's hard to keep track.

All these new systems are penetrating markets where traditional stucco is largely unknown, and where the details that make stucco work are not part of the local tradition. In place of the standard, generic water-management details that governed traditional stucco, which you could look up in the body of the building code, these new systems are regulated through evaluation reports ("ER reports") and proprietary specifications that you have to locate and study individually.

Without the base of experience and knowledge, and without simple references for proper detailing, installers have made a lot of mistakes with hard-coat stucco in new markets. Over many years in California, in the course of remodeling or adding on, I've opened up hundreds of homes clad with traditional stucco without finding significant mold or rot. But in recent years in Utah and Texas, I've been called in to remediate hundreds of homes clad with newer modified systems, where the lack of proper water-management details has caused major decay problems in homes that are practically new.

The good news is that any kind of stucco — traditional three-coat, proprietary one-coat systems, and even EIFS — can work well if you apply the flashing and drainage plane principles that have always been part of traditional stucco (see "Stucco Drainage Details: Three Systems, One Principle," pages 152 and 153). But before we get into those details, let's look at the differences between traditional "three-coat" stucco, the new proprietary "one-coat" systems, and EIFS (the polystyrene-based exterior insulation finish system).

Three-Coat Stucco

Conventional or traditional stucco is called three-coat stucco because it has a 3/8-inch scratch coat, a second 3/8-inch brown coat, and a thin "color coat" on top, for a total system thickness of about an inch. All three coats are mixed from portland cement, sand, water, and some lime for workability; the top coat has color powder and may include some polymer additives.

But the system starts with a drainage plane based on some type of building paper over the wood framing of the home. Building codes call for two layers of Grade D Kraft paper, which is made with virgin wood fibers. The paper is there to drain water, so it has to be carefully tied into flashings around all windows and doors. Metal flashing systems are also installed to divert roof water away from the stucco system and to protect any penetrations. The paper and flashings have to overlap each other in a way that creates a shingle effect.

Over the papers and flashings, a stucco netting or metal lath is fastened to the wall with staples. Stucco netting looks like chicken wire, but it is actually a heavier-gauge galvanized-steel wire. Expanded metal lath has the look of a heavier grating, but it serves essentially the same purpose.

Next comes the base coat, troweled into the lath mesh and tooled with grooves while wet, to provide keys for the second coat to lock into. The 3/8-inch-thick second coat is applied and tooled flat, and then both must cure for seven days before the color coat gets troweled on. Like all cement, stucco will shrink and crack; many traditional contractors will wait 14 days to make sure the first coats have completely "cracked out," so new cracks won't telegraph through the top coat.

Three-coat stucco is designed to be porous. Rain soaks into it, then drains out when the storm ends. The papers and flashings are vital to protect the house — without them, water will soak the wood and create conditions for rot.

One-Coat Stucco

Since the mid-1980s, a handful of manufacturers have introduced thin-coat stucco products that collectively are called "one-coat" (or sometimes "two-coat") stucco. One-coat is nearly identical to conventional stucco in concept and design, except that the base coat is applied in one layer instead of the original two-step scratch- and brown-coat process. The base coat is mostly sand and portland cement, as in conventional stucco, but it also includes synthetic polymers and fiberglass reinforcing strands that increase both the tensile and the compressive strength. The required total thickness is just 3/8 inch, instead of the standard 3/4-inch total for the three-coat base.

The idea behind one-coat systems was to save labor and time in the schedule. With the added components, base coat could be put on in just one layer, with no second plastering and no wait between them.

In practice, I'm not sure one-coat is all that economical. The proprietary mix ingredients add cost, and finding and following the special instructions for the proprietary systems add complexity. One experienced stucco contractor, whose work I respect, told me that he gave up working with one-coat because it was too complicated. His crews rebelled against the required special detailing, and he also found that with only 3/8 inch of thickness it was harder to achieve a nice, uniform finish over the usual irregularities in a house frame. (A common defect I see in one-coat installations is a base coat much thinner than the required 3/8 inch, at least in spots.)

The other big selling point for thin-coat systems is that the fiberglass and polymer additives help the stucco withstand the winter freeze/thaw cycle.

The thinner base coat is still applied over wire lath or expanded metal, and over a system of papers and flashing the same as we need for conventional stucco. The same screeds and expansion joints are also part of this system, although at different thicknesses. But unlike three-coat stucco, one-coat systems require a 48-hour moist cure. The applicator is responsible for keeping the base coat moist for the first 48 hours after application. The color finish is also required to go on within 72 hours of the base coat application.

Proper curing is more critical with one-coat than with traditional stucco, because the acrylics tend to isolate cement particles from water in the mix. If the coat isn't kept moist, it may dry out before the cement has a chance to react with water (hydrate), which it must do to form the strong cement compounds that give the cladding its strength. Without the correct moist cure, the base coat is likely to be weak and crumbly.

One-coat stucco usually receives one of the new acrylic color finishes, instead of traditional stucco's purely cementitious, textured color coat. It has a smoother and less porous look, because acrylics, rather than cement, bind the aggregates together — it's like sand mixed with latex paint. Many people perceive this acrylic top coat as the defining characteristic of one-coat stucco, but synthetic finishes are not really an essential component of a one-coat system — they just happened to be developed about the same time that one-coat was widely marketed. One-coat base-coat systems got code approval in ER reports without mention of any particular color finish. As long as the base coat is applied at least 3/8 inch thick, you can paint it or apply a color finish over it — either a conventional cement color finish or a synthetic acrylic type.

An acrylic coating's higher plasticity gives more resistance to cracking and creates a more closed, water- and stain-resistant surface. But one-coat stucco finishes are still porous enough to let rain enter the system — the perception that one-coat systems reliably repel water at the surface is incorrect. And even if the coatings were waterproof, one-coat systems do crack, and they can leak at all the joints and penetrations, so water is sure to get behind them. At the same time, they are less breathable and slower to dry out than conventional stucco. So they are less forgiving of any defect in the proper placement of building papers, flashing, and lathing staples — if water reaches the wood structure of the house, it is less able to escape by evaporation.

Figure 1. Flashing details frequently involve the interaction of two trades. Here, for example, the stucco crew members responsible for installing the building paper had to remove and reinsert a gable vent installed by the framers so that they could run building paper under the vent flange.

I've seen many failed stucco systems that someone has tried to repair by applying a thick polymer coat over the existing stucco, and by surface-caulking window and other joints. This is worse than useless — it actually accelerates the damage. Water will still enter the system somewhere, and then it's trapped next to the house. My company's educational video (available from our website at www.rambuilders.com) shows an example of a home just four years old, whose framing and sheathing is completely gone because of that kind of attempted "repair." Damage that might have taken 10 or 20 years to develop under normal, breathable stucco happened in one or two years after the sealer was applied.

Stucco Drainage Details:

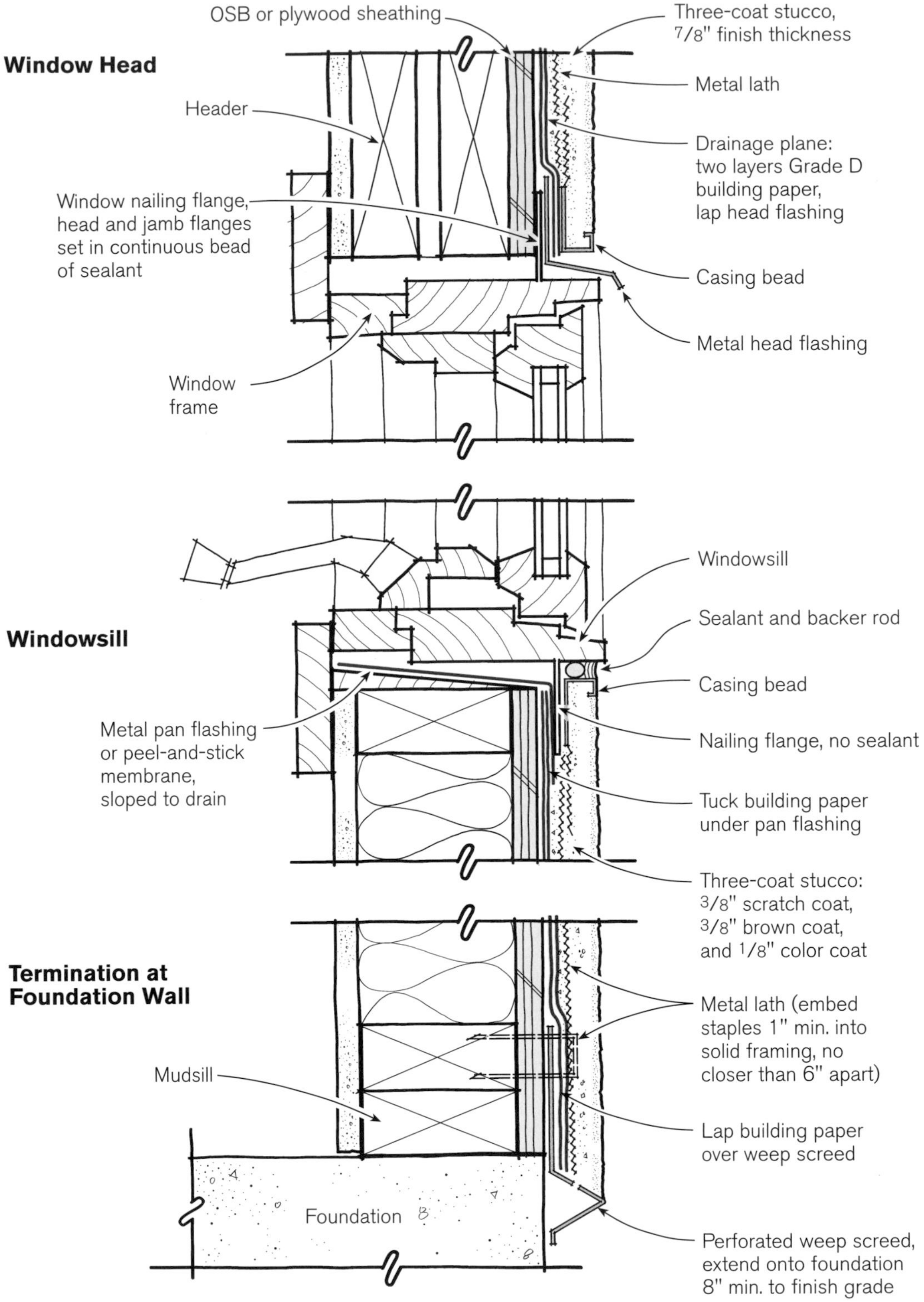

Traditional Three-Coat Stucco

Figure A. *Three-coat stucco relies on traditional details to keep water flowing down the wall and away from the building. Openings, transitions, and terminations are flashed to let water escape, while building paper, lapped over the flashings, keeps water away from the wood.*

Three Systems, One Principle

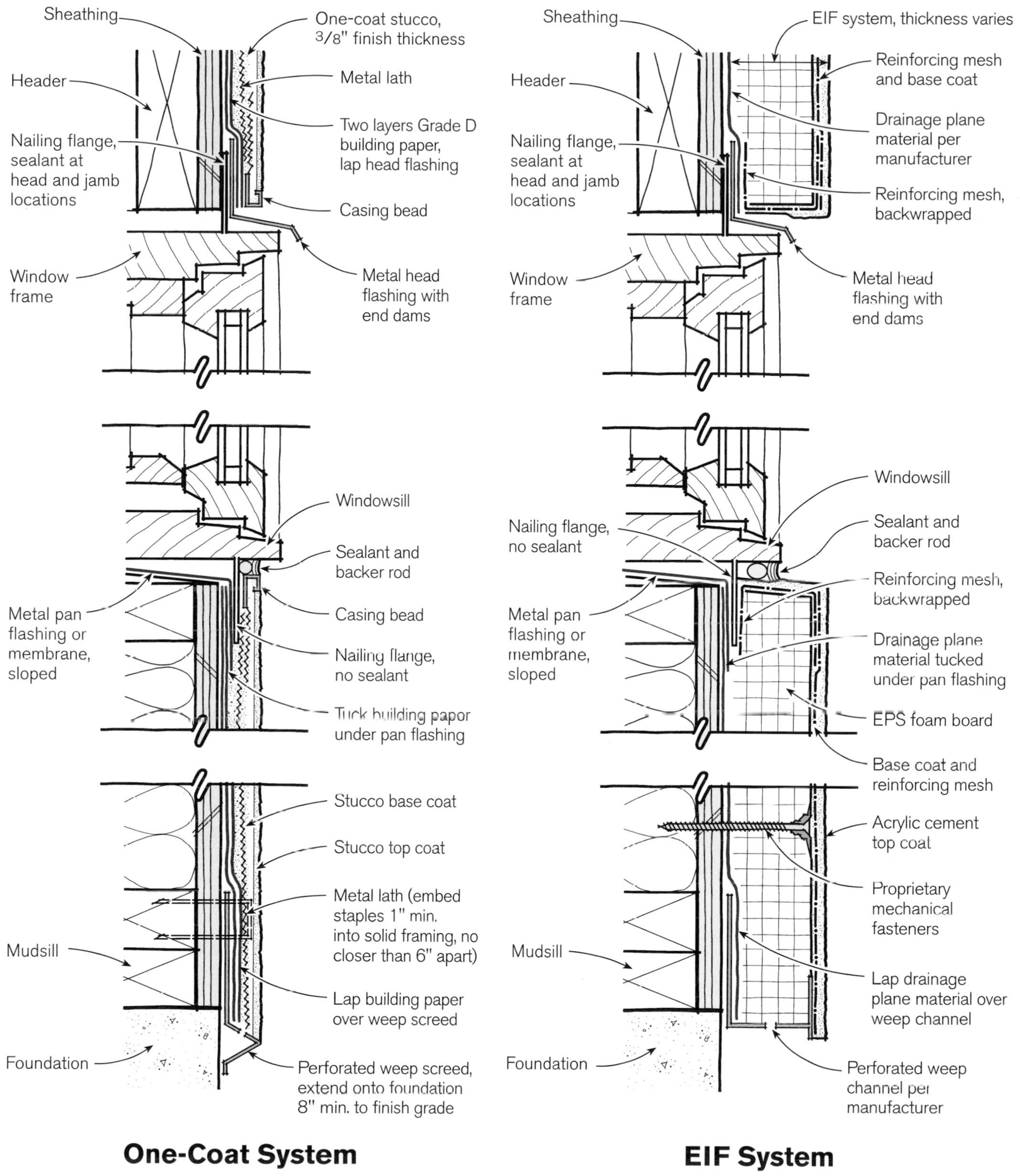

Sheathing

One-coat stucco, 3/8" finish thickness

Header

Metal lath

Nailing flange, sealant at head and jamb locations

Two layers Grade D building paper, lap head flashing

Casing bead

Window frame

Metal head flashing with end dams

Windowsill

Sealant and backer rod

Casing bead

Metal pan flashing or membrane, sloped

Nailing flange, no sealant

Tuck building paper under pan flashing

Stucco base coat

Stucco top coat

Metal lath (embed staples 1" min. into solid framing, no closer than 6" apart)

Mudsill

Lap building paper over weep screed

Foundation

Perforated weep screed, extend onto foundation 8" min. to finish grade

One-Coat System

Sheathing

EIF system, thickness varies

Header

Reinforcing mesh and base coat

Drainage plane material per manufacturer

Nailing flange, sealant at head and jamb locations

Reinforcing mesh, backwrapped

Window frame

Metal head flashing with end dams

Windowsill

Nailing flange, no sealant

Sealant and backer rod

Reinforcing mesh, backwrapped

Metal pan flashing or membrane, sloped

Drainage plane material tucked under pan flashing

EPS foam board

Base coat and reinforcing mesh

Acrylic cement top coat

Proprietary mechanical fasteners

Mudsill

Lap drainage plane material over weep channel

Foundation

Perforated weep channel per manufacturer

EIF System

Figure B. *EIF and modified thin-coat systems, while they have different substrates, rely on the same water-management details as traditional three-coat stucco.*

EIFS

Exterior insulation and finish systems use just a thin (1/8 inch to 3/16 inch) synthetic top coat over a substrate of expanded polystyrene foam. Originally designed as a barrier system with no water management behind the foam, EIFS in the residential market now has to have reliable paper and flashing assemblies behind it to allow water to drain. However, EIFS still requires surface caulking and sealing at joints (caulking is not part of a hard-coat stucco system).

The details for EIF systems are all specified by manufacturers in their specs and ER reports. In practice, I've found that EIFS applicators still mix and match in the field, using whatever components are cheap or easy to find, and assembling the system however they feel like doing it. With constant pressure on budgets and schedules, it's not surprising that we still find defective EIFS applications all over the market.

Even the new water-managed EIF systems use sealing top coats, so they lack the easy path for moisture escape that traditional stucco has. With EIFS, any water in the system has to make its way to weep exits — it can't readily bleed or evaporate out the face of the wall.

Drainage Detailing for Critical Spots

To make stucco work, you have to back it up with a drainage plane based on the shingle effect: water-resistant papers and flashings that direct the water down, out, and away from the wood structure of the home (see "Water-Managed Wall Systems," page 98). The failures that I see in hard-coat stucco are usually traced to a few common mistakes in the drainage plane details.

Proprietary one-coat stucco systems and drainable ("water-managed") EIF systems come with water-handling details supplied by the manufacturers. Some are better than others, but reading and understanding all the evaluation reports and company specs out there would be a daunting task for anyone — by now, the details for all the many systems amount to thousands of pages.

The good news is that every stucco system — even EIFS — can be made to work by applying the same principles that have always applied to traditional stucco. Stucco is a porous, drainable system. Rain penetrates it and drains through it.

As you look at the following examples, keep in mind that coordination and organization on site are keys to implementing them correctly. Most flashings and transitions occur at spots where more than one trade is involved (**Figure 1**, page 151). Terminations at grade may involve landscapers or foundation crews, window flashings can involve roofers as well as window installers, roof-to-wall connections of course involve the roofers, and soffit transitions can involve trim carpenters or framers.

It's the general contractor's job to make sure those transitions are built correctly, by managing the schedule, communicating with all the subs, supervising, and inspecting. Even on custom homes, it's easy to lose control of those critical areas; on tract homes where subs put in unrealistic bids based on incomplete plans, crews are untrained, everyone is in a hurry, and confusion reigns on site, we see many, many failures at spots where two trades were not coordinated.

Weep screed. Hard-coat installations start with the application of a "weep screed" at the bottom edge of all walls. This flashing, which is perforated at the bottom, defines the bottom edge of the stucco coats. It goes on first because it is lowest: The other papers will lap over it to begin the shingle-style layering.

Weep screed is a standard item in markets where stucco is established. In new markets, people may not have heard of it. But it's vital to the performance of the system. Rain will soak into any stucco coating; the water will head downwards, and it must escape at the bottom. Weep screed lets water out through its perforations, and it stops the stucco from bonding to the cement foundation and creating a dam where water might pool. The screed should span between the wood framing or sheathing and the concrete foundation, and it should terminate at least 8 inches above grade.

Other flashing assemblies are acceptable. In some places we use a perforated J-channel above a Z-flashing for a bottom termination. The key principle is simply that water must be allowed to escape and must be directed away from the building.

A common mistake is to pour a slab, patio, or step after the stucco is applied, and to trap the weep screed and the bottom edge of the stucco between the slab and the house. This traps water in the stucco at the bottom and ponds it against the building paper, which will eventually let moisture through. Of course, if there are reverse laps in the paper and flashings above this point, the water will already be behind the paper and in contact with the wood. This scenario can quickly destroy sills, wall plates, and studs.

Building paper. Lapping over the weep screed, as it must lap over all other flashings, is the water-repellent building paper, installed shingle-fashion from the bottom up. Code minimum is two layers of Grade D building paper.

Grade D paper is a tar-impregnated Kraft paper that comes in different thicknesses with different minute ratings, based on the time it takes for water to penetrate in standard tests.

The most common varieties are 15-minute and 30-minute papers. You can pull two layers off the roll at once; because of the space between them, paired sheets of 15-minute paper installed on the wall offer more than 30 minutes of weather protection, and

Figure 2. Integrating building papers with window flashings can be a challenge on site. In California, where this crew works, stucco contractors aren't typically licensed to install windows, so the paper crew must work with the existing flashing. Here, the window crew left the window perimeter protected by strips of flashing, with side strips lapped over the bottom strip and the head strip lapped over the side strips and the window flange. The paper installer lifts the bottom flap and runs paper under it (A), then seals the flashing to the paper with adhesive membrane (B). Next, he lays paper under the side window flashings and staples the flashing down before applying membrane to this joint as well (C). Paper-backed lath then butts directly to the window flange (D), but water that gets behind the stucco at the windowsill and jamb will be handled by the membrane, the flashing, and the first layer of paper.

doubled 30-minute paper provides more than 60 minutes. There is even 60-minute Grade D paper, which, doubled, gives more than 2 hours of water resistance. Rain takes a long time to soak into the stucco itself before reaching the papers, too; so the combination of good papering under a properly applied base coat and finish offers many hours of weather protection.

Plastic housewraps have approval for use under stucco, but I don't recommend any of them in single-sheet applications. Our experience shows that whatever sheet comes in direct contact with the stucco base coat will lose water repellency and break down over time. We use housewrap, but only with Grade D paper over it.

The latest building codes don't specify a "minute rating" requirement for paper under stucco. We adjust our paper choice to local climate conditions. In arid areas of Southern California, we use double 15-minute paper. In the Salt Lake Valley, we use double 30-minute paper. In the humid Galveston Bay region of Texas, we use double 60-minute paper. In some remedial work, where everyone is eager to be

Figure 3. Here, the window installers and the roofers have not coordinated their work. Roof flashing will effectively catch water coming off the main wall if stucco papers are applied to lap over it. However, the window flange dumps behind the roof flashing instead of onto it. The author's crew removed this window and reflashed the opening before reinstalling the window.

absolutely sure, I will even install wrinkle wrap first, then two layers of 30-minute or 60-minute paper — all lapped over or under any flashings as appropriate to achieve the shingle effect.

Builders should learn any local code requirements, and I would advise asking an experienced and reputable local stucco contractor what works in your area. If you can't consult the voice of experience, err on the side of caution: Heavier paper is cheap compared to removal and replacement.

Metal lath. Good installation of the metal lath over the papers and flashings is critical. Stapling is a big concern: I have seen bad leaks develop when the only mistake was that the lath was overstapled or stapled in the wrong places.

Lathing staples should be placed only at studs, plate lines, headers, or other solid framing members. Code requires the fasteners to penetrate 1 inch into the framing, so if the sheathing is 1/2-inch plywood, you need staples with a 1 1/2-inch leg. A wide-crown staple is the appropriate fastener, and the only way to get both legs of a 7/8-inch or 15/16-inch crown staple to consistently hit a 1 1/2-inch stud is to orient the staple vertically (this also prevents the staple from creating a water trap in the papers).

The staples should be placed no closer than 6 inches to each other. If you have to use a staple between studs — for instance, to fasten the edge of the lath near a vent penetration — use short staples that will not go all the way through the plywood. Locate all laps in the wire over studs or other solid framing members.

I've seen cases where poorly trained applicators have placed a hundred or more staples in a 1-square-foot area between studs, to pull lathing flat or to close a joint. The results can be disastrous. It seems to take a certain number of staples to break apart the wood flakes in an OSB piece enough to create a channel for water flow. Once you get above that critical mass of staples, you've opened a path. In heavy storms with turbulent winds, water in the saturated stucco gets forced through the paper and the OSB along the paths created by the staples, and flows down the inside of the OSB within the stud cavity. I've opened up walls from the inside and watched the water stream in. No wall system in the industry is designed to drain water out of the stud bays — when that area gets soaked, your wall is doomed. When I tear apart a wall like that after four or five years in service, what I find is a compost pile.

Window flashings. Many one-coat manufacturers supply window flashing details, but they aren't necessarily good ones. The key, as always, is to establish good overlapping for the shingle effect. We see many houses in Utah and Texas where the paper has been applied well, but the window flashings dump under the paper. Invariably this leads to rot.

Coordination on site can make or break this installation. Where window flashings dump under the paper, it's probably because the window installers put the flashings in before the stucco installers came to paper the building. The paper has to go on first, then the flashings, then the window, and finally the lath. Each trade has to wait for the one before, or you have to figure out a way to leave the flashings hanging so they can be integrated into the building paper later (**Figure 2**, page 155).

Another typical case is shown in **Figure 3**. Here, the window flange is likely to dump behind the roof flashings if someone is not careful. This situation was found on one of my company's retrofit jobs. My crew removed the window, papered the wall with papers lapping on top of the roof flashing, flashed the window opening so the flashing dumps on top of the paper, then reinstalled the window with flanges outboard of the papers and flashings so that water always moves away from the building as it heads downhill.

Bad window details damaged several spots on the building in the photos in **Figure 4**. Though it was less than ten years old, this building had been repaired twice previously with surface-sealing methods that did not work. After pulling out the window, we repapered the wall with DuPont's Tyvek StuccoWrap, then applied membrane and Tyvek FlexWrap to the opening to protect the wood structure if the window should ever leak (as many on this building have). We then replaced the window, sliding the top flange under the Tyvek and sealing the flange to the Tyvek on all four sides. Finally, we applied a second protective layer of Grade D building paper. More than a hun-

Figure 4. Less than 10 years old, this building had been repaired twice previously with surface-sealing methods that did not work. The author's crew first stripped the stucco. At this window corner (A), badly detailed flashing and paper let water soak the sheathing and framing, leading to rot. After pulling out the window, the author's crew repapered the wall with Tyvek StuccoWrap, then applied membrane and Tyvek FlexWrap to the rough sill to protect the wood structure even if the window leaks (B). The crew then replaced the window (C), sliding the top flange under the Tyvek and sealing the flange to the Tyvek all around the window (D) before applying a second protective layer of Grade D building paper (E).

Figure 5. Roof-to-wall intersections create particular problems. At top left, this bad detail held up the work: The rafter placed tight to the building wall does not allow paper to slip behind it, and the flashing left by the roofers will direct water behind the stucco and into the wall if used as configured. The photo above shows a water diverter (kick flashing) installed by the author's crew in a retrofit job: This design will lead water out away from the wall and dump it off the roof's drip-edge rather than into the wall. Papers installed on the main wall can readily integrate with the membrane and flashing between roof and wall at the rafter tail. At left, a wall-and-roof intersection built without the correct flashing detail shows discoloration and staining after a few years in service; the author typically finds significant rot in buildings with this detail, even though the wall surfaces may show only minor traces of trouble.

dred houses in this one neighborhood, built by different builders both large and small, need this treatment.

Roof-to-wall joints. The most damaging leakage we see in our work takes place where roofs intersect walls, either because a one-story roof meets a two-story wall, or because a chimney chase meets the roof. It takes work to keep the roofers and the stucco applicators coordinated so that their work interweaves correctly (**Figure 5**).

Every roof needs some kind of L-shaped flashing where the roof abuts the wall. Metal step flashing (or "step shingles," as we call it) is typical for asphalt or shake roofs; tile roofs usually get a continuous piece of metal J-flashing.

Where stucco is new in the market, the appropriate metal step shingles for stucco application can be hard to find. Folded flashings intended for use with asphalt shingles and vinyl siding are too small for stucco. In Salt Lake City, the typical step shingles on the shelf are 8 inches long, with a 2-inch leg for the wall and a 4-inch leg for the roof. Stucco requires a 2-inch reveal between the bottom termination of the stucco and the roof surface (many EIF systems need a 3-inch reveal), and a 2-inch lap of the building paper over the metal, so step flashings must have at least a 4-inch vertical leg.

Since you can't be sure of finding the right size metal flashings in all markets, I always use rubberized asphalt sheet material like Grace Ice & Water Shield as a backup.

However, the flashings are still important, particularly the water diverter or "kickout flashing" at the bottom of the roof, which kicks roof runoff away from the wall system (see "Kickout Flashing" detail, page 127). Where this is not installed, water from the roof will overwhelm the stucco system and cause at least a visual problem, and commonly a major structural problem.

Penetrations. Every penetration in the stucco — hose bibb, dryer vent, combustion air intake, or whatever — is a potential leakage point. Our solution for those spots is to use bent and soldered metal to make up a set of standard shrouds, like the hoods that cover dryer vents, in various sizes to meet the most common needs. We caulk the back side of the shroud to the paper below it, and caulk the paper above it to the shroud's top and side flanges. Then we terminate the stucco at a casing bead.

Homeowners Pay the Price

In Salt Lake, my stucco repair business is thriving. We also have a lot of work fixing homes with EIFS and cultured stone exteriors — the underlying drainage-plane problems are the same.

Recently, I started a company, RAM Exteriors, to install hard-coat stucco on new homes. But it's ironic — I can find plenty of work fixing bad stucco at four times the cost of applying stucco right in the first place.

The consequences can be tragic for homeowners who don't understand the issues. One house for sale we looked at recently lacked the right flashings and papers under the cladding. Even if we found no structural damage, I told the prospective buyers it would cost at least $30,000 to retrofit the home to provide good drainage details.

I worked for another couple who bought their home before they saw any problem. They called me because of leaks and musty odors. When my crew started to open the walls, the foreman called me from the site and said, "You better get over here. This house is about to fall down." When I got there, sure enough — the home's framing was almost gone. There was a risk of imminent collapse.

Utah has some of the weakest liability laws in the U.S. That couple's lawyer advised them to settle for $50,000. In other states, the builder would have been on the hook for the whole value of the house. If the builder is insured, that's a hit he can handle — once, and then lose his coverage. But I know some contractors who have thought they were covered and never were: Exclusions they hadn't read in their insurance policies ruled stucco out, and they didn't even know it.

Whether your insurance covers you for stucco failure or not, that isn't a road you want to go down. The way to prevent the human cost isn't with insurance. Insurance is for unavoidable disasters, one-time deals. If stucco is done wrong, failure is predictable: You can expect it. And the way to avoid stucco failure is simple: Provide the system of flashings and papers that will keep water away from the wood. If you do, you'll have something better than insurance: a weather-resistant home exterior that does its job.

Dennis McCoy owns and operates RAM Builders, based in Lindon, Utah, which specializes in remediation and repair work in Utah, Texas, Colorado, and California.

Storm-Resistant Stucco: Lessons from Florida

by Joseph Lstiburek

The four hurricanes that struck Florida in 2004 proved the effectiveness of the tough building codes passed by the state after Hurricane Andrew's strike in 1992. Hurricanes Charley, Frances, Ivan, and Jeanne killed dozens of people, but not one of those deaths was caused by failure of any structure built to the new codes.

Unfortunately, though, many stucco-clad homes in the state experienced a problem we would not be discussing if they had simply fallen down or blown away: They got wet.

After 20-plus inches of windblown rain soaked the whole region, there were hundreds of reports of water intrusion through stucco walls of otherwise undamaged homes. The Florida Home Builders Association hired my company, Building Science Consulting, to investigate the situation, identify causes, and propose solutions.

We applied a wide range of investigative techniques (**Figure 6**, next page): We inspected homes soaked by the storms as well as new homes built after the storms; we tested and experimented with new buildings and mocked-up assemblies; and we did bench-top testing of materials and components, including felt paper, plastic housewraps, and windows. We also reviewed relevant codes and standards, and interviewed builders, contractors, materials suppliers, manufacturers, and code officials.

Anyone who wants to keep rain out of a building might benefit from the lessons of Florida's wet walls.

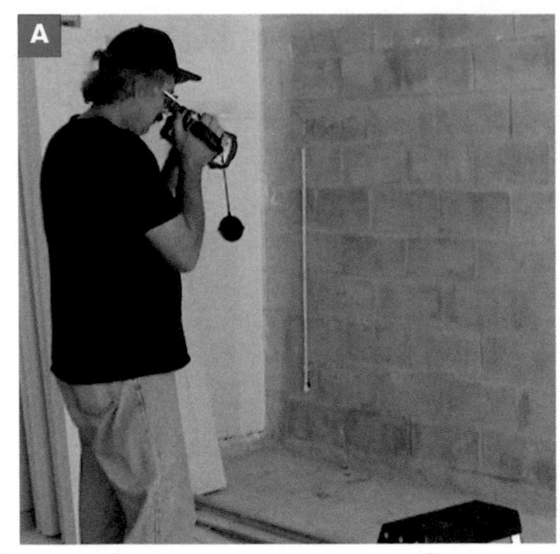

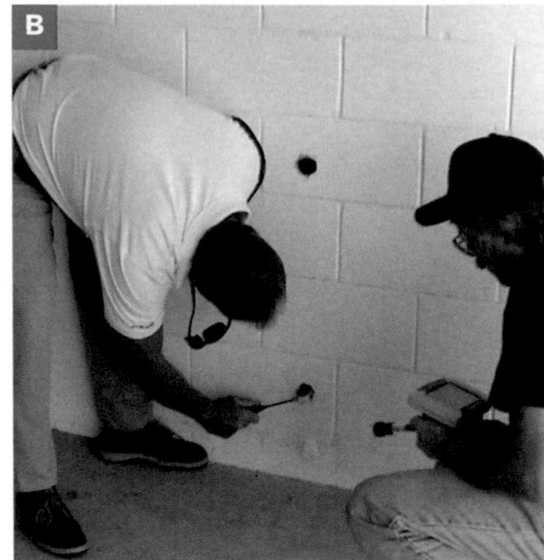

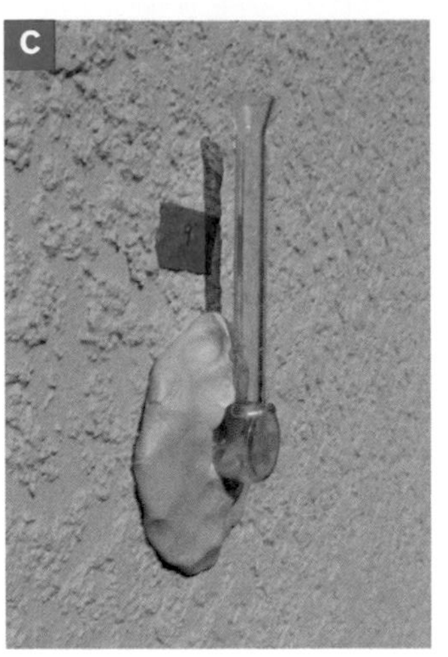

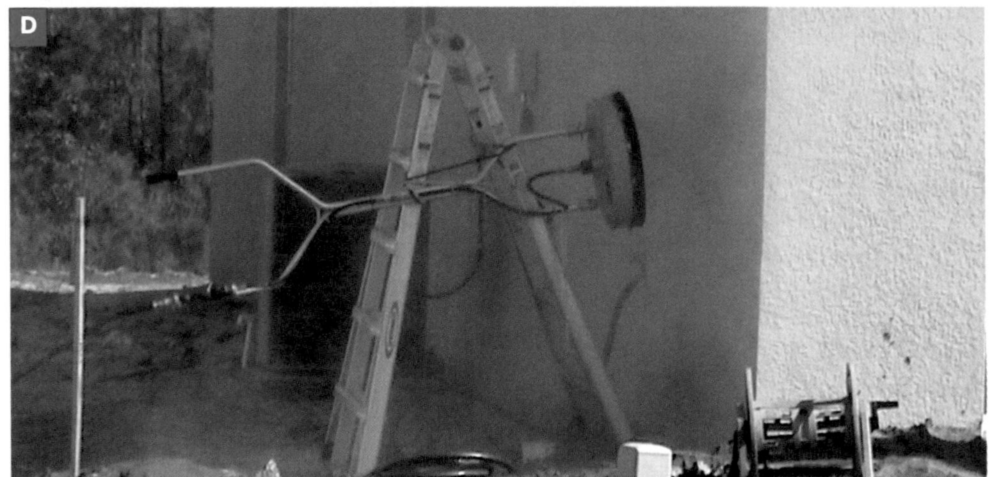

Figure 6. Members of the author's investigative team examined stucco walls with infrared cameras (A) and camera probes (B). To measure water leakage, they applied hydrostatic head tests (C) as well as simple water sprays and simulated wind-driven rain (D).

After all, whether you build in Florida or somewhere else, water is water, wind is wind, and the laws of physics are the same.

Why Stucco Leaks

We were asked to focus on stucco-clad homes. Actually, there are two kinds of stucco used in central Florida: traditional "hard coat" or "three-coat" stucco, and the modern "cementitious decorative finishes," popularly called "thin-coat stucco." Both types of cladding let water into homes during the storms.

Our testing of Florida homes confirmed what we already knew about stucco: It always cracks, and the cracks always leak. In homes we tested, stucco that was cracked leaked at the cracks; and where the stucco was not cracked, it did not leak (**Figure 7**). But there's a little more to the story than that.

Traditional stucco and thin-coat stucco aren't fundamentally different. Both are surface treatments applied to a substrate, and they behave in a generally similar fashion. Most important, neither can be considered waterproof or leakproof. On the contrary, when you use either, you can be sure it *will* leak. But with both decorative thin stucco and traditional three-coat stucco, there are ways to decrease the frequency of cracking.

Traditional stucco. This centuries-old coating is supposed to go on in three coats. The first is the scratch coat. It's applied about 3⁄8 to 1⁄2 inch thick and allowed to cure. Because it's cement, it shrinks as it cures, and as it shrinks, it cracks. Then, two or three weeks later, when it is done shrinking, you go back and apply the brown coat, which serves to fill in the shrinkage cracks in the scratch coat. After that cures, you go back yet again and apply the finish coat (the color coat), and you're done.

With each coat you apply, you change the mix of cement, lime, sand, and water slightly, so that each coat is a little weaker, more permeable, and more flexible than the one it covers. Thus the softer, outer coats have relatively more lime and sand — and less cement — than the hard inner coat.

But modern-day stucco applicators in Florida as well as in other places typically don't wait several weeks for the first coat to cure; they go back and apply the second coat the same day. That means, of course, that both coats shrink and crack at once — one reason the

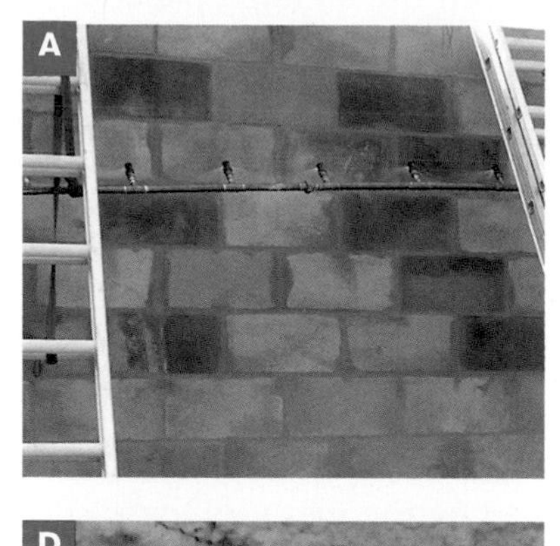

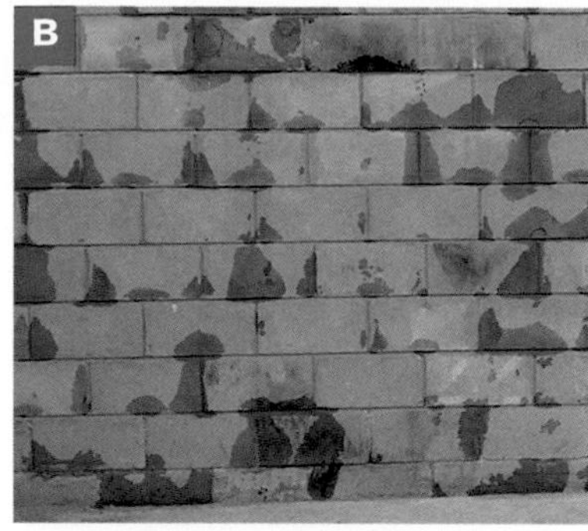

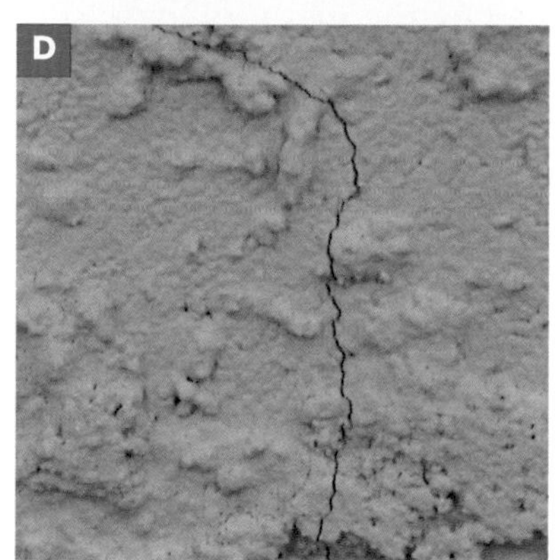

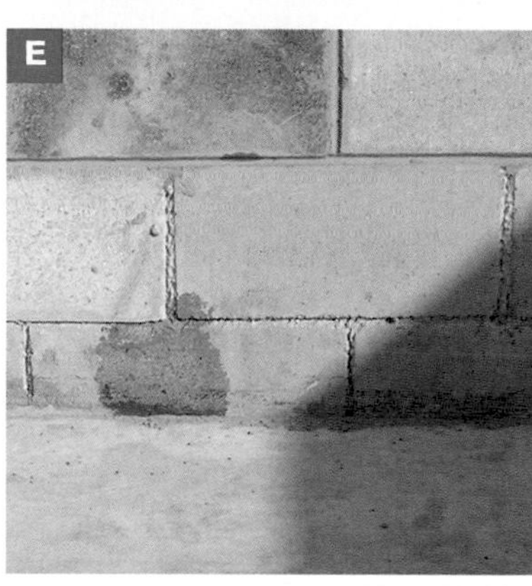

Figure 7. Using new garage block walls as test structures, the investigators compared the leak performance of bare masonry-block walls with that of various stucco claddings, with and without cracks. A water spray on a bare block wall (A) led to a characteristic leak pattern at mortar joints (B). Water sprays on unpainted stucco (C) did not cause leaks if the stucco was not cracked. However, when typical small stucco cracks (D) received the water spray, water intrusion occurred at mortar joints and at the wall base (E).

stucco in Florida leaked as much as it did.

Thin-coat stucco is applied in just one coat, so it's going to crack no matter what. However, with both thin-coat stucco and two- and three-coat applications that are not given time to cure between coats, it's possible to reduce the amount of cracking by using fiber mesh in the mix and by adding polymers to make the coats more flexible.

So why not change codes to require either a mandatory curing period between coats or the use of additives in the mix? That wouldn't really be a practical solution. Neither technique will prevent shrinkage cracks altogether. Nothing will. More to the point, there's another cause of cracking that we also can't prevent: settlement (**Figure 8**). Virtually all buildings move and shift enough in the first few years after construction to cause some cracking of the stucco — and no stucco, whether traditional or polymer-modified, is immune to that.

What, then, do we do? The answer is that you have to assume there will be cracks and that water will be able to get through them. Accordingly, you have to design wall systems that tolerate those leaks, and accept that some maintenance and crack repair by the occupants will be necessary over the years after the home is finished and occupied.

Two Kinds of Walls

The picture in Florida is complicated by the fact that builders there typically use two types of exterior walls on the same house. It's common to lay a concrete-block wall for the first story and then stick-frame second-story walls and gable ends; stucco is applied to both stories. Both types of walls leaked in the Florida storms, for somewhat different reasons.

Building paper and housewrap. Upper-story stick-frame walls, in principle, should function as drained assemblies. The stucco is applied over a "weather-

Figure 8. Houses shift after construction as supporting soils consolidate and materials change size with changing temperature and moisture content. This movement of substrates, though typical and expected, inevitably brings about some cracking in brittle surfaces like stucco, creating the need for ongoing maintenance and repair in the early years of a building's service life.

resistive barrier" — you can use housewrap, asphalt felt, or Grade D asphalt-saturated Kraft paper. Any water that penetrates to the weather-resistive barrier is supposed to drain down it until encountering a flashing that directs the moisture out to the exterior.

One reason Florida walls leaked was that the housewraps or papers installed beneath the stucco did not function effectively as a drainage plane (**Figure 9**). Stucco tends to bond to housewrap and building paper, eliminating the air space in which water is supposed to drain. Also, the housewrap or building paper itself loses water repellency when stucco adheres to it, or when it comes in contact with surfactants (soaplike chemicals that reduce the surface tension of water). In Florida, water that reached the housewrap or building-paper layer in the walls often bled through into the framing.

Reverse flashing. Even if the housewrap or building paper had worked as intended, however, there still would have been problems caused by incorrect flashing. At the base of the frame walls, where the upper-story cladding meets the lower-story cladding, builders typically install a metal expansion-joint over the building paper and run the building paper down into the top edge of the lower-story stucco coat (**Figure 10**). This detail allows water running down the upper-story drainage plane to flow into the lower-story mass wall, rather than move to the exterior. Builders can't be blamed for using this detail: The method is required by the code, as interpreted by local officials.

Lower-story mass walls. Masonry-block walls with stucco cladding aren't intended to function as drained assemblies. They are "mass assemblies." Water that penetrates the stucco through cracks is supposed to be absorbed by the masonry mass, which it doesn't damage, and then dry slowly to both the exterior and the interior during periods of dry weather (**Figure 11**, page 164). Central Florida's masonry walls, for the most part, were able to manage moderate amounts of rain but were simply overwhelmed by the huge water onslaught from three consecutive hurricanes.

Rather than suggest a modification of the stucco materials or installations, I've suggested a few small design changes that would enhance the ability of

Figure 9. Upper-story walls in central Florida are typically stick-framed, while lower-story walls are built with concrete block (A). Both wall types leaked, but for different reasons. Although designed to drain water, these frame walls were handicapped by the bonding of building paper or housewrap to the stucco coatings, which prevented free drainage (B). Forced into contact with trapped water, most housewraps allow some water penetration, as shown in table-top testing at the author's shop: Water dripped onto a horizontal housewrap surface (C) and soaked into the absorbent test material underneath (D). In the field, saturated stucco coatings over housewrap allowed water into sheathing and stud bays (E).

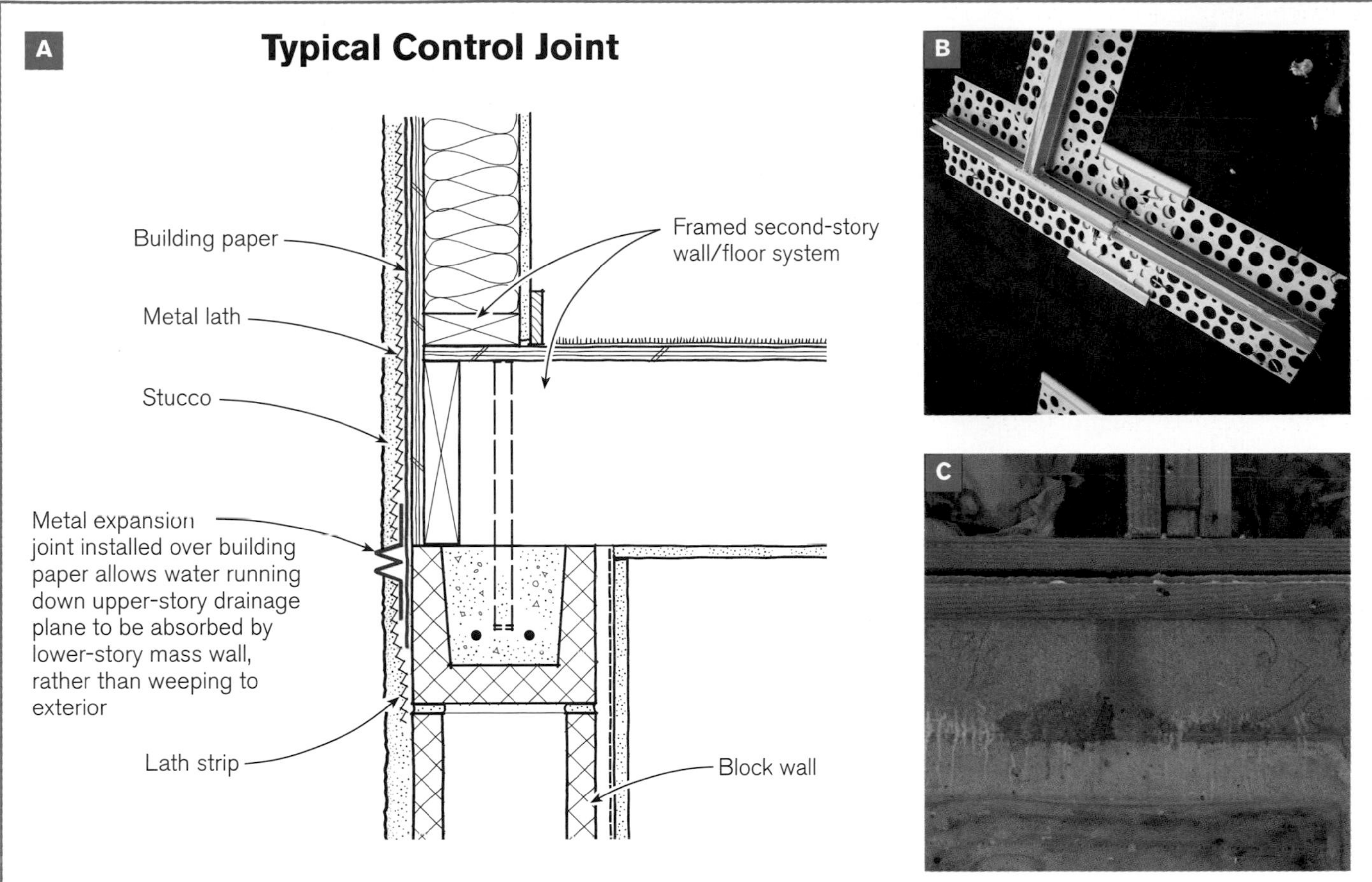

Figure 10. The joint detail, typically required in Florida between upper-wall and lower-wall stucco sections (A), does not manage water well. When the expansion-joint accessory is installed over the top of a continuous sheet of building paper or housewrap (B), water is not kicked out to the exterior but is allowed to pass behind the joint into the wall below (C).

these systems to absorb and dissipate water without allowing it to enter living space or damage finishes. But even improved masonry mass walls shouldn't be expected to handle rainwater that leaks in from windows, service penetrations, or other holes in the wall assembly — and it turns out that leaks at windows and other openings were a major source of water intrusion during Florida's storms.

Windows and Other Penetrations

The industry standards and building-code rules for windows don't require them to be leakproof when facing the kind of wind and rain that central Florida saw in 2004. Windows installed in Florida homes are rated for water holdout at 15% of the design wind load, or up to 140 pascals of pressure (approximately the pressure of a 35-mph wind). Clearly, these limits were exceeded during August and September of 2004. In a hurricane, the codes expect windows to stay in the wall, but not necessarily to hold out all the rain.

On the other hand, our testing of windows and window assemblies indicates that many of them leaked under conditions well below their listed, rated value. In fact, many tested windows leak under a simple water spray with no wind pressure at all. Factory testing of windows seems to be missing a widespread incidence of leakage at the window-assembly corners. Also, windows are tested as single units, but are often sold as preassembled "mulled" units, with two or more windows combined in a composite arrangement. Every preassembled mulled unit we tested leaked at zero wind pressure (**Figure 12**, next page).

From our visual inspections of windows in the field, and from a closer look at some randomly selected windows that we took apart, it seems clear that there is a widespread problem with the connections between the windowsill and the window jamb: Windows delivered to the site are likely to be leak-prone before installation.

Window installation is also an ongoing concern. The methods used in Florida, as elsewhere, often don't ensure reliable water management. In particular, precast concrete windowsill components sold into the Florida market are shaped in a way that directs some leakage into — rather than out of — the building (**Figure 13**, page 165).

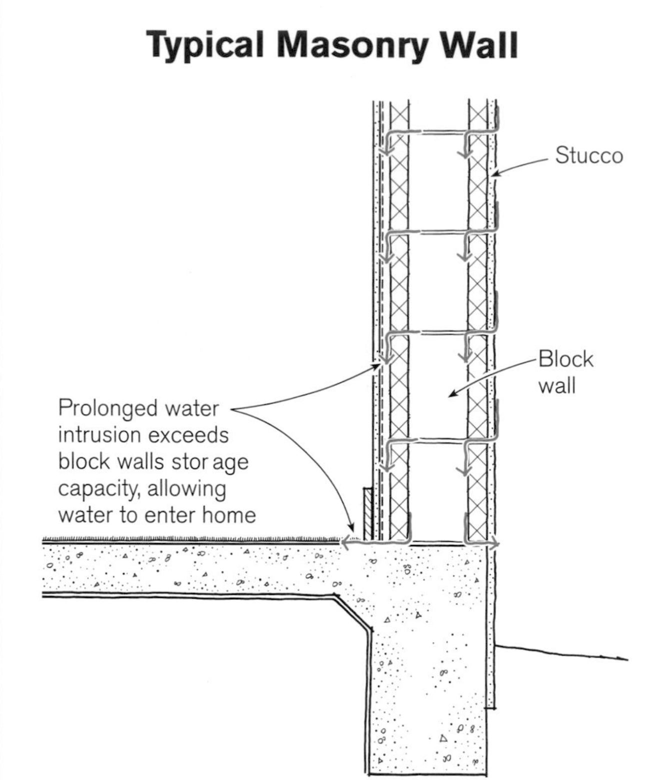

Figure 11. Masonry walls are intended to absorb and store minor amounts of penetrating water, and then allow the moisture to escape later during dry periods. But when their storage capacity is exceeded by continuing water intrusion, they can let water enter the home at the wall base or bleed through onto interior finishes.

It would be good if windows delivered to the job could be made to hold water out more effectively. But in the meantime, builders have to be aware of the limited water resistance of window units, and design walls that are tolerant of window leakage.

Paints and Coatings

When we first went to Florida, some people had the idea that we would focus on paints and coatings. Many observers had noticed that homes only a year or two old had shown more leakage than homes that had been around for five or ten years, and they thought perhaps this was because successive repaintings had sealed all the microcracks in the stucco. If we required a high-build elastomeric paint on new homes in the first place, the reasoning went, maybe we could prevent the whole problem.

That idea makes sense, but it doesn't hold up completely. For one thing, all those older buildings were repainted (and the cracks patched using other means as well) only after they had been through the process of shifting and had settled down to some kind of equilibrium. There are very few paints and coatings around that can span the shrinkage cracks in a new building and also stay intact as the building shifts and cracks over its first few years. So while patching and painting a stucco wall is a good idea — in fact, it's necessary maintenance — and it has to be done continuously over the life of a building, it is particularly important during the first two or three years.

Also, high-build paints and elastomeric coatings span microcracks most effectively when the surface is smooth. On rough-surfaced stucco, which is a very common finish in the industry, coatings are much less effective at sealing surfaces (**Figure 14**).

And to gain flexibility and crack-spanning ability in a coating, you often have to give up vapor permeability, so that the coating may tend to trap moisture within the stucco as well as keep bulk water out. That trapped moisture can cause coatings to blister. Modified stucco mixes may even re-emulsify and turn to goo when you trap moisture in them with a low-permeability coating.

That said, specialty elastomeric coatings hold great promise. The "holy grail" of coatings research has

Figure 12. Factory-assembled windows like this double unit (A) are frequently found to leak at the corners (B) and the center joint (C).

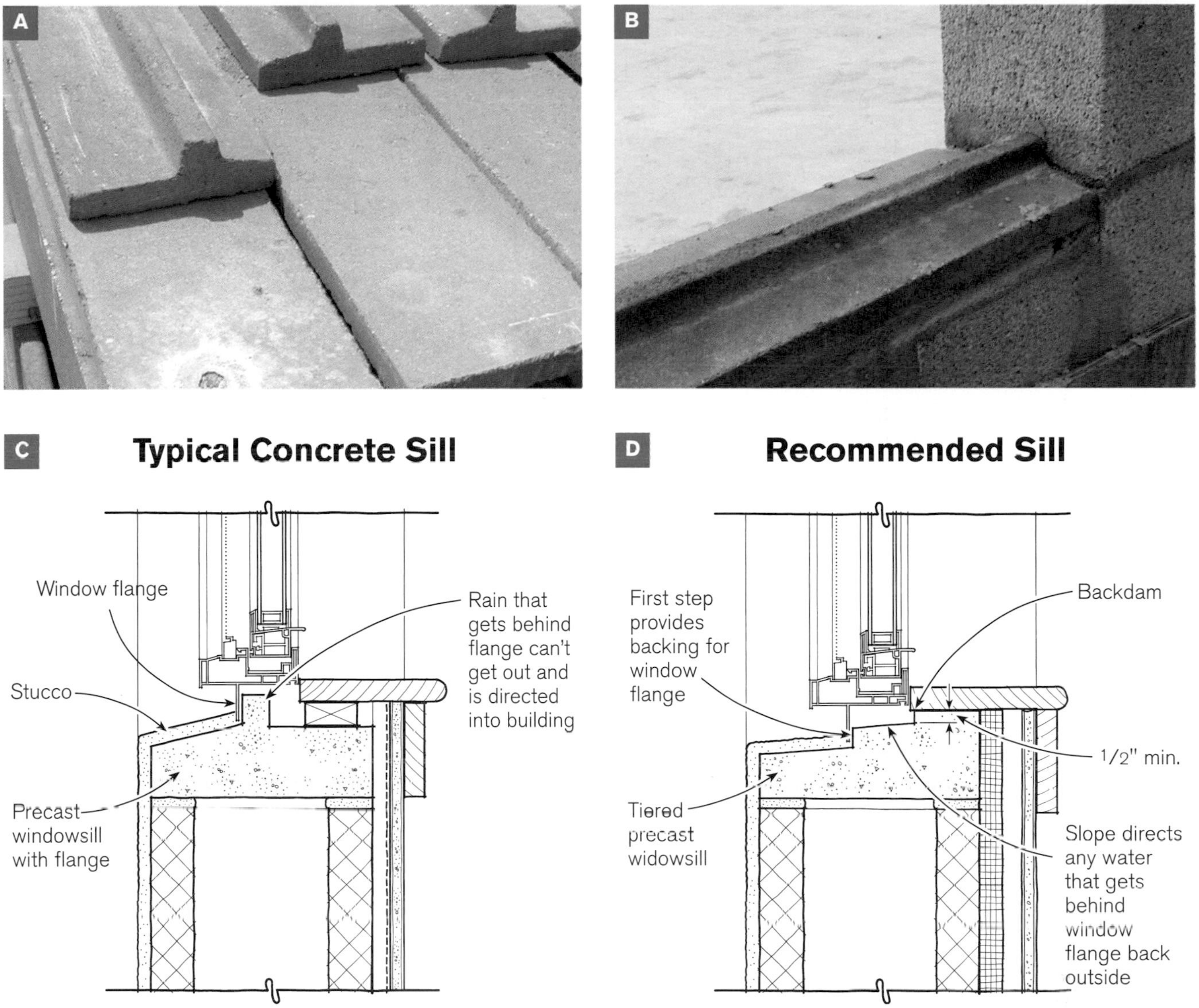

A

B

C **Typical Concrete Sill**

Window flange

Stucco

Precast windowsill with flange

Rain that gets behind flange can't get out and is directed into building

D **Recommended Sill**

First step provides backing for window flange

Tiered precast widowsill

Backdam

1/2" min.

Slope directs any water that gets behind window flange back outside

Figure 13. Precast concrete windowsills for block walls (A and B) have a profiled rib for attaching the bottom window flange. The rib directs some leakage toward the interior (C). A better windowsill design would direct water toward the outside (D).

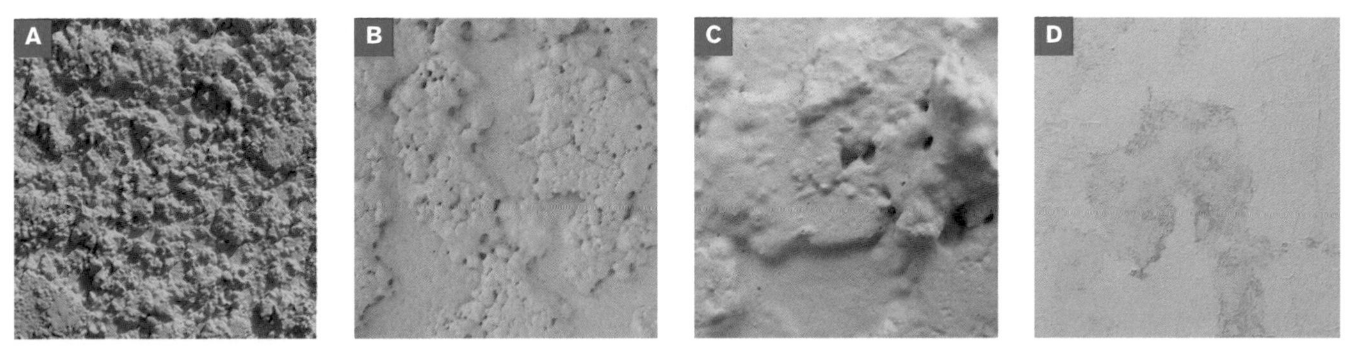

Figure 14. Paints and coatings are not highly effective at spanning cracks and pinholes in a rough stucco coating. Ordinary paint (A), a 3-mil high-build coating (B), and a 10-mil elastomeric coating (C) all leave pinholes that can be seen under magnification. Thick elastomeric coatings over stucco can also be prone to blistering (D).

Figure 15. To help block walls store greater amounts of incidental water and to direct the moisture back outside rather than allowing it to trickle into the home, foundations should have a stepped-down shelf at the slab edge. A weep screed at the lower termination of the stucco will allow accumulated water to get out.

Stepped-Down Foundation Detail

EPS insulation
Stucco
1x wood furring
Block wall
Drywall
Weep screed
Latex paint
Shelf prevents water from soaking interior materials
Extending vapor barrier under grade beam up to grade provides capillary break

always been to develop a highly elastic coating that also breathes. We're not sure how much it needs to breathe, but generally I think the perm rating should be 10 or higher. And, for the present, specialty coatings should be applied to stucco only by knowledgeable installers. "High build" acrylic paints that get you 5 to 6 mils of thickness at permeabilities of greater than 10 perms are pretty much the optimum performance limit with conventional coating systems.

Improving Masonry Mass Walls

Clearly, masonry-block walls — as commonly built in Florida and other places — have a limited capacity to hold and drain water. When cracks and crevices in the wall assembly are full, water trickles onto interior floors at the base of walls. Saturation of walls also leads to humid conditions on interior wall faces, sometimes allowing mold or mildew to grow.

Two proven methods would improve the performance of these walls. First, the foundation slab or footing should be built with a stepped-down seat or shelf where the first course of masonry block is set (**Figure 15**). This will direct water that reaches the base of the wall outward to the outdoors, rather than inward, where it can damage floors or cause humidity problems.

The interior-wall face will perform better if covered with a continuous layer of semipermeable rigid

Allowing Drying to the Interior

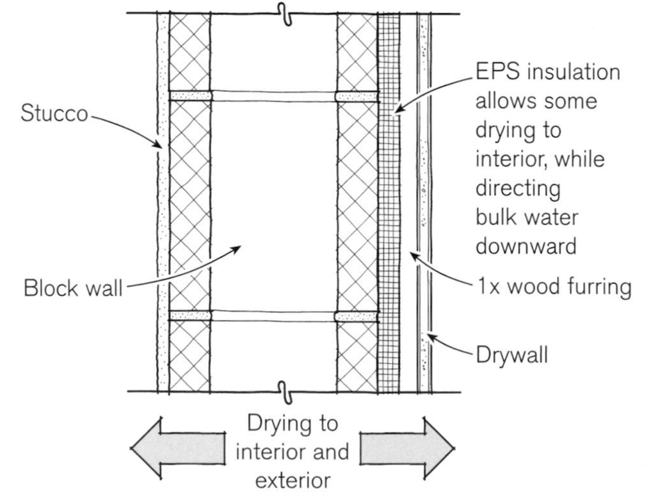

Figure 16. Extruded polystyrene insulation applied to the inside face of the block wall, with an air space under the drywall, will allow some drying by vapor diffusion to the interior, but will direct bulk water downward toward the base of the wall, where it can escape to the outside.

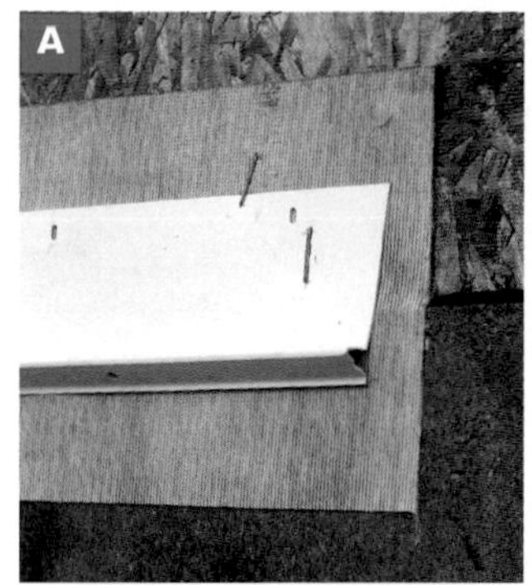

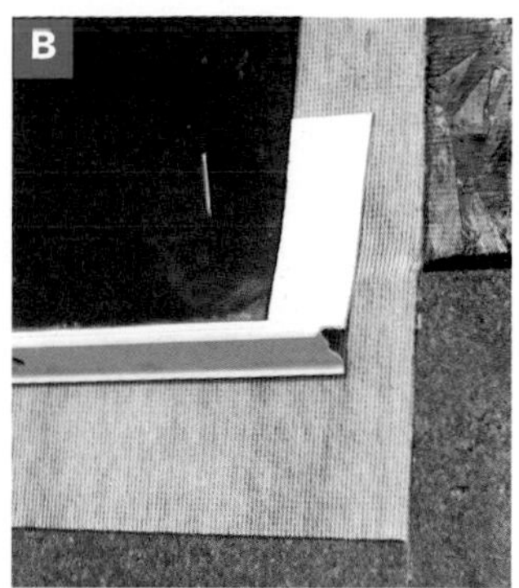

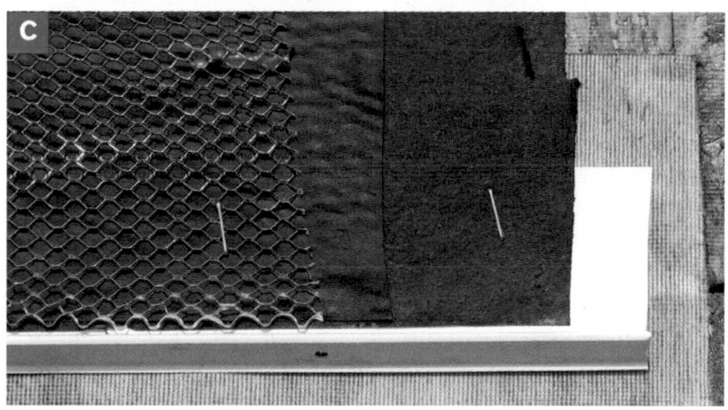

Figure 17. So that horizontal control joints between floors direct water to the outside of the wall, first apply a bridge flashing between the wood frame wall and the block wall below, and then attach a weep-screed flashing that overlaps the lower wall (A). The primary drainage-plane membrane should then be installed overlapping the weep screed (B) before a bond-break paper layer and wire lath (C) are put in place. Finally, stucco can be applied to both walls (D).

insulation, such as commonly available extruded polystyrene (**Figure 16**). This will reduce vapor migration into the home as well as condensation, preventing moisture from accumulating in the home's drywall.

Refining Drained Frame Walls

Wood-frame, stucco-clad walls should have a bond break layer installed between the stucco rendering and the drainage plane.

In practice, this means applying two layers of building paper, or one layer of building paper over a layer of plastic housewrap, before applying stucco. At the joint between drained upper-story assemblies and mass-wall lower-story assemblies, a weep-screed flashing should be installed (**Figure 17**).

Window and Flashing Recommendations

There is a problem in Florida and other states where high-wind codes are taking effect. The problem is caused by the conflict between two goals: ensuring structural integrity and the need to keep out water. In many cases, building officials are enforcing fastening schedules and structural connections at the expense of proper flashing and drainage details.

To fix this problem, all of us — including builders, code officials, and manufacturers — need to think through what we're doing when we attach a window or other component to a wall assembly. Here are a few things to consider:

First of all, whether it's a window, a dryer vent, or a hose bibb, when you install something through a wall, you have to flash the opening. Second, drainage assemblies for windows have to extend all the way to the back of the window, because windows can leak at any point. And, finally, flashings above windows and other penetrations have to catch water from all the way to the back of the cladding system, and have to direct it all the way to the building's exterior.

Maintenance and Crack Repair

Stucco cracks have to be addressed with ongoing homeowner maintenance. The best practice is to allow stucco walls a reasonable "breaking-in" period, from one to two years. By then, most if not all of the cracks that are going to appear will already be evident. At that point, cracks should be individually sealed with caulking or a brush-in cementitious crack-repair formula, and then the walls can be repainted.

Inspecting walls every few years, and repairing them in this fashion as needed, should be enough to keep a stucco wall performing well for many decades.

Joseph Lstiburek, PhD, PE, is a principal of Building Science Consulting (www.buildingscience.com) in Westford, Mass., and an investigator of moisture-related building problems.

Waterproofing Stucco Trim

by David Dobson

Every time it rained, water would soak the carpet under the windows of an acquaintance's Southern California condominium. Built about 20 years ago, this former apartment complex had a standard three-coat stucco and lath finish applied over building paper stapled directly to framing; 2x6 rough-sawn wood trim was nailed through the stucco around the windows and horizontally around the entire building. Because the window, trim, and surrounding stucco appeared to be undamaged on the exterior, I suspected that water was probably following the trim's nails right through the stucco and into the walls **(Figure 18).**

Hidden Bugs and Rot

When we went inside the house and opened up the gypsum wallboard underneath the window to expose the wood framing and the building paper, we found an enormous amount of damage. Not only were the framing members water-stained and starting to rot, they were also damaged and infested with termites. The king, trimmer, and cripple studs underneath both window jambs were almost completely destroyed, robbing each member of virtually all load-bearing capacity. And water damage had completely worn away the building paper in several places, exposing the back of the stucco (**Figure 19**).

Our architectural firm, Lohse2, specializes in investigating water leaks and other building failures. To locate sources of leaks in building envelopes, we often perform water tests on window and wall assemblies with a spray rack built to ASTM E1105 specs. In this project, as soon as we turned on our spray rack, water poured in around the window in several locations (**Figure 20**). Spray tests are normally conducted for 15 minutes, but we had to turn off the water after only a couple of minutes because so much water was pouring through the window and wall assembly.

When we removed the exterior trim from around the window, we found holes as big as 1⁄4 inch in diameter blown through the stucco where the nails attaching the wood trim had once been driven. We then removed the stucco 12 inches around the window, all the way down to the stucco screed. Our original hypothesis was correct: Everywhere there had been a trim nail driven through the stucco, there was corresponding water damage to the flashings, building paper, and wood framing.

The termites seem to have favored the wood that had been affected by water intrusion. We found the greatest termite damage on wood that was already stained and that got wet during our spray test. With the stucco removed, that damage was even more evident.

Considering the damage to the framing around the window, it was a wonder the wall was still standing. The king, trimmer, and cripple studs had not only been completely eaten away — they were not even bearing on the mudsill. Fortunately, damage to the wood framing in this part of the building was limited to the window area, but we suspected that other walls in the complex — which have both the same window trim detail and an additional horizontal trim detail — had similar damage.

Figure 18. Though there was no obvious damage, the window of this Southern California condominium complex leaked every time it rained (left). Underneath the traditional three-coat stucco exterior, water had caused severe rot (right).

Figure 19. Water stains and mildew behind the baseboard underneath the window hint at the damage in the wall (left). Removing the drywall revealed the extent of the damage (bottom left), including rotted framing and extensive termite infestation (below).

Figure 20. When the author directed his firm's spray rack at the window, water began pouring into the interior (left). Once the trim was removed (center), it became obvious that holes blown through the stucco by the trim nails were the path for the water intrusion; some were 1/4 inch or more in diameter (right).

Figure 21. To repair the wall, the author replaced the damaged framing and added blocking (far left), which provided solid backing for Moistop waterproofing membrane. The Moistop was first applied to the sill and jambs (left); later, after applying sealant to the flanges, the crew installed the window (below left) and then applied Moistop over the head flange (below).

Waterproofing Details

Needless to say, we had no choice but to replace the entire wall assembly. The trick was to rebuild it so that it looked the same as it had before we started, yet was still watertight.

As we reframed the wall, we added 2-by blocking around the window; this would provide solid backing for the waterproofing membranes we planned to install, since there would be no wall sheathing (**Figure 21**). And before reinstalling the window, we covered the sill and jamb framing with Moistop flashing, a 12-mil-thick fiberglass-reinforced membrane covered on both sides with water-resistant polyethylene (Fortifiber Building Systems Group).

After applying sealant to the window flanges and installing the window, we lapped Moistop over the head flange. For an additional layer of protection, we taped the window flanges with 12-inch-wide strips of 40-mil Jiffy Seal Ice & Water Guard (Protecto Wrap Co.), a self-adhering, rubberized waterproof membrane. Besides sealing the joint against water leakage, this thicker membrane does a good job of sealing around fasteners that penetrate it, helping to prevent the kind of damage we were repairing from recurring. In preparation for the stucco patch, we stapled 60-minute building paper to the framing, lapping it over onto the Jiffy Seal.

Next, we nailed primed 1x6s directly to the framing around the window, as a kind of sub-base for the window trim. With these in place, we could avoid having to nail the 2x6 trim directly through the stucco; also, they made it easier to create sealant joints between the window, trim, and stucco.

We left one ⅜-inch-wide gap between the window and the 1x6, and another between the 1x6 and the stucco J-mold surrounding the window. And we installed a primed G90 galvanized steel drip-edge over the trim at the head of the window. (If the original assembly had included drip metal over the trim at the head, it may have kept some of the water from getting into the wall assembly.) Then, after the ⅞-inch-thick three-coat stucco was applied, we inserted ½-inch-diameter closed-cell backer rod into the gaps.

Finally, we primed all surfaces of the new rough-sawn 2x6 Douglas fir trim and nailed it on over the 1x6s (**Figure 22**). (Because the original trim had not been back-primed before being installed, it had warped and twisted and couldn't be reused.)

To finish up, we caulked the sealant joints with a bead of SM7100 Permathane polyurethane sealant (Schnee-Morehead).

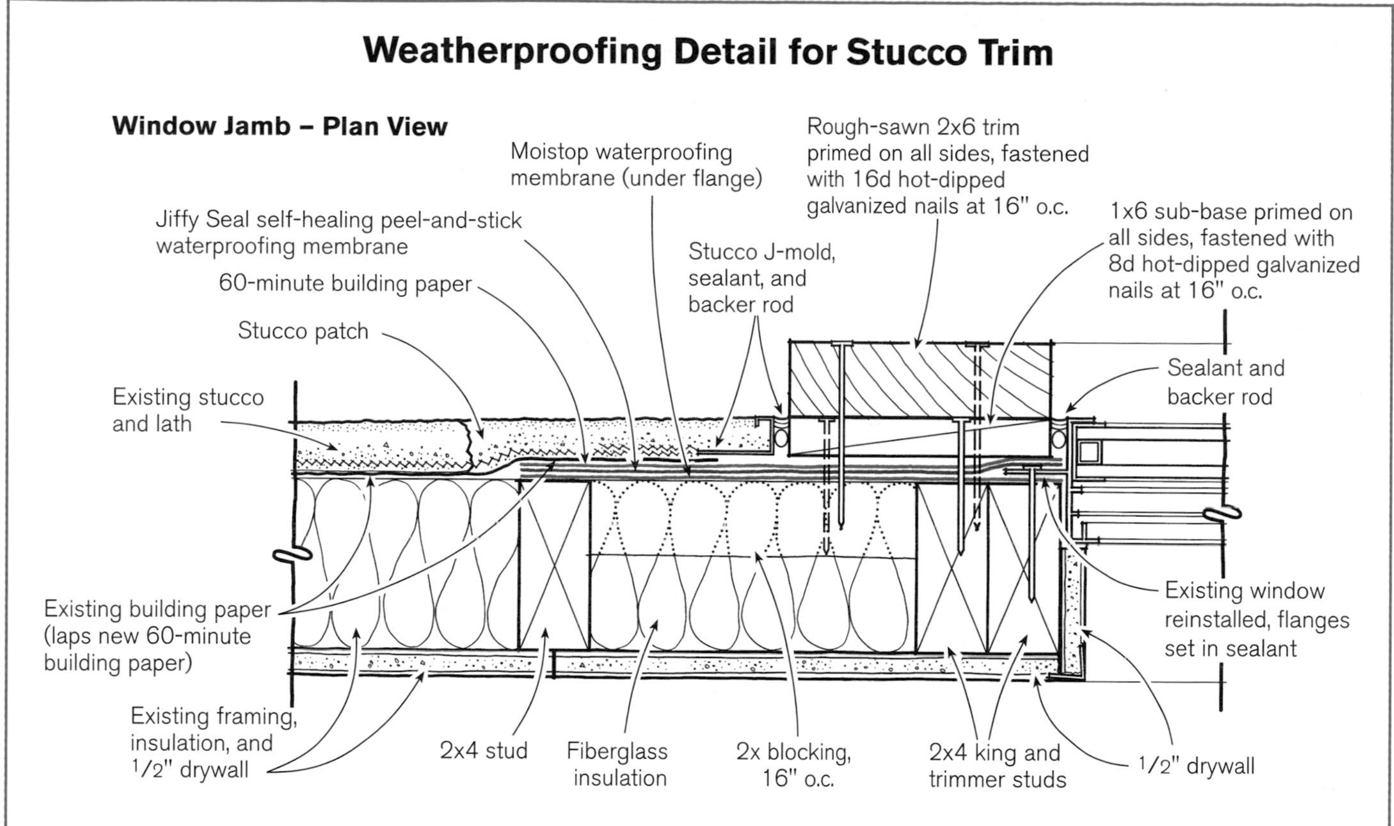

Figure 22. The reinstalled window trim relies on self-healing peel-and-stick membrane to prevent water from entering around the nail holes.

Looks Good, But Does It Leak?

To test the wall assembly, we set up our spray rack at the window and — because we wanted to be sure the assembly was watertight — sprayed it for an hour instead of the typical 15 minutes. We set the water pressure as high as we could, to get the greatest possible amount of water to hit the window and wall assembly. There was no leakage.

Two weeks later, the homeowner asked us to do the same repair on another window at his condo, which had the same damage. To his chagrin, I had to tell him that the damage we found probably exists throughout the entire condominium complex — anywhere trim is nailed through the stucco. Originally, we had thought that weather exposure had a lot to do with the amount of damage we found on the first window, since it was located on the south wall at the southeast corner of the building. But after we discovered that a neighbor had the same problem with windows facing to the north and west, we realized the problem wasn't an isolated one.

Since we performed this repair, Southern California has experienced heavy rains, and the homeowner called again to tell me that there was still leakage underneath the dining room wall. We went out to investigate one more time right after a rainstorm. Convinced that it wasn't our repair that was leaking, we went upstairs to examine the floor and wall in the closet above the window, and found that they were soaked, indicating that water was entering the wall higher up. We suspected that either the roof or a series of stucco cracks that we found in the same wall where we'd conducted our repair was the culprit.

So, on a dry day, I went back and sprayed the previously repaired window and wall assembly with a spray nozzle placed 18 inches away from the wall, to re-create the leaks that the homeowner saw during the rains. But, after spraying the wall for 20 minutes with a blast of water directed at the joints around the window and trim, I detected absolutely no water intrusion inside the condo. I then sprayed water on the wall over one of the stucco cracks, so that the water would sheet down the wall where the cracks occurred. Within just a few minutes, there was water leaking out of a soffit about 10 feet around the corner from where this crack was located, proving to me that water was also entering the wall assembly via cracks in the stucco.

Meanwhile, I also suspect that water damage from both nailed trim and stucco cracks is a widespread problem in this complex, and have recommended to the homeowners association that we conduct an investigation to determine the scope of damage.

David Dobson, AIA, is an architect, licensed general contractor, and glazing contractor in San Diego.

Watertight Details for EIFS

by Harrison McCampbell

As an architect and frequent consultant on waterproofing and building envelope failures, I see a lot of EIFS problems involving water leakage and resulting structural damage. Given the number of EIFS lawsuits involving homes built over the past decade, you'd think that builders would have learned the importance of water-shedding details (see "EIFS Details, pages 176 and 177). But it appears that surprisingly few have. That's unfortunate, because a little attention to a few key details can eliminate a huge amount of trouble down the road.

Caulk and Backer Rod

The key to a trouble-free EIFS application is the maintenance of a 1/2- to 3/4-inch gap wherever EIFS meets a non-EIFS material, such as roofing, trim, or doors and windows. The correct gap makes it possible to finish the exposed edges of the expanded polystyrene — which should be backwrapped with reinforcing mesh before the EPS is secured to the sheathing — with a waterproofing application of base coat when the rest of the finish goes on. Finally, the gap is filled with soft plastic backer rod and a bead of compatible caulk.

Good caulk, bad caulk. If it's going to last, the caulking has to be done right. The surface has to be clean and dry, the caulk space must be correctly filled with backer rod, and the caulk joint itself must be properly tooled (**Figure 23**). The backer rod serves two functions: First, it prevents the caulk bead from adhering to the back of the joint, allowing the caulk to flex in response to thermal expansion and contraction and other building movements. If the backer rod is omitted, the caulk will adhere to the back of the joint as well as the sides, limiting its ability to stretch and guaranteeing premature failure. Second, it controls the thickness of the finished application of caulk, which should ideally be about half as thick as it is wide.

It's in the truck. More often than not, though, the caulk and backer rod are never applied at all. (I'm always told, "They're in the truck.") That was the case in the repair job photographed here, where the polystyrene board was simply butted against the trim and other surfaces (**Figure 24**).

When you butt EIFS up against another material, the edge of the EPS board is now exposed to water absorption, since there is not enough space to apply the base coat. The caulking, if used at all, has less than 1/16 inch of EIFS surface to adhere to in order to seal against water entry.

I have even heard EIFS contractors try to defend themselves in a failed application by pointing out

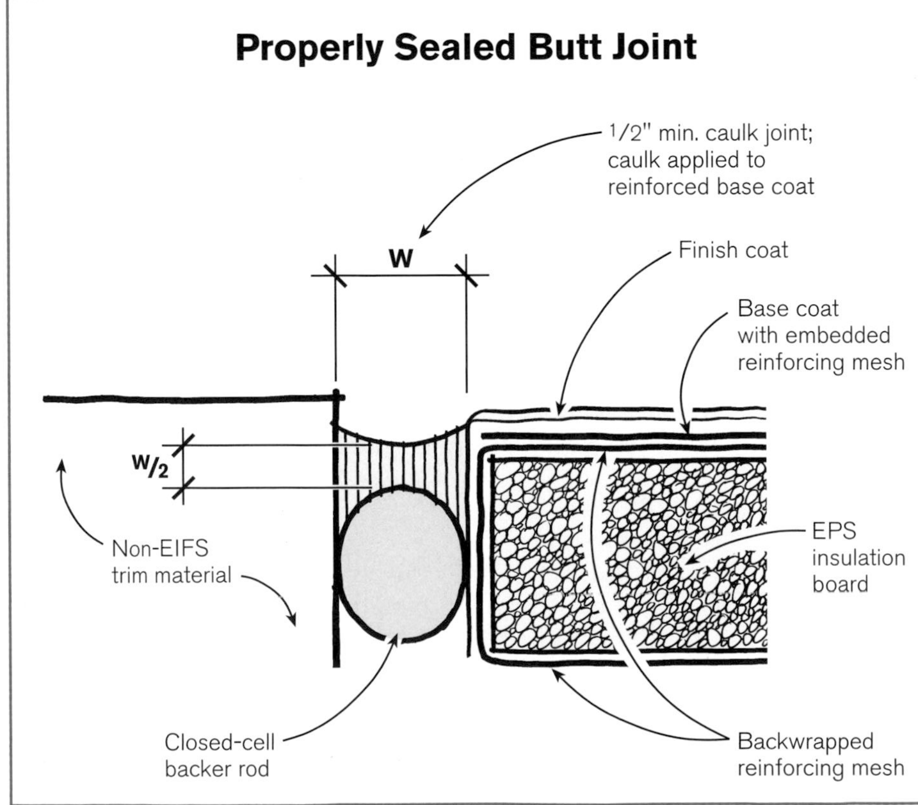

Figure 23. Wherever EIFS meets another material, backer rod must first be installed in the joint. This keeps the caulk from adhering to the back of the joint and allows it to stretch with building movements. A correctly tooled caulk bead has an hourglass shape that is about twice as wide as it is thick.

Figure 24. Moisture-soaked EIFS was butted directly against the gable-end trim in this photo. Water seeped through the resulting crack and penetrated the gypsum sheathing, which had turned to gray mud in some areas. Note the impression of the reinforcing mesh on the sheathing.

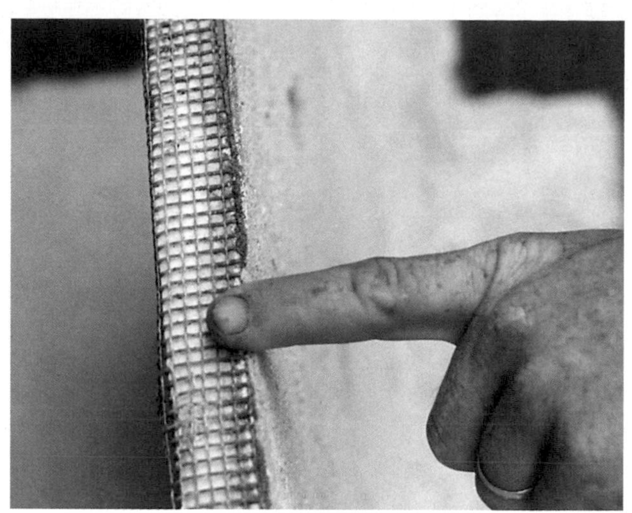

Figure 25. The EIFS applicator correctly backwrapped the edges of the polystyrene with mesh, as specified — a wasted effort, however, since the tight spacing made it impossible to apply EIFS to the edges of the sheets.

Figure 26. In a correctly executed butt joint — like the one in progress here — the edge of the insulation board is held back 1/2 to 3/4 inch, then backwrapped with mesh and base-coated. Note the backer rod and the well-tooled bead of caulk.

Figure 27. Headers and other horizontal surfaces must be protected with flashing. In this case, the damaged EIFS system has been stripped off, and a waterproof fiberglass-faced gypsum board screwed to the studs. The EPS board is attached to the sheathing with adhesive. Once the reinforcing mesh has been turned up at the front, the bottom edge of the sheet will receive a layer of base coat.

that they had diligently backwrapped the edges of the EPS board with mesh, as required. But unless the mesh-wrapped edges are also embedded in base coat, this does no good at all (**Figure 25**).

The solution in this case — as in so many others like it — was to tear off the improperly applied EIFS, repair the underlying water damage and rot, and reapply the EIFS system, this time leaving the required caulk spaces (**Figure 26**).

Flashing Details

Any joints between an EIFS wall and a flashed header should also include a suitable caulk space. I prefer soldered copper pan flashing in this application, because it's reliably leakproof and will last at least as long as the wall itself (**Figure 27**).

Better step flashing. Another common trouble spot is the joint where a wall meets step flashing at the edge of the roof. More often than not, the EIFS-covered

Incorrect Roof-to-Wall Installation

Finish coat
Base coat with embedded reinforcing mesh
Caulk joint
EPS insulation board
Roof shingles
Water migrates through failed caulk joint, soaking insulation and framing
Roofing felt
Step flashing

Correct Roof-to-Wall Installation

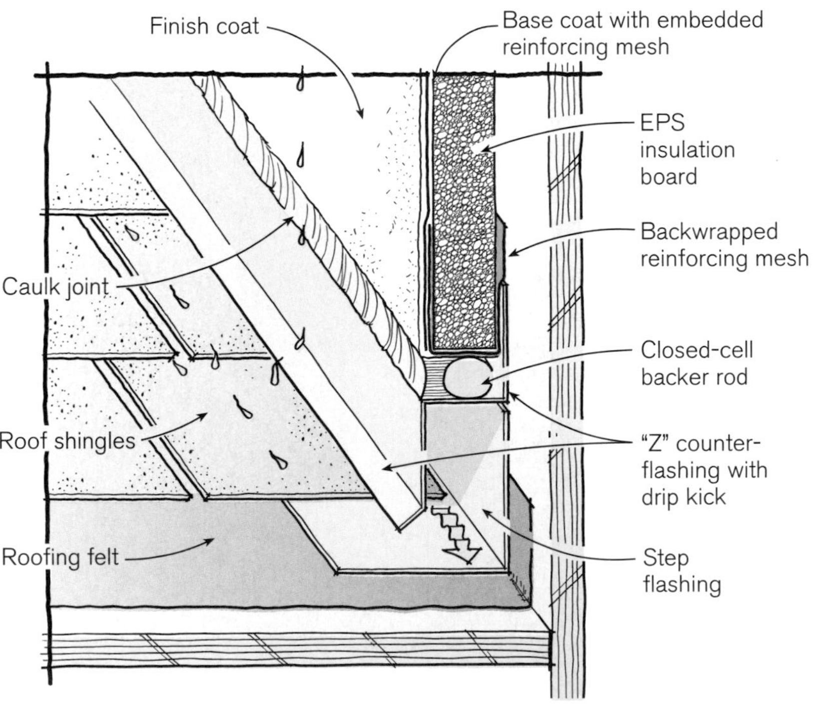

Figure 29. Where EIFS butts directly against the roof (top left), water will wick up into the foam board and eventually make its way past the flashing into the framing. The correct approach is to use a shaped counterflashing above the step flashing (above right). The additional vertical leg creates a ledge for caulk and backer rod, and it keeps the polystyrene board clear of water running along the roof.

Figure 28. Contrary to the manufacturer's recommendation and common sense, the EIFS applicator butted the edge of the polystyrene directly against the roofing, with no caulk space or counterflashing.

beadboard is simply butted and caulked against the shingles (**Figure 28**). Once this makeshift seal fails — as it soon does — the stage is again set for disaster as water wicks into the polystyrene, over the vertical leg of the flashing, and into the interior of the wall. Doing it right involves terminating the EIFS 2 inches above the roof, and including a run of counterflashing to provide a space for caulk and backer rod (**Figure 29**). When it's time to replace the original shingles, the roofer can slip the new shingles and step flashing beneath the counterflashing without damaging it.

Two-piece head flashing. In the case of head flashing — at the eaves wall of a dormer, for example — it's often impossible to replace the top course of shingles without bending the flashing up out of the way. When it's bent back into place afterward, the result can look pretty rough. Worse, bending and rebending the flashing can damage the caulk joint between the counterflashing and the EIFS, letting water seep through. A two-piece flashing like the one shown (**Figure 30**) allows the roofer to remove and reinstall the base flashing without affecting the counterflashing.

Harrison McCampbell, AIA, is a veteran EIFS troubleshooter in Nashville, Tenn.

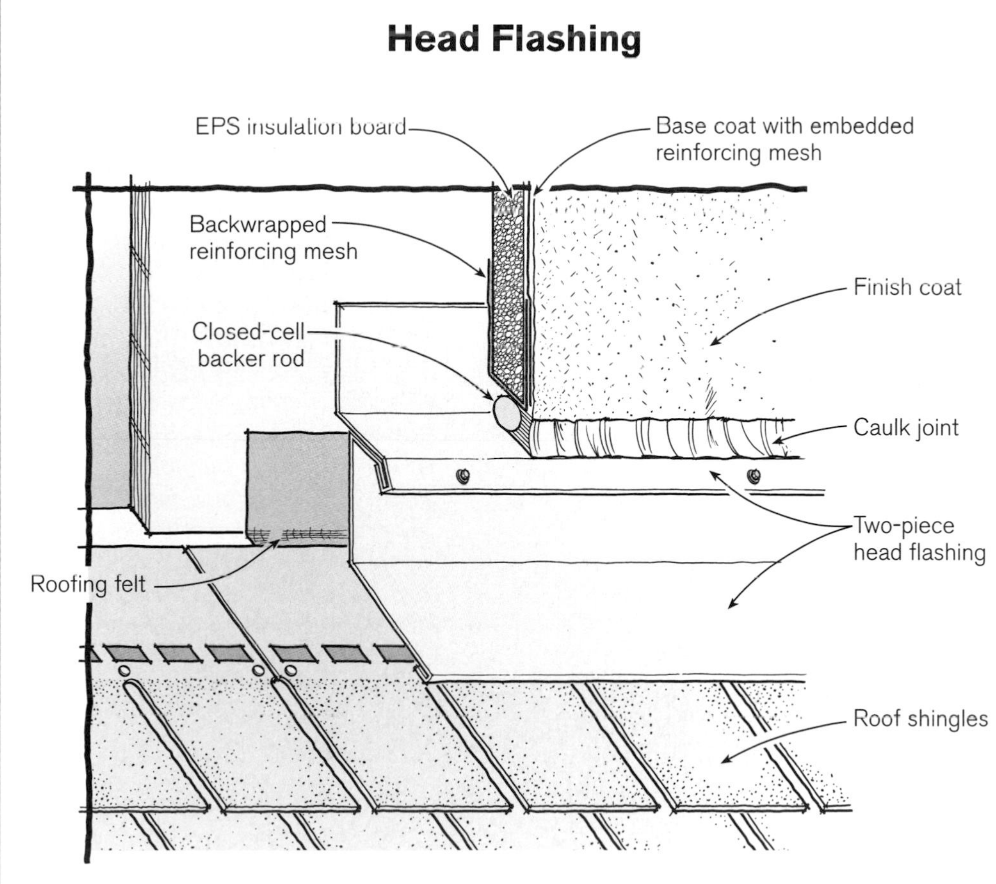

Figure 30. This two-piece head flashing provides a caulk space and makes it possible to renew the roofing without mangling the flashing. The counterflashing is secured to the base flashing with self-tapping sheet metal screws.

EIFS

Drainage EIFS Technique

Figure A. *A drainage EIFS relies on a drainage medium such as asphalt felt paper or housewrap to protect moisture-sensitive parts of the building against water that gets past the surface coatings. Foam board is attached over the drainage plane using mechanical fasteners; then base coat is troweled onto the foam, and fiberglass mesh is embedded in the base coat. Finally, a finish coat is applied over the reinforced base coat. Effective flashing details and joint sealing are critical to the success of the system.*

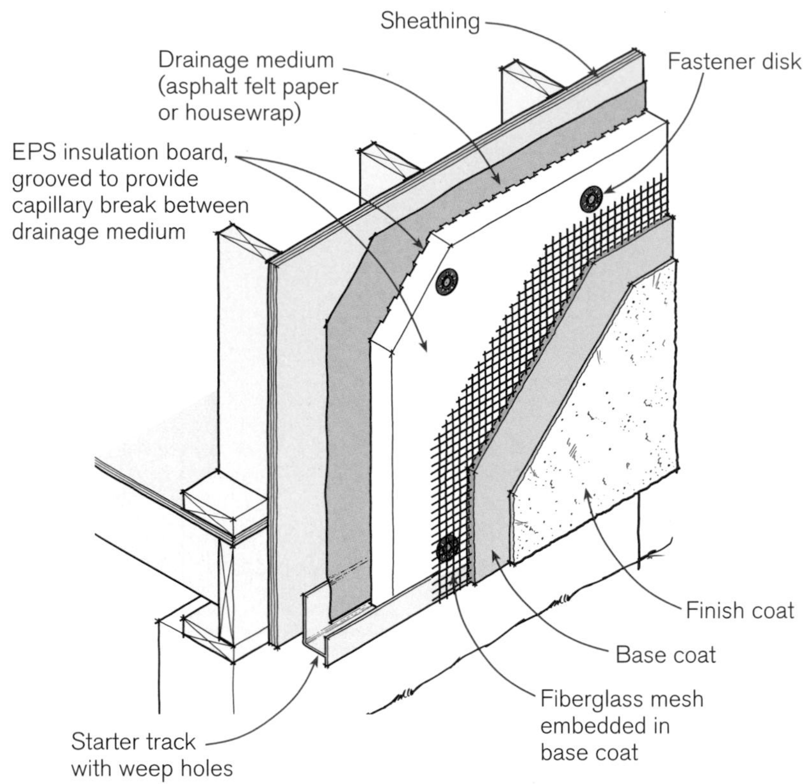

Grooved EPS insulation board
Sheathing
Drainage medium (asphalt felt paper or housewrap)
Peel-and-stick barrier membrane
Finish coat
Fiberglass mesh embedded in base coat
Fiberglass mesh
Finish coat
3/4" min. gap
Base coat
Sealant and backer rod
Peel-and-stick barrier membrane
Wrap reinforcing mesh
Base coat

EIFS Movement Joint

Figure B. *The EPS board in an EIFS can buckle when floor framing shrinks, causing cracks in the surface lamina, unless a movement joint is built into the system. There should be a 3/4-inch gap between the sheathing and EPS board, located at or above the midline of the band joist. A strip of peel-and-stick membrane should lap over the drainage medium on the lower floor and under the drainage medium on the upper floor. The expansion joint between EPS boards should be sealed with backer rod and silicone sealant.*

Details

Flashing Window Openings

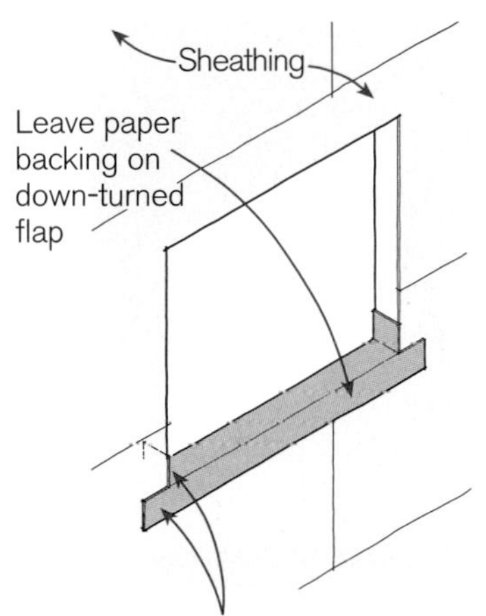

Step 1 – Peel and-stick membrane flashing cut on ends to allow one leg to turn up jamb and the other to continue onto sheathing.

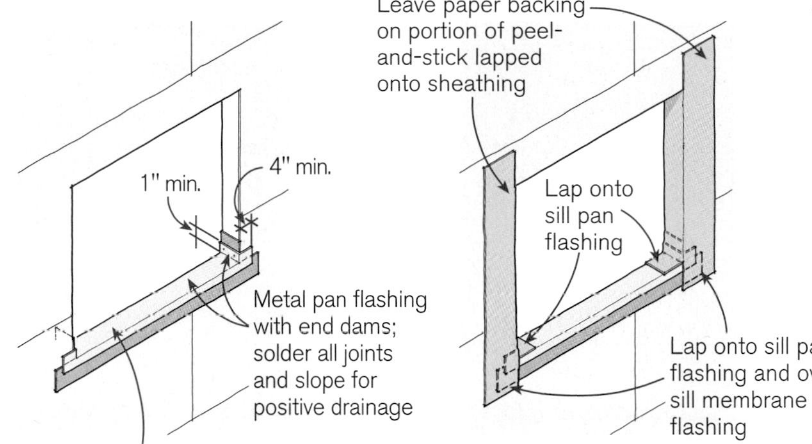

Step 2 – Place pan flashing at sill and fasten through jamb end dams.

Step 3 – Apply peel-and-stick membrane flashing to jambs.

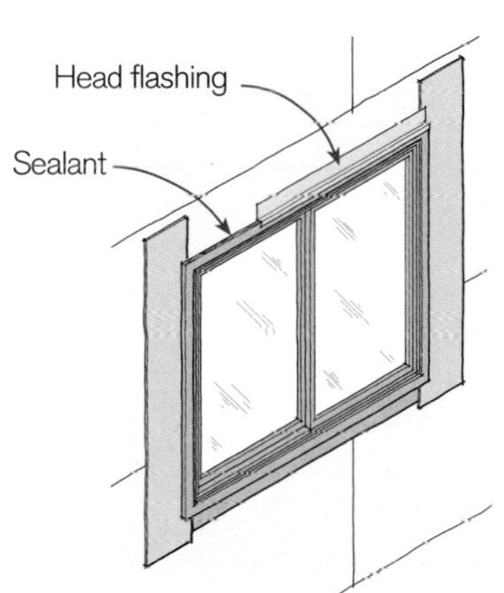

Step 4 – Install window in continuous bead of sealant (head and jamb locations only). Apply sealant to top of window flange and install head flashing.

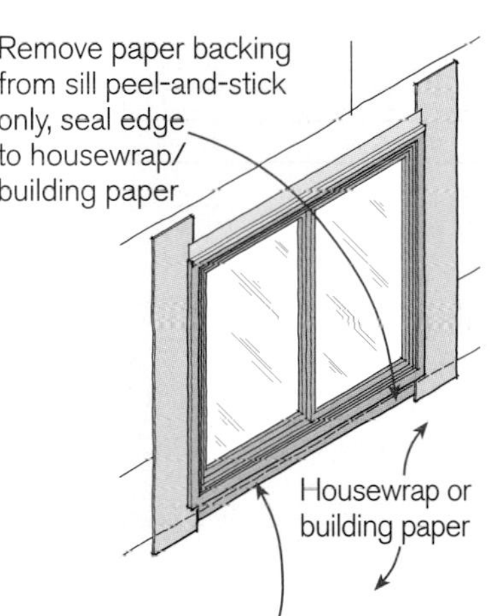

Step 5 – Install first course of housewrap or building paper under sill peel-and-stick flashing.

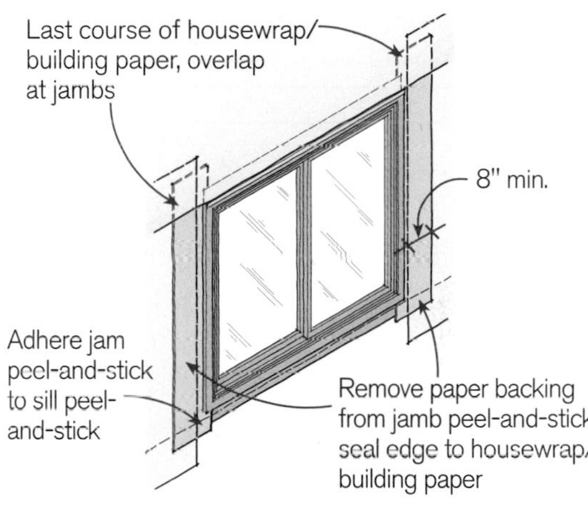

Step 6 – Install next course of housewrap or building paper under jamb peel-and-stick flashing. Install last course over head flashing.

Figure C. *Window openings for EIFS must be effectively flashed in a way that allows the flashing to tie into the building paper or housewrap that is applied after the window is set. The authors recommend covering the sill framing with a layer of peel-and-stick membrane, then placing a one-piece welded metal pan over the sill membrane. Next, side pieces of peel-and-stick can be installed to lap over the ends of the metal pan for a watertight assembly. The paper backing is left on the edges of the membrane, so that the membrane can later be sealed over the building paper or housewrap drainage plane used to cover the wall sheathing.*

Source: "Success With EIFS" by Russell J. Kenney & Michael E. Kenney

Chapter 10: Siding & Exterior Trim

- Durable Details for Exterior Trim
- Detailing Rain-Screen Siding
- Installing Cellular PVC Trim

Durable Details for Exterior Trim

by Paul Eldrenkamp

As a business owner, I try to minimize marketing and warranty costs. The most sensible way to do that is to build a finished product that looks as good in 10 years as it does right after completion. A good-looking job provides free advertising for my company, and the low maintenance of a durable exterior cuts down on callbacks and increases customer satisfaction.

I make it a policy to return to past projects regularly to see how the materials and techniques I use are faring. This practice has sometimes taught me more than I really wanted to know, but at least I've learned which exterior details do and don't work over time.

Good exterior work should weather gracefully and require a minimum of maintenance. Paint should gradually wear off rather than peel off, and discoloration from wear and grime should be even and unremarkable. Wood should never rot — where there is rot, there is poor craftsmanship or poor design. A durable exterior will need rejuvenation only every 10 years or so, and even then the work should be limited to simple, inexpensive preventive maintenance.

Flashing and Caulk

One key to long-lasting exterior finish details is proper flashing. Generally speaking, any piece of wood that sets more level than 45° should be flashed. Along skirtboards and cornice returns, I like to use lead flashing rather than water table or aluminum flashing because it performs well and ends up looking better in the long run. Cornice returns need flashing that continuously covers their entire tops and runs up and under the siding. And, although stock flashing profiles are good for many applications, I always have a metal brake on my job sites so that we can bend custom flashing when we need to.

One of the most common flashing failures I see is at the top of wall openings. When windows and doors are trimmed out, make sure that metal flashing caps off the trim to divert water that hits the siding. Behind the siding, make sure that the building paper overlaps this flashing. One related problem I sometimes see is siding that has been installed tightly against the window trim flashing or the skirt flashing. In these cases, the trim bends the flashing inward so that it forms a trough where water either gets trapped or drains out toward the vulnerable joints at the end of the flashing. To prevent problems, hold the siding up and away from the corner of the flashing. For even better results, bend flashing to 95° or 100° to ensure that water flows off the front edge.

Minimize caulking. If a joint doesn't look good without caulk, it will probably end up looking worse with caulk. Apart from being just about impossible to install well enough to act as a long-term water barrier, caulk can trap as much water in as it keeps out.

While most of us know how caulk is supposed to

Figure 1. Miter joints stay tight only when temperature and humidity match the day they were installed. When the weather changes, miters tend to open up and allow water to get in and cause rot.

Figure 2. Avoid miter joints on porch and deck stair trim. Instead, run stair risers long and butt the skirtboard into the risers.

be applied, few of us actually take the time and effort to do the job right. The result is an awful lot of wishful thinking, wasted effort, and hideous joints. It is far better to detail your work in such a way that it doesn't need caulk. The most obvious way to minimize caulking is to install even joints between pieces so they look good with no caulking at all.

Although I'm tempted to dismiss most uses of caulk as a band-aid approach to construction detailing, it's inevitably used. You'll do well, though, if you can limit caulk to uses where it acts as a behind-the-scenes sealant. Caulk works best when carefully applied to narrow joints between parallel surfaces that have been prepped with backer rod. It does not work at all when applied on top of an inside corner joint — which, of course, is how 90% of all caulk is applied.

Keep Joints Simple

My rule of thumb is to avoid fancy joints when installing exterior trim. Although I do advocate using scarf joints for corner boards and rakes, I steer clear of laps and rabbets. While these more intricate joints can increase strength and alignment in cabinetry, in exterior work they decrease durability by increasing the surface area and complexity of a joint. Joint strength and alignment are not problems with exterior details. Instead, the main objective is to avoid nooks and crannies where moisture can sit and collect.

Miters should be avoided because they fit tightly only at the humidity and temperature conditions at which they were first installed. In my New England climate, this is perhaps 25% of the time. The rest of the time, the joint is slightly open and the end grain soaks up moisture like a sponge (**Figure 1**). Premature paint failure and rot result. Try using butt joints that don't really butt — square ends with a 1/8-inch space between them. Spacing butt joints prevents water from getting trapped and will allow joints to dry out faster. Believe me, it requires as much skill and time to do a porch and stair with rigidly consistent 1/8-inch reveals between finish pieces as it does to do it with tight miters, so this should not be viewed as cheating. Furthermore, the 1/8-inch reveals will look good long after the "tight" miters are rotting and peeling.

There are also other trim-out tricks that avoid miter joints. For example, unlike interior stairs, which almost always have mitered joints between risers and an outer skirtboard, the risers on a porch stairway can run long past the skirt (**Figure 2**).

On corner boards and other wide trim, it's important to craft vertical and horizontal intersections in ways that prevent moisture from penetrating and getting trapped behind the exterior surfaces. I've found that stopping a vertical corner board on top of a properly flashed skirtboard makes for a more durable detail than the other way around. With this detail, it's important to keep a 1/8-inch space between the bottom of the corner board and the skirt flashing. A shallow back-cut will also help prevent wicking of moisture. The problem with corner boards that run down past the skirt is that water ends up getting into the butt end of the skirt. From there, moisture

Figure 3. The deep eaves on this remodel give extra protection to walls and windows beneath.

The Right Stuff

Paint protects exteriors by providing a renewable sacrificial wear surface. The paint takes the beating, and the underlying material is spared. With regular recoating, wood exteriors can last indefinitely. Compare this with vinyl, for example, which cannot be easily painted. Vinyl siding will start looking old and beat-up in about 20 years, and then the only realistic choice is to replace it. If you want the structures you build to last 50 to 100 years, as I think they should, use paintable materials, and install them in a way that allows the paint to adhere well over time.

Pine is commonly used as an exterior finish material, but it requires particular care because it rots very quickly through the end grain. If you have to use pine, make sure there's good draining and drying opportunity around pine end grain, and be sure to hit the ends with a thick coat of primer before installing. In fact, any piece of exterior wood you install should have a coat of primer or sealer applied on all faces and cut ends.

Wood Substitutes. Synthetic products or manufactured wood products that can be painted often hold up much better than wood over time.

For example, cellular PVC trim and moldings such as Celtec 550 (Vycom Corp.) or Azek (Azek Building Products), when painted, can only be distinguished from wood by the fact that they don't warp, check, rot, or bleed through. These materials can be used anywhere, including in direct rain and sunlight. Paint wears off rather than peels or flakes off, which is exactly what you want to happen. We use Celtec boards primarily for vertical trim such as corner boards (especially very wide ones) and casings (see photo). It also works well for frieze boards.

Wood substitutes, such as the Celtec 550 used for pilasters on this Greek Revival renovation, can look as good as wood while also lowering long-term maintenance needs.

MDO plywood, which is cheaper than cellular PVC, works well for soffits and other areas where edges are not exposed. I once used MDO plywood in a particularly grueling application: as a south-facing slide on a toddler playground. Even under these extreme conditions, all it has needed for maintenance is a coat of paint every two years. MDF also works in exterior applications as long as all faces and cut edges are sealed prior to installation.

But remember, joints need to be flashed — don't rely on caulk alone. I would not use either MDO or MDF in areas where they would be frequently hit with direct rain and sun unless I was willing to be particularly vigilant about maintaining a thick enough protective paint layer. For example, I often see people applying wood moldings to MDO panels to create a frame-and-panel effect, especially on storefronts. This detail doesn't wear well over time because water gets into the joint between the molding and the panel and stays there. Trapped moisture then penetrates the panel at nail holes and along the edges, leading to chronic paint failure and eventual rot.

Although I have not used fiber-cement products myself, everyone I've talked to who has finds them extremely durable as an exterior cladding material.

Windows and Doors. Ordering wood windows preprimed at the factory will pay for itself by protecting the wood and saving job-site prep time. When trimming out wood windows, the sill is most vulnerable to water damage, especially if it has finger joints.

Avoid wood storm doors, or carefully select which ones you use. I came to this conclusion with regret because I grew up in Iowa, accustomed to the slam of a spring-loaded wood screen door. But every time we've installed pine combination storm doors, we've had to come back repeatedly to adjust them. The pine expands and contracts excessively with seasonal moisture swings and is also prone to twisting and warping, especially when exposed to direct sunlight.

A quality wood-core clad storm door will perform much better because the cladding greatly improves the stability of the underlying wood. If a storm door has to be wood, go all out and get a good exterior wood like cedar or a hardwood. — *P.E.*

Figure 4. If drip-edge is installed too close to the fascia, rain runoff will drain over the boards and lead to discoloration. The author recommends spacing drip-edge slightly off of exterior trim to direct water outward.

soaks the sheathing and creeps upward.

Eaves and gutters. Always try for deeper eaves and rakes — 8 inches at a minimum — to help prevent water from sheeting down exterior siding (**Figure 3**, page 181). Drip-edge should also be spaced about 1/4 inch off the fascia to keep water from running down the fascia and discoloring it (**Figure 4**). Adding a second molding along the top of the fascia can help position drip-edge even further outward. Although it goes against what some people want to see, an even more durable design detail is to cut rafters square instead of plumb to lower the chance of roof runoff draining onto fascia boards.

Finally, install gutters so that there's no way for water to run between a gutter and the fascia. Use flashing rather than caulk to bridge this gap (**Figure 5**). Clogged gutters don't work and inevitably lead to water damage. In my experience there are two ways to handle this problem: Chop down all trees within 100 feet of the house, or clean the gutters regularly (four times a year or more). Stress to homeowners that they need to clean their gutters more frequently than they probably do now. It's a relatively cheap way to protect their investment.

Decks and Porches

Exterior living spaces must be detailed differently from interiors because everything must shed water and dry easily. If you install a pine baluster so that the bottom end butts tight to the bottom rail and the assembly is exposed to weather, I can almost guarantee that within five years you will be able to put your thumb clear through the bottom 2 inches of the baluster. A few subtle design changes can keep

Figure 5. Properly flashed gutters keep water out from between the gutter and fascia boards. Gutters should also be cleaned frequently to prevent clogging and overflow.

Figure 6. The bottoms of wooden porch and deck balusters are particularly prone to rot when they rest directly on a flat bottom rail. End-dipping balusters always helps, but it's best to use alternative designs such as running balusters through the decking (far left) or using a chamfered bottom rail that drains water (left).

Figure 7. Prevent water penetration where rails join newels by adequately priming the end cut of a rail. It also helps to avoid rails that are wider than 5½ inches. When newels posts are wrapped, butt the rails directly against the trim instead of running rails through to the post, where water will get trapped.

baluster bottoms relatively dry, such as running balusters through the decking or setting them onto a chamfered bottom rail (**Figure 6**). If you can't detail the railing to avoid a horizontal butt joint, soak the ends of the balusters in preservative or coat them heavily with primer before assembly.

You also have to be careful where sloping top and bottom rails hit a newel post. Although there is no way to entirely prevent moisture from collecting at this junction, there are ways to minimize the problem. First, avoid rails that are wide and flat on the top side. Second, if you're wrapping a post with trim boards, avoid running the rails through to the structural newel underneath, because water will also run through and become trapped in the void between the wrapping and the newel (**Figure 7**). Also make sure to adequately prime and coat the end of the rail to prevent excessive wicking of moisture.

Wide and flat or minimally pitched surfaces — like wide railings, wall caps, or newel caps — also present problems. My rule of thumb is to use metal flashing whenever the wood is wider than 5½ inches. For example, I run a piece of flashing completely over column caps (**Figure 8**).

Decking. The recent spate of nail-free wood deck fastening systems has developed in response to the fact that nails don't work so well over time. Big fat-headed nails create water-collecting depressions if you set them too deep; or they rip the skin off bare feet if you don't set them deep enough and the wood shrinks around the nail. Alternatively, you can use a

Figure 8. Flat surfaces are especially susceptible to water damage and require taking special precautions. On this porch, the column cap is completely capped with metal flashing, and the decorative trim above is also extensively flashed.

lot of finish nails, but they won't hold over time, yielding a creaky deck.

The deck fastener we like best is the Eb-Ty (Blue Heron Enterprises), which is installed using a biscuit joiner. You'll have to be careful estimating a job using these fasteners because they take three to four times longer to install than conventional fasteners. And, the Eb-Ty only works well with stable decking lumber. Don't try them with shrinkage-prone pressure-treated wood because shrunken wood can actually slip off the plastic biscuits. But for clients who are willing to pay the premium, nail-free decks are worth the extra hassle. A well-done deck or porch with no surface nails is about the smoothest and most glorious sight you'll encounter on a project (**Figure 9**). Waltz on it in your bare feet without fear.

Clear preservatives just don't work to control color even though they might work to preserve the wood. Clients often see a gleaming new wood deck and say, "I want it to keep looking just like that." So we obligingly put down a clear preservative. And the deck looks "just like that" for a few months, and then starts becoming a mottled gray-black that's not all that attractive. The only way to control the color of decks over time is with a pigmented preservative. I prefer to use a semitransparent stain and recoat every one or two years.

Paul Eldrenkamp owns Byggmeister Inc., a remodeling company in Newton, Mass.

Figure 9. Nail-free decking systems can dress up a job and reduce points of water penetration. Notice how the author's crew flashes off the newel tops before installing caps.

Detailing Rain-Screen Siding

by Gary Katz and Bill Robinson

Most of us have worked on old homes where the exterior trim and siding were still in great shape: no cupping, bowing, twisting, or rot. As often as not, the wood is old-growth Douglas fir, and none of it — the back of the siding, the back of the brick mold, the back and bottoms of the exterior jambs — is back-primed. In many cases, not even the bottoms of the doors were painted! Try that today.

Lumber these days is never old growth and hardly even "new growth" — a lot of it is more like "instant growth." Just look at the growth rings in a piece of siding or a 1x6 trim board. This new-growth wood is less durable, less dimensionally stable, and less able to hold paint than the material used a generation ago. This requires new building practices. We can no longer install doors without priming and finishing all six sides. In fact, most door manufacturers will no longer guarantee doors finished in dark colors or installed without adequate overhang protection.

Figure 10. Build-out blocks of pressure-treated plywood will provide an air space behind the wood window trim. To separate wood from wood, the authors covered the blocks with building paper before nailing up the trim.

New Products, Old Solution

The need for new building practices is most critical with siding and exterior trim — and not just because of new-growth lumber. There are also new manufactured lumber products on the market that perform differently than old-growth wood, and energy practices and housewrap technology have changed since those older homes were built.

Walls are no longer breathable cavities supported by let-in braces and wrapped with layers of felt paper. Instead, they've become sealed envelopes wrapped with plastic. Housewrap manufacturers are constantly improving their products by dimpling, creasing, and texturing them to encourage drainage. But the frac-

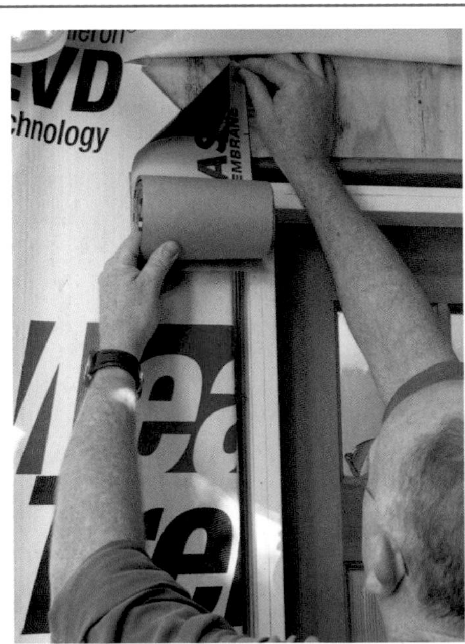

Figure 11. Peel-and-stick flashing tape seals the gap between the door jamb and the drainage plane.

tional stand-off space provided by bumps and wrinkles isn't always enough to offset the quality of marginal building materials, poor design and detailing, or the pressure differentials that drive moisture vapor through siding and housewrap and into wall cavities.

Oddly enough, one of the most effective moisture-control techniques has been used — at least in part — for decades. What carpenters once called furring strips are used today to build "rain screen" walls, which are the best way to ensure long-lasting trim and siding installations.

But there's more to a rain screen than simply nailing spacers on top of your housewrap. Here, we'll review the advantages of rain-screen walls and describe the details that make them work.

Reasons for Failure

Let's begin by looking at the reasons modern siding and trim fail. Growth rings are only part of this puzzle. First of all, except for vinyl siding, all exterior claddings are "reservoir" products. They absorb moisture even if they're primed on all sides.

For a variety of reasons, moisture will find its way into siding and trim through minute cracks and crevices no matter how tightly the siding and trim are sealed. Poor water-shedding designs, failure to prime end cuts, installation directly against pressure-treated or high-moisture-content substrates, and installation too close to grade are all obvious reasons why moisture penetrates siding and trim.

There are also a couple of less visible causes of excess moisture in siding and trim, namely the air-pressure difference between the outside of the wall and the back of the siding and trim, and the capillary action of water moving between materials tightly sandwiched together. Wind and wind-driven rain cause positive pressure against the exterior of a building — but there's no pressure on the back of exterior cladding.

This pressure difference creates a vacuumlike effect, so that moisture is both driven and sucked through capillary action into the exterior siding and trim. Even if proper water-shedding details are in place, capillary suction alone can draw water vertically up behind siding boards, and especially through small cracks at butt joints and even nail holes.

Once the exterior cladding absorbs enough moisture, the pressure differential can, in extreme cases, drive water vapor through the housewrap into the exterior sheathing and wall cavity. If this vapor ever reaches its dew-point temperature, it can condense inside the building envelope. Since liquid water cannot pass through plastic housewrap, it's trapped in the wall, where it can cause rot and mold.

Felt paper is the only housewrap that will absorb water within the wall and allow it to dry toward the outside, but the force of positive pressure will often prevent that. At the very least, saturated housewrap

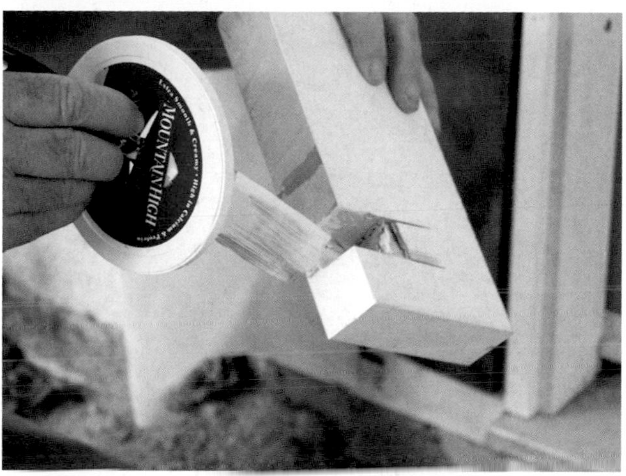

Figure 12. Covering the 1/2-inch plywood spacer with building paper (top) helps prevent water from moving between the wood trim and the plywood block. All cut edges should be primed before installation (center). Note the 1/2-inch jamb extension (bottom), which brings the back of the trim out flush with the top of the spacer blocks.

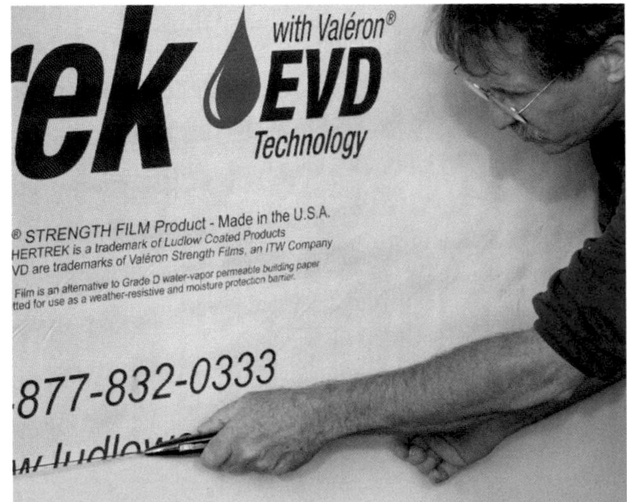

Figure 13. Custom-bent vinyl flashings tuck in beneath the housewrap above doors and windows (top) and at the water table (center and bottom), bringing any water that reaches the drainage plane back out to the surface.

and moisture-laden walls will accelerate the deterioration of exterior siding, trim, and paint.

A Ventilated Air Space

Rain-screen walls, sometimes referred to as "pressure-equalized assemblies," solve these problems because they provide a ventilated air space that defeats the air-pressure difference. Properly detailed, they also provide a drainage plane — a way for any water that does get behind the siding to escape. And compared with the cost of replacing trim and siding that have failed prematurely, building a rain-screen wall is by no means prohibitively expensive.

The requirements for an effective rain screen are

- a minimum 3⁄8-inch air gap between the back of the cladding and the drainage plane;
- ventilation to assist in drying and to partially equalize the pressure on the cladding;
- drainage at the bottom;
- a rigid drainage plane and air barrier.

In essence, a rain-screen wall — a ventilated gap or cavity providing drainage and a capillary break — works by promoting air circulation.

Prepping for Trim

As with most construction projects, the first step in building a rain screen is establishing the correct sequence. On the recent remodeling project shown here, we began by wrapping the wall, making sure that all window and door penetrations were properly flashed and sealed (see "Flashing a Flanged Window," page 198). The housewrap or drainage plane must be air- and watertight to prevent liquid water and air from passing through from outside to inside.

Rather than furring out the windows, which would create an offset in the drainage plane, we installed them against the sheathing and housewrap, then applied furring for trim and siding on top of the flashing (**Figure 10**, page 186). By leaving the trim — simple flat stock — slightly proud of the windows, we avoided creating a potential dam in the drainage plane.

To match the window trim, we chose to install a door with no brick mold; we added plinth blocks and flat casing afterward. This allowed us to run the drainage plane right onto the face of the door frame (**Figure 11**, page 186). Since we were using 1⁄2-inch-thick furring strips for the siding and furring blocks for the trim, we had to add 1⁄2-inch jamb extensions to the doors before installing the casing. We opted for the individual furring blocks instead of a continuous furring strip because we thought they would provide better air circulation behind the trim.

We covered the pressure-treated furring blocks with flashing or housewrap to isolate the trim from the blocks (**Figure 12**, page 187). We also sealed every

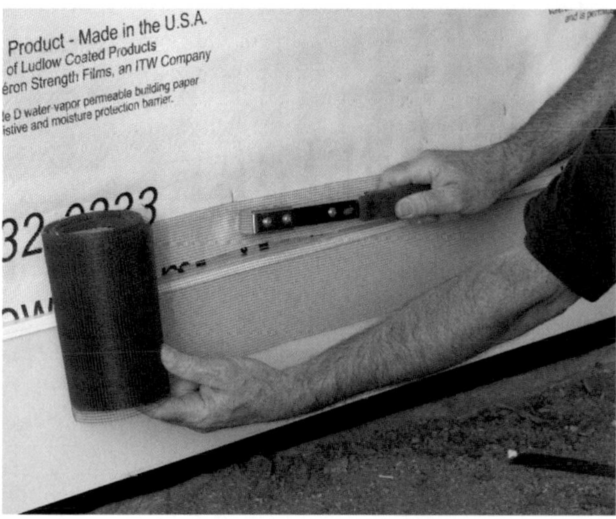

Figure 14. Two 3-inch-wide polypropylene-mesh vent strips — one at the top, one at the bottom — help provide continuous ventilation behind the siding (top and center). For good measure against bugs, the strips were first wrapped in insect screening (bottom).

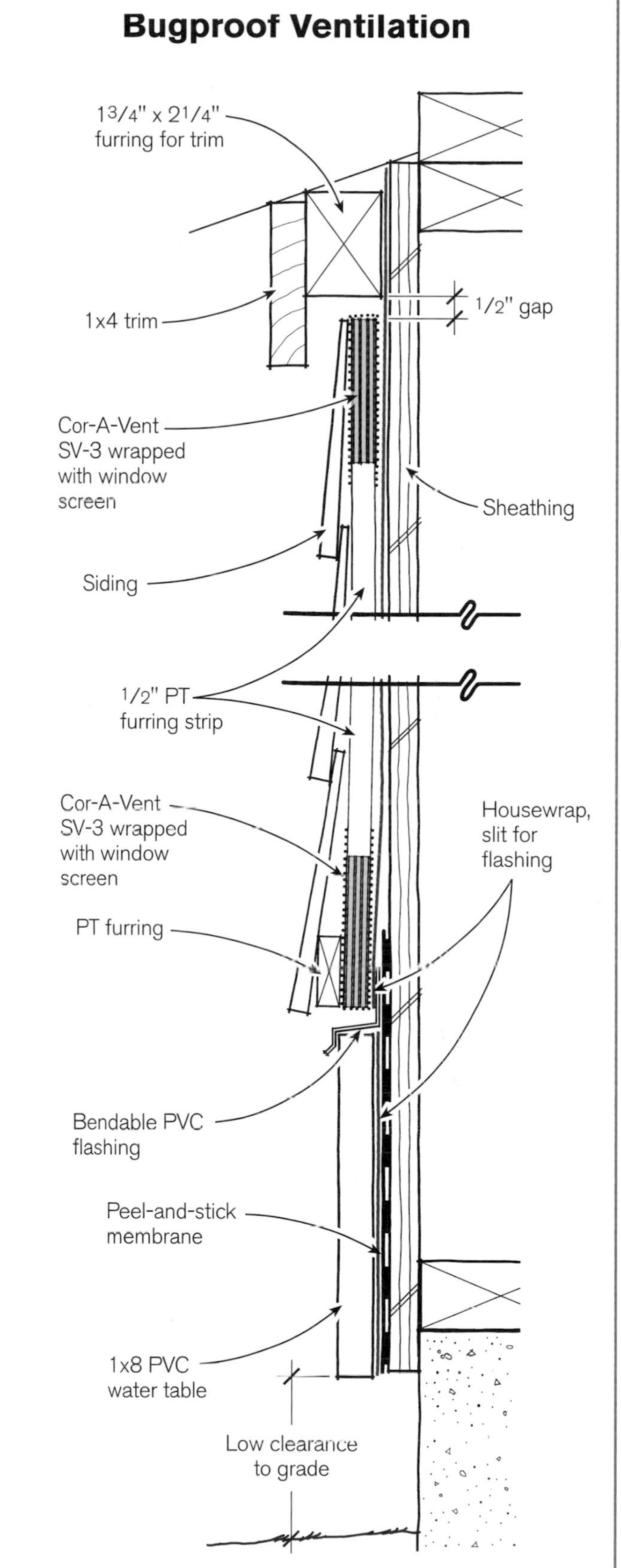

Figure 15. To allow air to circulate in the vent space but keep insects out, insect screening is needed along the top and bottom of the space.

Figure 16. With corner boards installed, along with the last $^1/_2$-inch furring strips, the wall is ready for the horizontal wood siding.

cut and notch in the trim with two coats of primer. The height of backing blocks above the doors and windows was determined by the upper trim detail, where head flashings were later installed (**Figure 13**, page 188).

Once the door and window trim was installed, we turned to the water table, where scant clearance to grade required special attention. Before wrapping the house, we applied a self-adhesive membrane at the bottom of the wall to protect the wood sheathing, then used PVC trim — a rotproof, nonreservoir material — for the water table.

After attaching the water table, we carefully sliced through the housewrap and inserted a custom-bent PVC flashing.

Vent Screening

To prevent bugs from infiltrating the rain-screen cavity, some type of screening is needed at the top and bottom of the ventilation cavity. For extra protection, we decided to combine Cor-A-Vent corrugated plastic venting material (Cor-A-Vent Inc.) with insect screening. First we attached a layer of ordinary window screening, and then we installed the Cor-A-Vent SV-3, wrapping the window screen over the SV-3 (**Figure 14**, previous page).

We repeated the same steps at the top of the wall, but because this overhang had no soffit, we installed backing for the eaves trim beforehand. This allowed us to hide the ventilation strip behind the trim at the top of the wall (**Figure 15**, previous page).

Finally, we installed corner boards and intervening furring strips (**Figure 16**), and the wall was ready for siding.

Well Worthwhile

Material and labor costs for the rain-screen wall were not excessive. On an average home, a rain screen might add $2,000 to the cost, but the savings in maintenance and the increased longevity of the exterior paint more than compensate for the additional investment.

Gary Katz is a finish carpenter in Reseda, Calif.

Bill Robinson is a general contractor in Arroyo Grande, Calif.

Installing Cellular PVC Trim

by Jim Blahut

My company, Perennial Homes, works exclusively in the affluent community of Beach Haven, N.J., which is known for its attractive Victorian-era homes. As a design/build firm, our niche is building new homes with attractive exterior details like flat casing, window and door pediments, and wide corner boards. My customers value these exterior details, and we take pride in creating exteriors that retain a historic look. Our biggest problem in the past has been that the elaborate wood trim that gives our homes their Queen Anne style simply rots away on New Jersey's weather-beaten coast. When composite and plastic trim became available several years ago, I thought it might be a good solution for the hardship of coastal weather and the limitations of wood trim. I hoped to find a trim product that wouldn't change the aesthetics of our popular homes and wouldn't require as much homeowner maintenance as painted pine or cedar.

In our first attempt to find a long-lasting and good-looking exterior trim, we tried a hardboard-type composition product that promised lifetime durability and low maintenance. But it became apparent shortly after installation that the product had some limitations. Where the factory surface was disturbed from cutting or fastening, the material would swell, resulting in extra surface preparation by our painter. The hardboard's dimensional changes from wet weather and high humidity also made paint adhesion difficult (**Figure 17**).

The next leg of our search led us to urethane, which has excellent dimensional stability and because of its composition should last a lifetime. But it wasn't right for us because it relies on its outer skin for an attractive appearance, and the exterior details on our homes require frequent ripping and machining of trim. When exposed, urethane's soft core looks a little spongy and inconsistent.

For almost three years now, we've been using Azek (Azek Building Products), which has held up well and retains the look of wood that our customers value. The PVC-based trim material is impervious to salt spray; it machines, cuts, and fastens like wood; and it's the only synthetic trim material we've found that can be machine-sanded. We've been happy with Azek's performance so far, but it requires some special installation techniques to take full advantage of its durability and good looks. This is because its plastic composition behaves a little differently than wood.

Special Techniques

One of the drawbacks of plastic trim like Azek is its greater expansion and contraction compared to wood. On cold days, gaps can develop at unglued butt joints and miters. On long lengths of trim like corner boards or fascia, those gaps can be obvious, so we overlap joints with opposing 45° bevels, glue them with PVC cement, and put some construction adhesive on the back side (**Figure 18**, next page). The adhesive securely attaches the joint to the house, and some extra nails at joints and board ends actually force the material to stretch in the center, preventing unsightly voids as the

Figure 17. This hardboard product started showing signs of swelling after a year, even though the manufacturer's installation instructions were carefully followed (far left). The Azek's PVC composition has held up better and still looks good three years after installation (left).

Securing PVC Joints

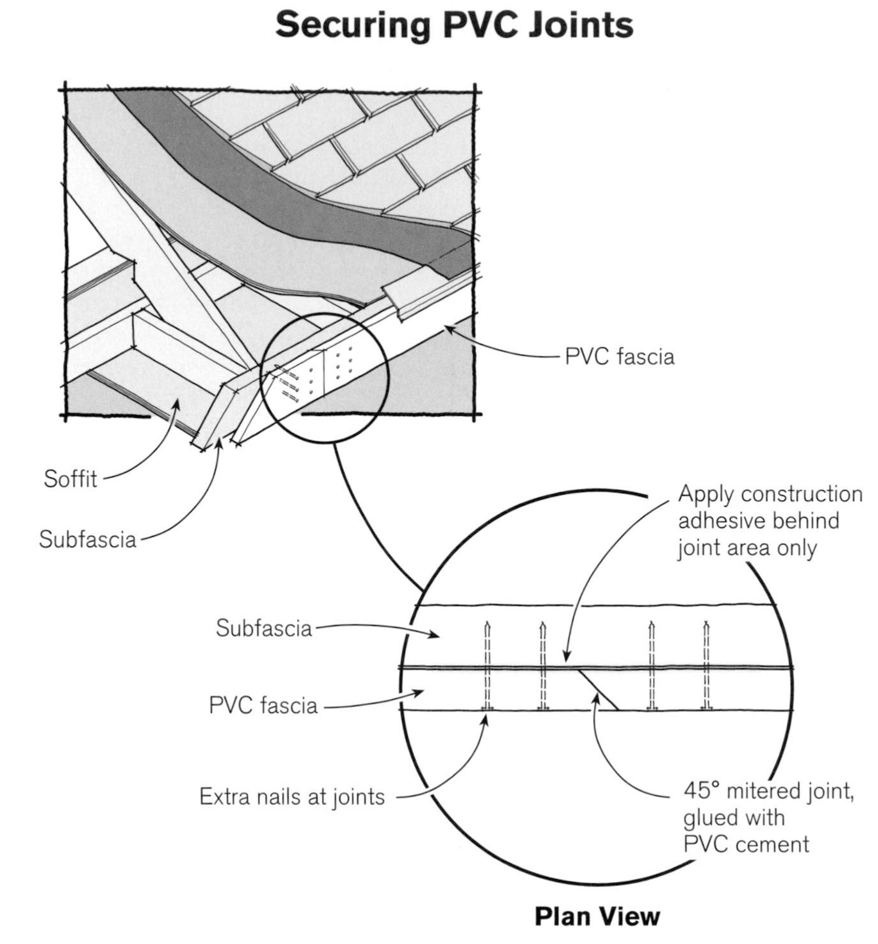

Figure 18. Because of PVC's tendency to expand and contract, the author uses extra nails and construction adhesive at joints so the gap will stay closed as the material moves.

Figure 19. Gluing corner boards with PVC cement keeps joints tight and makes installation easier. The author's crew hides expansion gaps with a slight back-cut on the bottom of corner boards where ordinary gaps would be more obvious.

material shrinks. Intersecting trim (corner boards terminating in a frieze, for example) should have a gap of 1/4 inch for every 20 feet of length, so we leave 1/8 inch at each end to make the gap less noticeable. Gaps aren't a big deal high up on the house, but in more visible areas, like the bottom of corner boards, we back cut the bottom edge to further hide the gap (**Figure 19**). Without a little room to move, warm temperatures can cause the trim to expand and buckle.

Plastic materials also get brittle in cold weather, so poorly placed fasteners might create a crack, especially if temperatures are close to freezing. We keep nails 3/4 inch away from board edges and stagger them slightly. Staggering fasteners also reduces the likelihood of a crack along the line of fasteners as the material contracts and tension increases.

Azek claims that its product won't yellow with age and doesn't require painting. Nevertheless, we always paint it because the brush strokes make it nearly indistinguishable from painted wood, and a couple of coats of acrylic-latex paint offer some additional protection from the elements. We use only 100% acrylic paints because they really stick to the material, and we prefer light colors rather than dark. Dark colors absorb more heat, resulting in greater expansion and

Figure 20. PVC cement actually fuses corners together. This keeps corners tight and eliminates a possible source of water infiltration. Joints must be held together tightly with nails or screws while the glue sets, because the cement can't bridge gaps like other adhesives.

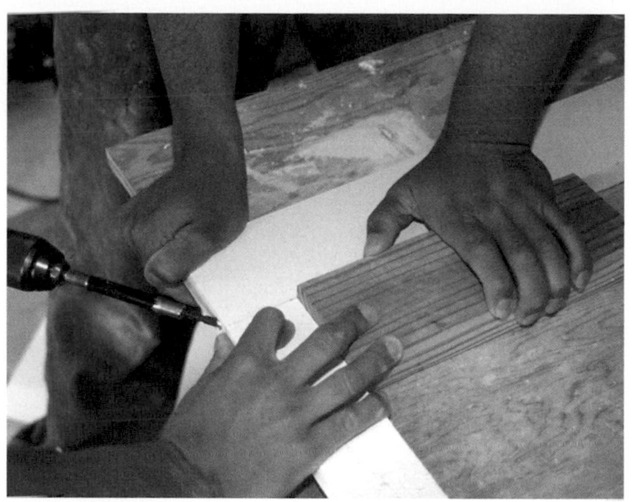

Figure 21. The author predrills at an angle and drives in some galvanized screws to hold the assembly tight while the glue dries. A scrap of 2-by makes for a true 90° angle and provides backup for drilling and fastening. To make several frames of the same size, cut the 2-by to the same dimension as the casing's inside length.

softening of the material. Although we've experimented with darker colors and had good results so far, in climates warmer than ours they could result in saggy or bulging trim. It's best to stick with light shades or try dark shades before committing.

Casing Windows

We always preassemble our window casing in a four-sided frame in the shop and then install it on site in one piece over the window's nailing fin. Framing up the casing in this way has several key advantages. Using windows with a nailing fin creates a surface that isn't perfectly flat for trim. Because the fin is proud of the sheathing, casings tend to roll back toward their outside edges. Some builders put a thin rabbet on the back of the casing or shim the outside edge to match the thickness of the nailing flange. Both methods work, but preassembling the casing into a frame eliminates the additional step. Our method literally fuses the corners together with cement, which eliminates a source of water infiltration as well as gaps caused by cooler temperatures. Finally, cutting and assembling the casing gives us a foul-weather project when coastal storms prevent us from working outside.

We start our casing process by making a cut schedule when the windows show up on site. I measure the frame and add about 3/16 inch to allow for caulking and contraction in cold weather. Large picture units get a little larger gap, and on twin and triple mulled units I add 1/16 inch for each additional window on top of the 3/16. I keep a file of measurements for future jobs; sometimes I have all the dimensions I need to make the frame assemblies without taking any new measurements.

The assembly process is straightforward. I start with a scrap of 2-by screwed to my workbench, which helps me get a true right angle and provides backup for predrilling and running in screws. If I'm making a few frames of the same size, it's easier if the 2-by is cut to the same length as the inside width of the casing frame. I make certain that both ends of my scrap are cut square, and I build the casing around it, starting at the bottom. I glue all joints with Gorilla's low-odor PVC cement (Gorilla PVC Cement), which cleans up with water. The cement works the same as plumber's PVC cement and keeps everything nice and tight during changes in temperature. But just like plastic plumbing fittings, the pieces need to be held tight, because the PVC cement won't bridge even small gaps (**Figure 20**). Then, I predrill at an angle and fasten the pieces with galvanized deck screws to hold the assembly tight while the glue sets (**Figure 21**).

After both bottom corners are fastened, I move on to the top. Our typical detail includes a 4-inch side casing with a 6-inch head casing to better reproduce older architectural styles. I fasten the top in the same manner, running it over the cut end of the side casing. The head casing gets a small piece of 1-by stock mounted on top, meant to replicate a traditional wood drip cap (**Figure 22**). I rip this out of a larger piece of Azek and

Figure 22. The drip cap used here is meant to reproduce a traditional wood cap and is ripped from a larger piece of Azek. One of Azek's strengths is that it allows you to sand out saw marks and other imperfections; other products "fuzzed," melted, or created extra work for the painter.

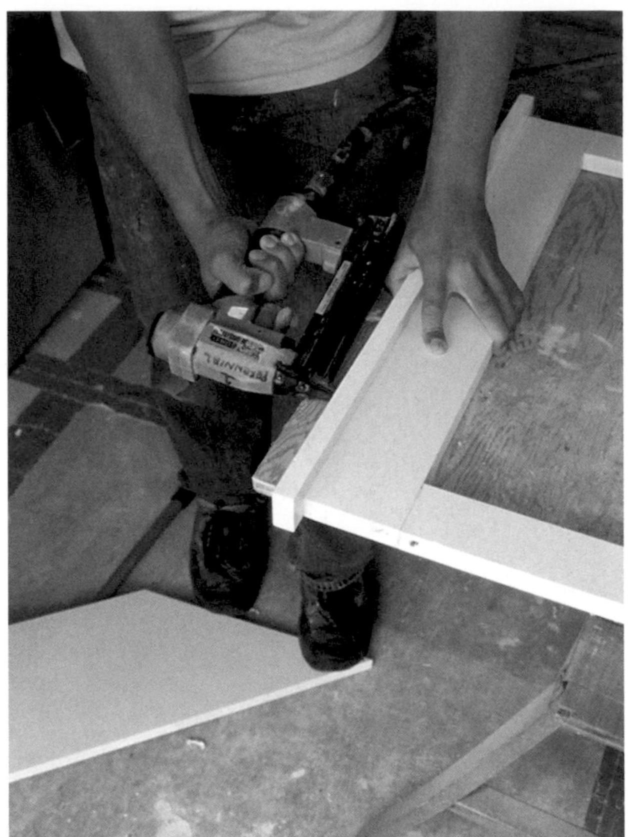

Figure 23. The author relies on the cement to bond Azek to itself. The fasteners simply keep everything tight while the glue sets. Here the author's crew places a few brads, keeping the cap in place while the cement sets up.

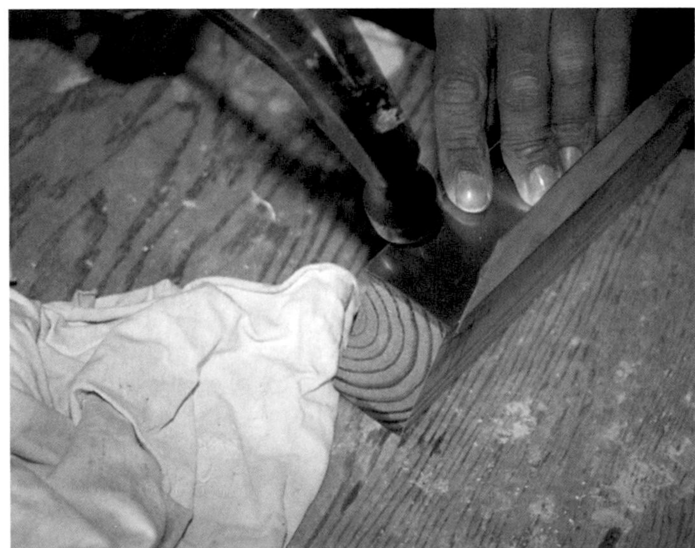

Figure 24. Copper drip cap adds a nice touch to the completed homes. It's cut about an inch longer than the head casing and bent over the ends with a hammer on a block of scrap wood (left). The completed cap is slid up behind the housewrap when the frame is installed (right).

Figure 25. After the preassembled casing is nailed in place over the window fin, the narrow expansion gap between trim and window is caulked. Although the manufacturer claims that the material can be left unpainted, two coats of acrylic latex leave subtle brush marks, for a thoroughly convincing "woodlike" appearance.

fasten it on the flat with some PVC cement and a brad nailer (**Figure 23**).

We typically use preformed 1 1/4-inch copper drip cap, which adds a decorative touch, lasts forever, and helps to weatherproof the assembly. I cut the cap about 1 inch longer than the head casing and put a 1/2-inch bend on both ends. I just use my framing hammer (not a waffle face!) and a block of wood to make the bends. When we install the casing frame, we make certain to slip the copper drip cap behind the housewrap so any water that gets behind the siding will run out when it reaches the top of the window (**Figure 24**).

We fasten the completed assembly to the wall with a pair of nails every 12 to 16 inches using a 15-gauge finish gun. The pneumatic finish nail's small wire size allows the material to move around with changes in temperature and reduces splitting. It also makes nail holes easy to fill and finish. After caulking and painting, the casing is indistinguishable from traditional wood trim, even under close inspection (**Figure 25**).

As with any new material, there is a learning curve with Azek, and some different techniques must be developed. But we've found the effort to be worth it, and our customers are happy with the results.

Jim Blahut, along with his brothers Don and Mike, owns Perennial Homes and builds in the Beach Haven community on New Jersey's Long Beach Island.

Chapter 11: Windows & Doors

BRETT HAGSTROM

- Flashing a Flanged Window
- Flashing Windows in Coastal Climates
- Flashing an Entry Door With Brick Mold
- Rot-Proofing Wood Windows and Doors in Wet Climates

Flashing a Flanged Window

by Carl Hagstrom

There's no such thing as waterproof siding. Over time, moisture will work its way behind even properly installed siding. Housewrap provides good protection against the moisture that does get in, but it must be detailed properly at windows and other penetrations to work.

The housewrap details I use when installing flanged window units prevent any water that gets past the siding from damaging the windows or rotting the framing.

Think Like a Roofer

For some reason, builders tend to work less hard at flashing details on a wall than they do flashing a roof. But when you think about it, a wall is really a roof with a very, very steep pitch, so a window is basically a skylight installed in a vertical roof. I flash windows in much the same way that I flash skylights: I start at the lowest point and work my way uphill, with each layer of flashing overlapping the previous layer, creating positive drainage laps and always avoiding reverse laps.

Cutting the Window Opening

I wrap my houses as soon as I can: The chance of rain is always present where I work, and I want to

protect the shell as quickly as possible. When it's time to install a window, my first step is to cut the wrapped window opening. I start by making a level head cut (**1**), then two 45° cuts upward from the lower corners (**2**). I finish with a vertical cut (**3**).

X-cutting the opening should be avoided: The head flap of an X-cut will direct any moisture that manages to get behind the housewrap into the structure. Instead use a modified Y-cut, as shown in the photos 1 through 7 and in Figure 2, page 206.

Next, I trim the flaps of housewrap just a bit shy of the interior face of the studs and tape them to the

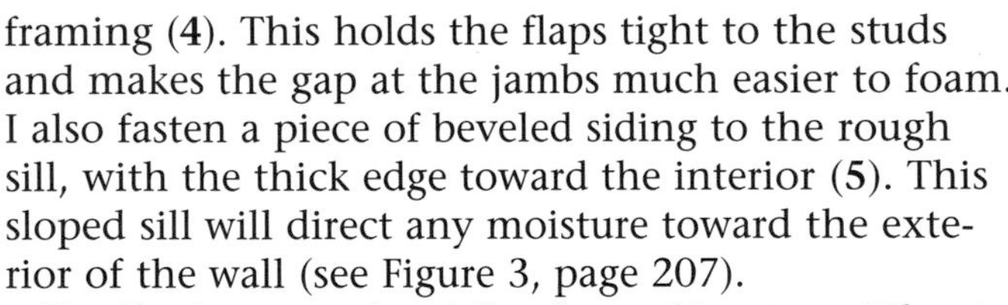

framing (**4**). This holds the flaps tight to the studs and makes the gap at the jambs much easier to foam. I also fasten a piece of beveled siding to the rough sill, with the thick edge toward the interior (**5**). This sloped sill will direct any moisture toward the exterior of the wall (see Figure 3, page 207).

Finally, I create a head flap by making two 45° cuts 6 inches long in the housewrap at the window head corners (**6**), and temporarily fold and tape this flap up out of the way (**7**).

Next Step, Sill Flashing

After I've taped the housewrap to the studs, I install the sill flashing. I prefer to use Tyvek FlexWrap (DuPont), a butyl-based self-healing flashing product I call "peel-and-stick on steroids." It has all the self-healing characteristics of generic peel-and-stick, but it also can be stretched to form seamless sill corners.

I cut the sill flashing one foot longer than the width of the window opening, so the flashing will extend up the jambs 6 inches. Then I peel off the release paper (**8**), center the flashing in the opening (**9**), and lower it onto the sill. I press it into place, working from the middle toward the corners (**10**), where I carefully stretch the flashing out to create seamless protection (**11**). The flashing has a memory, so to prevent it from curling back, I drive a cap nail (**12**) at the outer edge to hold it in place until the adhesive achieves its full grip (24 to 48 hours). Finally, I smooth the vertical portion of the flashing against the housewrap (**13**).

Installing the Window

Before installing the window, I apply a heavy bead of elastomeric latex caulk at the jambs and the head (**14**), but I never caulk the sill flange area. Should any moisture find its way into the rough opening, this caulk-free sill flange, coupled with the sloped sill,

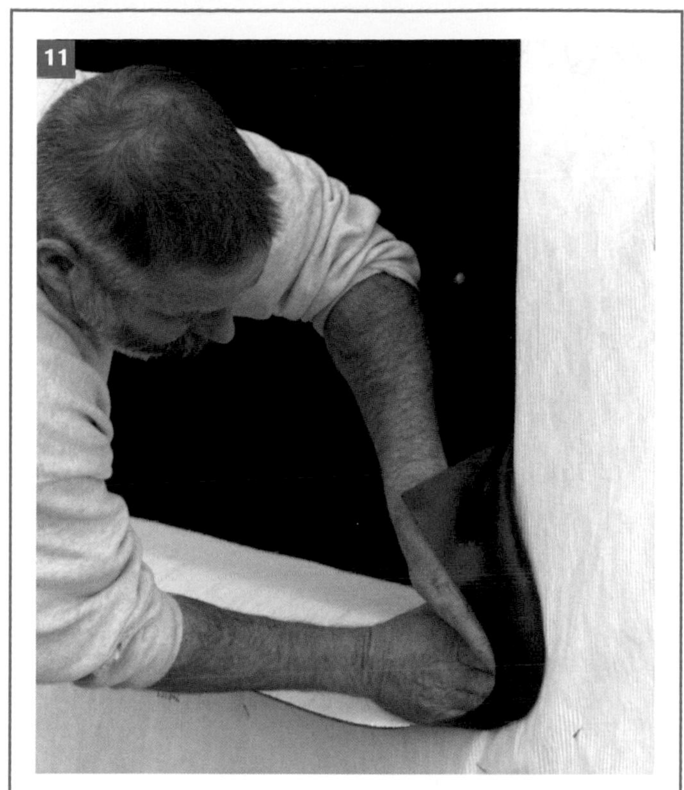

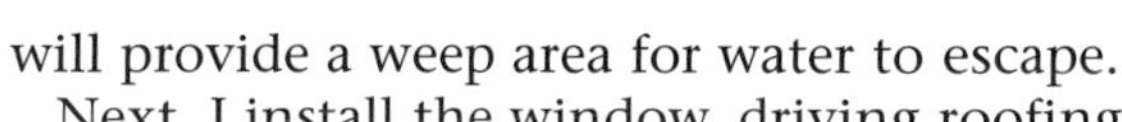

will provide a weep area for water to escape.

Next, I install the window, driving roofing nails through the preformed holes in the flanges, spacing them approximately 6 inches apart (**15**). Check your window manufacturer's specifications for the correct spacing.

Flashing the Jambs and Head

Starting 2 to 3 inches above the window head, I apply flashing membrane over the jamb flanges (**16**), letting the tape extend at least to the bottom of the sill flashing.

I like to use a J-roller (**17**) to apply strong, even

pressure to all flashing membranes and tapes. Although the tool is designed for countertops, it works great for this application.

I then apply flashing membrane over the window head flange (**18**), lapping it over the tops of the jamb flashings (**19**).

Applying the head flashing directly to the sheathing provides another level of protection. If any moisture were to find its way behind the housewrap and seep down to the window, it would encounter the head flashing and be directed over the window head flange, not behind it.

Once I've applied the head flashing, I fold the housewrap flap down over it (**20**, **21**), tape the 45° corners (**22**), and "skip-tape" (apply short pieces of tape with gaps in between) the lower edge of the flap in place (**23**). I also skip-tape the bottom (uncaulked) sill flange (**24**). These skip-taped gaps at the lower edges act as weeps, giving any moisture that gets to the window head a way to escape. Skip-taping also limits air leaks, though it's not entirely airtight. (For my money, I'd take an air leak over a moisture problem any day.)

Because I build in a cold climate, I apply a bead of

low-expanding foam in the gaps between the window unit and the rough framing, close to the face of the interior wall. I apply only enough foam to create a seal, not to fill the entire gap: Too much foam can distort the window unit.

Working in the Cold and Wet

The DuPont flashing membranes are meant to be installed at temperatures of 45°F or above. In cold-weather situations, I keep the flashing in a warm area and cut pieces as I need them. As the temperature drops, it sometimes becomes necessary to heat the area that will receive the flashing (I use a heat gun). In wet conditions, I get rid of any standing water and wipe down wet surfaces with a dry rag before applying the flashing membrane. Again, when in doubt, I'll dry things off with a heat gun.

In cold or wet conditions, I'll also use a hammer stapler along the edges of the flashing membrane to hold the material in place so the adhesive remains in contact with the sheathing or housewrap.

Just Do It

Flashing windows properly isn't difficult, and adds only about 15 minutes in labor and $15 in materials per unit. Some builders substitute less-expensive contractor's tape for flashing tape. The problem with this is that when the siding or trim is fastened at the window, every fastener becomes a potential leak, whereas the flashing membrane seals around the fastener.

As a builder, there's nothing I do in one day that puts more dollars in a house than installing the windows. Spending a little extra time getting things right sure makes sense to me.

Carl Hagstrom is a builder in Montrose, Pa., a JLC *contributing editor, and a speaker at* JLC Live. *All photos by Brett Hagstrom.*

Flashing Windows in Coastal Climates

by Clayton DeKorne

Regardless of the preferred housewrap material, most experienced builders agree that it is not a good idea to X-cut the housewrap across rough openings and fold the triangular flaps around the wall framing. Instead, use the modified I-cut shown in **Figure 1**. The critical detail here is the straight cut across the top of the window. There should not be a flap that gets folded around the window header.

Peel-and-Stick Tapes

The advent of peel-and-stick flashing tapes has revolutionized flashing methods. These materials come in widths ranging from 4 to 12 inches (9 inches is typical) and are made from either bituminous (similar to eaves flashing) membranes or from butyl rubber. Butyl-based flashing tapes are generally more expensive, but will stay flexible in cold weather and remain much more stable at high temperatures. Butyl products also bond better to difficult substrates. Perhaps most important of all, they can be peeled off and adjusted during installation.

Self-adhering bituminous products start to lose stickiness below about 50°F and will not bond well below 40°F. Problems may also arise with bituminous flashings in high temperatures. Under a dark-colored metal flashing in direct sun, for example, a bituminous flashing will soften and may begin to drip or ooze. Bituminous flashings should never come into contact with any caulk or sealant unless the sealant is specifically formulated for that use.

While peel-and-stick flashing has gained in popularity, there is still enormous confusion in the field about the correct procedure for applying these materials. Most builders agree that a head flashing must lap under the housewrap, but beyond this, application practices vary for the other flashings. We recommend the procedure shown in **Figure 2**, next page, which closely compares to the typical sequence used by builders such as Robert Criner, owner of Criner Construction in Yorktown, Va., Patty McDaniel of Boardwalk Builders in Rehoboth, Md., and Tim Cross of Merrick Construction in Monmouth, N.J.

Sill pan. The sill flashing may be the most important flashing of all, for it allows water that does seep through to drain to the outside (**Figures 3** and **4**, page 207). This piece goes in first, and the bottom flap must lap over the top of the housewrap below. A sill flashing can be formed easily in the field from flexible flashing tape. Tyvek FlexWrap (DuPont) has a wrinkled facing that allows it to be molded to the rough opening without any cutting and folding at the corners. This material is decidedly more expensive than most other flexible flashing materials, but the labor savings generally make up for the higher material cost.

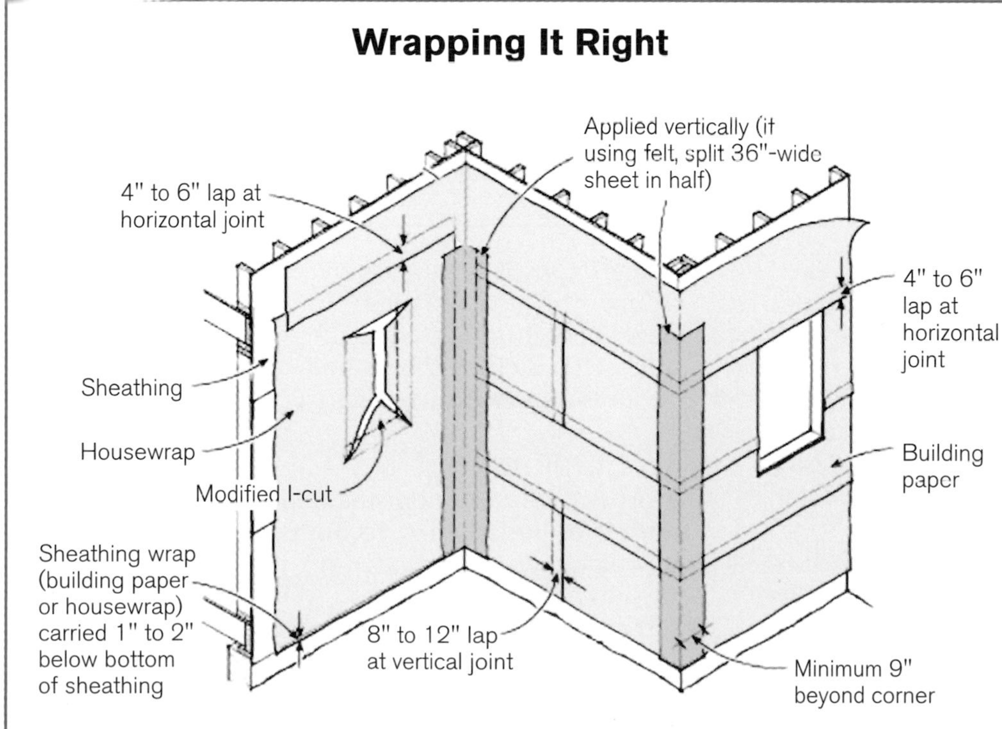

Figure 1. Any sheathing wrap should be applied from the bottom up. The wide overlaps shown here are recommended for coastal regions where increased wind pressures can pull water uphill, allowing it to leak past a narrow overlap.

Window Flashing Sequence

1. Apply housewrap and cut as shown (do not X-cut)

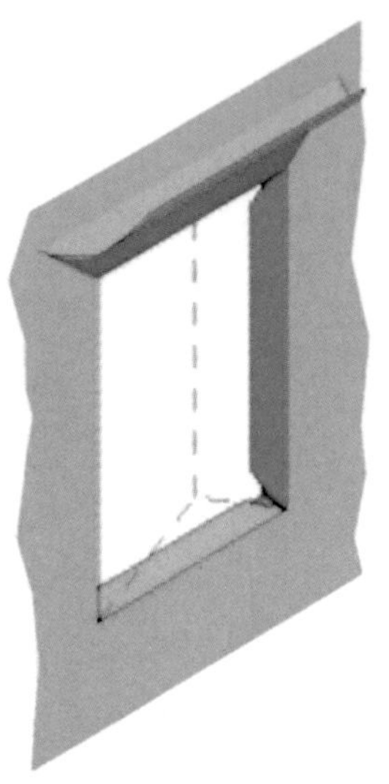

2. Sill flashing should wrap up the sides of the window at least 6". Caulk is optional, and should never be applied beneath bottom window flange.

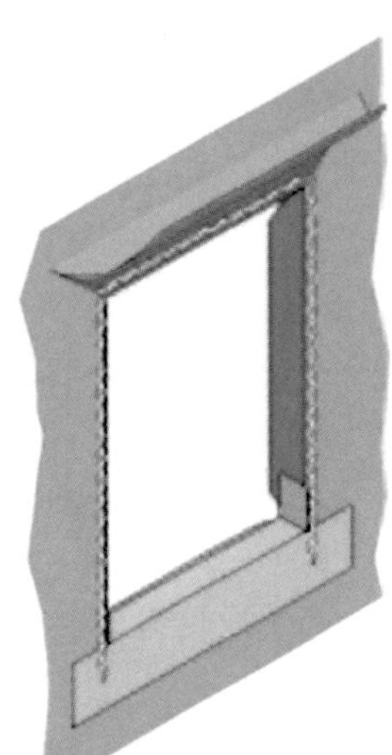

3. Install window and apply jamb flashing

4. Apply head flashing

5. Fold housewrap down and tape over cuts

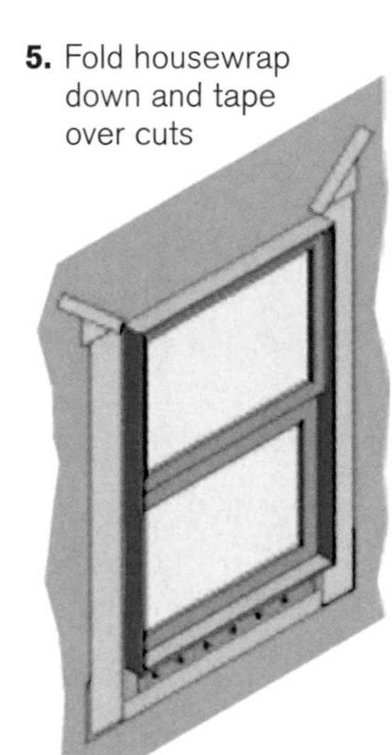

ILLUSTRATION COURTESY APA - THE ENGINEERED WOOD ASSOCIATION

Figure 2. It's not enough to caulk window flashings when installing a window. Instead, housewrap and flexible flashing tape should be interwoven with the flange, as shown in this installation sequence.

Side flashing. Side pieces should go in after the window has been installed. Some builders dispute this, arguing that these pieces should wrap the rough opening and protect the framing. Any water that gets past the window flange will presumably drain down to the sill flashing. While this theory sounds about right, intense wind pressure in coastal regions can pull water straight back to the interior drywall, long before it reaches the sill pan. Instead, Criner, McDaniel, and Cross all recommend applying the side pieces after the window is installed, lapping the flashing over the window flange to prevent water from getting into the rough opening in the first place.

When positioning the side flashings, don't butt the tape hard to the jamb. Leave 1/4 to 1/2 inch of the flange exposed, so the flashing tape won't show after siding or trim is installed. Trim or siding should never be tightly butted to the window but must have at least 1/4 inch to accommodate the expansion of window and cladding materials.

To Caulk or Not

Most window and door manufacturers, as well as the makers of housewraps, recommend bedding the window flange in caulk. Exterior trim details routinely include exterior caulking as well. However, a 2002 test conducted by NAHB Research Center demonstrated that caulk never lasts as long as the materials it is sealing. The report concluded, "Over time, all exterior wall sealant systems, including caulk, will

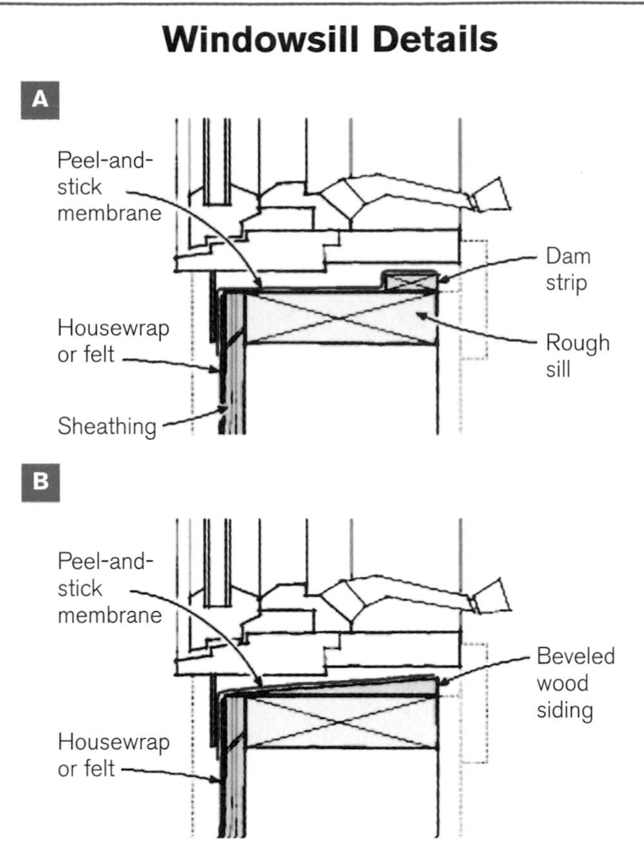

Figure 3. Water will leak through any window over time, so any sill flashing should allow this water to drain to the exterior. Using flexible flashing, this can be achieved by applying a dam (A) or a piece of bevel siding (B) over the rough sill before the pan flashing is put in place.

leak. Caulks work from a few days to a few years, which makes it impossible to predict when and where maintenance will be required." In short, caulking is largely a waste of time. Instead, the NAHB Research Center advocates caulkless siding systems, which rely on a well-detailed weather barrier and flashing system, similar to those described here.

Door Threshold Details

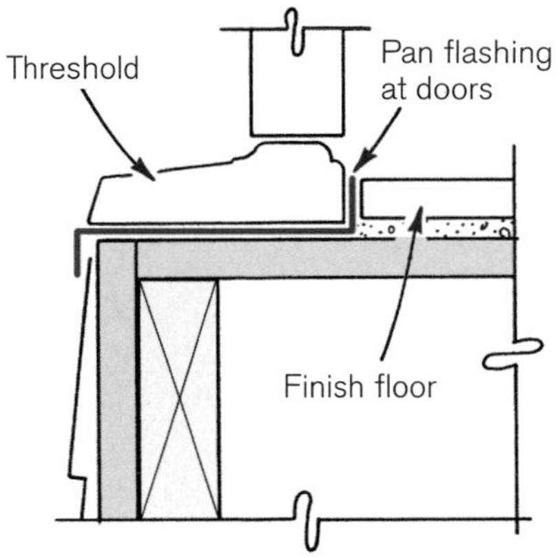

Threshold

Pan flashing at doors

Finish floor

Figure 4. As with windows, every door should include a pan beneath the threshold to prevent windblown water from seeping inside.

Some builders have argued that caulk helps to seal the window against air leaks. However, air sealing is usually best done from the inside using a spray foam such as Great Stuff (Dow Chemical Co.). This type of foam remains flexible and won't cause a window to jam as wall materials expand with climate changes. If air sealing is attempted on the outside, it would necessarily be incomplete because the bottom window flange should never be caulked. Windows will inevitably leak over time, and any water that leaks through the sill must be allowed to drain back out. In general, any horizontal caulking bead will create a dam that holds water, and this dam may prevent water from draining outside as it follows properly lapped membranes.

Clayton DeKorne is editor of Coastal Contractor *magazine. He is also editor of the* JLC Field Guide to Residential Construction *and a former senior editor at* The Journal of Light Construction.

Flashing an Entry Door With Brick Mold

by Carl Hagstrom

There's plenty of material available about how to flash windows and patio doors, but most of it seems to cover flanged units. Nearly every house I build, though, includes at least one "flangeless" unit — typically a standard entrance door with an applied brick-mold casing. The tricky part about flashing cased units is sealing the area where the back of the casing meets the housewrap. And door units present an added challenge: Since there's no sill flange, wind-driven rain has a straight shot at penetrating the area immediately below the threshold.

Here's how I use self-healing membrane to fabricate flashing flanges for the jambs and heads of cased units, and how I form a one-piece sill pan with flexible membrane.

Prepping the Opening

The days of X-cutting housewrap openings are long gone. The proper method is first to make a level cut at the door head (**1**), followed by two 45° cuts at the corners (**2**), creating a head flap that is folded up and out of the way (**3**). An inverted Y-cut is used to prepare the remainder of the opening.

As with most flashing details, I start at the lowest point and work my way uphill, making sure each layer overlaps the previous one and avoiding any reverse laps. In the case of an entrance door, this means I start with the sill flashing.

Self-Healing Sill Pan

To prevent moisture from working its way under the door threshold to the framing, I fabricate a sill pan using Tyvek FlexWrap (DuPont), a flexible self-healing membrane that can be stretched to form seamless sill corners.

In the past, I've tried both metal and plastic sill pans, but the upturned rear flange always made for nasty trim details, because the rear flange never fit snug against the back of the threshold. Also, I always felt that any fasteners I drove through those pans were potential leaks. Plus, the fabrication lead time for metal pans was a nuisance.

I cut a length of FlexWrap one foot longer than the rough-opening width, and with the piece upside

down on my sawhorses, I measure in 1/2 inch from the edge and carefully score the release paper with my utility knife (**4**). I make sure I've got a brand-new blade in the knife, and I score only the paper, being careful to avoid cutting into the membrane itself. (Before I developed the feel required to cut freehand, I found that I could create an effective blade-depth stop by pinching the end of the knife blade with a pair of small vise grips.)

After I score the release paper, I fold the FlexWrap back on itself, creasing the cut and finishing off any areas where I may not have cut completely through the paper (**5**).

I snap a line on the subfloor 1/2 inch behind where the interior edge of the threshold will rest; this marks the back (or inside) edge of the sill-pan material. I pull the release paper off the FlexWrap, leaving the 1/2-inch strip I scored (**6**). I center the membrane above the door opening (**7**) and lower it into place, making sure the back edge lands on my layout line (**8**).

I use a J-roller to apply pressure and ensure a good bond between the flashing and the housewrap (**9**). At the outside corners, I carefully push the flashing out to form a seamless corner (**10**). The flashing has a memory, so to prevent it from curling back I drive a cap nail (**11**) at the outer edge; that holds it in place until the adhesive achieves its full grab (24 to 48 hours).

Finally, I smooth the vertical portion of the flashing against the housewrap, and again use the J-roller to press things tightly in place (**12**).

Site-Applied Flanges

At this point, the opening is ready for the door. My next step is to apply peel-and-stick membrane (I typically use DuPont StraightFlash) to the back of the door casing and frame, creating my own sealed flanges to prevent moisture from working its way behind the brick molding. I stick the membrane to both the back of the casing and the side of the door jamb.

11
12
13
14
15
16
17
18
19
20
21
22

I cut the jamb pieces about 3 inches longer than the height of the door frame, and cut the head piece about 10 inches longer than its width. Since the aggressive adhesive backing is tricky to work with, I begin by scoring the release paper into thirds, lengthwise (**13**). As with the sill pan, I'm careful to cut only the paper, not the membrane. After scoring, I fold the membrane material back on itself and crease all the score lines to make sure the release paper is cut all the way through (**14**).

I lay the door frame facedown on sawhorses, and because I'm working from the back of the door, I install the head flange before the jamb flanges to avoid creating a reverse lap when the door is upright. I fold one-third of the flange back on itself, remove the release paper from the middle third of the flange, position the piece at the door head, and press it onto the back of the head casing (**15**). Then I remove the release paper from the folded-back portion of the flange (**16**), fold this outer third up against the doorframe head, and stick it in place (**17**).

With the J-roller, I press the head-flange adhesive tight against the frame and casing (**18**), then slice the flange material at the jambs and fold it down on the jamb casing (**19**). With the head flange in place, I install the jamb flanges in the same manner (**20, 21**), and at the door head, slice the material and apply it to the back of the head flange (**22**).

Counter Flanges Are the Final Step

I now install the door frame (**23**). First, I run a bead of elastomeric latex caulk along the interior edge of the threshold. (Caulk along the exterior edge of the threshold could trap moisture instead of allowing it to drain out.) I peel off the remaining release paper from the jamb flanges (**24**), peel back enough release paper on the head flange to expose the jamb portion (**25**), and then apply a StraightFlash counter flange over the jamb flanges (**26**).

I've got to stay on my toes when applying the counter flanges — I'm joining two adhesive faces of the membrane, and once they touch, they're stuck together for good. To make sure the counter flanges are positioned correctly, I remove a portion of the release paper from the top of the jamb counter flange and adhere that much to the head flange. Then I pull the jamb counter flange taut and slightly away from the wall, and work my way down the counter flange, pulling the release paper off in stages as I stick the upper portion to the flange (**27, 28**).

After the jamb counter flanges are in place, I peel off the remaining release paper from the head flange (**29**) and install a drip cap (**30**) — which I make from painted aluminum coil stock or bendable vinyl — directly on the adhesive of the head flange. Then I remove the release paper from the counter head flange (**31**) and install it over the vertical leg of the

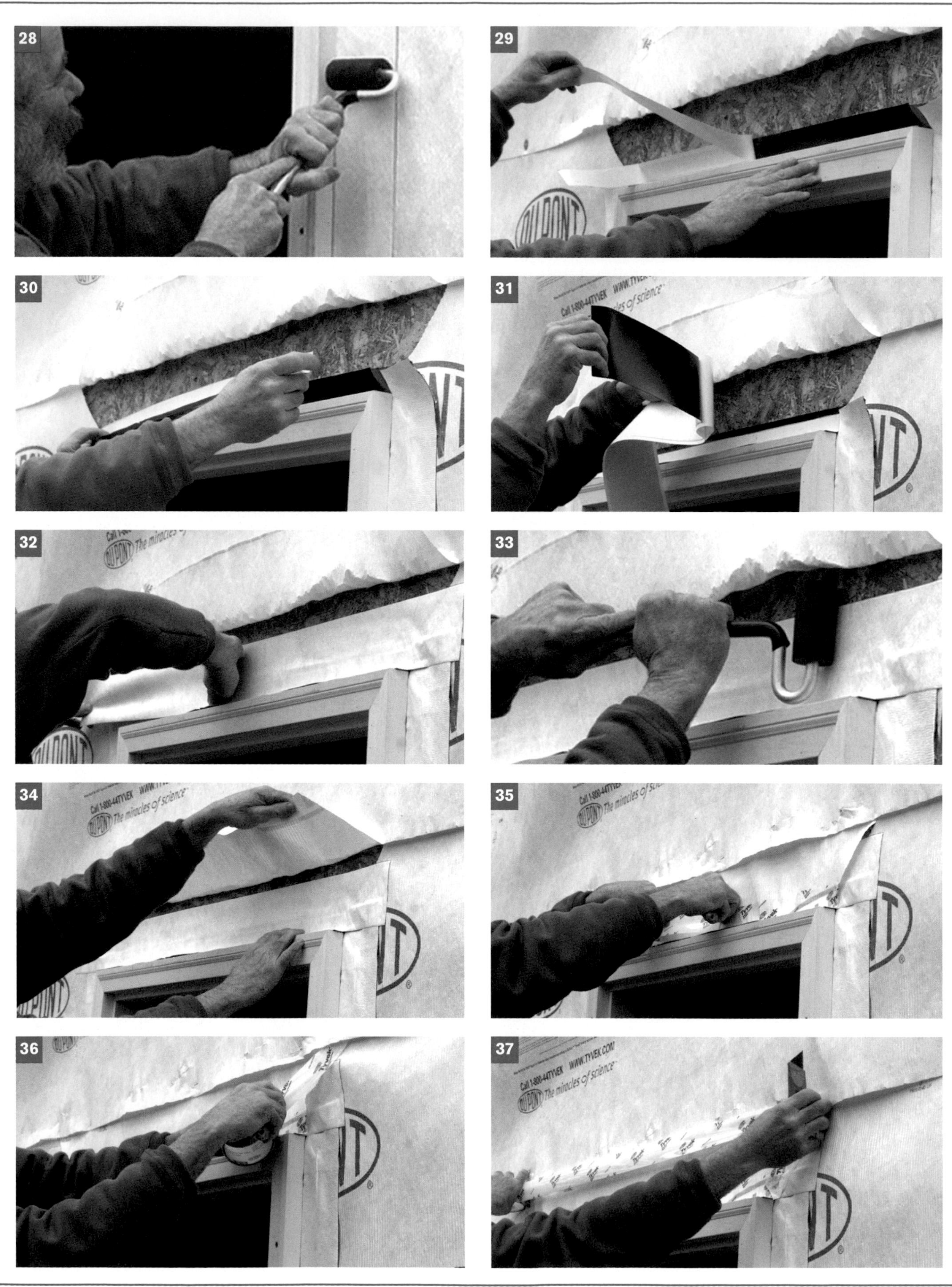
28
29
30
31
32
33
34
35
36
37
Call 1-800-44TYVEK WWW.TYVEK.COM
DUPONT The miracles of science

drip cap, with the upper portion adhering directly to the wood sheathing (32). I roll all the counter flanges tight to the wall to ensure a good bond to the housewrap and sheathing (33).

I fold the housewrap head-flap down over the door-head counter flange (34), skip-tape the flap in place (35), and tape the diagonal housewrap cut (36). The small gaps created by skip-taping allow any moisture that works its way behind the housewrap to drain off the drip cap. I also tape all horizontal seams in the housewrap (37).

Interior Threshold Trim Detail

On the interior of the threshold, I fold and tape the exposed portion of the sill pan against the interior edge of the threshold (38). This lip serves as a dam, preventing outside moisture from working its way under the sill and into the house. I run the finish flooring tight to the threshold and use a utility knife to cut back any portion of the sill pan still exposed. The result is a very clean flooring detail that requires no trim.

After the siding is installed, I sometimes apply a 1½-inch strip of membrane material to the underside of the sill and to the face of the siding. This added flange prevents wind-driven moisture from blowing beneath the sill, while still allowing the sill pan to drain out over the housewrap.

Carl Hagstrom is a builder in Montrose, Pa., a JLC *contributing editor, and a speaker at* JLC Live. *All photos by Brett Hagstrom.*

Rot-Proofing Wood Windows and Doors in Wet Climates

by Michael Davis

The Deep South is a great place to be a restoration carpenter. With 62 inches of annual rainfall and humidity levels that hover around 90% for much of the year where I live, I'm guaranteed a steady stream of jobs repairing rotted windows and doors. Much of my work involves 100-plus-year-old homes; fortunately, given the high quality of the old-growth wood commonly used in these homes, I can make most of these repairs with a little epoxy.

But the millwork in newer homes is often a different story. Some of my clients with relatively new homes require extensive repairs after only eight or 10 years. While fighting rot in this region's climate sometimes feels like a losing battle, I've developed some techniques — and adopted some specialized products — to help new millwork and repairs on existing windows and doors last as long as possible.

Protect Vulnerable Wood

One of the major reasons newer doors and windows start rotting so quickly, I believe, is that the quick-growing white pine (or its variants) used in most factory-made doors and windows is not suitable for the Deep South.

If the wood contains any treatment at all, it's a water-repellent, not a preservative, so when this fast-growing pine starts going bad, it takes off at a gallop (**Figure 5**, next page). That is why I carefully back-prime everything I can on new doors and windows, seal all end grain with paint or special epoxy coatings, and raise the units slightly so they're not sitting directly on horizontal surfaces that could hold water. Since the bottom 16 inches of jambs and casings are especially vulnerable, I focus most of my attention on this area.

Figure 5. After only eight years, this door frame is well on its way to becoming compost (far left). The damage to the window (left) is typical in New Orleans' hot and humid climate. The author uses a number of techniques — including treating with preservatives, back-priming, and epoxy-coating end grains — to prevent rot in both new and existing doors and windows.

If I have enough time and new doors and windows to justify building a dipping trough, I first soak the bottom 3 to 4 inches of each unit in a borax solution such as Tim-bor or Bora-Care (Nisus Corp.; **Figure 6**). Then I seal these areas with West System 105 Epoxy Resin and 207 Special-Coating Hardener (West System Inc.) or with Corlar 25P or 26P two-part epoxy coatings (DuPont Performance Coatings; **Figure 7**).

The two Corlar products are similar, but 25P — an epoxy mastic — contains more solids and goes on thicker than 26P. The 25P is great for protecting end grain, and I use it for applications like porch flooring, where a thicker coat is an advantage. The thinner 26P penetrates and brushes out better; I use it as the primer for almost all of my rot-repair work. One drawback to Corlar 26P, though, is its induction time. After mixing, you have to let it sit for about an hour. The 25P doesn't require the wait.

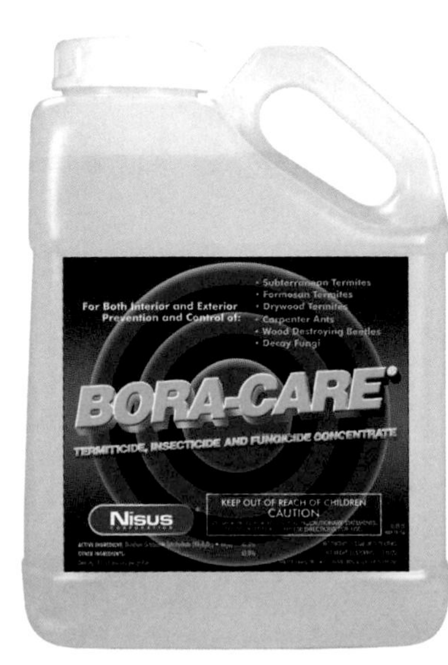

Figure 6. For added insurance against rot, the author often soaks new and repaired pieces in a borate-based preservative like Bora-Care.

(Note: DuPont has changed the names of all its industrial coatings. Corlar 25P is now Corlar 2.1 ST and Corlar 26P is Corlar 2.8 HG. However, the former names are still commonly used at the dealer level.)

Both types of Corlar are mixed one-to-one with their activators and thinned with MEK (methyl ethyl ketone). I buy the epoxy base and its activator in gallon containers from a DuPont Performance Coatings dealer for about $85, which makes two gallons of the coating. And I always wear a respirator and nitrile gloves while I'm using these substances.

I use Corlar 26P to coat the bottoms of frames and casings, usually up to about the first finger joint. Where finger joints are within 12 inches of a horizontal surface, I carve out a small "V" directly over the joint with a utility knife (**Figure 8**) and skim it over with WoodEpox epoxy putty (Abatron, Inc.).

I also like to pry factory-installed brick mold away from frames just enough to coat the back side of the bottom inch or two of the molding. Then I feather out the top edge and rough up the dried epoxy with 220-grit sandpaper, so an alkyd primer will bond.

Sometimes I use West System 105/207 epoxy in place of the Corlar because, depending on the hardener used, it dries in as little as a half-hour, making it a better choice when I have only one or two repairs to make. Otherwise, I prefer the Corlar because it sands more easily and has a longer working time.

Let Air In and Water Out

Whenever possible, I try to install new doors and windows in such a way that they have a chance to dry out. For example, I like to attach 1/4-inch-thick pressure-treated shims to the bottom of door thresholds, or place door and window units on strips of Cor-A-Vent S-400 (Cor-A-Vent Inc.). Designed primarily as a soffit vent, Cor-A-Vent S-400 is made from a

Figure 7. Two-part epoxies — like these from DuPont and West System — dry faster than conventional paints and provide better protection against water penetration. Because epoxies break down when exposed to UV light, it's important to cover them with a protective top coat of paint.

Figure 8. Finger joints on doors and windows are one place where rot can quickly gain a foothold, so the author creates a small recess over the joint with a utility knife and then fills the recess with two-part epoxy putty to create a more water-resistant joint.

Figure 9. Made from stacked sections of corrugated plastic, Cor-A-Vent S-400 is primarily designed for soffit venting (left). But once the staples are removed, individual sections can easily be separated from the stack and placed under windows or doors, where they promote drying (center and right).

1-inch-tall by 1½-inch-wide stack of plastic corrugations held together with large staples.

After prying apart the staples, you end up with six individual corrugations. Each corrugation can be used singly to create a 1/8-inch-high vent channel, or the stack can be left as high as needed (**Figure 9**).

Because Cor-A-Vent is made from rigid plastic, it also offers some structural support. To keep swarming Formosan and dry-wood termites from crawling through the holes, I wrap a piece of aluminum screen around the back of the Cor-A-Vent before installing it.

Figure 10. Before installing a door unit, the author likes to remove the brick molding, cut 1/8 inch to 1/4 inch off the bottom ends, coat them with epoxy, and staple bronze screening to them. Holes drilled in the trim at an upward angle and covered with small thimble vents allow interior moisture to drain while keeping out bugs.

When I'm working on a new installation and the door threshold has to sit on the floor for some reason, I commonly trim 1/8 inch to 1/4 inch off the jamb bottoms so they're not touching the subfloor, making them less likely to wick water. I don't remove the jambs from the threshold; I just take a little off the bottoms with a circular saw (or, if the door is already in place, a reciprocating saw). After coating the end cuts with Corlar 25P, I fill this gap with Cor-A-Vent or bronze screening (Blaine Window Hardware) to keep out bugs and create a combination weep and vent at the bottom.

On both new installations and repairs, I'll frequently remove the brick mold and cut it 1/8 inch to 1/4 inch short, then attach screening to the trimmed and coated bottoms, doubling it over and stapling it in place with stainless steel staples (**Figure 10**). Folding the screening over a round pencil before installation gives it a nice shape.

On repair jobs where removing the casing would be

Figure 11. The wood bottoms on steel doors are vulnerable to rot. The author first removes the damaged wood and replaces it with pressure-treated stock, then drills a series of holes in the interior side of the door to promote drying. Small thimble vents inserted into these holes prevent insects from nesting inside the door.

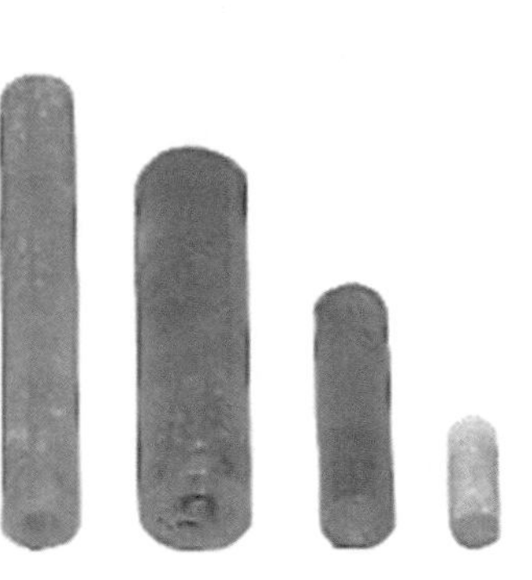

Figure 12. Made from compressed borax and available in different sizes, Impel rods (left) can prevent rot. Inserted into vulnerable areas in windows and doors, the dowel-shaped pellets slowly dissolve when they're exposed to moisture, protecting the wood (right). The author uses a two-part epoxy wood filler — the same material used for repairs — to cap the holes.

difficult, I trim it in place with a Fein MultiMaster, then pry it loose enough to back-prime the bottom inch or two with Corlar 25P. Then I insert a rolled piece of bronze screening or Cor-A-Vent.

Rot-Proofing Doors

Since the untreated wood stock under the aluminum threshold found on many inexpensive doors is bound to cause problems later on, I'll often replace it with pressure-treated stock or a piece of fiber-composite decking before installing the door. This isn't as much trouble as it sounds. After removing the sill from the door unit, I pry loose the rot-prone pine filler and replace it with a duplicate made from pressure-treated stock, which I secure to the aluminum sill with small stainless steel screws.

On metal exterior doors, the wood perimeter — especially at the bottom — will cause problems if exposed to water. If the door has a sweep with a solid plastic top, this further traps moisture inside the door. On both new doors and ones that I'm repairing, I usually pry the weather sweep loose at the ends, so I can epoxy-seal the end grain on the stiles and on the joint where the stiles meet the bottom rail. Then I bed the top of the sweep in caulking.

If I'm working on a number of similar doors, I remove their sweeps entirely and cut slots into their solid tops to promote drying, using a 1/8-inch straight-cutting bit in a die grinder guided by a jig. (You could also use a small router or laminate trimmer.) Another option is to drill a series of holes into the base of the sweep before remounting it.

To provide ventilation to the interior of the bottom rails, I drill 3/8-inch-diameter holes on 6-inch or 8-inch centers in the bottom rail from the interior side of the door. I cover the holes with 3/8-inch thimble vents (Midget Louver Co.; **Figure 11**).

Handy Protection

A good way to prevent rot at the bottom of doors and windows is with Impel rods (Chemical Specialties Inc.). Inserted into drilled holes, the compressed borax pellets remain inert as long as they stay dry; when they get wet, they slowly dissolve, protecting the wood from rot. The manufacturer claims they last a minimum of eight years.

Though expensive (a 24-count box of my favorite 1/3-by-1-inch size sells for $25), these little jewels offer protection in locations that would otherwise be very hard to address. For example, I'll insert two or three of them into a single hole drilled in each door stile, and use two or three more in another pair of holes drilled in the bottom rail. I also install rods at the bottom of jambs and casings, and in window sash and sill horns, covering the holes with either wood plugs and polyurethane glue or with WoodEpox (Albatron, Inc.). These rods allow you to put protection where it's needed most. If a rot-damaged area is addressed soon enough, you can usually repair it with epoxy and install the rods without removing the piece.

Window sash are like small doors: No matter how they operate, their bottom corners are vulnerable to rot. If their sash are fixed, I insert short Impel rods into face surfaces to protect the stiles' bottom end grain and the rails' side end grain (**Figure 12**).

Special Solutions for Windows

The area where jambs and casings meet windowsills is a potential trouble spot. In new construction or where it's possible to trim the casing short, I leave a 1/4-inch

Figure 13. The bottoms of doors and windows are natural collection spots for moisture, but tiny "thimble" vents allow the water to drain. Held in place by friction, the vents come in 3/8-inch and 1/4-inch sizes.

to 1/8-inch gap where the casing meets the sill and fill it with Cor-A-Vent or screening. Another option is to drain these joint intersections with 1/4-inch angled weep holes that come out just behind the casing and out the bottom of the sill just past the siding.

In locations with especially severe weather, I also drill a series of 1/4-inch holes in the bottom rail of sash to drain away any water that penetrates behind stops. I epoxy-coat drilled holes with a long cotton or foam swab or with a 1/4-inch flux or artist's brush, and then cap them with a small thimble vent (**Figure 13**).

To make a long-lasting caulk joint on long horizontal joints — for example, where a subsill meets a sill — I cut a slot with a special tool called a "corner grooving machine" that's designed for installing weatherstripping (Resource Conservation Technology). Instead of foam backer rod, I use bulb weatherstripping from the same company to fill the slot before caulking, which gives the joint flexibility and improves adhesion (**Figure 14**).

If any repairs to the sash are needed, I use either Abatron's LiquidWood/WoodEpox system or West System adhesive epoxy, depending on how structural the repair needs to be (West System is stronger, but harder to sand). After making repairs and sanding everything, I apply a coat of West System 105/207 epoxy and a coat of DuPont Corlar 26P epoxy enamel. The 26P is applied when the 105/207 goes into the "green" stage — that is, when it is tack-free, but not fully hard — which eliminates the need to key sand the fully hardened 105/207 for good adhesion of the subsequent coat. This technique also works when using West System 105 with alkyd or latex primers.

Replacing Window Stops

Some factory wood windows come with wooden glazing stops on the exterior. The ones I've seen aren't back-primed, and neither are the sash, a recipe for disaster in my climate. If the windows are getting enough weather for me to be there making repairs, I figure that at the very least I should pull off the bottom stops for inspection. If they are in good shape, I back-prime both surfaces with epoxy and reinstall them using stainless steel brads. If the stops show even a little rot, they go into the trash can.

While it would be best to replace all of the factory stops, the top and side ones are generally in much better shape because they dry more easily. Granted, it

Figure 14. Designed for retrofitting weatherstripping, this specialty tool cuts slots that are the perfect size for a caulked joint (left and inset). The same manufacturer also makes the weatherstripping that the author uses as a backer rod (right).

Figure 15. Mitered stops hold water, so the author copes new stops at the corners for better drainage, cutting the vertical stops — which are usually left in place — with a utility knife. Once installed, the new stops are sealed to the glass with silicone, the front edge is caulked with polyurethane, brad holes are filled with epoxy, and then the entire assembly is given another coat of Corlar 26P.

Figure 16. When the bottom stops on true-divided-light windows start showing the first signs of water damage, the author replaces them with wider versions cut from rot-resistant mahogany. Made with a steeper slope to aid in drainage, new stops are coated on all surfaces with two coats of epoxy. The black material on the front of the stop is a self-stick EPDM glazing gasket that the author uses instead of glazing putty.

would make sense to remove them, too, for back-priming, but the factory usually attaches them with staples, which are often rust-encrusted, making it difficult — if not impossible — to extract the thin stops without breaking them. If there is no obvious damage, I just leave them in place.

Discarded stops could be replaced with glazing putty, but wood stops look and perform better, so I usually make new ones out of mahogany. To aid drainage, I give them a steeper 10° or 15° pitch and increase their width as much as possible. After sanding the stops, I apply one coat of West epoxy and one coat of Corlar 26P to all sides. To eliminate the water pockets that miter joints create, I slide the bottom stop under the sides, essentially making a coped joint at the corners (**Figure 15**). I use a piece of new stop to mark the side stops for trimming, then cut them in place with a sharp utility knife. As I install the stops, I coat any exposed end grain with Corlar 25P epoxy. Gently bending the new stop upward in the middle lets it slip into place.

If windows have true divided lights, the mullions are a weak link. Since most failures occur when the putty pulls away from the glass, the upward-facing mullions are most at risk. Wherever I find failed glazing compound, I remove it, coat the underlying wood with epoxy, and replace the putty with custom-made wood stops.

I used to bed new stops in glazing putty, but lately I've been using Resource Conservation Technology's glazing gaskets, because I've never found a glazing putty that lasts more than two years (**Figure 16**).

After filling brad holes with epoxy putty and sanding, I give the top surfaces of the new stops another coat of 26P. When it's no longer tacky, I apply a coat of alkyd or latex primer so I don't have to key sand. (A word of caution: If you apply primer too soon, it will puddle and you'll have to key sand and apply another coat.) Then I caulk the front edges with polyurethane and, after the final top coat, run a bead of Dow 795 sealant (Dow Corning) where the stops meet glass. If I haven't used glazing gaskets for some reason, I apply 1/8-inch Scotch Fine Line masking tape (3M Center) to the glass as a bond breaker.

It's worth mentioning that all this extra effort to prevent doors and windows from rotting away is largely unnecessary when the building has sufficiently wide overhangs or some other protective cover for doors and windows — something I'm always stressing to architects and designers.

Michael Davis is a restoration carpenter in New Orleans.

Chapter 12: Decks & Porches

- Rot-Resistant Deck Details
- Building Durable Porches
- Rooftop Decks for Coastal Homes
- Repairing Cantilevered Balconies

Rot-Resistant Deck Details

by Kim Katwijk

Millions of wood decks are built every year. Unfortunately, many of them will deteriorate long before they should. As a deck builder in the Pacific Northwest, I have a lot of experience demolishing and replacing rotted decks. I want what I build to last, so when I tear down a rotting deck, I try to figure out what went wrong.

Know Your Enemy

Rot is a fungus, an organism that feeds on and destroys natural materials like lumber. The spores it uses to reproduce are nearly everywhere and will grow wherever conditions are right. There are many different types of rot, but they all require food and moisture to survive. If you understand how these organisms grow, you can build decks that are less hospitable to them.

Food source. Most decks — particularly the structural framing — are made from woods that are susceptible to rot. Because the companies that treat lumber use local materials, the wood you use depends on where you work. From Denver east, builders use pressure-treated southern pine, a kind of wood easily penetrated by chemical preservatives. On the West Coast, we use pressure-treated hem-fir, a species group that does not accept chemicals very well. Frequently, only the outer surface contains preservatives, so the interior of the lumber is unprotected and susceptible to rot (**Figure 1**).

Moisture. Wood won't deteriorate unless moisture is present. Green lumber often contains enough moisture to rot, but even materials that start out dry can become wet when they're exposed to the weather, washed, or used as a surface for potted plants.

Some kinds of rot fungi, the wet rots, require a wood moisture content of 30% or more to survive. But many types of rot will do just fine as long as the wood has a moisture content of at least 20%, a threshold easily reached in damp climates.

People often speak of "dry rot," but if lumber is dry, it will not decay. So-called dry rot fungi are a specific type of brown rot that sends out hyphae, strands of tissue that can transport moisture from surrounding wood. But this can't happen unless the surrounding wood is wet. If you can keep a deck below 20% moisture content, it won't rot.

Figure 1. Pressure-treated hem-fir lumber is incised to increase penetration, but often the colored preservative barely soaks in at all, as is evident on this piece of blocking. The end cut should have been coated with preservative; the brown staining visible on the end grain is a sign of rot.

Collection Zones

A typical deck harbors hundreds of places where organic matter can collect and sit. I call them "collection zones." Every time it rains or the wind blows, leaf litter — leaves, needles, twigs, dirt, dust, and grass clippings — finds its way into the gaps and cracks in the deck. The collected material holds moisture, so that a deck full of collection zones mimics the natural habitat of fungus: wet fallen wood on a forest floor.

A collection zone can be very small. For example, when a baluster is nailed to the face of a rim joist, the area where the two pieces meet is a collection zone. Poor deck design and building practices increase the size and number of these zones. Once the collected material becomes wet, rot will attack any unpreserved wood in the area.

The best way to prevent this is by limiting the size and number of the collection zones. If you prevent moisture and debris from getting into places they can't get out of, you reduce the potential for rot.

Fascia detail. Some common building practices create perfect collection zones. For example, many carpenters rim the deck with a fascia board (**Figure 2**). There is usually no airflow between the fascia and the framing, so the 20% moisture content required for rot can be maintained over long periods of time. Water takes debris down between the fascia and the rim joist. Once organic matter gets into this collection zone, there is no way to get it out.

It's best not to use a fascia at all, but if one is required, cantilever the deck boards one inch over it. This detail greatly decreases the likelihood of rot because it reduces the size of the areas that dirt and moisture can get into. One way to compare construction details is by looking at how many linear feet of collection zone each design creates (**Figure 3**).

Figure 2. On this deck (far left), water got between the fascia and rim, partially rotting the fascia and completely destroying the rim. When the fascia was removed, the rim collapsed. Here (left), the author installs composite decking on a pressure-treated frame that will completely cover the fascia and rim, avoiding this potential collection zone. The lattice separating the fascia and rim joist will also help to drain away water.

Avoiding Collection Zones

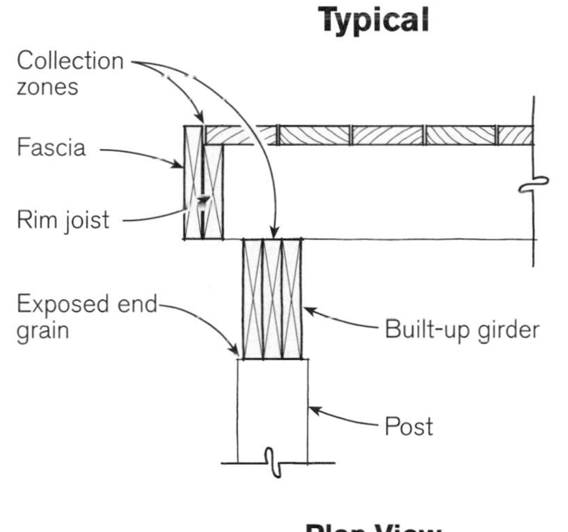

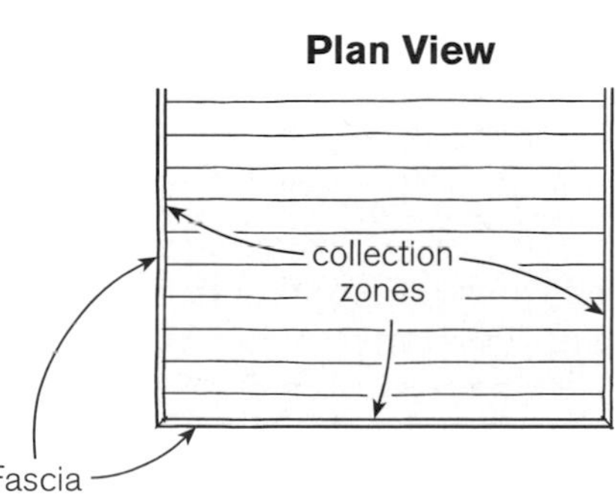

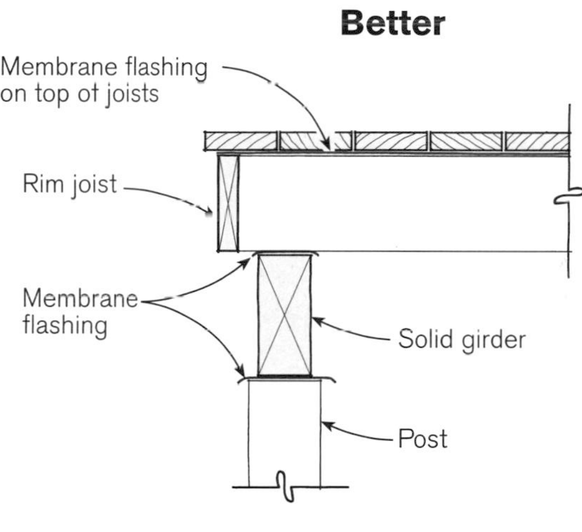

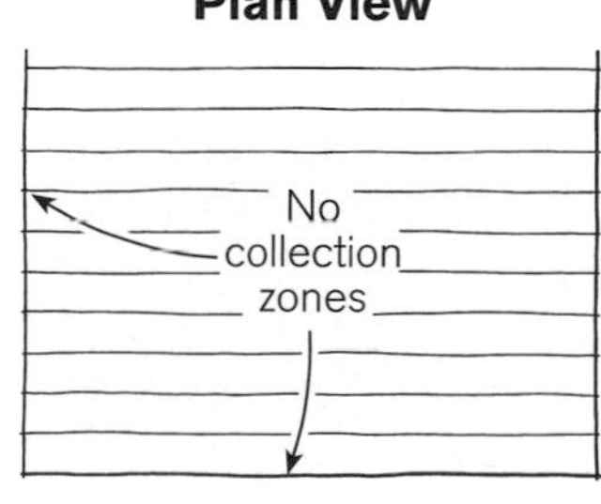

Figure 3. Wrapping a 12-by-16-foot deck with fascia (left) creates 40 linear feet of potential collection zones at the rim joist. Running the deck boards so they overhang the fascia (right) will reduce the collection zones at the rim joist to a cumulative 12 1/2 inches (1/4 inch per gap x 50 gaps = 12 1/2 inches). While some water and debris will still get in, the potential for rot has been greatly reduced. Membrane flashing on top of the joists provides additional protection.

Figure 4. Although it's common practice to bring an L-shaped flashing down the wall and kick it out over the ledger, the resulting pocket can collect debris — and rot both the decking and the siding above.

Built-up beams. It's common practice to double or triple up 2-by material to form beams. Unfortunately, the space between the pieces is a perfect collection zone. It's better to carry loads with solid 4-by or 6-by beams.

Attaching Ledgers

Another common building practice is to use flashing to keep moisture from getting between the house and ledger. Building codes require flashing, and many contractors meet the requirement by installing an L-shaped piece of metal. The horizontal leg covers the top of the ledger and the vertical leg goes up the wall and is lapped by the building paper and siding above. Most carpenters install the ledger in the same plane as the joists, so the deck surface ends up an inch or more higher than the horizontal leg of the flashing. This creates a perfect collection zone, because if something falls in toward the house, the flashing will prevent it from falling through to the ground (**Figure 4**). If enough organic matter collects on the flashing, it can induce rot in the adjoining deck board or invade the siding above.

There are many ways to deal with this problem, but whatever you do, you still need to flash the connection. The simplest method is to use a ledger that is taller than the joists and install it so the top edge will be in the same plane as the deck boards once they're installed. The flashing should come down the wall from behind the siding and building paper, run across the top of the ledger, and end in a lip that laps down the face (**Figure 5**).

Another option would be to space the ledger off the building so that there is a minimum 1/2-inch gap between the ledger and the wall. Most debris will fall through a 1/2-inch gap; any leaf litter that doesn't can be cleaned out. (Since it's impossible to eliminate every single collection zone, we tell clients that if they want the deck to last, they will need to maintain it by removing any leaf litter that collects.) This type of connection is trickier than it looks, so we hire an engineer to design it to support the necessary loads.

Deck Boards

Many carpenters use 16-penny nails to space deck boards. This creates a 1/8-inch-wide gap that forms a perfect collection zone between boards and on top of every joist (**Figure 6**). It's nearly impossible to remove leaf litter from such a narrow gap. Once the organic matter gets in, it will start to rot the deck boards and the joists below. Some contractors think they don't have to worry about this because they use redwood or cedar decking. Unfortunately, decking is no longer made from old-growth lumber. Most of the deck boards you can buy now contain a lot of sapwood, which, unlike heartwood, has very little resistance to rot.

The way around this problem is to install decking with a larger gap. We never use a gap less than 1/4 inch wide; a 3/8-inch gap is preferable. Organic matter will not collect in the larger space but instead will fall through. Where it does collect on top of joists, the space is wide enough to be raked clean with a screwdriver or deck-cleaning tool. The larger space also allows air to circulate and dry out the decking and structure below.

The same rules apply to composite decking such as Trex (Trex Company, Inc.). Captured organic matter may not affect the deck boards, but it will pile up on and rot the framing below.

Placement of boards. It's amazing how much leaf litter will fall through a 1/4-inch gap and land on top of a beam. It's good practice to plan where the decking will land and position beams and joints so they are not directly under a gap. Another way to minimize this collection zone is by running the deck boards at a 45° angle to the framing and beam. Less leaf litter will land on the beam because the gaps that pass over it will be farther apart.

Maintenance. We tell clients to maintain their decks by washing them with a deck-cleaning product like Defy TimberWash (SaverSystems) or Sun Frog

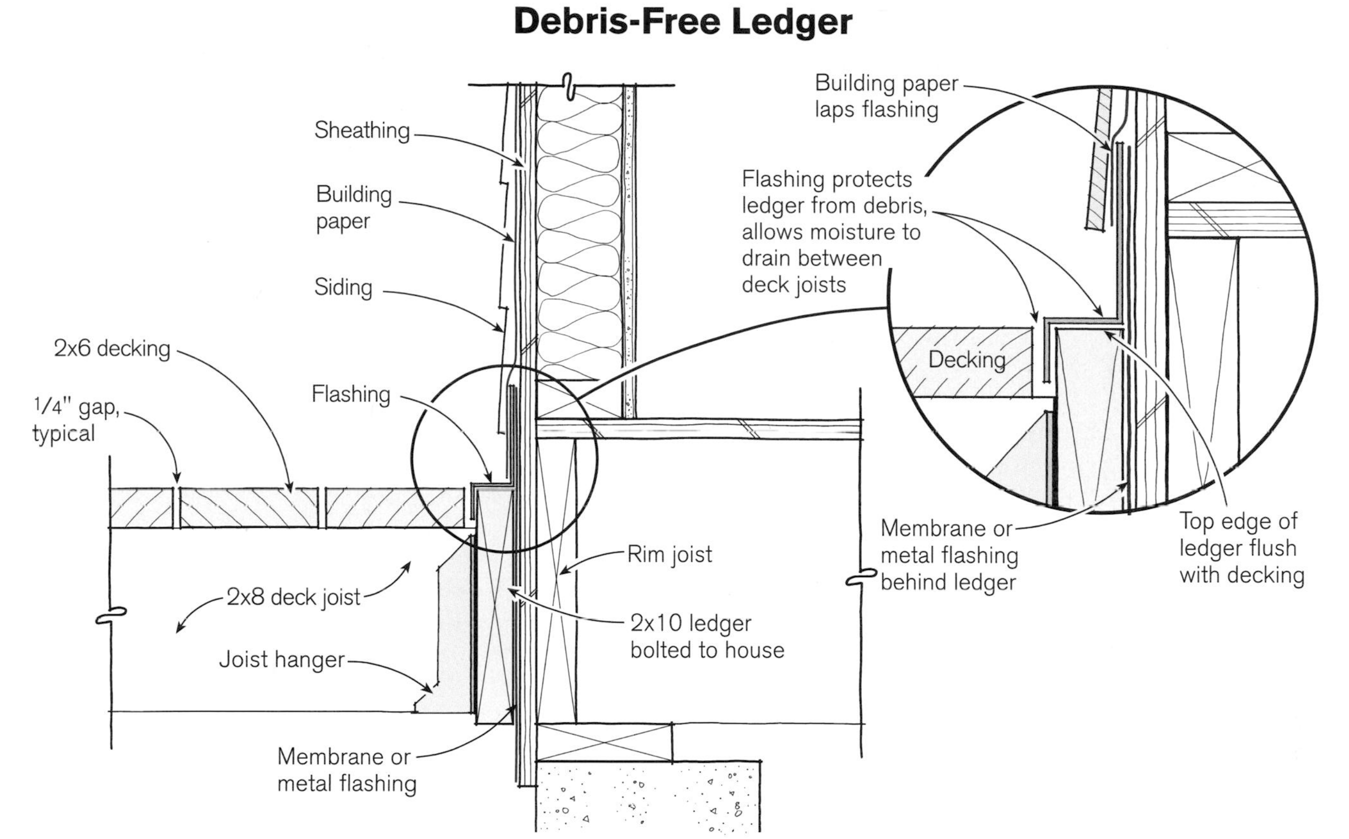

Debris-Free Ledger

Sheathing
Building paper
Siding
2x6 decking
1/4" gap, typical
Flashing
2x8 deck joist
Joist hanger
Membrane or metal flashing
Rim joist
2x10 ledger bolted to house
Building paper laps flashing
Flashing protects ledger from debris, allows moisture to drain between deck joists
Decking
Membrane or metal flashing behind ledger
Top edge of ledger flush with decking

Figure 5. To avoid creating a collection zone between the house and the deck, position the ledger flush to the deck boards. There are two pieces of flashing, one behind the ledger and another over the top of it.

Figure 6. Most carpenters space deck boards too tightly (left), leaving enough room for debris to get in but no way to clean it out. On this deck, organic matter collected at every gap and joint (far left, top), as well as between a rim joist and blocking that landed under a gap in the deck boards (far left, bottom).

Membrane Deck Flashing

by Andrew Hutton

We always protect pressure-treated deck (**A**) and stair (**B**) framing by flashing edges where water might collect and cause rot. This is vital here in the West, because the preservatives don't penetrate very well into the hem-fir lumber used in this part of the country.

Several companies have recently released products designed for this purpose; probably the best known is Grace's Vycor Deck Protector (Grace Construction Products). For 10 years, though, we've been using Polyken 626-35 Foilastic, an aluminum-foil–faced adhesive tape (Covalence Adhesives). Like other peel-and-stick membranes, it grabs well and self-seals around fasteners. It is also more resistant to UV rays than similar membranes (for up to a year in direct sun, according to the maker) and can be painted.

We put it on the top edges of deck joists, where fasteners are concentrated and water tends to sit. We also put it on the vertical cuts of stair stringers (**C**), where the notches go right to the untreated center of the material; merely painting the cuts with preservative can't provide the same level of protection. Foilastic comes in 50-foot rolls in widths as narrow as 2 inches and as wide as 36 inches.

Andrew Hutton is a site supervisor for Moroso Construction in Pacifica, Calif.

Deck Cleaner (Sun Frog). I recommend doing this twice a year after major pollen events, which in this area land in October and March.

Wood decks should be stained and sealed to prevent sun damage and to repel moisture. To increase absorption, this work should be done during the driest months of the year. We use Wolman F&P Finish and Preservative (Wolman Wood Care Products), Sun Frog Deck Sealer (Sun Frog), or one of the TWP deck and furniture finishes (MFG Sealants.).

Wood Railings

Many carpenters install 2x2 balusters by nailing them to the rim joist and then lapping over them with a fascia. This is easier than other methods, but it's poor practice because it creates two rot zones, one where the baluster hits the rim and another where the baluster hits the fascia (**Figure 7**). There are so many nails in the rim that it ends up looking like a pincushion. The large number of fasteners can split the balusters or rim and allow water to get into the wood.

To prevent rot, it's better to install posts every 5 feet or so and span between them with rails that support the balusters. Avoid notching posts, but if a post must be notched where it hits the rim, the notch should extend high enough to lap onto the deck boards. This is better than butting deck boards into the side of the post, because it takes what would have been a vertical crack and turns it into a horizontal one that debris has a hard time getting into. Lap or no lap, the joint between the post and decking should be sealed with caulk.

Pressure-Treated Lumber

The substructure of a deck needs to survive the harshest conditions, so in most cases it should be made from pressure-treated lumber. Currently, alkaline copper quat (ACQ) is the most common chemical for pressure-treating wood. Pressure-treated lumber is graded on the basis of how much chemical preservative is retained by the material. Retention is measured in pounds per cubic foot (pcf); the higher the pcf of

Figure 7. The common practice of nailing balusters to the rim joist (left) creates pockets that trap moisture and debris, which can cause rot (right).

preservative, the better the lumber will be able to resist rot. With ACQ, standard practice is to use .25 pcf material above ground, .40 pcf material for lumber that will be in contact with the ground, and .60 pcf material for pilings and marine applications.

To be on the safe side, we frequently frame substructures with .60 pcf lumber. Even so, there is no guarantee that the structural members won't rot. This is because the chemicals are unlikely to penetrate all the way through the material, especially large structural members like 4x4s, 4x6s, and 4x8s. This problem is more common on the West Coast, where hem-fir is used, but it can also happen with southern yellow pine.

Figure 8. It's a good idea to coat end cuts in pressure-treated yellow pine with extra preservative. With hem-fir, which doesn't accept pressure treatment well, it's an absolute necessity to do so.

To help the chemicals penetrate more deeply, the pressure treaters incise (cut slits in) the surface of hem-fir. But wood expands and contracts as it gains and loses moisture, and this can cause cracks to open and admit water and organic matter to areas that aren't preserved. Under certain conditions, the lumber will rot from the inside out.

Sealing cuts. There's not much you can do about checking and cracking, but you *can* protect the untreated wood that is exposed when you drill or cut pressure-treated hem-fir. We treat cuts with a liquid preservative that contains 9% copper naphthenate (**Figure 8**). There are many such products on the market. Two of the better-known brands are Jasco Termin-8 Wood Preservative (Jasco Chemical Corp.) and Wolman Wood End Cut Preservative (Wolman Wood Care Products). We brush this material onto all end cuts and into any holes we drill in the wood.

Untreated lumber. Pressure-treated lumber is not very attractive, so there are times, especially for upper-level decks, when we use untreated lumber for beams. You should do this only when there will be enough airflow to discourage the growth of rot.

To prevent the material from rotting, we take a couple of precautions. First, we contaminate the food source by treating the wood with a borate product such as Tim-bor (Nisus Corp.). Frequent wetting may cause the borate to leach out of the wood, so it's necessary to coat borate-treated surfaces with a water-repellent sealant.

We also create a moisture barrier by sealing the top edges of joists and beams with strips of torch-down roofing material (**Figure 9**, next page). Torch-down roofing is designed to stand up to UV rays and will self-seal where nails penetrate it. We make the membrane stick by heating it with a torch, and produce a drip-edge by allowing it to project about 1/2 inch beyond the edges of the lumber. Grace Construction Products recently introduced a product designed specifically for this purpose, Vycor Deck Protector (see "Membrane Deck Flashing," page 226).

Other Details

Lumber won't rot if you keep it dry. We try to keep posts up off the ground by installing them on piers formed with sonotubes. The piers extend 6 inches above grade; to prevent moisture from wicking up the post, we seal the lower end with torch-down roofing material. We also use this material to seal the top ends of posts, especially when they're made from untreated lumber.

It's important to create opportunities for airflow under low-level decks. If the design calls for skirting, we enclose the area below with open lattice or vertical boards with gaps of at least 3/4 inch between them. To encourage airflow, we space the deck boards 3/8 inch apart. When the deck is low and air circulation is limited, we frame the substructure with .60 pcf treated lumber.

Figure 9. To keep this deck — which is framed with untreated lumber — from rotting, the author coated it with a borate preservative and covered the upper surfaces with torch-down roofing membrane.

Kim Katwijk is a deck builder in Olympia, Wash.

Building Durable Porches

by Harold Chapdelaine

During my 30-plus years in the building business I've replaced a lot of rotted decks and porches. Some of these were less than ten years old; a few were less than seven. Many of the homes in question were otherwise well built, with solid framing and quality interior trim. But the builders failed to provide two key elements: good water-shedding details and air spaces to allow the porch lumber to dry after it got soaked by rain or snow.

The secret to a long-lasting deck or porch lies in keeping water out of the joints between the various layers of lumber and ensuring that those joints can dry out if water does get between them. Here are some simple techniques I use to accomplish this.

Porch Design and Materials

Resistance to water damage starts with the design. To give protection against windblown rain and accumulated snow and ice, I always include as large a step as possible between the decking and the door sill (or the sills of any full-height windows that open onto the deck).

I use only pressure-treated lumber for girders, posts, joists, and decorative aprons. I use select pine for fascia boards, and stock pine moldings. To make sure that the pine lumber will hold paint, I prime all surfaces (front, back, and ends) before installation.

One useful material for building decks and porches is peel-and-stick flexible membrane — the black, rubbery membrane originally developed to protect roof edges against ice dams (see "Choosing Flexible Flashings," page 113). One product specifically marketed for decking applications is Grace's Vycor Deck Protector (Grace Construction Products). I use it to keep water out of all joints where one piece of lumber is sandwiched flat against another — a common spot for decay to set in (**Figure 10**). Unlike tar paper or metal flashing, the membrane seals around any nails that pass through it, forming a tight barrier against unwanted water.

Ledger Details

Porch construction usually starts with the installation of a ledger board against the house (**Figure 11**). Some builders install their ledger boards over wood spacer blocks applied to the siding; others fasten the spacers directly to the sheathing and flash them. I prefer different, more durable methods. My crew and I use one

Figure 10. Doubled framing members (left) are good candidates for rot because water that seeps between them cannot drain. In a typical deck repair, the author covers the new double joist with bituminous flashing membrane to keep the water out (right).

Porch Ledger Details

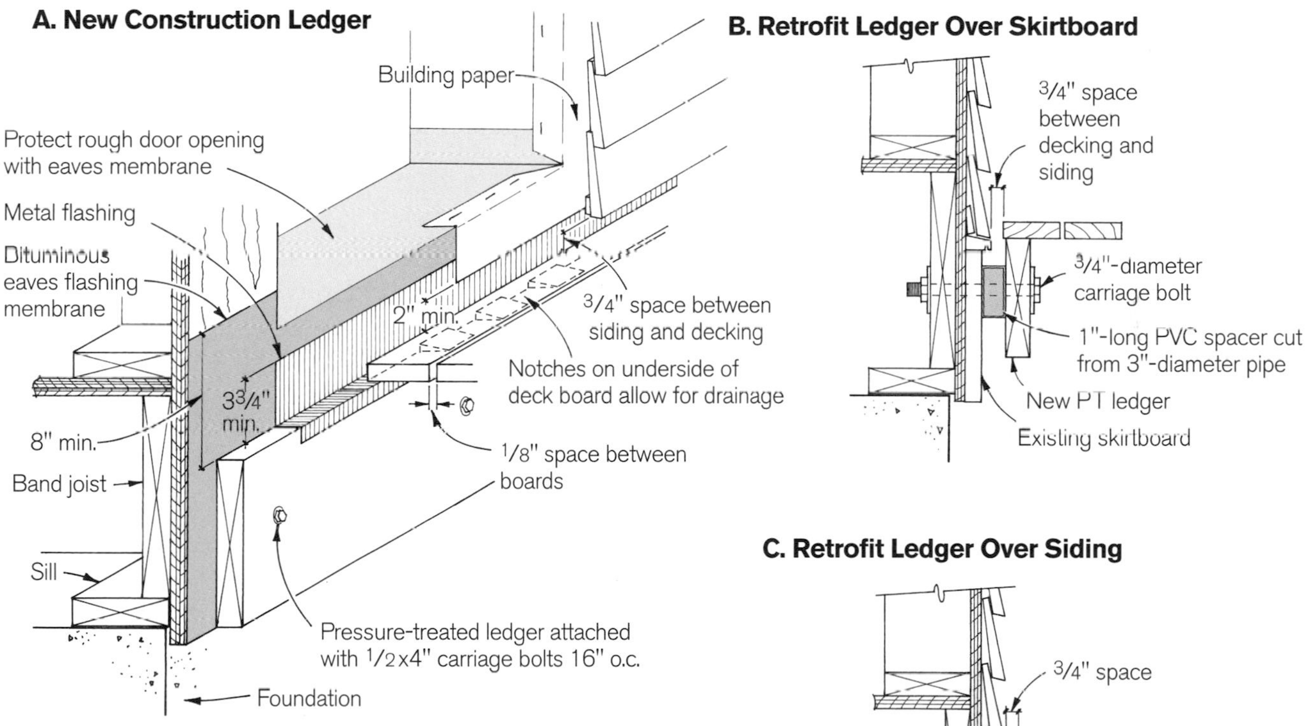

A. New Construction Ledger

Building paper
Protect rough door opening with eaves membrane
Metal flashing
Bituminous eaves flashing membrane
2" min.
3/4" space between siding and decking
Notches on underside of deck board allow for drainage
3 3/4" min.
8" min.
Band joist
1/8" space between boards
Sill
Pressure-treated ledger attached with 1/2x4" carriage bolts 16" o.c.
Foundation

B. Retrofit Ledger Over Skirtboard

3/4" space between decking and siding
3/4"-diameter carriage bolt
1"-long PVC spacer cut from 3"-diameter pipe
New PT ledger
Existing skirtboard

C. Retrofit Ledger Over Siding

3/4" space
1" long PVC spacer cut from 3"-diameter pipe
3/4"-diameter carriage bolt
Spacer cut at angle of siding
New PT ledger
Existing skirtboard

Figure 11. When adding a porch to new construction (A), the author first installs a protective layer of bituminous flashing over the sheathing. He then attaches the porch ledger several inches below interior floor level, bolting it through the band joist. Site-bent metal flashing, slipped behind the sheathing wrap above, covers the top of the ledger. For retrofit ledgers, the author uses PVC spacers to create a drainage gap behind the ledger. When installing the spacers over a finish skirtboard (B), he cuts them square at both ends; over siding (C), he angles one end of the spacer.

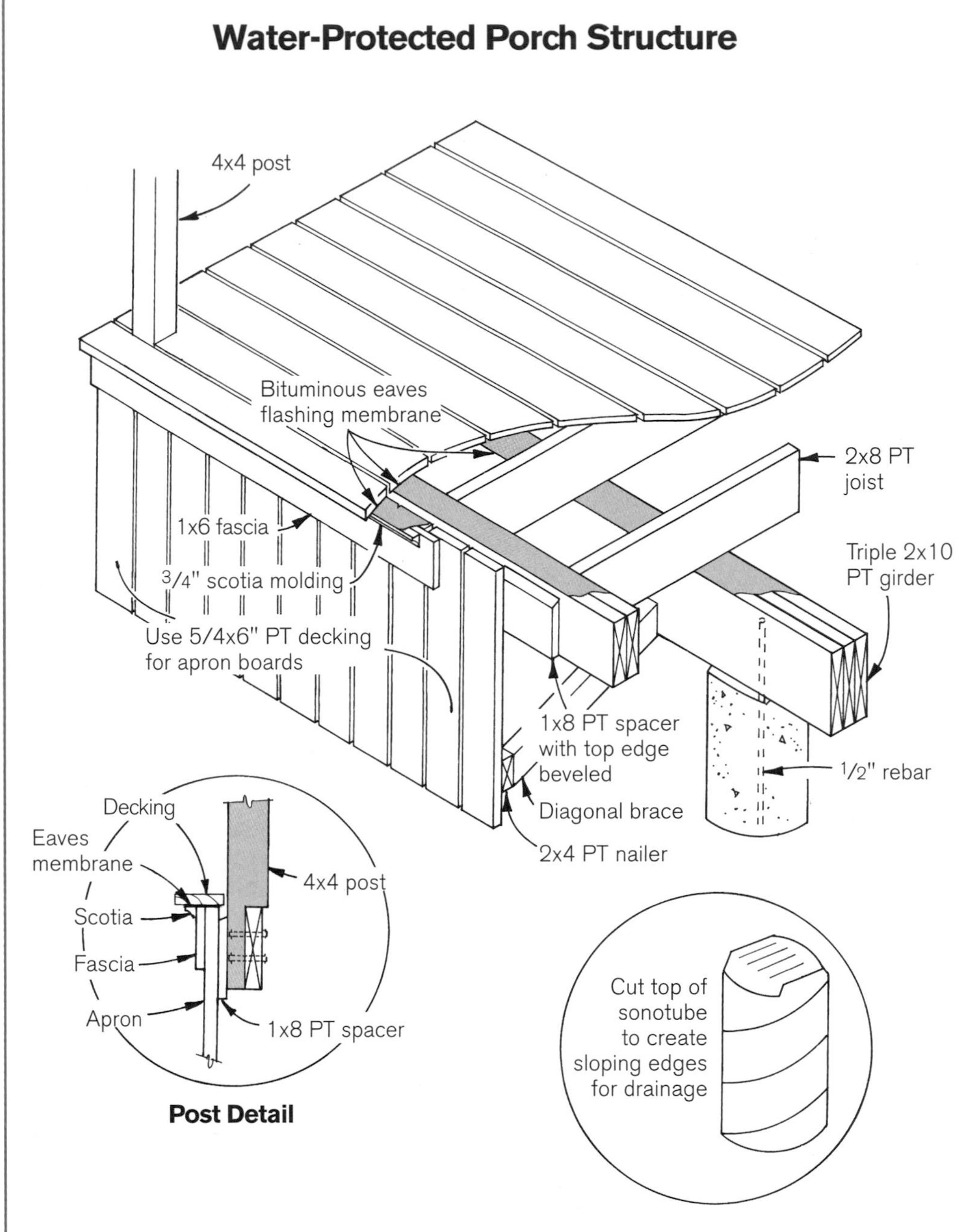

Figure 12. To provide protection against decay, the author covers all sandwich constructions, like the triple 2-by girder, with peel-and-stick flashing membrane. A beveled 1-by spacer directs water through the spaces between the vertical apron boards. Even the sonotube is fashioned to create a water-shedding surface at the top.

approach for new homes and additions, and another when adding a deck to an existing structure.

New construction. On new work, we fasten the ledger directly to the sheathing, then flash it properly. The installation is tight and clean, though it takes a little more time than using wood spacers.

Before installing any doors and windows that open onto the deck, we apply a strip of bituminous membrane to the exterior wall sheathing. The membrane extends from the bottom edge of the sheathing to at least 8 inches above where the top of the deck ledger will be; it also extends past each end of the deck by at least 6 inches. We run it over the subfloor at door openings as well as over the rough sills of any windows, taking care to fold the material up the 5 1/2-inch face of the jack studs. Where necessary, we use small pieces of membrane to seal any joints or slits.

We fasten the ledger using 1/2 x4-inch carriage bolts 16 inches on-center, extending all the way through the band joist of the house. Centering the bolts in the house's floor joist bays makes the nuts and washers easier to install and to retighten after the treated ledger dries and shrinks.

Next, we fabricate a standard metal flashing, using 6-inch roll stock (copper, zinc, or aluminum, depending on the budget), and making sure that it extends at least 3 3/4 inches up the side of the house. When using more than one piece of flashing, we overlap joints at least 6 inches. The flashing also extends far enough past the ledger to cover the end joists and apron boards.

Before installing the siding, we lap the housewrap

or felt 2 to 3 inches over the top of the flashing. It's important not to bunch up the paper on the top of the ledger, as this will trap water. We hold the bottom of the siding back 1/2 inch from the top of the finished deck height.

Retrofits. When adding a deck to an existing house, we use a method that incorporates 3/4-inch carriage bolts and 1-inch-long spacer rings cut from 3-inch PVC pipe.

The first step is to snap a line on the existing siding or skirtboard where the top of the ledger will be. We then drill a 1/4-inch-diameter reference hole below the chalk line from the outside, being careful not to hit any wiring or plumbing. We use this reference hole to locate the interior floor joists. We then transfer the layout to the ledger, and the holes where the center of the joist bays will be, making sure they're far enough above the interior sill to allow installation of the nuts and washers on the inside. When installing the ledger over siding, we try to keep the holes roughly in the middle of a course. We drill 3/4-inch holes through the ledger and temporarily tack it in place as a template to drill through the siding, sheathing, and band joist.

Now it's time to cut the PVC rings. If you're installing the apron over bevel siding, you'll have to cut one end of the ring at an angle — usually between 5° and 10° — to compensate for the siding angle. Getting the angle right is important. If the ledger is out of plumb, the ends of all the joists will have to be cut at an angle. When mounting the ledger over a skirtboard, cut the PVC spacer square at both ends.

With the holes drilled, we lay the ledger on the ground so that the side that will face the house faces up. Then we run a bead of silicone sealant over the end of each ring and center the rings over each hole on the ledger. We let the silicone cure before attaching the ledger to the house.

Girders, Joists, and Railing Posts

Most of our decks are framed with 2x8 pressure-treated joists cantilevered over a triple 2x10 girder.

The girder's sandwich construction makes it a potential water trap, so we top it with a layer of membrane flashing (**Figure 12**). For high decks, we support the girder on 6x6 posts, but for decks within 24 inches of grade, we lay the girder directly on top of concrete piers. We cut the sonotubes so that there's a level area in the middle equal to the width of the girder, while sloping the sides away to provide drainage (a 1/2-inch slope is enough). After filling the tubes with concrete, we pull a string across the top to locate the centers, then insert a length of 1/2-inch rebar. The rebar penetrates 3 feet into the pier and about 8 inches into the girder.

We use a double band joist at the ends, covering the joint with bituminous membrane, and notching and bolting the 4x4 railing posts as shown in Figure 12.

Decorative Aprons and Fascia Boards

Decorative aprons are another problem area. Most of the trouble I've seen has been with unprimed aprons nailed directly to the deck joists. This looks fine when it's first completed, but it won't stand the test of time.

To encourage airflow behind the apron boards, we first install a 1x8 pressure-treated horizontal spacer. We rip a 15° bevel on the top edge of the spacer, and nail it to the deck's band joist, holding it down 3/4 inch from the top of the joist. Next we install the apron — vertical, 5/4x6-inch pressure-treated boards spaced at least 1/4 inch apart. We install the apron boards flush with the top of the band joist. The bevel on the spacer directs water to the gaps between the boards. We finish with a primed 1x6 select pine fascia and stock 3/4-inch scotia molding. As insurance, we cover the top of the apron with bituminous flashing.

Decking

Once the aprons, girders, and all double joists have been covered with bituminous flashing, it's time to lay decking. The type of decking we use depends on whether we're building an open deck or a roofed porch. For open decks, we use square-edge boards with at least 1/8 inch between them. For covered porches, we frame the deck with a 1/4-inch-per-foot slope and install 1x4 tongue-and-groove flooring. While this slope won't drain like a roof, it will prevent standing water. We prime the flooring on all sides with a high-quality, mildew-resistant exterior primer, install it with tight seams, and finish it with at least two coats of a high-quality deck enamel. The finished floor effectively locks out water penetration.

When laying square-edge decking, we carefully adjust the spacing so that the last full piece stops 1/2 to 3/4 inch from the flashing. On new construction, we cut a series of 1/2-inch-deep by 1 3/4-inch-wide notches on the underside of this last piece of decking, placing the notches so they fall between the joist bays. These notches provide drainage above the ledger flashing. For retrofit ledgers, the clear space created by the PVC spacer rings ensures free drainage at the ledger.

Fiberglass Columns

For some jobs we use columns, rather than 4x4 wood railing posts, to support a porch roof. Over the years we have switched from factory-milled wood columns to structural fiberglass. Costs for clear lumber seem to rise weekly, and the expense of repainting every couple of years can eventually match the price of the columns. We have also been seeing a lot of quality problems with wood columns, including deteriora-

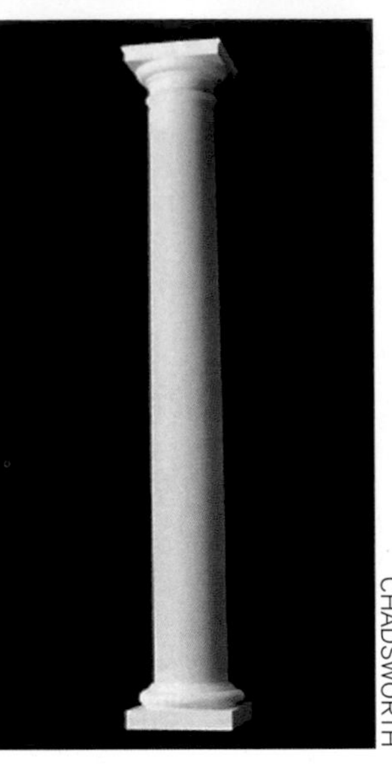

Figure 13. Because wood columns often delaminate (left), the author prefers to use composite columns. They're strong, durable, and easier to install (right).

tion of the pine bases (no matter what we do to seal and paint them), constant bleeding of pitch in the lumber, and occasional delamination of the vertical seams (**Figure 13**).

The two fiberglass or composite column suppliers I'm familiar with are Chadsworth (Chadsworth, Inc.) and Marbleine (Kavanaugh Sales Co., Inc.). Both are easier to install than wood. They require no special tools; the fiberglass cuts cleanly with a fine-tooth saber saw, hacksaw, or handsaw and grinds and smooths with a rasp, belt sander, or disc grinder. Small dents and nicks can be repaired with two-part epoxy. Wood railings are also simple to fasten to the columns. We just scribe the railing to the contour of the column, predrill the screw holes, and fasten with self-tapping, stainless steel screws.

Half-Lap Railing Joint

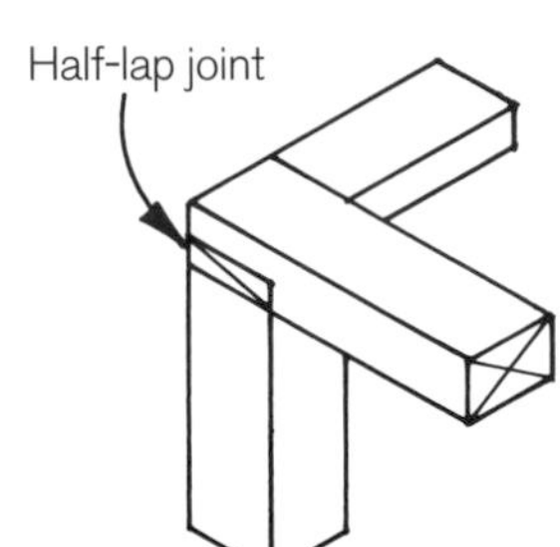

Figure 14. When joining handrails above 4x4 posts, the author avoids mitered corners, which inevitably open with time. He prefers a half-lap joint, which looks neater and will remain tight.

Composite columns are extremely strong; some are rated for loads as high as 18,000 pounds. They weigh about one third as much as comparable wood columns, come in a wide variety of sizes and styles, and cost about the same as wood columns.

Railings

Most of our projects don't have fancy railing details. Most decks have 2x4 railings, sometimes with a profile routed along the edge. A lot of builders miter their 2x4 railings directly over the posts. Over time, the resulting joint is almost guaranteed to absorb water and open up. A neater way is to join them with a half-lap, as shown (**Figure 14**). This joint will absorb water too, but it will remain closed.

Selling Quality

Details like these do raise the cost of a project. But when I explain the consequences of doing otherwise, I've found that most clients will pay the price. If they're in doubt, I just show them the repair bills for rotten decks I've replaced. When they see that the repairs often cost more than the deck I'm proposing to build, they're usually persuaded.

Harold Chapdelaine is a builder in West Tisbury, Mass.

Rooftop Decks for Coastal Homes

by Andrew P. DiGiammo

In the coastal area where I design and build homes, a rooftop deck is often the best way to reveal a beautiful ocean view, or perhaps just to catch a glimpse of the water over dunes or neighboring buildings.

Working primarily in the Shingle style, which typically involves a lot of dormered spaces under roofs, I often end up setting those decks into the roofline above a lower-story room. It's also convenient in many cases to build a deck on top of one of the many-sided projecting rooms I like to use for catching light, views, and breezes. It makes sense to me that the "widow's walk" has been such a popular element on homes in this area throughout the years.

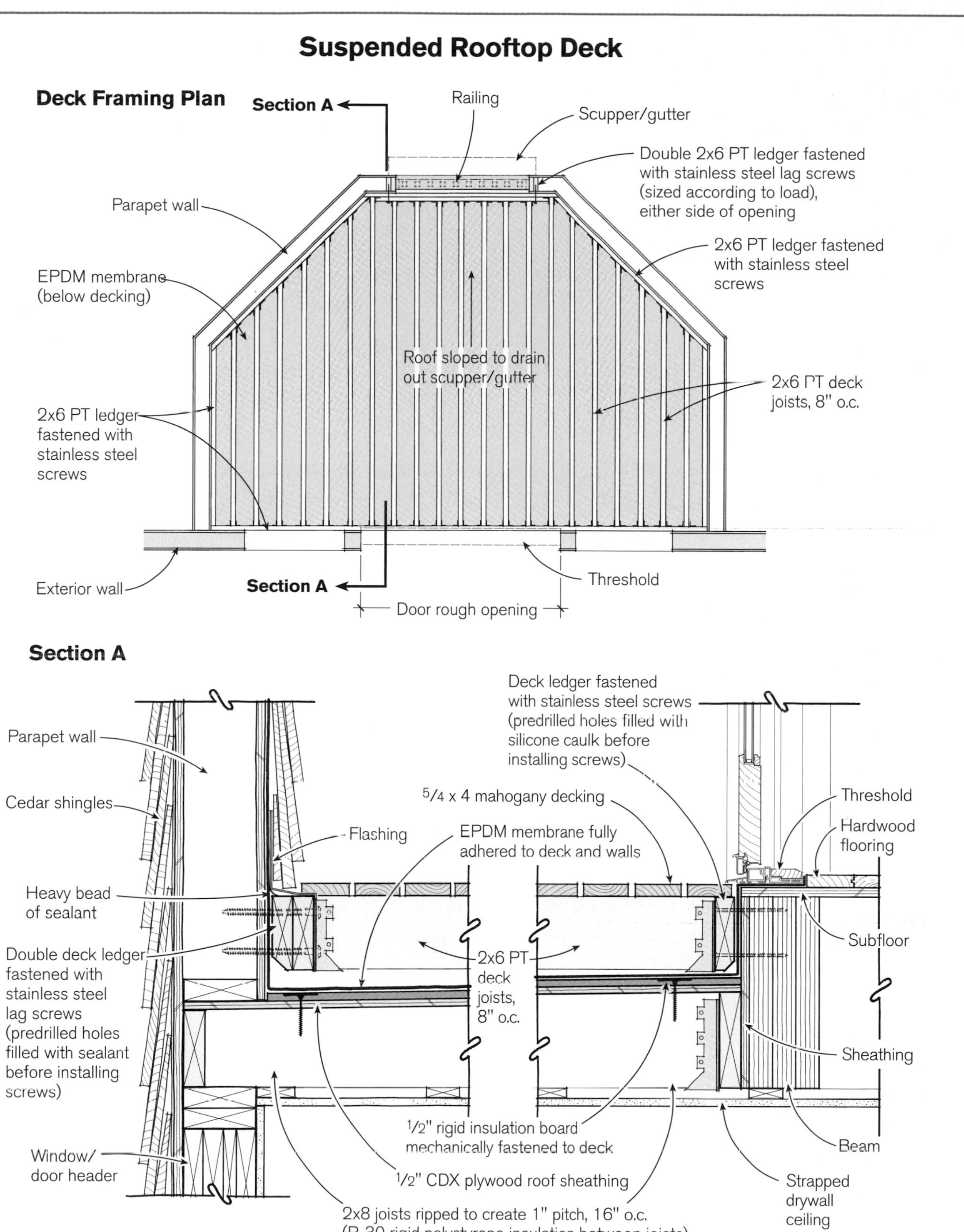

Figure 15. The author's design for rooftop decks protects the structure and living space of the room below with a continuous EPDM roof. To allow free drainage and protect the roofing, the deck frame is suspended from the parapet walls.

When I started to use rooftop decks more than 15 years ago, I looked around at some examples built by others. EPDM rubber membranes make an excellent low-slope roof covering, and it's not hard to build a deck sitting on sleepers that rest on the membrane itself; but I've never liked that method. For one thing, the sleepers tend to compress the foam-board underlayment used for those EPDM systems, creating a slight trough or depression in the roof surface. And they tend to dam up the water that should flow freely off the roof. Debris and grime quickly start to collect in the low spots around the sleepers and, after a few years, accumulate on the roof just below the walking surface.

To avoid those problems, I worked out a design that suspends the deck frame an inch or two above the rubber roof, supported by parapet half-walls that rise above the roof plane as a continuation of exterior or interior house walls (**Figure 15**, previous page). That way, the deck structure never contacts the roof surface at all — instead, a continuous drainage space lets water (and dirt) flow freely off.

On the other hand, the deck still shades the watertight EPDM surface and protects it from damaging sunlight. That extends the service life of the rubber (which is good for 30 years or more, even when it isn't shaded). I've built at least 25 roof-and-deck combinations using this design over the last dozen or so years, all exposed to harsh seaside conditions that can eat the enamel off a doorknob in about three months — and I haven't had a single callback.

For an example of how it's done, I'll use the deck we installed over a bump-out room on a custom home we designed and built on the coast of Rhode Island. On that house, a projecting octagon room facing the ocean provided nice views, light, and air; it also helped stiffen the house frame against coastal windstorms. With parapet walls, a rubber roof, and a deck assembly placed above it, the room also supports a protected but open upper-story deck, graced with a nice view and plenty of sunshine.

Roof Framing

The room's ceiling-roof framing really resembles a floor frame more than the usual roof frame (**Figure 16**). The house walls do the work of supporting the above-roof walking deck, and the deck framing itself is sized to carry the design dead and live loads for our area, including snow loads. So although it is capable of considerably more, the roof-ceiling frame for the room isn't actually subjected to loading much beyond its own weight. Depending on the dimensions of the space, I'll use 2x8s or 2x10s for joists, with 1x4 strapping on the underside and 1/2-inch plywood sheathing on the upper side. We rip the tops of the joists to provide a pitch of about an inch, creating a gentle slope away from the house.

Parapet Wall

We frame the parapet wall with 2x6 plates and studs, and sheath it on both faces with plywood (**Figure 17**). The parapet wall supports the deck and also serves in place of a railing; it needs to be high enough so that when the depth of the deck framing and decking is considered, the wall cap will reach the required height for a deck rail. Because the roof edge it sits on is sloped away from the house, the studs for the wall have to be individually measured and cut to the proper length, so that the wall height will be uniform above the level walking deck.

The main room walls beneath the parapet walls are mostly full of windows and doors. The headers in those openings are sized to support both the uppermost deck, with its allowable live loads from snow and people, and the more lightly loaded lower-room ceiling frame.

Rubber Membrane

EPDM roofing is a known quantity, with billions of square feet in service and decades of accumulated installer experience. There are several ways to attach EPDM to roofs in the commercial market; for our jobs we use a fully adhered system. First, we screw a rigid insulation board to the plywood roof sheathing, then we apply adhesive to the foam board and lay the rubber over it (**Figure 18**, page 236).

It takes several pieces to completely cover the whole shape of our roof and its parapet walls; seams are formed according to manufacturer specifications, with either applied adhesive or a special seaming tape. We also run the rubber roofing up the main house wall and into the rough window and door openings — when all the seams have cured, we're left with one continuous, integrated waterproof membrane protecting not just the roof, but also all the vertical walls around the deck, as well as the main house wall and its rough openings (**Figure 19**, page 236).

The contractors I use for my rubber roofs come out of the commercial roofing industry, of course — that's where most EPDM is used. These little jobs are attractive to them, however: They can make good money on a weekend, and some of my smaller roofs they could just about cover with scraps left over from one of their regular commercial jobs.

Deck Frame and Decking

I build my deck frames with pressure-treated southern yellow pine (**Figure 20**, page 237). We fasten the ledger to the parapet wall with lag screws sized to more than handle the load. We predrill for the lags, and before we drive in the screws, we fill the drilled holes with a manufacturer-recommended caulking that's compatible with the EPDM membrane (**Figure 21**, page 237). That completely seals those holes, so

Figure 16. The ceiling joists of the room below the deck are ripped to provide a slight pitch away from the house, then sheathed with 1/2-inch plywood (left). Strapping helps ensure a flat drywall ceiling (right).

Figure 17. Half-height parapet walls framed on top of the sheathed roof (far left) enclose most of the deck area, with just a small front panel left open (left). The front opening will receive a cedar railing and copper roof-edge flashing, draining into a copper-lined wood gutter.

water won't get into the wall structure where the screw penetrates the rubber. We caulk the top edge of the ledger to keep water from getting behind it.

For decking boards, I prefer to use a heavy, durable, rot-resistant tropical hardwood. I've used mahogany on some of my older decks, and currently I like to use ipe. Alternatively, I'll use a plastic composite decking material such as Trex (Trex Company, Inc.). I don't ever use treated southern yellow pine for decking. It doesn't deteriorate, but I've found that the juvenile wood, with its flat grain, twists, checks, and splinters, just isn't suitable for my projects.

One caution to keep in mind: Coatings commonly used on wood decks may contain solvents that will eat through EPDM. I always warn my clients that they can't apply an oil-based stain to their deck, unless they want to burn big holes into their roof. I prefer to use lumber that's naturally resistant to weather and rot and needs no stain, but if the customer wants a deck stain, we prestain the wood before we install it.

Figure 18. A roofer lays out the specified fasteners for the rigid-foam underlayment (left). After the screws are driven in (top right), the EPDM is adhered to the deck (bottom right).

Figure 19. At left, the roofing contractor rolls adhesive onto the back of the EPDM in preparation for covering the parapet walls. Lapping and seaming the rubber into wall openings and at intersections and transitions (photos at right) creates a continuous watertight drainage plane capable of protecting vulnerable points in the building envelope against brutal oceanfront weather.

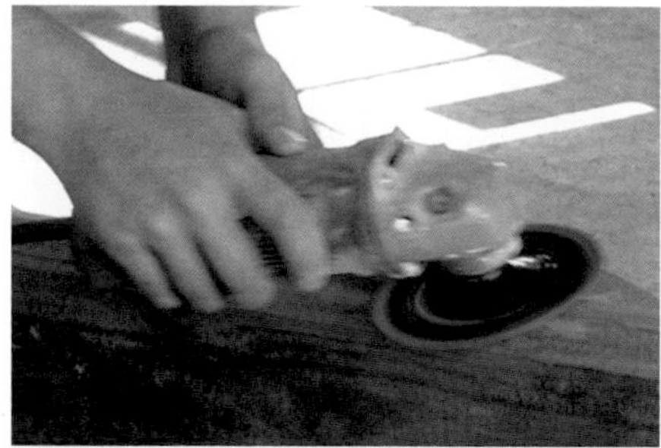

Figure 20. The crew first bevels the back of the ledger (photos at right) to promote free drainage around the edges of the deck. Because the roof surface slopes, the ledger board has to be leveled (left) — the drainage space along the bottom of the ledger gets wider toward the front of the roof.

Figure 21. A heavy bead of sealant keeps water from getting behind the ledger (left). The crew also puts sealant on the back of the ledger (left) before screwing it into place (photos at right). The lags are driven through predrilled holes filled with a manufacturer-recommended caulking that's compatible with the EPDM membrane. The caulking completely seals each hole, so water won't get into the wall structure where the screw penetrates the rubber.

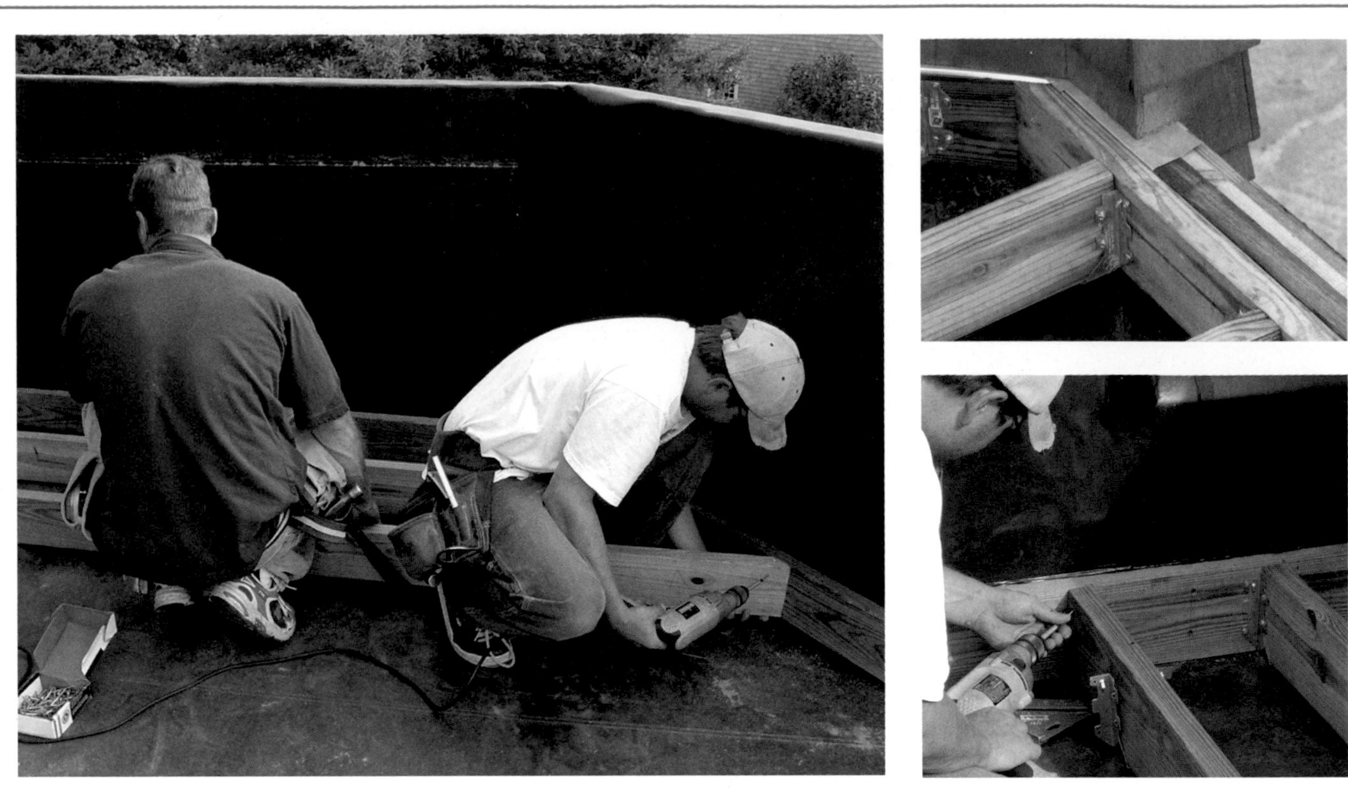

Figure 22. Deck joists are first screwed into place (left), with hangers added after (photos at right).

Figure 23. A cedar rail will finish off the opening at the front of the deck (left). The copper flashing will drain runoff from the roof surface into a painted and copper-lined wooden gutter. The author sometimes uses scuppers to carry the runoff into a gutter, as in this small deck with a plexiglass rail (top right). Note the height of the scuppers (bottom right), which are at roof level, relative to the decking.

Also, I often assemble my deck frames in smaller panels, or modules, that can be unfastened and lifted out in sections if the deck needs recoating, or, more important, if the roof membrane has to be repaired or modified. Sometimes we fasten our deck hangers to the ledger, or even send the fasteners for the hangers all the way into the framing of the parapet wall; but instead of fastening the joists into the hangers in the usual way, we just set the joists into the stirrup of the hanger and put a hold-down strip across the top. That way, someone can remove the strip later and lift the joists up out of the hangers, if need be — the deck comes free in panels.

Railing

If I'm putting a deck over a rectangular room, I'll suspend the deck frame between two half-wall side parapets and run a railing across the whole front opening. More commonly, though, the deck rests above an 8-sided or 12-sided room. In that case, we frame up the parapet walls around almost the whole circumference of the polygon, as we did in the example shown here, and we frame the deck with joists running from the main house wall out to the parapet half-walls. With the roof itself pitched gently toward the outside, the angling polygon half-walls naturally catch the rainwater and funnel it toward the outermost segment of the polygon. There, we leave a gap and install a railing across the opening, letting the rainwater drain out over a copper drip-edge and into a gutter (**Figure 22**). Or, sometimes, I will close in that wall as well, installing just one or two scuppers for drainage.

Scuppers and Gutters

We have copper scuppers custom-bent at a metal shop for each job, and we let the roofer attach the membrane to the metal. Then we drop the metal right into a fir gutter. I like to use wood gutters, because they look like a piece of the woodwork — almost like a cornice or a piece of crown molding. You can get fir gutter stock at most lumberyards, but if appearance is critical, I order it from a specialty supplier who carries high-quality material. We always preprime and prepaint the gutter before installing it, and we line it with copper (**Figure 23**). The big key is to make sure that you space the gutter away from the fascia when you attach it. We use stainless steel screws to fasten the gutter to the fascia, but we attach it through predrilled spacer blocks of pressure-treated plywood (sawn lumber would be more likely to split).

Andrew P. DiGiammo is a design/build contractor and a partner in an architectural firm in Assonet, Mass.

Repairing Cantilevered Balconies

by Angus Smith

My company specializes in condominium maintenance and repairs. In California, homeowners have up to 10 years to bring suit against the original builder for faulty workmanship. Condo associations are often awarded settlements for remedial projects that can run into the millions of dollars — work that is usually undertaken by companies much larger than mine.

We're most often hired by associations that have already passed the 10-year limit, which means that the work must be paid for out of a maintenance budget. Our most common job involves repairing water-damaged framing, especially in the cantilevered balconies that are so popular in multifamily buildings here. The jobs we tackle are awarded in quantities from 1 to 50 balconies at a time.

Anatomy of a Balcony

The typical condo balcony we encounter is framed with cantilevered joists that project about 6 feet from the face of the building, or from one-fourth to one-third of their overall length. The remainder of the joist is buried inside, an integral component of the interior floor system. A fractured or delaminated balcony surface (typically plywood, covered by one of several possible waterproofing systems) is usually the first tip-off to greater problems; all too often, the unseen damage is extensive and poses a hazard to the occupants (**Figure 24**, next page). Stucco, a common exterior finish in this part of the world, can also conceal a multitude of problems. Although the surface seldom reveals underlying rot, staining and discoloration should raise suspicions.

Water, water everywhere. We rarely encounter cantilevered joists with a deliberate, taper-sawn slope to drain water away from the structure, despite the minimum 1/4-inch-per-foot slope requirement specified by most waterproofing manufacturers. These flat decks permit water to pond on the surface, leading to premature failure of the waterproofing membrane. In

Figure 24. Surface cracks in a balcony's waterproofing are often the first sign of hidden structural damage. Cracks typically appear above joints in the plywood deck sheathing.

addition, we often find poorly detailed or missing flashing at the balcony perimeter, which allows wind-driven water to enter the framing.

Railing systems are usually solid half walls rather than open assemblies, which makes for easy construction and provides privacy for the residents. It also prevents runoff from a balcony from dripping directly onto one below, but at a cost: The rainwater that falls onto each balcony must be collected and directed outside. This is usually handled by a floor drain or an open, floor-level scupper draining to a gutter. Either drainage method can lead to rot unless the spout that passes through the framing is properly installed and sealed (**Figure 25**).

Inadequate flashing and finishing at railing post penetrations often allow water to run down into the framing cavity, making those common points of failure as well. We frequently find railings that are attached to the building without proper flashing, allowing water to become trapped against the wall. As the framing decays and the fasteners corrode, the railing provides little support, and the condition is often dangerously invisible.

Joist Repair

Repairing rotten joists is particularly difficult because we can't go inside to tear up the floor or open the ceiling over the occupant below. We've had to devise effective techniques for repairing damage and preventing future problems while working almost entirely outside.

Bolted sisters. The first order of business is to expose the bare joists by tearing off the railing, the plywood deck, and any soffit paneling underneath. In most cases, we find enough sound wood to permit repairing the joists, rather than replacing them. Rot is often concentrated in the outermost 6 inches of the joists and along the upper edges, where nail penetrations have allowed water in. We cut the damaged ends back to healthy wood and sister new, 6-foot-long joists of equal dimension alongside, using two carriage bolts at the center and two at each end to tie the joists solidly together. To make a neater-looking repair and provide full nailing for the deck sheathing and trim, we fill in the end cuts with blocks of lumber.

Any top-edge rot gets ripped away to undamaged wood and replaced with a new ripping, which we simply gun-nail into place. We treat all cuts with a termite and rot repellent, Jasco Termin-8 (Jasco Chemical Corp.), a green, oil-based copper-naphthenate solution that helps prevent future infestation. If the original joists didn't incorporate a drainage slope, we'll rip a full-length, 1/4-inch-per-foot taper on the top edge,

Figure 25. Improperly flashed scuppers (left) and floor drains (right) often allow water into the framing, leading to hidden rot.

Figure 26. To eliminate puddling, the author rips a 1/4-inch-per-foot taper from the top edge of the cantilevered joists, creating a positive drainage slope. A power planer cleans up the cut.

Figure 27. Joists that are too far gone to repair must be replaced between the wall plate and the new double rim joist (far left). The rim hangs at the ends of the intact cantilevered joists on upside-down joist hangers. The replaced "cripple joists" are hung conventionally (left).

cleaning up the cuts afterward with a power plane (**Figure 26**).

Shifting the load. Joists that are too far gone to repair must be replaced. With no practical way to insert a new cantilever, this can pose a real problem if the rot is extensive. Fortunately, we usually find that only one or two of the original joists are rotted to the point of being unusable. In such cases, we rely on the remaining members for structural support by installing a new, double rim joist at the outboard edge and tying it to each solid joist with an upside-down joist hanger (**Figure 27**).

This beefed-up rim hangs from the sound joists, providing outboard support to the few joists that must be completely replaced. The inboard ends of the replaced joists rest on the wall plate, while the outboard ends are supported by conventionally installed joist hangers at the rim — an approach that shifts the load from these replaced "cripple joists" to the repaired and sistered joists through the rim.

I gleaned this detail from a structural engineer many years ago, and it has proved to be reliable in practice. But obviously, it demands common sense and good judgment. If more than two in ten joists must be replaced, I'll consult an engineer. That also applies to another situation we sometimes encounter, where the damaged cantilever framing consists of a heavy beam at either end of the balcony with perpendicular infill joists running between them. In either case, it will usually be necessary to tear up the floor inside or post the balcony to the ground, but that's another story.

Figure 28. Flexible membrane flashing, tucked behind existing building paper and overlapping a sheet-metal skirt flashing, provides positive wall drainage onto the new balcony surface.

Buttoning Up

Once the joists are repaired, we apply a 3/4-inch T&G plywood deck, glued and screwed to the joists, to help create a strong, unified structure. It's important to observe the prescribed 1/8-inch spacing between plywood sheets; otherwise, this is the area where a waterproofing membrane will first show signs of stress.

In replicating the original closed or open railing system, we pay strict attention to the sequence and detailing of the flashing. (Incredibly, we often find that the original flashing was mindlessly installed to trap rather than shed water.) Where the railing abuts the building, we break back the stucco or siding and weave Moistop flashing (Fortifiber) a polyethylene-fiberglass composite membrane, behind the existing building paper to protect all framing transitions from water penetration. The top of the railing gets a sheet-metal cap flashing, followed by Moistop, woven behind the existing building paper.

California condo framing typically has no sheathing over the wall studs, except where a shear panel is required. Instead, stucco lath is applied directly to the studs over 60-minute building paper. To make

Figure 29. Galvanized expanded metal lath, thoroughly stapled to the plywood deck, reinforces the cementitious waterproofing membrane. Plywood expansion joints are isolated and protected from filling by a proprietary seam tape.

Figure 30. Stucco siding repairs follow the original three-layer process of scratch coat, brown coat, and color coat. A narrow strip of the sheet-metal flashing is left exposed to allow crack-free movement between wall and deck.

Figure 31. A final, acrylic color coat seals and protects the multilayered deck system from water absorption.

sure that the transition from deck to side wall is watertight, we break the stucco (or other siding) back about 6 inches up the wall and run a 9-inch-wide Moistop strip over the side-wall framing, behind the original building paper and over the flange of the 26-gauge bonderized, galvanized sheet-metal (C&J Metal Products) transition flashing that runs onto the deck surface (**Figure 28**).

Waterproofing

To prevent future problems in the repaired balcony, proper waterproofing is essential. I rely on Life Deck AL (Life Deck Specialty Coatings), a reinforced three-coat cementitious product made for exterior plywood walking surfaces. We handle the installation ourselves, paying close attention to the manufacturer's specifications.

First, we install bonderized sheet-metal wall flashing and drip-edge, nailing it directly to the plywood and sealing overlaps with an approved polyurethane caulk. To prevent the expansion joints between plywood sheets from filling up, we cover them with self-adhesive, 40-mil-thick Life Deck Seam Tape. Then we install a layer of galvanized expanded metal lath over the plywood and flashing and thoroughly fasten it with a pneumatic stapler, using at least 16 staples per square foot (**Figure 29**). The base coat — a thick, soupy mix of cement and acrylic polymer — is poured on and troweled into the lath. After the base coat cures, we trowel on a similar, slurry layer to build up the membrane and fill any voids. The third, texture-coat layer is splattered on using a hopper-fed texture gun, at about a 70% coverage rate, and knocked down with a steel trowel while wet.

Once the texture coat can be walked on, we complete the patching of the stucco siding, following the original steps of 60-minute building paper, stucco lath (wire), scratch coat, brown coat, and a color and texture coat (**Figure 30**). Usually, we're patching small areas, so we use a quick-drying mortar mix to help expedite the job. We take the stucco down over the apron flashing but not all the way to the deck, leaving a narrow band of metal exposed. This allows for some necessary structural movement and eliminates cracking at the junctions.

A proprietary acrylic color coat seals and completes the deck surface treatment (**Figure 31**). The deck can be walked on within about 4 hours, but it's best to wait 24 hours before putting the surface to regular use.

Angus Smith owns Angus Smith Construction in Aliso Viejo, Calif.

EXTERIORS

Chapter 13: Paints & Stains

- Finishing Wood Siding and Trim
- Keeping the Paint on Wood Windows
- Paint and Moisture Q&A

Finishing Wood Siding and Trim

by Bill Feist

Here's a plausible scenario: You've just completed a new custom home — the clients are ecstatic, the project looks great. With fresh paint on the outside, the house's curb appeal promises to bring new client referrals. Then, within six months or a year, the phone call comes: "The paint is peeling; can you do something?"

Premature paint failure on wood siding has become commonplace in recent years. The reasons cited are varied. Some blame paint quality, claiming that paints are not as durable since the lead content was banned. Others point to the declining quality of the wood siding itself. Still others argue that the high interior moisture levels in today's tight houses cause water vapor to move through the exterior walls into the back of the siding, which eventually causes the paint to peel and blister.

All of these arguments have some merit. There is often a complex combination of causes behind a particular paint failure. But paint failure is not inevitable: In most cases, if the job had been designed and executed properly in the first place, the failure could have been prevented.

Success with painted siding starts with an understanding of how the siding you choose will perform under local weather conditions. Next, it's necessary to match the finish to the siding — a given finish performs differently on different types of siding.

Here, I'll look mainly at two areas: (1) the properties of wood that most affect paint durability; and (2) varieties of paints, stains, and other finishes, and how they perform on various types of siding.

Although it's not covered in this discussion, ventilation details are critical to good paint performance. This includes proper roof venting as well as using adequate indoor exhaust ventilation to remove excess moisture from the building. When the budget allows, vented siding — where an air space is created between the sheathing and siding — is unquestionably one of the best details for ensuring long-term paint performance (see "Detailing Rain-Screen Siding," page 186).

Table 1
Paint-Holding Ability of Selected Softwoods

	Weight per cubic foot at 8% moisture content	Paint-holding ability (I best, IV worst)
Western red cedar	22.4	I
Redwood	27.4	I
Eastern white pine	24.2	II
Ponderosa pine	27.5	III
Western hemlock	28.7	III
Spruce	26.8	III
Douglas fir	31.0	IV
Red pine	30.8	IV
Southern yellow pine	38.2	IV

Note: Lighter-weight woods shrink and swell less than denser woods, so tend to hold paint better. Besides being lower density, redwood and cedar have narrow bands of latewood compared with southern yellow pine and Douglas fir, which are higher in density and have wide bands of latewood.

The Wood Makes a Difference

How wood siding performs varies not only from one wood species to another but within the same species. These natural variables, and the variables created during the manufacturing processes, have important influences on wood's finishing properties and its durability.

Density. The density of wood, or its "weight," is one of the most important factors affecting paint life, for a simple reason: "Heavy" woods shrink and swell more than "light" woods with changes in moisture content (**Table 1**). Excessive dimensional change constantly stresses a film-forming finish, such as paint or a solid-color stain, and may result in early failure. Finishes that don't form a film, such as penetrating stains, are not affected by these dimensional changes.

Flat grain vs. edge grain. Softwood lumber is referred to as either flat-grained or edge-grained (*plainsawn* or *quartersawn* in hardwoods). Most standard lumber grades contain a high percentage of flat grain. Flat-grained lumber shrinks and swells more than edge-grained lumber (**Figure 1**), so edge-grained lumber will usually hold paint better than flat-grained material. Some bevel sidings are produced in both a flat-grained standard grade and an edge-grained premium grade (sometimes called "vertical grain").

Earlywood and latewood. Another reason that edge-grained siding holds paint better is that edge-grained wood has narrower bands of latewood. Earlywood and latewood form in two distinct bands within an annual growth ring. Latewood is denser, harder, smoother, and darker than earlywood. Although new paint or solid-color stain will adhere well to both earlywood and latewood, old alkyd paints and solid-color stains that have become brittle with age and weathering will peel first from the smooth, hard surface of the latewood.

Heartwood and sapwood. Mature trees have a darker central column of wood called heartwood, surrounded by a lighter cylinder of wood called sapwood. Heartwood is formed as the individual cells die and are impregnated with extractives, pitch, oil, and other extraneous materials. These natural materials give the heartwood of some species, such as redwood, cedar, and cypress, a natural resistance to decay and insects as well as an attractive color. Extractives, however, can sometimes cause discoloration problems when the heartwood is finished with paints or solid-color stains. Because the extractives are water soluble, they can dissolve when water is present in the wood and be transported to the wood surface. When the solution of extractives reaches the painted surface, the water evaporates, and the extractives remain, showing through as a reddish brown mark.

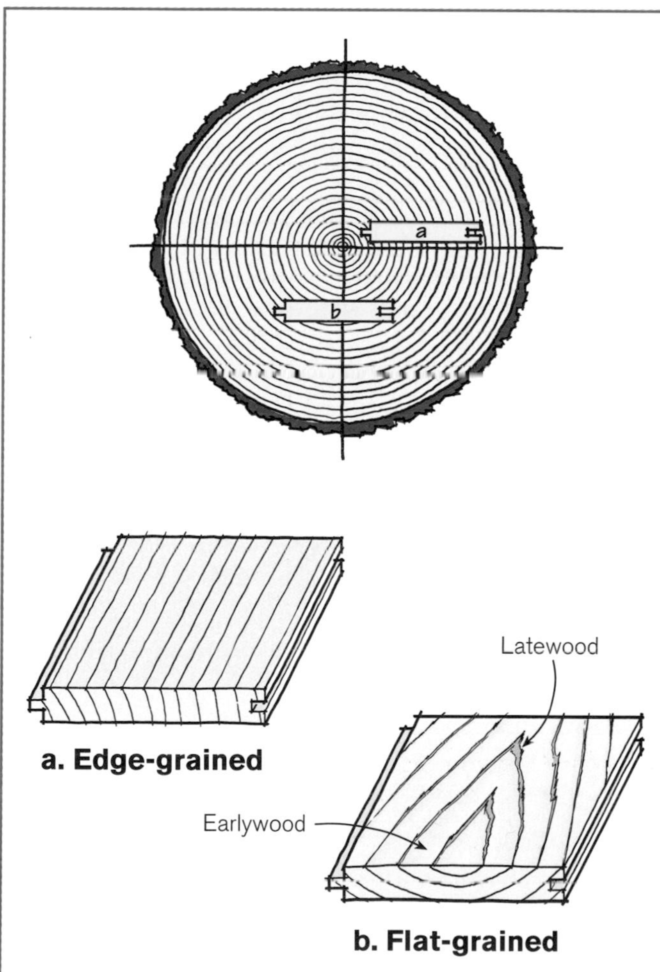

Figure 1. Flat-grained lumber shrinks and swells more than edge-grained (quartersawn) lumber and also has wider bands of dark latewood. Therefore, edge-grained siding will usually hold paint better than flat-grained material.

Table 2
Optional Moisture Content for Wood Siding and Trim

Geographical area	Moisture content: Average	Moisture content: Individual pieces
Most areas of United States	12%	9–14%
Dry southwestern areas	9%	7–12%
Warm, humid coastal areas	>12%	9–20%

Note: It's best to paint exterior wood when its moisture content is within the prevailing range for the region.
Source: Williams, Knaebe & Feist, "Finishes for Exterior Wood"

Sapwood is not decay resistant, but also does not normally cause discoloration problems through paints or solid-color stains.

Knots and other irregularities, such as bark, splits, pitch pockets, and insect damage, also affect paint adhesion. Knots are mainly exposed end grain. End-grain wood absorbs more finish than flat- and edge-grained lumber, which will affect the appearance of paint. In pine, knots often contain a high percentage of resin, which may cause the paint over the knot to discolor. Furthermore, large knots usually check and crack, and can leave a noticeable split in the wood surface. Good painting practices can eliminate or control brown stain over knots. First apply a primer recommended for blocking the extractives in the knot, then follow with two top coats. Some manufacturers recommend orange shellac for controlling knot bleed.

Wood Properties You Can Control

So far, we've been talking about properties of wood that vary from species to species and grade to grade. But once you've selected and bought wood siding or trim, there are a few variables under your control that will affect the life of the finish.

Moisture content is critical in determining the service life of paint. The best time to paint wood is when its average moisture content is about the same as that expected to prevail once the wood is put in service (**Table 2**). Wood above 20% moisture content should never be painted, as the paint will most likely peel.

Surface roughness. Paint lasts longer on smooth edge-grained surfaces than on smooth flat-grained ones. However, paint will last longest on roughsawn or rough-sanded wood, whether the wood is edge-grained or flat-grained. To roughen the surface, sand smooth siding with 60-grit paper before painting.

Avoid weathering before painting. Much research has been done that indicates that whenever wood is to be painted, stained, or finished in any manner, weathering of the unprotected wood before finishing may be detrimental to the service life of the finish. The USDA Forest Service's Forest Products Laboratory in

Madison, Wis., recommends that any dry, unprotected wood should not be allowed to weather for more than two weeks before it is protected with some finish that will prevent photodegradation and water damage.

Choosing a Finish

Wood finishes range from opaque, film-forming paints and solid stains to penetrating semitransparent stains, which impart a rustic appearance and allow some wood grain to show through, to clear finishes, which accentuate the grain and natural beauty of the wood. The choice of finish should be made at the same time that the siding treatment is chosen. For example, while an expensive all-acrylic latex paint may perform well on a clear grade of siding, it may not be the best choice for a roughsawn, knotty grade.

For a rundown of the available types of products, with comments on their suitability for various types of sidings, see **Table 3**, page 250.

Paints

Paints form a film, and provide the most protection against weathering and wetting. It's possible to get up to 10 years from a top-quality paint applied as

Wood Siding Q&A

Sealing Siding Before Painting

Q. *How much benefit is there to applying a water sealer and wood preservative to clapboard siding before priming and painting?*

A. There are many advantages to using a paintable water-repellent preservative (WRP) on unpainted clapboard siding before priming and painting. The treatment reduces raised grain, checking, warping, and splitting, and it also improves paint adhesion. A WRP inhibits mildew growth on both painted and unpainted wood, and it will retard decay in above-ground applications. A paintable preservative will help improve paint performance on the more difficult-to-paint woods, like flat-grain southern yellow pine and other flat-grain wood species.

Use WRPs only on dry, bare wood. The treatment must be done when the temperature is above 50°F. You can apply the treatment by brush or by dipping. When brushing, allow two days of warm, favorable drying weather before painting. When dipping, a full week of favorable drying weather may be necessary before painting. If you don't allow enough time for most of the solvent to dry from the wood and for the wax in the preservative to be absorbed, the paint may not cure or bond properly.

If you want to apply a WRP to previously painted wood, remove all loose paint, then brush the preservative into joints and unpainted areas only. Remove excess WRP from the painted surfaces with a rag. Again, allow two days of favorable warm drying weather before repainting.

Commercially available WRPs include Clear Wood Preservative (in the Cuprinol Group) from Sherwin-Williams and DAP's Woodlife Classic II wood preservative (Wolman Wood Care Products). When shopping for a WRP, the key word to look for is "paintable." There are many WRPs that are meant to be used as wood deck treatments and natural finishes, but these are generally not paintable. — *B.F.*

Back-priming vs. Sealing

Q. *I have often read that wood siding should be back-primed before installation. But I believe that a primer without a finish coat is of no value, because I don't think a primer can slow down moisture movement. Has there been any research or testing on this question?*

A. Some architects and wood trade associations advise priming the back side of solid wood siding with paint or a water repellent. Research performed at the U.S. Forest Products Laboratory (FPL) in Madison, Wis., during the 1950s conclusively indicated that back-priming the siding with a paintable water-repellent preservative (like DAP's Woodlife) improved the paint retention and overall performance of horizontal wood lap siding. However, the benefits of back-priming solid wood siding with paint have not been experimentally verified, and I am not aware of any published information on studies on this subject.

Recent FPL publications describing studies on back-priming hardboard siding conclude that "back-priming did not improve the performance of this particular hardboard siding nor did it lower in-service moisture content." The studies indicated that there was a possibility that back-priming the lower half of the hardboard siding was beneficial.

Keep in mind that if only the lower portion of the back of wood siding is primed, it is likely that the siding will absorb less moisture, and this would be beneficial. However, it is also possible that if the entire back face of the siding is primed with paint, water that has been

two top coats over a primer coat.

Oil-based vs. latex. The most durable house paints are the all-acrylic latex paints. Although oil-based paint films usually provide the best protection from liquid water and water vapor, they are not necessarily the most durable, because they become brittle over time. No matter how well sealed, wood still moves with seasonal humidity changes, thus stressing and eventually cracking the brittle paint film. On the other hand, latex paints, particularly the acrylic paints, remain more flexible with age. Even though latex paints allow more water vapor to pass through, they hold up better by swelling and shrinking with the wood.

Gloss. Paints are available in different degrees of gloss, including flat, matte, semigloss, and gloss. Generally, high-gloss paints contain more paint resin and less pigment, and will perform better and last longer than the low-gloss or flat paints. Flat paints tend to pick up dirt and absorb water more readily than do the high-gloss paints. Because of this, mildew growth is often greater on the flat paints.

Back-prime. Paints do not penetrate the wood deeply but rather form a film on the surface. This film can blister or peel if the wood is wetted or if

absorbed by the siding will be retarded from evaporating. Back-priming with paint retards water vapor from leaving the wood, and the FPL hardboard research suggests that back-priming the entire back with paint may have more negative effects than positive. Unlike paint, a water-repellent preservative will permit drying (loss of water vapor) and also reduce wetting (liquid water).

If I were installing new solid wood siding, I would treat the entire board with a paintable water-repellent preservative, as discussed in the previous question. Best of all, dip the siding before installation (redipping any cut ends), then dry, prime, and top-coat. If that is not possible, I would treat the back, the ends, and the bottom edge of the siding with water repellent preservative.

Finally, if a paintable water-repellent preservative is not available, I would back-prime the lower half, ends, and bottom edge of the board with a single coat of alkyd primer paint. — *B.F.*

Paint vs. Stain on Clapboards

Q. *I plan to install radially cut spruce clapboards on a new house and want to stain them with a white semitransparent or opaque stain. What type of finish appearance should I expect, and how often will the finish need to be renewed? Although stained siding looks better to me than painted siding, I know that some people say that stain is "just thinned paint."*

A. Semitransparent stains are most effective on roughsawn and weathered wood because more finish can be applied. The best exterior house stains are usually described as semitransparent, penetrating, and oil- or alkyd-based (solvent-borne). The better alkyd-based penetrating stains contain a fungicide (preservative or mildewcide), an ultraviolet light stabilizer, or a water repellent. Check the label for these important ingredients.

The alkyd-based, solvent-borne stains actually penetrate the wood surface to a degree, and do not form a surface film like paint does. Thus, they don't totally hide the wood grain and will leave a soft, flat appearance. They will not trap moisture that may encourage decay. Since they penetrate and don't form a film like paint does, the stains cannot blister or peel even if moisture penetrates the wood. Alkyd-based stains normally require only a light cleaning with a stiff bristle brush and water before refinishing.

Latex-based (waterborne) stains are also available, but they do not penetrate the wood surface as do their oil- and alkyd-based counterparts. These are essentially "thinned paints." On spruce clapboards, a latex stain probably won't perform as well as an oil- or alkyd-based stain, and could also be more difficult to refinish.

How long the stain will last depends on weather exposure and the roughness of the wood. When used on new smooth-planed siding that is fully exposed to the weather, semitransparent penetrating stains generally last only about two to three years. When refinished after weathering, a smooth-planed siding should accept two coats of stain, and the finish will last much longer than the first application.

Since a rough surface will usually accept two coats of stain, even on the first application, it is preferable to a smooth surface. Stain on roughsawn siding may last six to eight years, depending on the amount of exposure. However, such durability often requires applying the stain at a rate of 100 to 150 square feet per gallon, a much greater amount than is usually required for paint, which is typically applied at a rate of 400 to 450 square feet per gallon. — *B.F.*

Table 3. Suitability and Expected Life of Exterior Wood Finishes

Type of exterior wood surface	Water-repellent preservatives and penetrating oils: Suitability	Water-repellent preservatives and penetrating oils: Expected life (years)	Semitransparent stain: Suitability	Semitransparent stain: Expected life (years)	Paint and solid-color stain: Suitability	Paint and solid-color stain: Expected life (years) Paint	Paint and solid-color stain: Expected life (years) Solid-color stain
SIDING							
Cedar and redwood							
Smooth (vertical grain)	High	1-2	Moderate	2-3	High	4-6	3-5
Roughsawn	High	2-3	High	5-8	Moderate	5-7	4-6
Pine, fir, spruce							
Smooth (flat-grained)	High	1-2	Low	2-3	Moderate	3-5	2-4
Rough (flat-grained)	High	2-3	High	4-7	Moderate	4-6	3-5
Plywood (Douglas fir and Southern Pine)							
Sanded	Very Low	1-2	Low	2-4	Moderate	2-4	2-3
Textured (roughsawn)	Low	2-3	High	4-6	Moderate	4-6	3-5
Medium-density overlay	—	—	—	—	Excellent	6-8	5-7
Hardboard, medium density							
Smooth or Textured	—	—	—	—	High	4-6	3-5
MILLWORK (often pine)							
Windows, shutters, doors, exterior trim	High	—	Moderate	2-3	High	3-6	2-4
DECKING							
New (smooth)	High	1-2	Moderate	2-3	Very Low	2-3	1-2
Weathered (rough)	High	2-3	High	3-4	Very Low	2-3	1-2

*These data were compiled from the observations of many researchers. Expected life predictions are for one and two coats of each finish at an average location in the continental United States. Expected life will vary in extreme climates or exposure, such as desert, seashore, and deep woods.

water vapor from inside the house moves through the exterior wall into the siding because of the absence of a vapor barrier.

It's important to back-prime the siding with one coat of primer or a paintable water-repellent preservative before installation. This helps reduce wetting up the back of the siding. Carefully coating butt ends and cut ends is also important.

Solid-Color Stains

Solid-color stains (also called hiding, heavy-bodied, or opaque stains) are essentially thin paints, not true stains. Solid-color stains have a higher concentration of pigment than semitransparent penetrating stains, but a somewhat lower concentration of pigment than standard paints. As a result, solid-color stains obscure the natural wood color and grain, while the wood's surface texture is retained. They are often the finish of choice on textured or roughsawn siding products. They can also be applied over existing paints and solid-color stains, and normally leave a flat finish appearance.

Like paints, solid-color stains protect wood against UV degradation. Lifetimes of three to six years can be expected for two-coat applications.

Water-Repellent Preservatives

A penetrating water-repellent preservative may be used as a natural wood finish. This type of finish contains a preservative (a fungicide), a small amount of wax (or similar water repellent), a resin or drying oil, and a solvent such as turpentine, mineral spirits, or paraffinic oil. Some may be lightly pigmented, and waterborne formulations are also available. The unpigmented finishes provide minimal protection for wood and may last only one to three years depending on exposure. Water-repellent finishes reduce warping and checking, prevent water staining at the edges and ends of wood siding, and help control mildew growth. Wood treated with preservative is easily refinished and usually requires minimal surface prep.

Paintable water-repellent preservatives (such as DAP's Woodlife II, available from Wolman Wood Care Products) are also an excellent treatment for bare wood before priming and painting or in areas where old paint has peeled, exposing bare wood. This pretreatment keeps rain or dew from penetrating the wood, especially at joints and on end grain, thus decreasing the shrinking and swelling of the wood. As a result, less stress is placed on the paint film, and its service life is extended. While these treatments protect against liquid water, they do not protect wood from water vapor.

Oils

There are many penetrating oil-based and alkyd-based finishes available, most using linseed or tung oil. However, these clear or lightly pigmented oils may serve as a food source for mildew if applied to wood in the absence of a mildewcide. The oils will also perform better if a water repellent is included in the formulation. All these oil systems will protect wood, but their average lifetime may be only one to three years.

Semitransparent Stains

Semitransparent penetrating stains are pigmented water-repellent preservatives with higher resin or binder content. Lifetimes may vary from three to six years, depending on wood surface texture and quantity of stain applied. The solvent-borne stains (oil or alkyd-based) penetrate the wood surface to a degree, are porous, and do not form a surface film like paint. Thus, they do not totally hide the wood grain and will not trap moisture that may encourage decay. As a result, the stains will not blister or peel even if moisture penetrates the wood.

The better solvent-borne penetrating stains contain a fungicide (preservative or mildewcide), ultraviolet radiation stabilizer or absorber, and a water repellent. Latex-based (waterborne) stains are also available, but these do not penetrate the wood surface as do their oil-based counterparts. Newer latex formulations are being developed that may provide some penetrating characteristics.

You Get What You Pay For

When buying paint and other exterior wood finishes, it is best to use the top-of-the-line product of a supplier you know and trust. For example, the top-of-the-line and most expensive latex house paint of most manufacturers is usually the all-acrylic latex type.

Consider a factory finish. Many wood siding products are available either factory-primed or factory-finished (primed and top-coated). Factory finishing offers many advantages. Because of the controlled environment, it's easier to apply the correct amount of finish and to have it dry and cure under optimal conditions.

Bill Feist is a former wood-finishes researcher with the Forest Products Laboratory in Madison, Wis., and coauthor of Finishes for Exterior Wood. *This article was adapted with permission from* Wood Design & Building magazine.

Finishes for Treated Wood

by David Bowyer

Treated wood is safe from bugs and rot. But it will still warp, split, and deteriorate prematurely unless you finish it correctly. This kind of damage is caused by water and sunlight, not biological activity. To shield the wood's surface from water and sunlight, and keep it looking good, you need to protect it with sealers, and stain or paint.

Sealers

Sealers are penetrating coatings, generally clear or lightly tinted, that repel moisture. Their effective service life is only one to two years, with most manufacturers recommending an annual reapplication. Sealers make good undercoats for stains or good preprimers for paints. Many paint manufacturers are now recommending sealing before priming. A few sealers cannot be stained or painted over, so check the label before you buy.

Some sealers have preservatives added. Even though you're sealing treated wood, these are worth the small extra cost if you have a lot of site-cut ends (of course, you should seal all site-cut ends with full-strength preservative first).

USDA FOREST SERVICE, FOREST PRODUCTS LAB

Figure A. *The wood surface at left was brush-treated with a water repellent. The untreated wood surface at right absorbs water quickly.*

Another extra worth paying for, especially if you want the wood to keep a fresh-looking appearance, is an ultraviolet (UV) inhibitor and other transparent solids. These are found in the higher quality clear or lightly tinted finishes that have traditionally been used to protect

(continued)

Finishes for Treated Wood *(continued from previous page)*

natural wood sidings like cedar. They last longer than standard waterproofing sealers, with some manufacturers claiming an effective life of six years and longer.

Application. Sealers can be applied to treated lumber as long as the surface of the wood is dry (**Figure A**, previous page). Do not allow new wood to weather for more than a couple of weeks before applying the sealer, since a weathered surface will not hold finishes as well. Don't worry about the wood having a high internal moisture content. Sealers let the wood dry to the moisture content of the environment. Because they slow the drying process, stress in the wood is minimized.

You can brush, roll, or spray on the sealer, but dipping works best. The size of the pieces limits what you can dip, but for a project with small pieces, such as 2x2 porch balusters, you can use a section of gutter with two end caps for a dipping tank.

For large projects, I prefer a sprayer to get the sealer on and a brush to work it in. Because of their low solids/pigment content, sealers can easily be applied with a low-pressure sprayer like the one you would use in your garden (**Figure B**). I work with a spray wand in one hand and a brush with a 2- to 3-foot handle extension in the other. The chemical makeup of some sealers may gum up internal workings of some types of sprayers, so check the directions, and make sure you have solvent on hand before you fill the spray tank.

Where to use. I recommend using a waterproofing sealer on every treated wood project because it controls the initial drying and eliminates cracking, splitting, warping, and cupping. Another option is purchasing premium treated lumber with water repellents factory-applied under pressure at the time of treatment. Factory-applied waterproofing treatments penetrate the wood to a much greater degree than a surface application, and they can be a real timesaver for contractors.

HICKSON CORPORATION

Figure B. *For large surfaces, use a low-pressure garden sprayer, followed by brushing, to apply sealer.*

Stains

Like sealers, oil-based stains penetrate the wood. They have varying levels of pigment but still allow the grain and texture of the wood to show through. Stains are relatively permeable to moisture and are not as effective as sealers in protecting the wood. For better protection, you can apply an undercoat of sealer followed by a penetrating stain.

Stains can be applied to treated lumber as long as the surface is dry — preferably at least 1/8 inch deep — to get maximum penetration. I recommend a waiting period of a couple of weeks on new projects, depending on exposure and weather: longer in cool, damp weather; shorter in hot, dry weather. However, make sure the wood is sealed within a couple of weeks to prevent degradation of the surface.

A finish consisting of a coat of sealer, followed in a couple of weeks by two coats of stain, with the second coat being applied before the first is completely dry, will give you a finish that will last six to eight years. The lighter the stain and the more limited the exposure, the longer the life. Darker stains won't last quite as long, because they absorb more solar radiation.

Application. Again, a low-pressure sprayer followed by brushing works very well. Keep the stain well mixed by giving the sprayer a gentle shake now and again. With darker stains, the higher solids content could plug the sprayer, but I've never had a problem with this.

When you're applying semitransparent stains, watch out for lap marks. These are caused where you overlap a "dry edge" with wet stain. A sprayer lets you work faster, and it's easier to maintain a "wet edge."

Where to use. Semitransparent stains are not ideal for horizontal surfaces like decks, since they are not very resilient to abrasive wear. If you use a dark stain, wear patterns develop quickly. Stick to lighter shades if you're staining a deck.

Beyond this slight limitation, semitransparent stains are an excellent way to protect treated lumber. Their ease of application, good service life, and the fact that they never peel make them my favorite.

Paint

Oil or latex paints and latex stains form a film on the surface of the wood. Whether latex or oil, paint offers the greatest protection against weathering because of its high pigment content. However, paint performance can be a problem for two reasons: moisture content and surface grain.

First, the wood's high moisture content can cause paint to peel. Moisture gets trapped behind the paint film, especially during the initial drying period. Even though latex paints are supposed to be "breathable," the paint just can't release the moisture fast enough.

Ideally, you should wait for the wood to dry out completely, but if you do, direct sunlight will degrade the wood, creating an unstable surface for paint. You can get around these problems by sealing the wet treated wood and then waiting for the surface to dry out just enough for painting. This is typically two to three weeks, depending on weather conditions.

A quicker technique is to use kiln-dried treated lumber, which you can prime and paint immediately. Although time-consuming, you can also let the treated wood air-dry. If you keep some stock pieces on hand, drying in a sheltered area, you'll have dry lumber for those small remodeling projects.

Even with dry lumber, you may have problems with paint adhesion because of the high proportion of flat grain on the wide face of the lumber (**Figure C**). The problem is not unique to treated lumber. All construction lumber is flat sawn, making the surface a poor substrate for paint.

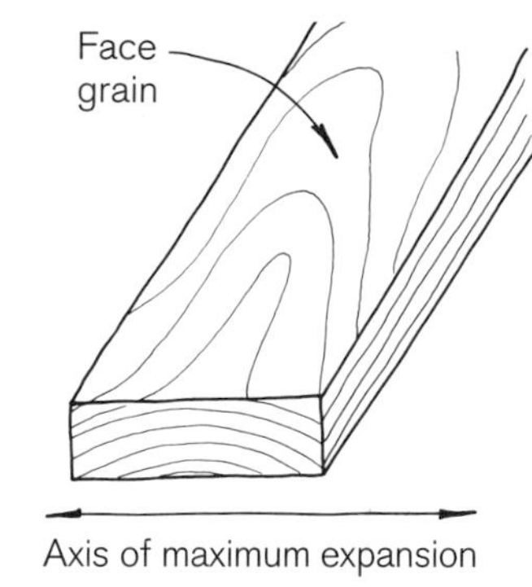

Figure C. *Construction lumber has a higher proportion of exposed face grain than you find in siding or trim. This makes construction lumber dimensionally unstable and a poor substrate for paint.*

Application. A brush, roller, or conventional sprayer is the way to go here. Low-pressure sprayers cannot handle the high amount of solids and pigments.

For maximum durability, start with kiln-dried lumber with as much vertical grain as possible. Use a sealer followed by a compatible primer after the sealer cures. Use two coats of top-quality acrylic-latex house paint for the finish. This will give you an extremely durable finish that may outlast the same finish on untreated wood.

Where to use. Painted surfaces work best when the wood is not exposed to foot traffic. A fence, deck railing, arbor, or woodshed can be protected with paint.

A project built from treated lumber is going to last a long time. But how it looks while it's there depends on how well it is protected from moisture and sunlight.

David Bowyer has worked as a remodeling contractor and as a rep for treated-wood products manufacturers.

Keeping the Paint on Wood Windows

by Jon Tobey

When I lived in New England, I was surrounded by decades-old traditional wood windows that still held paint quite well. But where I live in Seattle, it's not unusual to find expensive, recently manufactured windows being replaced before they're even five years old. I know of a three-year-old house that didn't sell until all of its wood windows were replaced — with vinyl. Modern wood windows seem to have earned a bad reputation as being notoriously difficult to keep intact. What gives?

Why Does Paint Fail?

The sash of a traditional wood window — that is, a window with panes of glass held in place with glazier's points and glazing putty — is essentially composed of four single, dimensionally stable pieces. But a modern window, with insulated glass sandwiched into a wooden frame, can have two or three times as many pieces, which are often smaller and frequently made from finger-jointed wood. This results in a number of joints, edges, and end grains

Figure 2. Some wood windows are built with sills that have no slope — or even a reverse slope — which means water can't easily drain away from the glazing (left). Instead, it gets absorbed by the end grain of vertical window components that sit on the sill, quickly leading to paint failure and rot (right).

that all move in different directions at different rates, presenting openings for moisture penetration and offering a tricky substrate for paint.

Compounding the problem, modern windows sometimes seem as if they're designed to attract — rather than repel — water. Often, they'll have vertical joints that act as channels, collecting water and transporting it onto the sill. If the window's sill has an inadequate or negative slope, water will pool on it or even be directed toward the house and against the window frame's vertical end grain (**Figure 2**). Some windows substitute wooden trim for glazing compound. Narrow and dimensionally unstable, these pieces can trap water on their unprimed back sides, bow out, and eventually rot. In other cases, a window manufacturer will substitute an adhesive for glazing compound, but it, too, quickly rots out and forms water-holding channels.

Other manufacturing practices only make these problems worse. Some windows are built with acute angles that look great to the designer but are too sharp to hold paint well. In addition, factory-primed windows are generally primed with an alkyd primer that rapidly oxidizes and dusts up if not top-coated in 10 to 14 days. This dust prevents bonding of future coats of paint to the surface. Sometimes, the window's sash and frame aren't completely primed or painted, leaving bare wood that invites airborne moisture to enter the window. Even unprimed windows present a problem: They're subject to mill glazing, a condition where the cellulose in machined surfaces gets plasticized, removing the "tooth" necessary for paint to adhere properly.

When it comes to top coats, many painters who work with a brush prefer oil-based paint because of its self-leveling properties. Unfortunately, oil-based primers and top coats are too brittle for exterior applications. Modern windows, which are made up of many parts, are vulnerable to temperature extremes, expanding and contracting with changes in the weather. This thermal cycling causes inflexible oil-based paint to crack and eventually fail, which is why you generally see much greater failure on the south sides of houses. In fact, even on the same side of a house, I've seen differences in paint durability between the first-floor windows and the eaves-shaded second-floor windows. In every exterior application, 100% acrylic latex paints are superior to oil paints today. This is especially true on modern wood windows, where flexibility is crucial.

Proper Installation Comes First

Wood windows can be doomed by shoddy installation practices. For example, head flashing is so rarely installed these days that I'm actually amazed when I find a window that has it. Without flashing, storm-driven water can get under clapboards or other types of siding and start rotting the top of the frame. I see this over and over again, especially on first-story windows that don't get protected by the second-story eaves.

Flashing is even more important when wood windows are mounted in walls clad with brick, stucco, or other types of nonwood siding. Because the wood window and the siding material expand and contract at different rates, a gap forms that can trap water against the window's wood frame. In every case where I've found an unflashed window in this situation, I've also found rot. Typically, windows that aren't flashed don't get caulked around the edges, either, presenting yet another entry point for water.

Water vapor is also a problem. Even when a window's interior and exterior surfaces are properly sealed with paint or lacquer, often the window's edges never get finished. Especially in a tight house, the gaps around windows and doors are among the few places interior moisture — in the form of water vapor — can escape. Because there's no impermeable membrane (in the form of paint) to prevent it, moisture can be drawn from this vapor path into the bare wood edge of the window, right around the weatherstripping. Sunlight then pulls the moisture through the wood; when it reaches the wood's surface, it sits between the wood and the paint. The result is disbonded paint. Frequently, you'll find the interior paint peeling on these windows as well.

Proper flashing and caulking are the best ways to avoid rot, of course. But another strategy that will prevent — or at least slow — rot is to prime the exterior of the frame all the way around, including the edges, before the window is installed.

Prep Before Painting

Whether a window is newly installed or old and peeling, the key to getting paint to stick is proper preparation. In some cases — for example, old windows that are in really bad shape or new unprimed wood windows — I'll remove the sash from the frames to do this work. If the interior surface is already painted, I'll immediately mask it off to protect it.

On houses with badly peeling windows, it's fair to assume that paint that hasn't peeled yet will peel eventually. Even so, most people cannot afford to have all of their windows stripped to the bare wood simply as a precautionary measure. So I concentrate on the worst windows, which are typically found on the south side of the house. I'll work on them until I can no longer remove any paint, which usually takes about an hour.

To remove paint, I use a combination of ProPrep molding scrapers (Preservation Resource Group), a palm sander, and putty knives. The fact that most of the failures noted above cause disbonding and failure down to the bare wood makes paint removal somewhat easier (**Figure 3**).

Once I've thoroughly scraped the window, I use Sherwin-Williams' resin-based spackling to putty any fastener holes made during the manufacturing or installation process (**Figure 4**). If there is any rot or even serious checking on the sill, I do repairs with epoxy (**Figure 5**, next page).

Next, I sand the entire surface with a palm sander loaded with 50- or 60-grit sandpaper. This removes any oxidized layers, roughs up the bare wood, and feathers the old paint. The feathering is crucial, as sharp edges from old paint will cut right through new paint, continually expanding the peeling area. (Look at any house with a problem paint job and you'll see that the new failure starts right where the paint was last scraped.) I also round over any acute corners just enough to remove the factory knife edge that guarantees paint failure but not enough to be noticeable from the yard (**Figure 6**, page 257).

Finally, I scuff the exteriors of all unprimed new windows to remove mill glazing. I use a dry trim brush to clean off the dust, then wipe down every

Figure 3. Scraping wood windows before they are repainted removes disbonded paint and reveals areas where rot has taken hold.

Figure 4. After scraping, the author fills small holes and minor gouges with a quick-drying spackling compound.

Figure 5. Rot damage needs to be repaired. Using liquid epoxy, the author saturates and consolidates areas that have minor rot (top left). Where damage is more extensive, he first removes as much damaged wood as possible, then rebuilds the affected area with a two-part epoxy putty (top right and below).

surface with a rag lightly dampened with mineral spirits, which quickly evaporates to leave a clean, dry surface ready for paint. (Don't use a water-dampened rag, because it might raise the grain and lift the carefully feathered paint edges.)

Even when I'm planning to spray the top coat, I generally hand-prime bare wood with Sherwin-Williams' A-100 latex primer, particularly when repairs are minor. While many manufacturers claim that their top-of-the-line 100% acrylic latex paints can be used without priming, priming at this stage prevents dew from getting under the newly feathered edges and lifting them before I get a chance to paint. Besides, I figure that if these paints will work over bare wood, having a primer coat certainly won't hurt them.

Caulk Is Cheap Insurance

The step that gets missed most often in painting wooden windows is the caulking. Because the joinery on modern wood windows is almost as complex on the exterior as it is on the interior, both sides should be caulked with the same care. On the interior, you caulk mainly for looks; on the exterior, you caulk mainly for protection. For both, I use White Lightning (White Lightning Products), a 100% acrylic caulk with a 40-year warranty.

I first carefully caulk each joint and seam where water can get into the trim and gain access to unprimed surfaces. Then I look for any horizontal surfaces that lack the proper slope for draining water. On these, I use caulk to build a little fillet between the horizontal and vertical sections to drain water away

(Figure 7). Water wicked up by the end grain in these joints is one of the most common causes of failure.

In most cases, it's enough just to fill in any acute angles and slope the water to the edge of the sill. In extreme cases, where the sills are so rotted they need replacing, I'll shape the new sill correctly so that it will drain — but I still caulk it very thoroughly. (Fortunately, we have a carpenter on our crew, because we replace a lot of rotten sills.)

And in cases where windows lack proper head flashing, I'll gob caulk into the gap between window and siding (sometimes an entire tube's worth), again forming a fillet to act as flashing.

Finally, I run a bead of caulk around the glass pane, just where glazing compound would traditionally be. I apply a steady 1/8-inch bead, then smear it slightly with the edge of my dampened little finger. When done right, the caulk bead can't be seen from inside; but without it, there's nothing to prevent water from running down the glass and behind the wood trim holding the glass in place. Many windows come from the manufacturer with a bead of adhesive extruded into this gap. Because this adhesive quickly weathers away and leaves a channel where the water can sit,

Figure 6. After the scraping and epoxy repair work, a palm sander loaded with 60-grit paper smooths the wood surface, feathering out the old paint and rounding over sharp edges. New unprimed windows should also be scuff-sanded to remove mill glaze.

Figure 7. Careful caulking helps protect exterior joints and seams from water intrusion and future paint failure (left). Because horizontal surfaces are especially vulnerable, the author creates a fillet with caulk to help shed water: First, he applies a generous bead of caulk (top right), and then he smooths out the surface with his dampened finger (bottom right).

Figure 8. To prevent water from running behind the glazing trim, the author caulks this joint around all four sides of each window (left), paying particular attention to the bottom rail, where water intrusion is most likely (above). A slightly dampened little finger is useful for tooling this joint smooth.

on new windows I remove the extra adhesive with a razor blade before running the caulk line. All of this is especially important along the bottom of the pane, where water constantly runs down and into the joint (**Figure 8**).

Figure 9. Using a 3½-inch angled sash brush, the author laps the paint slightly onto the glass, creating a final barrier against water intrusion.

Painting the Windows

The windows are now ready for painting. Usually, I paint siding and windows at the same time, in which case I use spray equipment. But if I'm doing just the windows, I break out my short-handled 3½-inch angled sash brush. A good latex brush has synthetic bristles that are much softer than those of natural-bristled oil brushes, which makes it easier to lay out the paint.

I paint windows from the center out and from the top down. Starting at the top, I first paint the glazing compound moldings surrounding the panes, then work outward toward the frame. I dip 1½ inches of the bristles into the paint and clean one side off on the lip of the can. The clean side of the brush goes on the glass side of the sash, allowing me to draw a perfectly straight line along my caulk/glaze line. The paint should just barely lap onto the glass, just as if you were painting a traditionally glazed window (**Figure 9**).

Spraying paint. Compared with brushing, it may seem that masking a houseful of windows in order to spray-paint them is a lot of extra work. But I can mask an average 35-window house in less than one day and spray it in four hours — a savings of days over traditional brushing. Plus, it's easier to hire and train a good masker than it is a good hand-painter. And by spraying latex paint rather than brushing it, I can get a thicker, brushstroke-free finish.

To mask, I use a 3M dual-tack tape dispenser (3M Center), laying tape on the glass 1/64 to 1/32 inch

Figure 10. Spraying is considerably faster than brushing when windows, siding, and trim are being painted at the same time. The author begins by using a dual-tack tape dispenser to mask the window glass (top left), being careful to leave a slight, even gap between the tape and glazing trim (bottom left). Then he lays painter's plastic onto the tape, trimming it to size with a razor blade (right).

inside my caulk/glaze line. This slight gap allows some paint to lap past the caulk just onto the glass, creating a further seal against water getting behind the caulk. Then I lay a piece of 0.31-mil painter's plastic on the tape and trim it to size with a razor blade. If the window is unprimed and removed from the frame, I do the same to the inside glass, so that I can spray both sides of the window (**Figure 10**).

If I'm working on new unprimed windows or completely reconditioning older windows, I'll remove the sash from the frames and lay them flat on short painter's horses to prime the exterior side and the edges. When they're dry, I flip them and prime the interior. This way, any blemishes from sitting on the horses will end up on the exterior. I like to use Sherwin-Williams' A-100 latex primer for the edges and exterior, and a sandable, fast-drying alkyd primer for the interior (where flexibility isn't as crucial). I shoot all of my trim using a 213 reversible tip and the lightest possible pressure that will give me an even fan without "fingering" — those stripes you see from a poorly adjusted sprayer or a worn tip.

For the finish coat, I use Sherwin-Williams' Duration satin latex. One coat goes on and dries twice as thick as SuperPaint, the paint it replaced at the top of the company's product line. (Some homes I painted with SuperPaint still look great after 20 years.) Plus, Duration has a lifetime warranty.

I first spray around the window's edges and let them dry. If the windows are new, I'll paint the interiors, then thoroughly caulk and reinstall the window so that I can spray the face and frame together. Duration is thick, so I try to use vertical strokes and avoid crossing horizontal and vertical passes; I spray carefully, using quick, light passes. On a complex piece like a 15-pane French door, for instance, I'll

Figure 11. To minimize sag-producing crossing patterns, the author makes quick vertical passes with his spray gun and sprays lightly, sometimes applying two thinner coats rather than a heavier one that may need to be brushed out.

spray the entire door with overlapping vertical strokes, changing the angle of the gun slightly to get the top and bottom of the muntins and the left and right sides of the mullions.

I prefer to spray two light coats rather than risk runs. Over the years, I've found that there's no advantage to back-brushing smooth surfaces, especially prepainted ones. Besides, brushstrokes won't level out completely with the new latex paints (**Figure 11**).

After 20 minutes or so, I check each window in case any sags have developed that need brushing out. If I spray carefully, runs will be rare, but if I find more than a few, it means that I need to go lighter with the spray gun. After all, with the windows already masked, a second coat of paint is a piece of cake.

If I'm spraying the siding, too, the windows should be dry enough to mask over after about 24 hours in warm weather. I lay 3M 2040 1 1/2-inch yellow masking tape flat around the face of the window frame and flush to its edge, burnishing the outside edge down and leaving the inside edge unburnished. Then I tuck plastic under the loose edge and trim it to fit with a razor blade. (I've found that yellow dual-tack tape doesn't hold as well for extended periods in this application.) Then the siding can be sprayed with abandon (**Figure 12**). Again, it takes less than a day to spray a typical 3,500-square-foot house.

Jon Tobey is a painting contractor in Monroe, Wash.

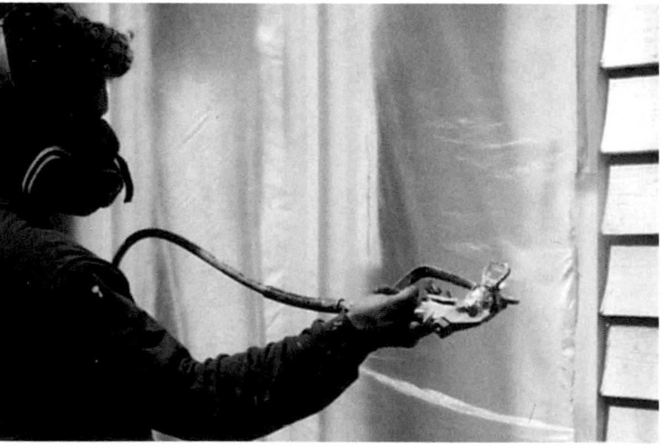

Figure 12. After spraying on the window's finish coat (left) — and allowing enough drying time, so that the tape won't lift the paint — the author masks around the frame with regular tape, tucking plastic underneath (top right), before finishing the rest of the siding (bottom right).

Paint and Moisture Q&A

by Charles Gilley Jr. and Charles Owens

When to Power-Wash?

Q. *When you prep an existing house for repainting, should you power-wash before you scrape and sand, or power-wash to remove dust after sanding?*

A. Always wash first, then scrape and sand. And wash just to clean off the surface dirt, not to remove paint — blasting hard enough to remove paint with a power-washer typically tears up the wood, and it also can blow water into the walls under the siding.

A thorough job of scraping takes off any paint that no longer has good adhesion to the wood, but it leaves sharp edges where the remaining areas of well-attached old paint meet the newly exposed wood. We sand after scraping in order to feather those edges into the bare wood and create the smoother surface required for fresh paint to go on at a consistent thickness. Power-washing after you sand would get water under the feathered edges and lift them up, so you wouldn't have a sound surface. And then you'd have to wait for the wet wall to dry, when it really is preferable to prime the newly exposed wood as soon as possible.

If you just wash with moderate force before scraping, the wood will be protected by whatever sound paint is still on the wall. The wall won't get so soaked and won't take so long to dry. So after sanding, just dust off the surface with rags or a blower, and prime as soon as your wood is dry.

Drying Time

Q. *How soon after power-washing will the wood be dry enough to paint?*

A. It might take a week, or it might take less than a day. There is no standard time to wait — it depends on the wind, the rain, the sun, how hard you sprayed the wall, the condition of the existing paint, and so on. But a moisture meter can give you a firm answer in every case. We use one on every job, because it eliminates guessing and arguments. Wood will dry out and stabilize at about a 10% to 12% moisture content in the outdoor air, but 15% or lower is acceptable for paint. If it's higher than 15%, moisture will be trying to get out of the wood, and that will prevent the paint from adhering properly.

Pin-type moisture meters (see photos, below) that sell for around $200 are okay for rough lumber, or for areas of a trim board that will be covered up. For about $300 you can get a nondestructive model that doesn't make any holes in the wood — just hold it against the surface, and it will read the moisture content as deep as 3/4 inch into the piece. Both types give a more accurate reading on dense hardwoods than on softwoods like pine or cedar — softwood may read 15% on the dial when the true moisture content is a little higher. But the manufacturers of the devices supply charts of correction factors, so you can interpret the moisture readings for different types of wood.

Moisture Meters

Q. *Do you need to use a moisture meter for inside work? Is moisture a problem for inside the house as well as outside?*

A. A moisture meter is always useful on a painting job, indoors or out. It's the only way to be sure that the wood is dry enough to hold paint — a leak or a humid environment could have left the wood close to its saturation point. And it tells you whether your wood is likely to shrink or expand dramatically after you paint. Wood inside a house cycles from

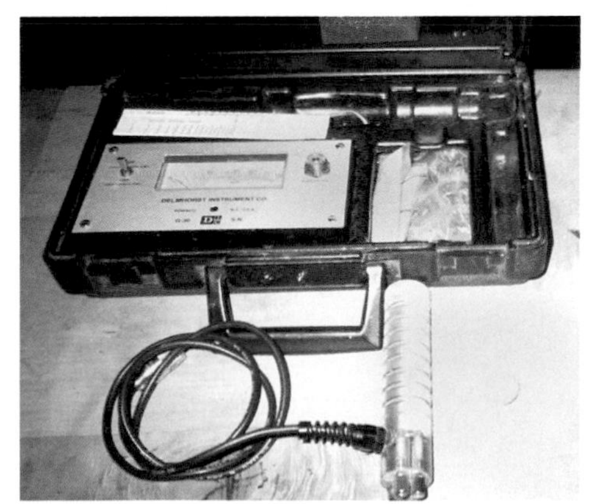

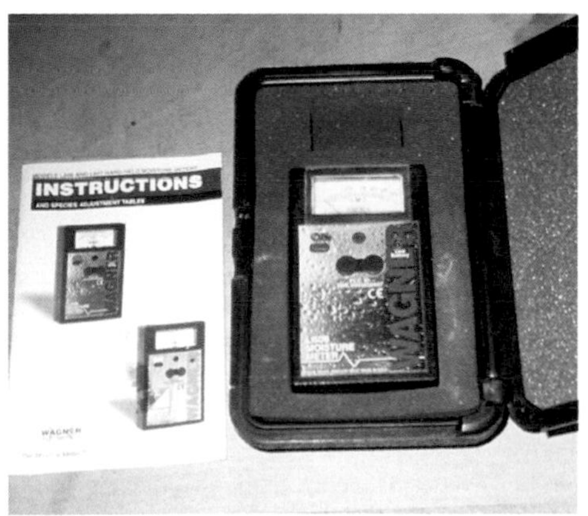

Pin-type moisture meters (far left) leave holes in the wood, while the slightly more costly nondestructive type (left) can read interior moisture 3/4 inch beneath the surface without marking the piece. Readings from either should be interpreted for different wood species according to charts supplied by the instrument suppliers.

Alligatoring occurs when paint loses flexibility and can't accommodate the seasonal expansion and shrinkage of wood (left). Latex paints stay flexible longer than oil paints, prolonging their service life. A new coat of paint applied over tight alligatored paint (right) will perform well if the wall has been properly prepared. The authors recommend washing to remove dirt and mildew, scraping to remove loose alligatored paint, sanding to feather the edges of the remaining well-adhered paint, and dusting the sanded wall. Oil primer should then be applied as soon as possible, followed without delay by a latex top coat.

12% or higher moisture content during the hot, humid summer season down to as low as 4% or 5% in a dry, heated house in winter, and that can cause shrinkage of 1/4 inch across an 8-inch door panel or trim board. The painter needs to take that movement into account.

Painting Unheated Interiors

Q. *Can you paint a new house in winter if it has no heat or only temporary heat?*

A. For inside work, we still need a minimum temperature of 50°F in order for the paint to cure properly. We'd prefer it a little warmer — not only because it's uncomfortable to paint when it's that chilly, but also because the paints may not flow as nicely or leave as nice a finish at 50°F as at 65°F or 70°F.

Temporary heat is another matter. Sometimes we have to paint in houses where propane heaters are running, but it doesn't work well at all. The moisture in the burner exhaust makes the air humid and keeps the wood from drying out. You'll get a much better paint job if you let the permanent heating system operate in the house for a while, monitor the indoor humidity with a hygrometer, and check the wood moisture content with a moisture meter until you get down to the low end of the seasonal range. Paint will have many fewer problems down the road if it's applied to trim that has adjusted to dry winter conditions in a heated house.

Oil vs. Latex

Q. *What are the big differences in the way latex and oil paints perform?*

A. Oil's penetrating ability is its main advantage for repainting work. But latex has advantages that make it a better choice for a top coat. For one thing, latex coatings stay flexible longer, and that gives them a longer service life. When paints fail with age, it's because they've lost flexibility — you see alligatoring when paint has gotten brittle and can no longer expand and contract along with the wood (see photos, left). Latex paints take longer to reach that point. Also, latex coatings breathe better than oil coatings, so they are less prone to peeling: Moisture in the wood can escape more easily, instead of getting trapped under the coating at the surface and stressing the adhesive bond. And finally, the acrylic colorants in latex paints hold longer than the alkyd pigments in oil paints do. We see a lot more fading with oil paints. So there are good reasons that latexes tend to be preferred for top coats in general, and for primers in cases where the superior penetration of an oil primer isn't a significant factor.

Panel Shrinkage

Q. *How do you deal with panel shrinkage when painting wood doors?*

A. If you paint a door in summer, you'll often see exposed wood the following winter at panel edges when the wood shrinks due to lower indoor humidity levels (see photo, below). Masonite or other composite doors don't have this problem, but the only way to prevent it on a solid wood door is to paint the panels before the door is assembled, and

Shrinkage of wood panels in winter's dry indoor air can reveal unpainted edges on wood door panels or on raised-panel or beadboard wall surfaces, almost guaranteeing callbacks for jobs done during the humid months of summer.

Repainting Questions

Paint Over Stain?

Q. *Is it okay to use an exterior latex house paint over stained wood siding?*

A. *Bill Feist responds:* That should work fine, as long as the substrate is properly nailed and in good condition and there are no obvious moisture problems.

Treat the old finish the way you would any coat of paint: Remove loose and peeling finish, then sand the surface, taking care to feather sharp edges left over from scraping. Any bare wood should be sanded, too. And if the old surface is shiny or glossy, sand it or treat it with a deglosser so the new paint will adhere.

As usual, the siding must be cleaned to remove chalking, oils, mildew, and other contaminants. The best approach — though labor-intensive — is to scrub all of the siding with a detergent-and-water mixture and then rinse it thoroughly. Simple power washing can also be effective, but if there is a mildew-and-dirt problem, spray first with detergent and rinse, then spray with mildew cleaner (usually a bleach) and rinse again.

After everything has dried, the surface can be recoated. Use an all-acrylic paint. If the old finish is an opaque oil-based stain, apply a coat of alkyd (oil-based) primer to ensure good adhesion and provide a base for the top coat (two coats are preferable).

If the original finish is a solid-color latex stain that adheres firmly to the wood, it probably isn't necessary to prime the finish before painting, though all of the prep work is still important.

One caution: Some semitransparent and transparent penetrating-oil finishes contain water repellent that can interfere with the adhesion of the new top coat (whether paint or opaque stain). These finishes should be thoroughly cleaned with a strong detergent, then rinsed and dried.

In really troublesome cases, the old stain may have to be removed (stain removers are available from a number of deck-stain manufacturers). I'd recommend using two coats of an alkyd primer to provide a good base for future paint.

Bill Feist is a former wood-finishes researcher with the Forest Products Laboratory in Madison, Wis., and coauthor of Finishes for Exterior Wood.

Repainting Aluminum Siding

Q. Does faded aluminum siding with a chalklike residue on the surface require any special preparation before repainting?

A. *Jon Tobey responds:* Most of the time, a pressure washing with detergent solution is adequate for removing chalking and dirt from aluminum siding. Kill any mildew that's present with a 3-to-1 water-bleach mixture before washing.

If there is some water-activated staining that won't wash off, lightly fog the siding (at the rate of about 3 gallons per house) with a quick-drying alkyd primer. If you're brushing, you can buy aerosol cans of the primer and spray the stains with a very light coat (one you can still see the stains through). In rare cases, there may be some bare aluminum; if so, I'd try to find out why the paint is peeling. But in general, aluminum doesn't require any primer, as latex adheres tenaciously to the metal.

Then the siding can be painted with a high-quality 100% acrylic paint by brush or roller, or by spraying. I've had good success with Sherwin-Williams' SuperPaint; aluminum siding that I painted 10 years ago with this product still looks good.

Jon Tobey is a painting contractor in Monroe, Wash.

---

that's not going to happen except on the occasional high-end custom job. If the customers want wood doors painted in summer, we warn them that the painter will probably have to come back and touch up the paint, and we charge for that as an extra.

These touch-ups are trickier when the coating is a clear finish over stained or natural wood, especially if the finish is spray applied. The wet finish tends to creep into the dado and dry as a little thickened ridge. On the callback, that ridge has to be sanded smooth, and then the touch-up stain and finish have to be blended in carefully.

You also get shrinkage that exposes unpainted wood on paneling such as beadboard. But you can preprime or even prepaint those pieces before installing them, so the shrinkage won't expose any uncoated wood.

Shrinkage can also make a caulked joint look terrible in six months, even though it looked fine when the job was done. When the wood shrinks, the caulk pulls off and splits with an ugly "fingering" appearance.

Charles Gilley Jr. is the owner of Restoration Painting of South Woodstock, Vt. Charles Owen is the president of Two Dogs Painting, Inc.

Chapter 14: Roof Ventilation

- **Roof Ventilation: Research Update**
- **Sizing Ventilation to Prevent Ice Dams**
- **Eaves Ventilation Details**
- **Venting Cathedral Ceilings**
- **Unvented Attics With Spray Foam Insulation**

Roof Ventilation: Research Update

by William B. Rose

I've gotten many calls over the years about attics and attic ventilation. Most of the callers say that they hear different things from different people. Here, I address the performance of attic systems and why the issue has so many different points of view.

An "attic assembly," for the purposes of this discussion, consists of a ceiling, insulation, structure, roof deck, and roofing materials. For the most part, this article addresses truss-framed, steep-pitch attic assemblies, but the same principles apply to cathedral ceilings.

Research Findings

The temperature of a northern-climate roof we monitored throughout the 1990s is shown below (**Figure 1**). Here is a summary of the study: The roof gets cold at night and is hot during the day. It gets hotter on a sunny day than on a cloudy day. Attic assemblies with openings to the outdoors ("vented" attics) stay a bit cooler during the daytime than unvented assemblies. They also stay slightly warmer at night.

Many factors influence the temperature on the roof. A prioritized list might include hour of the day, outdoor air temperature, cloud cover, color of the roof, roof orientation, where the measurement is taken (sheathing or shingles, top or bottom), latitude, wind speed, rain or snow on the roof, heat conduction across attic insulation, roof framing type (truss or cathedral), and attic ventilation to the outdoors. As you can see, ventilation falls pretty far down the list.

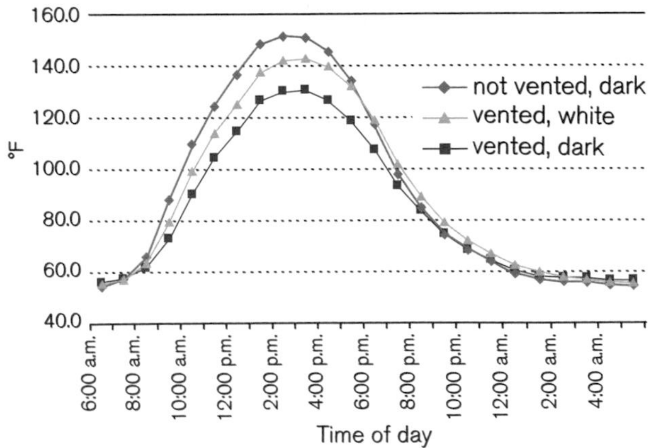

Figure 1. Sheathing temperatures are affected somewhat by roof ventilation, but many other factors play a bigger role.

Source: Data from the Attic Performance Project, University of Illinois.

To better understand how wind affects roof ventilation, Canadian researchers T.W. Forest and I.S. Walker measured the air exchange rate in attic assemblies using tracer gases. **Figure 2** gives us a feel for what they found. That is, air change rates in the attic tended to increase with wind speed, but the amount of air change at a given wind speed was unpredictable. In fact, even with specific information about climate, construction type, and wind speed and direction, the resulting air change rates may vary by a factor of 10 or more. Whether air flows out through a roof opening or in through that opening, and whether this airflow induces flow from indoors into the attic or helps dilute and remove moist air from the attic, can never be pinned down very well, except to say that wind is a more powerful factor than buoyancy (the "stack effect").

For the most part, roof assemblies behave like any wood structure — they are wetter when cold and drier when warm. Roof assemblies tend to be hot, thanks to the sun, so they tend to be dry. Of course, if the roof leaks, that becomes the biggest source of wetness. High moisture levels indoors or in basements or crawlspaces can also increase moisture levels in the roof. Roof members can become particularly wet or covered with frost near holes in the ceiling or leaks in attic ductwork, where humid air enters the attic. It was the formation of local frost "walnuts" like those shown (**Figure 3**) that led researchers in the late 1930s to recommend attic ventilation. (If only they had offered to seal up the ceiling instead!)

Many attic assemblies are built with vents to the outdoors on the presumption that outdoor air will enter the attic and dilute moisture coming from indoors or from the foundation. The further presumption is that indoor air is wet and outdoor air is dry. Both of these assumptions are often false. If there are openings in the ceiling, then air movement in the attic can induce airflow from below, or dilute air from below, or do nothing, in ways that are just plain unpredictable no matter how much research is thrown at it. It can also induce flow into the living space from the attic above, which is a nasty problem when the air conditioning is running.

Observations in the Field

Suppose that the picture of attic ventilation provided by physics, described above, doesn't quite cut it. Too many qualifications; nothing pinned down. Then we

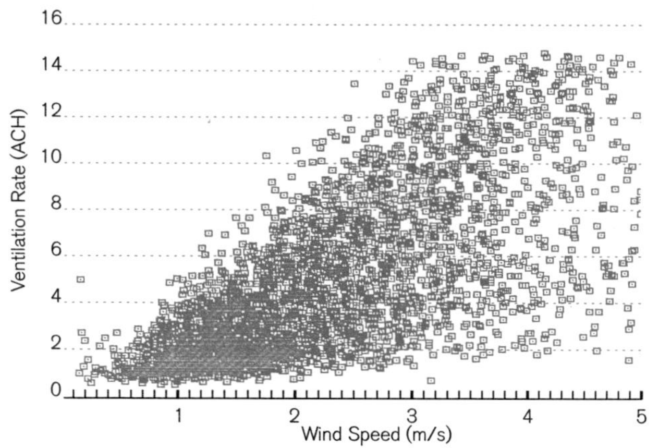

Figure 2. While higher wind speeds tend to increase attic ventilation, the relationship is a weak one: ventilation rates at a given wind speed can vary by a factor of 10.

Source: Forest and Walker, "Attic Ventilation and Moisture," 1993, summarized at www.cmhc-schl.gc.ca/publications/en/rh-pr/tech/93-201.pdf

can go to our own observations and experiences, subjective and incomplete as they may be. Here's my main finding: Attic assemblies built over the last 15 years or so are pretty good. Attics may be a crapshoot in building physics terms, but the crapshoot is *heavily* biased toward good performance.

Let's look at the assemblies by component:

Truss construction seems to do quite well. There are disasters that occur during construction. Truss uplift continues to be a problem requiring cosmetic fixes (see "Truss Uplift Solutions," page 366). The industry has, for the most part, discontinued the use of fire-retardant treatment of truss members, thereby avoiding what was a serious concern for several years. The truss heels in many cases still fail to provide the height necessary for good insulation. Attics have become a forest of truss webs, and thus are less usable for attic storage space. But the overall picture is good (at least by my observations).

Gypsum wallboard ceilings have shown improvement. The message seems to have gotten out that ceilings must be airtight — there is no justification, summer or winter, for allowing indoor air or foundation air to pass into attic cavities. The common culprits, such as framed soffits over kitchen cabinets, open oversized plumbing or mechanical chases, and leaky can lights, are going away in most construction where the word has gotten out. Weatherization of existing buildings has maintained a valuable focus on closing off any ceiling bypasses. In my experience, most truss-framed attics do fine without special vapor barrier membranes in the ceiling, but in cold locations, cathedral ceilings may need vapor protection just as walls do.

Insulation. Regarding insulation, most areas of the country have healthy amounts in the attic — R-30 in general and R-38 in northern areas. Cellulose provides good insulation and helps block airflow. Fiberglass, in sufficient density and with good installation, also provides good thermal insulation. Foam insulation is finding much more use. It has been the material of choice for residential air-sealing. Structural insulated panels (SIPs) work fine, as long as the airflow problem at joints is addressed. Foam insulation has been sprayed at the underside of board and wood-panel sheathing with great success. Insulated panels (often polyisocyanurate) make for good roof-deck assemblies, as we know from commercial low-slope construction, where the foam insulation is often sandwiched between the structural roof deck and the roofing membrane. All foam needs fire protection, of course. Open-cell foams such as Icynene (Icynene Inc.) may need more vapor protection than closed-cell foams, which have greater resistance to vapor flow.

Vapor barriers still cause squabbling, but most builders know that moisture flow from below comes through holes in the ceiling for the most part (**Figure 3**). Cathedral ceilings require special care in insulation placement and vapor protection. But the new code provisions (see "IRC No-Vent Provision," page 269, and "Code Provisions for Unvented Attics," page 282) should encourage insulated sheathing materials or insulated "sandwich" assemblies that resist moisture transport and heat flow as a package. With such a roof assembly (I call them "insulated vapor retarders" or "fat vapor retarders"), the inside surface stays close to indoor conditions, the outside surface stays close to outdoor conditions, and nothing bad happens in the middle. Our laboratory has

Figure 3. Moist interior air leaking through a hole in the ceiling can produce moldy sheathing or frost on a roof truss. This photo by the author shows results from the Attic Performance Project.

had such an assembly in place for more than 15 years, with one inch of foil-faced polyisocyanurate insulation directly beneath the OSB decking; the sheathing gets hot during the day, but the OSB above the foam insulation is the driest sheathing of all. Remember — hot means dry.

Ductwork in unconditioned attic assemblies always has room for improvement. It is best to place all ductwork in conditioned spaces.

OSB has become the universal sheathing material, by economic and environmental necessity. We know too little about the moisture performance of this material, such as under what conditions the material will begin to fail. In my laboratory, we have seen the material swell by 50% or more, under extreme conditions. Will it begin to show signs of sagging between trusses, or will workers be putting their feet through it at the time of re-roofing? I don't know, but the absence of signs of product failure in the field, at least to my drive-by observations, is reassuring. Nevertheless, I look forward to the day when the marketplace provides a product with more clearly established performance characteristics. I'll be a strong supporter.

Shingles. I'm reviewing the condition of the shingles installed on our research laboratory in 1989, and, after 18 years, signs of aging are appearing. We hope to conduct laboratory tests to pin down and better quantify the shingle performance and the factors that influence it. The aging we see shows some temperature effect: The white shingles are in better shape than the dark, and a few of the most aged-looking shingles are found on the hottest bay, the one with foam directly on the underside of the sheathing. Without the numbers to go by, we must rely on observation, and our observations suggest that performance depends on other factors besides the presence or absence of ventilation and whether the assembly is truss-framed or cathedral ceiling.

Of course, natural weathering tests that began 18 years ago say little about shingles that are made today. I sense that the shingle industry is currently producing dimension shingles that seem to lie quite flat, resist wind uplift, and hang onto their UV-protecting granules. I don't know how to re-roof over dimension shingles, and it does seem unfriendly to the landfill to have that much more mass in the shingle. Nevertheless, my drive-by observations show a lot of good-performing shingles on the roofs of the last couple decades, and that is very reassuring.

Roof vents. Many years ago, we measured the "net free area" of about a dozen ridge vent materials using an apparatus that measures the pressure drop across a vent device with great accuracy. We found that ridge vents with large openings (minimum opening dimension around 1/4 inch) had an equivalent net free area very close to their rated capacity. Vent devices with small openings, or with filter fabrics, or scrims, performed much worse, as much as 75% less than their rated area. (If you want to know how restrictive a vent device is, use your imagination — if it looks like air would have a hard time moving through, it probably does.) This discrepancy would be a big deal, I suppose, for someone who felt that vent regulations were critical to attic performance. I don't, so for me, having vent devices with less airflow than advertised is not a cause for concern.

Building Codes

You (and your building code inspectors) may be unaware that the 2006 version of the International Residential Code for One- and Two-Family Dwellings permits attic construction with no ventilation of the attic cavity. This new provision, R806.4 (see "IRC No-Vent Provision," facing page, and "Code Provisions for Unvented Attics," page 282), is largely due to the efforts of Joseph Lstiburek, Armin Rudd, and their colleagues. In brief summary, unvented conditioned attic assemblies are permitted when an air-impermeable insulation such as rigid foam is applied in direct contact to the underside/interior of the structural roof deck, with sufficient thickness given the climate to prevent condensation on the underside.

This new provision is a direct challenge to the rule of thumb that has been in place for 50 years, saying that you have to vent a steep-roof attic so the ratio of net free vent area to the projected roof area is 1:300 (or 1:150 when using "cross ventilation" rather than soffit and ridge vents). This ratio arose from observations of frost on protruding nail points in Wisconsin homes by researchers at the Forest Products Laboratory in 1937, and frost on aluminum plates in research "doghouses" at the University of Minnesota in 1938, under "outdoor" conditions of -13°F.

The Federal Housing Authority turned these findings into the famous 1:300 ratio in 1942, to be applied as a minimum building requirement for the small homes in its financing program. The requirements were picked up by model codes and others following WWII, and the rest, as they say, is history. Shingle manufacturers did not begin piggybacking their warranties on venting regulations until reports of shingle problems began piling up following the change in asphalt sources in the early 1980s.

To Vent or Not

Every designer and builder should be able to produce good attic and roof assemblies, both with and without ventilation — and even between the two — with just part of a conventional ventilation system. For example, from our studies, roof assemblies that have holes but not necessarily straight airflow paths (one gable end vent, or soffit-only) should also be candi-

IRC No-Vent Provision

R806.4 Conditioned attic assemblies. Unvented conditioned attic assemblies (spaces between the ceiling joists of the top story and the roof rafters) are permitted under the following conditions:

1. No interior vapor retarders are installed on the ceiling side (attic floor) of the unvented attic assembly.
2. An air-impermeable insulation is applied in direct contact to the underside/interior of the structural roof deck. "Air-impermeable" shall be defined by ASTM E283. **Exception:** In Zones 2B and 3B, insulation is not required to be air impermeable.
3. In the warm humid locations as defined in Section N1101.2.1:

3.1. For asphalt roofing shingles: A 1-perm (5.7 x 10-11 kg/s Å m2 Å Pa) or less vapor retarder (determined using Procedure B of ASTM E96) is placed to the exterior of the structural roof deck; that is, just above the roof structural sheathing.

3.2. For wood shingles and shakes: a minimum continuous 1/4-inch (6 mm) vented air space separates the shingles/shakes and the roofing felt placed over the structural sheathing.

4. In Zones 3 through 8 as defined in Section N1101.2, sufficient insulation is installed to maintain the monthly average temperature of the condensing surface above 45°F (7°C). The condensing surface is defined as either the structural roof deck or the interior surface of an air-impermeable insulation applied in direct contact with the underside/interior of the structural roof deck. "Air-impermeable" is quantitatively defined by ASTM E283. For calculation purposes, an interior temperature of 68°F (20°C) is assumed. The exterior temperature is assumed to be the monthly average outside temperature.

Source: International Residential Code 2006: For One- and Two-Family Dwellings.

dates for good performance. There are good reasons to vent: The truss-framed, steep-roof attic with an insulated ceiling has been the workhorse of single-family construction, and ventilation works well with this construction, at least in the northern U.S.

In some cases, there are also good reasons *not* to vent: in wildfire areas, in complex cathedral ceiling assemblies, in existing and historic buildings that have never had ventilation, in shed roofs beneath clerestory windows, with foam insulation (foam and ventilation do not go together — think fire), and in complex roof assemblies that combine steep and low-slope construction. I've also heard persuasive arguments against venting in hurricane-prone areas, but I'm not an expert in that area. In short, since critical performance doesn't hinge on ventilation, then either vent, no-vent, or an in-between "kinda"-vent can be taken as the starting point. Whether they work or not depends on design and execution of the other factors.

So you should vent where venting is appropriate and not vent where it is not appropriate. As it turns out, the worst-performing, most mold-ridden attics I have seen were vented — with a flooded crawlspace and a direct path for air movement from the crawlspace to the attic. You can mess up a vented attic by allowing such airflow. You can mess up an unvented attic as well, usually by not providing vapor protection appropriate to the climate and indoor moisture levels. Tight ceilings would be a great first step toward moisture control, summer and winter.

Conclusions

The father of a colleague of mine says that when the word "ventilation" comes out, people stop using their heads. Vented assemblies often perform well, but sometimes they don't. Sometimes roofs appear to be vented, but they actually aren't vented at all! Still, we can take comfort in the observation, based on years of experience, that our attic assemblies are pretty darn good, and, in my opinion, they're getting better. We need to constantly be on the lookout for new conditions and new problems, as they crop up.

For those working in the trenches, you should continue to build in a way that complies with code and that you know works for your climate. Concerns of ice damming, summer cooling load, shingle service life, and moisture problems have been dealt with elsewhere (TenWolde and Rose, "Issues Related to Venting of Attics and Cathedral Ceilings," www.fpl.fs.fed.us/documnts/pdf1999/tenwo99a.pdf). For all four of these concerns, ventilation makes a contribution that is generally more positive than negative, but ventilation hardly ever makes the difference between success and failure.

For the most part, the focus of codes, researchers, designers, and builders on roof ventilation is misplaced. Instead, the focus should be on *building an airtight ceiling,* which is far more important than roof ventilation in all climates and all seasons. The major causes of moisture problems in attics and roofs are holes in the ceiling and paths for unwanted airflow from basements and crawlspaces. People should focus first on preventing air and moisture from leaking into the attic. Once this is accomplished, roof ventilation becomes pretty much a non-issue.

William B. Rose is an architect with more than 20 years of research experience at the Building Research Council, University of Illinois Urbana-Champaign, and author of Water in Buildings: An Architect's Guide to Moisture and Mold.

Sizing Ventilation to Prevent Ice Dams

by Ted Cushman

Most builders in the snowy North take pains to ventilate their roof systems, even when it's not easy. One important reason is to prevent the formation of damaging and dangerous ice at the eaves. Deep snow insulates a roof and traps heat inside the attic, but a well-vented attic will allow the heat out before it can melt the snow.

So how can a person determine how much venting it takes to keep a given roof free of ice? Code requirements like the 1:300 rule (one square foot of free vent area per 300 square feet of attic floor area) and the 1:150 rule are a good start, but in some cases they may provide either less or more ventilation than is strictly necessary. However, recent research by the U.S. Army Corps of Engineers has produced a more precise design tool: a set of attic and outdoor temperature limits that building designers can plug into a simple formula to calculate the required vent area. The formula will also help you figure out if upgrading an attic's insulation will help solve an ice dam problem.

Researchers Wayne Tobiasson, James Buska, and Alan Greatorex, of the Corps of Engineers Cold Regions Research and Engineering Laboratory (CRREL), in Hanover, N.H., developed their attic venting guidelines based on studies of army buildings at Fort Drum, an installation in upstate New York. For several winters, the team recorded outdoor temperatures and attic air temperatures in five buildings: one building with no ice dam problems and four with problems ranging from slight to severe. The findings allowed the engineers to define the temperature conditions in which icing would occur and to prescribe methods to keep attics within a safe temperature range. By installing passive vents in some attics and a combination of passive vents and thermostatically controlled exhaust fans in others, the team was able to eliminate severe ice dam and icicle problems.

Deeper Snow Requires More Insulation

CRREL staffers generated this graph based on computer modeling of heat loss from an insulated, *unvented* attic through a roof covered with varying depths of snow. The graph shows the levels of attic insulation required to keep the snow from melting as the outdoor temperature rises to 22°F. (Above 22°F, snow melt runs off before it can refreeze into an ice dam at the eaves.) Attic cooling slows as the outdoor temperature rises, and more slowly still with deeper snow levels. More insulation is needed to counteract the increasing amount of heat that would be trapped in the attic. For example, the chart shows that an unvented roof with a 1-foot blanket of snow would need nearly R-50 insulation in the attic to prevent an ice dam when the outdoor temperature is 22°F. If the snow were 2 feet deep, the amount of insulation required would be almost R-90.

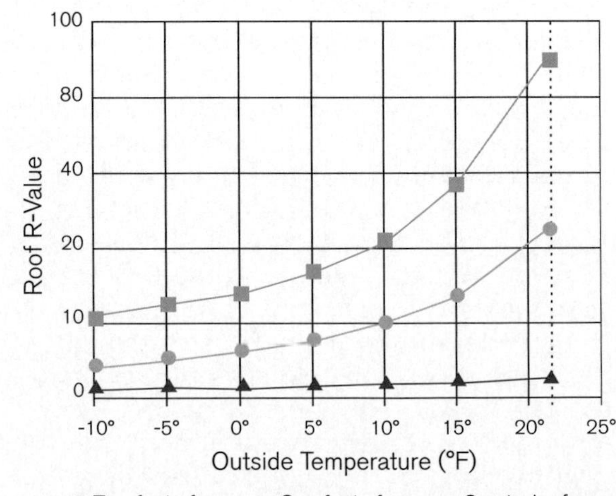

How Much Vent Area Is Enough?

This graph shows required vent area as calculated by the 1:300 and 1:150 ventilation rules compared with CRREL calculations based on building size, roof slope, and insulation levels. In most cases, the 1:150 rule provides more than adequate venting area, even at lower insulation levels; the 1:300 rule also works well for well-insulated attics. However, for small buildings, such as those depicted at the extreme left end of the chart, these rules of thumb may fall short.

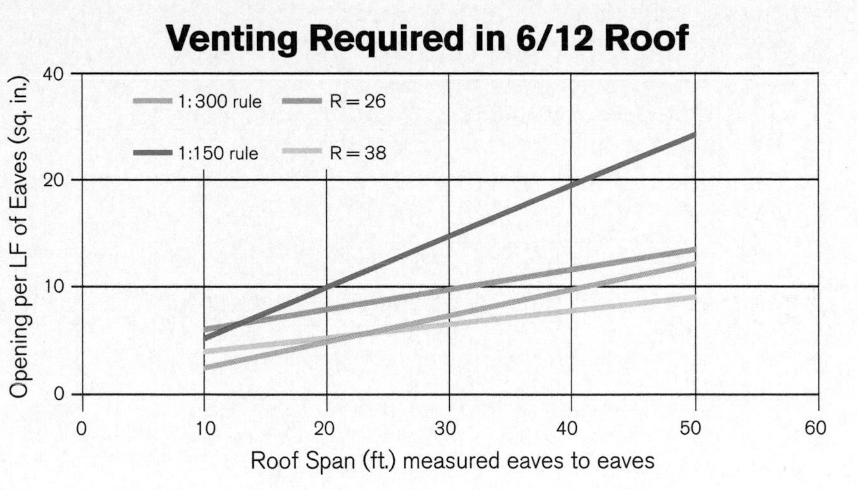

The icing envelope. Ice-ups are a combination of two events: First, snow on the roof melts; and second, the melt water refreezes at the eaves. Heat escaping from the building into the attic (along with heat contributed by ductwork or heating equipment located in the attic space) is the main cause of the melting, and the reason for the refreezing is low outdoor temperatures. As it warms up outside, snow over a warm attic is more prone to melting; but when the outdoor temperatures rise above a certain point, the melt water will drain off without refreezing.

The CRREL team's observations showed that snow on the roof would begin to melt at the roof surface anytime the attic temperatures went much above 30°F, but would refreeze on the eaves only when the outdoor temperature was below about 22°F. The researchers called this set of conditions the "icing envelope" and concluded that ice dams could be avoided if attic ventilation could maintain the attic at 30°F when the outdoor temperature was 22°F or below.

By plugging those values into ASHRAE formulas for airflow and heat removal, the team was able to design vents of the right capacity for the situation. The same method is broadly applicable to many buildings.

But what about insulation? In theory, of course, if the quantity of heat escaping into the attic could be reduced enough by heavily insulating the ceiling below, the vent area required to remove the heat would approach zero. But Tobiasson has concluded that in roof systems with no cooling ventilation at all, very high levels of insulation would be needed to prevent icing.

Tobiasson and Greatorex did a thermal analysis to show a superinsulating company how much insulation would eliminate melting on an *unvented*, snow-covered roof under different weather conditions and snow depths (see "Deeper Snow Requires More Insulation"). "As it warms up outside, more insulation is needed to prevent melting," wrote Tobiasson. "The critical condition is when it is just a bit colder than 22°F outside. It takes a massive amount of insulation to prevent icings then. For example, if 2 feet of snow is present on the roof, the R-value of the roof (to prevent icings) would have to be around R-90.

"This is not an exact answer," Tobiasson continued, "but it is a good indication that insulation alone, even big piles of it, is seldom the way to stop icings at eaves. The best strategy is to insulate the roof sufficiently for energy conservation reasons, then ventilate the space above the insulation and below the snow with outdoor air to create a cold-ventilated roof."

Calculation vs. rule of thumb. At *JLC*'s request, Tobiasson and Buska compared the results of their calculation method with results given by the standard 1:150 and 1:300 ratios, in a simple house design with a 6/12 roof pitch and attic-floor R-values ranging from R-25 to R-38 (see "How Much Vent Area Is Enough?").

The rule-of-thumb approach based on attic area means bigger vents for larger attics, regardless of insulation R-values. But when the required openings are calculated using CRREL's design criteria, buildings with wider spans (or steeper roofs) turn out to need proportionally smaller vent openings, because higher peaks generate a greater stack-effect airflow. And the better the attic insulation, the smaller the necessary vents.

There's good news here for home builders: Simple houses built with today's standard methods usually have more venting than they need for ice dam protection. In most houses, standard ridge and soffit vents actually provide more vent area than even the generous 1:150 rule calls for. And for tricky designs where code-required venting is hard to achieve, calculations may show smaller openings to be sufficient.

Ted Cushman reports on the building industry from Great Barrington, Mass.

Eaves Ventilation Details

by Gordon Tully

A challenging place to design insulation and ventilation details is the intersection of roof and wall. I have written in *JLC* about the visual importance of the exterior roof-wall intersection. What goes on inside is equally important and often influences the exterior appearance. In fact, solving the insulation details may lead you to better exterior eaves details.

Eaves at Unoccupied Attic Floors

In the typical one- or two-story house with an unoccupied attic, the eaves are at the same level as the attic floor (**Figure 4**). The rafters rest on the top plate of the wall and nestle alongside the attic or floor joists. If a roof truss is used, the lower and upper chords often intersect at the top of the wall. This joint is troublesome, because if not done properly it squeezes the insulation (just where you want it thick to prevent ice dams) and invites cold air from the roof ventilation system into the ceiling insulation.

If you are using trusses, make sure you request shop drawings from the truss manufacturer. In my experience, no matter what you draw, the manufacturer will send through the design cheapest to build. But for a modest extra amount, they can easily create a "raised-heel" truss, either by blocking between the bottom and top chords, or by adding another member underneath the top chord (**Figure 5**). Try for as much depth as you can at the eaves, ideally the full dimension of the attic insulation.

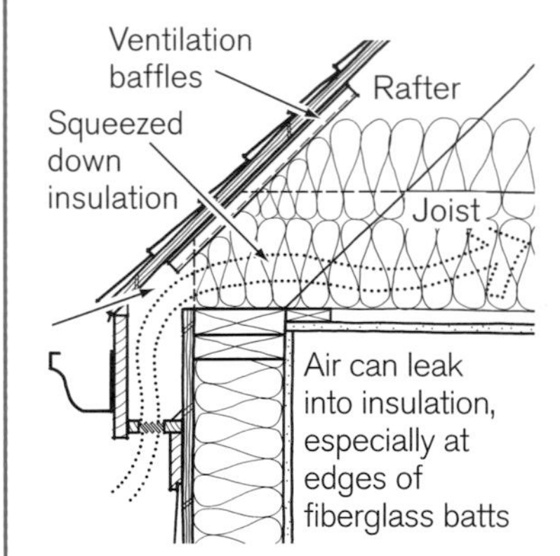

Figure 4. When the eaves are at attic floor level, the rafters squeeze the insulation just where you want it thick to prevent ice dams. This also invites air from the roof ventilation system into the ceiling insulation.

If you are using rafters, put a band joist around the attic floor, and add a shoe on top of the joists to receive the rafters (**Figure 6**). This will add the depth of the rafter to the depth of the joists and greatly improve the insulation at the eaves. However, don't overlook the structural requirements of the connection of the rafter ends to the eaves (see "Raised Rafter Plate Connections").

Eaves at Occupied Attics

When the attic is used for living space, as in a Cape Cod or a gambrel-roofed house, where do you run the insulation? When possible, run it between the rafters, because experience shows that insulated cathedral ceilings are much more airtight than insulated attic floors.

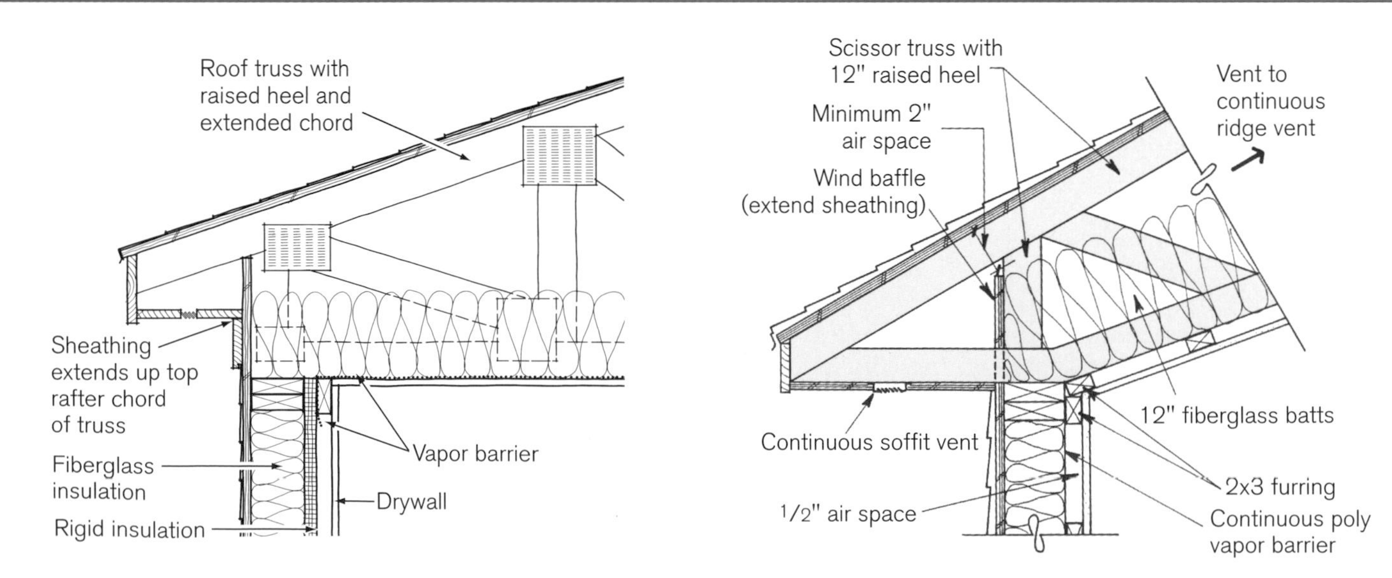

Figure 5. When using trusses, have the manufacturer add depth for insulation at the eaves, creating a "raised-heel" truss (left). For cathedral ceilings, use a raised-heel scissor truss (right).

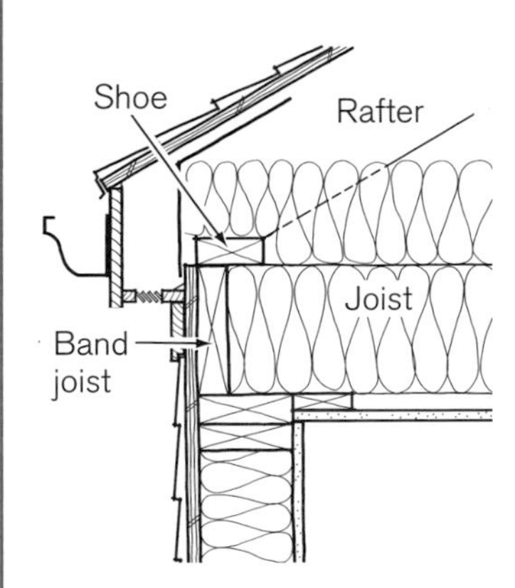

Figure 6. When using rafters, put a band joist around the attic floor and add a shoe on top of the joists to receive the rafters. This allows room for a full depth of insulation. However, structural reinforcement of the rafter-end connections is usually required.

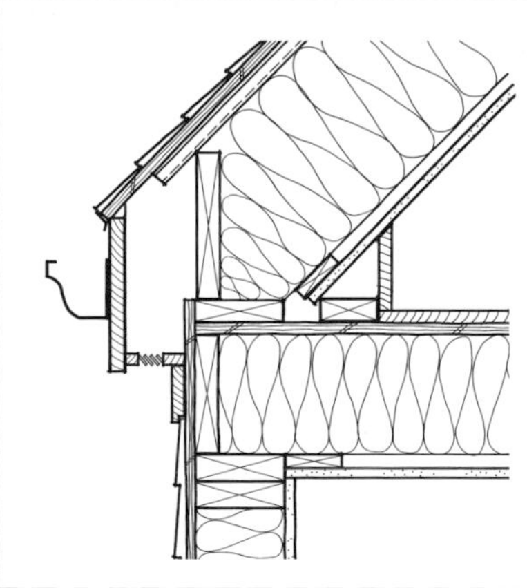

Figure 8. Leaving out the knee wall or making it very short can make interesting interior spaces. Thicker-than-usual rafters allow for sufficient insulation.

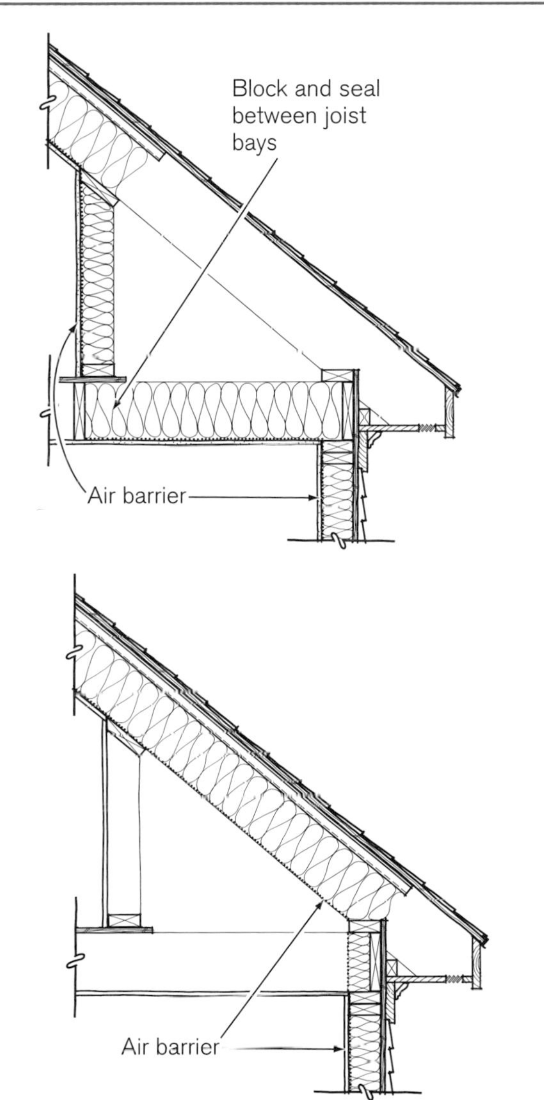

Figure 7. Avoid insulating knee walls, but where the detail is required, it's especially important to maintain a continuous air barrier by installing blocking between the joists directly below the knee wall (top). Whenever possible, run the insulation between the rafters instead (above), making it easier to maintain a continuous air barrier and thermal boundary.

Raised Rafter Plate Connections

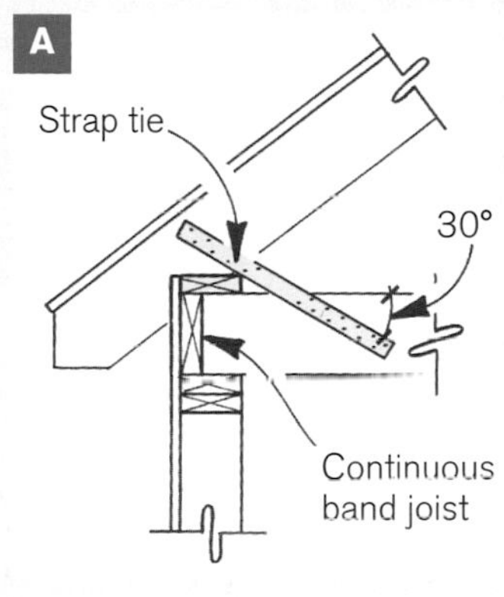

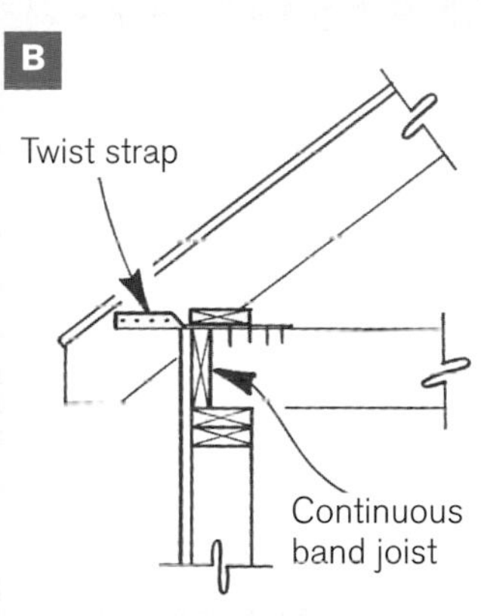

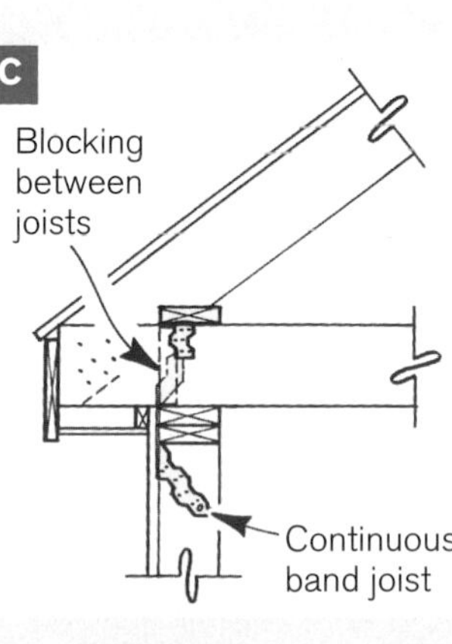

The raised rafter plate allows room for insulation above the wall plate, but the lateral thrust of the roof must be accounted for in the design. When using a raised rafter plate, Simpson strap ties (A) are the easiest way to resist roof thrust. When an attic floor is in the way, twist straps will work (B). Extending the attic joists beyond the walls (C) provides a strong rafter-joist connection, but may require additional hurricane ties to resist wind uplift. — *Robert Randall*

Insulating the cathedral ceiling creates the most continuous vapor retarder possible, and you also avoid the air leakage that inevitably occurs through the floor system from inside the knee wall area where the floor insulation ends (**Figure 7**, previous page). By insulating at roof level, you also avoid the nasty problems created when the homeowner insists on using the uninsulated space behind the knee wall for storage. Finally, it is often nice architecturally to leave out the knee wall, or make it very short, as shown in **Figure 8** (previous page).

Notice that the rafters are thicker than needed for structure in order to accommodate a sufficient thickness of blown-in (my preference) or batt insulation. The floor deck runs right to the outside of the building, as in a normal second floor, and prevents air from entering the floor system.

To create the most continuous vapor retarder possible, and more important, to avoid drafty spaces between knee walls and roof, it is best to keep the insulation and retarder running in the plane of the roof, not in the knee wall.

Gordon Tully is an architect in Norwalk, Conn.

Venting Cathedral Ceilings

by Robert Hatch

As a builder in the Northeast, where cold, snow, and ice are the main course on the winter menu, roof ventilation is one of my top concerns. The primary reason is that without good ventilation, most roofs in snowy climates will suffer from destructive ice dams.

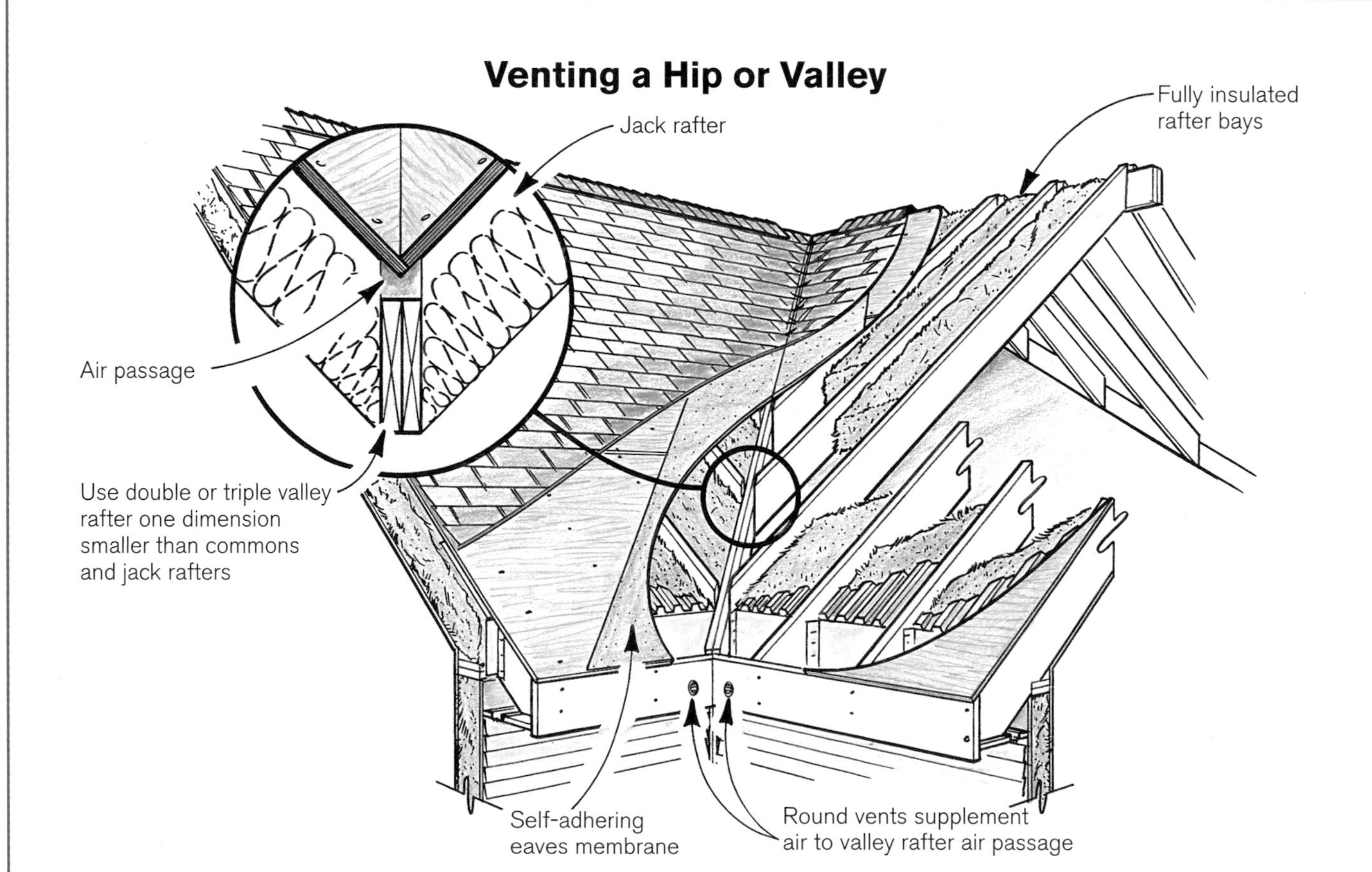

Figure 9. To create an air inlet channel in valley systems, the author aligns the jack rafters flush with the bottom edge of the valley rafter. Doubling or tripling up the valley rafter strengthens the beam and widens the air channel.

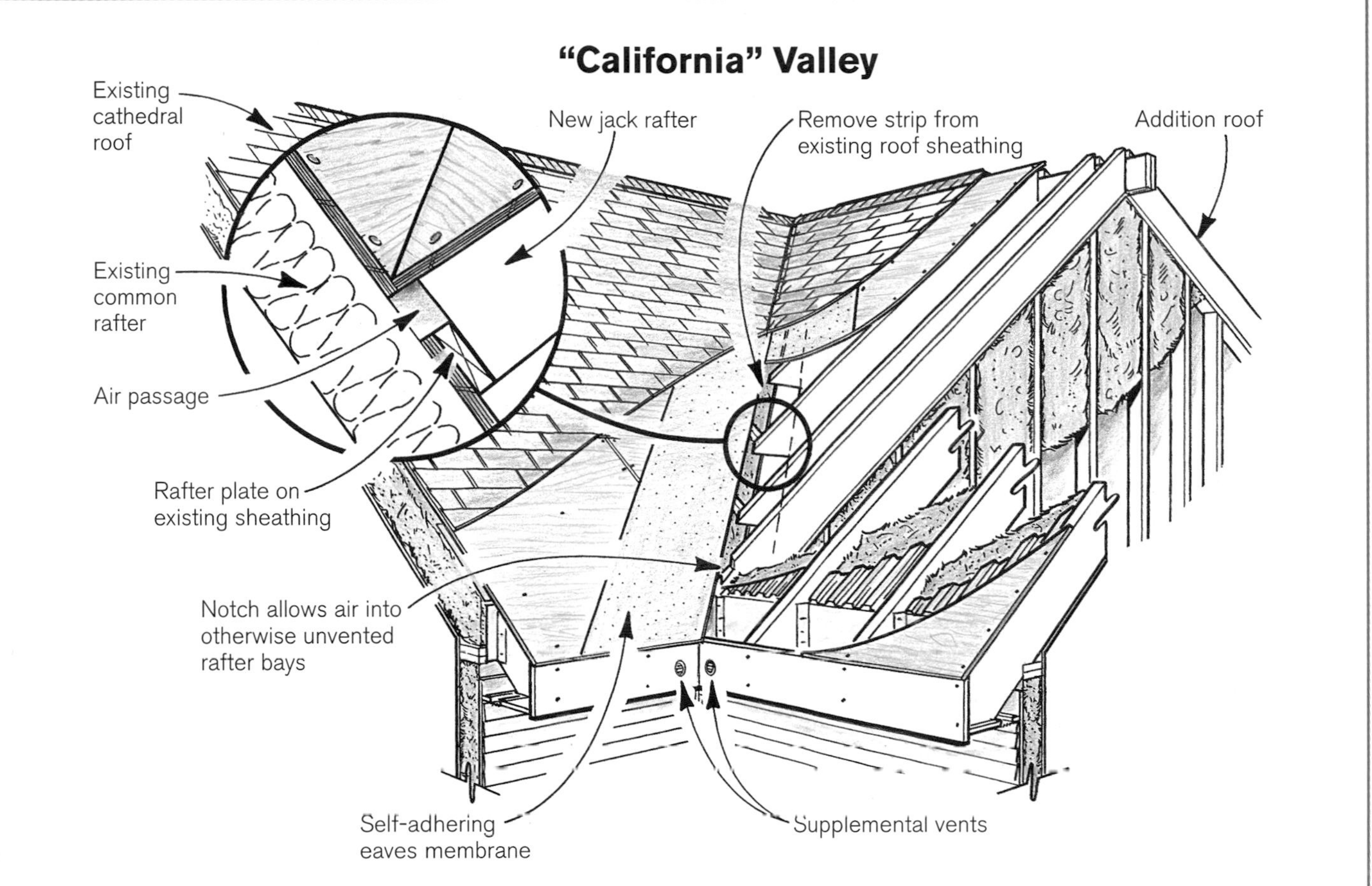

Figure 10. When framing a valley atop an existing roof, the author allows the top edge of the jack rafter seat cuts to extend beyond the flat valley plate, creating a space for airflow. A gap in the sheathing in front of the plate allows air into the rafter bays that have no soffit venting.

I've chipped away at my share of ice dams, and in my experience the cause is always the same: Heat loss through the roof causes the snow on the roof to melt. The melted snow trickles down the roof slope and refreezes as an ice dam at the eaves. The result: Water backs up behind the ice dam and leaks into the roof.

To protect the roof against this backed-up water, I always apply a 3-foot width of bituminous membrane continuously along eaves and valleys. That's the industry standard, but I can say from experience that the membrane by itself is not always enough. It makes more sense to attack the source of the problem — the melting — than to wrestle with a subsequent refreezing and water backup. Venting allows you to get warm air out of your roof system before it starts melting the snow. On a simple attic roof, it's no sweat to install soffit and ridge vents, and additional gable vents where appropriate (see "Cathedral Ceiling Details," page 278). But start with a cathedral roof and add details like skylights, a clerestory, hips, valleys, and dormers, and you've got to get creative. Terminate a cathedral roof against a wall, or join it to an upper roof of a different pitch, and you've got another set of problems. Dealing with tricky spots like those is the focus here.

Hips and Valleys

Cathedral hips and valleys commonly create a venting puzzle. With valleys, the problem is giving air a way in at the bottom; with hips, the problem is giving it a way out at the top. The solution varies from case to case, but here are a few techniques that have worked for me.

On traditional textbook valleys and hips, the plumb cuts on jack and common rafters will always be longer than the width of the valley or hip rafter. If you align the hip or valley rafter with the bottom edge of the jacks and ridge (**Figure 9**), you will create an air passage the length of the valley or hip, and allow each subsequent bay to breathe.

On roof pitches of 8/12 or greater, this will create a trough at least 1½ by 1½ inches — the minimum air passage I would allow for a hip or valley. On roofs pitched less than 8/12, the space is smaller. For these applications, I either install a smaller-depth hip or valley rafter or double up the hip or valley rafter to provide a wider air passage. On shallow pitches (under 4/12), I'll do both.

On roofs where a valley is created on top of a run of common rafters, the process is much the same.

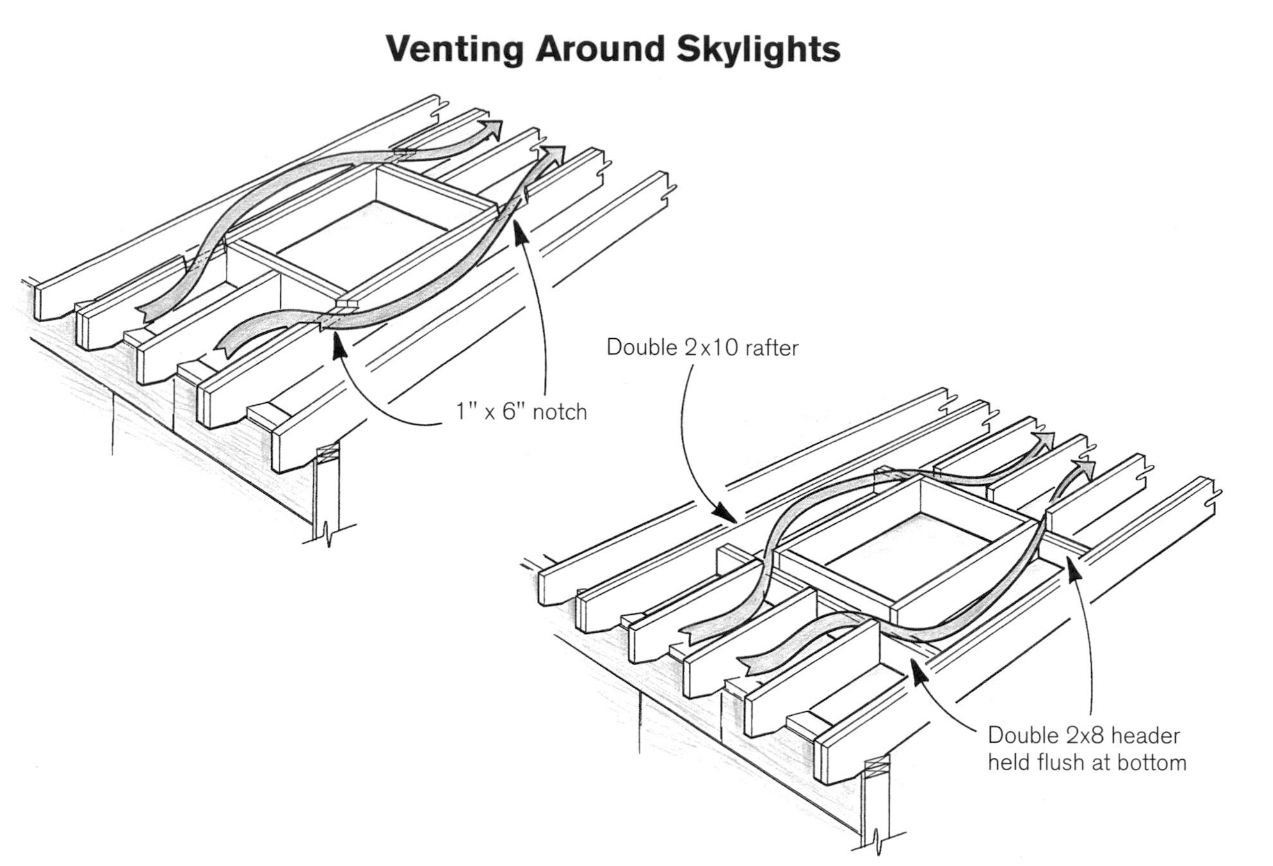

Figure 11. To allow ventilation of the rafter bays above and below a skylight, the author sometimes notches the top edge of rafters around the rough opening (left). Check with your building official before you do this to be sure the remaining rafter is strong enough to meet code. If you can't notch the rafters, use narrower lumber for the headers, doubling or tripling as necessary. Install the rafters flush to the bottom edges of the headers (right).

Make sure that the plate the jack rafters rest on is narrower than the seat cut of the jacks, and cut away or hold up the sheathing on the main roof deck to allow airflow to enter these bays (**Figure 10**, previous page). On a remodel, make this vent cut on the main roof's sheathing before the valley jacks are installed; otherwise, the tails of the seat cuts will get in the way and make cutting out the sheathing awkward.

At the eaves end of hip and valley rafters, I try to supplement the soffit vent if possible. If I'm running strip vent or ventilated drip-edge and I can sneak in a few round louver vents on the fascia adjacent to a hip or valley, I will. These narrow passages are asked to feed and vent a number of rafter bays, and they need all the airflow they can get.

On steep-pitched hips, I hold back the sheathing and install shingle ridge vent, just as I would on a ridge — except that the lower 3 feet is for aesthetics only. It's not a good idea to carry a hip vent all the way to the eaves, where an ice dam may be lurking later on in the season. Instead, I install bituminous membrane along the eaves and over the lower portion of the hip to safeguard against a possible backup.

Skylights

Any time you install a header in a rafter bay, you effectively block the vent and allow a hot spot to develop. This is true for most skylights and chimney openings, as well as at dormers that project through the roof. I routinely notch the tops of rafters above and below such openings to allow airflow into adjacent unrestricted bays (**Figure 11**). I cut these notches on an angle that expedites upward airflow.

In my area, we routinely use 2x10 or 2x12 rafters for the sake of installing R-30 batt insulation, even when 2x6 or 2x8 rafters would be adequate for the span. So a 1x6 notch on the top edge of a 2x12 doesn't jeopardize the structural integrity of that portion of the rafter required by code — I'm substantially overframing to begin with. Since my purpose is to enable air to flow for venting, I have yet to encounter a building inspector who wouldn't give his blessing to this procedure. But technically, it could be considered a code violation, so always check first, and never notch a rafter unless it is significantly wider than required for the span. If you're not certain, don't cut it.

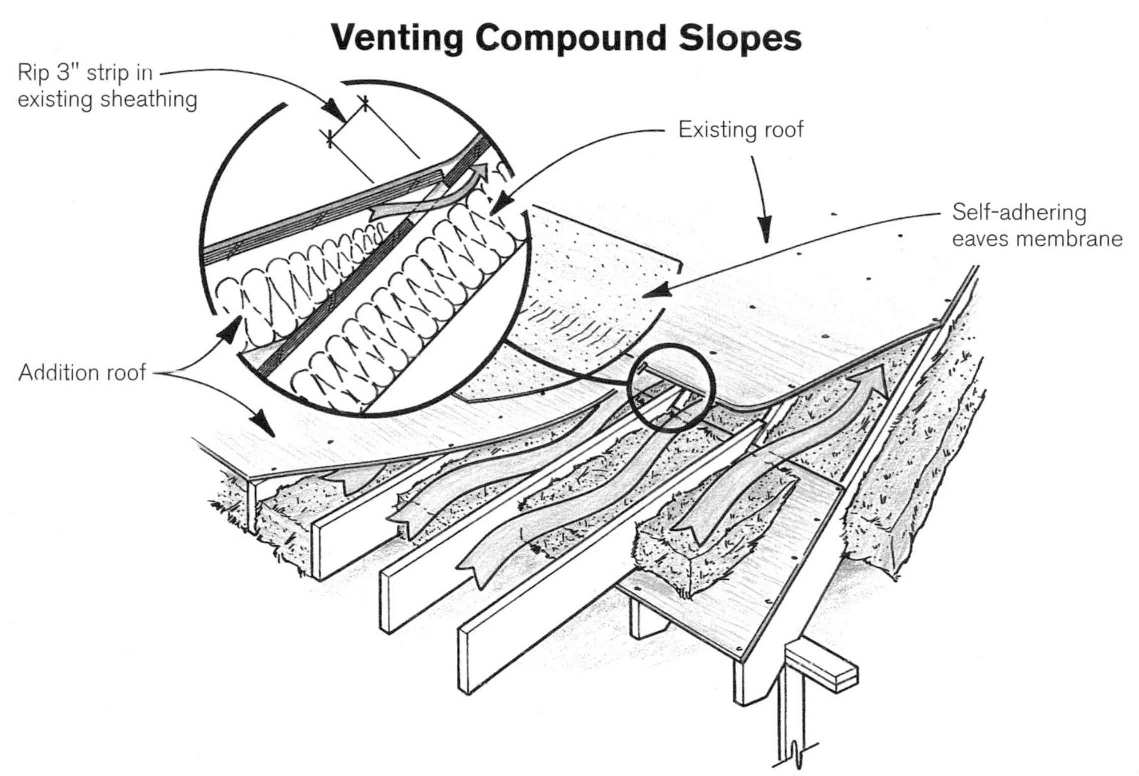

Figure 12. Where a low-pitched roof below adjoins a higher-pitched roof above, the author removes a 3-inch strip of sheathing from the upper roof and connects the vent channels in the lower system to those in the upper system, allowing free airflow through the entire roof assembly. Even with the venting, he applies a 6-foot width of bituminous membrane, 3 feet above and 3 feet below the joint, to protect against backed-up ice and water.

Also, watch out for knots in the area of the notch. Under accepted lumber grading rules, knots near the edge of a board will disqualify the piece for joist and rafter structural grades, because the knots weaken the wood. However, boards are allowed to have knots as large as 1$^{1}/_{2}$ inches in diameter toward the centerline, where the stresses aren't as great. If notching your rafter would bring the edge close to one of those big knots, don't make the cut.

If you can't notch the rafters, here's another technique, similar in principle to the method of using smaller-dimension stock for hip rafters. When you head off above and below the skylight, use stock one size smaller than the rafters, doubling or tripling the headers as needed for strength. Hold the headers flush with the bottom edge of the rafters, not the top. The 2-inch space between the header and the sheathing will allow air to move through.

Compound Roofs

Wherever a low-pitched roof merges with a higher-pitched roof, as with shed dormers and some porch or room additions, look for water to back up at the intersection line. Because this configuration commonly occurs as an add-on, there is likely to be a lot of difference in thermal and moisture protection between the upper and lower roof sections. For example, the lower roof may cover an uninsulated porch, or it may be well insulated and merge with an uninsulated attic.

When working on this kind of configuration, I insist that the lower roof be continuously vented into the upper roof (**Figure 12**). If the design or budget won't allow that, I won't guarantee the roof — I've repaired too many leaks on roofs of this shape, and a few out of my own pocket.

I prefer that the rafter layout be the same between the upper and lower roof. On a retrofit, we cut a slot in the roof deck of the main frame to pick up the venting of the lower roof. If it's a full cathedral we're tying into, and there's no room in the rafter bays to perfect a vent, then we strap the upper roof section and resheathe it to create the vent chase, like the way we treat cathedral roofs. It doesn't matter if the lower roof covers an uninsulated porch — it should still vent to the upper roof.

As further insurance, I always apply a 6-foot width of bituminous membrane at the intersection of these two roof sections (3 feet above the joint and 3 feet below). Even with correct venting, I've seen a few cases where in the spring there was a good layer of

Cathedral Ceiling Details

Few components in low-energy homes produce more diverse approaches — and more disagreement — than cathedral ceilings. The reason is simple: Trying to satisfy the insulation and ventilation requirements in such a tight space is a real challenge.

It's often impossible to fit the required amount of insulation into the depth provided by a 12-inch rafter. A common solution for an R-40 ceiling is to use fiberglass batts between the rafters and then nail an inch of rigid insulation underneath the rafters. The seams of the foam board can be taped so that it doubles as a vapor barrier. An alternative is to use deeper (but more expensive) engineered beams such as I-joists or trusses and avoid the use of foam insulation.

Another problem is providing adequate roof ventilation. Most roofs are designed to have an eaves-to-ridge flow of air. These are called "cold roofs" because they keep the underside of the sheathing cold in winter. In a heating climate, the flow of cold air under the sheathing discourages interior moisture buildup and ice damming. In a cooling climate, ventilation relieves heat buildup.

To complicate matters, not all builders and researchers agree that ventilation space above the insulation is necessary in heating climates. Cathedral ceilings that aren't ventilated are referred to as "hot roofs," and rely on a well-sealed air and vapor barrier and ample insulation to keep moisture out of the roof. Solid foam roof systems, such as stress-skin panels, are a type of hot roof.

Shown here are details used by energy-conscious builders and designers from different locales, along with the pros and cons of each approach.

Deep I-Joists

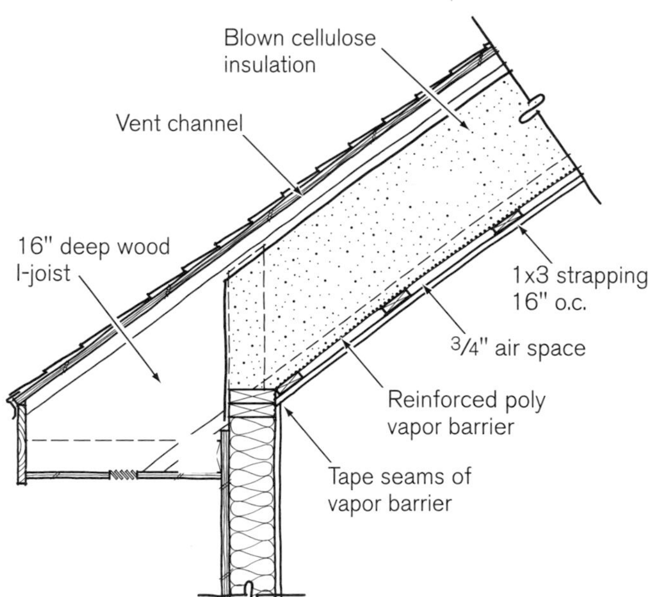

Sixteen-inch-deep wood I-joists insulated with dense-blown cellulose create a high-R cathedral ceiling. However, the high cost of the I-joists and the complicated ridge and eaves details associated with I-joists make this the builder's least favorite system. — Paul Bourke, Leverett, Mass.

Foil-Faced Foam

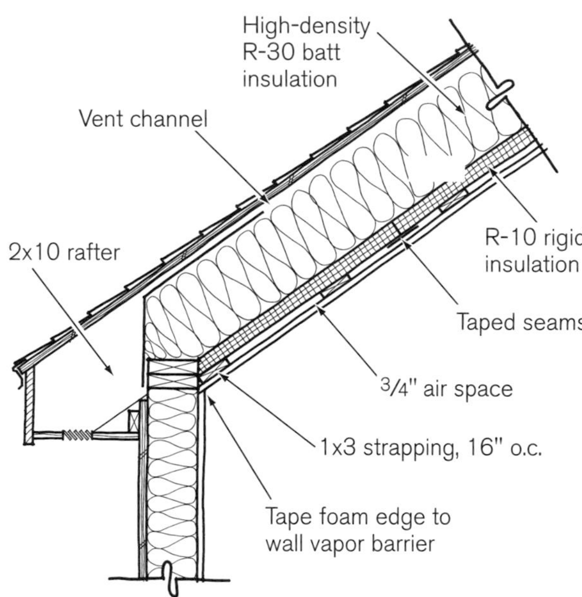

If space is limited, leaving no room for build-downs, or on a small area of ceiling that the builder wants to complete quickly, the builder applies foil-faced foam sheets to the bottom faces of the rafters for added R-value and a thermal break. Taping the seams where sheets meet creates a good air and vapor barrier. Using high-density batts, you can pack a touch over R-40 into 10 3/4 inches. Don't use cellulose over foam board, because the foam can't resist the pressure the dense cellulose exerts. — P.B.

2x12 Rafters With BIBS

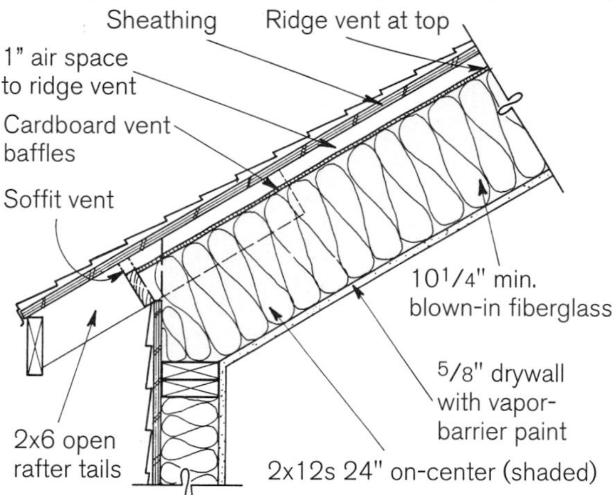

This method achieves R-38 to R-40 with standard framing and blown insulation, making it fast and efficient. It requires 2x12 rafters, typically larger than are required for structural reasons. The insulation is blown-in fiberglass (BIBS), which achieves a higher R-value than batt insulation and is not subject to settling. The only drawback is the higher costs of the oversized framing and BIBS system. — John Raabe (designer), Langley, Wash.

2x12 Hot Roof

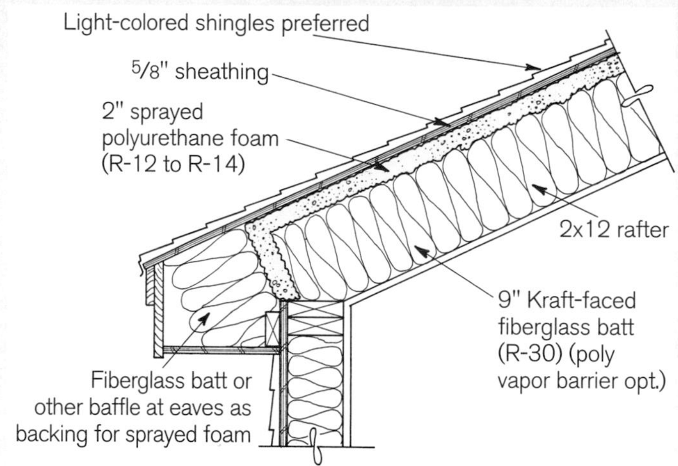

Hot roofs are beginning to gain acceptance by building designers and codes. The simplified framing approach is useful for complex roofs with hips, valleys, skylights, etc. Condensation inside the roof cavity should not be a problem as long as the foam insulation is thick enough to keep the underside of the foam above the dew point of the interior air. The colder the climate, the thicker the foam insulation must be. An airtight air barrier is required below the insulation to keep moist air out of the roof assembly. In high-snow areas, ice damming may be a problem. — P.B.

Scissor Trusses

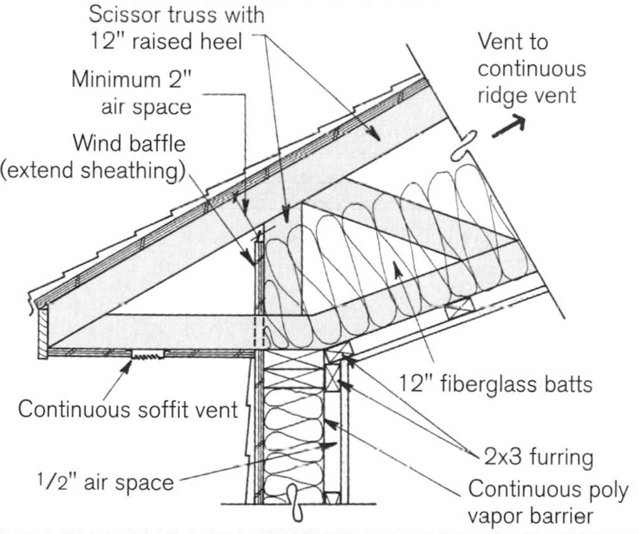

Scissor trusses provide a fast, cost-effective way to frame cathedral ceilings with ample space for insulation and ventilation. Standard fiberglass batts can be used, but the batts must be carefully fitted to minimize short circuiting at truss chords. Make sure the trusses are designed with raised heels to allow full insulation at the eaves. — William Baldwin, Johnston, R.I.

Crisscross Build-Down

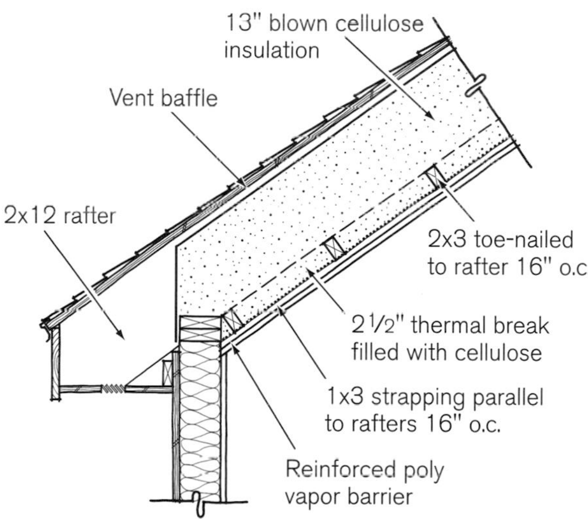

This method is quick and simple as long as you plan ahead for vapor barrier and strapping details. In the case shown, a knee wall complicated the vapor barrier installation. To prevent that, the author recommends first insulating the entire roof plane down to the eaves, then building the knee wall. Besides giving a 13-inch-deep insulation cavity, the crisscross build-down also provides a 2 1/2-inch thermal break below the rafters. — P.B.

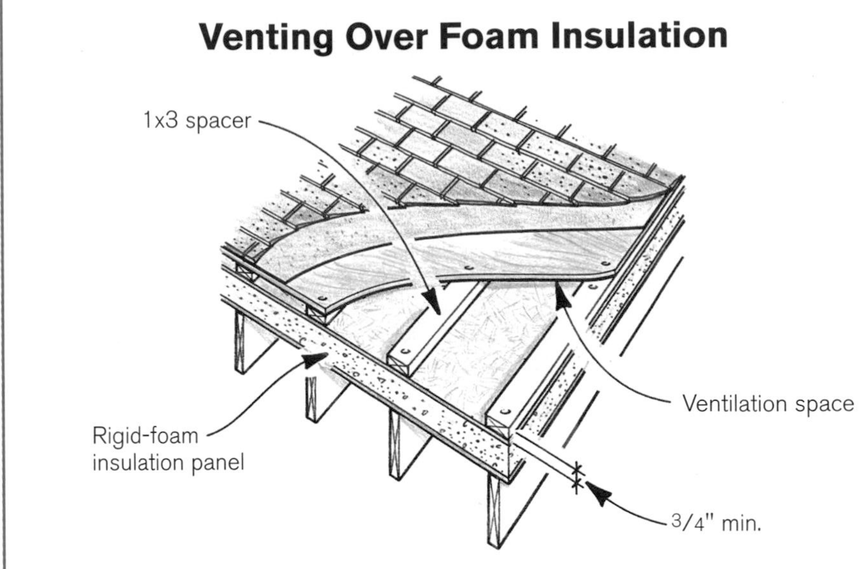

Figure 13. The author ventilates foam-insulated cathedral roofs by attaching strapping through the foam into the deck below, 16 inches on-center, using 6-inch screws. With structural foam panels, shown here, the strapping can be installed directly to the panel's OSB face. Sheathing nailed to the strapping forms a 3/4-inch-thick vent channel.

snow on such a roof, followed by a heavy spring rain, and the lower roof become saturated and backed up at the juncture.

Venting Over Foam Roof Decks

Many New England vacation homes feature a cathedral ceiling framed with exposed timbers, 3 to 4 feet on-center, with 2x6 tongue-and-groove sheathing, a 2-inch layer of foam insulation, and shingles installed with 3-inch roofing nails. If no vent is provided, there's trouble brewing. I get to see a lot of these roofs, because they leak like sieves.

For a retrofit, we strip the roof to the decking to inspect it for soundness and allow it to dry. Then we install a double layer of 2-inch rigid foil-faced insulation, staggering the joints to provide half-laps on these panels. All roof projections or penetrations are tightly sealed with spray foam. Next, we apply 1x3 strapping in vertical rows 16 inches on-center, securing it with 6-inch screws through the insulation and into the decking. We then nail 1/2-inch plywood to the strapping to create 3/4x14-inch continuous vents (**Figure 13**). At the eaves, we install a vented drip-edge over a band of bituminous membrane. Then we shingle the roof and apply a vented ridge cap. With 4 inches of foam run-

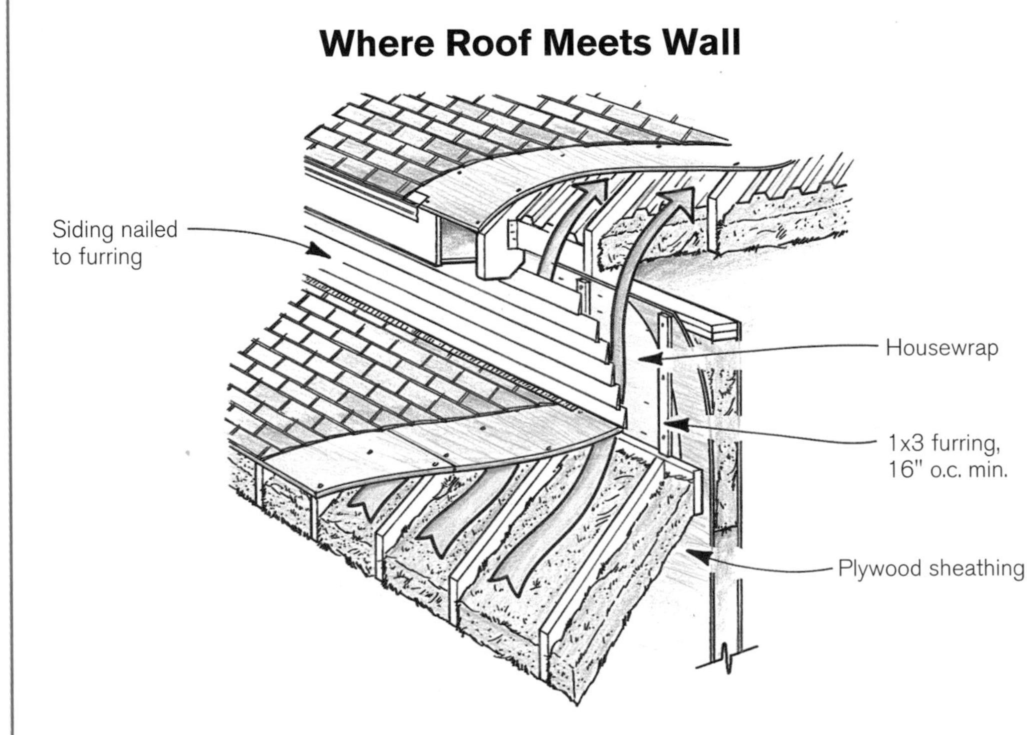

Figure 14. To vent roofs that terminate against a wall at the top, the author prefers to connect the roof venting channel to a vent channel in the wall, which he forms by nailing strapping to the wall studs. The wall vent system allows air to move up into the upper roof system and exit the building via the upper ridge and gable vents.

ning continuously, there is little opportunity for thermal bridging or the transfer of heat to the roof deck. Even in the worst of winters, I've yet to see any significant ice dams occur on this type of roof system.

On a remodel, this system requires that the fascia be supplemented or replaced with wider trim to cover the raw edge of the built-up insulation. On a budget, the end caps of commercial metal roofing will work as well, and you can pick a color to match the rest of the building.

Roof-Wall Junctures

The juncture of a roofline and a side wall is a likely spot for warm air and moisture to become trapped. I typically use one of two methods to provide venting to these roofs (**Figure 14**). On new construction, if the side wall above isn't too cluttered with window openings, the trick is to apply lengths of strapping to the outside edge of the dormer or clerestory stud wall before sheathing is applied. This creates a 3/4-inch vent chase at the top plate of the dormer for venting to continue into the upper roof. If there is a window or two in the side wall, I strap the perimeter of the rough opening. The vertical strapping applied to cripple studs below any openings are held short about 6 inches from the sills to allow lower rafter bays to vent up and around window openings.

The other method I've used is to leave a 2-inch gap in the sheathing of the lower roof deck where it butts into the side wall. I split lengths of rigid ridge vent and install it across this gap, then cover the ridge vent with a bend of roll flashing that is incorporated into the side wall. Commercially made metal side-wall flashing will do the same, but most lumber companies don't stock it. Rather than deal with special orders and lead time, I find it simpler to make up the vent as I've described. (Also, the ridge vent/flashing system offers the opportunity to create a wider drip cap than is provided by the commercial vents I've seen. This reduces the chance that backup or wind-driven rain will enter the vent.)

On an addition or retrofit, it's more practical to use the second method. Where possible, though, I prefer the furring method because it provides sealed venting and vents the dormer or clerestory side wall as well as the roof. Otherwise, snow lying where the roof meets the wall melts and gets drawn into the wood of the side wall, causing the wood to rot and paint to blister and peel. Venting the side wall goes a long way toward remedying this problem.

Builder Robert Hatch lives in Freedom, N.H.

Unvented Attics With Spray Foam Insulation

by James Morshead

As a general contractor, I was taught that attic and cathedral ceiling assemblies should always be vented. Since then, however, studies have shown that properly designed and installed unvented attic assemblies outperform vented assemblies. They reduce energy loss and protect against rot and mold by preventing moisture from passing through the insulation and condensing on cold surfaces. Although many builders — and even some building inspectors — are unfamiliar with them, unvented assemblies are already part of the 2006 IRC and will soon be allowed by most building codes (see "Code Provisions for Unvented Attics," next page, and "IRC No-Vent Provision," page 269).

I work for a company in northern California that installs spray polyurethane foam or "SPF" insulation, and we are frequently asked to insulate unvented assemblies. Sometimes the building has a flat roof or a cathedral ceiling that would be difficult or impossible to ventilate (**Figure 15**). In other cases, the existing framing cavities are too shallow to accommodate a sufficient amount of insulation plus a vent space. And occasionally customers request unvented attics because they make the building more comfortable and energy efficient.

Why Install Roof Venting?

Traditionally, venting has been used to deal with problems that occur when heat or moisture escapes into the attic.

In cold climates, the escaping heat can cause ice dams by melting the snow on the roof. Venting the space above the insulation helps keep the roof cool by carrying this heat away. If moisture enters the attic through the ceiling (usually as an air leak), the vents are supposed to allow it to exit before it condenses on something cold.

However, ventilating above fiber insulation comes with an energy penalty. Fiber insulation is designed to be enclosed in an airtight cavity. When air flows

Figure 15. Spray foam is a good choice for roofs that are difficult to vent, like a turret with converging rafters (far left) or a flat roof with its rafters hung between flush beams (left).

over and through fiber insulation, there is a substantial loss of thermal performance (**Figure 16**).

Also, most HVAC ducts and air handlers leak to some degree, so when these are installed in vented attics, conditioned air is lost to the exterior. And because vented attics are subject to extreme high and low temperatures, additional energy is lost through the thin insulation on the HVAC equipment.

In cooling climates, venting the attic can bring humid outdoor air into contact with attic ductwork. If the ducts are not properly insulated, they can be cold enough to cause condensation.

Venting and shingle temperature. It's a common misconception that code-required venting significantly lowers the summer temperature of the roof surface. In fact, tests have shown that it lowers the

Code Provisions for Unvented Attics

Every state except California and Hawaii has adopted some version of the IRC. And California is expected to adopt it in 2008.

Until recently, the IRC required all attics and enclosed rafter spaces to be vented. But the latest version allows unvented attic assemblies if certain conditions are met.

According to Section R806.4 of the 2006 IRC, unvented assemblies are allowed if "no interior vapor retarders are installed on the ceiling side (attic floor) of the unvented attic assembly" and if "air-impermeable insulation is applied in direct contact with the underside/interior of the structural roof deck."

There is an exception that allows air-permeable insulation (fiberglass and cellulose) to be used in unvented assemblies in certain parts of the South (climate zones 2B and 3B).

It has long been possible to get an unvented assembly approved by the inspector as an "alternate construction method." But once states update their codes to the 2006 IRC, it will no longer be necessary to get special approval for unvented assemblies.

In the meantime, the fact that the 2006 IRC allows unvented assemblies should make it easier to get special approval in states that have adopted earlier versions of the code.

Do not build an unvented attic assembly without first talking to the local building inspector. Unvented assemblies are new in the IRC, and your state might be using an older version of the code. Also, the committee that wrote this section is still working on it, so more changes may be on the way.

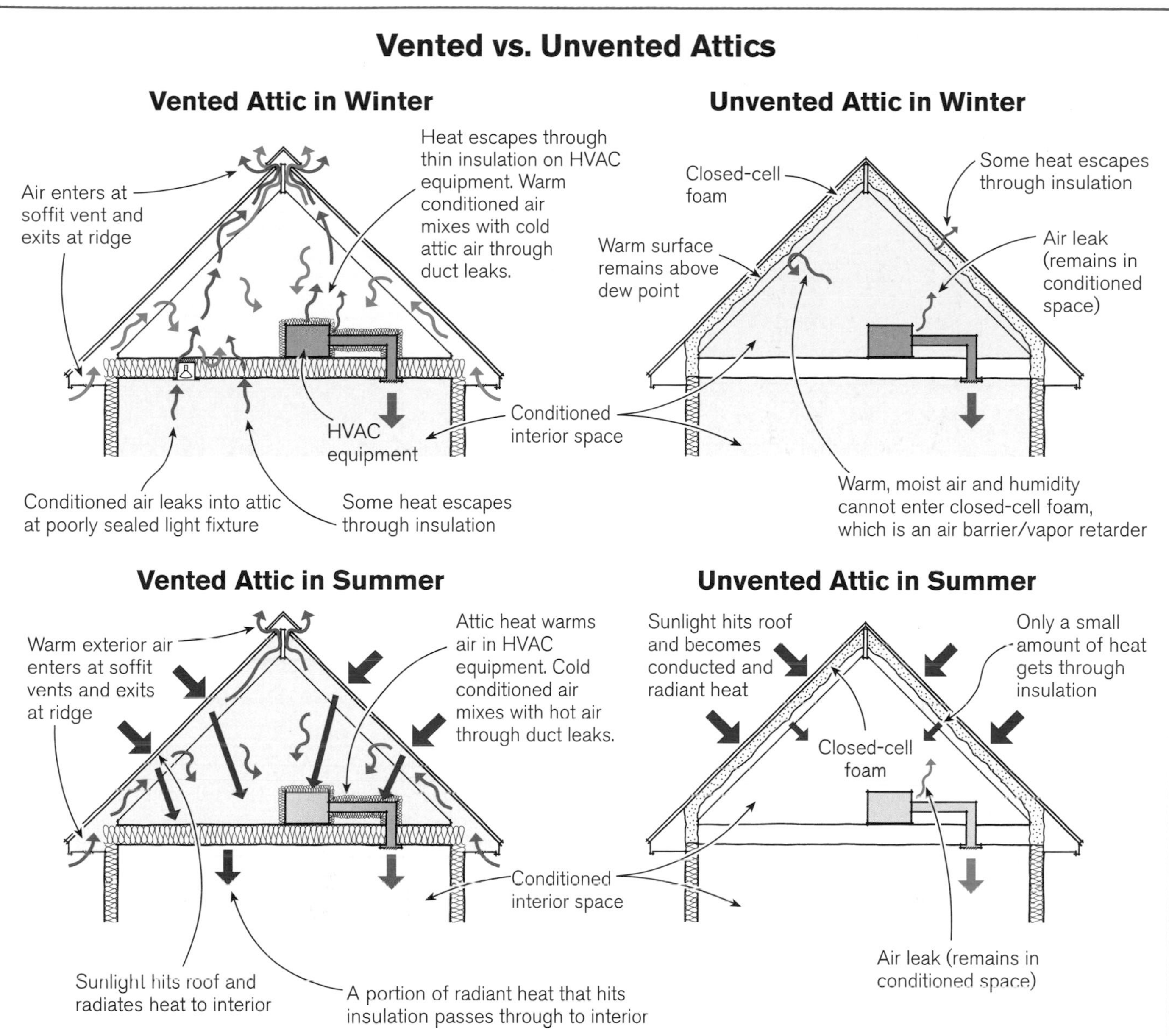

Figure 16. While attic ventilation can mitigate problems caused by ineffective insulation, air leaks in the ceiling, or inadequate vapor retarders, a better approach is to build the attic as an unvented assembly. The foam insulation used for unvented attics stops air movement and with it the transport of moisture. Any HVAC equipment located in the attic is within the conditioned shell of the house, which also cuts energy losses.

surface temperature of asphalt shingles by at most about 5°F.

For many years, roofing manufacturers required that shingles be installed over vented substrates, but today, several companies — including Elk and CertainTeed — will guarantee shingles installed over properly constructed unvented roofs.

How Unvented Assemblies Work

A properly constructed unvented attic is immune to the moisture problems that occur in vented assemblies and is much more likely to be energy efficient.

In an unvented assembly, anything below the insulation — including an attic — is considered conditioned space. Turning the attic into conditioned space saves energy; if heat or air escapes from the HVAC equipment, it remains within the conditioned space (**Figure 17**, next page).

If enough energy is saved in this manner, the HVAC system can actually be downsized, reducing installation and operating costs.

A number of insulation materials can be used in an unvented assembly, but the one with the greatest applicability across the country is spray polyurethane foam (SPF). It's an extremely effective insulation and air barrier all in one, and since it's spray-applied, it

Figure 17. The ducts visible in this unvented attic will be concealed after drywall is installed. But because they are in conditioned space, they won't be subject to the extremes of temperature typical of attics.

conforms to irregular shapes that otherwise might be difficult to insulate and seal (**Figure 18**).

Despite the multiple brands of SPF, there are only two main kinds: open-cell foam and closed-cell foam. Chemically, all brands are nearly identical — contrary to some advertising claims — and contain about the same proportion of agriculturally derived resin from corn, sugar beets, sugarcane, or soybeans. None of the spray foams contain formaldehyde or use toxic or ozone-depleting blowing agents.

The important differences between products have to do with density, R-value, and permeability.

Open-cell foam. The typical open-cell foam weighs 0.5 pound per cubic foot and has an insulation value of R-3.5 per inch of thickness. This type of foam is relatively permeable; at 5 inches thick it is rated at about 10 perms. Open-cell foam is an air barrier but not a vapor retarder.

When sprayed, open-cell foam expands to about 100 times its liquid volume, so it usually has to be trimmed flush to the framing. Fortunately, it's soft and easy to trim.

Closed-cell foam is denser and less permeable than open-cell material. The typical closed-cell foam weighs 2.0 pounds per cubic foot and provides R-6.6 per inch of thickness.

When sprayed, closed-cell foam expands from 30 to 50 times its liquid volume, making it easy to apply without completely filling the framing bay. If the bay must be filled completely, the applicator can overfill it and then trim off the excess.

Trimming closed-cell foam is not as easy as trimming the open-cell material, but it can be done.

Advantages of Closed-Cell Foam

Both types of SPF are excellent insulation materials, but our company uses closed-cell material in unvented assemblies because we think it provides the best overall performance. With it, we can pack more R-value into a small space, which is helpful when the existing rafter bays are shallow; for example, we can get R-30 into a 4 1/2-inch space.

In our climate zone, it's important to avoid excessive vapor diffusion, and we think the best way to do this is to use closed-cell foam. One of the great benefits of closed-cell foam is that if you install it to a thickness of at least 2 to 2 1/2 inches, it will have a permeance of 1.0 perm or less.

This means that in addition to being an air barrier, closed-cell foam is a vapor retarder. It's actually a vapor retarder from both sides, so it ends the debate about which side of the insulation to put the vapor retarder on in climates where interiors are both heated and cooled.

Some companies that make both open-cell and closed-cell foam advise insulation contractors not to use the open-cell material in unvented assemblies —

Figure 18. This barrel ceiling (left) would be difficult to insulate and seal with traditional materials. It's an ideal candidate for spray foam, which conforms to its irregular surfaces (right).

Figure 19. Open-cell foam, which expands to about 100 times its liquid volume, typically has to be trimmed flush to framing members — an easy task, since the foam is so soft. Because of its lower expansion rate and higher R-value per inch, closed-cell foam doesn't usually have to be trimmed. When it does, as in this shallow rafter bay (left), the author's crew uses a scraper — in this case a horse curry comb — to clean the framing in preparation for drywall (right).

or to do it only in certain climates where vapor diffusion will not be a problem.

In conditions of extreme vapor drive — an indoor pool or spa, for instance — it may be necessary to further reduce the permeability of closed-cell foam by coating it with a spray-applied liquid vapor barrier.

Cathedral Ceilings

In a vented cathedral ceiling, the insulation is in contact with the back of the drywall and there's an air gap (the venting space) above. But in an unvented assembly, the insulation must be against the bottom of the sheathing.

Sometimes, if the rafter bays are unusually shallow, we have to fill them all the way up with closed-cell foam (**Figure 19**). But because this type of foam has such a high R-value, in most cases we have to fill the cavities only partway.

Contractors often ask about the air space below the foam; most were taught that it's bad to leave an air

Figure 20. Fiberglass and cellulose insulation are usually installed in contact with the back of the drywall; the concern is that leaving a space on both sides of fiberglass insulation allows convective air currents to degrade the insulation's thermal performance. Because closed-cell foam is unaffected by air movement, the space between it and the drywall is not a problem.

space below insulation. This is true of fiber insulations because convection currents can form in gaps and degrade the insulation's thermal performance, particularly if there is an air space on both sides of the insulation. But this is not true of foam, which can't be infiltrated and is relatively unaffected by surrounding air currents.

Any space left below the foam is considered conditioned space (**Figure 20**, previous page).

Dealing With Can Lights

It's easier and more energy efficient to build a cathedral ceiling as an unvented assembly, but dealing with recessed light fixtures can be a real challenge.

There are two issues: how to insulate and seal the area above the fixture, and how to provide enough space around it so it doesn't overheat. Even if the fixture is an IC unit, you can't embed it in foam.

Insulating above. If we're lucky, there will be room to spray a full thickness of foam above the fixture and still maintain the desired 2 to 3 inches of clearance between foam and fixture.

If there isn't enough space or access to spray above a fixture, we sometimes install a piece of nonperforated foil-faced rigid foam above it instead. Before spraying, we mask the fixture to keep it clean, then create an airtight seal by lapping the SPF onto the rigid foam (**Figure 21**). If the rigid foam butts to framing, we caulk that joint with polyurethane sealant.

Clearances. Few building codes contain specific requirements about clearances between foam and can lights, so it's a good idea to talk to the building inspector about the issue. SPF is such a good insulator that it can cause a fixture to overheat, tripping the temperature-limit switch and cutting power to the light. Excess heat could also damage the wire sheathing or even the foam itself.

In California, new code provisions are being developed that will require builders to take one of three measures with recessed lights: leave 3 inches of clearance around a fixture, box around it, or wrap it with 2 inches of mineral fiber. A 3-inch clearance is already required around hot appliance vents.

SPF is compatible with PVC and CPVC, so it's okay to spray it on Romex, PVC pipe, and CPVC sprinkler pipe.

Air Sealing

Any surface we spray will be sealed against the movement of air, but there are always some surfaces we can't spray.

For example, the gaps between doubled-up framing members are too small to spray with foam, yet a significant amount of air can leak through at these spots. It's best to seal these joints during framing by installing compressible foam gaskets between the members. If that isn't done, you can caulk the joints after the foam is installed.

When the gaps are too wide for caulk, we fill them with foam from a can. The canned foam should be the low-expansion type; it contains more closed cells than the high-expansion material. We stay away from the latex foams because they're very permeable.

Figure 21. Code requires that a space be left between can lights — even IC-rated cans — and spray foam insulation. In shallow bays, the author's crew installs foil-faced rigid foam above fixtures and creates a seal by lapping the spray foam onto it (left). An alternate method, which may soon be required in California, is to isolate fixtures from the foam by installing them in metal boxes (right).

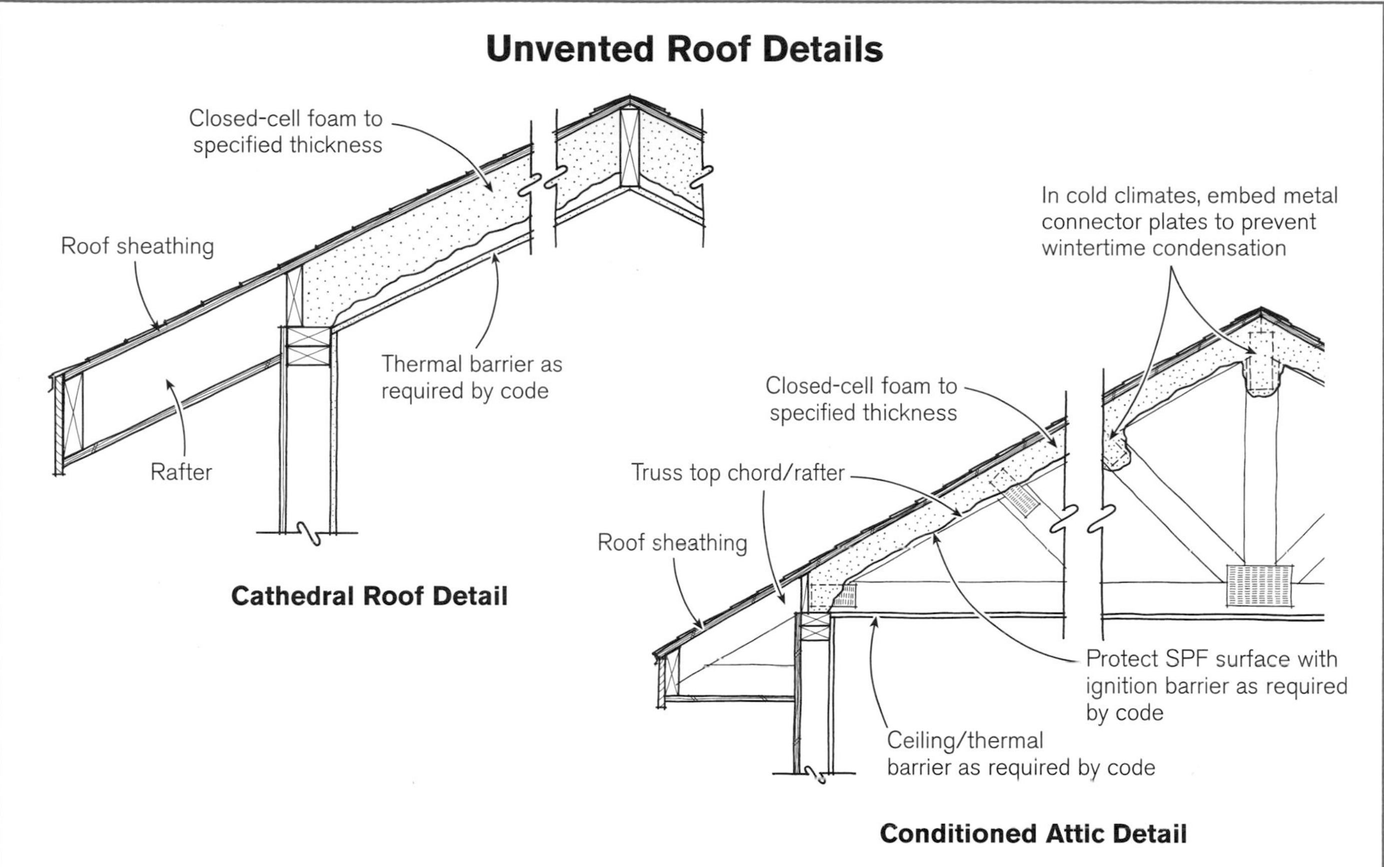

Figure 22. When insulating an unvented roof assembly, the author prefers closed-cell to open cell foam because it's both an air barrier and a vapor retarder. To finish an unvented cathedral ceiling insulated with closed cell foam, most codes require a layer of 1/2-inch drywall or an equivalent thermal barrier (left). Depending on local code, the spray foam in an unvented, or "cathedralized," attic (right) may not require drywall covering unless the area is accessible for servicing equipment. In some cases, the foam may have to be sprayed with an intumescent coating.

Fire Resistance

When the unvented assembly is a cathedral ceiling, the foam will be covered with drywall, which is a code-approved thermal barrier. In an attic, though, the rafter bays are not normally covered by drywall, so the issue of fire-resistance comes into play (**Figure 22**).

This can be a gray area in the code, so be sure to check with your building department before building an unvented attic space. Most codes state that if the attic is accessible for the service of utilities, the foam must be covered with an ignition barrier. Certain water-based intumescent coatings qualify as ignition barriers.

If the attic area is not accessible or is not "accessed for the service of utilities," it may be possible to leave the SPF exposed. Many contractors are confused about how to treat this enclosed attic space. Providing access through a ceiling hatch is okay but not necessary; venting to the room below is prohibited by the fire code.

Other Issues

Unlike fiber insulation, which can be blown through a hose or stuffed into hard-to-reach areas, SPF can't be installed without sufficient access. The applicator must be able to get close enough to the sheathing to spray from 16 to 24 inches away — and do it from pretty much straight on.

Cost. In our area, the installed cost of an average-size closed-cell foam insulation project is between $1.10 and $1.40 per board foot of material.

For R-30, that comes to about $5 per square foot of roof area. That's more than other insulation materials would cost, but not much more if you factor in all of SPF's advantages — future energy savings, increased comfort and moisture control, the greater design flexibility that comes with being able to fit the necessary R-value into small framing cavities, and the possibility that the mechanical system can be downsized.

James Morshead is senior project manager and technical director for American Services Co. in Dublin, Calif.

Chapter 15: Sealing & Flashing Roofs

- Troubleshooting Roof Leaks
- Leakproof Valley Flashing
- Skylight Installation and Flashing

Troubleshooting Roof Leaks

by Harrison McCampbell

As an architect who has worked with the roofing industry since 1977, I often inspect leaking roofs. I have found that poor flashing details — at penetrations, at roof edges, or where a roof changes planes — are much more likely to be the cause of a leak than the roofing itself. Similarly, many leaks are caused by the use of insufficient or inadequate fasteners for sheathing, flashing, or roofing, and by the attempt to substitute caulk or roofing cement for flashing.

The cost of installing the roof on a new building usually amounts to less than 5% of the total construction cost. Yet some lawyers estimate that 60% to 80% of construction lawsuits involve roof failures. Often, it's a small leak that quickly grows into a big, expensive problem.

The following problems are among the most common I encounter. In every case, the leak could have been avoided had the installer used common sense and paid more attention to detail.

Fasteners

Problem: No support at sheathing edges. The plywood sheathing on this flat roof was installed without blocking under the edges. If someone walks on the roof, the roofing may crack when the sheathing flexes at the plywood joints.

Solution: Use H-clips or solid blocking at plywood edges, or use tongue-and-groove plywood roof sheathing.

Problem: Smooth-shank nails don't hold. Smooth-shank common nails used to fasten roof sheathing can work themselves loose over the years, especially if a roof deck is walked on. Rising nail heads can eventually poke through the roofing.

Solution: Use ring-shank nails for roof sheathing.

Fasteners

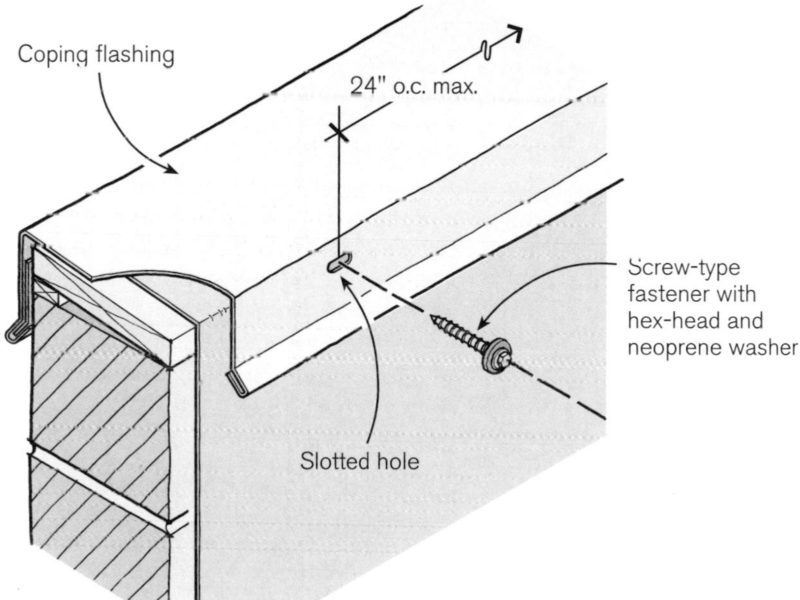

Problem: Flashing is incorrectly fastened. There are three problems with the coping flashing on this parapet wall:

- **The flashing has been fastened on the horizontal face**, instead of the vertical.
- **The flashing has been nailed** instead of screwed.
- **No allowance has been made for expansion and contraction** of the metal flashing, nor for differential movement between the metal flashing and the wood nailer, which expand at different rates.

An exposed fastener on the horizontal surface of the flashing is a potential leakage point. If flashing is attached with nails instead of screws, the last hammer blow can leave a concave dimple in the flashing, encouraging ponding around the nail hole.

If long runs of flashing are installed without allowing for expansion and contraction, the moving flashing can work nails back and forth until they loosen.

Solution:

Attach flashing on a vertical surface rather than a horizontal surface.

Use hex-head screws with neoprene washers rather than nails if it is necessary to use exposed fasteners.

Install fasteners in slotted holes, which allow the flashing to move with changes in temperature.

Some Rules of Good Roofing Practice

- Never permit ponding on flashings or roofing. All roofs and flashings should have positive drainage, with a slope of at least 1/4 inch per foot.
- Install flashing to accommodate anticipated movement, either by building settlement or by expansion and contraction from temperature swings.
- Install counterflashing at a height of at least 8 inches above the roofing surface.
- Plan generous overlaps (at least 4 inches) of flashings to limit the entry of wind-driven rain. Overlaps on shallow-pitched roofs need to be more generous than on steeply pitched roofs.
- Use minimum 24-gauge flashing, which is better able to resist wind damage than the code-required 26-gauge.
- Locate roof drains either at the midspan of a structural member, which will be the low point when the member has deflected, or along an exterior wall. — *H.M.*

Flat Roofs

Problem: Because no gravel stop was installed, the asphalt flood coat and the roofing gravel from the built-up roof are migrating down the face of the shingle roof.

Solution: Install a 3/4-inch-high sheet-metal gravel stop, with a flange at least 4 inches wide, under the edge of the built-up roofing. The stop should also include a bottom flange, extending at least 4 inches over the top course of asphalt shingles.

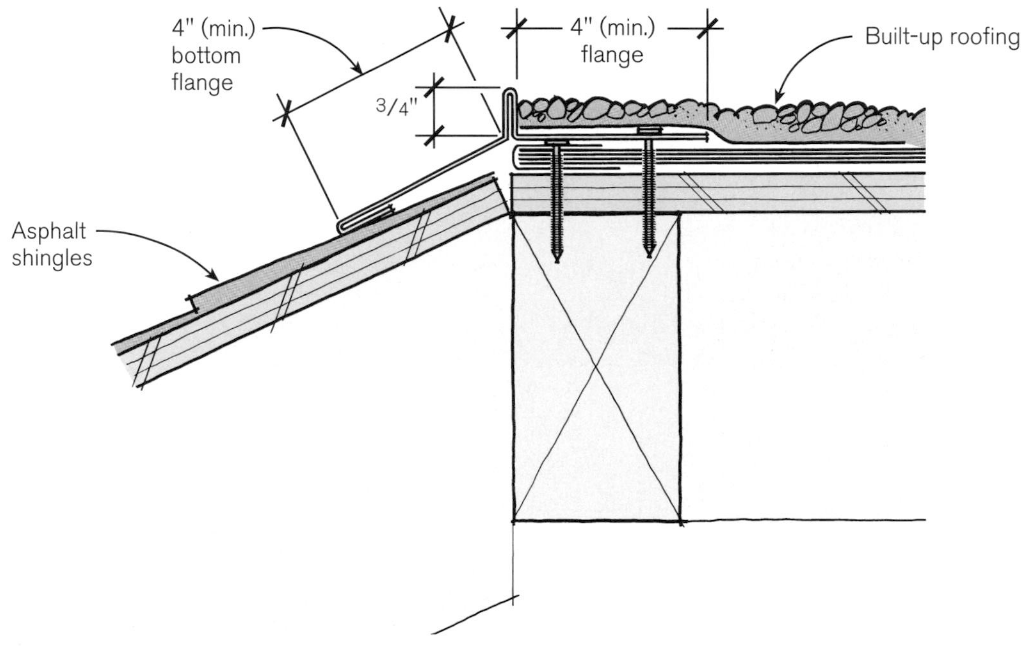

Problem: Edge flashing was not nailed. The installer forgot to attach the edge flashing to the roof before the built-up roofing was installed. When the roofing material later contracted, it pulled the entire flashing away from the edge of the roof.

Solution: Don't forget to fasten the flashing to the sheathing or nailer with nails or screws.

Flat Roofs

Problem: No overflow scupper. The parapet wall around this roof has only one scupper on each side, with no overflow scupper. If the primary scupper becomes blocked — by a tennis ball, for example, or in this case, a soda can — then not only are leaks likely to occur, but ponding water on the roof could get heavy enough to threaten the structural integrity of the roof framing.

Solution: Install a secondary scupper 2 inches higher than the primary scupper to drain excess water in case the primary scupper becomes blocked.

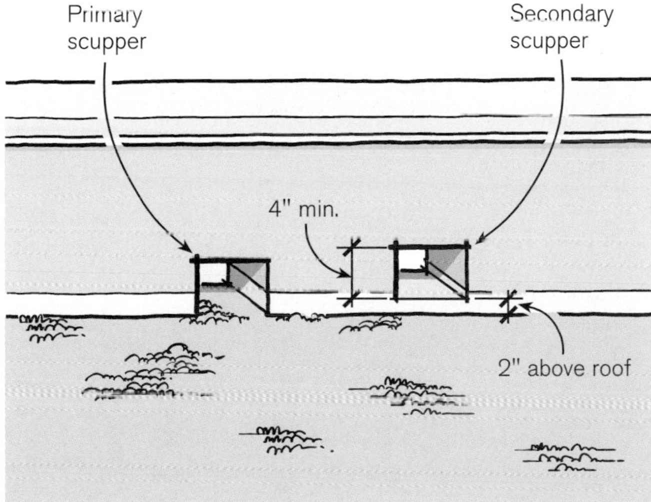

Problem: Clogged roof drain. Failure to clear away leaves from a drain strainer can cause ponding.

Solution: Remind homeowners to check roof drains and scuppers regularly, and to clean them at least once a year — preferably more often. An overflow scupper is needed here, as well — no roof should ever depend upon a single drain.

Counterflashing

Problem: Counterflashing is pulling away from the chimney. In the top photo, expansion and contraction have caused a failure of the caulk used to seal the surface-mounted counterflashing to the chimney. In the bottom photo, a too-shallow flange in the counterflashing has allowed water to get behind the flashing when the brick gets saturated in a heavy rain.

Solution: Install the counterflashing between courses of brick as the chimney is being laid up. The minimum width flange for counterflashing inserted into a brick chimney is 1 1/4 inches.

For existing masonry, cut a 1 1/2-inch-deep kerf into a mortar joint with an abrasive blade. Run a bead of caulk along a 1/4-inch hem turned up on the back edge of the flange, then slide the flange into the kerf. The hem will compress slightly, holding the flange in place. Finally, caulk the top of the flange where it enters the kerf to keep excess water out.

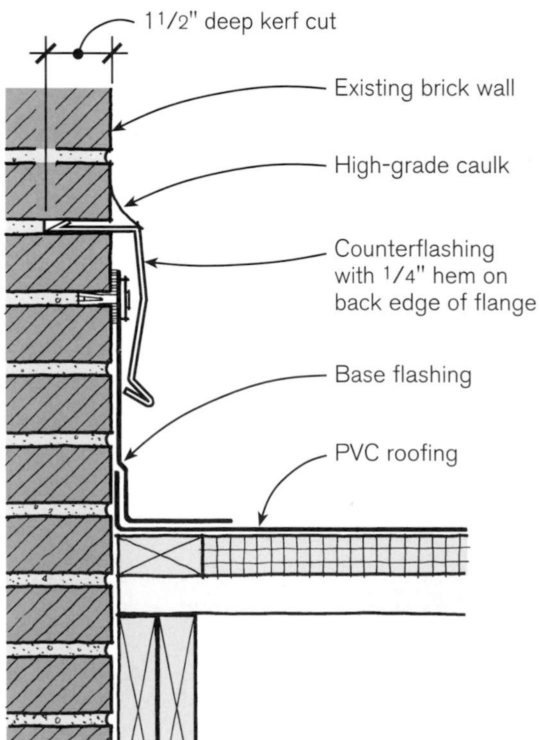

Counterflashing

Problem: Failure of caulk between stucco and flashing. Don't depend on caulk or roofing cement to keep water out of a crack anywhere on a roof, especially if the crack is between dissimilar materials, which expand and contract at different rates. Caulk has its uses, but it should not be relied upon as the primary barrier against water entry.

Solution: Install overlapping flashings that permit some movement. When stucco will be used above counterflashing, the counterflashing should be installed first, behind the stucco, and the felt underlayment should be lapped over the counterflashing.

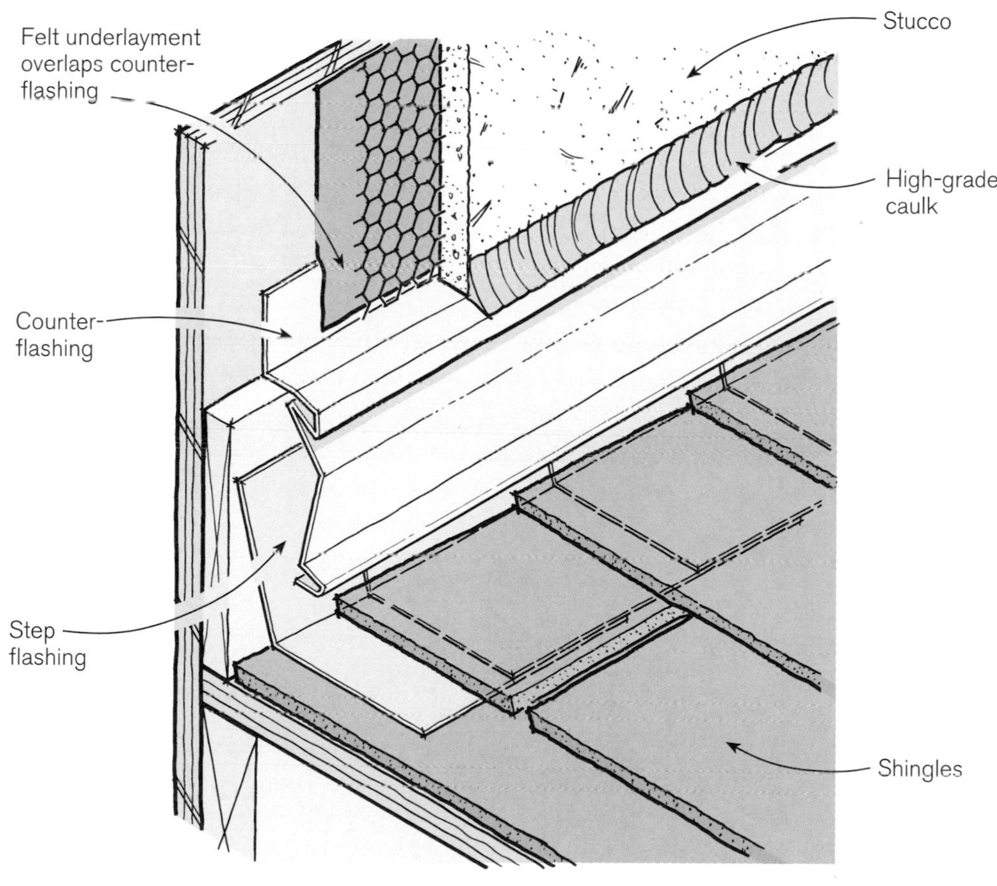

Asphalt Shingle Roofs

Problem: No drip-edge. If asphalt shingles are installed without a drip-edge, it's only a matter of time before the plywood sheathing and fascia begin to rot. Water dripping off the edges of the roofing is drawn by capillary action to the exposed edges of the plywood sheathing.

Solution: Install a metal drip-edge at rakes and eaves. The main purpose of a metal drip-edge is to interrupt the wicking of water to the sheathing edges.

Problem: Felt underlayment incorrectly lapped under (instead of over) the metal drip-edge. Any water that may get under the shingles — for instance, from wind-driven rain — should be carried by the felt underlayment over the top of the drip-edge.

Solution: Lap the felt underlayment over the drip-edge.

Asphalt Shingle Roofs

Problem: Valley shingles were not tabbed or spotted with roofing cement. The large volume of water that collects in a valley can back up under uncemented shingles.

Solution: In a closed valley, embed valley shingles in roofing cement. Always clip the top corner of the valley shingles at a 45° angle. This prevents debris from getting caught in the shingles and accumulating in the valley, and it also directs water toward the valley centerline. For extra protection, install a self-adhering eaves membrane under valleys.

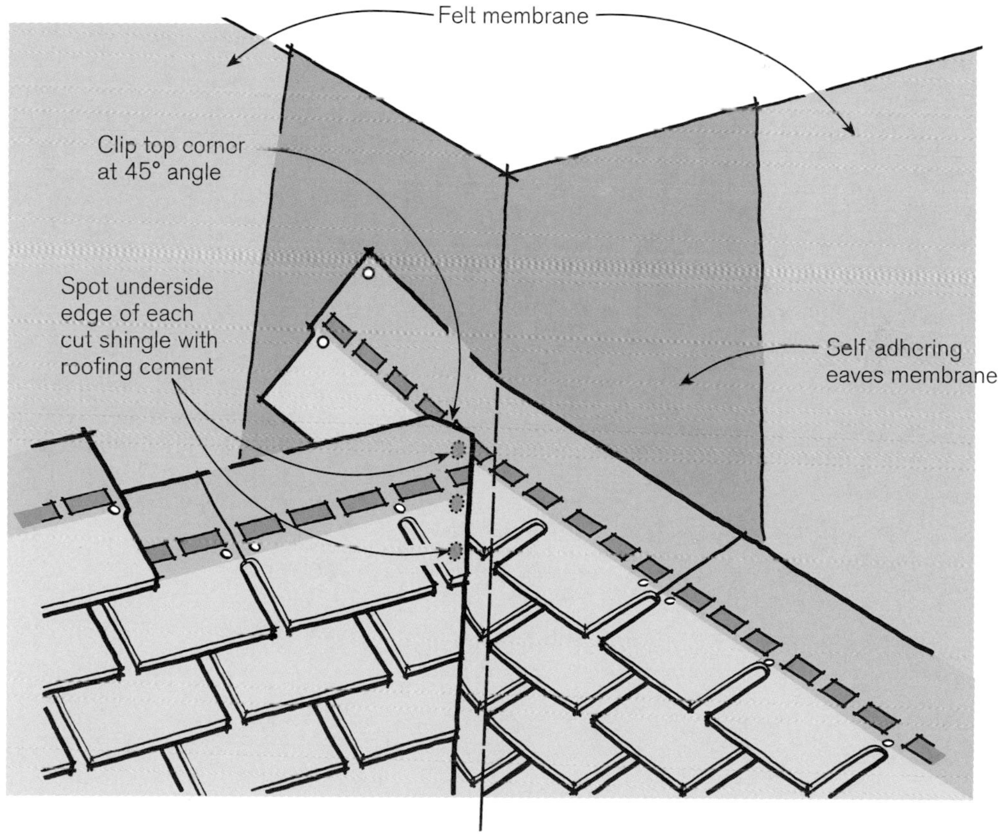

Asphalt Shingle Roofs (continued)

Problem: Exposed roofing nails. Exposed roofing nails are sometimes a source of leaks.

Solution: Cover exposed nail heads with a dab of roofing cement, when exposed nails can't be avoided — as on cap shingles.

Problem: Excessive shingle overhang. This installer apparently believed that increasing the overhang on the first course of shingles would help direct the water into the gutter, and would substitute for metal drip-edge. Eventually, however, the shingles crease under their own weight and break off, exposing the edge of the sheathing beneath.

Solution: Shingles should overhang 1/2 inch to 3/4 inch beyond the metal drip, according to recommendations from the Asphalt Roof Manufacturers Association.

Asphalt Shingle Roofs

Problem: Slipping shingles. Shingles can slip when the manufacturer's fastening instructions are not followed. Improper practices include using too few fasteners, and overdriving and underdriving the fasteners.

Solution: Follow the shingle manufacturer's fastening instructions as printed on the bundle wrappers.

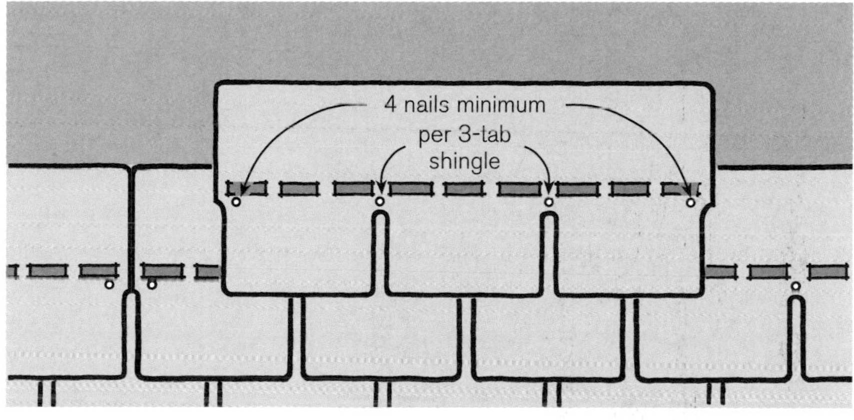

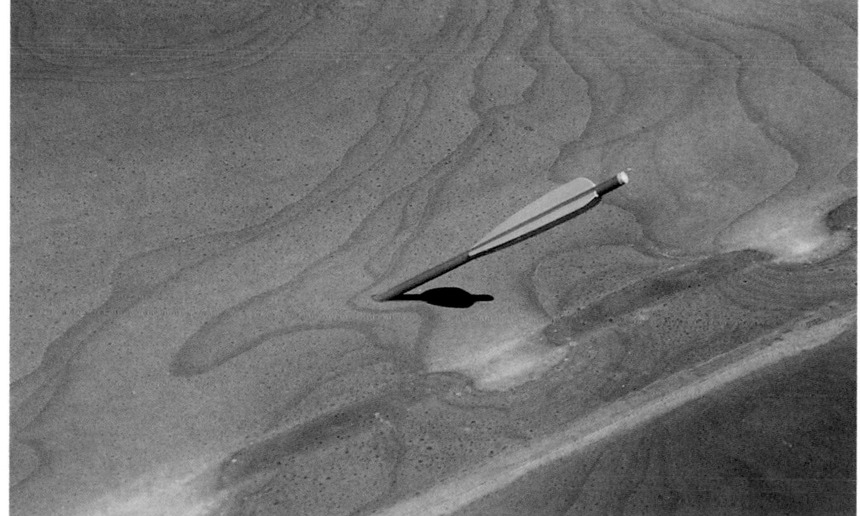

Problem: The owner calls to report a roof leak.

Solution: Not every leaky roof is the fault of the contractor.

Harrison McCampbell, AIA, is an architect and roofing consultant in Nashville, Tenn., specializing in construction defects.

Protecting Shallow Roofs

by Charles Wardell

Minimum slopes for shingle, shake, and tile roofs range 3/12 to 4/12, depending on the specific material and climate. Below those slopes, single-ply roofing material, such as EDPM, is the best choice. But in many cases, putting a single-ply roof on a shallow slope — a porch or a shed dormer, for example — clashes with the shingles used on steep areas of the same room. Builders who want to use shingles, shakes, or tiles on a shallow roof need to take extra precautions against leaks.

Underlayment

The most important factor in devising a watertight roof at shallow slopes is the type of underlayment you use. Underlayment is a backup watershed installed beneath the shingles that prevents water from reaching the sheathing. On a shallow roof, it's wise to lavish some extra care on this part of the job.

Most roofers agree that the best underlayment for low slopes is a self-adhering bituminous membrane, such as Grace's Ice & Water Shield (Grace Construction Products) — a 4-mil polyethylene film backed by a 36-mil layer of rubberized asphalt adhesive. Bituminous membranes are fast becoming standard fare for lining valleys and for ice protection at eaves (**Figure A**), but they're also a good option for protecting the entire surface of a shallow roof.

Compared to glued, double-layer felt systems, permitted by code, membranes are easier to install and are relatively foolproof. They're also self-healing in that they automatically seal nail penetrations. And because membranes are fully adhered, water can't travel beneath them, so any leaks remain localized.

Roofers who start using bituminous membranes are easily hooked. "We cover the entire roof with Ice & Water Shield whenever the slope is 5-in-12 or below," notes Joe Cazeault, a Weymouth, Mass., roofing contractor with more than 30 years in the business. It may not be required by code, he says, but there's just too much chance that water or snow will back up under the shingles. Cazeault recommends laying the membrane from the edge of the roof to the ridge or to a point 12 to 18 inches above a change to a steeper pitch (**Figure B**).

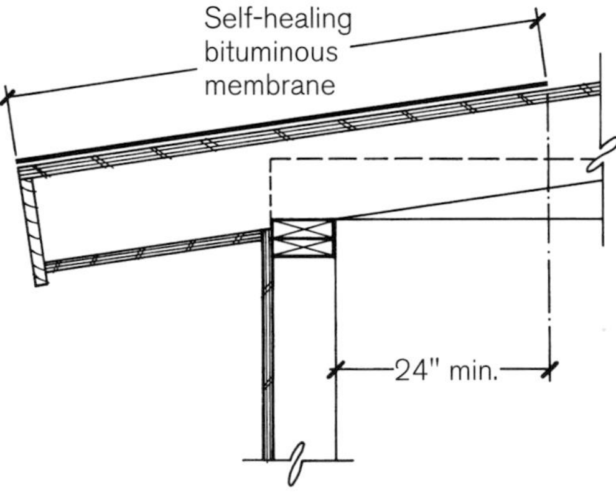

Figure A. *In cold climates, eaves protection is recommended for all slopes, but is especially important on low slopes. To prevent water behind an ice dam from entering the building, place a self-adhering bituminous membrane from the edge of the roof to a point at least 24 inches inside the living space.*

Membrane Tips

Properly installing self-adhering membranes takes practice. First, roll the membrane out and cut it into 10-foot to 15-foot lengths, then reroll it. Sweep the roof clean and apply the membrane by peeling off the paper while unrolling the membrane across the roof. This takes at least two sets of hands: one to work the roll, and a second to smooth the membrane onto the roof. The membrane should be applied with a 6-inch top lap and a $3^1/_2$-inch side lap. Peel-and-stick membranes are more slippery than felt systems, so rubber-soled shoes are a good idea.

Wrinkles. A big problem with membranes installed by inexperienced workers is excessive wrinkling. "It's like putting up wallpaper for the first time," says Larry Shapiro, a product manager at Grace. The membrane sticks to the sheathing on contact, so there's little room for error. A

Full Membrane Underlayment

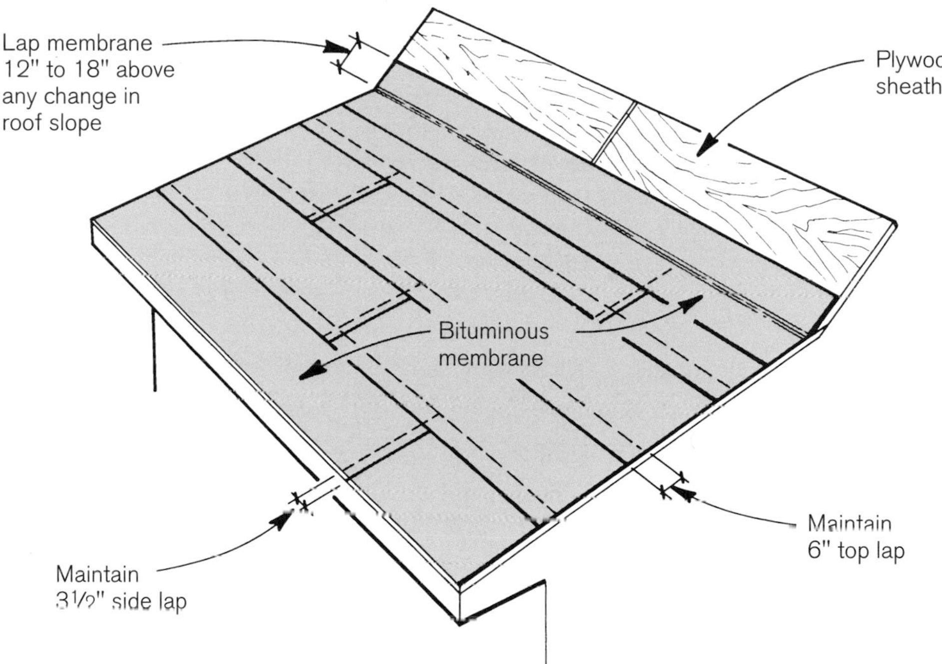

Figure B. *For best protection on shallow slopes, cover the roof from eaves to ridge with a bituminous membrane. Where the shallow slope meets a steeper roof, continue the membrane to a point 12 to 18 inches above the change in slope.*

nail driven through a wrinkle won't seal properly and may leak. Wrinkles can be repaired by cutting them away with a utility knife, then patching them with a small piece of membrane.

Temperature. Manufacturers stress the need to adhere to minimum installation temperatures. Membranes don't stick well below 40°F, making them more vulnerable to leaks. Some products may also have upper temperature limits, above which the adhesive tends to melt. In the worst cases, a gooey mess can seep out from beneath the membrane at the eaves. To prevent seepage during peak summer temperatures, make sure the product you choose is rated for at least 180°F.

UV damage. Membranes are also subject to damage from the sun's ultraviolet rays. While short-term exposure to the sun — up to several months, depending on the product — doesn't harm them, long exposure can cause the polyethylene film to become brittle and crack. Some brands of membrane last longer in the sun than others, but none is designed as a finish roof material.

Nailing. The self-healing properties of bituminous membranes effectively seal smooth-shank roofing nails, but you'll need to be more careful with other types of fasteners.

Ring-shank nails, for example, may tear the membrane instead of slicing cleanly through it. The result may be a slew of isolated leaks.

Ventilation. Membrane manufacturers also caution that their products should be installed over a well-ventilated roof deck. On inadequately ventilated roofs, a membrane acts as a cold-side vapor barrier, making it more apt to trap heat and moisture. In the worst cases, this can result in damage to the roof sheathing and framing.

Charles Wardell is a freelance construction writer and former associate editor at The Journal of Light Construction.

Leakproof Valley Flashing

by Tom Brewer

During the decades I've been roofing, I've learned to pay attention to valleys. Valleys are the high-mileage areas of the roof: They have to be able to withstand a steady stream of runoff during heavy rains and, during the winter, are parking lots for melting snow and ice.

Look on the back of any bundle of shingles and you'll find instructions on how to flash a valley. Generally, the multilayer flashing system I use exceeds these manufacturer specifications. The methods I describe here pass my most important test: the "no leaks, no callback" test.

Membrane Protection

I use a built-up multilayer flashing system for valleys — a "belt and suspenders" approach. Typically, by the time I detail the valleys, I've already "dried in" the entire roof by installing #15 roofing felt.

In the old days, before self-sticking membrane materials were readily available, I used to run an additional two layers of #30 roofing felt in the valleys. Nowadays, I lay in a 3-foot-wide sheet of Ice & Water Shield (Grace Construction Products). It's sticky stuff to work with, but well worth the aggravation.

Since the membrane seals itself around any nail shanks, I feel it goes a long way toward preventing leaks from any nails that end up too close to the center of the valley. I'm always careful not to drive any nails within 12 inches of the valley centerline, but sometimes roof-mounted antennas are installed by less conscientious people.

Before I install the membrane, I look for loose nails lying in the valley. Dropped nails tend to collect in valleys and will puncture the membrane (and the flashing that follows) as it's installed.

Aluminum Backup

For added protection, I next install a 2-foot-wide layer of aluminum coil stock directly over the membrane. The coil stock I use (.019 inch) can be purchased at most lumberyards and is available in a number of colors.

While the membrane material is very flexible and molds itself to any irregularities in the valley, the coil stock is not as pliable. I use a bending brake to crease the center of the aluminum so that it will fit snugly in the center of the valley.

Allowing for movement. Many builders nail the aluminum valley flashing along the edges to hold it in place. But metal flashing that is loaded with nails will buckle as it expands, making for an unsightly valley. In my area of northeastern Pennsylvania, for instance, a 10-foot length of aluminum coil stock will change up to 1/2 inch in length between the cold of winter and the heat of summer.

To allow for this movement, I fold a hem along the edge of the valley flashing and use site-bent clips to hold the flashing in place (**Figure 1**).

To prevent the flashing from creeping downhill, I drive one nail at the top edge of the flashing. Before I position the flashing, I again clear out any loose nails that have found their way into the valley.

Figure 1. To allow aluminum flashing to expand and contract, the author uses a site-bent hem-and-clip system to secure valley flashing. He places the hem clips every 2 to 3 feet along the edge of the flashing.

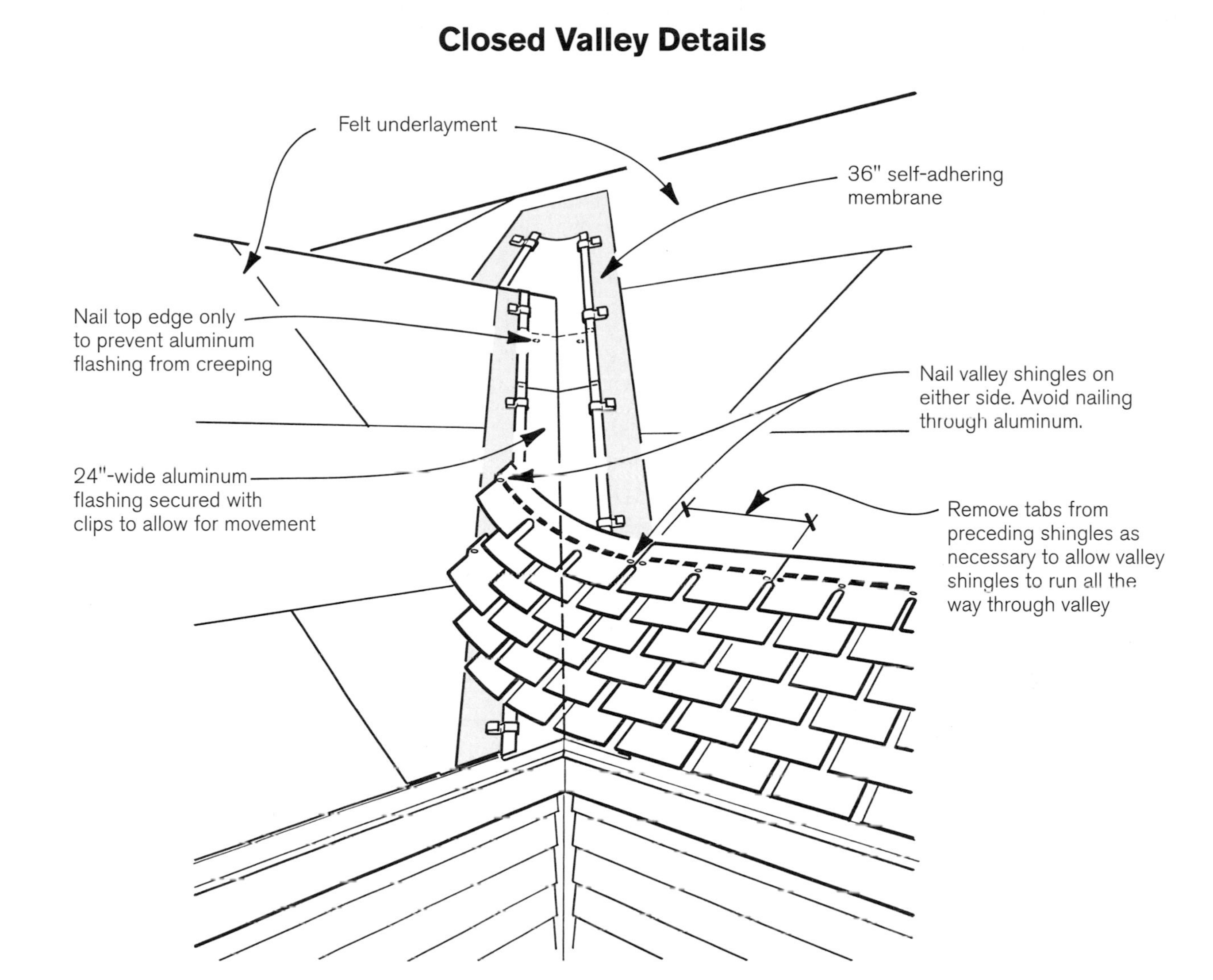

Figure 2. When shingling a closed valley, the author tries to avoid nailing through the aluminum flashing, so that it's free to expand and contract with temperature changes. The shingles that run through the valley are laid out so that nails can be placed on either side of the aluminum.

Laying a Closed Valley

There are three generally accepted methods for shingling a valley: the closed valley, the open valley, and the woven valley. I use the same underlying flashing details for all three methods, and any of the methods will perform satisfactorily when installed properly.

Closed valley. I prefer the closed valley. It's the quickest and easiest to install, it protects the valley with a double layer of shingles, and, to my eye, it's the best looking.

After I've installed the valley flashing, I begin shingling the main roof. When I reach the valley, I run the first layer of valley shingles *all the way through* the valley and onto the secondary roof plane (**Figure 2**). The trick here is to avoid driving any nails through the aluminum. Nails driven at the edge of the flashing may not cause a leak, but they will not allow the expansion clips to do their job and may cause the flashing to buckle.

At some point, however, the shingle coursing will naturally end in the middle of the valley. In this case, I remove a full tab or two from the preceding shingle so that the "run-through" valley shingle falls where it can be nailed on either side of the flashing.

Once the run-through shingles are in place, I shingle the secondary roof plane, trimming these shingles at the centerline of the valley. The line formed by the cut shingles is a strong visual cue, so I make sure my cuts are straight and the finished valley line is crisp (**Figure 3**, next page). Homeowners and superintendents will quickly complain about a wavy valley.

Open valleys. In an open valley, the shingles stop short of the valley centerline, leaving the flashing exposed. I'm not sure why open valleys are used so

Figure 3. The finished valley has a crisp appearance — and three layers of protection.

often. Twice as many shingles must be cut at the valley, and the exposed flashing is not protected by a layer of shingles.

When a customer insists on an open valley, I install the membrane and flashing as though it were a closed valley. I lay out my shingle cuts so the open portion of the valley is slightly wider at the bottom than the top. The widening trough allows ice and snow to creep out of the valley.

Woven valleys. A woven valley is essentially a closed valley formed by alternating the shingles that run through the valley. The good news is that none of the through shingles need to be cut to length. But for some reason, I'm always frustrated by shingles that creep up on the coursing lines as I weave the valley. The finished valley also has a "mushy" appearance. For these reasons, I try to avoid woven valleys.

Whichever style of valley you choose, take the time to install it correctly. A leaky roof leads to a leaking wallet.

Tom Brewer is a roofer in Hallstead, Pa.

Skylight Installation and Flashing

by Dennis Bates

I design and build custom sunroom additions in Vermont. Many of these rooms include skylights as a practical way of adding glazing overhead. I install around 20 skylights each year, so I need to be certain that I don't get called back to fix leaks. So far, I've never had a leak, which I attribute primarily to closely following the manufacturer's installation instructions.

I prefer Velux skylights (Velux America Inc.), simply because they've never given me any trouble, I'm comfortable with their flashing system, and I have the installation instructions memorized. The VS model is my favorite; it provides good ventilation and comes in a wide variety of sizes. Although I've used other manufacturers with success in the past, the distribution wasn't as extensive in my area, making their products harder to get and increasing lead times.

Square Framing First

During framing, I make an extra effort to get the openings perfectly sized and square. It makes setting the skylight — not to mention the trim — go more smoothly.

I leave the units boxed for transport and on the job site to lessen the chance of damage and to keep all the parts together. A few days before the scheduled installation, we remove the manufacturer labels and prefinish the frames and sash. Prefinishing is neater and faster than working from a ladder after the units are installed. I'm seldom asked to paint the skylights, because the engineered beams that form the structural frame of our sunrooms are naturally attractive, and my customers usually want to continue the look of natural wood to the trim and millwork. We typically use a couple of coats of water-based polyurethane. It provides good protection from humidity and condensation and cleans up easily.

Setting the Unit

In preparation for the skylight installation, the roof is sheathed and covered with #30 felt. I hold the felt back from the openings about 6 to 8 inches, so the waterproof underlayment can adhere directly to the roof sheathing. Up to this point, I've temporarily covered the openings with plywood to keep rain out of the room. Before bringing the skylights out onto the roof, I shingle up close to the openings. On hot days, I'll stop shingling a little lower on the roof so the shingles don't get scuffed while the skylights are being installed.

Figure 4. Removing the sash makes handling safer and easier. Narrow strips of ceiling between skylights make layout mistakes really obvious, so special attention is given to accurate spacing during framing.

Figure 5. An improvised tool helps center the unit in the opening. The speed square rides along the rafter, and the combination square indicates the space between the unit and the rough opening. Note the layer of polystyrene insulation installed beneath the roof sheathing.

I start the skylight installation by first bending out the L-shaped mounting brackets and removing the cladding and sash, making the unit lighter and easier to handle. I pass the frame through the roof to a helper and stand inside to center it in the opening (**Figure 4**). Centering ganged skylights is especially important, because trim and narrow sections of drywall will show up the discrepancy inside if the roof windows aren't spaced equally.

I've improvised a simple tool to help with centering: A speed square clamped to a combination square with a set of locking pliers makes it easy to check the reveals quickly and get them just right (**Figure 5**). I rest the units on a temporary cleat nailed to the roof, which makes positioning easier and safer (**Figure 6**). It also keeps multiple units in a straight line and prevents expensive skylights from sliding to an untimely demise.

Fastening

When I'm certain the skylight is centered, we nail through the mounting brackets in two opposite corners, using the heavy-duty ring-shank nails included with the skylight (**Figure 7**, next page). We try to get them into the roof framing, but the annular rings resist pull-out even if they're driven only into the roof sheathing. Next I reinstall the sash to check operation and ensure that the unit's frame is square

Figure 6. Tacking a 2x4 cleat to the sheathing keeps units in a straight line and prevents them from sliding off the roof. Once the units are secured, the cleat will be removed so shingling can continue.

Figure 7. After the carpenters nail down two of the four mounting brackets, they reinstall the sash to make sure that the unit is square (far left). Necessary adjustments are made; then the other brackets are nailed off (left).

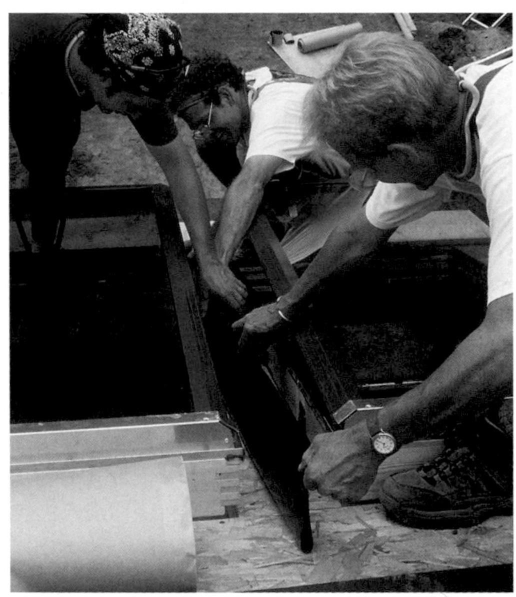

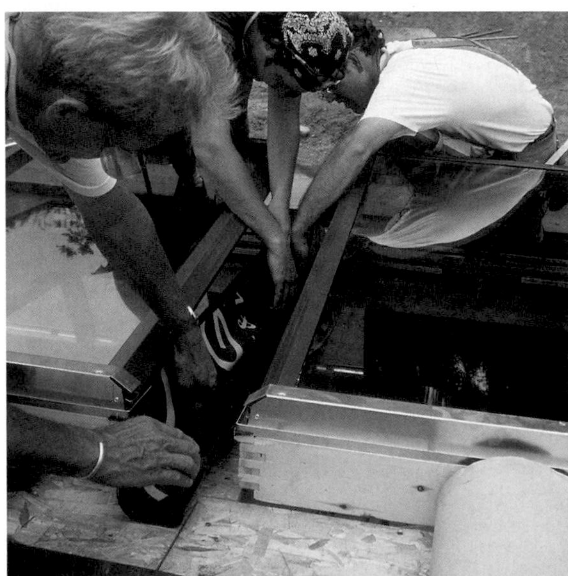

Figure 8. To reduce the chance of leaks, the author uses a single piece of membrane in the space between skylights. Folding the membrane in half helps to keep it from sticking to itself (top left). Aligning the membrane's edge on the first unit and smoothing toward the roof deck and back up the second unit minimizes wrinkles (bottom). Cutting the corner allows the vertical leg to wrap around the top corner (top right).

Figure 9. The top piece of membrane laps over the sides (far left), and a slit cut outward forms a flap that folds around the corner (left). The membrane's leading edge is adhered to the roof deck under the felt.

and will remain so. Once the unit is in its final position and the sash operates without binding, we fasten through the other brackets, locking the skylight in place.

When we have all the skylights secured in their final position, I remove the cleat that helped with placement and we cut 10-inch-wide strips of self-adhering membrane for a secondary water barrier. This is the last defense against water infiltration, and the manufacturer requires it. The skylight manufacturer makes its own membrane, but we generally use Grace Ice & Water Shield (Grace Construction Products) because it's readily available, less expensive, and it sticks better than other products I've tried.

We start at the bottom, attaching the membrane to the skylight and smoothing it onto the roof. The sides are next, with the areas between adjacent skylights the biggest challenge. To install the membrane between adjacent skylights, we get all hands on deck and take positions at top, bottom, and middle, trying to keep the membrane from sticking to itself and making a mess. The piece is cut so that it extends about 6 inches beyond the skylight, top and bottom. We adhere the membrane to one skylight and smooth it down toward the roof and back up onto the other skylight (**Figure 8**).

Finally, we install the top piece of membrane. It laps over the side pieces and is stuck directly to the roof sheathing under the felt (**Figure 9**). We use a hammer stapler to better secure the membrane to the skylight, stapling as close to the membrane's top edge as possible. This isn't as critical in warm temperatures, but I had one occasion where the membrane separated from the skylight and had to be redone. Since then, I always staple the membrane as extra insurance.

After the membrane is installed, we continue shin-

Figure 10. When the shingling reaches the skylight, the sill flashing is slid up from the bottom and fastened at the top corner with the manufacturer's special nails (far left). The first piece of step flashing overlaps the sill flashing 3 1/2 inches. Where adjacent sill flashings overlap, urethane sealant provides extra insurance against leaks (left).

Ice Dams and Skylights

by Henri de Marne

Skylights are vulnerable to ice dams — even in a well-ventilated roof. Cold roofs are designed to prevent ice dams. Cold air enters through continuous soffit vents and exits through a ridge vent, carrying away any heat escaping through the insulation. Ice dams are prevented because the snow pack never melts until temperatures rise safely above freezing.

Heat loss around a skylight, however, is usually greater than on other parts of a roof. With very cold temperatures, water from melting snow around the skylight can get trapped between a layer of snow and a very cold vented roof, and rapidly freeze. The resulting ice can work its way up the roof from the eaves, with new snow melt freezing close to the skylight. Water pooled immediately below the skylight can back up under the skylight flashing and enter the house (**Figure A**).

To guard against this problem in areas of high snowfall, I recommend shielding the entire area around the skylight with self-sticking bituminous membrane. I advise the following procedure, even on cold roofs.

After the skylight is installed, but before the counterflashing is in place, cover the area around and below the skylight with a self-adhering bituminous membrane, such as Ice & Water Shield (Grace Construction Products). Begin at the eaves, and lay the membrane so that it extends 3 feet to each side of the skylight, with a 6-inch overlap at the seams (**Figure B**). Extend the membrane 3 feet above the skylight as well. To prevent water from leaking into the skylight, roll strips of membrane up the sides of the curb, lapping the main membrane by 6 inches. Finally, apply the skylight counterflashing and roofing in the normal manner.

While you may not need this kind of protection every year, the extra cost of the protective membrane layer is a small price to pay for peace of mind. And it's a lot easier than standing at the top of a ladder in the middle of winter, chipping away at an ice dam.

Henri de Marne works as a home inspector, consults on energy issues, and writes a nationally syndicated home repair column.

Ice Dam at Skylight

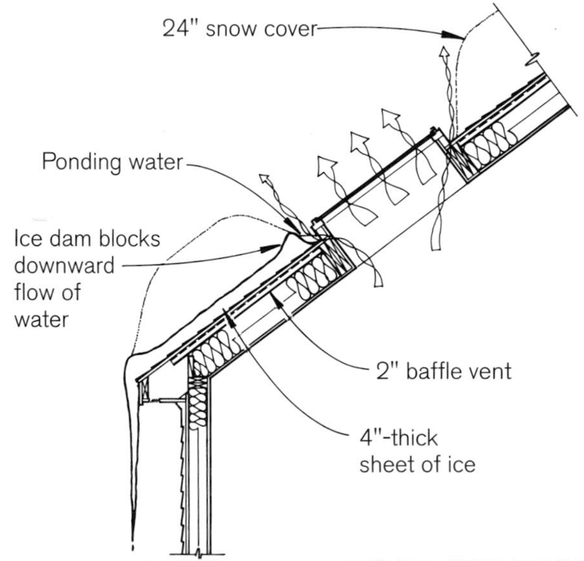

Figure A. *In extremely cold temperatures, water from melting snow at the skylight is trapped between the cold, vented roof and the snow, freezing almost immediately. A thick sheet of ice can form between the skylight and the eaves, causing water to back up into the building.*

Protecting Skylight With Membrane

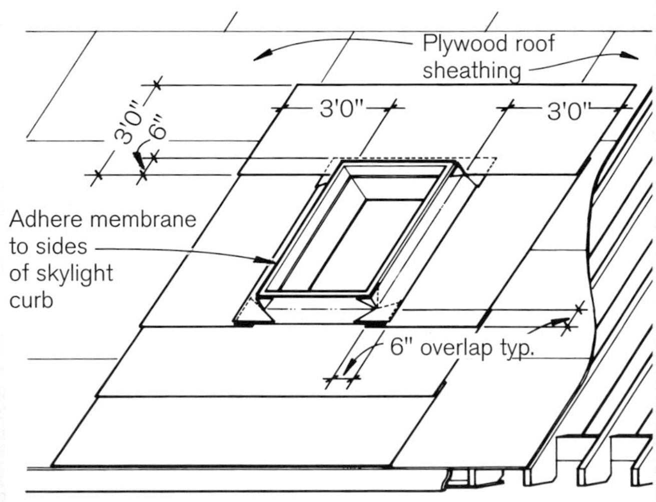

Figure B. *When ice dams can't be prevented, protect against leaks with a continuous bituminous membrane applied before the skylight counterflashing. Extend the membrane 3 feet on all sides of the skylight, and run it all the way down to the eaves.*

gling up the roof to the bottom edge of the skylight. We know we have shingled far enough when the sill flashing, the bottom piece of flashing, covers up some of the shingles' 5-inch exposure (**Figure 10**, page 307). Special nails are provided for attaching the flashing: They're 3/4 inch long so they won't poke through the frame, and they're noncorrosive to the aluminum.

We shingle up the sides, weaving the step flashing into the courses. The manufacturer specifies at least a 3 1/2-inch overlap on every piece, and the pieces are nailed near the top on the downhill edge. The last piece of step flashing is slit so it can bend around the top corner (**Figure 11**).

The small section of roofing between ganged units gets a U-shaped piece of flashing rather than step flashing. We bend our own in the shop out of high-quality

Figure 11. Cutting the last piece of step flashing at the fold allows it to be bent around the skylight's top and nailed like the others to the side of the frame.

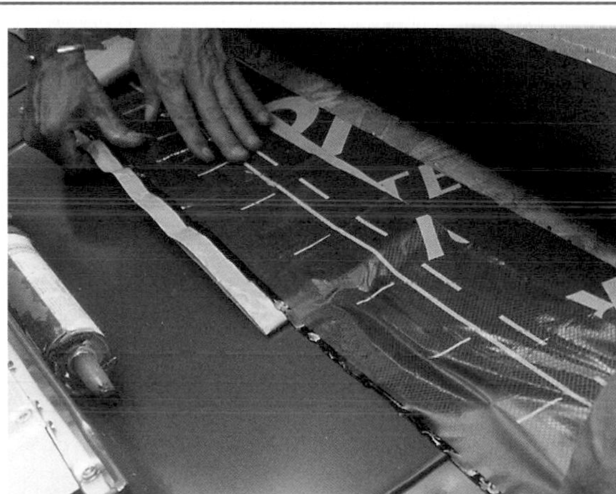

Figure 12. The leading edge of the head flashing (top left) gets covered with a second strip of eaves membrane (top right). Note that the felt is lifted so the membrane can be adhered to the roof deck. Notching the shingles around the skylights maintains a 4-inch exposure (bottom).

Figure 13. Reinstalling the skylight's cladding completes the process. The bottom goes on first (top left). Slots in the bottom receive the side pieces (top right). Plastic inserts in the sides receive the screws inserted through the head flashing (bottom left). Finally, the top cladding piece is slipped over the head flashing and secured with two screws (bottom right).

bronze aluminum trim coil; if you don't have a brake, the manufacturer offers a pre-bent U-shaped flashing as well. We make our own flashing because I like to have flexibility in spacing the units. The U-shaped metal is held in place by the cladding when it's reinstalled.

Next, we install the head flashing over the step flashing and shingles, but we don't install the screws (**Figure 12**, previous page). We put a strip of eaves membrane over the head flashing and under the felt. Shingling is easier now because we no longer have to cut and fit around the skylights, but it's important to leave a 2 3/8- to 4-inch space between the top of the skylight and the shingles. That space prevents roofing nails from punching holes in the head flashing and allows water and debris to get around the skylight unimpeded. Next we reinstall the cladding that was taken off when the sash was removed (**Figure 13**). Those pieces, held in place by screws, give the skylight its finished look and act as counterflashing for the U-flashing and step flashing. We start at the bottom, continue up the sides, and finish with the top piece.

Dennis Bates is owner of Vermont Sun Structures in Williston, Vt.

Chapter 16: Masonry Chimneys

C. BATES

- Leakproof Chimney Flashing
- Troubleshooting Common Chimney Problems

Leakproof Chimney Flashing

by Tom Brewer

A properly flashed chimney is protected by the overlap between the base flashing and the counterflashing. This two-part system absorbs any building movement that may occur (when new house framing shrinks, for example). Base flashing is installed as the shingles are applied, and generally consists of the lower base pan, step flashing, and the upper pan or cricket. Most builders are comfortable installing the base flashing, because the roof sheathing provides a solid nailing base. But what about the counterflashing?

In the Groove

Many contractors make the mistake of using masonry screws to fasten the counterflashing to the side of the chimney, then applying a bead of caulk at the top of the flashing (**Figure 1**). As daily temperature changes cause the flashing to expand and contract, the adhesive bond of the caulk joint is constantly stressed. This type of flashing detail will fail — sometimes in less than a year. Roofing cement doesn't last any longer.

Properly installed counterflashing is "let in" to a groove in the chimney and overlaps the upturned sides of the base flashing, as shown in Figure 1. No fasteners are required. I've used these methods for both aluminum and copper flashing.

New construction. In the case of new construction, this groove should be about 1¼ inches deep and can easily be made by raking out a portion of the mortar joint before the mortar has set. To determine which joints get raked out and where, I choose a mortar joint that's at least 8 to 10 inches above the point where the chimney first penetrates the roof (**Figure 2**). On block chimneys, this is usually the joint just above the first full course on the down-slope face of the chimney. (For brick chimneys, this joint is above the third or fourth course.) I rake this joint out horizontally until the groove is within 3 inches (measured vertically) of the roof surface. Then I move up to the next mortar joint (one 8-inch course for block, three

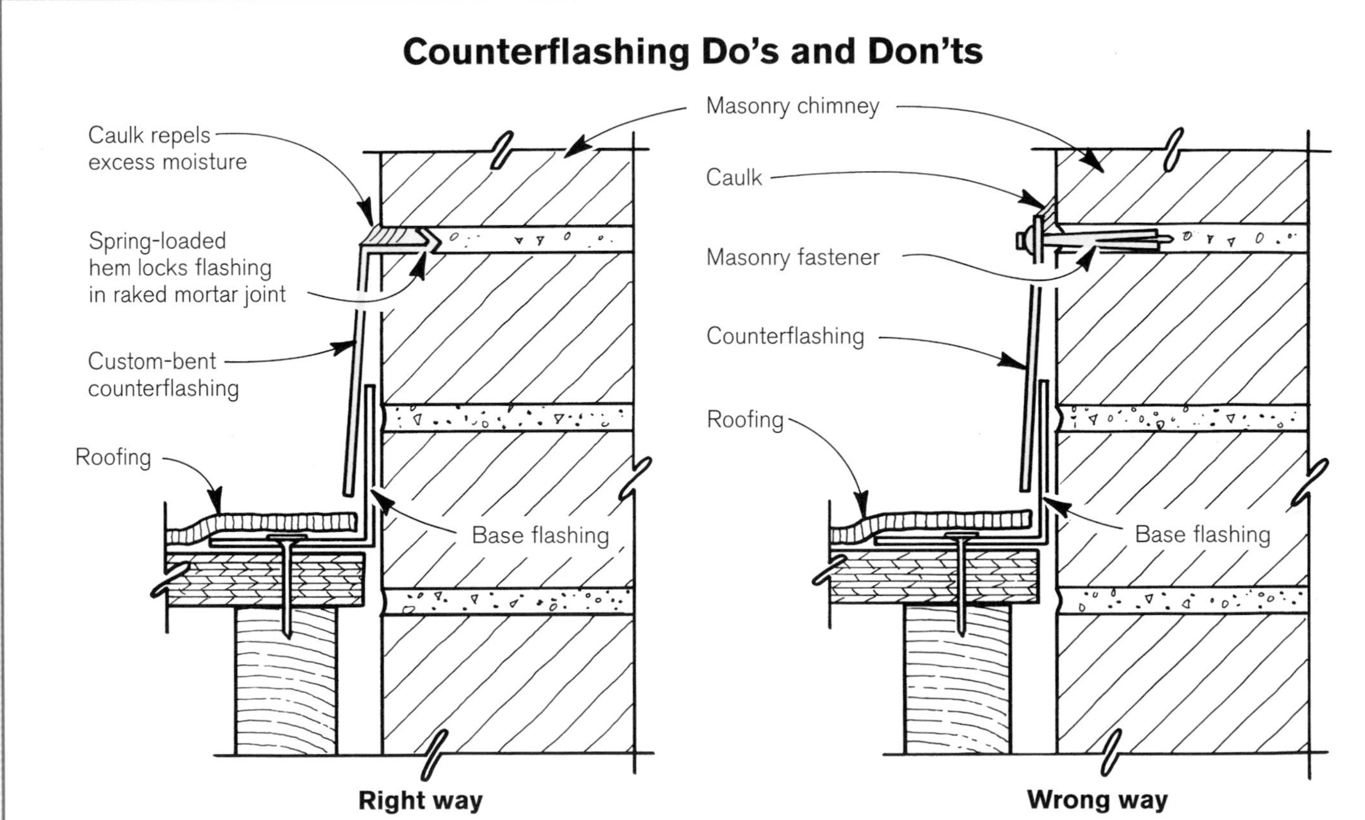

Figure 1. The proper way to counterflash a chimney is to insert the counterflashing into a raked joint (left). A small bend in the horizontal leg of the flashing ensures that no water can run behind the flashing. Caulk provides a secondary line of defense against moisture intrusion. Flashing fastened directly to the face of the chimney relies entirely on caulk to maintain a watertight joint (right); in time, the caulk will fail, allowing water to penetrate the house.

Raking Joints for Counterflashing

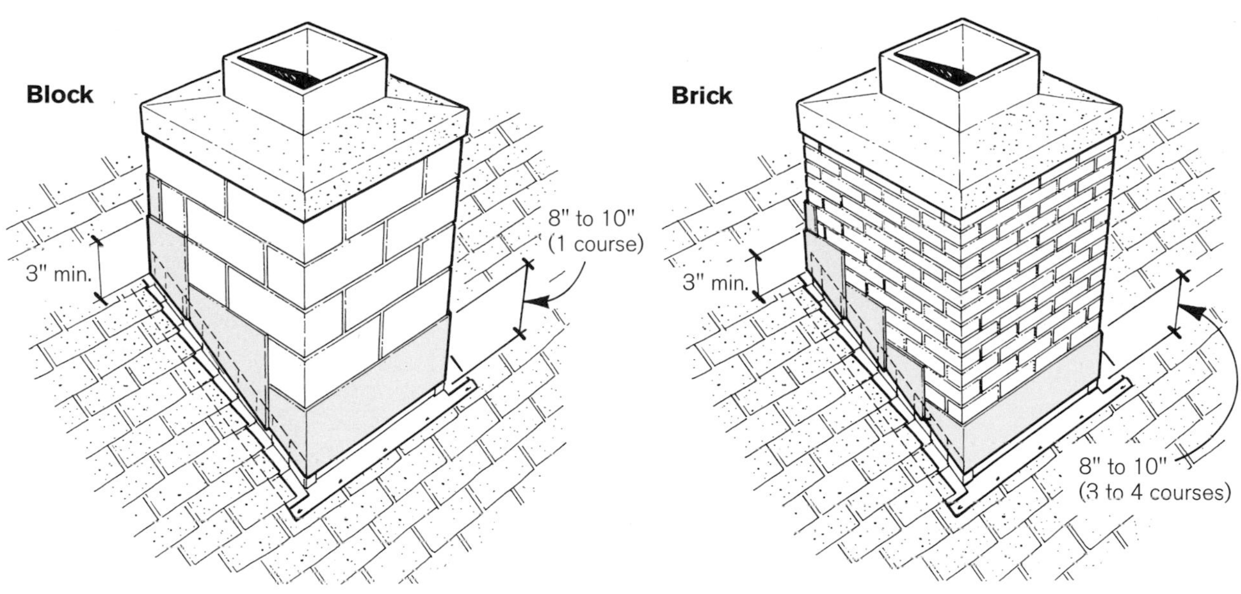

Figure 2. Rake the mortar joints to leave a 1 1/4-inch-deep groove for the counterflashing. On the down-slope side of the chimney, choose a joint that is 8 to 10 inches above the roof deck (one course for block chimneys; three to four courses for brick). Rake the joint along the down-slope face of the chimney and along each side, until the joint is about 3 inches above the roof deck. Then measure up 8 inches vertically to start the next course of counterflashing.

courses for brick), and rake it out until it comes within 3 inches of the roof surface. I repeat this process until I reach the back corner of the chimney and the joint is at least 3 inches above the roof. The first time you try this, don't worry about raking out more joint area than you think you'll need. The "excess" will get covered by the counterflashing or can be pointed after the flashing is installed.

Existing chimney. If you're working on an existing chimney, you've got no choice but to get out your goggles and dust mask and saw the joint (**Figure 3**). You can use a circular saw equipped with a masonry blade, a heavy-duty concrete saw, or a hand-held grinder equipped with a diamond blade. The groove

Figure 3. To prepare an existing chimney for counterflashing, a mason cuts a 1 1/4-inch groove in the mortar joints using a gas-powered concrete saw.

Figure 4. The author cuts the upper and lower pieces of counterflashing from painted-aluminum coil stock (.019 inches thick). The tapered cuts match the roof pitch; layout lines mark the folds at the chimney corners.

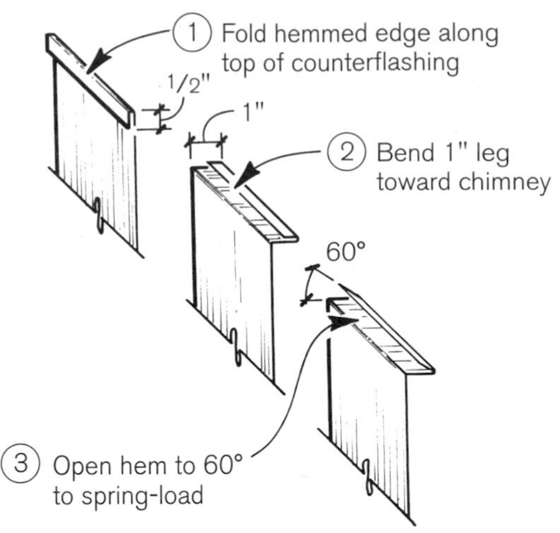

Figure 5. First, make two simple bends along the top edge of the counterflashing, then pry open the hem to "spring-load" it: The V-shape will form a strong mechanical "lock" in the raked joint.

Figure 6. The author cuts pie-shaped pieces in the folded hem so that the counterflashing can be bent around the chimney corner.

should be 1¼ inches deep and the width of a saw kerf. Make sure you do your cutting before the new shingles are installed. Otherwise, you'll be cleaning masonry dust off the newly installed roof — a tough chore when working with dark-colored shingles.

Custom Counterflashing

For counterflashing, I like to use painted aluminum coil stock (.019 inches thick). If you have access to a break, forming the metal will be easier, but I've shaped flashing for more than one chimney using a 2x6 and a brick hammer. To prepare the flashing, follow these steps:

- ***Lay out the dimensions on the flashing stock and cut to size*** before making any bends (**Figure 4**, previous page). Be sure to mark the fold lines where the counterflashing will turn the corner of the chimney.
- ***Fold a ½-inch hem, then a 1-inch leg,*** along the top edge of the counterflashing (**Figure 5**). Cut away a pie-shaped piece where the flashing must wrap around a corner of the chimney (**Figure 6**).
- ***Pry open the hem to "spring-load" it.*** This creates both a water stop and a mechanical "lock" that holds the flashing in place. Test-fit the flashing before opening the hem; removing the flashing once it's locked in place can be difficult.

Before inserting the counterflashing, make sure the groove is free of debris, and is cut or raked out at least ¼ inch deeper then the length of the angled leg. Then insert the V-shaped edge formed by the leg and the open hem into the groove (**Figure 7**) and seal the joint with caulk. I use Sikaflex-1a (Sika Corp.), a high-quality one-component polyurethane sealant. It's gummy stuff, but forms a tenacious bond with masonry. Since the joint is watertight, the caulk serves to keep out excess moisture and wind-driven rain.

Figure 7. In this mock-up, the V-shaped leg of both the upper and lower pieces of counterflashing is locked into the joint between chimney blocks. A bead of caulk in the joint will keep out excess water and wind-driven rain.

Tom Brewer is a roofer in Hallstead, Pa.

Troubleshooting Common Chimney Problems

by Stephen Bushway

During the more than 20 years I've been repairing chimneys, I've found that most chimney problems can be traced to a handful of causes. Here, I identify the problems I most often encounter and explain the techniques I use to repair them.

Up-Close Inspection

Typically, the exterior of a chimney will deteriorate first. A few minutes spent inspecting a chimney will often reveal telltale signs of problems.

I start at the top, and check to see that the crown is sound and free of cracks. Next, I examine the joints, looking for any missing mortar, hairline cracks, or soft, eroded mortar. I also check the integrity of the mortar bonding by tapping the bricks or blocks with a hammer. A well-bonded wall will transmit the vibration to your hand; compromised bonding will not.

It's also important to examine interior chimneys below the roofline. The portion of the chimney that passes through an unheated attic is subject to mortar erosion from flue gas condensation. I look for soft or sandy mortar and black stains (evidence of leaking soot). If I see any of these conditions, I recommend bringing in a seasoned professional to advise on chimney relining.

Figure 8. This chimney crown dried too quickly, causing the edges to curl and pull away from the masonry, allowing water to penetrate. This crown also bonded to the flue liners. When the liners expanded, they lifted the top of the chimney, causing the top three courses of brick to crack.

Leaky Crowns

Failed chimney crowns are by far the most common problem I encounter. The crown serves as the roof of the chimney, and a leaky crown can damage a chimney — and the surrounding structure — in many ways. In freeze/thaw climates, the problems are compounded when infiltrating water freezes and expands. Here are some of the most common problems I encounter with crowns.

Inadequate curing. When a freshly cast crown dries too quickly, the exposed top surface sets more rapidly than the interior portion. As the surface dries,

Figure 9. Excessive shrinking caused this crown to crack at the weakest point — the area where a flue penetrated the surface. Proper curing of the crown reduces the amount of shrinkage, and reinforcing fibers added to the concrete mix add tensile strength.

it also shrinks, pulling at the outer edges and causing the crown to curl (**Figure 8**, previous page). The resulting gaps will allow water to penetrate into the interior of the chimney.

Bonded flues. The photo in Figure 8 illustrates another common problem. As flue liners heat up, they expand. If the crown bonds to the flue liners, the liners can actually lift the top of the chimney as they expand, stressing the mortar joints and creating cracks that allow water to infiltrate the chimney.

Lack of reinforcement. Even properly cured crowns will shrink as they harden. Flues reduce the cross-sectional area where they penetrate the crown, creating weak links. As the crown shrinks, improperly built crowns will pull apart and crack at the weakest point (**Figure 9**, previous page).

Feathered crown. The mortared "wash" on the top of the chimney in **Figure 10** is guaranteed to fail. My guess is that the mason ran out of flue liners before bricks. The feathered edge of the mortared wash broke down quickly, and the recessed flue liners allowed rain to penetrate the interior of the chimney.

Efflorescence. The whitish haze that appears on the outside surface of the chimney in Figure 10 is called *efflorescence*. The staining occurs when water within the chimney works its way to the exterior surface and evaporates, leaving behind soluble salts.

While efflorescence itself is a cosmetic problem, the water penetration that causes efflorescence can lead to serious structural problems in colder climates.

Figure 10. Flue liners should project at least 3 inches above the crown. Here, a thin crown and recessed flue liners caused this chimney crown to leak. As the water worked its way out of the chimney and evaporated, soluble salts remained behind, leaving a whitish stain called efflorescence.

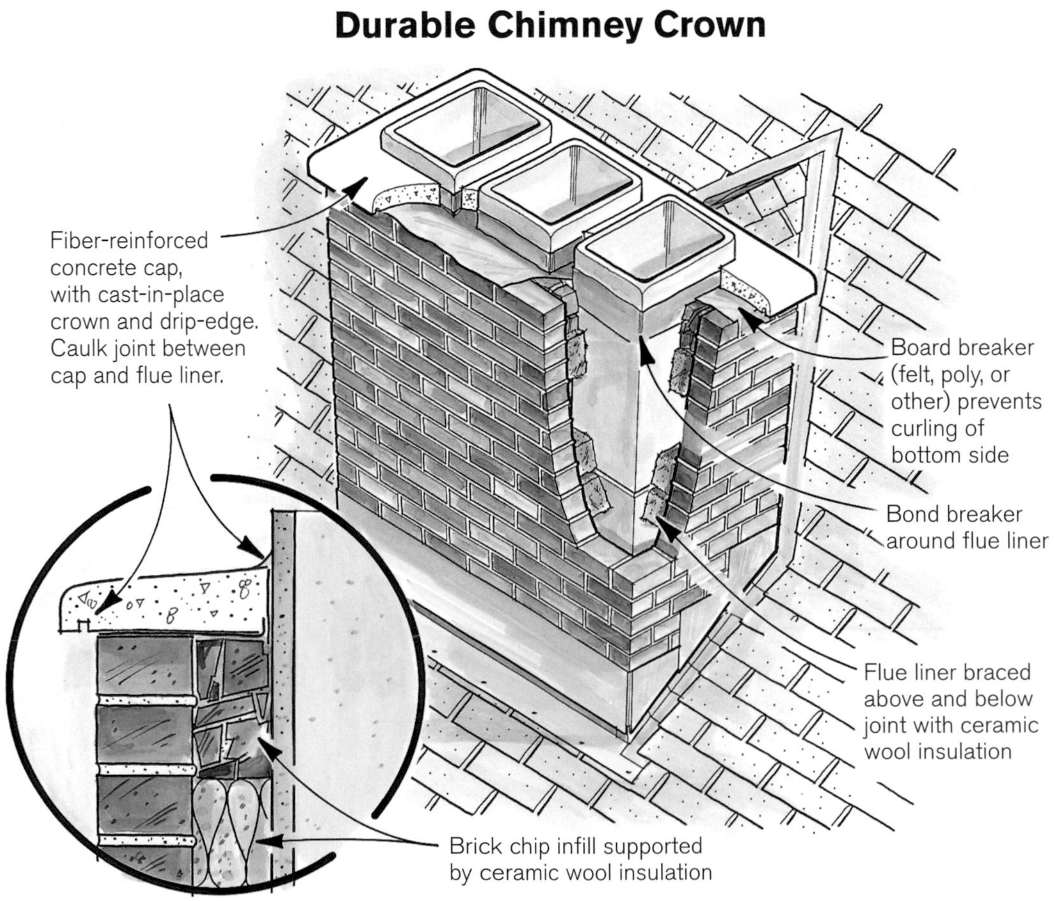

Durable Chimney Crown

Fiber-reinforced concrete cap, with cast-in-place crown and drip-edge. Caulk joint between cap and flue liner.

Board breaker (felt, poly, or other) prevents curling of bottom side

Bond breaker around flue liner

Flue liner braced above and below joint with ceramic wool insulation

Brick chip infill supported by ceramic wool insulation

Figure 11. A bond breaker isolates the chimney crown from the masonry below and from the flue tiles. The drip-edge on the underside of the overhang prevents water from running down the face of the chimney.

When the penetrating water freezes, it expands, and will eventually break the chimney apart.

Proper Crown Construction

I use the following techniques to prevent or repair the crown failures I've just described.

Mud recipe. To achieve a dense, watertight surface, I cast crowns that are at least 3 inches thick. Crowns are essentially small concrete slabs, and the size of the aggregate used in the mix controls the minimum thickness. I prefer a mix of 1 part portland cement, 2 parts sand, and 1 1/2 parts pea gravel. To increase the tensile strength of the crown at flue penetrations, I add about 1/4 cup of "angel hair" (chopped fiberglass) reinforcing fibers to the mix. The fibers, which are available from local concrete suppliers, tie the crown together so it shrinks as a unit.

The mix must be workable, but to minimize shrinkage, I keep it as stiff as possible.

I detail my crowns with a generous overhang that includes a formed drip groove on the underside of the overhang (**Figure 11**). I use adjustable steel crown forms from Ahrens (Ahrens Chimney Technique). They cost about $150, and eliminate the need to custom-form each chimney crown.

A sure cure. I place a bond breaker between the bottom of the crown and the top course of masonry.

Figure 12. The code-required air space between the flue liners and the chimney walls allows the liners to expand and contract freely. In this chimney, the void between the bricks and the flue liners was filled solid with mortar, resulting in a 7-foot-long crack when the liners expanded.

This prevents the masonry units from wicking moisture from the crown mix, and functions as a slip joint, allowing the crown to shrink as it dries. I use either a lightweight sheet of poly or aluminum flashing material.

After I've mixed and placed the crown, I mist the surface for a few hours to prevent it from drying pre-

Getting There Is Half the Work

When it comes to chimney repair, it can take longer to set up shop than to make the actual repair. Since scaffolding is such a large part of the equation, I've developed efficient staging strategies that make setup costs more predictable. If the roof configuration isn't straightforward, I take photos or make a sketch, then analyze the layout for a few days before submitting a bid.

Two products that I have come to rely on are Ultimate Ridgehooks, which I developed for my own work and now manufacture (Deer Hill Enterprises), and Vanguard chimney brackets (Lynn Ladder & Scaffolding). The ridge hooks provide a secure nail base that is hung from the ridge of the roof, and is independent of the finish roofing material (see photo). The adjustable chimney brackets provide a level launch base for my tubular steel scaffolding frames.

Before I started using these products, I was custom-building rickety wood staging (nailing into the roof where I could), or adapting ladder hooks and hoping for the best.

When repairing chimneys, it's easy to cause more damage than you repair. To protect the roof I'm working over and walking on, I lay 1/4-inch lauan plywood under roof ladders, and heavier plywood over skylights and at the base of the chimney where a falling brick could damage the roof.

Coming up with a safe, efficient scaffolding method significantly affects the cost of the repair — on a recent job, my bid was exactly half my competitor's, and we still covered our labor costs. — *S.B.*

Roof-supported scaffolding increases safety and provides a more efficient work area. The heavy-duty ridge hooks (inset) are attached to 2-bys, which provide a nail base for the adjustable scaffolding brackets (visible to left of chimney).

Figure 13. On removing a loose brick during a repair, the author discovered that the standard-type mortar used to set the flue liners had eroded (left), allowing creosote to leak in between the liners and the chimney wall (right). Flue liners should be set in non-water-soluble refractory cement, which can tolerate high heat.

maturely. During the time it takes for the crown to make its initial set, I keep busy installing counterflashing and starting the general job-site cleanup. After the crown has set, I cover it with a tarp and wet burlap. This extends the drying time and ensures a slow, strong curing process.

Bond breakers at flues. At crown level, I wrap the flue liners with a bond breaker. I use "caution" tape, the yellow-poly tape I use to keep traffic away from the work area. The point is to prevent the crown mix from bonding to the flue liners, allowing the liners to move independently through the crown. I seal this joint with a high-quality urethane caulk. I include a stainless steel chimney cap (RMR Products) to keep weather, leaves, and small animals from getting into the flue.

No Room to Move

While faulty crowns cause a lot of the chimney damage I see, they're just the tip of the iceberg. Flue liners that cannot expand freely can also cause serious damage to a chimney.

Recently, I was called in to repair a chimney that had a 1/2-inch-wide vertical crack 7 feet long, starting at the crown (**Figure 12**, previous page). I discovered that the space between the bricks and the flue liners had been filled solid with mortar. The homeowners had adapted a wood stove to the existing fireplace, and creosote accumulated on the walls of the oversized flue liners. At some point, the intense heat of a chimney fire caused the flue liners to expand, literally pushing the chimney walls apart.

The NFPA 211 Standard (National Fire Protection Association, www.nfpa.org; 800/344-3555) requires a 1/2- to 1-inch free air space between the flue liner and the chimney wall. To stabilize the liners within this free air space, I cut strips of ceramic wool insulation (available from Sleepy Hollow Chimney Supply) and wrap the liners above and below each flue joint.

Faulty Flue Joints

I was recently replacing spalled bricks on a chimney, and after removing one of the damaged bricks, I discovered that the flues had been set in conventional mortar. Portions of the joint were missing entirely (**Figure 13**).

Upon deeper inspection, I found that creosote had leaked into the interior of the chimney walls, causing extensive damage to the chimney.

The problem was in the mortar. Flue liners and joints need to be able to withstand the intense heat of a chimney fire and resist corrosive condensation. If standard mortar is used, the joint will eventually deteriorate.

I always set flue liners in a non-water-soluble refractory cement from Ahrens Chimney Technique. Whenever possible, I use round, lap-joint refractory flues or stainless steel liners designed for solid fuel appliances (wood stoves, for example). The stainless liners I use are available from Heatfab (Heatfab Division).

Figure 14. The decorative, deeply raked joints in this chimney allowed water to pool and soak into the brick. When the saturated brick was exposed to extended sub-freezing temperatures, the water froze and expanded, causing the brick to spall.

Figure 15. Older chimneys with deteriorated lime-and-sand mortar must be torn down to the roofline and rebuilt.

Poor Joint Profiles

Improperly designed mortar joints can also create problems. The brick chimney in **Figure 14** was built using raked mortar joints that were recessed nearly 1/2 inch, forming a shelf at each horizontal course. Rainfall tends to collect on these ledges, and if the brick happens to tilt toward the chimney core, the water can be absorbed by the brick. When a heavy rain is followed by an extended stretch of sub-freezing temperatures, the absorbed water freezes and expands, and can cause spalling.

If the damage is extensive, replacing all the spalled bricks can be expensive. In cases where the customer cannot afford to have the chimney rebuilt, I've used a water-based product called ChimneySaver (Saver-Systems). It's a vapor-permeable siloxane treatment that usually prevents further spalling by imparting an electrostatic charge to the bricks. I'm always careful to advise my customer that some bricks may have already experienced internal damage that has yet to become visible.

In new work or rebuilds from the roofline up, I prefer to use a concave mortar joint. It's attractive, holds up well in my climate, and the concave striking tool compresses the mortar into a dense, weather-resistant surface. I'm careful to wait until the mortar is "thumbprint hard" before striking. Mortar that's tooled too early will not compress properly.

Old Age

Sometimes, the problem with a chimney is just plain old age. Many older chimneys were built with weak lime-and-sand mortar (**Figure 15**). In most cases, I tear the chimney down to the roofline, install new flashing, and rebuild the chimney. Typically, these chimneys come apart very easily. I was able to dismantle the chimney shown in less than an hour, with hardly the need for a chisel blow.

I've developed a good rule of thumb for assessing the condition of a chimney over the phone. If the homeowner tells me that they can see the problems from the ground, chances are I'll be rebuilding the chimney from the roofline up.

Stephen Bushway is a certified heater mason. He owns and operates Deer Hill Masonry and Deer Hill Enterprises in Cummington, Mass.

MECHANICAL VENTILATION

Chapter 17: Kitchen & Bath

- Bathroom Ventilation Options
- Ventilating Ranges and Cooktops

Bathroom Ventilation Options

by Andrew Shapiro

On a visit to a house to solve a heating problem, I had the chance to look at the bathroom. Moisture was causing the paint to peel, and decay had set in on the window sash and trim and probably in the structure behind the drywall. This house was not airtight by any stretch of the imagination, but the bathroom had no fan — and the lack of ventilation was causing a major maintenance problem.

I recommended installing a fan and specified one that ran quietly. I've learned that most people find it annoying to be in a small room while a loud fan is running; if the fan is quiet, it's more likely to be used. That translates into fewer moisture-related problems and lower maintenance costs over the life of the house. Also, if the owners later decide they want an automatic ventilation system for the whole house, an appropriate fan will already be in place (see "Installing Simple Exhaust Ventilation," page 340).

In recent years, several manufacturers have come out with very quiet bath fans. Here, I describe the types of fans available, take a look at the pros and cons of each, and look at some of the installation practices that will help you and your clients get the most out of the fan you put in.

Defining "Quiet"

The Home Ventilating Institute (www.hvi.org, 847/526-2010) certifies and publishes independent laboratory sound test results for most of the fans on the market. The sound levels are listed in "sones," a unit of sound in which one sone roughly equals the loudness of a typical refrigerator. By comparison, a typical range hood is 5 or 6 sones, and many common bath fans — the ones that rattle your teeth — are as loud as 4 sones.

For this discussion, I refer to fans with ratings of up to 1.5 sones, because there are a number of these on the market that are labeled "quiet" or "ultra-quiet." However, if you are looking for the best quality, I recommend a fan rated at 1 sone or less. For about the same price, the result will be much more satisfying.

One caution about sone ratings: The noise level of fans is measured at the relatively low duct pressure of 0.1-inch water pressure. This is about what you'd expect from a 50-cfm fan with 6 feet of 4-inch-diameter rigid duct with one 90° bend — a shorter and straighter duct run than is typical. If your ducts increase pressure above this level, the noise from the fan will increase as well.

What's available? Manufacturers have used three basic designs to lower the noise level of bath fans:

1. Room-mounted fans, with improved design to lower noise
2. In-line fans, which locate the fan outside the bathroom but still inside the house — usually with the duct run in the attic or basement
3. Exterior-mounted fans, which move the fan entirely outside the house as part of the hood or duct termination.

Let's look at the advantages and disadvantages of each.

Room-Mounted Bath Fans

Fans mounted in the bathroom ceiling (or sometimes in the wall) are commonplace — a fact that is per-

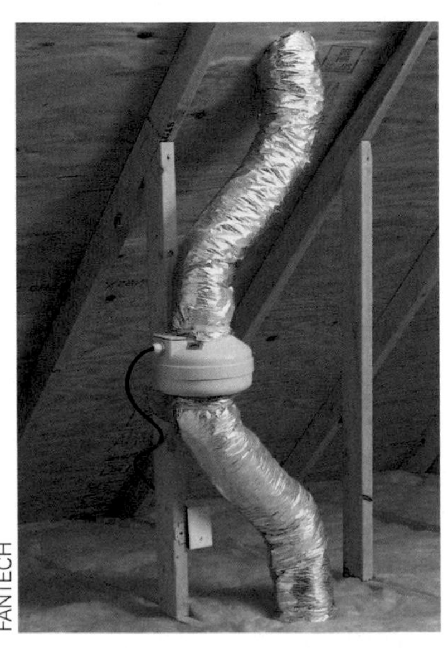

FANTECH

Figure 1. In-line fans are mounted in the attic (shown) or basement, between a grille in the bathroom and the outside wall jack. The insulated duct helps reduce sound transmission and prevents condensation.

CONTINENTAL FAN

Figure 2. Some in-line fan manufacturers supply special registers and fittings for various sizes of round duct.

haps their greatest advantage. Everyone on the job, including the electrician, knows how they work, so there are no surprises. Room-mounted fans are typically ducted a short distance through the ceiling framing to the outdoors. Attic ducting is also common, although the duct run may be longer because the exhaust port is usually mounted on a gable end.

Another advantage of room-mounted units is that it's easy to find and get access to the fan for maintenance. The big disadvantage is that the fan and motor are right in the space with the occupants, who are going to hear any noise that the fan makes. For a room-mounted fan, the quieter the better. Manufacturers of low-sone fans include American Aldes, Panasonic, and Broan-NuTone (see Sources of Supply, page 397).

In-Line Fan Systems

An in-line bathroom ventilation system consists of a register in the wall or ceiling and ductwork leading to the outside, with the fan mounted somewhere between (**Figure 1**). HVI does not certify sound ratings for exterior-mount and in-line fans or heat-recovery ventilators because their perceived noise levels vary greatly depending on installation (see "Kitchen and Bath Venting Recommendations," page 327). Informal testing by some in-line fan manufacturers indicates that the noise level in the bathroom is typically 1 sone or less, depending on the installation details and type of ducting.

The in-line fan is usually located in the basement or attic. An in-line system may be unfamiliar to carpenters and electricians, but a basement-mounted fan is easy to get to for installation and maintenance; the opposite is true, however, of a fan in the attic.

One drawback of a basement location is the need for a slightly longer duct run. If ducts are sized improperly, the result may be a louder fan and reduced airflow. (Don't worry about the ability of the fan to pull air down into the basement: In-line fans are plenty strong enough to overcome this small resistance.) Another drawback is that ceilings and walls with finish drywall amplify sound like the head of a drum. If you do end up hanging the fan from the floor joists in the basement, use rubber straps to hang it. Alternatively, mount the fan directly to the foundation, where vibration will be absorbed by the concrete rather than transmitted through the framing.

Duct runs for attic-mounted fans are often shorter but require insulation in almost all climates to avoid condensation inside the fan. Kraft-faced R-11 fiberglass batts can easily be wrapped around the fan and tied with cord. (One advantage of basement mounting is that the duct can go out through the band joist, with no need for duct insulation.)

At the bathroom end of the duct, you can use standard grilles and boots, or you can use the nifty fittings made by some fan manufacturers that fit right in the end of a 4-, 5-, or 6-inch round duct (**Figure 2**).

Another advantage of the in-line system is that a single fan can serve more than one bathroom (the switch in either bathroom turns on the fan). This dual use helps you get the most out of the higher price you will pay for a quiet in-line fan. All of the in-line fan manufacturers and the suppliers listed in **Table 1** sell kits that include the fan, flow-adjustable grilles, the wye fitting, and some other parts that simplify a split duct.

One minor disadvantage of a single fan serving two bathrooms is that some unnecessary ventilation takes place, because air is drawn from both rooms even when only one room is being used. Also, duct runs of different lengths can result in uneven airflow. To balance the airflow when the lengths of the duct runs to the two bathrooms are unequal, you can put a damper in the shorter duct or use a damping grille.

You can also avoid overventilation by using a speed control to slow the fan down and further decrease noise levels. But the owners may slow down the fan too much and not get enough airflow.

Table 1. In-Line and Exterior-Mounted Fans

Manufacturer/series Model	Airflow cfm@.1"	Capacity cfm@.25"	Sound Rating[1]	Draw (watts)[2]
REMOTE IN-LINE				
Fantech/FR & CVS				
FR-100	108	94	n/a	43
FR-125	130	110	n/a	48
FR-150	240	222	n/a	93
CVS-275	280	256	n/a	197
Broan-NuTone				
SP-100	115	107	n/a	
MP-140	140		n/a	
Continental Fan				
AXC-100A	115	85	n/a	35
AXC-125A	159	80	n/a	40
American Aldes[3]				
VMPS	n/a	85 – 120	n/a	n/a
SPV-200	n/a	50 – 250	n/a	90
EXT. MOUNTED				
Fantech/RVF				
RVF-4	122	105	n/a	48
RVF-4-XL	178	158	n/a	90
RVF-6	235	211	n/a	90

1. Sound rating is not yet available for in-line fans.
2. At 0.1" pressure.
3. Designed to operate at high pressure (above 0.25").

Multiport fans. One variation on in-line fans, called a multiport, has built-in collars for attaching more than one duct (**Figure 3**). Several manufacturers make these, including American Aldes, Broan-NuTone, and Fantech.

BROAN-NUTONE

Figure 3. Multiport fans, such as this one from Broan-NuTone, are simple to install when ducting exhaust from more than one bathroom.

Exterior-Mounted Bath Fans

The third strategy used to reduce fan noise is to locate the fan entirely outside the house, with ductwork running from one or more bathrooms. Fantech has some models with large enough capacities to serve several baths (**Table 1**, previous page).

As with in-line systems, exterior-mounted fans have the same minor disadvantage of being a nonstandard installation. And if the fan is mounted outside a second-floor bathroom, maintenance requires working from an extension ladder. Also, unless these fans are located under an eaves or gable overhang, they will need to be flashed on the outside to keep out water.

Control Options

Most bathroom fans run off of a separate switch, but they are sometimes coupled with the bathroom overhead light. It is a mistake, however, to assume that ventilation is only needed when the light is on. It often takes longer to clear moisture or odors out of the bathroom than the time that the room is occupied. And in bathrooms with more than one light, the fan may not get turned on at all.

Timers. One solution is a 60-minute crank timer, which I have found works well once people become accustomed to using it. Humidity controls are another option, but they have a big disadvantage: Proper operation requires seasonal adjustments that homeowners probably won't make. For example, in cold-climate winters when the air is dry, the humidistat should be set to turn on the fan at a relatively low humidity level; but in the higher humidity of summer, the fan would run constantly at that same setting.

Another option is the Airetrak (Tamarack Technologies), a push-button control that runs the fan for 20 minutes at full speed whenever the button is pressed (**Figure 4**). This control can also be set to run the fan at a lower speed for some portion of each hour. (This works well when the fan is part of an automatic whole-house ventilation system.)

Occupancy sensors. A third control option is an

Ductwork Do's and Don'ts

Do:

- Use ductwork that is the same size or larger than the fan outlet.
- Seal all duct joints with foil-backed tape, silicone caulk, or duct mastic.
- Use a plastic wire-tie or other mechanical connection at joints between flexible and rigid ducts, then seal the joint. (Foil-backed tape is great for air-sealing, but *not* for mechanical connections.)
- Use rigid duct where possible or be sure the fan is rated for the required flow at higher pressures inside flex duct.
- Use short lengths of flex duct at the connection to the fan to reduce noise.
- Insulate all ducts and fans in unheated attics or unheated crawlspaces to a minimum of R-5.
- Undercut the bathroom door 1 inch above finished floor level.
- Support ducts at frequent intervals to keep them straight; pitch ducts down slightly (1/4 inch over 4 feet) toward the outside for drainage. Place metal duct seams facing upward so they do not leak any condensed water (see Figure 9, page 341).
- Provide ventilation to every bathroom that has a shower or a tub. Windows are great for light, but often are not opened when ventilation is most needed.

Don't:

- Reduce the duct size below the fan outlet size.
- Seal ducts with cloth duct tape — it doesn't hold up over time.
- Use long lengths of 4-inch flex duct, unless you're using a fan rated to pull enough air at higher duct pressures.
- Terminate the ductwork in the attic. Always take it to daylight. — *A.S.*

Sizing a Bath Fan

The Home Ventilating Institute (HVI) guidelines recommend approximately 8 air changes per hour (ACH) for small bathrooms of up to about 100 square feet. The guidelines call for 1 cfm of exhaust ventilation for each square foot of floor area, with a minimum rate of 50 cfm. For larger bathrooms, lower rates may be suitable. The formulas for larger baths are shown in "Kitchen and Bath Venting Recommendations," page 327.

Note that a room with a hot tub may need a more powerful fan to remove the additional moisture. Note also that a long duct run will reduce the actual airflow that is listed on the fan. HVI listings are for 0.1-inch water static pressure. For longer duct runs, use airflow ratings for higher static pressures.

Table 2. Sizing Ducts

Duct Length (feet)	Airflow (cfm)	Static Pressure (inches of water)				
		4" Flex	4" Rigid	5" Rigid	6" Rigid	6" Flex
10	50	.12	.10	.04	.02	.02
10	75	.29	.19	.08	.04	.05
10	100	.50	.39	.16	.07	.09
10	150	1.20	.87	.35	.16	.20
20	50	.16	.12	.05	.02	.03
20	75	.39	.27	.10	.05	.06
20	100	.65	.45	.18	.08	.10
20	150	1.62	1.00	.39	.18	.24
30	50	.19	.13	.05	.02	.03
30	75	.49	.31	.12	.05	.07
30	100	.00	.52	.20	.09	.12
30	150	2.03	1.13	.43	.20	.28

Note: Values in chart assume all ducts include two 90° elbows; values for flex duct assume an additional two 45° bends. Pressure drop due to inlet and outlet terminations is included.

To find the correct duct size: In the column labeled "Airflow," find the cfm of the fan you plan to use and match it with the Duct Length you expect to use. Use any duct size that corresponds to a static pressure value of less than 0.15 (highlighted). If no value meets this criterion, increase the cfm of the fan.

Figure 4. Tamarack's Airetrak (far left) combines a single switch with a timer — the fan runs for 20 minutes at full speed whenever the button is pressed. Sensor Switch's Passive Dual Technology occupancy sensor (left) turns the fan on whenever it "sees" or "hears" someone enter the room.

Figure 5. Built-in humidity controls in Broan-NuTone's QTXE110S Sensaire fans turn the fan on when humidity rises rapidly.

occupancy sensor, which automatically turns on the fan whenever it detects the motion of someone entering the bathroom, and can be used in place of a wall switch. An adjustable time delay can be set so that the fan will run for a specified amount of time (usually from 5 minutes to an hour) after a person leaves the room. This is a good control strategy for rental or commercial bathrooms as well as residences. Occupancy sensors are available from control manufacturers such as Sensor Switch, Watt Stopper, and Leviton. Some fans are available with built-in occupancy sensors, but few of these qualify as low-sone models.

Humidistats. Some fans, such as Broan-NuTone's Sensaire series, are available with built-in humidity-sensing controls (**Figure 5**). You can omit the wall switch altogether, or substitute a three-stage (on/off/automatic) switch available with the fan. The Broan humidity-sensing model looks for a fast rise in humidity, but must be set for a base humidity — again, be aware of the need for seasonal adjustment. Some humidity-sensing units, such as the Broan QTXE110S, operate at less than one sone.

Ductwork Details

Depending on the design of the fan and motor, some quiet fans do not maintain a high airflow when pushing against excessive duct pressure. Airflow ratings for room-mounted fans are listed by most manufacturers and by HVI at 0.1 inch static pressure, but ratings at 0.25 inches of static pressure, a more realistic measure for many installations, are also available from some manufacturers. It doesn't take much ductwork to bump the pressure above the 0.1 level, especially if 4-inch flex is used. Washington State has recognized that most bathroom fan ductwork has a higher back pressure and now requires all fans to have the minimum required airflow at 0.25-inch pressure. However, if you can keep the resistance down by picking proper duct size and materials, and by minimizing the total duct length and number of elbows, your installation will pull more air more quietly. And it will use less electricity.

The specs for the many fans including those listed in Table 1 show airflows at both 0.1-inch and 0.25-inch static pressure. If the airflow drops off too much at 0.25-inch pressure, it means the fan is sensitive to duct pressure. Don't avoid these fans — they often use the least energy and are usually quieter — but pay closer attention to ductwork details.

Duct selection critical. Use **Table 2**, previous page, to pick the duct diameter and material for your particular installation. I have seen many jobs where duct selection and sizing is left up to the electrician with the lowest bid. The result was cheap rattler fans attached to 30 feet of flex duct held up with an occasional piece of duct tape. These are the homes that end up with moisture problems in the bathrooms, the ducts, or the attics. Providing a clear specification to bidding electricians as to fan make and model, duct material, and location can avoid this problem (see "Ductwork Do's and Don'ts," page 324).

Notice in Table 2 that 4-inch-diameter flex duct is only recommended for duct runs of 10 feet or less and for flows up to 50 cfm, unless the fan is capable of supplying the needed airflow at higher pressures. On the other hand, rigid 4-inch duct can be used for 50 cfm of flow up to 30 feet and still maintain relatively low pressure (0.13 inch).

Another point to note is that 6-inch flex (I prefer the preinsulated type that comes in 25-foot lengths) can be used for quite a long distance without much increase in pressure. Remember, however, to avoid sharp bends and to stretch out the duct as much as possible: Kinks and bends will restrict airflow. If the fan outlet is too small for 6-inch duct, use the appropriate duct adapter.

My favorite 4-inch duct material is rigid thin-wall PVC drainpipe, the kind used for foundation drainage. It's inexpensive and readily available, the joints and fittings glue up easily, and the smooth surface minimizes pressure drop.

Replacement air. No matter how good the fan or the duct, however, you can't get air out of the room if there is no way to get replacement air in. Remember to undercut the bathroom door 1 inch above finished floor level.

In unheated attics and unheated crawlspaces, be sure to insulate all the ducts and in-line fans. I have seen condensation in uninsulated ducts that was so heavy during cold periods it was mistaken for roof leaks. A side benefit of the insulation is further sound reduction, particularly with insulated flex duct.

Andrew Shapiro is an energy and sustainable design consultant and principal of Energy Balance, in Montpelier, Vt.

Kitchen and Bath Venting Recommendations

For adequate ventilation, The Home Ventilating Institute (HVI) recommends the following guidelines for ventilation rates:

Bathrooms (intermittent ventilation)

- ***Small Bath*** — 1 cfm per square foot, providing approximately 8 air changes/hour. Minimum of 50 cfm.
- ***Large Bath*** (over approximately 100 square feet) — Add up the needs of each fixture to determine the total ventilation rate:
  - Toilet 50 cfm
  - Shower 50 cfm
  - Bath tub 50 cfm
  - Jetted tub 100 cfm

An enclosed toilet should have its own exhaust fan. Fans should be located over the shower or tub area. Bathroom doors need to have at least 3/4" clearance to the finished floor to allow entry of makeup air. Using a timer or other control ensures that ventilation continues for a minimum of 20 minutes after use of the bathroom. For steam showers, we recommend a separate fan in the steam room that you can turn on after use.

Bathrooms (continuous ventilation)

When supplied on a continuous basis, ventilation should be 20 cfm at a minimum in lieu of an intermittent 50-cfm fan.

Kitchen Range Hoods

Recommended kitchen range hood ventilation rates vary greatly and depend on the type of cooking performed. The minimum rates are 40 cfm per lineal foot for a kitchen range hood placed along a wall and 50 cfm per lineal foot for island hoods. However, HVI recommends

- 100 cfm per lineal foot for wall-mounted kitchen range hoods.
- 150 cfm per lineal foot for island kitchen range hoods.

For a 30-inch-wide kitchen range hood along a wall, a kitchen range hood should be rated at 250 cfm at full speed. Kitchen range hoods with multiple speed settings allow low-level, quiet ventilation for light cooking with the ability for higher-level ventilation when needed. For "professional"-style cooktops, HVI recommends following the cooktop manufacturer's advice to estimate the approximate cfm requirements. Look for range hoods with HVI-Certified Performance Ratings. Inflated performance ratings are common on range hoods that are not HVI certified.

Downdraft vents. Kitchen range hoods capture contaminants with their canopy shapes. Downdraft exhausters require a higher volume and velocity of air to capture contaminants and their performance cannot equal that of hoods that capture the rising column of air above the cooking surface. When considering a downdraft kitchen exhauster, consult the range manufacturer's recommendations. Whether using kitchen range hoods, fans, or downdraft exhausters, always use equipment that vents directly outside the home.

Noise Control

While HVI certifies and publishes independent test results for most room-mounted residential exhaust fans on the market, it does not certify sound ratings for exterior-mount and in-line fans, or heat-recovery and energy-recovery ventilators. Although different remote-mount fans produce different amounts of sound energy, the perceived sound level can vary greatly depending on the installation. However, remote-mounted fans can be extremely quiet if installed properly.

For bathroom and other exhaust- or supply-air applications using remote-mount fans, HVI recommends using insulated flexible ducting (same as used for HVAC ducting). Insulated flexible ducting has very good noise-attenuating properties and minimizes condensation. With 8 feet of insulated flexible duct between the ceiling grille and the remote-mount fan, almost no fan noise should be evident in the bathroom. Ensure that the ceiling grilles are large enough to not induce significant air noise. For bathroom applications, an automatic timer is recommended in order to keep the fan from being left on inadvertently.

For range-hood exhaust ducting, rigid metal duct should always be used. Rigid ducting does not attenuate sound effectively. With the very powerful remote-mount fans often used for residential range hoods in "professional"-style kitchens, a silencer designed for the purpose will significantly lower the sound level.

Adapted with permission from Home Ventilation & Indoor Air Quality Guide, *2004, published by the Home Ventilating Institute (www.hvi.org).*

Ventilating Ranges and Cooktops

by Wanda Olson

Range-top cooking produces, among other things, water vapor, grease, smoke, and cooking odors. In addition, gas ranges produce nitrogen dioxide, carbon monoxide, and carbon dioxide. Left in the house, these gases pose health risks, while excess moisture poses risks to the house itself.

For all these reasons, most new and remodeled kitchens these days have some sort of ventilation. But some of these units aren't up to the task before them, and they fail to remove moisture and contaminants.

Here at the University of Minnesota, we tested the two main types of kitchen exhaust systems — overhead range hoods and downdraft fans — to see how well they capture cooking contaminants. We used steam from boiling water to simulate the exhaust gases, cooking odors, and moisture produced from typical cooking uses.

We found that the standard overhead range hood, properly installed, best meets the whole spectrum of exhaust needs that a kitchen might create. The two downdraft options, on the other hand, meet some exhaust needs very well while meeting others very poorly. Before getting into the details of how hood and downdraft units perform, it's worth mentioning one type of "exhaust" fan that hardly performs at all: the so-called "recirculating" range hood. These simply filter the gases, moisture, and contaminants rising from the range before blowing them back into the room. While these units trap some grease and odor in their filters, they don't remove any moisture or noxious gases from the house. They are inadequate in any kitchen. Over a gas range, they give a false sense of security while leaving potentially dangerous gases inside the house.

Typical Airflow Rates for Range Hoods

Wall-mounted range hood	150–600 cfm
Island hood	400–600 cfm
Microwave hood	200–400 cfm
Downdraft hood	300–500 cfm

Hoods

The full-size overhead range hood is the only fan design that will remove all moisture and combustion gases from all conventional cooking uses. It succeeds because hot gases and moisture rising from the range top naturally move into the fan's most effective collection area, rather than away from it, as happens with downdraft systems.

Overhead hoods can be either wall mounted, hung over an island, or included as an integral part of a microwave appliance mounted over the range. Most overhead hoods have a canopy to aid in capturing contaminants. Hoods without canopies include the new pull-out "silhouette" models and microwave hoods. Our tests did not include the silhouette models.

Wall-mounted hoods. Among overhead fans, properly sized wall-mounted hoods work best because the back wall provides an effective capture area and because wall-mounted hoods avoid the problems of other types, which are described below. Wall-mounted hoods should draw at least 150 cfm (see table above). The hood should be as wide as the range it is venting and should be at least 20 inches deep, rather than the 17 inches common in many

Installation of Wall-Mounted Range Hood

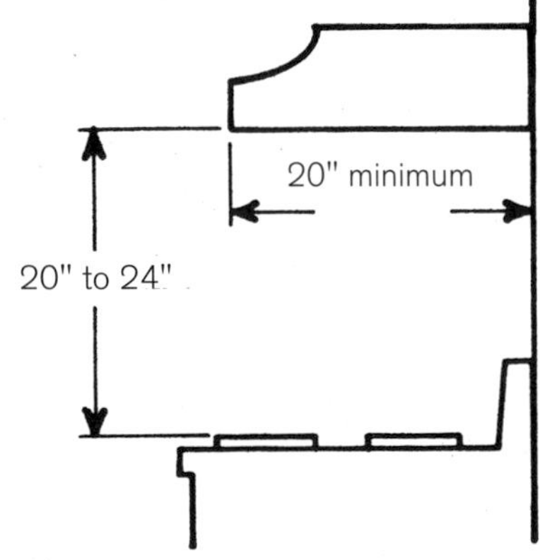

Figure 6. A hooded overhead fan captures steam from both short and tall pots, even those placed on the front burner (far left). To maximize effectiveness, use a range hood that extends at least 20 inches from the rear wall, and install it between 20 and 24 inches over the rangetop (left). The hood should be the same width as the cooktop.

Sizing Kitchen Ductwork

Few exhaust fans deliver the airflow promised by the cfm rating. A Canadian study of kitchen exhaust fans found that their actual airflow ranged from 14% to 92% of the rated capacity; over a third of the fans produced airflows below 40% of their rated levels. These reductions are typical of many installed fans.

Why the difference between rated and actual airflows? Usually, the fan is not the problem — the ductwork is. Most leading fan manufacturers have their fans' flow rates certified by the Home Ventilating Institute (www.hvi.org, 847/526-2010). HVI has fans independently tested to verify that the fans operate at the advertised flow rates under a standard pressure of 0.1 inch of static pressure. This is roughly equivalent to 30 feet of 3¹/4- by 10-inch duct venting a 200-cfm fan. Fans perform poorly when the ductwork creates resistance much greater than this.

To avoid this problem, you must keep ductwork as short and with as few elbows as possible, keeping the ductwork's total "equivalent length" to 30 feet or less. Use the accompanying chart to find the size and shape of the fittings you plan to use. When calculating the equivalent length of your proposed duct run, add the straight-length equivalent of the fittings to the lengths of straight duct. If you have more than one duct size in the run, use the size that corresponds to the majority of the duct used.

When planning a duct run, place a length of straight duct between fittings, if possible. In new construction, plan the path of ductwork before the framing is completed so you won't have to add fittings just to avoid a stud or joist that's in the way. When it's not possible to keep the total equivalent run to under about 30 feet, it's best to consult with the fan manufacture's technical staff to come up with a workable plan.

Equivalent Lengths for Common Duct Fittings

3¹/4 x 10-Inch Rectangular Fittings

90° elbow

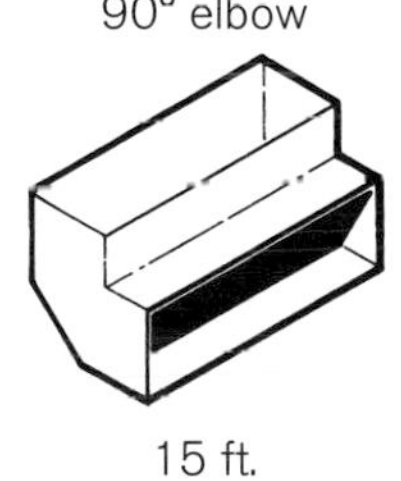

15 ft.

45° elbow

7 ft.

Wall cap

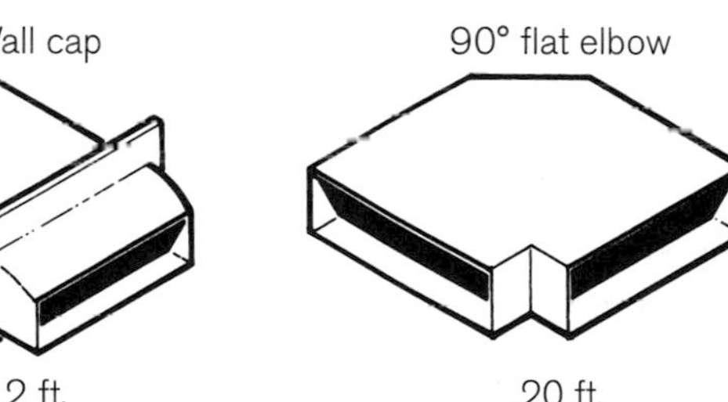

2 ft.

90° flat elbow

20 ft.

3³/4 x 10-Inch-to-Round Transitions

Straight transition

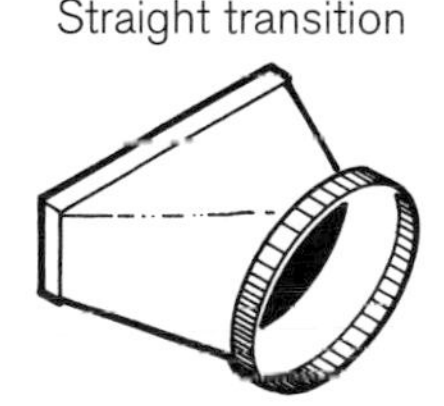

6-in. to 8-in. round = 4 ft.

90° transition

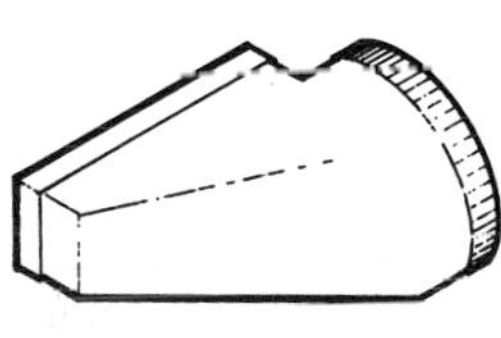

8-in. round = 25 ft.

Round Fittings

45° elbow

6-in. round = 6 ft.
7-in. round = 5 ft.
8-in. round = 3 ft.

90° elbow

6-in. round = 12 ft.
7-in. round = 10 ft.
8-in. round = 7 ft.

models. For best performance, it should be mounted 20 to 24 inches over the range top. Raising the hood above 24 inches, which is high enough even for tall cooks, reduces effectiveness (**Figure 6**).

Island hoods. Most island hoods work well because of their combination of high power and complete coverage of the cooking surface. However, because they are usually in the room's center and are installed at a higher distance above the cooking surface (27 inches is typical to preserve the line of sight across the room), room air currents can diminish their effectiveness. That is why these hoods usually have such powerful fans, up to 600 cfm.

Microwave systems. The hoods that come mounted beneath microwave ovens are similar to ordinary range hoods, with two important exceptions: They don't project as far from the wall (typically only 13 to 15 inches), and they don't have a collecting canopy, only vent openings. They do a good job of exhausting rear burners, but they miss

Surface Downdraft

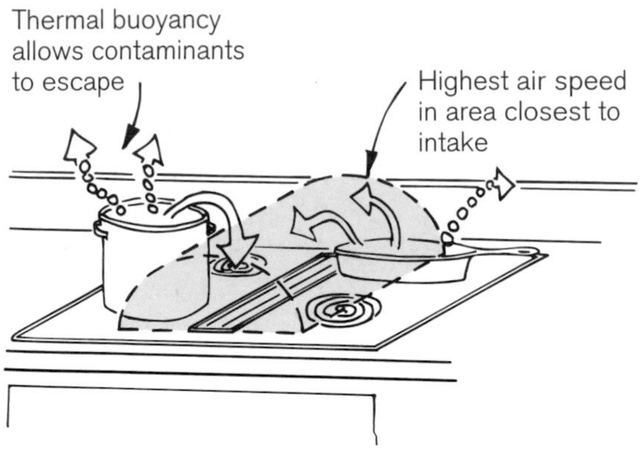

Thermal buoyancy allows contaminants to escape
Highest air speed in area closest to intake

Figure 7. Counter-level downdraft models, whether center- or side-mounted, work well only with pans shorter than 3 inches.

most of the gases and vapors rising from the front burners, even if lowered as close to the cooktop as 15 inches. Because of this, their overall performance isn't that good. If cooking is limited and clients will keep the steamy stuff on the back burners, these fans can be an acceptable solution. But in most homes, you're probably better off installing the microwave elsewhere and using a conventional wall-mounted hood.

Silhouette fans. A new type of wall-mounted fan is the sleek-looking pull-out silhouette model. This has a flat horizontal shelf that pulls out for use; it stores by sliding back into a shallower cabinet. We didn't test these, but I would guess that they're more effective than hoodless microwave units because they come out farther but not as effective as true hoods, which have canopies to aid in collecting steam and gases.

Downdraft Systems

Downdraft systems come in two types:

- counter-level downdraft units, which have vents mounted either in the center or at both sides of the range-top; and
- rear-mounted pop-up units, which have vent scoops that typically rise 8 inches from the rear of the unit to pull exhaust back and then down.

Both types are usually powered by strong fans. While neither unit performs as well as an overhead hood does for all heights of pots and all cooking loads, their relative strengths and weaknesses differ.

Counter-level units. Counter-level units, whether center- or side-mounted, successfully remove combustion gases, grease, and moisture from grills, pots, and pans shorter than 3 inches (**Figure 7**). But they capture very little rising from pans more than 3 inches high, such as spaghetti pots. If the household's cooking habits create considerable moisture from tall pots (do they cook a lot of pasta?), these hoods should be installed only if the kitchen is otherwise well ventilated, such as by a whole-house system.

Rear-mounted units. Rear-mounted pop-up units, because their vents are located at roughly the height of typical tall pots (about 8 inches), perform well for pots on the rear burners (**Figure 8**). For the front burners, the capture rate for tall pots is poor, though that for pans under 3 inches is adequate with the fan on high.

This performance isn't ideal, but can be made to work. If a client wants a downdraft unit rather than an overhead hood, ask about cooking practices. If they use tall pots, your best bet is installing a rear-mounted pop-up unit capable of at least 400 cfm — and telling the client to cook the noodles and lobsters to the rear.

About High-Powered Fans

Island and downdraft models have two potential drawbacks you should watch for, both due to the high-powered fans these models use.

First, powerful fans are often loud when run at full speed. Most manufacturers list the sound level of their fans in sones. Unlike decibel ratings, sone ratings are linear: A sone rating of 4 means twice as much noise as a sone rating of 2.

A few range hoods operate at around 2.5 sones. Most fans, however, particularly downdraft and island hoods, range between 4 and 7 sones or higher at full power. Homeowners should use these fans at their lowest effective setting to reduce noise and household negative pressure.

Pop-Up Downdraft

Thermal buoyancy allows contaminants on front burner to escape
Some contaminants escape from tall pots on rear burners
Highest air speeds close to intake
Contaminants from shallow pots on rear burners are captured well

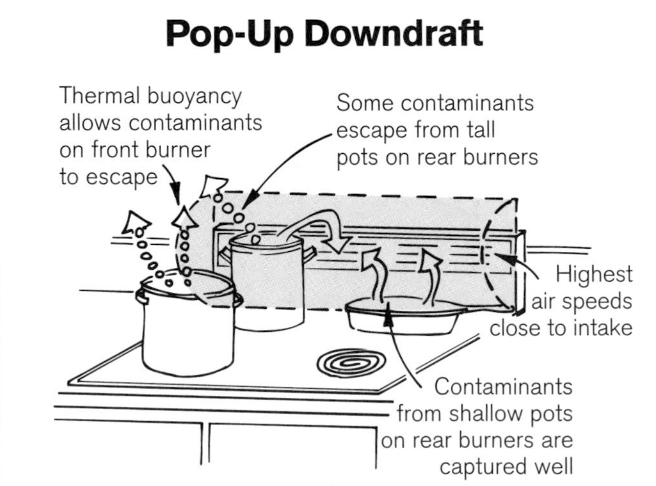

Figure 8. Rear-mounted pop-up units work well with pots on the rear burners. Pots on the front burner must be under 3 inches tall with the fan on high for adequate performance.

Clearly, you're best off with the quieter fan, all other things being equal. Fans over 6 or 7 sones may not get used by the client. If the fan has a variable control rather than a simple two-speed switch, the clients can find a happy medium between low and high settings that is quiet enough to use and strong enough to adequately ventilate.

Getting a quiet fan will probably mean getting a centrifugal blower, sometimes called a "squirrel-cage" fan. The alternative, the prop-like axial fan, is generally noisy even at lower airflow rates. Fortunately, most quality exhaust fans are centrifugal models, since they better overcome the resistance caused by ductwork (see "Sizing Kitchen Ductwork," page 329).

Backdrafting risks. The other potential drawback to powerful exhaust fans is that they pose a serious health risk in tight homes. Large-volume fans can depressurize tight homes and cause backdrafting of noxious fumes. Backdrafting occurs when negative indoor pressure pulls combustion gases down natural-draft chimneys venting furnaces, fireplaces, woodstoves, or water heaters. The tighter the home and the larger the exhaust fan, the greater the risk is of backdrafting. If you suspect that a backdrafting danger exists, you should test and, if necessary, provide an adequately sized fresh-air intake before installing the exhaust fan. If you are unsure about how to test for problems or how to provide adequate make-up air, have the situation evaluated by a qualified HVAC professional.

Wanda Olson is an associate professor and extension housing-technology specialist in the Department of Design, Housing, and Apparel at the University of Minnesota, in St. Paul.

Chapter 18: Whole-House Ventilation

- Choosing a Whole-House Ventilation System
- Installing Simple Exhaust Ventilation
- Installing a Heat-Recovery Ventilator

Choosing a Whole-House Ventilation System

by Judy Roberson

Increasingly, because of either code changes or customer demand, builders are having to take a closer look at whether the new, tight houses they build have adequate ventilation. Many builders would like to provide something better than just a few bath exhaust fans but aren't sure how to design a simple ventilation system that is reasonably priced and meets the needs of the homeowner.

Most whole-house ventilation systems rely on either exhaust fans or the fans in forced-air heating and air conditioning systems, because these fans are cheap, ubiquitous, and familiar to builders and homeowners. Yet just because these fans can be adapted for whole-house ventilation doesn't mean they do the job well. In many areas of the country, *supply ventilation* systems or *balanced heat-recovery ventilation* systems make more sense than either *exhaust ventilation* or *forced-air supply* systems.

While building codes typically require that only bathrooms be ventilated (with either an operable window or a spot exhaust fan), the trend in recent years is toward whole-house mechanical ventilation. ASHRAE's new residential ventilation standard (Standard 62.2) has been incorporated by reference into many building codes. Washington State has required mechanical ventilation in all new residential construction since 1991, and Minnesota instituted similar requirements in 2000. Many other states have taken note as well.

The Purpose of a Ventilation System

The purpose of a whole-house ventilation system is to maintain indoor air quality, which means supplying people with fresh air — and, in some cases, lowering the indoor humidity level. Ventilation is accomplished by regularly exchanging indoor air with outdoor air. People perceive indoor air quality differently, but, in general, complaints relate to odors, high humidity, and "stuffiness." The key to an effective and efficient ventilation system is to remove indoor air from rooms where the majority of moisture and odors are generated (kitchen, laundry, and bathrooms) and reliably distribute outdoor air to all habitable rooms, particularly bedrooms, where people spend most of their time.

Sources of indoor air pollution. Besides the moisture and odors that people constantly generate as they breathe, bathe, and cook, there are other sources of indoor air pollution to consider. Volatile organic compounds (VOCs) are emitted by some building materials and furnishings, including engineered wood (such as MDF and particleboard), carpet, paint, vinyl, and synthetic fabrics. Odors from these materials, which are strongest when they are new, may subside after a few weeks or months, but they can continue to outgas for much longer. By far the best way to control these pollutants, besides keeping them out of the house in the first place, is to ventilate continuously (nonstop) at a low rate.

Other sources of indoor air pollution vary, depending on occupant activities and lifestyle. These include chemicals in cosmetics, clothing, and household cleaning products. When designing a ventilation system, consider whether the occupants smoke, entertain frequently, have indoor pets, or engage in hobbies requiring chemicals. To deal with such pollutants, consider providing a higher level of continuous ventilation, additional spot exhaust fans, or a second, higher ventilation speed.

The most dangerous air pollutants are those that should never be allowed indoors — radon and most combustion gases. Combustion gases from water heaters, furnaces, boilers, fireplaces, and automobiles can all include carbon monoxide. A ventilation system cannot protect occupants from these pollutants. In fact, a poorly designed ventilation system can actually bring these pollutants into the house.

Qualities of a Good Ventilation System

Homeowners should be well informed about their ventilation system but should not be aware of it in their daily lives. If the ventilation system makes noise, creates drafts, or raises the electric bill, people are likely to disable it, in which case indoor air quality will deteriorate. To avoid that, you want to install ventilation systems that are quiet, continuous, and automatic.

Quietness counts. The best way to ensure a quiet system is to select a ventilation fan with a noise rating of less than one sone. Remotely located fans don't have to be as quiet, but they should be installed to isolate noise or vibration. Quality ventilation fans are designed for continuous operation for at least 10 years. Using a quality fan that is sized correctly is also the best way to minimize operating cost. Look for the EPA Energy Star label on quality home ventilation fans.

Good controls. Ventilation controls should be located in such a way that the system can't be shut off accidentally. The simplest control is an on/off

Figure 1. For homeowners who are away from the house according to a predictable schedule, a programmable timer, like this one from Leviton, works well for controlling ventilation rates.

switch, located in a basement or utility closet and clearly labeled, "This switch controls the ventilation system. It should be ON whenever the home is occupied." A better idea is to install a programmable control that operates the ventilation system continuously on low but allows residents to schedule a higher ventilation rate (cfm) during hours of higher activity (Figure 1).

Good distribution. It's not enough to introduce outdoor air into a home; that air must be distributed to people where and when they need it. This is one of the challenges of ventilation system design. Remote in-line fans that are ducted to several rooms provide better air distribution than ceiling-mounted fans. All ventilation systems should be tested at installation to verify that they deliver adequate air to all rooms.

Filtration. The ability to filter incoming air is an important aspect of indoor air quality and ventilation systems. Fans that supply outdoor air to a building make it possible to push the incoming air through a filter, but the fan must be sized to accommodate the additional resistance of the filter, even when clogged. Ventilation fans should be located where they are readily accessible for maintenance and easy replacement of filters.

Ventilation and Indoor Pressure

The tighter the house, the more easily it can be pressurized or depressurized (relative to the outdoors) by fans, particularly large fans such as kitchen range hoods (100 to 1,000 cfm), clothes dryers (100 to 500 cfm), or forced-air handlers (1,000 to 1,500 cfm). Although ventilation fans are relatively small (50 to 200 cfm), they have a disproportionate importance, since they operate continuously rather than intermittently. Builders need to understand indoor pressure because of its implications for safety, health, moisture transport, heating and air conditioning performance, energy consumption, and ventilation airflow.

From a safety and health standpoint, positive indoor pressure is better than negative indoor pressure. Negative indoor pressure as low as 3 Pascals (25 Pascals = 0.10 inches on a water gauge) can cause backdrafting of natural-draft combustion appliances and fireplaces, pull auto exhaust from an attached garage, or pull radon (if present in the soil) through cracks or holes in the foundation. Positive indoor pressure, on the other hand, does not interfere with combustion gas venting and helps prevent these and other outdoor air pollutants from entering a home.

In cold climates, however, positive indoor pressure can cause problems, since indoor air is pushed out through the exterior walls of a home. In very cold weather, moisture in this warm air can condense on cold surfaces inside the wall cavity, where it could cause framing to rot. Similarly, negative indoor pressure pulls outdoor air in through exterior walls, and in hot, humid climates, moisture in this warm air can condense on cold, air conditioned surfaces within the wall. Properly designed wall systems (see Part 2: Water Vapor Control) can minimize these types of moisture problems but, in general, builders should avoid positive indoor pressure in very cold climates and negative indoor pressure in hot, humid climates.

Three Types of Ventilation

Mechanical (or active) ventilation uses electric fans to move air into or out of a building, or both into and out. There are three basic types of home mechanical ventilation systems: exhaust, supply, and balanced. Regardless of what a particular system is called, it is always one of these basic types, and you can save yourself a lot of trouble by learning to recognize them.

Exhaust ventilation uses a fan to remove indoor air from a building. In a tight house, this creates a negative indoor pressure that pulls outdoor air in through openings in the walls, floor, and roof. Supply ventilation uses a fan to deliver outdoor air to a building. In a tight house, this creates a positive indoor pressure that pushes indoor air out through these openings. Balanced ventilation uses two fans to supply and exhaust similar volumes of air, so it does not affect indoor pressure.

Exhaust Ventilation

In homes where depressurization does not pose a safety, health, or structural durability risk, exhaust ventilation can be very effective. Its success depends on the ability of the exhaust ventilation fan to pull air from all parts of the house, a job made difficult

Exhaust Ventilation

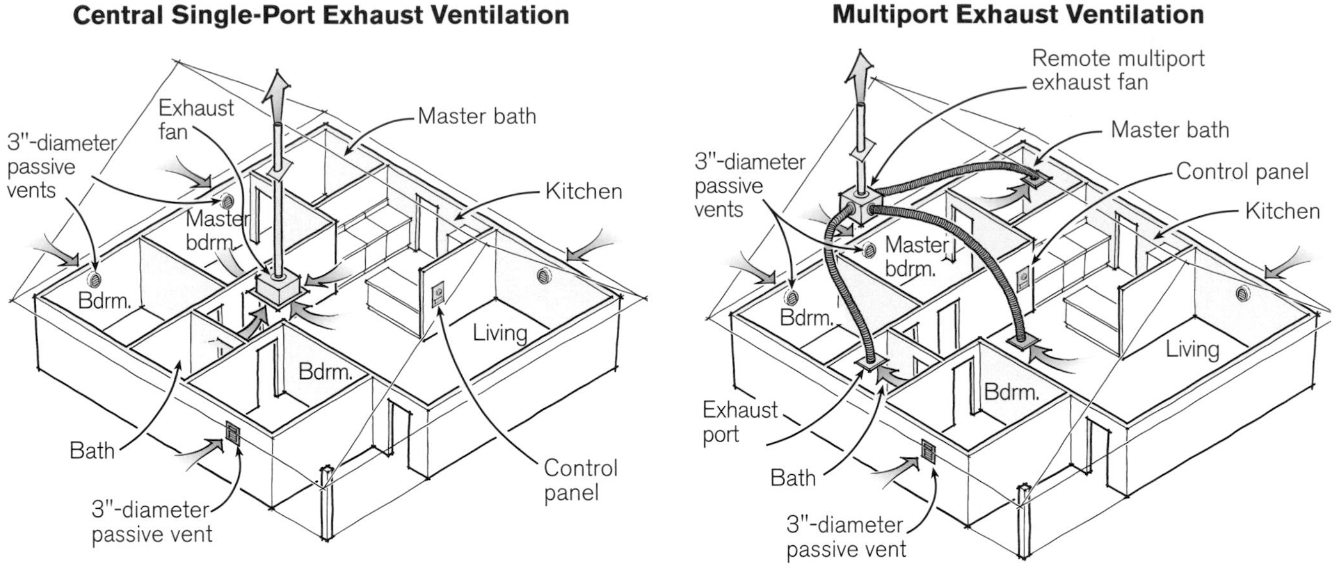

Central Single-Port Exhaust Ventilation

Multiport Exhaust Ventilation

Figure 2. Exhaust ventilation systems remove stale air, either from one location (left) or from several locations (right). Fresh supply air is drawn into the building passively, either through miscellaneous cracks or through installed passive vents. Note that passive vents are only effective in very tight houses.

by closed interior doors, air leakage sites, and the stack effect, which increases with building height and severity of climate. Therefore, exhaust ventilation is most effective in small, very tight homes with open floor plans (**Figure 2**).

Single-port versus multiport. Exhaust systems vary according to the location of the fan and the number of exhaust points, or ports. Locating the exhaust ventilation fan in a bathroom saves the cost of one spot fan but makes it harder for the fan to pull air from all the other rooms, especially when the bathroom door is closed. Locating the exhaust fan in a central hall or stairway improves its ability to pull air from all rooms (**Figure 3**). The multiport is the most effective exhaust system. It uses a remote fan, located in a garage or attic, connected by small (4- to 6-inch-diameter) ventilation ducts to several rooms, usually each bathroom (**Figure 4**).

Figure 3. Bath exhaust fans, like this model from Panasonic, can be used for whole-house ventilation if they are wired for continuous operation.

With exhaust ventilation systems, it is not possible to filter incoming air or to control the source of that air, so negative indoor pressure is as likely to pull air from a moldy crawlspace or dusty attic as from outdoors. Exhaust systems sometimes include several passive vents, which are small (4- to 6-square-inch) screened openings installed in exterior walls or windows. These vents are designed to provide some control over the location of incoming air but require 10 to 20 Pascals of negative indoor pressure to be effective. In other words, the exhaust fan must significantly depressurize the building to ensure that air enters the home through the vents. Otherwise, they are uncontrolled leakage sites, and the wind and stack effect determine the direction of airflow (as it does when there is no ventilating fan).

Supply Ventilation

With supply ventilation, the fan not only draws incoming air from one uncontaminated location, but it can also filter the incoming air, which is important to the growing number of people with asthma, allergies, and chemical sensitivities (**Figure 5**). Supply systems always include spot exhaust fans in the bathrooms and kitchen for removing excess moisture and odors.

Forced-air supply systems use the fan and ductwork of the forced-air heating or cooling system to distribute ventilation air. Typically, a 6- to 12-inch-diameter supply air duct runs from outdoors to one

Figure 4. Multiport ventilators, like these models from American Aldes (far left) and Broan-NuTone (left), use a single fan to exhaust air from several locations.

of the plenums of the forced-air handler. When the forced-air fan runs, outdoor air is drawn into the plenum, mixed with recirculated indoor air, and delivered to the house. But while the need for heating or cooling is intermittent, ventilation is needed all the time, so a control must be used to operate the forced-air fan at regular intervals (usually about 20 minutes each hour) for ventilation whenever the fan is not operating for heating or cooling.

Because a standard forced-air fan cannot be operated continuously, it doesn't maintain positive indoor pressure. And since forced-air systems are designed to move ten times as much air as is needed for ventilation (about 1,200 versus 120 cfm), these systems are noisier and more expensive to operate than those designed for ventilation only. Besides the noise, residents may also object to untempered air coming out of the supply registers. These problems can be addressed by installing an efficient, variable-speed (ECM) forced-air fan that can operate continuously. Such a fan increases forced-air supply installation costs by about $1,000.

As an alternative to using the HVAC supply system, an independent, multiport supply ventilation fan can distribute outdoor air to living room and bedrooms through a set of 4- to 6-inch-diameter ventila-

Supply Ventilation

Forced-Air Supply Ventilation

Outside air duct with motorized damper
Forced-air furnace and/or central air conditioner
Master bath
Forced-air return duct
Forced-air fan control
Kitchen
Master bedroom
Bdrm.
Bath
Bdrm.
Living
Forced-air supply duct

Multiport Supply Ventilation

Forced-air fan with screened air intakes supplies outside air
Master bath
Forced-air fan control
Kitchen
Master bdrm.
Bdrm.
Bath
Bdrm.
Living
Forced-air supply ducts

Figure 5. Supply ventilation systems introduce fresh outdoor air into a house, slightly pressurizing the building. A forced-air supply system (left) uses the same fan as the furnace or central air conditioner, blending outdoor air with return air in the return plenum. A multiport supply system has a dedicated fan (right) and filters and distributes outdoor air through dedicated 4- to 6-inch-diameter ducts.

tion ducts. This provides all the benefits of supply ventilation, including quietness, efficiency, air filtration, and positive indoor air pressure, without the drawbacks of using forced-air fans and ducts. Surprisingly, multiport supply is the least common type of ventilation system currently used, partly because builders and homeowners are more familiar with exhaust fans and forced-air systems.

Balanced Ventilation

Balanced ventilation systems use two fans, one for exhaust and one for supply. The fans move similar volumes of air, so indoor pressure is not affected (**Figure 6**). The primary advantage of balanced ventilation, however, is not neutral pressure but the ability to transfer energy from the exhaust air to the incoming supply air. This reduces the operating costs somewhat and also increases comfort by preheating the incoming supply air in cold climates or precooling the incoming air in hot climates. Thus, the appeal of balanced systems varies according to whether they incorporate heat recovery and how well they do it.

Balanced systems are more expensive than unbalanced systems, because the installation and operation of two fans is required. Balanced ventilation can be used in any climate but is most common in very cold or hot, humid climates, where heat recovery is most cost-effective.

In winter, heat-recovery ventilation systems (HRVs) use heat from the exhaust air to raise the temperature of incoming supply air (**Figure 7**). Energy-recovery ventilation systems (ERVs) are similar, except they exchange moisture as well as sensible heat energy. ERVs transfer moisture from the more humid to the less humid airstream. In arid climates, moisture is transferred from outgoing to incoming air; in humid climates, moisture is transferred from incoming to outgoing air, until the ERV's capacity for moisture transfer is reached. ERV moisture transfer is passive, and neither the amount nor the direction of transfer can be controlled.

HRVs and ERVs vary according to the type and efficiency of the heat recovery mechanism and the efficiency of the ventilation fans. When selecting a unit, refer to the Home Ventilating Institute's annual *Certified Home Ventilating Products Directory*, which reports HRV and ERV efficiencies (available online at www.hvi.org or by calling 847/526-2010). HRVs and ERVs provide excellent distribution of air because both fans are usually ducted to several rooms. The main disadvantages of HRVs and ERVs are their high initial cost and the fact that considerable expertise is required to properly install and maintain them.

Choosing the Right System

Choosing a ventilation system requires balancing cost and performance. For example, forced-air supply ventilation, which uses the fan and ductwork of the heating or cooling system, is popular among

Balanced Ventilation

Balanced Heat-Recovery Ventilation | **Multiport Supply Ventilation Balanced by Single-Port Exhausts**

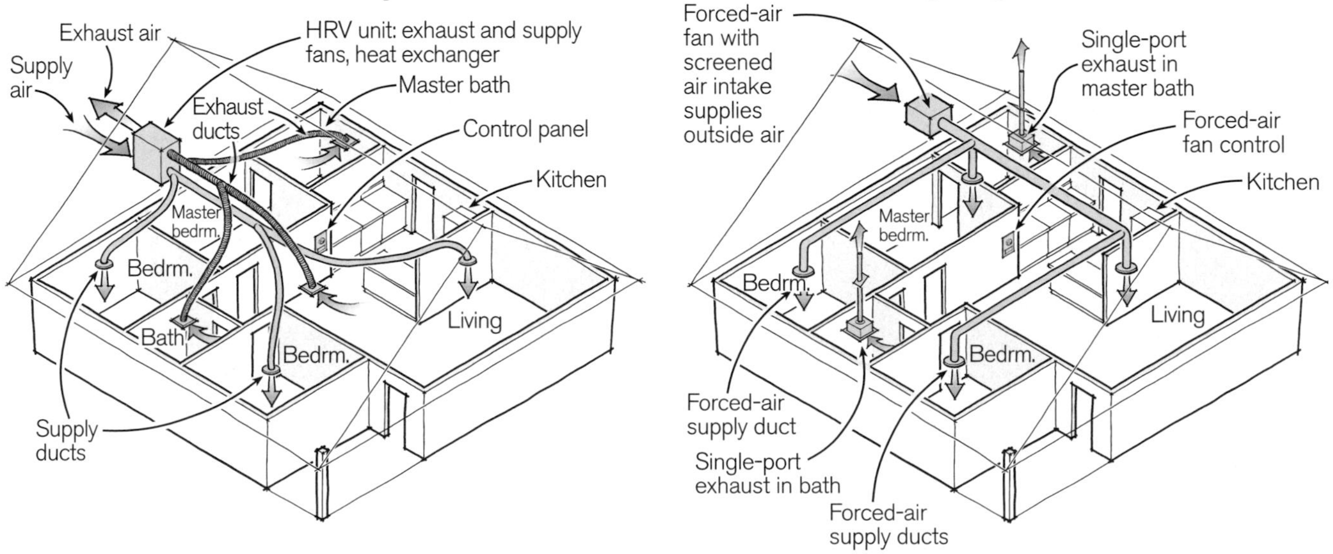

Figure 6. A balanced ventilation system uses two fans — one to supply fresh outdoor air, and another to simultaneously exhaust stale air. A heat-recovery ventilator (left) provides balanced ventilation, as does a multiport exhaust system balanced by a single-port exhaust fan (right).

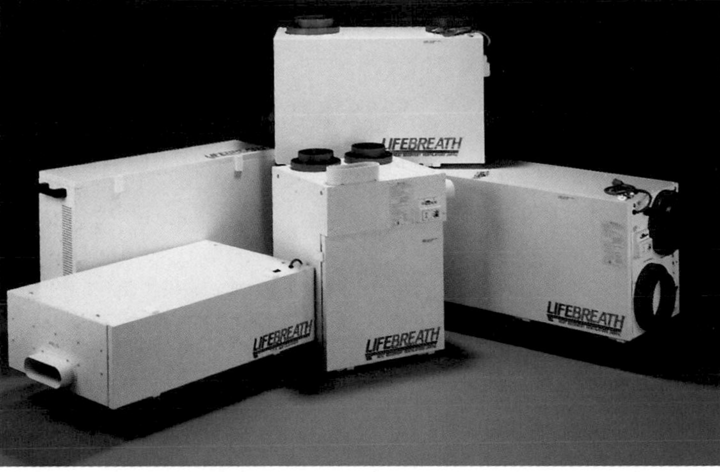

Figure 7. Although heat-recovery ventilators, like this model from Stirling Technology (left) or these units from Nutech (right), have a high initial cost, they reduce the cost of tempering the ventilation air.

tract home builders because it's very inexpensive to install; however, it's expensive to operate a standard forced-air fan for ventilation. On the other hand, balanced heat-recovery systems are expensive to install but save on operating costs. The more severe the climate, the greater the operating cost savings with heat-recovery ventilation. Single-port exhaust systems have low installation and operating costs, but often do not distribute air as well as ducted systems. Multiport supply and multiport exhaust ventilation have moderate installation and low operating costs.

At Lawrence Berkeley National Laboratory, we devised a ranking system in order to compare the cost and effectiveness of various residential ventilation systems. Our results were intended for production home builders, whose decisions are driven primarily by lowest first cost, but the information provided is useful to any builder or homeowner trying to select a ventilation system.

Recommended strategies. We evaluated nine ventilation strategies, including three types of exhaust systems, three types of supply systems, and three types of balanced systems. These nine systems were then scored and ranked for four different climates (cold, mixed, hot-humid, and hot-arid, represented by Boston, Washington, D.C., Houston, and Phoenix). Scores were based on three criteria: installation cost, long-term operating costs, and effectiveness of ventilation provided by each system. The lower the costs and the more effective the ventilation, the higher the score. Our criteria for effectiveness included air distribution and indoor air pressure, but they did not include air filtration or source of air.

In all four climates, the ventilation system with the highest score was multiport supply. However, since positive indoor pressure can cause moisture problems in exterior walls in cold climates, we recommend that in cold climates, a multiport supply system be balanced by single-port exhaust ventilation, and that heat recovery ventilation be offered to home buyers as an optional upgrade.

Exhaust systems, which usually are not ducted, are as affordable as ducted supply systems, but are less effective. Balanced HRVs and ERVs are the most effective systems, but their high installation cost is difficult to justify, at least in production homes. The full report, entitled *Recommended Ventilation Strategies for Energy-Efficient Production Homes*, is available on-line at http://enduse.lbl.gov/Projects/ESVentilation.html (click on the link under "Publications").

Judy Roberson is a senior research associate at Lawrence Berkeley National Laboratory in Berkeley, Calif.

Installing Simple Exhaust Ventilation

by Andrew Shapiro

Indoor air quality has aroused increasing concern in recent years, with home buyers worried about everything from carpet fumes and formaldehyde to excess moisture and dust mites. These problems have been compounded by improved building practices that, in many cases, have created tighter homes. But a house doesn't have to be airtight, or even close to it, to have poor indoor air quality.

Of course, the best solution to indoor air problems would be to eliminate from the home all the products that emit air pollutants, but this is impractical and costly. And moisture from people, plants, pets, cooking, and bathing is a fact of indoor life. The most practical way to remedy problems from moisture and pollutants in a home is to install a simple ventilation system. Adding good ventilation is also an easy way to reduce callbacks from excess moisture on windows in cold climates.

Here, I focus on a system I've used that relies on a quiet fan from Panasonic (see Sources of Supply, page 397).

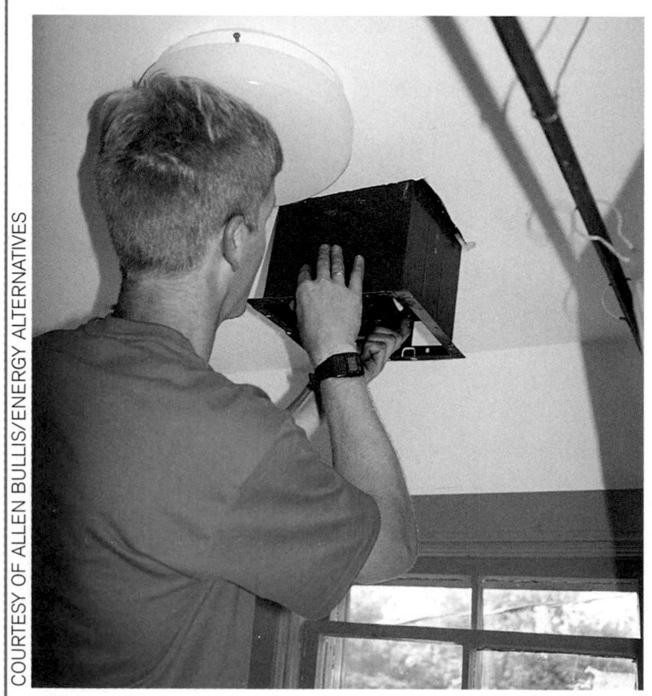
COURTESY OF ALLEN BULLIS/ENERGY ALTERNATIVES

Figure 8. An energy contractor installs a Panasonic FV-08 bath fan. These quiet, energy-efficient fans are deeper than most, but the housing still fits in a 2x8 joist bay.

New Fan on the Block

Many manufacturers now offer relatively quiet exhaust fans. I typically use the Panasonic FV series of bathroom fans (**Figure 8**) because they're affordable, extremely quiet, *and* energy efficient. This combination is critical for a ventilation system for a couple of reasons. First, most low-cost fans are so noisy you can't wait to turn them off, if you ever turn them on at all. If you expect a fan to be used, it must run quiet. The Panasonic fans run at 1/2 sone for the 50-cfm model, and 1 sone for the 90- and 110-cfm models. (One sone is about as quiet as a relatively new refrigerator.) Compare this with 3 sones for many cheap fans with similar capacities.

Also, since the fan is going to run for long periods to exhaust a whole house, it must not consume too much electricity. The Panasonic FV-08 fans use 17 watts, compared with 100 or even 150 watts for some cheap fans of similar capacity. A 100-watt fan used for 8 hours per day would cost about $29 per year to operate (at 10¢/kWh), while the 17-watt Panasonic fan would cost $5.

Ventilation System Components

A fan by itself does not make a whole-house ventilation system. A complete system consists of a way to get stale air out, a way to get fresh air in, and a way to control the fans.

Out with the old. One FV-08, installed with less than 20 feet of smooth-wall duct and no more than two elbows, will deliver about 70 cfm. Just one of these is enough ventilation for a one-story, 1,800-square-foot house if the fan runs at least part of each hour that the house is occupied. Larger houses will require two or more fans (see "Sizing Ventilation Fans," page 342).

Fresh air in. Whenever you have this much air exhausted from a house, you must provide a way for fresh air to get in — and get in where you need it. Cracks around windows and doors, and other unavoidable air leaks, will also let in air, but this may not always provide enough fresh air in the occupied areas of the house.

I use through-the-wall inlets to do the job. I place one inlet in each bedroom, usually near the ceiling, where the colder outside air will mix with the warm house air before it contacts occupants.

Controls. One key difference between a simple bath fan and a whole-house ventilation system is the

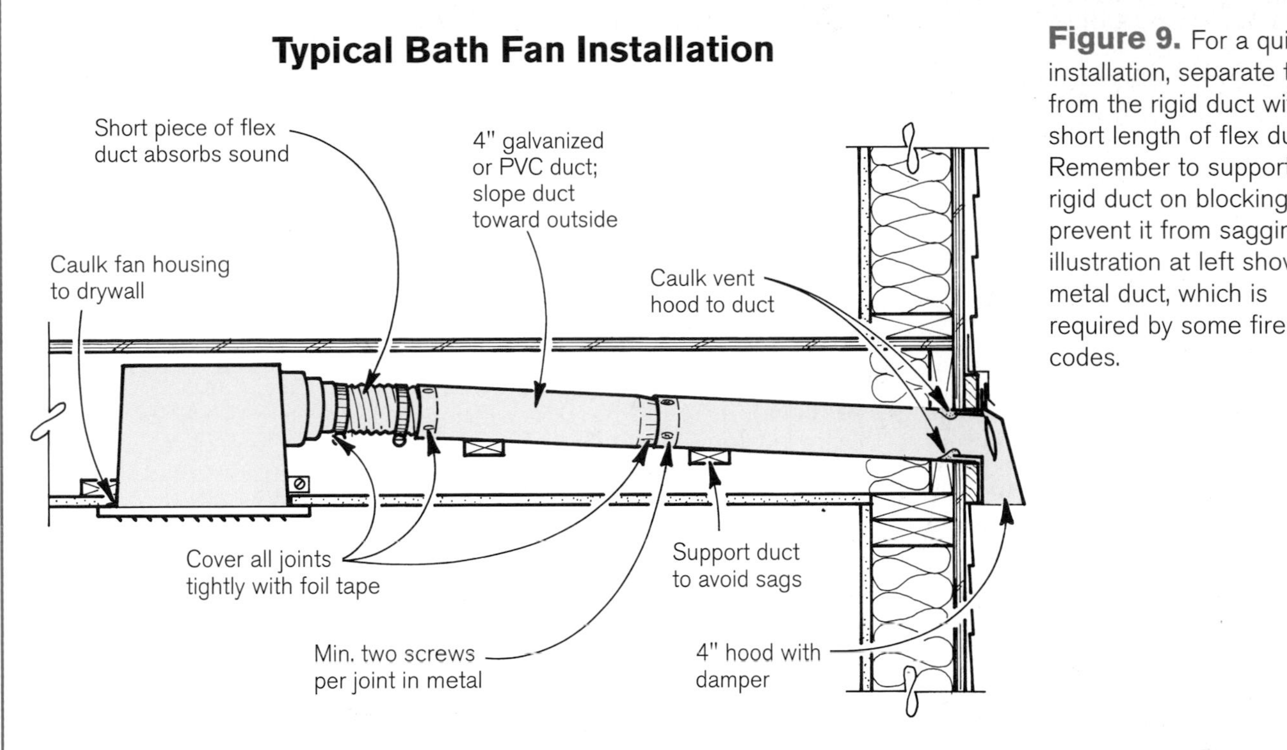

Figure 9. For a quiet installation, separate the fan from the rigid duct with a short length of flex duct. Remember to support the rigid duct on blocking to prevent it from sagging. The illustration at left shows metal duct, which is required by some fire codes.

length of time the fan runs. In most cases, the fan will run for 6 to 8 hours per day. Also, since most houses have more than one fan, the fans should be coordinated to run at different times to provide ventilation where and when it's needed. This requires reliable automatic timers.

Fans will need to run longer for people with "wet" lifestyles — lots of houseplants, cooking, Jacuzzis, or the like — and more during the first winter of occupancy in a new house when there is still a lot of moisture coming out of the building materials. This assumes that the occupants don't smoke and that there are no unusual sources of moisture or air pollution inside the house.

Sources of supply. Good mail-order sources for all the components of a whole-house system, including the Panasonic fans, fresh air inlets, and automatic timers, are Energy Federation, Positive Energy, and Shelter Supply (see Sources of Supply, page 397).

Fan Installation

The Panasonic fan installs in the bathroom ceiling just like any other bath fan (**Figure 9**). Be aware that the fan housing is larger than that of typical bath fans — 9 inches square by 7⁷/₈ inches deep. This will fit in a 2x10 floor joist bay above the drywall. In a 2x8 floor system, however, you have to plan the installation so that the lower lip of the fan housing is flush with the bottom surface of the drywall. Panasonic provides a trim collar that can be secured with two thumbscrews from inside the fan housing.

Filters. Since the fan is going to be running frequently, it will collect a lot of lint and dirt. This can eventually clog fan blades and cooling holes in the motor, lowering air delivery and shortening the life of the fan. To protect the fan, use an ordinary cut-to-fit air conditioner filter. Cut a square that fits just inside the grille and push the grille springs through the filter before pushing the grille in place. Explain to the owners that this filter will need periodic cleaning or replacement. Also, if you run the fans during drywall finishing to help the mud dry faster, be sure the filter is in place during sanding and plan on replacing the filter before the owners move in.

Ductwork. If there is any "fine print" about Panasonic's FV series fans, it is that they cannot move air against a lot of back pressure, which is resistance to airflow caused by ductwork and other obstructions. This means the ductwork needs to be full 4-inch-diameter rigid duct. A little flex duct — up to 2 feet or so — to connect to the fan and to the termination outside helps reduce noise and makes the installation easier without decreasing airflow too much.

For ductwork, I often use 4-inch thinwall PVC pipe — the nonperforated type used for foundation drains. This material is easy to work with and the joints can be sealed tight with PVC cement.

If you use galvanized ducts, put at least two screws per joint. Then use foil duct tape — the type with a peel-off paper back — *not* cloth duct tape. Conventional cloth duct tape will eventually deteriorate, releasing moist air into the attic or floor structure.

Flexible duct should be clamped first with metal hose clamps or straps, then taped to the rigid duct. Do it right from the start so you don't ever have to get in there again.

Sizing Ventilation Fans

Ventilation fans are sized to provide specific airflow rates in cubic feet per minute (cfm). The size of the fan needed for ventilation depends on the size of the house and the number of occupants. The ASHRAE Standard recommends a minimum of 0.35 air changes per hour (ACH), but not less than 15 cfm per occupant during the time the house is occupied. You should calculate minimum whole-house fan size based on both house size and number of occupants, then use the higher number.

Here's how to calculate 0.35 air changes per hour:

1) Multiply the exterior square footage of the house or apartment by the average ceiling height to calculate total volume. Then multiply by 0.85 to account for the wall and partition thicknesses.
2) Multiply the volume by 0.35.
3) Divide by 60 (minutes per hour) to get the required cfm.

So, for example, an 1,800-square-foot, three-bedroom house with 8-foot ceilings would need a ventilation rate of 71 cfm to ensure 0.35 ACH.

Now compare this with the other ASHRAE recommendation of 15 cfm per occupant. Since the number of occupants in a house or apartment changes over time, the assumption is made that there are two occupants in the master bedroom and one occupant in each of the other bedrooms. So a three-bedroom house requires 60 cfm of ventilation by this measure. Because the ACH measure — 71 cfm — is higher, that is the one to use. In this case, one Panasonic FV-08 will meet the required ventilation needs.

Most fans' airflow ratings are usually listed at 0.1 and 0.25 inches of water. When choosing a fan, use the cfm rating at 0.25 inches of water, which approximates the static pressure of a typical duct installation. — *A.S.*

Panasonic FV-08 Fan Curve

Static Pressure (inches of water): 0.52, 0.50, 0.45, 0.40, 0.35, 0.30, 0.25, 0.20, 0.15, 0.10, 0.05, 0.00

Airflow Volume (cfm): 0, 8, 16, 24, 32, 40, 48, 56, 64, 72, 80, 88, 96, 104, 112

The fan curve shows how much air a fan will move as the static pressure increases with longer duct runs, elbows, grilles, and dampers. The 0.25 measure approximates the static pressure of a typical duct installation.

Keep the total duct run to no more than 20 feet, and use no more than three elbows or 2 feet of flex duct. In most cases, this will be plenty of duct to get to an outside wall. If you need more, reduce the number of elbows and eliminate as much of the flex duct as possible.

If at all feasible, avoid running duct inside 2x4 walls. However, running down and out may sometimes be the shortest route to the outside. If you run the duct in partition walls, use 4-inch *oval* duct. Don't reduce the duct size below 4 inches.

Vent termination. As a termination outside, I use a simple low-cost dryer vent with a flap-type backdraft damper. The dryer vent terminations with three louvers can freeze up in the winter, so I recommend the hood-type outlet instead.

Insulation. If the duct is in the attic, it should be under the attic insulation; otherwise, condensation will form on the ductwork and leak into the house. If

Figure 10. A whole-house ventilation system needs effective controls. The author uses a Grasslin automatic timer that can be set to run at 20-minute on/off cycles, with manual overrides.

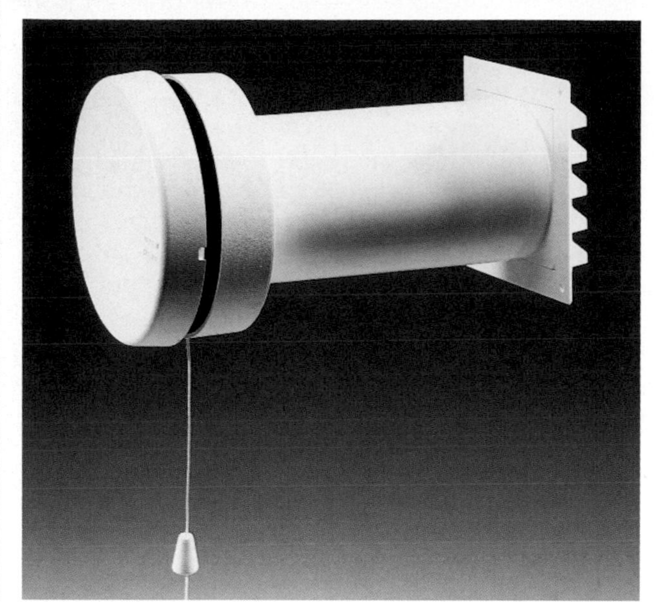

Figure 11. To provide makeup air to bedrooms and prime living spaces, the author uses through-the-wall Fresh-80 inlets. These are only effective, however, in a tight house.

this is not possible (as when the duct runs across the top of the ceiling joists), insulate the duct separately. If you are using blown-in attic insulation, you can put up "dams" using any available material, such as drywall, plywood, cardboard, or window screen. Fill the dammed-off area with insulation, mounding it over the ductwork to the proper insulation depth.

Support the duct with blocking to prevent any sags, and slope the rigid duct down toward the exterior as much as possible. With metal duct, face the long seams upward and "nest" the joints in the direction of flow, as a further hedge against water leakage from condensation problems.

Controls

An automatic timer gives occupants the most options for controlling the fans. I install one timer for each fan (up to two fans). If there are additional fans located away from normally occupied areas (a guest-room bathroom, for example), a switch for each of these is adequate.

Don't wire the fan into the light switch. Doing so makes it impossible to turn the fan on long enough for good ventilation without leaving the light on and wasting electricity.

I use the Grasslin KM2/I 24-hour in-wall timer (Grasslin Controls Corp.). The Grasslin timer I use (**Figure 10**) fits into a standard electrical box, and can be programmed to turn on in 20-minute intervals. It can also be manually turned on and off. The timer needs a separate 2x4-inch electrical box, as the cover doesn't fit a ganged box.

Another good option is the Tamarack Airetrak timer (Tamarack Technologies). This timer is a bit more expensive, but it allows the fan to cycle for part of every hour at full or reduced speed. You select the fraction of the hour, plus the speed of the fan. A single push-button allows you to bump up the fan to full speed for 20 minutes when the bathroom is being used.

Inlet Installation

Since the fans are exhausting air from the house, makeup air must be supplied through inlets. Although there are other air inlets on the market, I use Fresh-80s (Therma-Stor, **Figure 11**). These are relatively inexpensive, easy to install, and have several good features, including an adjustable damper and an easy-to-get-to filter to keep out dust.

Install one air inlet in each bedroom and in any "extra" rooms such as home offices, dens, or other perimeter rooms that will be occupied. The goal is to move air from perimeter rooms toward the bathrooms. If the living room doesn't have any exterior doors, install an inlet in the living room as well. A typical small house will have three or four inlets.

Locate the inlet as near the ceiling as possible, and keep away from beds, couches, or other locations where cool, incoming air might be uncomfortable to occupants. Over a window is ideal, but this may mean drilling a big hole in a header, which isn't a great idea. If there isn't room over the header, locate the inlet anywhere in the exterior wall near the window. Keep the inlets near operable windows so that the vent's outside louver and screen can be cleaned (as often as once a year) by sticking a vacuum cleaner hose out the window.

These inlets install easily by drilling a 3 1/4-inch hole through the drywall, sheathing, and siding. The plastic duct that goes through the wall telescopes to fit various wall thicknesses. Caulk the duct to the drywall to keep moist air from getting into the insulation, and to the siding or trim to keep water out. For retrofit work, it's worth taking the time to align the hole so the outside grille, which is 4 1/4 inches square, fits on one clapboard. For new construction, install the inlet before the siding goes on so you can plan a 1-by block to go under the grille.

Be sure the inlets are away from garages, exhaust vents, or any other source of noxious fumes. Also be sure the doors in rooms with an air inlet and in the bathrooms are undercut a minimum of 3/4 inch (1 inch is better) above finish floor height (including carpet) so that air can move through the room with the door closed.

Once the inlets are installed, adjust the inlet for maximum opening. With the filter, the outside screen, and the inside diffuser, these inlets don't let in very much air, and they don't do much at all if they are only partially open. The Fresh-80 has a string to open and close the inside diffuser. I usually open the diffuser, then wind up the string and stick it inside, so no one closes the inlet.

Backdrafting Cautions

An important caution about any exhaust-only ventilation system is the potential for backdrafting fireplaces, wood stoves, and natural-draft appliances, such as gas boilers and furnaces. While the negative pressure created by the Panasonic fans is quite low — much lower than that induced by a clothes dryer or most range hoods — there is still a chance for backdrafting when the bath fans, the dryer, and the range hood all run at once. The best way to avoid this is to use only sealed-combustion fuel burners and to supply combustion air to wood stoves and fireplaces.

Also, if the house is leaky, the fan will draw air from the nearest air leak. In this case, the inlets will not do their job, and the ventilation effect will be very localized. Dropped ceilings in the bathrooms can be a disaster — a leaky dropped ceiling can provide all the air the fan draws, leaving the rest of the house without any ventilation. In general, exhaust-only ventilation works well with houses with a natural leakage rate of about 1/4 to 1/2 ACH (air changes per hour). This includes most reasonably tight new homes, built with vapor barriers and good seals around windows, band joists, and ceiling penetrations, such as vent stacks, chimney chases, and attic hatches. Older homes that are not built to these tightness standards should be air-sealed by a qualified weatherization contractor before retrofitting a ventilation system.

Andrew Shapiro is an energy and sustainable design consultant and principal of Energy Balance, in Montpelier, Vt.

Installing a Heat-Recovery Ventilator

by David Hansen

Poorly ventilated homes can have high levels of humidity, pollutants, and mold. Most homes depend on random cracks or exhaust-only systems for ventilation, but today's techniques for building tighter homes have made random cracks less common, and exhaust-only ventilation systems have a few disadvantages: They can contribute to backdrafting problems in combustion appliances, and they may draw their supply air from undesirable locations like basements or crawlspaces.

The best way to improve indoor air quality is to provide a balanced ventilation system that includes a heat-recovery ventilator, or HRV. Such a ventilation system will create a gentle circulation of fresh air throughout the home, will lower the levels of indoor air pollutants, and will eliminate odors and window condensation.

How They Work

An HRV exhausts stale air from a house at a calculated rate, while simultaneously bringing in the same amount of fresh makeup air. The two airstreams pass each other in the heat-exchange core, allowing much of the heat energy in the stale air to be transferred to the fresh incoming air, without any mixing of the airstreams (**Figure 12**). In an air conditioned home in a hot climate, an HRV lowers the temperature of the incoming air by transferring some of its heat to the cooler exhaust air.

Core design. The heart of an HRV is its heat-exchanger core. Today's residential HRVs use one of three different core designs: a parallel-plate counterflow core, a parallel-plate crossflow core, or a rotary wheel core (**Figure 13**). Parallel-plate cores, whether counterflow or crossflow, are made of aluminum, plastic, or, in the case of an energy-recovery ventilator, a moisture-permeable membrane (see "Hot Climate Ventilation With ERVs," page 348).

Some manufacturers tout the theoretical superiority of one core design or material over another. In practice, however, HRV efficiency depends upon many design factors, not just core geometry or material type. The best resource for comparing HRV efficiencies is the *Certified Home Ventilating Products Directory* published by the Home Ventilating Institute (available online at www.hvi.org, or by calling 847/526-2010). When choosing an HRV, small differences of efficiency may be less important than the level of service provided by a local ventilation contractor.

Frost formation. When the outdoor temperature drops below about 20°F, the incoming air is so cold that frost can build up in an HRV core. All HRVs have a defrost cycle to avoid frost problems. When

Figure 12. In an HRV with a parallel-plate core, like this model from Venmar, the incoming fresh air and outgoing exhaust air pass through alternating layers of the core, which is composed of stacked air channels separated by thin plates of plastic or aluminum. Although there is no mixing of the airstreams, heat is transferred from one airstream to the other.

an outdoor temperature sensor detects cold weather, a control module activates a defrost damper, which shuts for about six minutes every half hour. When the defrost damper is shut, the stale air recirculates through the HRV, thawing the core.

Energy performance. Because an HRV recovers some of the heat from exhaust air, it uses less energy than a ventilation system without heat recovery. Nevertheless, a home with an HRV uses more energy than a home without a ventilation system.

An HRV draws between 85 and 225 watts of electrical power. Most HRVs are only about 60% to 75% efficient at recovering the heat from exhausted air, although some models can achieve efficiencies of up to 90%. HRV operating costs, including the cost of the electrical power and the cost to temper the ventilation air, range from about $160 to $200 a year or more, depending on climate and electricity costs.

Ducting Options

An HRV system can be ducted one of several ways, depending on the existing heating system and the customer's budget. The three most common types of systems are simplified systems, modified systems, and fully ducted systems.

In a simplified system (installed in a home with forced-air heating or air conditioning), the HRV unit pulls stale air out of the main return duct of the forced-air system and introduces the fresh air downstream a few feet, in the furnace's return plenum. A

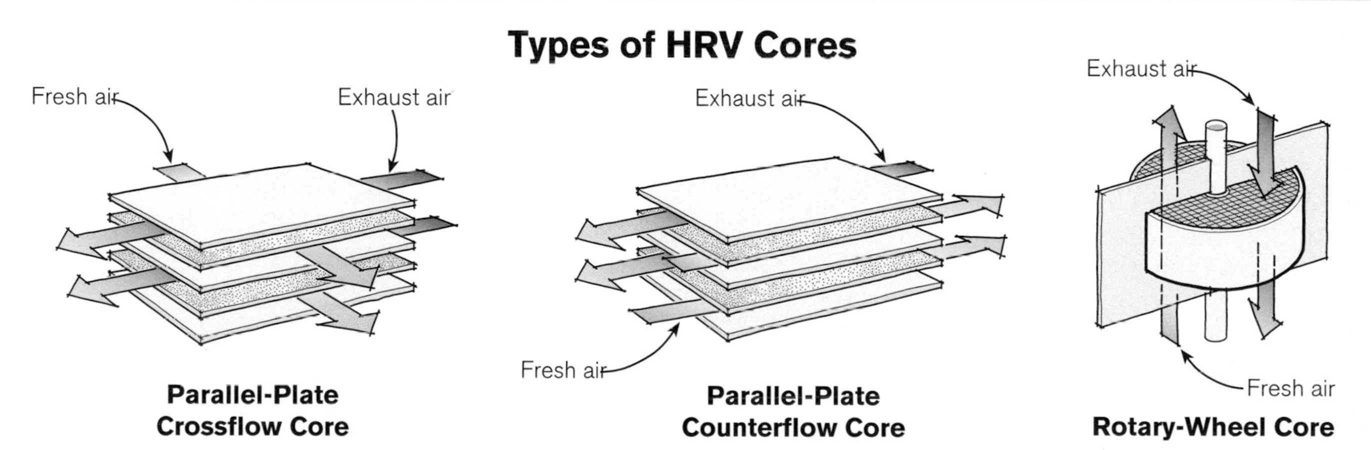

Figure 13. All three types of HRV cores are designed to encourage some of the heat from the exhaust air to be transferred to the incoming fresh air. There are two types of parallel-plate cores: In a crossflow core (left), the airstreams cross at right angles, while in a counterflow core (center), the airstreams travel in opposite directions. Parallel-plate cores can be made from either aluminum or plastic. A rotary-wheel core (right) has enough thermal mass to absorb and release heat as the wheel turns through the two separated airstreams.

Figure 14. Each wall-mounted fresh-air and stale-air register requires a rectangular duct fitting called a stackhead. Stackheads are installed 1/2 inch proud of the joists, like electrical boxes.

simplified system does not provide point-source control of moisture or pollutants.

A modified system, which is an improvement over a simplified system, introduces fresh air into the forced-air duct system while exhausting stale air from the bathrooms.

A fully ducted system — the type described here — is typically installed in a home with hydronic heat, and requires two duct systems dedicated to ventilation: one to exhaust stale air from areas that produce most of the moisture or pollutants, and another to supply fresh air to the living spaces.

Sizing an HRV

To size an HRV unit, first check whether any local ventilation code applies. My company generally uses ASHRAE Standard 62-1989, which recommends between 0.35 and 0.5 air changes per hour (see "Sizing Ventilation Fans," page 342). To apply this standard, we start by calculating the volume of the house, using the following formula: square feet x ceiling height x .85. (This formula reduces the house's gross volume by 15% to account for interior walls and furniture.) To find the necessary ventilation airflow, we multiply the net volume by the design air-change rate (0.5 ac/h) and divide by 60 (to convert cubic feet per minute to air changes per hour). With this information, we can select an appropriate HRV, using the airflow fan curves supplied by the manufacturer for specific HRV models. The fan curve represents the amount of air a specific fan can move, depending on the resistance of the duct system.

Residential HRV systems move relatively small volumes of air. In most homes up to about 3,500 square feet, the total design airflow will be less than 200 cfm, with each bedroom receiving 25 cfm or less. For the main ducts, 6-inch round duct, which has a maximum airflow capacity of 180 cfm, is usually sufficient. When moving such low volumes of air, it's important for ducts to be as short, smooth, and airtight as possible. Every extra foot of duct and every elbow or transition adds resistance (or static pressure) to the airflow. If plans are available, the ducts can be laid out on paper, although their final locations are best determined on site.

Laying Out the Ductwork

Ventilation ducts can be installed once the interior walls are framed. We try to be on site during the plumbing rough-in. Sometimes locating a pipe just a few inches to one side can make enough of a difference to allow a duct to fit into a tight joist bay. In a pinch, a wall can be shimmed out to make room for ducts to get past the plumbing or a chase can be located inside a closet, but by communicating with the plumber, we usually avoid such steps.

Locating the registers. Stale air is exhausted from bathrooms, the laundry, and the kitchen. (An HRV is not intended to handle grease or smoke, so a range hood should be separately exhausted to the exterior.) Fresh air is supplied to the bedrooms, living room, and other living areas. We try to locate bedroom registers away from the bed.

When we rough-in our duct drops, we always work from the top floor down. We locate both the fresh-air and the stale-air registers high on a wall or in the ceiling. After choosing tentative locations for the registers, we follow the intended duct routes down to the basement, to be sure there are no unworkable obstacles.

Figure 15. Because this is a fresh-air duct, the crimped end of the duct points toward the stackhead. The photo shows two styles of 90° ells that can be used to make the transition from oval duct to round: The ell at the top of the photo is a longways ell, while the ell at the bottom is a shortways ell.

Figure 16. Ventilation systems remove relatively small volumes of air, so ducts should be as airtight as possible. All galvanized duct connections should be secured with sheet-metal screws and aluminum tape.

Figure 17. Where an oval duct penetrates a floor, aerosol foam helps secure the stack to the framing.

In most cases, all the fresh- and stale-air registers are wall-mounted 6x10 registers, and each gets its own separate duct down to the basement. To keep airflows as high as possible, we use 6-inch duct for stale-air pickups. For fresh-air supplies into bedrooms, 4-inch ducts are usually adequate.

We use mainly 30-gauge galvanized ductwork. In 2x4 partitions, we use 6-inch oval duct, which measures 3 1/2 x 7 1/2 inches and comes in 5-foot lengths. Oval duct has a smaller airflow capacity than round but is perfectly adequate for the individual wall stacks. Each register mounts in a 6x10-inch stackhead, a duct fitting that makes the transition from a rectangular register to oval duct.

Installing the Ducts

Stackheads are installed 1/2 inch proud of the studs, like electrical boxes (**Figure 14**). On most jobs, the top of the stackhead is installed about 4 1/2 inches down from the top of the wall. If the room will receive crown molding, we install the stackhead lower.

The crimped end of a stale-air duct always points toward the HRV unit, while the crimped end of a fresh-air duct points the opposite way, toward the stackhead (**Figure 15**). By consistently following this system, we can distinguish between stale-air and fresh-air ducts in the basement just by looking at which direction the crimped end is pointing.

We secure every galvanized duct connection with two or three 1/2-inch sheet-metal screws and aluminum duct tape (**Figure 16**). We've had good success with #1520 CW foil HVAC tape (Venture Tape Corp.), which is easy to apply because it has a paper release backing.

We extend all the stacks, both fresh and stale, down from the stackheads into the basement. Wherever an oval duct passes through the top plate of a wall, we use a piece of plumber's strapping to secure the duct to the plate. Because sweep ells for oval pipe take up too much room, we transition from oval to round duct as soon as possible, using straight transition fittings or transition elbows. Once the stacks are installed, we use aerosol foam to seal the gaps between the ducts and the bottom plates. This helps stop air leakage between floors and secures the stack to the framing (**Figure 17**).

PVC ducts. In houses where the installation of wall-mounted registers is difficult, we often install round ceiling-mounted diffusers, working from the attic. Since attic ducts, being cool in winter, are prone to condensation, we use 4- or 6-inch thin-wall PVC (sewer and drain pipe, type ASTM D 2729) for all attic ducts. (Because PVC is available in 10-foot lengths, it's also useful wherever a long section of straight duct is needed.) If condensation occurs, the glued joints of the PVC will prevent leaks. We always insulate any ducts that run through unheated space.

We like to use PVC pipe made by Flying "W" Plastics because it is thinner than some other brands, making it easier to slide 6-inch galvanized duct into the pipe. To ease the transition, we chamfer the inside edge of the PVC pipe with a utility knife. The connection is then secured with screws and sealed with aluminum tape.

Wiring

Once we've roughed-in the stacks to the basement, we install the low-voltage control wiring, following the manufacturer's instructions. Usually, we run 4-conductor wire from the location of the HRV unit to each bathroom and laundry for an override timer, which permits the exhaust ventilation fan to be controlled from the bathroom. These override timers are located next to the room's light switch. We install a separate run of wire for the main control, which is usually located near the central thermostat on the first floor, about 5 feet from the floor.

Most residential HRV units come with a cord and a plug, so we coordinate with the electrician for the installation of a standard duplex receptacle near the HRV unit. When the stacks are installed and the wiring is complete, the first stage of our work is finished. We usually return later to complete the basement ducts and install the HRV unit.

Basement Ducts

In the basement, the various stale-air wall stacks are connected to a main round duct running to the HRV. A second main duct connects all of the fresh-air supply stacks. For most residential jobs, all basement ducts, galvanized or PVC, are 6-inch round ducts.

We determine the main duct run locations and then position a wye along this line with the leg of the wye pointing up into the joist bay of the stale-air stack nearest the unit. For galvanized ducts, we use #160 wyes, which come with three uncrimped ends, and crimp the ends as required. Because galvanized wyes aren't airtight, we seal all joints in a wye with silicone caulk, duct mastic, or aluminum tape before installation (**Figure 18**).

We then fasten the wye to a length of duct and use perforated nylon strapping to hang the duct from the floor joist. By adding adjustable elbows as necessary, we aim the branch of the wye toward the oval stack boot. The main duct runs should end near, but a little short of, the HRV unit. Once the ducts have been installed, we seal all connections not secured by aluminum tape, including the joints in adjustable elbows, with duct sealant or silicone caulk.

Hot-Climate Ventilation With ERVs

An energy-recovery ventilator, or ERV, is a special type of HRV that tempers the extremes of humidity in the incoming fresh air. Like an HRV, an ERV transfers heat between the two streams of air passing through the ERV core. But an ERV also transfers some of the moisture from the more humid stream of air to the drier stream of air.

In winter, when outdoor air is usually dry, an ERV increases the humidity of the incoming air, while in summer, when outdoor air is usually more humid, an ERV can lower the humidity of the incoming air, as long as the house is air conditioned. (In a house without air conditioning, the humidity levels of the indoor and outdoor air are essentially the same, so an ERV can't help lower humidity.)

ERVs are recommended for air conditioned homes in hot, humid climates. In cold climates, where winter indoor air can be humid enough to cause window condensation, one of the main goals of a ventilation system is to lower indoor humidity levels. For that purpose, an HRV makes more sense than an ERV. For the same reason, ERVs are not recommended for pool or spa rooms, where HRVs are more appropriate.

An ERV core, sometimes called an *enthalpic* core, can be either a fixed core or a rotary-wheel core, and is usually made of treated paper or polyester fiber. Rotary ERV cores are often impregnated with a desiccant to improve moisture transfer. — *D.H.*

Installing the HRV Unit

The HRV unit is generally located inside the tempered space of the building, usually in the basement mechanical space close to the outside ports. Other possible locations include a closet, laundry room, workshop, top-floor knee-wall area, or even a garage. We usually hang it from the ceiling joists.

We avoid the use of flex duct as much as possible, because its interior corrugations impede airflow. However, because insulated flex duct prevents problems with condensation drips, we use it to connect the HRV unit to the outside vent hoods. The flex duct needs to be sealed to both the HRV unit and the house vapor retarder. We also use short lengths of noninsulated vinyl flex duct to connect the HRV unit to the house ducts.

We keep our flex duct runs as short as possible, and we always seal any rips or tears in the outside cover of the flex duct. (If moist interior air comes in contact with the cold fresh air in the intake duct, condensation will saturate the duct insulation.) Where flex duct connects with the HRV unit, we seal the connection with silicone caulk and screw the duct to the collar on the HRV.

Outside vent hoods. Exterior vent hoods protect the intake and exhaust ports from weather and animals (**Figure 19**). A 6-inch exhaust duct needs a 6-inch or equivalent exterior hood, not a 4-inch dryer vent. The vent hood should include a cleanable rodent screen made from 1/4-inch hardware cloth. We usually install Jenn-Air wall caps (see Sources of Supply, page 397).

The two outside vents are typically installed through the basement rim joist, level with one another. They should be located at least 6 feet apart to minimize the chance of the fresh-air intake pulling back any stale air. Sometimes a corner of the building can be used to better separate the fresh-air intake from the exhaust port. The fresh-air port should be as far as possible from any combustion flues, dryer exhaust vents, and places where cars may idle. An exhaust vent can be located under a deck or porch, but we avoid pulling fresh air from an enclosed space.

Since we usually install the vent hoods on trim blocks, we prefer to schedule this part of the work before the siding is on. We use a short (about 6- to 12-inch) section of 6-inch PVC pipe (including a bell end) to connect the insulated flex duct to the vent hood. We cut a series of 1-inch slots, about $1^1/_2$ inches apart, in the male end of the pipe section, and then slip the flex duct over the PVC. The connection is sealed with aluminum tape and screws. We insert the bell end of the PVC through the hole in the building, flush with the outside face of the trim block. The Jenn-Air hood is then inserted into the PVC. We always seal the gap where the PVC duct penetrates the building with aerosol foam.

Registers. Once the drywall has been painted, we install the various controls and registers. The controls are installed according to the manufacturer's instructions.

Both stale-air and fresh-air registers require a damper to allow airflow balancing. For wall-mounted registers, we use either a Lima 12V register (Lima Register) or a Hart & Cooley 661 register (Hart & Cooley). We check the registers with a level before fastening them with screws through the ears of the stackhead. To provide better air distribution and hide the inside of the stackhead, we always adjust the register dampers to direct the airflow up toward the ceiling.

For round ceiling registers, we use molded plastic Scandinavian-style diffusers. These are secured to the inside of the round PVC duct with sheet-metal screws. Then we spin in the trim ring, making a friction fit, and adjust the damper rings to about three-fourths of the full opening size.

Figure 19. An HRV system requires two exterior ports, an intake port and an exhaust port. These identical 6-inch ports are protected by vent hoods and are usually located at the rim joist. Locate them at least 6 feet apart to avoid cross contamination.

Figure 18. Galvanized #160 wyes come with three uncrimped ends and are crimped as required on site. As purchased (left), the wyes are not airtight, so all seams should be sealed with caulk before installation (right).

Balancing. Once the installation is complete, the system must be tested for airflow balance. Small airflows are hard to test, but most manufacturers provide a recommended balancing procedure, generally requiring the use of an airflow measuring station or unit-mounted pressure taps and a calibrated magnehelic gauge.

The final step of any job is an important one: homeowner instruction. We provide the homeowner with the operation manual and an on-site orientation, explaining:

- control operation (most HRVs can be set for intermittent operation, low-speed continuous operation, or high-speed continuous operation);
- humidistat function (most HRVs include a humidistat that automatically operates the fan at high speed when the indoor humidity rises above a user-adjustable level);
- the filter cleaning schedule (every three months, HRV filters should be vacuumed, washed, or replaced); and
- the importance of keeping the outside intake and exhaust ports free of leaves and mulch.

David Hansen is the owner of Memphremagog Heat Exchangers, a ventilation contractor in Newport, Vt.

TROUBLESHOOTING

Chapter 19: Wood Moisture Content

C. BATES

- Wood and Moisture: Facts and Fiction
- Framing Details for Wood Shrinkage
- Wood Shrinkage and Interior Finishes

Wood and Moisture: Facts and Fiction

by Paul Fisette

As builders, we spend much of our time cutting wood, carrying it around the job site, or pounding it full of nails. We think of ourselves as wood experts. But even experts can be mistaken, and you may be surprised to learn that some of what you know about wood and moisture is wrong. Here, we'll consider some common notions about wood, and see how they compare with the cold, hard facts.

MYTH: KD (kiln-dry) and S-DRY (surfaced-dry) means dry lumber.

Virtually all problems with wood-based building materials are moisture related. Peeling paint, rot, warping, cracks, and general shrinkage can all be attributed to the presence of water in wood. Wood swells and shrinks in response to liquid water and relative humidity. Conventional wisdom tells us that when wood absorbs water it swells, and when wood dries it shrinks. But this will occur only when the wood is below its fiber saturation point, which is around a 28% moisture content.

We don't normally work with "green," fully swollen lumber. Part of the price we pay for lumber includes the manufacturer's cost to remove at least some of the moisture. The lower cost of S-GRN (surfaced-green) lumber may look like a good deal, but you're actually buying shrinkage problems and callbacks. The S-GRN designation indicates that the wood was surfaced to its finished shape when the moisture content was above 19%. How much above 19% is anyone's guess. I've been called in to examine rotten joists in brand-new homes (**Figure 1**). In a case I saw recently, S-GRN Douglas fir 2x10s were shipped from the West Coast, stacked for months, and then installed in a rotted state. The installed moisture content was over 50%, and the remedy was very expensive.

It's important to match the moisture content (MC) of the wood you're using with the equilibrium condi-

Ideal Moisture Content for Exterior Wood (% EMC)

	Temperature °F (°C)						
	30 (-1.1)	50 (10.0)	70 (21.1)	90 (32.2)	110 (43.3)	130 (54.4)	150 (65.6)
5% RH	1.4	1.4	1.3	1.2	1.1	1	0.9
10% RH	2.6	2.6	2.5	2.3	2.2	2	1.8
15% RH	3.7	3.6	3.5	3.4	3.2	2.9	2.6
20% RH	4.6	4.6	4.5	4.3	4	3.7	3.4
25% RH	5.5	5.5	5.4	5.1	4.9	4.5	4.1
30% RH	6.3	6.3	6.2	5.9	5.6	5.2	4.8
35% RH	7.1	7.1	6.9	6.7	6.3	5.9	5.5
40% RH	7.9	7.9	7.7	7.4	7	6.6	6.1
45% RH	8.7	8.7	8.5	8.1	7.7	7.2	6.7
50% RH	9.5	9.5	9.2	8.9	8.4	7.9	7.4
55% RH	10.4	10.3	10.1	9.7	9.2	8.7	8.1
60% RH	11.3	11.2	11	10.5	10	9.4	8.8
65% RH	12.4	12.3	12	11.5	11	10.3	9.7
70% RH	13.5	13.4	13.1	12.6	12	11.3	10.6
75% RH	14.9	14.8	14.4	13.9	13.2	12.5	11.8
80% RH	16.5	16.4	16	15.4	14.7	14	13.1
85% RH	18.5	18.4	17.9	17.3	16.6	15.8	14.9
90% RH	21	20.9	20.5	19.8	19.1	18.2	17.2
95% RH	24.3	24.3	23.9	23.3	22.4	21.5	20.4

If exterior wood is applied while it is too dry or too wet for local temperature and humidity, it will swell or shrink more than usual. To prevent excessive movement, find the intersection of the temperature (top row) and relative humidity (left column). Compare the resulting number, which is called the equilibrium moisture content (EMC), to a moisture meter reading of the wood you intend to install. For example, at a temperature of 70°F at 45% relative humidity, the EMC of the wood is 8.5%. Wood drier than that will swell after installation; wetter wood will shrink.

Figure 1. The S-DRY stamp (top) doesn't necessarily guarantee this wood is dry — just that the wood's moisture content was below 19% when it was surfaced. Even a KD stamp doesn't necessarily mean much: Lumber stored in moist conditions (center) can reach the job site with moisture levels above 50%. These joists (above), stamped S-DRY, began to rot before the house was completed.

tions it will see in service. Framers usually work with lumber stamped S-DRY (surfaced-dry) or KD (kiln-dry), which means that the lumber was surfaced when moisture content was at or below 19%. Some material is stamped MC-15 or KD-15, for lumber surfaced at 15% moisture content or lower. But these designations only indicate the moisture content of the lumber when it was manufactured, and not necessarily its current percentage. The moisture content of lumber can soar when it's stored at a lumberyard without a protective cover, stacked over wet ground, or stored in a very humid environment, like next to a body of water. A KD stamp doesn't mean much if the lumber has been stored under these conditions. To avoid problems, spot-check the lumber you're using with a moisture meter before you put interior wallboard up.

Wood used for interior finishes such as trim, cabinets, and flooring, should be installed at an MC close to 8%. Wood used in exterior applications is a different story — it depends on where you live. In New England, 14% MC is a good target. In Tucson, a 6% MC would be a better mark. The USDA Forest Products Laboratory in Madison has a pamphlet (FPL-RN-0268) listing the outdoor equilibrium moisture content (EMC) for about 350 cities worldwide. To be certain that you're working with sufficiently dry lumber, benchmark the in-service moisture content to the relative humidity of your area (see table, facing page).

MYTH: Wood is destroyed by dry rot.

There really is no such thing as dry rot. Wood decay has three requirements: water, oxygen, and favorable temperature (40°F to 105°F). Wood can be too wet to decay. Marine pilings kept fully submerged may never rot, for instance, because waterlogged wood won't allow oxygen in to support the growth of fungi. And wood can be too dry to decay. Keep wood below 22% MC and you are generally safe. But the fact remains: Wood needs water to rot.

Carpenters replacing a sill or corner post in an old house often find a brown, crumbly rot they call dry rot. It may be dry when it's discovered, but don't be fooled. There was or is a moisture problem that needs fixing. Most likely there is intermittent wetting. A source of moisture is to blame, so inspect carefully for signs of leakage, dampness, or chronic condensation. There are a few strains of fungi that have water-conducting strands that carry water from soil into building elements, but these forms are quite rare.

MYTH: Rot is catchy.

If you install a new stick of lumber against a piece of rotted wood, the new piece of lumber may begin to rot. But it won't be because the rot is "contagious"; it will rot because the new lumber is now exposed to the conditions that caused the existing wood to rot. Rot fungi are "seeded" by the spread of single-celled spores. These spores are everywhere. Essentially all wood is exposed to the seed stock, but only when conditions are right will the infection develop into rot. The moisture content of wood needs to be above 28% to be initially infected. Since all lumber is above 28% moisture content at some point in its life, all lumber is infected. When the moisture content of wood drops below 22%, the rot fungi goes dormant. It's harmless, but it will be reactivated when the moisture content rises above 22%. The solution: Keep wood dry or kill the fungi with a chemical treatment.

MYTH: Install decking boards bark-side up.

There's no shortage of conflicting advice on this topic. Some manufacturers insist that boards should be installed with the bark-side up. An equal number say bark-side down. The truth is, it depends.

The moisture content of the board when it's installed and its exposure after installation control a board's shape. Wood shrinks and swells twice as much in the direction parallel to the growth rings as it does perpendicular to them. The combined effect of these different rates of movement causes lumber to warp, twist, and deform. Deck boards are typically flat sawn, so they are very likely to cup. A good way to remember how wood cups is to imagine that growth rings try to straighten out as a wet board dries. So if you install a wet piece of lumber (like most treated decks) with its bark-side up, it will cup to hold water as it dries. However, a dry board moves in the opposite direction when it gains moisture. Dry lumber installed bark-side up will arch up to shed water as it gets wet.

Figure 2. It makes little difference whether growth rings are installed up or down — the wood will cup either way because the bottom dries more slowly than the top. Install the best-looking face up.

Decay resistance is a consideration, too. Heartwood is more resistant to decay than sapwood. Clearly you would want to install lumber bark-side down to expose the more resistant heartwood portion of the board to the elements. But heartwood is difficult to treat with wood-preserving chemicals, and sapwood is easy to treat. It follows that treated wood should be installed bark-side up.

Growth rings are made of earlywood and latewood layers. The more central layer of each growth ring is made during the early part of the growing season. Repeated cycles of wetting and drying can cause the earlywood to separate from latewood. Known as "shelling," it's most likely to occur in flat-sawn yellow pine and Douglas fir that is installed bark-side down.

Knots originate at the center of the tree. They sometimes show on the pith side of a board and not on the bark side. So if you want to see fewer knots, install all boards bark-side up. But wane results on the bark side of a board. To reduce the probability of exposed wane, install boards bark-side down.

Fluctuating humidity and exposure affects the stability of wood. The underside of a deck sees damp ground and high humidity. The upper surface is baked by the sun and dried by prevailing winds. This action causes boards to cup and hold water, whether installed bark-side up or bark-side down.

The soundest advice is to pick the best-looking surface and install the decking best-face up (**Figure 2**). Securely fasten the deck boards and apply an annual coating of water repellent.

MYTH: Cedar and redwood are rot-resistant.

Unfinished cedar is widely hailed as a low- to no-maintenance exterior finished surface. Don't get me wrong; cedar is my choice for siding, too. But let's get something straight: Not all lumber with a reputation for durability is actually rot-resistant. Only the heartwood of certain species is naturally decay-resistant, while untreated sapwood, regardless of species, has very little decay resistance (**Figure 3**).

Large old-growth trees are a thing of the past. We now harvest smaller, second-growth material that contains a high percentage of sapwood. Heartwood lumber is all but unavailable in many species — specify "all-heart" and you may be in for a dose of sticker shock. But if durability is important to your design, you should make heartwood part of your budget.

It's difficult to rate precisely the decay resistance of heartwood for different species, but broad groupings have been made, based on years of research and field performance. Common woods considered to be decay-resistant include: all cedars, old-growth redwood, old-growth bald cypress, white oak, and locust. The heartwood of these species generally provides rot-free performance in the untreated state.

Figure 3. It may be cedar (top), but the abundance of sapwood means it's not highly rot-proof. To improve rot resistance, specify "all heartwood" (above).

Water-repellent treatment is still a good idea on all species of wood exposed to the weather, because it helps keep wood dimensionally stable.

MYTH: It's best to let siding weather for several weeks before painting.

Simply put, weathering is the deterioration of wood. Don't allow wood to weather before you paint. Research conducted by the Forest Products Laboratory clearly shows that even a three-week exposure to sun and rain is too much for new wood (**Figure 4**). Ultraviolet radiation from the sun alters chemicals in the wood and destroys lignin — the natural glue that holds wood cells together. Loosened wood fibers and decomposition of the surface prevent good bonding between paint and wood.

Figure 4. Don't let the wood "weather" before painting. For long-term adhesion, paint exterior wood immediately if not sooner — and don't fail to back-prime.

In addition, when raw wood sucks moisture from rain, dew, and high humidity, it swells. When the sun quickly dries surface fibers, they shrink. As a result, the surface is stressed, so when it's painted at a later time, the paint is much more likely to peel.

Siding must be dry and clean before it is painted. Weathered wood should be sanded and washed. On the other hand, weathered wood is not such a bad idea if you plan to stain the siding, because loose fibers and the roughened texture absorb penetrating stains better.

MYTH: A deck built with pressure-treated wood will last a long time.

Promotional literature promises lifelong performance for pressure-treated wood. The Forest Products Laboratory and other research groups have shown that treated wood stakes placed in the ground for more than 40 years remain rot-free. Nevertheless, young pressure-treated deck surfaces, many less than 10 years old, are being shoveled into landfills. In fact, a technical report in the *Forest Products Journal* (Nov./Dec. 1998) indicated that the average pressure-treated deck lasts only nine years. Why?

CSI ULTRAWOOD

Figure 5. Just because it's pressure-treated doesn't mean it will last forever (top). For wood that is less likely to cup, warp, and split, use PT wood that is dried after treatment — stamped KDAT (above).

Pressure treating does make wood rot-resistant, but it doesn't make wood water-resistant. Pressure-treated wood still absorbs and loses moisture. As a result, the wood moves, cracks, twists, cups, and can eventually tear itself apart. However, a pressure-treated deck can last a long time; all it takes is a little extra care during installation and a yearly dose of maintenance.

Keep the wood stable by applying a coat of water repellent onto all surfaces before installation. Securely fasten the deck boards with corrosion-resistant screws, such as double-dipped hot galvanized or, better yet, stainless steel. Brush-treat raw wood that's exposed when cutting and drilling. Advise your customers to re-treat the tops of the boards with a new application of water repellent every year. The water repellent will keep the boards looking bright and will minimize the uptake of water. As a result, the boards will have fewer cracks, splits, cups, and twists.

Better yet, buy treated wood that has water-repellent chemicals included as part of the pressure-treating process. UltraWood (Chemical Specialties Inc.) and Wolmanized Extra (Arch Wood Protection) are two examples of this product. The repellent gets injected deep into the wood along with the preservative. This type of decking is likely to perform better for a longer period of time. In fact, UltraWood guarantees water repellency for 50 years. I'm a skeptic, but that is quite a promise.

It's a great idea to purchase KDAT lumber (kiln-dried after treatment) whenever the budget allows (**Figure 5**). You will have less initial shrinkage, and the deck will look much nicer for years. These recommendations are good for all wood decks, but apply in particular to pressure-treated southern pine.

MYTH: When you buy mahogany, you get mahogany.

Order mahogany at your local lumberyard and you'll probably get a pretender. True American mahogany (*Swietenia* spp.) comes from the West Indies, Mexico, Central America, and South America. It is a premium furniture and shipbuilding material, and it's prized for its beautiful dark red appearance, dimensional stability, termite resistance, machining qualities, and decay resistance. A related African mahogany (*Khaya* spp.) is also available, but it is not as durable as true mahogany.

The real problem is that many lumberyards sell you meranti (*Shorea* spp.) as mahogany (**Figure 6**). Merchants separate 125 species of *Shorea* into 4 groups according to color and weight: dark red, light red, white, and yellow. The grain is usually interlocked, which makes grain direction unpredictable. White meranti dulls cutters because it has a high silica content. The dark red and yellow varieties tend to warp. Dark red is only moderately resistant to rot, and light red, white, and yellow versions are not durable in exposed conditions. So if you buy mahogany clapboards or decking, beware. Ask about the species.

Figure 6. A durable mahogany deck? Actually, it's meranti, a wood from the Philippines that is often sold as mahogany. Unlike Honduras mahogany, it has to be maintained with water repellent to resist movement and decay.

MYTH: Durability is the same as strength.

Technically, durability refers to the ability of wood to resist rot. It can describe the ability of a finish to protect wood products from the exposures that cause rot, or it can describe the wood itself. The term is also used to explain the character of a glued connection, as in the durability rating of a glue-laminated beam. But durability should not be confused with strength. Rot-resistant species are not particularly strong.

MYTH: Pressure-treated lumber is resistant to attack by termites and carpenter ants.

This assumption is half-true. Entomological studies have shown that arsenical treatments like the CCA commonly used in pressure-treated lumber do repel and can kill termites. However, termites may also decide to tube around CCA-treated wood and survive to enjoy the more delicate studs and joists that lay beyond the poisoned barrier.

Arsenical treatments do not repel or kill carpenter ants. Ants are attracted to wet and decayed wood because it's soft, weak, and easy to chew. That's why ants also like foam insulation. Ants don't ingest wood, they simply hollow out wood and nest in it. CCA is fixed tightly to wood fiber, so it's not accessible to ants.

Borate-treated wood is a different story. Borates are very soluble and can be picked up by ants as they work their way through the treated wood. The borates are ingested when ants groom themselves, and this poisons them. The characteristic differences of borates and CCA are significant in other ways. Since CCA is held tightly by wood fiber, it provides very permanent protection from rot in moist environments. Borates will leach out of wood that's in contact with wet surfaces, eventually leaving it unprotected.

Paul Fisette is a wood technologist and professor with the Building Materials and Wood Technology program at the University of Massachusetts in Amherst.

Framing Details for Wood Shrinkage

by David Frane

Early in my carpentry career, I was asked to remove all the trim from the third-floor hallway of a 140-year-old house we were renovating. All the baseboards in the hallway were touching the floor, except for one piece, which was 2 inches off the floor. It didn't make sense until I had removed the baseboard in the hallway. While most of the walls consisted of plaster and lath over studs, the wall behind the base that didn't touch the floor was plaster over a brick chimney. When the house was originally built, the air-dried framing lumber dried and shrank, and all of the third floor dropped except for that one piece of baseboard fastened to the chimney.

Today, most builders frame with kiln-dried stock. But if you think that means you don't have to be concerned about wood shrinkage, think again: Kiln-dried lumber will definitely shrink. How much depends on its moisture content at the time of installation (see "Calculating Shrinkage," next page). And as the lumber shrinks, it tends to twist and bow, causing humps and nail pops in walls, and bumpy, squeaky, out-of-level floors.

Understanding Wood Shrinkage

Moisture affects wood the same way it affects a sponge. If you take a sopping-wet sponge and wring it out, you'll remove some of the water, though not enough to change the sponge's size. But if you let the damp sponge dry out, it will shrink.

In a piece of wood, moisture resides both in the cell cavities and in the cell walls. Green wood is like a sopping-wet sponge: As it dries, the moisture in the cavities is the first to go. But, as with the sponge, this doesn't cause the wood to shrink. The point at which there is moisture in cell walls, but not in cell cavities, is called the *fiber saturation point*. Below this level, the wood (like the sponge) will shrink as it dries, and then swell as it absorbs moisture.

The amount of moisture in a piece of wood is referred to as its *moisture content* (MC). Moisture content is the ratio of the weight of the moisture in a piece of wood to the weight of the piece of wood if all of the moisture were removed. Because the water in a piece of green wood can easily outweigh the wood fiber, wood can have a moisture content of more than 100%. The fiber saturation point of most wood species is 25% to 30% MC; kiln-dried framing lumber is supposed to have no more than 19% MC. Since this is well below the fiber saturation point, the wood will swell and shrink with changes in moisture content.

Wood stored at a constant humidity eventually reaches a stable MC, called the *equilibrium moisture content*. For most of the U.S., the equilibrium MC of wood that's inside a building is around 8% (see table, page 352). In arid climates like Arizona, it's closer to 6%, while in moist climates like Florida, it's closer to 11%. This means that a piece of kiln-dried lumber will lose 8% to 13% MC after installation.

Start With Dry Lumber

Kiln-dried framing lumber is stamped KD or S-DRY (surfaced-dry). Lumber stamped S-GRN (surfaced-green) has not been kiln dried. Its MC was higher than 19% at the time it was milled — probably a lot higher. Avoid S-GRN lumber anywhere you're concerned about shrinkage. Also be aware that anything larger than a 4x4 isn't available in KD. The outside of these timbers may be somewhat dry, but assume that the inside is pretty green. When using a large solid beam, like a 6x6 or a 6x10, keep in mind that it will shrink a lot more than a comparable built-up beam made from kiln-dried stock.

You can minimize the effects of moisture swings by ensuring that all your framing lumber has the same MC. This means storing it up off the ground and protecting it from sun and rain with a tarp. It's just as bad to let the joists on top of the lift dry out in the sun as it is to let the bottom ones soak in a puddle. The idea is to make sure that all of the members in a given component — all of the joists in a floor, for instance — shrink the same amount.

Dry the Frame

Studs that are straight at 19% MC can do a lot of twisting and bowing as they dry to 8%. The USDA Forest Products Laboratory (FPL) recommends that a frame be within 5% of its final moisture content before walls and ceilings are closed in. At the company I work for, we try to dry the frame to 10% or 12% MC before installing drywall or plaster. This gives us a chance to fix or replace any pieces that bow.

In cold weather, drying the frame may require some heat. A few winters back, I used a moisture meter to record how long it took the frame of a house I was working on to dry out. It was cold, but the humidity was low and the house was weather-tight. After three weeks, most of the frame was stuck at 15%. We then set up an old gas furnace as a tem-

Calculating Shrinkage

Because wood shrinks and swells at a predictable rate, it's possible to calculate how much a building, or any part of a building, will shrink as it dries. Let's say we want to find out how much a kiln-dried hem-fir 2x12 at 19% MC will shrink if it's dried to 8% MC. We need something called the coefficient for dimensional change — the shrinkage coefficient — which expresses the percentage change in the size of a piece of wood for each percentage change in its MC. Although different wood species have slightly different shrinkage coefficients, an average number for flat-sawn framing lumber is .0025. You can safely use this to calculate the shrinkage for average 2-by stock.

With that in mind, we can use the following formula:

Shrinkage (or swelling) = Width of wood x change in MC x Shrinkage Coefficient

So a typical 2x12 will shrink about 5/16 inch as it moves from 19% MC to 8% MC (11.25 inches x (19-8) x .0025). A 2x6 would shrink half as much (see chart, below). The formula can also be used to calculate how much wood swells as MC increases. — *D.F.*

Predicted Shrinkage of Dimension Lumber

Lumber Size	Actual Width	Width @ 19% MC (at Delivery)	Width @ 11% MC (Humid Climates)	Width @ 8% MC (Average Climates)	Width @ 6% MC (Arid Climates)
2x4	3 1/2"	3 1/2"	3 7/16"	3 3/8"	3 3/8"
2x6	5 1/2"	5 1/2"	5 3/8"	5 5/16"	5 5/16"
2x8	7 1/4"	7 1/4"	7 1/8"	7 1/16"	7"
2x10	9 1/4"	9 1/4"	9 1/16"	9"	8 15/16"
2x12	11 1/4"	11 1/4"	11"	10 15/16"	10 7/8"

Note: *Framing lumber shrinks primarily across its width; shrinkage along the lumber length is insignificant. Actual shrinkage varies depending on the lumber's moisture content when delivered and the area's climate.*

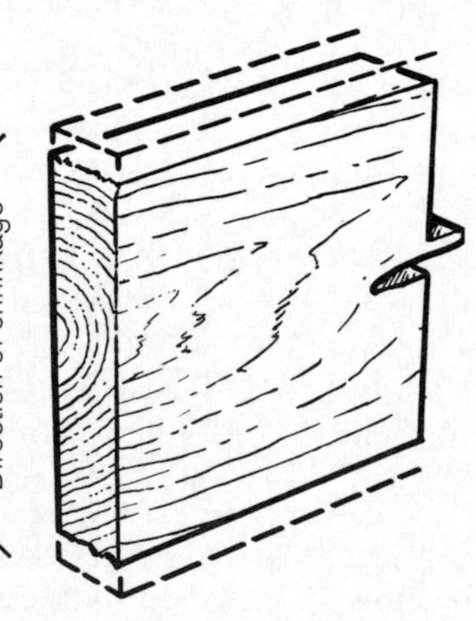

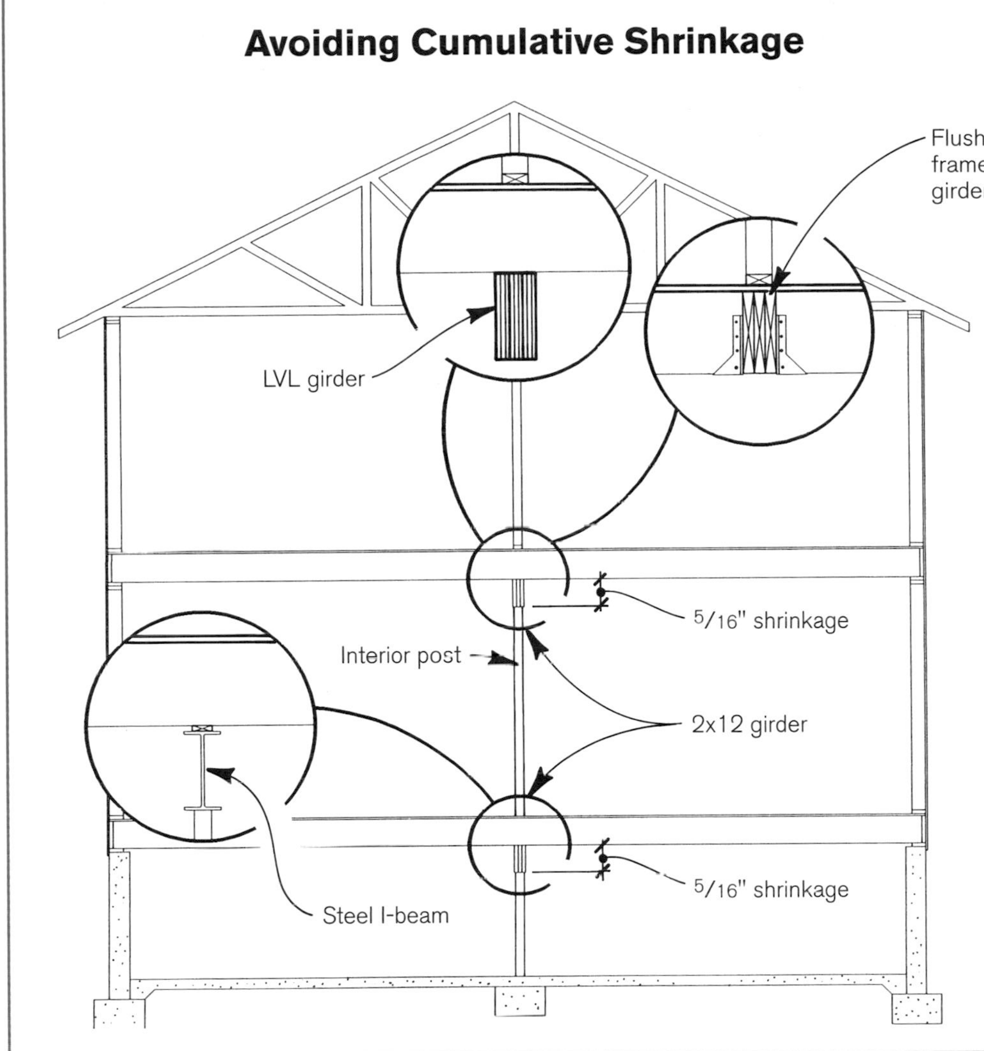

Figure 7. Watch out for situations where wood shrinkage can compound to create noticeable problems. In the house shown here, the two built-up 2x12 girders will cause the center bearing wall to shrink much more than the exterior walls. This will result in a 1/2-inch drop at the second floor level — enough to cause nail pops and cracks in the finishes. Using a steel I-beam in the basement and engineered lumber or flush framing at the second floor will alleviate the problem.

porary heater. A week and half later, everything had dried to around 10%. Of course, it's not cheap to use heat to dry out a house. But if you're doing a high-end job, it beats coming back later to repair drywall, tile, and trim. And the heat doesn't have to be all that high. The FPL says that you need to keep the inside of the building only 10° to 15° warmer than the outside.

Pay Attention to Framing Details

Even if you purchase high-quality framing lumber and protect it after it arrives, you still won't be able to prevent the wood from shrinking altogether. But if you use framing details that *allow* for the shrinkage, you will avoid most of the problems that can occur when the frame shrinks.

Problems occur when one side of the building has considerably more headers and plates than the other side, when there's an improper connection to masonry, or when solid lumber is mixed with steel or engineered lumber without compensating for the materials' different shrinkage rates. The symptoms include sloping floors, and lumps and dips in floors and walls. Although this sounds complicated, it's fairly easy to design a frame that will shrink evenly.

Avoid Lopsided Shrinkage

It's important to recognize situations where a structure will shrink unevenly. Look at the example in **Figure 7**. Here, the first-floor joists are supported by a built-up 2x12 girder. The upstairs features an open floor plan, with the second-floor joists also resting on a 2x12 girder.

The problem with this configuration is that the two girders may shrink as much as 5/16 inch each as the lumber dries from 19% moisture content to 8%. This is much more than the shrinkage that would occur in the exterior walls. The first-story ceiling and the second-story floor will then drop by 1/2 inch or more, wreaking havoc with the drywall finish and possibly leaving noticeable dips in the floor.

The solution is to use girder material that doesn't shrink — either steel or LVL — or to flush-frame the girders.

Whenever you're flush-framing a floor system where solid wood joists meet an engineered lumber

Flush-Framed Floor Joists

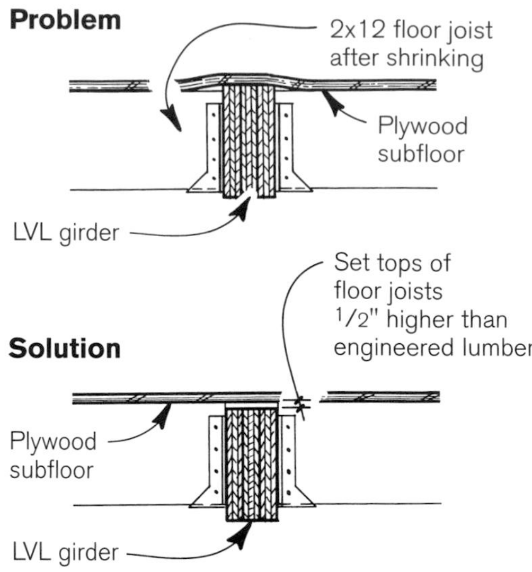

Figure 8. Floor joists laid flush with the top of engineered or steel beams will create a bump in the floor when they shrink (top drawing). In these situations, install the joists 1/2 inch high to accommodate the anticipated shrinkage (bottom drawing). Where I-joists meet an engineered lumber beam (right), you can install them flush since shrinkage is not an issue with I-joists.

or steel beam, don't set the tops of the joists exactly even with the top of the beam (**Figure 8**). Otherwise, when the joists shrink, they'll leave a bump in the floor. When I'm faced with this situation, I drop the beam approximately 1/2 inch in relation to the joists, so the joists can shrink without the top of the beam contacting the subfloor.

Foundation Details

Some designs call for the first-floor joists to bear on an interior foundation ledge, as in **Figure 9**. The problem here is that when the joists shrink, the ends pull away from the subfloor, leaving a slope at the exterior wall. I once installed a refrigerator in a kitchen that was framed this way; the floor sloped so badly that I couldn't level the refrigerator with the leveling feet.

A better detail is to keep the subfloor off of the sill plate. When the floor joists shrink, the subfloor will move with them. When installing a wood floor, you can prevent a gap from opening beneath the baseboard by installing the flooring after the baseboard and using a shoe mold that's attached to the floor.

Sloping Subfloor

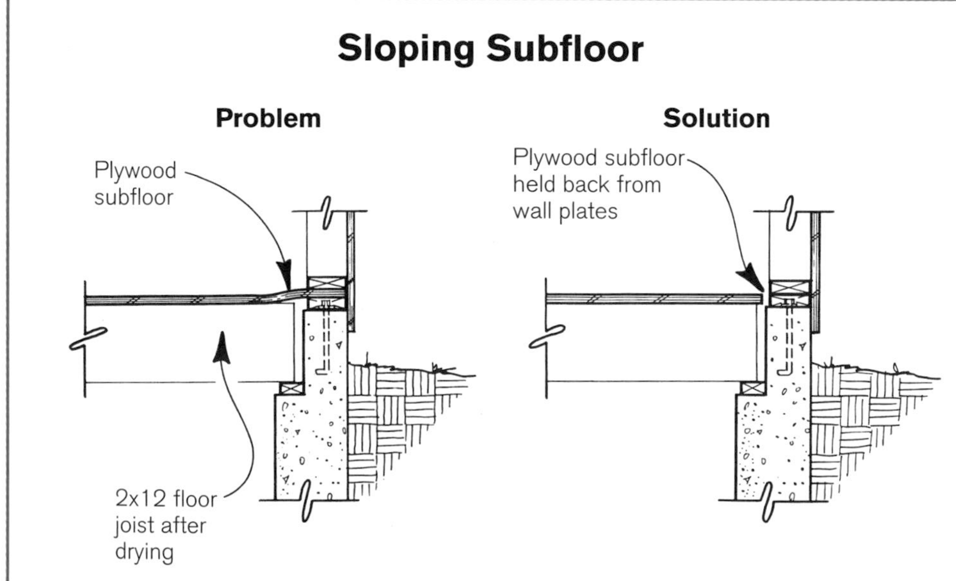

Figure 9. Subflooring that is installed underneath the exterior wall framing (far left) will cause a slope as the floor joists shrink. Where floor joists bear on a foundation ledge, the subflooring should stop short of the exterior wall (left). This allows the subfloor to move with the joists as they shrink.

Where Wood Meets Masonry

If the framing isn't dry when a concrete hearth is poured, the framing will shrink so that the hardwood floor surface ends up slightly below the hearth. Because hearths are usually set late in the job, after the framing has had time to dry, this is seldom a problem. But if the hearth is set earlier — or if cold weather prevents the frame from drying — you should anticipate shrinkage and set the hearth a bit lower.

David Frane is a senior editor at The Journal of Light Construction.

Wood Shrinkage and Interior Finishes

by Paul Fisette

Complaints about misaligned wood moldings, floor squeaks, and drywall cracks are like fingernails on a blackboard to a builder's ears. Callbacks can lead to customer dissatisfaction that will threaten a builder's reputation. Regardless of how you resolve these problems, you can always count on one thing: The cure will cost you money. Prevention is always the least expensive and most effective remedy.

Here is a selection of callback complaints that builders ask us about over and over again. Each time the questions remain the same: What is causing this problem and how can it be prevented?

Gaps in the Floor Boards

Six months after a new home is occupied, large gaps may open up between the floor boards. The gaps are rarely uniform. Usually several individual boards appear to have shrunk significantly while large areas of flooring remain tight. The separations run in a connecting zigzag pattern across the room.

Cause: Fluctuation in relative humidity causes wood to absorb and lose moisture and, consequently, to expand and contract. Wood shrinks and swells most in the direction tangent to the growth rings (across a typical flat-grained board) and about half as much perpendicular to them. Shrinking and swelling along the length of a board are insignificant.

Even if the flooring is delivered at a low moisture content and installed correctly, and the indoor humidity at the time of installation is kept at a reasonable level (between 40% and 60%), moisture can still be a problem. The floor can absorb moisture from the basement slab, fresh paint, and curing drywall mud. The wood expands as it takes on this moisture and the edges of the boards press against each other and compress. As indoor humidity drops, the boards shrink to a size smaller than their installed size — a condition known as *compression set* (**Figure 10**). Furthermore, polyurethane finish drips between the floor boards during finishing, gluing portions together, so areas of the floor shrink as a monolith. When this happens, it appears that only a few boards have shrunk, when in reality all the boards have swelled and then shrunk.

Cure: Contrary to conventional wisdom, leaving a 3/4-inch gap around the perimeter of the room does not solve the problem. Flooring nails would have to be sheared off or pulled out of the subfloor in order for flooring to fill the recommended 3/4-inch perimeter gap.

In this case, the only cure is prevention. Relaying the floor is the only fix.

Figure 10. If a new hardwood floor picks up too much moisture from curing concrete or drywall mud, it will swell. This crushes the wood fibers and leaves gaps in the floor when the wood dries out again. To prevent this, acclimate the wood to a dry job site, which may require ventilation or dehumidification of the site.

To avoid similar problems with a new floor, only install wood flooring after the building is reasonably dry and after the wood flooring has equalized to its in-use moisture content (see "Acclimate the Floor or Dry the Job Site?"). Ideally, according to the National Oak Flooring Manufacturers Association, you should buy wood flooring at 6% to 9% moisture content. But even if the flooring arrives at the job site at 10% to 12% moisture content, it should still acclimate to job-site conditions in a few days, as long as indoor humidity at the site is controlled by mechanical ventilation and, if necessary, dehumidifiers. The floor may take on additional moisture from curing construction materials after you have left the job, but at least the chances for compression set are reduced. Advise your customers that continual ventilation during the first year after construction will reduce the swelling as long as no large sources of moisture are introduced into the home. Keep records showing the moisture content of the wood when it arrived and what the humidity conditions in the home were during storage and installation. Good recordkeeping will help reduce your liability if problems arise.

Miters Open Up

Often the miters on window and door casings are tight when you install them, but they open up at either the long point or the short point after you leave the job, so the angles look as if they were miscut.

Cause: A dry piece of wood casing, tightly mitered and installed during the winter months, can look much different during the summer months as the humidity in the home rises. Indoor relative humidity can drop to 20% during cold periods and rise above 75% during humid summer months. Under these conditions, the moisture content of the wood casings

Acclimate the Flooring or Dry the Job Site?

by Howard Brickman

Excessive moisture at the job site is the leading cause of problems with wood floors. All of the expense and effort to properly kiln-dry and precisely manufacture wood strip flooring are for naught if it is later exposed to excessive moisture and swells before, during, or after it is installed.

Much of the wood flooring industry literature is misleading because it emphasizes acclimating wood flooring to job sites. In reality, the reverse is true: A job site needs to be dried out before any wood flooring arrives. There is nearly always excessive moisture on new construction sites and major remodeling job sites.

Wood flooring should never be delivered to the job until all excessive moisture has been eliminated. The quickest and most effective method for removing job-site moisture is to run the heating system and increase fresh air ventilation.

Wood flooring should be installed only after the interior MC level of a structure has been reduced to within the range that will prevail during the life of that structure *after it is occupied.* Typical interior MC levels throughout the United States are shown on the USDA map (right). Today most manufacturers kiln-dry wood building materials to an MC of 7.5% at a corresponding RH of 40% — roughly the national average.

Installing the flooring after the structure has been dried to its normal range prevents the excessive moisture present during any major renovation or new construction project from being absorbed into a kiln-dried wood floor. If the wood subfloor over which the wood floor is to be installed contains excessive moisture, then the wood flooring will absorb the moisture and swell.

One of the biggest lies I've been told over my years as a flooring contractor is "This job is as dry as a bone — you can start laying the floor next Monday."

Even if there is no intent to deceive, you need to confirm that a job site is dry by measuring the moisture content of the subfloor. If you're acting as the flooring sub, don't rely on the contractor to control site moisture. In the end, it's the installer who needs to take responsibility for checking MC levels.

Water vapor is colorless and odorless, so it can only be reliably measured with moisture meters. Electrical resistance meters are the simplest type to use and provide the only practical non-destructive way to determine moisture content in wood frame construction. Two pins are driven into a wood surface parallel to the grain and the meter gives an MC reading. Small pocket versions are available from several manufacturers for less than $200.

To Acclimate or Not?

Ideally, the proper moisture content for the installation of any wood floor is midway between the seasonal high humidity, which occurs during the summer, and the seasonal low humidity, which occurs near the end of the first winter heating season after construction is completed. In

can swing from 4% to as much as 16%. A 6-inch-wide casing can expand more than 1/8 inch. Because wood swells by different amounts in each direction, mitered connections remain tight at the bottom, but separate at the top as the casing swells. Similarly, the miters open near the short points as the wood shrinks (**Figure 11**, next page).

Cure: To prevent miters from opening up, first install high-quality wood casing that has an 8% to 12% moisture content. The easiest way to check the moisture content is with a moisture meter (see "About Moisture Meters," page 367). At the very least, acclimate the casing material to indoor humidity conditions. You might try using biscuits at the joint. But beware that if the indoor humidity fluctuates too much, the wood will have to move somewhere. If the miters are held rigid, the casing may pull away from the window stool, warp, or, in extreme cases, split.

The best prevention is to educate your customers about controlling indoor humidity. Encourage them to maintain indoor humidity levels between 40% and 60% year-round. This range is healthy and will help keep your work looking good. Finally, be sure to lead your customer on a careful walk-through after the job is complete and point out the level of craftsmanship. Again, record and document humidity levels in the home and the moisture content of the trim stock during storage and installation.

Squeaky Floors

Squeaky floors rank high in nuisance value. Customers usually hold their complaints until the squeak has frayed their nerve endings. Then, when you attempt to fix it, they watch you like a hawk.

Cause: Squeaks result from wood rubbing against wood. Often the squeak occurs when a floor joist

Ideal Flooring MC Levels

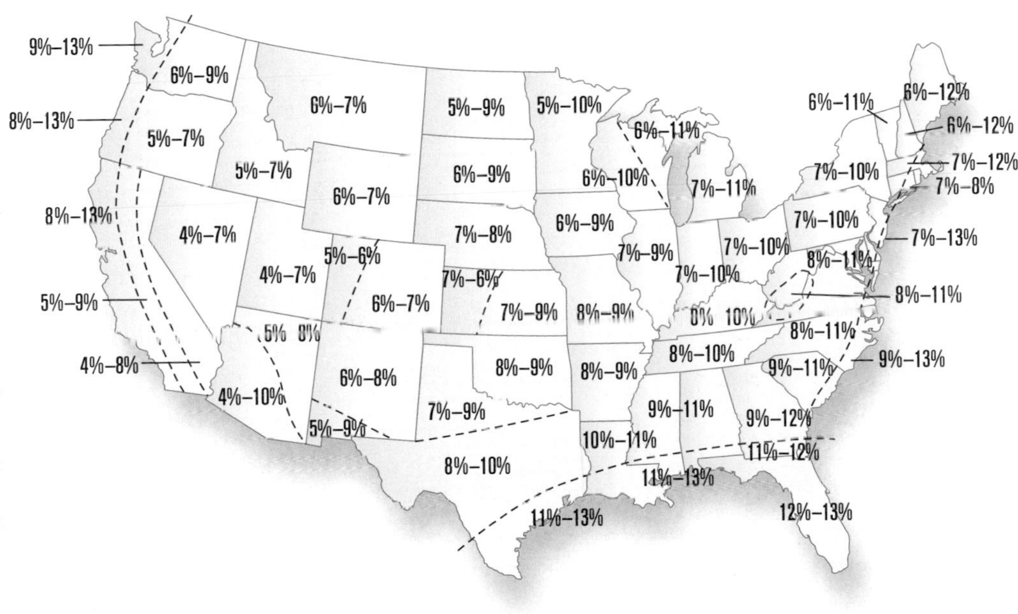

Seasonal ranges in RH vary across the U.S. Optimally, both the subfloor and the strip flooring should be at mid-range MC levels shown on this map during installation. This means drying out new construction sites before delivering materials, and acclimating materials only if you are in extremely dry or moist areas of the country.

USDA

my more than 25 years of consulting in the wood flooring industry, I have often seen damage done to wood flooring from "acclimating" the flooring to the job before installation.

Because the quality of kiln-drying within the wood flooring industry is high, acclimation is only appropriate in extreme climates where interior relative humidity levels are substantially above or below the 7.5% MC/40% RH manufacturing specifications. This includes the arid regions of the western U.S. and the humid southeastern U.S.

Acclimating wood flooring in other regions actually risks exposing it to the high levels of relative humidity and moisture present during summer or on a new construction site. This will cause the wood flooring to swell before and during installation. Then, during the first heating season, it will shrink and permanent spaces will be left between the flooring strips. Instead, dry out the building before bringing the flooring on site.

Howard Brickman is a flooring contractor and consultant based in Norwell, Mass.

Why Miters Open

Miter opens at top as casing swells

Miter opens at bottom as casing shrinks

Figure 11. As indoor humidity fluctuates, wood casings shrink and swell, causing miters to open up. As the casing swells, miters separate at the top but remain tight at the bottom (far left). As the wood shrinks, the opposite occurs (left).

shrinks after it is installed. A space develops between the subfloor and the top of the floor joist, and when the homeowner walks over this spot, the subfloor moves against the joist and squeaks.

Cure: The best cure for floor squeaks is prevention. Use dry wood, keep it dry, and apply construction adhesive between all wooden surfaces. Also, use screws — not nails — to fasten subfloors and underlayment.

In theory, fixing floor squeaks is simple — stop the movement of the wood. But accomplishing this is often difficult.

If the squeaks are located in the first floor, you're in luck because you can usually get at the floor frame from the basement or crawlspace. One cure is to sister a length of 1x3 to the side of the offending floor joist. Holding it tight to the underside of the subfloor, attach the strip along the top edge of the joist using screws and glue. Make sure you also spread adhesive between the top of the 1x3 strip and the subfloor. The adhesive will help prevent future rubbing.

There are also a couple of products on the market designed to fix floor squeaks. One is Squeak-Relief (ATCI Consumer Products) — a metal bracket with inclined screw slots that pulls the subfloor tight to the floor joist. Another device, the Squeak-Ender (E&E Engineering) has a carriage bolt, which is secured to the subfloor, and a bracket, which hooks under the joist. When the nut on the carriage bolt is tightened down, the framing and decking are pulled together (**Figure 12**).

The solution is not so simple when the squeak is located on an upper level of a home. To fix these adds the extra step of opening and repatching the finished ceiling.

Cracked Drywall

Drywall cracks when the framing moves. This happens most often at the upper corners of windows and doors.

Cause: If the drywall joints fall at the edges of a window, the finished joint will crack when the header shrinks. Headers with a moisture content of 19% can shrink 1/4 inch across their width.

Cure: Don't break drywall sheets at the corners of

ATCI CONSUMER PRODUCTS

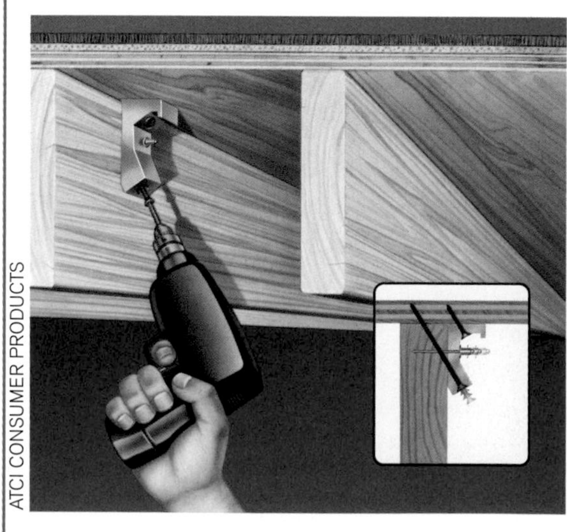

Figure 12. Two ways to fix squeaky floors: The Squeak-Relief bracket (far left) has inclined screw slots, so as you drive in the screws, the floor joist and subfloor are drawn together. The Squeak-Ender (left) hooks under the joist, and pulls the subfloor down as the nut is tightened.

Installing Drywall Around Doors and Windows

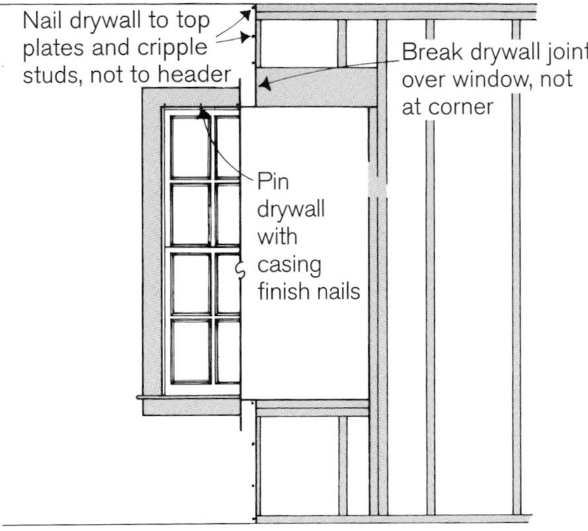

Figure 13. To prevent drywall joints from cracking at the corners of windows and doors, place the sheet so the joint falls in the center of the opening, and then cut out the waste. Also, do not fasten the drywall to the header, but use the interior casing to secure the loose edge of the drywall.

an opening. Instead, lap the sheet over the corner so the joint falls in the center of the window or door span, and then cut out the opening (**Figure 13**). Also, do not fasten the drywall to the header. Screw the drywall into the cripples and wall plate above the headers. This lets the wallboard float down over the header. Use the interior window casing to hold the loose edge of the drywall secure.

Faux Truss Uplift

Have you ever seen drywall cracks at a ceiling corner or a center partition separate from the ceiling? This is often caused by truss uplift (see "Truss Uplift Solutions," next page) but not always.

Cause: In many cases, the triple-2x12 girder in the basement that supports the floor joists is the cause (**Figure 14**). Since the beam is located directly beneath the center partitions and the partition sole plates are nailed securely to the deck, shrinkage of this beam can pull the partitions downward, opening a crack at the ceiling. This happens frequently with lumber that is grade-stamped "S-DRY," meaning that it was surfaced at a moisture content of 19% or lower. Yet once the house is occupied and heated, the moisture content of the girder, joists, and partition studs can fall to 11%. The cumulative shrinkage of all these members can easily equal 3/8 inch.

Cure: While the cause is not true truss uplift, the effect is the same. Fasten trusses to partitions with hardware such as the Truss-Float-R (Stud Claw), which allows the ceiling drywall and wall partition to float independently. Use dry framing lumber, especially for girders. Lumber stamped "MC 15" is a good choice.

The fix is the same as with truss uplift. Install a molding in the corner at the ceiling. Attach the molding to the ceiling only, allowing the wall to move.

By the way, this problem can occur in houses without roof trusses, too. To prevent this, break ceiling joists over a center bearing partition. As the partition settles, this break will act like a hinge, allowing the ceiling to drop as the center bearing shrinks.

Interior Doors Won't Close

The doors closed properly when they were installed, but after a couple of months the doors began to rub against the strike jamb and now they are too wide to be forced closed.

Cause: The doors have absorbed moisture, but to find the exact source requires a bit of investigation. Determine whether all doors have swollen or if just certain ones have, like the bathroom or basement doors. Isolated swelling suggests local humidity problems.

Cure: Wood doors should be delivered and installed at a moisture content between 6% and 12%. But even

(continued on page 367)

Drywall Cracks From Shrinking Framing

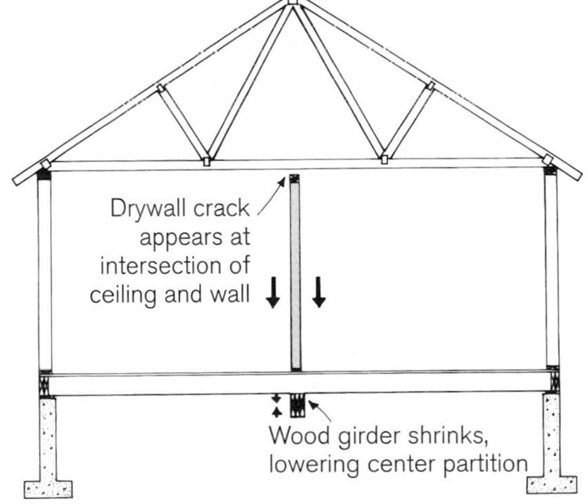

Figure 14. Drywall cracks at the ceiling can open up when the basement girder shrinks and pulls the partition downward. The only fix is to install crown molding over the crack. Attach the molding to the ceiling but not to the wall.

Truss Uplift Solutions

by Henry Spies

Truss uplift is caused by differential shrinkage between the upper and lower chords of a truss. In a well-insulated house, the bottom chord is buried in ceiling insulation. In the winter, that chord is kept much warmer, and tends to dry to a lower moisture content than the top chord, which is exposed to the ventilated attic air. This dry bottom chord shrinks. Most of the shrinkage takes place across the grain, but there is some lengthwise movement as well.

In a triangular structure, such as a truss, if the bottom member of the triangle is shortened while the two top chords remain the same length, the peak of the triangle rises, pulling up the bottom chord, which is attached by webbing or a king post. As the ceiling rises, unsightly corner cracks may open up. If the partition is firmly attached to the bottom chord, the partition may even be lifted off the floor deck. *This is not a structural problem,* just a cosmetic one.

In the summer, when the temperature and moisture content of the top and bottom chords are nearly the same, the truss will come back to its original position, closing any cracks that have formed. In many instances, this cycle will occur only once. In others it will occur on an annual basis.

How can you keep this from happening? You can't fool Mother Nature. A truss manufacturer can select chord members that come from the outer parts of the tree, which helps. The "juvenile wood" near the center of the tree moves more with changes in moisture content than the mature wood. But the most practical thing a builder can do is to use details that will prevent the cracks from showing.

A connector such as the Truss Float-R (Stud Claw) can be used to connect the top plate of an interior partition to the truss. A single nail that slides in a groove is tacked into the bottom truss chord, allowing the truss to move vertically with seasonal changes (**Figure A**).

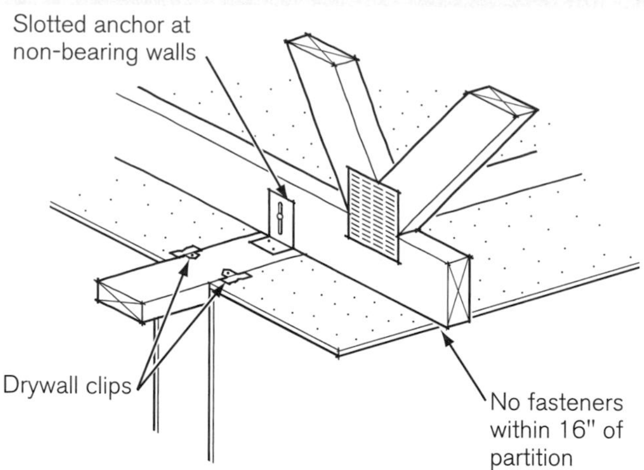

Source: Drywall, Wood & Truss U plift" / www.buildingscience.com

Figure A. *Slotted anchors fasten the partition to the truss, while allowing the truss to move vertically. Keep all drywall fasteners at least 16 inches away from the partition, allowing the ceiling corner to "float."*

The ceiling drywall should not be nailed to the bottom chord of the truss within 16 inches of an interior partition. Instead, it can be supported by corner clips nailed to the wall studs, or nailed to a wider top plate, as shown (**Figure B**). This allows the drywall to flex in the 16-inch space between the last nail in the chord and the partition. The corner is held solid, so the tape does not break. The deflection of the drywall is usually unnoticeable.

Henry Spies is a building consultant formerly with the Small Homes Council-Building Research Council of the University of Illinois.

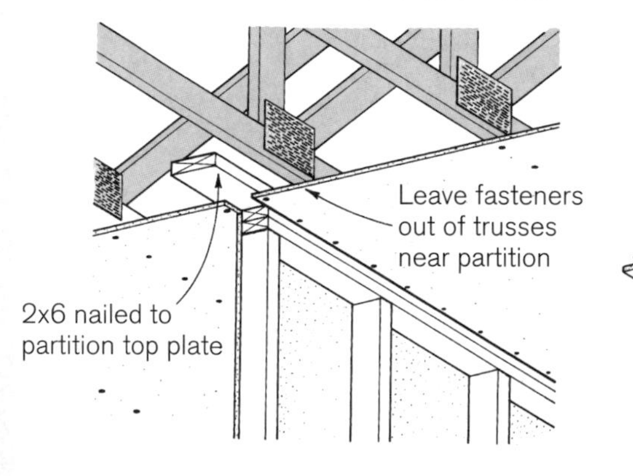

Parallel Partitions

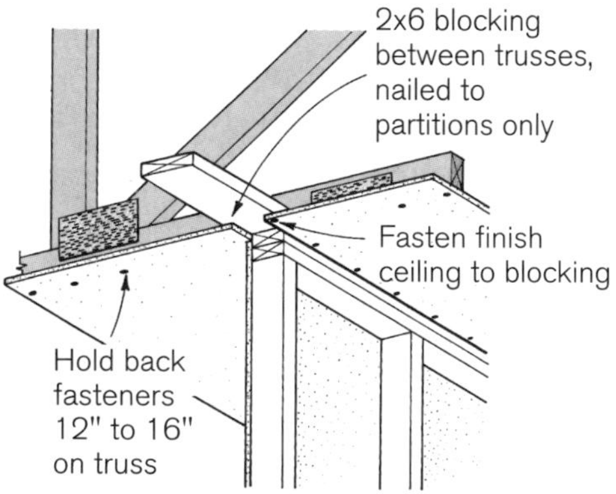

Perpendicular Partitions

Figure B. *When trusses are parallel to partitions (far left), install 2x6 nailers for fastening the ceiling drywall. Do not nail the drywall to the bottom chords near partitions. When trusses are perpendicular to the partitions (left), install "dead wood" blocking to attach the ceiling drywall, and hold the nailing back 12 to 16 inches on either side of the partition.*

About Moisture Meters

by Clayton DeKorne

There are two types of meters for measuring the moisture content in wood — *electric resistance* meters and *dielectric* meters.

Dielectric Meters

Dielectric meters send out a radio signal that passes through the wood. The meter reads the return signal and measures either the power loss or the capacitance of the signal. These properties will vary depending on the moisture in the wood. Dielectric meters tend to be expensive ($350 and up) but they have one distinct advantage: You need only pass the device over the surface, so you can measure moisture content without damaging finished materials.

Electric Resistance Meters

In most cases, however, an electric resistance meter will be sufficient. You can tell an electric resistance meter by its two short, sharp metal prongs. To use the meter, stick these prongs about 1/4 inch into the back face of a board, which will leave two small holes. The meter passes a low-voltage electric current from one prong to another through the wood and measures the resistance. The wetter the board, the less resistance to the current it will have. Thus, an electric resistance meter is essentially an ohm meter, but instead of reading out in ohms of resistance, the meter translates the reading into percentage of moisture content. Readings will be slightly different for different species of wood; when you buy the meter, find out if there is some way to adjust for this.

There is a wide variety of electric resistance meters, ranging in price from under $100 to more than $400. The less expensive models have built-in prongs, and read out at whole number percentages of moisture content. Most of these are only accurate between a 6% and 25% moisture content, but this is suitable for on-site use. Better low-end meters will provide a chart for calculating an adjustment for different wood species. The more expensive models have external electrode prongs that are connected to the meter by a cord, can be recalibrated for different species, and have a wider range of accuracy. For use on site, a medium priced (under $200) meter with a durable shell is your best buy, as it will inevitably get dropped. Manufacturers include Delmhorst, Lignomat, and Wagner (see Sources of Supply, page 399).

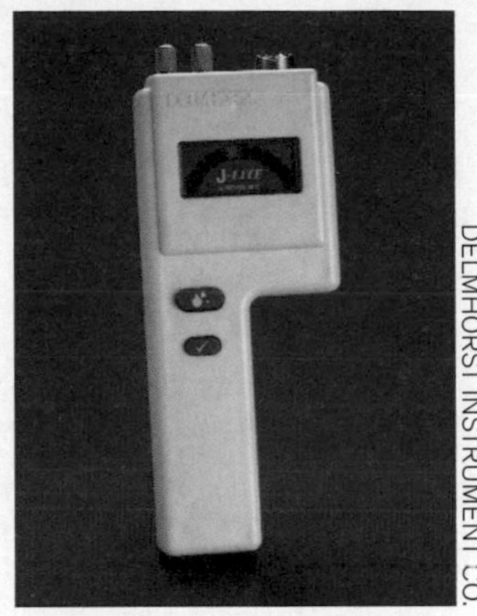
DELMHORST INSTRUMENT CO.

A moderately priced electric resistance meter with a strong shell, such as this one from Delmhorst, is adequate for gauging the moisture content of lumber on site.

Clayton DeKorne is the editor of Coastal Contractor *magazine and a former senior editor at* The Journal of Light Construction.

(continued from page 365)

those doors can become unstable in houses with fluctuating humidity levels. For best results, doors should be sealed as soon as they are delivered (right after they are made would be even better). If the doors are prehung units, remove all the hardware and seal the undercut edge and all hardware cutouts, including hinge mortises and the inside of lock bores. End grain is very absorbent. An unsealed edge will suck up moisture rapidly under humid conditions. If doors arrive at the job site unsealed, check the moisture content by inserting the probes of a moisture meter into the end grain. Then seal it when conditions are right. To solve the immediate problem, plane the door to size and reseal the edges. Also, as with all wood movement problems, control the indoor humidity.

Paul Fisette is a wood technologist and professor with the Building Materials and Wood Technology program at the University of Massachusetts in Amherst.

Chapter 20: Mold & Wood Decay

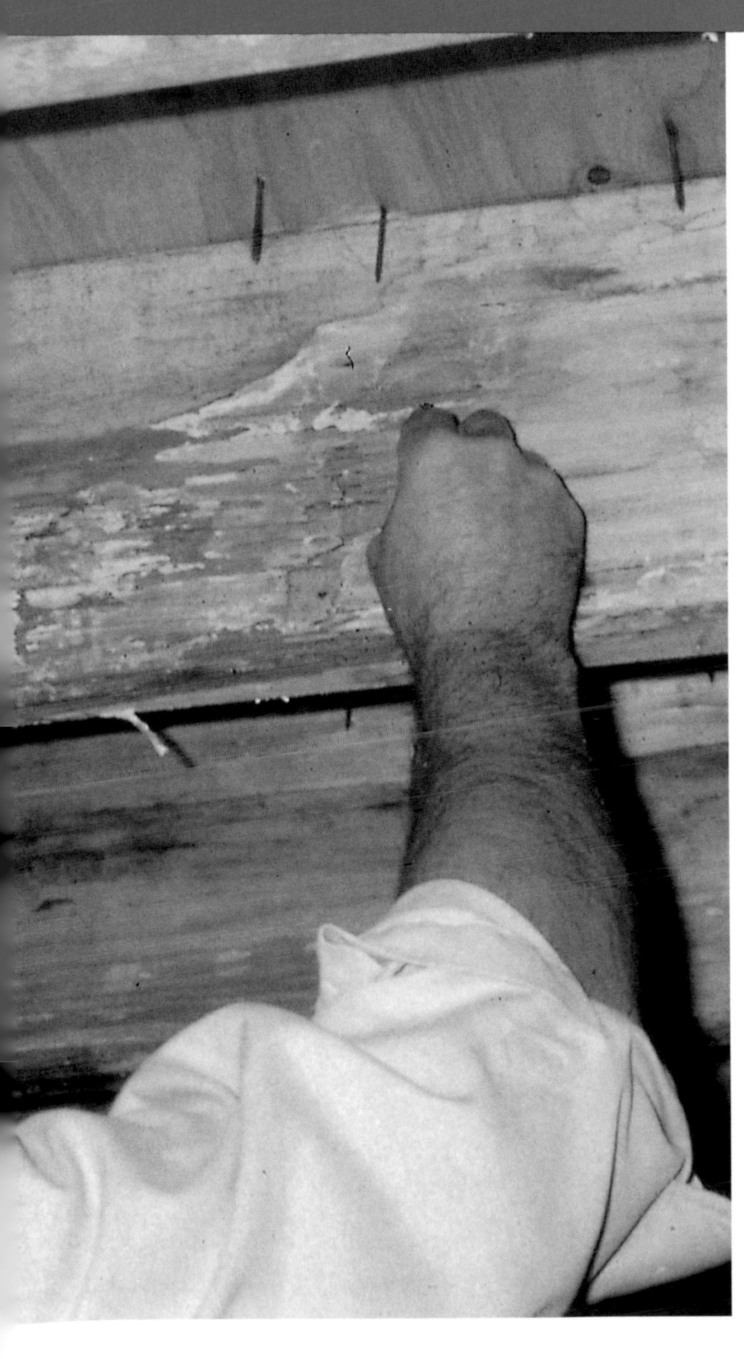

- **Building Details That Fail**
- **Wood Fungi Causes and Cures**
- **Indoor Mold Remediation**

Building Details That Fail

by Martin Holladay

After working as a builder for 20 years, I changed gears and set up shop as a home inspector. Most of the houses I inspected were only five to ten years old. I was surprised to learn how quickly some building components can deteriorate. In house after house, I found it frustrating to see certain poor building details, all leading to similar types of early failures.

In most cases, these details were built wrong not so much because of an intentional trade-off between cost and longevity, but because the builder didn't realize how quickly building components can deteriorate. If the deterioration happens after the normal new-home warranty expires, a builder may never have the chance to discover that some details almost always fail prematurely. Let's face it, we have all thought, as we contemplated a shortcut on the job site, "I know the recommended way to do it — but does it really matter?" I offer these descriptions of failures as a reminder of the importance of building it right the first time.

A building without roof overhangs leaves the siding exposed to the weather.

Stingy roof overhangs, whether at the rakes or the eaves, greatly reduce the longevity of most types of siding. When siding receives the full brunt of the weather, it is alternately soaked by rain and baked by the sun. These humidity changes cause nails to loosen, paint to peel, and siding to rot prematurely (**Figure 1**).

Figure 1. The clapboard siding on this building has no roof protection. It is curling and splitting, and requires repainting every three years.

Figure 2. Locate clapboard siding joints over studs so that the nails penetrate the framing.

In many cases, a difference of just a few inches in the width of a roof can make a big difference in protecting the siding.

Smooth-shank siding nails that miss the studs don't hold.

Smooth-shank siding nails that penetrate the sheathing but not the framing, cannot hold clapboards for long. After just a few years, normal variations in humidity cause the siding to swell and shrink, ratcheting out the smooth-shank nails. Inadequately nailed clapboard siding soon begins to curl (**Figure 2**).

The solution is to use ring-shank siding nails, nailed into the studs. Most siding manufacturers recommend that ring-shank nails penetrate 1¼ inches into the nailing base, and that smooth-shank nails penetrate 1½ inches. If you are installing ½-inch bevel siding, that means using 5d ring-shank nails or 6d smooth-shank nails. But if you aren't going to bother to locate the studs, it hardly matters how long your nails are: Since they'll only be hitting the sheathing, they'll only hold as well as 2d nails.

Exposed exterior doors deteriorate quickly.

Exterior doors should be protected from rain by a roof that extends at least 3 feet beyond the door. A roof located high above the door — for instance, the rakes on the gable end of a two-story house — offers little, if any, protection against wind-driven rain.

Unroofed exterior doors can begin to deteriorate just five years after installation. They are vulnerable

Figure 3. When an exterior door has no roof protection, the lower sections of the jambs and door are vulnerable to rot or rust.

to direct wetting as well as splashback. Usually, the first signs of deterioration are jamb rot and rust spots near the bottom of the door.

Steel door proponents sometimes say that "unlike wood, steel doesn't rot." Steel doors can rust right through, however, and it happens particularly quickly when the builder fails to paint them. The factory-installed primer on a steel door is not intended to be a finish coat of paint (**Figure 3**).

Wood siding installed too close to the roofing rots quickly.

When an exterior wall with wood siding rises above a roof — for example, where a two-story house extends above the roof of an attached one-story garage — the siding and corner trim nearest the roofing can rot quickly. Rain bounces off the roofing onto the adjacent wall. Snow may sit on the roof for weeks at a stretch.

In the case of asphalt shingle roofs, siding is usually installed over step flashing formed from 8-inch aluminum squares. This gives 4 inches of flashing on either side of the crease. Some siding installers pride themselves on covering as much of the flashing as possible, bringing the end grain of the clapboard close to the roofing (**Figure 4**). On the contrary, the more exposed metal, the better.

Ideally, step flashing should be at least 12 inches wide, with 8 inches on the vertical side of the crease, and 4 inches on the roof slope side. That way, the siding and corner trim can lap the flashing by 4 inches, and still leave a gap of 4 inches between the siding and the roofing.

High grade causes splashback.

Some design and workmanship problems are easier to fix than others. One of the most frustrating errors to encounter, years after construction, is a high grade. Ideally, the final grade should be at least 8 inches lower than the lowest wooden components of a building — usually, the water table or lowest course of siding. Unfortunately, far too often a builder

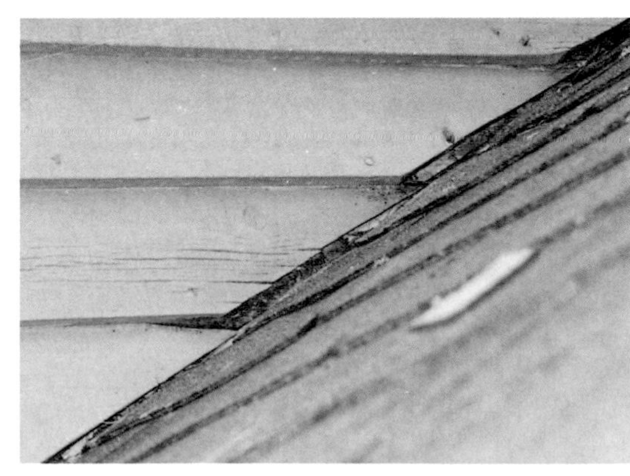

Figure 4. Instead of butting wood siding and trim up to the roofing, it should be held back to prevent the wood from wicking up water, and to allow for drying.

Figure 5. If the grade is too high, the water table and corner trim are kept constantly wet from splashback and damp grass.

establishes the final grade within an inch or two of the lowest course of siding (**Figure 5**).

By the time the wooden components nearest grade are beginning to rot — due to splashback or damp vegetation — landscape plantings are usually well established, and concrete walkways may have been poured. At this point, lowering the grade is very expensive. Worse yet, the builder didn't save any money by doing it wrong in the first place. Usually, establishing a lower grade at the time the foundation is backfilled won't cost the builder an extra penny; in fact, if it saves bringing in some fill, it might even be cheaper.

Figure 6. Because it catches water from the windowsill above, the pine trim on this house began rotting after only five years.

"Picture frame" window trim catches water.

These days, many windows come from the manufacturer with nailing flanges and no casing. You can get into trouble if you try to dress up such windows with exterior casing.

How far the manufacturer's windowsill will project from the plane of the sheathing depends on the type of window, the type of sheathing used, and how the window is installed. In some cases, the sill will not project enough to permit the installation of a 3/4-inch-thick exterior apron or trim piece under the sill.

A window should never have exterior casing installed like interior "picture-frame" trim. If the trim ends up proud of the sill lip, as was the case at one five-year-old house (**Figure 6**), it acts as a sponge to receive all of the water dripping off the windowsill.

Miters in post-formed countertops that are too close to the sink cause the substrate to swell.

There are two basic types of laminate countertops: post-formed and custom self-edged. A custom top can be formed in an L-shape in one piece, avoiding miter joints. However, with post-formed laminate, the inside corners are usually joined with a site-glued miter joint.

In theory, mitered joints in post-formed laminate countertops can work — if they are kept dry. (As we all know, kitchen countertops never get wet!) If these miter joints do get wet, the particleboard substrate begins to swell (**Figure 7**). If you prefer to use post-formed laminate for kitchen countertops, at least plan the kitchen to keep the miter joint as far from the sink as possible. If the sink is within 4 feet of the miter joint, you had better hope the homeowners don't use their sink very much.

Figure 7. Over time, water will enter a mitered joint on a laminate countertop, causing the particle-board substrate to swell and deteriorate.

Figure 8. Whenever a bath exhaust duct terminates in the attic, the warm, humid exhaust air can cause mildew and ice dams.

Bath exhaust fans ducted to the attic cause mildew, rot, ice dams.

The bath exhaust fan should always be ducted to the exterior, never terminated in the attic (see Figure 9, page 341). To be charitable, this is one of those items that is not so much a deliberate error as a forgotten detail. "Sure, I was going to get back up in the attic, as soon as the siding was done, to take care of that bath exhaust duct ..."

What's wrong with blowing the bath exhaust (or the range hood, or the dryer vent) into the attic? After all, the attic has soffit and ridge vents, so it shouldn't be a problem, right? Actually, there are two problems with this idea: warm temperatures and high humidity. The warm interior air from the exhaust duct raises the temperature of the roof sheathing, melting the snow and leading to ice dams. And since the interior air (especially bathroom air) is very humid, that moisture will want to condense on the cold surfaces in the attic (**Figure 8**).

In houses with a bath exhaust fan vented to the attic, the underside of the roof sheathing is often black with mildew. The soffit and ridge vents do not provide enough ventilation to handle the added warmth and moisture from an exhaust duct.

Martin Holladay is the editor of Energy Design Update.

Wood Fungi Causes and Cures

by Stephen Smulski

More than 5% of all construction lumber manufactured in the U.S. each year is used to replace wood that has decayed in existing structures. This need not be the case. Damage to wood-frame buildings by mildew, mold, staining, and decay is entirely preventable. Their presence points to design flaws, poor workmanship, and neglected maintenance.

The Culprits: Microorganisms

The microscopic organisms that cause mildew, mold, staining, and decay in wood belong to a huge group of primitive plants known as fungi. Unable to produce their own food, fungi feed instead on natural substances that make up organic materials like leather, cloth, rattan, paper, and wood.

Mushrooms that spring from lawns and tree trunks are fungal "fruits." They release millions of dust-size "seeds" called *spores* that are scattered helter-skelter by wind. When conditions are right on the surfaces where they eventually settle, the spores germinate, sending out thread-like filaments called *hyphae*. Enzymes secreted by hyphae break down organic matter so fungi can use it for food.

Before fungi can colonize wood, four requirements must be met: an oxygen supply, temperature in the 40°F to 100°F range, sufficient moisture, and a food source (wood). Infection can be prevented by eliminating any one of the requirements. Obviously, it's hard to limit oxygen. Temperature control is tough too, since most living things thrive in this range. And even at subfreezing temperatures, many fungi don't die; they just go dormant. Since you can usually control moisture to some extent, the most effective way to prevent fungal deterioration of wood is to keep it dry. Most fungi need a wood moisture content of at least 20% to grow. Since the moisture content of interior wood throughout most of the U.S. fluctuates between 6% and 16%, it's usually too dry for most microorganisms to get started.

In exterior or other situations where wood can't be kept dry, you can use naturally rot-resistant woods like western red cedar and redwood. Nature has partially protected these woods from fungi by depositing toxic extractives in their heartwood. But the supplies of nat-

Detecting Decay

I use several methods when looking for decay in wood. When wood is suspiciously wet or discolored, but otherwise looks okay, I first determine its subsurface moisture content with a moisture meter. If it's 20% or below, I know that there's no active decay present. If it's between 20% and 28%, existing decay can continue merrily on its way. If it's over 28%, conditions are ripe for fungi to get started.

The pick test is also useful (see photos). I judge the soundness of the wood from the way a large splinter breaks when I pry it with an awl or ice pick. Sound wood emits a sharp crack as the splinter is pried up. The splinter is typically long, with one end still attached to the wood. Sometimes it breaks in the middle over the tool, but the fracture will still be splintery.

A splinter pried from wood with incipient decay lifts quietly from the surface and almost always fails directly over the tool, with both ends still anchored to the wood.

The pick test is highly subjective; natural characteristics of sound wood can produce misleading results. Accurate interpretation comes only with experience and consideration of other clues.

Pick test. *A short splinter pried from decayed wood (top) typically breaks quietly over the tool with both ends still anchored. When pried from sound wood (bottom), the splinter cracks sharply, is longer, and remains attached at only one end.*

To find decay hidden inside timbers, I take a small-diameter boring and examine the shavings. Discolored, wet, and musty shavings signal decay. I always plug the hole with a preservative-treated dowel. — *S.S.*

urally durable woods are shrinking, so to meet the demand, less naturally durable woods are impregnated with pesticides like ACQ (alkaline copper quat) that extend their service life by 30 to 50 years or longer.

Mildew

Mildew grows both inside and outside houses. Most mildews are black, but reds, greens, blues, and browns are possible. The familiar gray color of weathered wood is the work of mildew. Masses of dark spores and hyphae give mildews their characteristic splotchy look. But although they discolor the surface they grow on, mildews have no appreciable effect on wood itself. Some mildews that feed on airborne organic matter can even grow on inorganic vinyl and aluminum sidings. Dew and rain supply the needed moisture.

Exterior mildew. Outside, mildews appear most often on unheated, projecting parts of buildings that cool quickly after sunset, like eaves, decks, and porch ceilings. North-facing walls and walls shaded by trees and other obstructions that restrict sunlight and airflow are also candidates. You often find mildew in the same places where dew forms. While mildew won't grow where siding crosses studs and other thermal bridges, mildew may thrive over the cooler, insulated bays between studs, where the dew persists to provide the needed moisture.

Interior mildew. Mildew occurs indoors most frequently in baths, basements, and other areas prone to high relative humidity. It also shows up in places with poor air circulation, such as behind furniture against exterior walls, and in closets and closed-off rooms. Mildew can form whenever the relative humidity of air near a surface exceeds 70%. This can happen when warm air near the ceiling cools as it flows down colder wall surfaces. The relative humidity of 70°F air, for example, rises from 40% to 70% when it's cooled to about 52°F.

Gaps in the insulation or "thermal bridges," where solid wood, metal, or masonry bleed heat through a wall, create "cold spots" inside where mildew can form. Exterior corners are notoriously mildew-prone because of poor air circulation inside and heat-robbing wind outside. In summer, water vapor from warm, humid air entering crawlspaces and basements below air conditioned rooms may condense on cooler joists and subflooring, creating good conditions for mildew, as well as mold, stain, and decay. In winter, moisture condensed as ice from heated air leaking into attics can wet rafters and sheathing when it melts.

Stopping mildew. Not only is mildew unsightly, its spores and odors indoors can trigger allergic reactions. Fortunately, ridding wood of mildew is easy. But first, do a simple test to see if the splotches are mildew or just plain dirt. Place a drop of fresh household bleach containing sodium hypochlorite on the suspected area. The dark color of mildew will fade in a minute or two, while dirt is unchanged.

Once you've determined the stain is mildew, clean it by brushing or sponging the surface with a solution of one-third cup household detergent, one to two quarts household bleach, and two to three quarts of warm water. Or use commercial cleaners. Wear eye protection and gloves, and rinse surfaces with water.

Virtually all exterior finishes — paints, solid color and semitransparent stains, and water repellents alike — are susceptible to mildew. Oil-base formulations, especially those with linseed oil, are particularly vulnerable. Among water-base coatings, acrylic latexes have proven the most mildew-resistant. Defend against mildew on siding and trim by using only primers and top coats that contain mildewcide, or by mixing in the add-it-yourself types that paint shops sell. Finishes with zinc oxide pigments also deter mildew. But beware: Finishes applied over mildewed surfaces that are recoated without first killing the fungus will soon discolor.

The amount of moisture generated inside a home may be beyond your control, but you can encourage use of the bath exhaust fan, for example, by wiring it to the room light switch or to a timer. Install louvered doors to ensure airflow in closets. Use a soil cover and vent and/or insulate crawlspaces as site and climatic conditions dictate. Always install a vapor retarder and an air barrier, use plenty of insulation in walls and attics, and provide adequate roof ventilation.

Molds

Molds need a wood surface moisture content of about 20% to get started. To provide that, simply surround wood with air at 90% relative humidity at any temperature from 40°F to 100°F, and presto! That's why mold and mildew sometimes suddenly appear on furniture during the dog days of summer.

While most molds are green, black and orange molds are not uncommon. The color comes from spores strewn across the surface. Though hyphae reach deeper into wood, discoloration in softwoods tends to be limited to the surface of the sapwood. It can usually be planed, sanded, or even brushed off. Brown, gray, or black patches penetrate more deeply into hardwoods and can't be machined away. Discoloration aside, molds generally have little effect on wood's integrity.

Some molds are surprisingly tolerant of wood preservatives. This explains the fuzzy growths occasionally found between boards in banded shipments of pressure-treated southern yellow pine. Molds die once lumber dries, but can be washed off beforehand with the same solution used for mildew.

Preventing mold. Flourishing in damp crawlspaces and basements and in poorly vented attics, molds form a living veneer on framing and sheathing.

Fungi Field Guide

A guide to fungus identification and habitat

(All case studies photographed in southern New England.—*S.S.*)

Mildew

Dark stains, usually black, on surface of wood. Needs 70% relative humidity at surface to grow. Primarily a visual problem. Will lighten from bleaching.

Location: *Cedar siding on shady side of house.*
Cause: *Persistent wetting from dew.*

Location: *Bottom side of roof sheathing, new home.*
Cause: *Dryer vented into attic.*

Brown Rot

The most common decay fungi in softwoods. Requires 28% moisture content to start, but once established, needs only 20%. Turns wood brown and crumbly, with cross-grain and cubical checking. May sprout cottony mycelia and mushroomlike fruiting bodies.

Location: *Behind shower stall in 22-year-old home.*
Cause: *No vapor retarder, no bath exhaust, cold outside wall corner.*

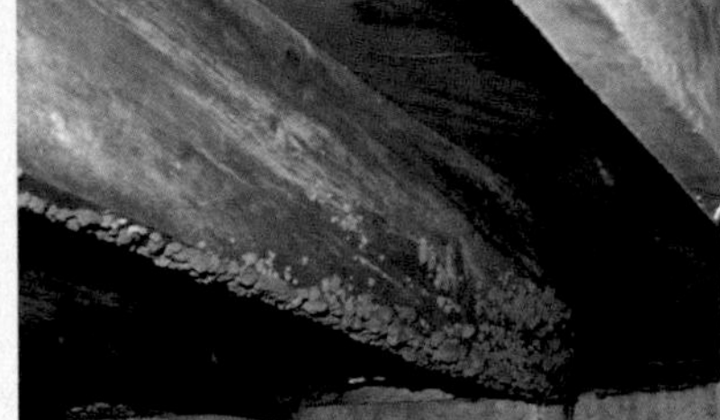

Location: *Crawlspace of 20-year-old apartment building.*
Cause: *Standing water and poor ventilation. Note mycelia (left) and fruiting bodies (right).*

Location: *Sill in direct contact with concrete in five-year-old home.*
Cause: *Untreated wood on concrete slab-on-grade.*

Location: *Trim at entrance to three-year-old home.*
Cause: *Splashing water from unguttered eaves two stories above. Exposed end grain sitting on metal flashing.*

Mold

Green, black, or orange discoloration on surface of wood. Can penetrate below the surface of hardwoods and cause permanent stain. Needs a surface moisture content of 20% to get started.

Location: *Douglas-fir floor joists in basement.*
Cause: *High humidity in basement.*

Staining Fungi

Discoloration of wood in logs or freshly sawn lumber, primarily softwood. Can also occur on pine windows wet from condensation. Steel-gray to blue-black color, commonly called blue stain. Stain is indelible.

RICHARD B. NEWTON

Photo: *Eastern white pine lumber, sawn green during humid summer months, discolored by blue stain.*

White Rot

Most common in hardwoods, giving them a whitish, gray, or yellow bleached appearance. Turns wood spongy and stringy.

RICHARD B. NEWTON

Photo: *Partially decayed, or "spalted" rock maple. Spalted maple is prized by woodworkers for its figure.*

Prevention lies wholly in controlling air moisture levels and condensation potential through proper site drainage and dampproofing, and again, the proper use of soil covers, vapor retarders, insulation, and ventilation as required in your area.

Staining Fungi

Discoloration of wood by staining fungi happens almost exclusively in logs and freshly sawn lumber. As a precaution, rough lumber is often dipped in a fungicidal bath immediately after sawing.

Also called sap stains, these fungi are most troublesome in softwoods, where they cause a steel-gray to blue-black color commonly called blue stain. In hardwoods, staining fungi may create blue or brown hues. The stains result from dark hyphae that permeate sapwood in search of stored starches and sugars. You can often spot inactive blue stain in doors, millwork, and other pine products. Active staining fungi sometimes discolor the bottom rails and corners of pine windows that are kept wet by condensation. These stains are indelible and will not wash off.

In their search for food, staining fungi destroy certain wood cells. As a result, the wood becomes more permeable and more susceptible to decay. Its strength and toughness are slightly reduced as well.

Decay Fungi

While discoloration by mildew, mold, and staining fungi is only an appearance problem, decay fungi threaten the structural integrity of wood. Aptly termed the "slow fire," these fungi eat the very cellulose and lignin of which wood cells are made.

Moisture content is the critical factor that makes wood susceptible to decay. It must exceed 28%, and liquid water must be present in cell cavities before decay fungi can gain a toehold. Once established, some fungi can carry on their destruction at a moisture content as low as 20%. When moisture content falls below this level, all fungal activity ceases. That's one reason why framing lumber is dried to 19% moisture content or less.

In its early, or *incipient*, stages, decay can be difficult to detect, even with a microscope, yet strength loss can still be appreciable. As the slow fire advances, wood's luster fades. Surfaces become dull and discolored, and a musty odor is often present. The rate at which decay progresses depends on moisture content, temperature, and the specific fungus.

It doesn't take a trained eye to recognize decay in its advanced stages. Wood is visibly discolored, spongy, and musty. Surfaces may be stringy, shrunken, or split across the grain. Cottony masses of hyphae called *mycelia*, as well as fruiting bodies, may be present. Decay extends deep into wood; strength loss is significant.

Brown rots and white rots. Decay fungi fall into three major groups: brown rots, white rots, and soft rots. Soft rots are rarely found inside homes, though they occasionally degrade wood shakes and shingles on heavily shaded roofs in wet climates.

Brown rots are so-named because infected wood turns dark brown. They usually colonize softwoods, consuming cellulose but hardly touching the darker lignin, which is the natural glue that holds wood cells together. Mycelia appear as white growths, either

Figure 9. After only four years, the corner posts and other main timbers of this timber-framed house showed extensive damage from brown rot. The cause: excessive moisture from green timbers trapped behind foil-faced foam sheathing.

sheetlike or fluffy, on the wood's surface. Brown-rotted wood shrinks excessively and splits across the grain as it dries. The surface becomes friable and crumbly, and shows cubical checking (**Figure 9**, previous page).

Water-conducting fungi are a special type of brown rot that shows up infrequently in the Southeast, Northeast, and Pacific Northwest. These fungi are unique in their ability to pipe moisture from the soil over long distances. They do this through rootlike fusions of hyphae called *rhizomorphs*, wetting otherwise dry wood in advance of their attack. Water-conducting fungi are sometimes called dry rot fungi. Unfortunately, this name suggests that dry wood can decay. Dry wood can't decay, period! What builders, inspectors, and homeowners alike routinely mislabel

Wet Wood and Insects

by Terry Amburgey

In addition to causing mold and decay, wood with a high moisture content is attractive to a wide range of insects that damage wood. And once the wood is softened from decay, it is readily infested by carpenter ants, which can cause extensive damage. The most common pests are described below.

Termites

Subterranean termites (**Figure A**), though most common in the South, live as far north as Canada. In colder states, they are found mostly in urban areas where they can migrate from house to house — places that we conveniently keep warm for them all year long.

Termites feed most actively on wet wood. Areas of wood-soil contact provide easy access to a house, but subterranean termites can also get into a building through "earthen tubes." They build these on foundation walls or in voids in foundation materials, such as foam insulation.

USDA

STEPHEN SMULSKI

Figure A. *Termite workers (left) are 1/4 inch long and wingless. They avoid light and thus are rarely seen. After several years of colony growth, winged adults emerge briefly and swarm to establish new colonies. Termites will tunnel in all wood products, except for pressure-treated, and can cause serious structural damage (right).*

Once they've built the tubes, the termites carry moisture to otherwise dry areas.

Termite shields slow down termites, but can't be relied on for full protection. Termites will find any breaks or seams — and they can build tubes *around* the shields.

The most effective protection against termites is a toxic barrier around a building. In termite-prone areas, treat the soil under all concrete slabs (including porches, patios, and carports) with a long-lasting *termiticide.* Also apply it next to all foundation walls and piers down to the footings.

The soil adjacent to wood foundations should be treated also. Termites can build tubes over the treated wood to get to the untreated wood. Treat slab and foundation perimeters after the grading and landscaping have been completed.

In homes with crawlspaces, soil treatment can be a problem if the crawlspace is used as an airflow plenum. Experts fear that chemicals applied to the soil can enter the air stream and be carried into the living space. Sub-slab heating or cooling ducts can also pick up chemical treatments — if they are penetrated by drilling rods during re-treatment. Sub-slab ductwork should be avoided anyway.

Carpenter Ants

Controlling wood moisture content in structures also reduces the likelihood of carpenter-ant damage (**Figure B**). Although carpenter ants do not feed on wood, they frequently burrow through wood that is partially decayed in order to nest. Thus, they are usually found in rafter ends, sills, or other building components frequently wetted by rain or other sources of moisture. Ants often are mistaken for termites in the spring during dispersal flights. If one looks closely, however, the two groups can be distinguished from each other.

These groups also can be differentiated by the damage they do. Whereas both tend to remove only the springwood from each annual ring, subterranean termites usually carry some soil in the tunnels. In contrast, the tunnels of carpenter ants are clean and free of debris.

as dry rot is almost always, in reality, wood that got wet, rotted, and dried out before discovery.

Water-conducting fungi infect both softwoods and hardwoods. Their light-colored mycelia look like large, papery, fan-shaped sheets. Damp crawlspaces and wood in contact with the ground are avenues for entry.

White rots give wood a white, gray-white, yellow-white, or otherwise bleached appearance. They most often infect hardwoods, feeding on both cellulose and lignin. In advanced stages of decay, white-rotted wood is spongy, has a stringy texture, and lacks the cubical checking of brown-rotted wood. A thin black line often marks the advancing edge of incipient white rot in hardwoods. Ironically, this partially decayed, or *spalted*, wood is coveted by woodworkers for its unique figure.

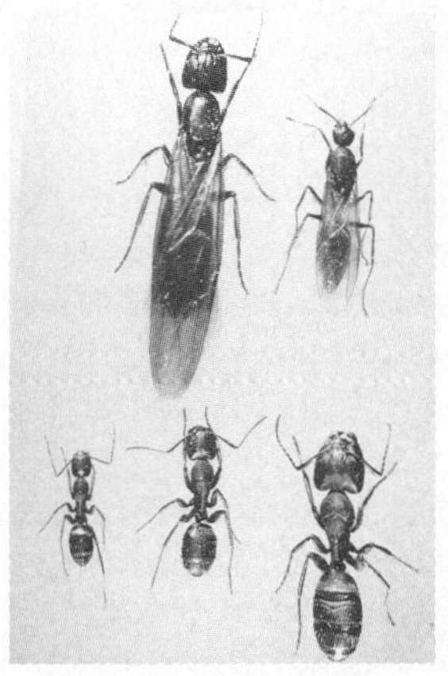

Figure B. *Carpenter ant queens and males are winged and up to an inch long (left). Workers range from 1/8 to 1/2 inch long. Carpenter ants don't eat wood, but carve tunnels for nesting — preferring moist decayed wood or foam insulation. Tunnels in wood (right) run parallel to the grain.*

Wood Borers

Wood borers do most of their damage in wet crawlspaces. Like termites, they are most common in the South and in metropolitan areas in colder regions.

The most common wood borers, anobiid beetles (**Figure C**), feed on seasoned hardwoods and softwoods. They typically infest crawlspace timbers in homes more than 10 years old. Adult anobiids range from 1/8 to 1/4 inch long. When they emerge, they leave a 1/16- to 1/8-inch-diameter hole. Anobiid larvae will not survive in wood that has less than about 12% moisture, and will thrive only in moist wood.

Lyctus powderpost beetles infest recently seasoned hardwood sapwood, often damaging new homes. The 1/8- to 1/4-inch-long insects leave tiny holes of less than 1/16 inch in diameter. Lyctus damage is on the rise because more plywood products use tropical hardwood veneer for the inner plies.

Another species, old-house borers, which are up to one inch in length, prefer recently seasoned softwoods. They typically infest the framing and trim of houses less than 10 years old, leaving holes of up to 3/8 inch in diameter. This damaging insect is spreading throughout the mid-Atlantic and southeastern states, and is best controlled by fumigation.

Wood in crawlspaces and basements can be protected from wood borers by applying a finish, such as a water-repellant preservative (WRP). The finish seals the pores and fissures where wood borers lay their eggs. If the crawlspace is kept dry and well vented, the finish should not be necessary.

The untreated, unfinished, and unseasoned wood that is currently popular in log homes provides prime housing for beetles, as well as for fungal decay. Deep checks and cracks in the logs hold water and invite pests. Wide roof overhangs and periodic treatment of log exteriors are essential in decay-prone areas.

Terry Amburgey researches and teaches wood preservation at the Forest Products Utilization Laboratory at Mississippi State University.

STEPHEN SMULSKI

USDA

Figure C. *Anobiid beetles (left) are 1/8 to 1/4 inch long. Attracted by moist conditions, they fly into the house and lay eggs in cracks and checks in wood. The larvae attack the sapwood for three or more years, then emerge as adult beetles from 1/16- to 1/8-inch round exit holes (right, enlarged in inset).*

Dealing With Decay

Like mold, mildew, and staining, existing decay can be stopped by drying up the moisture. But remember that to make the remedy permanent, you've got to cure the disease (water infiltration) not just treat the symptoms (mildew, mold, and decay).

Stopping decay. The first and most important step when you find decay is to figure out where the water is coming from. Check for the obvious — roof and plumbing leaks, and missing or punctured flashing. Look for stains and drip tracks caused by ice dams. Are the eaves wide enough to prevent water from cascading down sidewalls? Are gutters poorly maintained or missing? Do finish grades slope toward the foundation? Are foundation cracks admitting water? Is untreated wood in direct contact with concrete, masonry, or soil?

Check to see if crawlspaces have soil covers and if venting and/or insulation is adequate and properly installed. Look for adequate attic ventilation as well.

Peeling and blistering paint often signal inadequate interior ventilation or a missing vapor retarder. Water stains on framing and sheathing inside walls suggest condensation from excessive indoor humidity.

Once the source of water has been shut off, remove as much decayed wood as is practical and economical. Decayed wood absorbs and holds water more readily than sound wood, inviting further decay and insect attack (see "Wet Wood and Insects," page 378). This is especially important with girders, columns, and other critical members whose load-carrying ability may have been compromised. There's no known way to accurately determine the remaining strength of decayed wood left in place. Cut back rotted members to sound wood, keeping in mind that difficult-to-detect incipient decay can extend well beyond visibly rotted areas.

When a partially decayed structural member can't be replaced, reinforce it with a sister anchored to sound wood. Let any rotted areas you don't remove dry out before making repairs. Otherwise, you're just adding fuel to the slow fire.

In damp crawlspaces or other places where water is likely to reappear, replace decayed members with preservative-treated wood. The major model building codes require that treated wood be used for sills and sleepers on concrete or masonry in contact with the ground, for joists within 18 inches of the ground, for girders within 12 inches of the ground, and for columns embedded in the ground that support permanent structures.

Borates. Dormant fungi can be reactivated when dry, infected wood is rewetted. Consider treating infected but otherwise serviceable wood left in place with a waterborne borax-based preservative such as Tim-bor or Bora-Care (Nisus Corp.) that will not only kill active fungi but guard against future infection as well. Borates have low toxicity to humans and are even approved for interior use in food processing plants. They don't affect wood's strength, color, or finishability, don't corrode fasteners, and don't outgas vapors. Widely used in treating new timbers for log homes, they're the preservative of choice for remedial treatment of wood in service. Because of the decay hazard posed whenever wood bears on concrete or masonry, solid borate Impel rods (Chemical Specialties, Inc.) are often inserted into holes bored near contact areas. Should wood ever get wet, the rods dissolve and ward off infection.

Epoxy. Sometimes replacing rotted wood isn't an option. In conserving historic buildings, for example, the goal is to preserve as much of the original "architectural fabric" as possible. Stabilizing deteriorated wood with epoxy is often the only choice. Epoxies consist of resin and hardener that are mixed just before use. Liquids for injection and spatula-applied pastes are available (see Sources of Supply, page 399). After curing, epoxy-stabilized wood can be shaped with regular woodworking tools and painted. Epoxies are useful for consolidating rotted wood, restoring lost portions of moldings and carvings, and for strengthening weakened structural members. In the last case, they're used to bond concealed metal reinforcement inside holes or channels cut into hidden timber faces. Epoxies aren't preservatives and won't stop existing decay or prevent future infection. They can also be tricky to use; follow the manufacturer's mixing, application, and safety instructions to the letter.

Editor's note: See "Rot-Proofing Wood Windows and Doors in Wet Climates," page 213, for tips on using epoxies and borate-based preservatives to repair and protect wood building components.

Stephen Smulski, PhD, is president of Wood Science Specialists Inc., a consulting firm in Shutesbury, Mass.

Indoor Mold Remediation

by Doug Garrett

Over the last few years, "mold" has turned into the ugliest four-letter word on the job site. The mold monster has become the bane of builders, insurers, realtors, and homeowners from coast to coast.

The effects of mold on human health are not fully known, and there's a lot of debate about it. But whatever the effect on personal health, there is no doubt that mold can threaten the health and even the survival of your business. To prevent problems, all builders need to know what mold is, how to prevent it from growing indoors, and how to get rid of it when it gains a temporary foothold.

There's no real mystery to this. As a building science consultant based in Texas, I've gotten pretty familiar with mold, and I've come to see the issues in terms of elementary building performance principles. The practical solutions are found in simple good construction practice.

Many of today's mold problems are related to recent changes in building materials and techniques. Every house is actually a complex system made up of interacting components, materials, and subsystems. Change one, and others may change in unanticipated ways. In some of today's houses, this has resulted in conditions that favor the growth of mold.

But while many types of construction problems can lead to mold, mold prevention starts with one basic principle: Keep the building dry. Build it dry to begin with, design it to stay dry, and make sure it can dry out if it does get wet. And if you tangle with a building that has an existing mold problem, remember that every mold problem is a water problem first. To fix the mold, you have to fix the water problem.

Some of the answers are as simple as drains that work and pipes that don't leak. We also need to pay careful attention to water-shedding exteriors, air and vapor barriers, insulation details, and HVAC system design, and consider how those systems affect one another. Here, I touch upon a few high points of dry building details, then discuss ways of tackling existing mold problems. To start, let's take a look at the beast itself: the mold organism.

Why Mold Grows

Molds are fungi, a group that includes 100,000 known species. Mildew in an old trunk, mushrooms in the woods or fields, brown and white rot in a woodpile, and black mold growing in a basement are all closely related organisms.

Fungi exist for a reason: They serve to recycle organic material on earth. They help keep the planet in balance, because for life to continue, everything that grows must decay and break down again.

Mold and other fungal spores are everywhere: Every cubic foot of air contains thousands of them, and every surface — natural or manmade, indoors or out — is covered with thousands more. When the environment is right, the spores sprout and grow. They need only three things: food, water, and the right temperature conditions.

Food. Anything that was once alive can serve as food for one fungus or another. In the wild, molds invade dead trees and grasses and consume the sugars stored in their cells. Mold colonies can live on the surface of sawn lumber, but they really thrive on products in which the wood has been prechewed and predigested, like OSB, particleboard, and paper-faced drywall.

Water. To germinate and grow, mold needs high levels of moisture — meaning greater than 60% relative humidity, or a surface that stays damp for about three days. Without water, molds die or go dormant (but only after releasing millions of spores into the air). From the builder's perspective, this need for water is where mold is most vulnerable: If we can keep the building dry, we can stop mold in its tracks. But if we build any part of the building wet, or let it get wet in service, we're inviting mold to move in.

Temperature. Molds can handle temperatures from 40°F to 100°F; their ideal zone is 50°F to 90°F. Generally speaking, if the temperature is reasonably comfortable for you, mold will be happy, too.

Mold in the Modern World

Builders at my training sessions often ask why we seem to hear so many more reports of mold problems these days than in the past. Several factors are involved. For one thing, houses are tighter now than in the old days. Tighter homes also tend to dry more slowly, so they may accumulate more moisture.

Increased levels of insulation also play a role. Heat flow through walls and ceilings is expensive, but it does dry out wet assemblies. The uninsulated or poorly insulated homes of a generation ago could dry before mold had a chance to begin growing. Better insulation cuts heat flow and slows the rate of drying, so even a minor leak in a home insulated to modern standards can lead to persistent wetness that can allow mold to flourish.

The other big consideration is that today's building materials are better mold food. We're using less brick, stone, and concrete (substances mold can't process); when we use wood, we're using juvenile lumber that

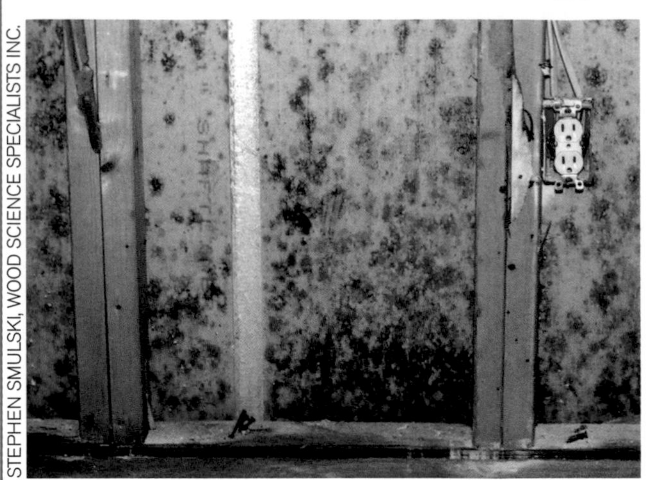

STEPHEN SMULSKI, WOOD SCIENCE SPECIALISTS INC.

Figure 10. Paper-faced gypsum board is ideal mold food. This photo shows a firewall between two multifamily units that stood in the rain before the building was closed in. After odor complaints from residents, every firewall in the project had to be removed and rebuilt. Wet conditions during construction are a major cause of mold in buildings.

contains a higher proportion of mold-prone sapwood than the lumber of years past. Sawn lumber has been replaced by OSB and particleboard — materials that are easy for water to penetrate and that have lots of the sugars and starches that molds can readily break down and absorb. And instead of traditional plaster, which is a hostile environment for mold, we're using paper-faced gypsum, which amounts to mold candy (**Figure 10**).

To these factors you can add all the small things that contribute to moisture in homes: air conditioners that achieve greater energy efficiency at the price of reduced dehumidification, exhaust-only ventilation systems that suck in moist humid air in warm climates, leaky air ducts, vinyl wallpaper that acts as a wrong-side vapor barrier in hot climates — the list goes on and on.

All of these problems are avoidable, but they won't take care of themselves. We need to actively address each one.

STEPHEN SMULSKI, WOOD SCIENCE SPECIALISTS INC.

Figure 11. Bad flashing at a deck ledger attachment allowed water to soak this walkout basement wall. The OSB sheathing shows both mold growth and white rot fungus.

Preventing Mold in New Houses

Stopping mold in homes is mainly a matter of attending to a few key elements, starting with the building envelope. Remember that there's no such thing as a waterproof wall. Windows, doors, brick, and wood siding leak; every joint leaks, and all caulks and sealants eventually leak, too. So water protection in walls is not about waterproofing — it's about drainage (see "Water-Managed Wall Systems," page 98). If you don't want mold, you can't let wall cavities get wet and stay wet.

Many leaks result from bad flashing details (**Figure 11**). For roof leaks, poorly detailed chimneys and wall-roof intersections are major culprits. Make sure your employees and subs handle those details right, and you'll avoid most roof leaks.

Foundations. Basements and crawlspaces are notorious for being damp and smelly, and they are a common location for mold growth (**Figure 12**). Moisture in the basement or crawlspace often moves directly into the home above and then into the attic. It's a common source of condensation on air conditioner supply grilles in the South and of frost under roof sheathing in the North.

Building codes may say otherwise, but from the standpoint of building science, the best way to keep crawlspaces dry is to stop ventilating them with outside air. Seal them up, insulate the perimeter, cover the floor with a continuous vapor barrier, and introduce a small amount of conditioned air from the main house. The ground cover is key: Left bare, the soil in a crawlspace evaporates 12 gallons of water per thousand square feet of exposed soil per day. Ventilating a crawlspace with damp exterior air only adds more moisture. Whether your crawlspace has vents or not, sealed crawlspace expert Jeff Tooley warns that you must place an effective barrier to block ground moisture *before* you close in the building. Otherwise, you create humid conditions while the house is still under construction, inviting fungi to attack (see "Building a Sealed Crawlspace," page 38).

Research also tells us that we should insulate a cold-climate basement on the outside of the wall, because this keeps the wall interior warm and dry. And in any climate that gets rain, gutters, downspouts, and good foundation drainage are important to protect the foundation against water intrusion (see "Foundation Drainage," page 2).

Warm-side vapor barriers. In the northern U.S., the primary vapor flow in homes takes place in the winter, as warm-humid interior air moves toward the

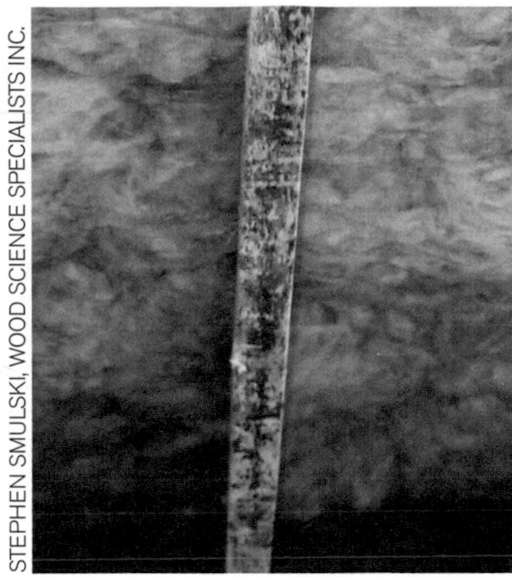

Figure 12. Damp basements are a friendly environment for mold. Extensive mold growth is visible on a drywall panel in a humid basement (far left). The sawn lumber, which is less moisture absorbent and has less available nutrition for mold, has not been colonized. At left, high relative humidity has allowed mold to grow on engineered I-joist floor framing in a basement.

dry exterior. But in the South, the forces switch sides of the wall: The warmer, more humid conditions are found on the outside of the home during most of the year, and the vapor drive is toward the dry, air conditioned inside. Literally speaking, northern homes dry out, but southern homes "dry in."

Vapor barriers should be positioned accordingly: on the interior wall face in cold climates, and on the exterior face in hot climates. In the South, vapor barriers on the inside of the wall actually tend to cause condensation, mold, and rot (**Figure 13**). Building codes in many areas are starting to catch up with this reality.

Ventilation. Tight homes do trap moisture. We don't need to build homes leaky again, but we do need to install mechanical ventilation in homes, as we have for decades in commercial buildings.

Figure 13. In hot, humid climates, vinyl wallpaper forms a vapor barrier on the cool, air-conditioned side of the wall, causing exterior moisture to accumulate under the wallpaper and support the growth of mold. Walls should be vapor-permeable on the side facing dry air, and vapor barriers should be placed on the side facing moist, warm air.

In the North, you want to create a neutral or slightly negative air pressure inside, so any air leakage will be cool, dry exterior air leaking in, not moist, heated air pushing out. Exhaust ventilation works well in cold climates. But be sure to use sealed-combustion appliances, or conduct a "worst-case depressurization test" to make sure any natural-draft appliances draw properly, even when all other equipment that can cause negative pressures is running.

In the South, we need to pull in extra air and pressurize the home to keep the humid outside air at bay. One solution is an outdoor air intake into the plenum of the air conditioner, which leads incoming air through the air filter and cooling coil before introducing it to the indoor space. Even better, install a whole-house dehumidifier, ventilator, and filtration system in parallel with the air conditioner. This will do a better job of maintaining year-round moisture control without overcooling the house.

It's very important not to oversize the air conditioner, because oversized units do a poor job of reducing humidity. Always have the equipment sized using the Air Conditioning Contractors of America *Manual J* (www.acca.org).

Bathrooms. The bathroom is a wet place by definition, which makes it a common place to find mold (**Figure 14**, page 386). Contrary to popular belief, "moisture-resistant" drywall ("green board") is not a mold-resistant substrate for tile. Use a cementitious backerboard instead. An even better approach is to skip the tile and use a nonporous sheet material like solid surfacing. The fewer cracks and gaps you have to seal, the better the odds of keeping the system dry.

Always install a good bathroom ventilation fan, even if you have a window. There are plenty of quiet, efficient models on the market, with controls that can respond to humidity or motion. Timer-linked controls are also effective. Vent the fan to the outside, not into the attic, or things have a way of turning ugly overhead (**Figure 15**, page 386).

Plumbing. Let's not forget the pipes. According to insurance industry statistics, plumbing leaks are the biggest source of water damage claims. Don't put pipes where they might freeze and burst. Pans under water heaters and washing machines are good insurance. Leave easy access to drains under sinks or in cellars, so leaks can be quickly detected and easily fixed. And be absolutely sure that plumbing is tested for leaks before anything is closed in.

Mold in Existing Buildings

What if you encounter mold during a remodeling job, or get a mold-related complaint in a home you've built? Now you're looking at cleanup (or to use the modern 50¢ word, "remediation"). Your cleanup methods have to keep the mold from spreading by minimizing dust and spore dispersal. You also have to provide personal protection for people who are exposed to the mold (including the building occupants and your crew) and protect yourself from any greater liability.

Know the standards. In particular, you must not leave yourself open to an accusation that you made the situation worse by not exercising due diligence (see "Mold the Law: Murky Business"). I'm no lawyer, and I won't go into details about liability issues, but I can say that it's a good start to know and apply well-accepted national standards for handling mold in buildings. If a case goes to court, it's nice to be able to tell the plaintiff's attorney, "We got there as

Mold and the Law: Murky Business

by Quenda Behler Story

Here's a quick rundown on the medical, scientific, and legal aspects of dealing with mold and construction.

Medical Issues

Let's start with the medical part. Mold is everywhere, and there are thousands of kinds. Most molds can cause trouble for people with allergies, but a few molds are also toxic. Some of the worst are members of the Aspergillus, Penicillium, and Stachybotrys families. Stachybotrys has gotten a lot of press because it attacked the homes of several high-profile victims, including Erin Brockovich. The resulting lawsuits got the insurance industry worried about paying claims and led to much higher insurance rates.

Unfortunately, there is no consensus among experts about what levels of mold-spore concentrations are acceptable inside a house or even which species of mold cause the most problems. According to some medical researchers, the types of mold mentioned above are a life-threatening danger to small children, the elderly, and people with impaired immune systems. The symptoms of a reaction to mold often resemble those associated with asthma but can also include rashes, fatigue, nausea, and vomiting. In severe cases, people have died because their lungs were bleeding.

Science Issues

What enables mold growth? Moisture. I bet you already knew that. There is no mold without moisture. Does that mean every moldy building has leaks? Not necessarily. You can get moisture through condensation, which is one of the reasons there have been more problems since we started constructing airtight buildings.

Suppose you're being sued because a building you worked on is now full of mold. Are you going to wind up paying big bucks to a kid with asthma? Maybe. Maybe not. Legally, there are very few definitive answers to that question.

So, what exactly are you supposed to do about mold? Again, there are no good answers. No one can tell builders exactly how to prevent mold. No one can tell them how much mold is too much mold. And there are no national mold standards.

Existing Legal Standards

Fewer than 10 states have adopted mold standards. This is a case in which people who don't like government regulation may want to reconsider their position, because there's substantial legal protection in being able to say, "I'm sorry you're sick, but I did what the law and the regulatory agencies required me to do."

Asbestos is a good example. There are specific legal standards that spell out how much asbestos is allowed in the air and what you're supposed to do if you find asbestos in a building. Because asbestos standards exist, asbestos isn't the big legal problem it once was.

Insurance problem. When it comes to mold, about the only thing I can say with certainty is that your insurance company has probably excluded mold problems

quickly as possible, did a thorough visual and moisture meter investigation to determine the extent of the damage, identified and stopped the water intrusion at its source, and then proceeded according to nationally respected guidelines."

Those guidelines are out there, and it's your business to know about them. If you ignore the guidelines or, worse, knowingly violate them, your position is very weak.

A panel of national experts convened by the New York City Department of Health issued mold remediation guidelines in 1995. New York's guidelines have served as a template for the Environmental Protection Agency (EPA) and other groups in creating their published guidance materials. All these organizations agree on the main points, and the rules aren't hard to follow. New York's guidelines are available from the city's Department of Health website at www.ci.nyc.ny.us/html/doh/html/epi/moldrpt1.shtml. EPA's guidelines are posted at www.epa.gov/mold.

Let's go over the key points.

Act fast. Timing is critical. Treat every water intrusion complaint like a report of a small house fire — because just like a fire, the problem will quickly get worse if you ignore it. Don't say you'll be over when you have time: Get there now!

You won't see or smell mold for the first 48 hours after the materials get wet. If you can get to the job before mold starts to grow, stop the water at its source, and remove or dry all the wet material quickly, mold may never be an issue.

Try to keep the relative humidity levels in the area

from your coverage. In other words, if you're sued for mold damage, forget your insurance: You're on your own. Insurance companies don't want to deal with mold because the legal answers are still so uncertain.

How to Protect Yourself

There are steps you can take to protect yourself — and if at all possible, you should take every single one of them.

Use disclaimers. In their warranties, your insurance company and your material suppliers disclaim responsibility for mold. You should, too. Include language in your contract that limits your liability for mold problems to those you created yourself by not meeting industry standards or by not following the plans. The reason I don't suggest excluding every single mold problem is that judges and juries are more likely to ignore that broad, boilerplate language than they are to ignore language that is a genuine effort to limit your liability to the problems you actually created.

Whatever you say, don't forget to include language that states you're not liable if you built according to the design and standards given you by the owner or the architect.

Follow industry recommendations. Be aware of industry recommendations about moisture abatement and water infiltration, and unless you're living in a very dry climate, follow them.

Actually, after reading some of the lawsuits out of the Southwest, let me amend that advice: Follow the recommendations regardless of how dry it is where you are. This means that whenever you install a building product, you need to read and follow the instructions. If the installation of this product leads to mold growth, you might be able to shift some of the blame to the manufacturer, but only if you followed the instructions.

Disclose and document. Don't limit yourself to advising the homeowner about potential problems with only the parts of the building you are working on. If you're working on an existing building, you should document every water infiltration and condensation problem you find.

For example, if you're replacing a window and happen to look up and notice moisture damage from a past ice dam, tell the owner and architect. In fact, tell them in writing and mention that the conditions you observed can lead to mold problems. Be sure to keep copies of these notifications for yourself. If mold is discovered after you work on a building, you want to be able to prove that it was there before you started.

Why would I tell you to be so careful about something that isn't even part of your window-replacement job? Because you were up there and you saw the problem, and at this time, the legal outcome of mold lawsuits is in such a state of flux that it's impossible to say with certainty who will be left holding the bag. All we can be sure of is that it won't be the insurance companies.

Quenda Behler Story has practiced and taught law for more than 25 years. She is the author of The Contractor's Plain-English Legal Guide.

AEROTECH LABORATORIES, INC.

Figure 14. The bathroom is a naturally humid environment and is also prone to plumbing leaks that create continual wet conditions. Drywall, whether moisture-resistant or not, supports thriving mold colonies in moist conditions. Use backerboard and tile instead, or a synthetic material like solid surfacing.

below 60%, because mold has a difficult time growing beneath that threshold. In fact, to speed the drying of materials, the drier you can keep the air, the better.

By eye and nose. If you don't arrive on the scene until things have already been wet for several days, you may well have a mold problem. Do a thorough visual examination of the area and all associated areas where the water might have gone. You need to determine the source of the water and the extent of the damage. Don't start repairs or remediation until you find and eliminate the source of the water — rebuilding or cleaning the damaged area is useless unless you're sure it will stay dry. Remember to look in the HVAC system, the ceilings of areas below the source, and walls associated with the general area, too.

A good moisture meter is vital for the initial investigations. There are good pinless meters now available that don't leave holes in the wallboard, tile, or other finish materials.

Don't ignore your sense of smell. Molds have a distinct odor, and our noses are finely tuned for detecting it. If you notice a "moldy" or "musty" smell, track it down. Odds are it is mold.

Don't test the mold. Somebody may suggest testing the mold to find out what type it is. Don't do it. Identifying the species doesn't serve any purpose in the cleanup process. No matter what mold species it is, we want it out of there, and you will proceed with your remediation the same way regardless. Air sampling for spores is also not helpful in most cases.

Whether there's mold or not, you need to stop any leaks or condensation problems. If you do find mold growth, consult the remediation guidelines and decide whether the cleanup is a job your crew can handle or whether it's time for a specialist to take over.

How much is too much? The New York guidelines lay out a graduated response that depends on the amount of mold present. The goal is the same — stop the water, protect the occupants and workers, and get rid of the mold — but for larger amounts of mold, the guidelines call for qualified supervision and more stringent measures to isolate the work area.

The guidelines recognize four levels of contamination, which are defined in terms of the square footage affected by mold. These range from "small isolated areas" of 10 square feet or less to areas of "extensive contamination," which cover 100 contiguous square feet or more. There are two intermediate classifications — "mid-sized isolated areas" of 10 to 30 square feet, and "large isolated areas," which cover 30 to 100 square feet.

The appropriate cleanup procedure for any given case will depend on the contamination level. Levels 1 and 2 — areas of mold less than 30 square feet, or about the area of a sheet of plywood — can be handled by a general contractor's crew or a building owner's maintenance staff, as long as the workers get appropriate training, have the correct equipment, and follow the steps laid out in the standard.

Areas of mold covering between 30 and 100 square feet (Level 3) require "personnel trained in the handling of hazardous materials and equipped with respiratory protection, gloves, and eye protection." When contamination exceeds 100 square feet (Level 4), the standards require full containment under HEPA-filtered negative air pressure, complete isolation of the work area, and airlocks. This is unquestionably a job for professionals (see "Remediation Methods," facing page).

STEPHEN SMULSKI, WOOD SCIENCE SPECIALISTS INC.

Figure 15. A dryer vent and bath fan were improperly vented into this attic, causing condensation to form on the sheathing and support mold growth.

Remediation Methods

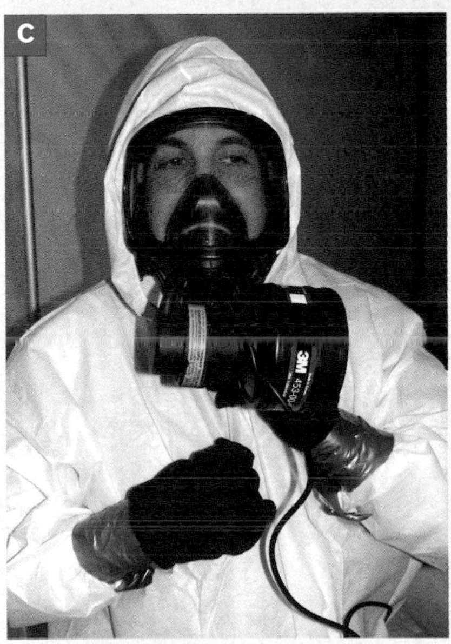

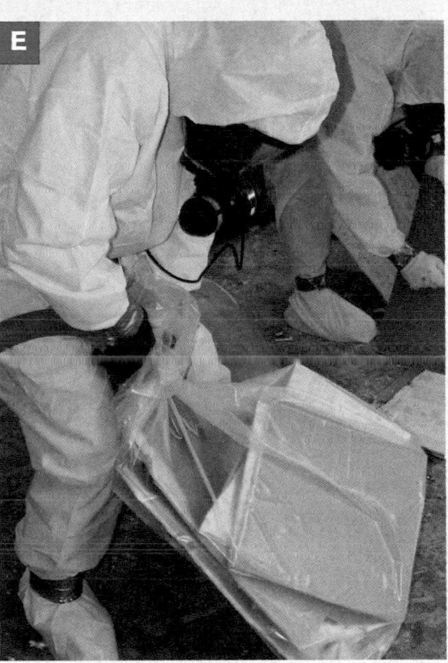

Large areas of mold growth call for crews trained in hazardous materials handling.

The area should be depressurized with a HEPA-filtration blower (**A**) and entered through a sealed "clean room" (**B**). This crew wears protective suits with hoods, booties, and gloves, along with full-face positive-pressure powered respirators (**C**) equipped with activated carbon filters to remove VOCs. "But this is not HAZMAT gear," according to the crew leader. "It's not good enough for asbestos or a chemical spill. It's really just very good dust protection. We use the charcoal canisters because we don't like the smells, not for safety reasons. And the blowers help keep us cool inside our hoods."

Careful dust-control practices prevent mold or anything else from being spread around during demolition. These trained mold remediators carefully cut away drywall with knives (**D**) and place it in plastic bags for disposal; they use a shop-vac to suck the air out of the bags and close them with duct tape. The bags of debris (**E**) are not toxic waste, however, and can be taken to a regular landfill — the purpose of the containment and dust control is just to avoid exposure to allergens and irritants. — *D.G.*

The square-foot thresholds are somewhat arbitrary, and the standards don't claim to be based on any proven relationship between area of mold growth and alleged health effects. It's really a judgment call: Can a crew get rid of the mold without spreading it or exposing anyone to elevated levels of spores or contaminated dust in the air? The more mold there is, the harder it is to contain the pollution; every contractor has to make his or her own decision on where to draw the line.

Cleanup Basics

Let's look at the minor jobs that can be undertaken by a building owner's regular maintenance crew. The standards recommend that the crew should "receive training on proper cleanup methods, personal protection, and potential health hazards." You can do this yourself with the help of some publications available free from the EPA (www.epa.gov/mold).

Protective gear. You need to be very strict about personal protection — you're open to a comp claim or lawsuit if anyone starts to feel sick. The crew should wear masks that meet the N95 disposable respirator standard. These are now widely available at all of the big-box hardware stores for a couple of dollars each. (Don't confuse these with much cheaper "nuisance dust" masks.) The crew should also wear latex gloves and goggles, because some people may get allergic skin reactions to the many substances molds produce.

Who should move out? The work area should be unoccupied, but with certain exceptions, the family can stay in adjacent areas. The exceptions include children under one year old; people with chronic lung diseases like asthma, severe allergies, or emphysema; and anyone with a compromised immune system (such as chemotherapy patients, people with AIDS, and transplant patients). People who fall into one or more or these groups should move out of the building until the work is complete.

Containment. Disturbing moldy materials can greatly increase the levels of spores and contaminated dust in the air. Contaminated materials must not be allowed to spread beyond the work area. The key to preventing this is something called containment — essentially a matter of isolating the work area with overlapping sheets of plastic that are sealed at their edges. Containment is not required for small moldy areas under 10 square feet but is recommended for areas between 10 and 30 square feet.

I recommend that containment with plastic be employed on all cleanup or demolition jobs. It's cheap and effective. At this level, there's no need to create a negative pressure field by exhausting the air from the work area through a HEPA filtration unit. That's not a bad idea, but the guidelines don't direct you to do it.

To depressurize the workspace on small jobs, I sometimes buy an inexpensive box fan and a 1-inch pleated-media filter (such as a 3M Filtrete filter) the same size as the fan. I tape the filter to the fan and seal the fan in the window, creating a simple exhaust system with a filter that will easily capture mold spores. The air is drawn from the house, pulled through the contaminated work area, then filtered and exhausted to the outside.

In any case, do what you can to suppress dust during your work. One effective way is to mist the areas before cutting into them. You don't want to soak them, just dampen them enough that you don't stir up a cloud when you work.

Reuse or discard? Some building materials can be easily cleaned and reused, while others can't. Porous materials that can't be easily cleaned, including insulation, drywall, carpet pads, carpet, and ceiling tiles, should be discarded. Any materials you remove must be placed in plastic bags and sealed before being removed from the work area. Moldy possessions — furniture and the like — also have to be cleaned or discarded; but if antique or valuable fabric or carpet has mold growth on it, a professional cleaning and restoration contractor may be able to save it.

Nonporous materials such as metal, glass, and hard plastic, and the semiporous materials like wood and concrete, can be cleaned instead of removed. But in the case of wood, decide whether it is still structurally sound. Processed wood products like particleboard and OSB are more sensitive to water damage than solid lumber. No materials of any kind should be left in place unless they are sound, dry, and visibly free of mold.

Cleaning. People often think they should use bleach on mold, but the industry standards recommend against it. Bleach does not kill mold spores, and the bleach itself is an irritant and can be harmful to workers and building occupants.

In any case, sanitizing or killing the mold is beside the point. Mold is an allergen whether it's dead or alive. If the area is clean and dry, mold will not grow; if it's wet, mold will grow back even if you wash with bleach.

The answer is to use a good strong soap and water solution. Mold spores have a waxy surface that repels water; the soap is a surfactant that breaks the water's surface tension and lets it pick up the spores and dirt for effective cleaning.

When you're finished, the surfaces should be clean and free of mold growth. All surfaces must pass a white-glove inspection. Any wood should then be allowed to dry completely. Test wood with a moisture meter to make sure it's below 15% moisture content before enclosing it again. When you're sure everything is white-glove clean and dry, and will not become wet again, you can rebuild the area.

Communication. Before you take on mold, it's vital to make sure you have the owners' full understanding and full agreement. The owners need to be comfortable. Communication is critical to this: You must talk to the clients frankly about what you've found, and what you are about to do in their home. Show them the guidelines, explain what you intend to do and how long it will take, and answer their questions regarding safety and other issues affecting their family. Important communications should be supported by a written follow-up. The NAHB has some good guidance on this issue.

To be frank, the customer may not fully trust you. I am often hired by builders to work as an independent third party to ensure compliance with the standards, and property owners often speak to me about their concerns. I've found that even people who like their builder often suspect — rightly or wrongly — that his real goal is to cover his own butt. You need to do whatever you can to dispel this idea, and full disclosure is the best available remedy. Remember, suspicion can lead to a lawsuit.

The best method is to assign one person to be the customer's point of contact on this job. This should be an individual who has good people skills, and who knows the remediation process front to back. Ideally, this contact person should be on the job regularly, overseeing the process and checking on details. This way, the residents can see that the person they're dealing with knows what's actually going on. This extra care will pay off in successful conclusions for you.

Doug Garrett is the president of Building Performance & Comfort in Leander, Texas, a building performance contractor serving both the residential and commercial markets.

Part 1: Foundations & Drainage

Armtec
800/265-7622
www.systemplaton.com
Manufacturer of Platon, an air-gap waterproofing membrane system for foundations

Basement Systems Inc.
800/638-7048
www.basementsystems.com
Supplier of IceGuard, RainChute, and WaterGuard basement-drainage products

BASF Building Systems (including ChemRex, Inc. and Sonneborn Building Products)
800/433-9517
www.chemrex.com
Manufacturer of cementitious foundation coatings Thoroseal 551 and Thoroseal Foundation Coating

Carlisle Coatings & Waterproofing
800/527-7092
www.carlisle-ccw.com
Manufacturer of foundation waterproofing products MiraDrain 860 (sheet membrane), MiraDri (drainage mat), and MiraClay (bentonite)

CertainTeed Corp.
800/233-8990
www.certainteed.com
Manufacturer of Form-A-Drain integrated footing form and drain tile

Colbond Geosynthetics
800/365-7391
www.colbond-usa.com
Manufacturer of Enkadrain, a foundation drainage board

Cosella-Dörken Products, Inc.
888/433-5824
www.deltams.com
Manufacturer of Delta-MS, an air-gap waterproofing membrane for foundations

D.A. Fehr
800/325-8999
www.dafehr.com
Distributor of a flapper valve used to drain water from a crawlspace

Epro Waterproofing Systems
800/882-1896
www.eproserv.com
Manufacturer of Ecobase II foundation waterproofing membrane (asphalt emulsion)

Grace Construction Products, a division of W.R. Grace & Co.
800/327-3962
www.na.graceconstruction.com
Manufacturer of foundation waterproofing products Procor (liquid rubber), Bituthene (sheet membrane), Hydroduct (drainage board), Grace Ice & Water Shield

HouseGuard
800/560-5701
www.houseguard.com
Supplier of foundation waterproofing systems TruDry (asphalt emulsion and, HouseGuard (TruDry + Dow Styrofoam drainage board)

Icynene Inc.
800/758-7325
www.icynene.com
Manufacturer of Icynene spray foam insulation

ITW Ramset/Red Head
630/350-0370
www.ramset-redhead.com
Manufacturer of TrakFast, a gas-fueled concrete nailer

Karnak Corporation
800/526-4236
www.karnakcorp.com
Manufacturer of foundation waterproofing products #229 AR-Elastomeric (modified asphalt), One-Kote (liquid polyurethane)

Koch Waterproofing Solutions, Inc.
See Tremco Barrier Solutions

Mar-flex Waterproofing and Basement Products
800/498-1411
www.mar-flex.com
Manufacturer of foundation waterproofing products

MFM Building Products Corp.
800/882-7663
www.mfmbp.com
Manufacturer of SubSeal 40 and SubSeal 60 waterproofing membranes

Nisus Corporation
800/264-0870
www.nisuscorp.com
Manufacturer of borate-based wood preservatives Tim-bor and Bora-Care

Owens Corning
800/438-7465
www.owenscorning.com
Manufacturer of Warm-N-Dri (foundation insulation/drainage board)

Pecora Corporation
800/523-6688
www.pecora.com
Manufacturer of foundation waterproofing products Duramem 500 (polyurethane), Duramem 700-SM (sheet membrane)

RCD Corporation
800/854-7494
www.rcdcorp.com
Manufacturer of low-VOC mastics, duct sealants, and barrier coatings, including PS-1 water-based, nontoxic duct-sealing mastic

Rubber Polymer Corporation
800/527-0238
www.rpcinfo.com
Manufacturer of foundation waterproofing products Rub-R-Wall waterproofing (liquid rubber), Rub-R-Wall Plus waterproofing (liquid rubber), Graywall waterproofing (liquid rubber)

Sealoflex Waterproofing Systems
843/554-6466
www.sealoflex.com
Manufacturer of Coraflex, a reinforced synthetic stucco system with an elastomeric top coat, and the base coat of Corabase Onepack, both made for EIFS applications

Part 1: Foundations & Drainage *(continued)*

TClear Corporation
800/544-7398
www.tclear.com
Manufacturer of ThermaDry foundation drainage panels (drainage/insulation)

Tremco Barrier Solutions (formerly Koch Waterproofing Solutions, Inc.)
800/876-5624
www.guaranteeddrybasements.com
www.tremcobarriersolutions.com
Supplier of foundation waterproofing systems Tuff-N-Dri (asphalt emulsion), Watchdog Waterproofing (asphalt emulsion), Warm-N-Dri (insulation/drainage board), Full System (Tuff-N-Dri + Warm-N-Dri)

Tremco Global Sealants
800/321-7906
www.tremcosealants.com
Manufacturer of foundation waterproofing products Tremproof 60 (liquid-polyurethane), Paraseal (bentonite)

W.R. Meadows
800/342-5976
www.wrmeadows.com
Manufacturer of foundation waterproofing products Meadow-Pruf Seamless (asphalt emulsion), Mel-Rol (sheet membrane), Mel-Drain (drainage system)

Zoeller Pump Co.
800/928-7867
www.zoeller.com
Manufacturer of high-quality sump pumps

Part 2: Water Vapor Control

ADO Products
866/240-4933
www.adoproducts.com
Manufacturer of Durovent heavy-duty polystyrene attic ventilation baffles

Advanced Foil Systems
800/421-5947; 909/390-5125
www.afs-foil.com/
Supplier of the radiant barriers and foil insulation

Canam
See Zerodraft

Carlisle Hardcast Inc.
800/527-7092; 888/229-0199
www.hardcast.com
Manufacturer of mastic for sealing ducts and transitions

CertainTeed Corp.
800/233-8990
www.certainteed.com
Manufacturer of MemBrain, a polyamide film whose permeability changes with ambient humidity conditions

Denarco Inc.
269/435-8404
Supplier of polyurethane foam sealants, weather strips, sealant tapes, and gaskets

DuPont
800/448-9835
www.tyvek.com
www.dupont.com
Manufacturer of Tyvek weatherization products and tapes

Energy Federation Inc.
800/876-0660
www.efi.org
www.energyfederation.org
Distributor of energy conservation products, including RCD mastics, Venture tape, Pur Fill aerosal urethane foam/Pur Fill foam guns, and Astrofoil reflective insulation

Fortifiber Building Systems Group
800/773-4777
www.fortifiber.com
Manufacturer of Moistop flashing

Grace Construction Products, a division of W.R. Grace & Co.
800/327-3962
www.na.graceconstruction.com
Manufacturer of Grace Ice & Water Shield self-adhering membrane roofing underlayment

Hanes Industries
800/699-6898
www.hanesindustries.com
Manufacturer of vapor-permeable InsulWeb fabric

Lennox International Inc.
972/497-5000, 800/953-6669
www.lennox.com
Manufacturer of the CompleteHeat water heater plus fan-coil unit for hot-air heat

Louisiana-Pacific
800/299-0028
www.lpcorp.com
Manufacturer of TechShield (formerly Kool-Ply) radiant barrier structural roof sheathing

Low Energy Systems Supply Company (LESSCO), Inc.
920/533-8690
www.lessco-airtight.com
Manufacturer of the Lessco airtight electrical box

Nudo Products, Inc.
800/826-4132
www.nudo.com
Manufacturer of Ground Breaker fiberglass panels for protecting exterior rigid foam wall insulation

Panasonic
800/211-7262
www.panasonic.com
Manufacturer of quiet efficient exhaust fans

ParPAC, Inc.
877/937-3257
www.parpac.com
Manufacturer of par/PAC

Pella Corporation
800/374-4758
www.pella.com
Manufacturer of windows and doors, including aluminum-clad energy-efficient wood windows

Poly-America
800/527-3322
www.poly-america.com
Manufacturer of flame-retardant polyethylene sheeting, which can be left exposed in a basement

Raven Industries Inc.
800/635-3456
www.ravenind.com
Manufacturer of Rufco-Wrap perforated housewrap

RCD Corporation
800/854-7494
www.rcdmastics.com
Manufacturer of RCD #7 Mastic and other RCD mastics, air-duct sealants, and coatings

Resource Conservation Technology
800/477-7724
www.conservationtechnology.com
Distributor of Tenoarm, a 10-mil polyethylene air-vapor barrier from Sweden

Sto-Cote Products, Inc.
888/786-2683
Manufacturer of Tu-Tuf, a white-colored cross-laminated polyethylene air/vapor barrier

Tamarack Technologies, Inc.
800/222-5932
www.tamtech.com
Manufacturer of exhaust fans and ventilation controls, including the Airetrak microprocessor control system, and distributor for a variety of ventilation products for exhaust fans ventilation

3M Center
888/364-3577
www.3m.com/us
Manufacturer of construction sealing tape

Todol Products
508/651-3818; 800/252-3818
www.todol.com
Distributor of Pur Fill aerosol urethane foam and Pur Fill foam guns

Tremco Global Sealants
800/321-7906
www.tremcosealants.com
Manufacturer of Tremco acoustical sealant

Venmar Ventilation
800/567-3855
www.venmar.com
Manufacturer of HRVs

Weather Shield Mfg., Inc.
800/222-2995
www.weathershield.com
Manufacturer of windows, doors, and hatches

Zerodraft, a division of Canam Building Envelope Specialists, Inc.
877/272-2626
www.zerodraft.com
Manufacturer of building envelope improvement materials, including a two-component polyurethane foam for sealing ducts and transitions

Part 3: Exteriors

Abatron, Inc.
800/445-1754
www.abatron.com
Manufacturer of epoxy systems

ADCO Products, Inc.
800/248-4010
www.adcocorp.com
Manufacturer of butyl-rubber/EPDM flexible flashing

Alabama Metal Industries Corporation (AMICO)
800/366-2642
www.amico-lath.com
Manufacturer of Tilath paper-backed stucco lath

Albion Engineering
865/235-6688
www.albioneng.com
Manufacturer of caulking guns and tools

American Saturated Felt, Inc.
800/292-6728
www.asfelt.com
Manufacturer of asphalt felt

Ashland Inc.
800/322-6580
www.ashland.com
Manufacturer of butyl-rubber/EPDM flexible flashing

Atlas Roofing Corporation
770/933-4479
www.atlasroofing.com
Manufacturer of asphalt felt

Avenco
865/525-6336
www.avenco.com
Distributor of butyl-rubber/EPDM flexible flashing

Azek Building Products, Inc., a division of Vycom
877/275-2935
www.azek.com
Manufacturer of Azek Trimboard and other expanded vinyl trim products

Part 3: Exteriors *(continued)*

Bakor Inc.
800/523-0268
www.bakor.com
Manufacturer of rubberized asphalt/polyethylene flexible flashing, including Blueskin flashing membrane

BASF Building Systems (including ChemRex, Inc. and Sonneborn Building Products)
800/433-9517
www.chemrex.com
Manufacturer of joint sealants and water repellents

Blaine Window Hardware Inc.
800/678-1919
www.blainewindow.com
Manufacturer and distributor of specialty window hardware

Benjamin Obdyke
800/346-7655
www.benjaminobdyke.com
www.homeslicker.com
Manufacturer of Home Slicker, a self-ventilating, draining housewrap

Blue Heron Enterprises, LLC
800/438-3289
www.ebty.com
Manufacturer of the Eb-Ty Hidden Deck Fastener

Carlisle Coatings & Waterproofing
800/527-7092
www.carlisle-ccw.com
Manufacturer of rubberized asphalt/polyethylene flexible flashings; EPDM and rubberized asphalt "Thru-Wall" flashings

CertainTeed Corp.
800/233-8990
www.certainteed.com
Manufacturer of asphalt felt

Chadsworth Inc.
800/265-8667
www.columns.com
Manufacturer of durable, weather-resistant columns

Chemical Specialties Inc., a division of Viance
See Viance

C&J Metal Products Inc.
800/500-8660
www.cjmetals.com
Manufacturer of galvanized sheet metal, waterproofing, roofing, and ventilating products

Cor-A-Vent, Inc.
800/837-8368
www.cor-a-vent.com
Manufacturer of corrugated plastic ridge and wall vents

Covalence Adhesives
800/343-7875, 800/248-7659
www.covalenceadhesives.com
Manufacturer of butyl-rubber flexible flashing; Polyken flashing tapes

Covalence Coated Products (formerly Simplex Products and Ludlow Coated Products)
877/876-3119
www.covalencecoatedproducts.com/
Manufacturer of Barricade and R-Wrap plastic housewraps

Dayton Superior Corporation
888/977-9600
www.daytonsuperior.com
www.polytite.com
www.dur-o-wal.com
Manufacturer of Polytite flashing and sealant products, Dur-O-Wal masonry products

Davis Wire
800/350-7851
www.daviswire.com
Manufacturer of Grade D Kraft paper

The Dow Chemical Company
800/800-3626
www.greatstuff.dow.com/
Manufacturer of foam insulation products, including Styrofoam insulation and Great Stuff spray polyurethane sealant

Dow Corning
989/496-7881
www.dowcorning.com
Manufacturer of high-performance sealants

DuPont
800/448-9835
www.dupont.com
Manufacturer of Tyvek, FlexWrap, StuccoWrap, and other butyl-rubber flexible flashings and tapes

DuPont Performance Coatings, a division of DuPont
800/438-3876
www.performancecoatings.dupont.com
Manufacturer of Corlar line of epoxy coatings

Dur-O-Wal, a division of Dayton Superior Chemical Division
630/898-1101
www.dur-o-wal.com
Manufacturer of rubberized asphalt/polyethylene flexible flashing

Fein Power Tools
800/441-9878
www.feinus.com
Importers of the Fein MultiMaster and other precision power tools

Fiberweb
800/284-2780
www.typar.com
Supplier of Typar

Firestone Building Products
800/428-4442
www.firestonebpco.com
Manufacturer of EPDM through-wall flashing.

Firstline Corporation, a division of Fortifiber Building Systems Group
800/773-4777
www.firstlinecorp.com
Manufacturer of FirstWrap plastic housewrap

Fortifiber Building Systems Group
800/773-4777
www.fortifiber.com
Manufacturer of Grade D Kraft paper and Moistop; rubberized asphalt/polyethylene flexible flashing; nonstick flexible flashing

GE Silicones
877/943-7325
www.gesilicones.com
Manufacturer of joint sealants

Geocel Corporation
800/348-7615
www.geocelusa.com
Manufacturer of butyl-rubber/EPDM flexible flashing

Gorilla PVC Cement LLC
888/367-4583
www.gorillapvc.com
Manufacturer of Gorilla low-odor PVC cement and other adhesives

Grace Construction Products, a division of W.R. Grace & Co.
800/327-3962
www.na.graceconstruction.com
Manufacturer of rubberized asphalt/polyethylene flexible flashing; Perm-A-Barrier fully adhered through-wall flashing; self-adhering membranes including Vycor Deck Protector and Vycor Plus

HAL Industries, Inc.
800/663-0076
www.halind.com
Manufacturer of Grade D Kraft paper

illbruck Sealant Systems
See Tremco Global Sealants

International Diamond Systems
800/248-1558
www.internationaldiamond.net
Manufacturer of butyl-rubber/EPDM flexible flashing

Jamsill, Inc.
800/526-7455
www.jamsill.com
Manufacturer of Jamsill Guard door and window sill pan flashing

Jasco Chemical Corp.
888/345-2726
www.jasco-help.com
Manufacturer of site-applied wood preservatives

Johns Manville
800/654-3103
www.jm.com
Distributor of ProWrap plastic housewrap

Kavanagh Sales Company, Inc.
508/485-6320
www.kscinc.com/
Distributor of Marbleine composite columns

Life Deck Specialty Coatings
800/541-3310
www.lifedeck.com
Manufacturer of Life Deck AL metal lath reinforced deck waterproofing system and Life Deck seam tape

Ludlow Coated Products
See Covalence Coated Products

Marbleine
See Kavanagh Sales Company, Inc.

Master Wall, Inc.
800/755-0825
www.masterwall.com
Manufacturer of rubberized asphalt/polyethylene flexible flashing

MFG Sealants
800/297-7325
www.woodsealants.com; www.mfgsealants.com
Manufacturer of TWP stains and sealants (formerly Amteco)

MFM Building Products Corp.
800/882-7663
www.mfmbp.com
Manufacturer of rubberized asphalt, butyl, and nonstick flexible flashings

Midget Louver Co.
800/643-4381
www.midgetlouver.com
Manufacturer of thimble louvers

NEI Advanced Composite Technology
800/998-4634
www.nei-act.com
Manufacturer of rubberized asphalt/polyethylene flexible flashing

Nisus Corporation
800/264-0870
www.nisuscorp.com
Manufacturer of Tim-bor and Bora-Care borate-based wood preservatives

Owens Corning
800/438-7465
www.owenscorning.com
Distributor of PinkWrap and PinkWrap Plus

Pactiv
800/241-4402
www.pactiv.com/green-guard
Manufacturer of AmoWrap, AmoWrap-VW, and AmoWrap Ultra

Pecora Corporation
800/523-6688
www.pecora.com
Manufacturer of joint sealants and water repellents

Polyguard Products
800/541-4994
www.polyguardproducts.com
Manufacturer of rubberized asphalt/polyethylene flexible flashing/aluminum-foil flexible flashing

PRG (Preservation Resource Group)
800/774-7891
www.prginc.com
Distributor of molding scrapers and other tools and materials for building restoration and preservation

Protecto Wrap Company
877/271-9661
www.protectowrap.com
Manufacturer of Jiffy Seal Ice & Water Guard, a rubberized asphalt flexible flashing, and building tape

Raven Industries
800/635-3456
www.ravenind.com
Distributor of Rufco-Wrap plastic housewrap

Reemay, a division of Fiberweb
800/321-6271
www.reemay.com
www.typar.com
Supplier of Typar
See Fiberweb

Resource Conservation Technology
800/477-7724
www.conservationtechnology.com
Distributor of energy conservation products for builders

RGM Products, Inc. (formerly Ridglass Manufacturing Co., Inc.), a division of Elk Premium Building Products, Inc. (ElkCorp)
888/743-4527
www.ridglass.com
Manufacturer of various rubberized asphalt/butyl rubber/polyethylene/aluminum foil flexible flashings

Ridglass Manufacturing
See RGM Products, Inc.

Part 3: Exteriors *(continued)*

Sandell Manufacturing Co., Inc.
800/283-3888
www.sandellmfg.com
Manufacturer of several kinds of through-wall flashing, including Sando Seal (self-sealing rubberized asphalt flashing), Copper Coated, Copper Kraft, Copper Kraft Duplex, and Nuflex Plastic; manufacturer of rubberized asphalt/ polyethylene flexible flashing

SaverSystems
800/860-6327
www.saversystems.com
Manufacturer of Defy deck cleaners

Schnee-Morehead, Inc.
800/878-7876
www.schneemorehead.com
Manufacturer of SM7100 Permathane polyurethane sealant

Senergy, a division of BASF Wall Systems, Inc.
800/221-9255
www.senergy.cc
Manufacturer of stucco products and Senergy drainage mat

Sherwin-Williams
800/832-2541
www.sherwin-williams.com
Manufacturer and distributor of paints, water-repellent preservatives, and spackling compounds

Sika Corporation
800/933-7452
www.sikaconstruction.com
Manufacturer of joint sealants

Simplex Products
See Covalence Coated Products

Sun Frog
866/786-3764
www.sunfrog.com
Manufacturer of deck cleaner, stains, and sealers

System Three Resins, Inc.
800/333-5514
www.systemthree.com
Manufacturer of resins and distributor of Impel rods

Tamko Building Products, Inc.
800/641-4691
www.tamko.com
Manufacturer of asphalt felt; rubberized asphalt/polyethylene flexible flashing

3M Center
888/362-3550
www.3m.com
Manufacturer of contractor's tape

Tremco Global Sealants
800/321-7906
www.tremcosealants.com
Manufacturer of joint sealants and flexible flashings (rubberized asphalt and butyl)

Tremco-illbruck, a division of Tremco Global Sealants (see above)
Manufacturer of rubberized asphalt/aluminum foil/ butyl rubber flexible flashings

Trex Company, Inc.
800/289-8739
www.trex.com
Manufacturer of Trex composite decking and railing products

Tyco Adhesives
800/343-7875
www.tycoadhesives.com
See Covalence Adhesives

Valéron Strength Films (formerly Van Leer Flexibles)
800/825-3766
www.valeron.com
Manufacturer of Valéron Strength Films, which is distributed by Johns Manville as ProWrap, by Raven Industries as Rufco-Wrap, and by Weyerhaeuser as ChoiceWrap

Viance, combining Chemical Specialties, Inc. (CSI) with Rohm and Haas
800/421-8661
www.treatedwood.com
Manufacturer of pressure-treatment chemicals and products, including Impel rods

Vycom Corp.
800/235-8320
www.cpg-vycom.com
Manufacturer of Celtec expanded vinyl trim products
See also Azek Building Products, Inc.

West System Inc.
866/937-8797
www.westsystem.com
Manufacturer of epoxy systems

Weyerhaeuser
253/924-2345
www.weyerhaeuser.com
Distributor of ChoiceWrap

White Lightning Products
800/241-5295
www.wlcaulk.com
Manufacturer of 100% acrylic caulk and other sealants

Wire-Bond
800/849-6722
www.wirebond.com
Distributor of various through-wall flashings, including Aqua-Flash (self-sticking rubberized asphalt), Copper Aqua-Flash (copper bonded to rubberized asphalt), and Fiberweb (a sandwich of polyester film, fiberglass, and vinyl film)

Wolman Wood Care Products, a division of Zinsser Co., Inc.
800/556-7737
www.wolman.com
Manufacturer and distributor of stains, sealers, and preservatives

Wood Care Systems
800/827-3480
www.ewoodcare.com
Distributor of borate-based wood preservatives including Tim-bor, Bora-Care, and Impel rods

W.R. Meadows, Inc
800/342-5976
www.wrmeadows.com
Manufacturer of rubberized asphalt/ polyethylene flexible flashing

York Manufacturing
800/551-2828
www.yorkmfg.com
Manufacturers of flexible copper through-wall flashing

Part 4: Roof Systems

Ahrens Chimney Technique
800/843-4417
www.ahrenschimney.com
Manufacturer of chimney repair products

Deer Hill Enterprises
413/634-0029
www.ultimateridgehook.com
Manufacturer of Ultimate Ridgehooks

Grace Construction Products, a division of W.R. Grace & Co.
www.na.graceconstruction.com
800/327-3962
Manufacturer of Grace Ice & Water Shield rubberized asphalt roofing membrane

HeatFab, a division of Selkirk Corporation
800/772-0739
www.heatfab.com
Distributor of stainless steel chimney liners

Icynene Inc.
800/758-7325
www.icynene.com
Manufacturer of Icynene spray foam insulation

Lynn Ladder & Scaffolding Co., Inc.
800/225-2510
www.lynlad.com
Manufacturer and distributor of ladders and scaffolding

RMR Products
800/366-8677
Manufacturer of stainless steel chimney caps

SaverSystems
800/860-6327
www.saversystems.com
www.chimneysaver.com
Manufacturer of ChimneySaver masonry sealers and repair products

Sika Corporation
800/933-7452
www.sikaconstruction.com
Manufacturer of construction sealants

Sleepy Hollow Chimney Supply, Ltd.
800/553-5322
www.bellfiresusa.com
Distributor of fireplace and chimney components

Velux America Inc.
800/888-3589
www.veluxusa.com
Manufacturer of Velux skylights and roof windows

Part 5: Mechanical Ventilation

American Aldes Ventilation
800/255-7749
www.americanaldes.com
Manufacturer of bath exhaust fans, inline fans, multi-port ventilators, exterior-mount ventilators, HRVs, and ERVs

Aprilaire
800/334-6011
www.aprilaire.com
Manufacturer of Aprilaire HRVs

Broan-NuTone LLC
800/558-1711
www.broan.com
Manufacturer of bath exhaust fans, multi-port ventilators, and Guardian HRVs

Brock Engineering & Manufacturing, a division of Wolseley Canada
888/344-1323
www.wolseleyexpress.com
Distributor of HRVs

Bryant Heating & Cooling Systems
800/428-4326
www.bryant.com
Manufacturer of HRVs

Carrier Corp.
800/227-7437
www.carrier.com
Manufacturer of HRVs and ERVs

Continental Fan
800/779-4021
www.continentalfan.com
Manufacturer of inline fans and bath exhaust fans

Des Champs Technologies
800/265-6921; 540/291-1111
www.deschamps.com
Manufacturer of HRVs

Energy Federation Inc.
800/876-0660
www.efi.org
www.energyfederation.org
Distributors of whole-house ventilation systems and energy conservation products

Fantech
800/747-1762; 800/565-3548
www.fantech.net
Manufacturer of inline duct fans, multi-port exhaust fans, exterior-mount fans, controls, and timers; Enviro HRVs

Flying "W" Plastics, Inc.
800/327-4735
www.flyingwplastics.com
Manufacturer of thin-wall PVC pipe

Grasslin Controls Corporation
800/272-1115
www.grasslin.com
Manufacturer of timers for ventilation control

Hart & Cooley, Inc.
800/433-6341; 616/392-7855
www.hartandcooley.com
Manufacturer of heating registers, grilles, and diffusers

Honeywell
800/345-6770; 800/328-5111
www.honeywell.com
Manufacturer of HRVs and HVAC controls

Jenn-Air, a division of Whirlpool
800/688-1100
www.jennair.com
Manufacturer of self-ventilating cooktops and accessories

Part 5: Mechanical Ventilation *(continued)*

Lennox International Inc.
800/953-6669; 972/497-5000
www.lennox.com
Manufacturer of HRVs

Leviton
800/323-8920
www.leviton.com
Manufacturer of switches/timers for ventilation control

Lima Register, a division of American Metal Products Group
800/423-4270
www.americanmetalproducts.com
Manufacturer of heating registers, grilles, and diffusers

Memphremagog Heat Exchangers
800/660-5412
Distributor of HRVs

Nu-Air Ventilation Systems Inc.
902/798-2261
www.nu-airventilation.com
Manufacturer of HRVs

Nutech Brands Inc.
519/457-1904
www.lifebreath.com
Manufacturer of LifeBreath HRVs

NuTone
See Broan-NuTone LLC

Panasonic
800/277-1860
www.panasonic.com/building
Manufacturer of bath and whole-house exhaust fans

Positive Energy Conservation Products
800/488-4340
www.positive-energy.com
Distributor of energy conservation products, including in-line exhaust fans and HRVs

Powrmatic of Canada Ltd.
800/966-9100; 418/683-2708 (Quebec); 416/744-7206 (Toronto)
www.powrmatic.com
Distributor of HRVs

Raydot
800/328-3813
www.raydot.com
Manufacturer of HRVs

RenewAire
800/627-4499
www.renewaire.com
Manufacturer of bath exhaust fans and HRVs

Rheem Air Conditioning Division
479/648-4900
www.rheemac.com
Manufacturer of HRVs and ERVs

Ruud Air Conditioning Division
800/848-7883
www.ruudac.com
Manufacturer of HRVs

Sensor Switch Inc.
800/727-7483
www.sensorswitch.com
Manufacturer of switches and electronic controls

Shelter Supply, Inc.
800/762-8399
www.sheltersupply.com
Distributors of whole-house ventilation systems and energy-conservation products

Spruce Environmental Technologies
800/355-0901
www.spruce.com
Developer of ventilation and air filtration products, including the Dyna Vent in-line fan

Standex Air Distribution Products (formerly Snappy)
800/328-2044
www.standexadp.com
Distributor of HRVs

Stirling Technology, Inc.
800/535-3448
www.stirling-tech.com
Manufacturer of HRVs

Tamarack Technologies, Inc.
800/222-5932
www.tamtech.com
Manufacturer of exhaust fans and ventilation controls, and distributor for a variety of ventilation products, including the Airetrack timer

Therma-Stor LLC
800/533-7533
www.thermastor.com
Manufacturer of ventilation heat pumps and dehumidifiers, and distributors of ventilation equipment and components

United Air Specialists, Inc.
800/252-4647
www.uasinc.com
Manufacturer of HRVs

Venmar Ventilation Inc.
800/567-3855
www.venmar.ca
Manufacturer of HRVs and ERVs

Ventamatic Ltd. (formerly NuVent Products)
800/433-1626
www.nuventproducts.com
Manufacturer of NuVent bath exhaust fans and HRVs

Venture Tape Corporation
800/343-1076
www.venturetape.com
Manufacturer of foil HVAC tape

Watt Stopper/Legrand
800/879-8585
www.wattstopper.com
Manufacturer of switches and electronic controls

Part 6: Troubleshooting

Arch Wood Protection, Inc.
866/789-4567; 770/801-6600
www.wolmanizedwood.com
Manufacturer of pressure-treatment chemicals and Wolmanized lumber

ATCI Consumer Products, a division of Accuset Tool Co. Inc.
800/343-6129
www.squeakyfloor.com
Manufacturer of Squeak-Relief floor repair hardware

Chemical Specialties, Inc.
See Viance

Delmhorst Instrument Co.
877/335-6467
www.delmhorst.com
Manufacturer of moisture meters

E&E Engineering, Consumer Products Division
800/854-3577
www.squeakender.com
Manufacturer of Squeak-Ender and Squeek No More hardware for wood floors

Lignomat USA Ltd.
800/227-2105
www.lignomat.com
Manufacturer of moisture meters

Nisus Corporation
800/264-0870
www.nisuscorp.com
Manufacturer of Tim-bor and Bora-Care borate-based wood preservatives

Rio Tinto Borax (formerly U.S. Borax)
800/729-2672
www.borax.com
Manufacturer of boric acid and borates

Stud Claw
905/844-9173
www.studclaw.com
Manufacturer of Truss Float-R framing brackets and drywall backer clips

3M Center
888/364-3577
www.3m.com/us
Manufacturer of 3M Filtrete filter

Viance, combining Chemical Specialties, Inc. (CSI) with Rohm and Haas
800/421-8661
www.treatedwood.com
Manufacturer of pressure-treatment chemicals and Impel rods

Wagner Electronics
800/585-7609
www.wwwagner.com
Manufacturer of moisture meters

A

B

F

S